A HISTORY OF WORLD THEATER

A HISTORY OF

Gillot inv. *Arlequin Soupirant* Joullain Sculp

WORLD THEATER

Margot Berthold

WITH 363 HALFTONES
AND 85 LINE DRAWINGS

Frederick Ungar Publishing Co. / New York

Translated by Edith Simmons from the original German

Weltgeschichte des Theaters

Published by arrangement with Alfred Kröner Verlag, Stuttgart

Printed in the United States of America
Designed by Irving Perkins
Library of Congress Catalog Card Number 70-127203
ISBN 0-8044-2037-8

PHOTO CREDITS

With the exceptions listed below, all photos are courtesy of the libraries, collections, and museums mentioned in the captions. Photos not otherwise credited are from the archives of Alfred Kröner Verlag.

Bayerische Versicherungskammer, Munich: p. 449; M. Berthold, Munich: p. 189 top and bottom; E. Betz, Munich: p. 107; Picture Archive Foto Marburg, Marburg: pp. 237, 246, 247 top; I. Buhs, Berlin: p. 669 bottom; L. Burrows, London: p. 660; Callwey-Verlag, Munich, E. Baur (Photo: H. Schmidt-Glassner): p. 363; L. Chmel, Vienna: pp. 278, 279; Deutsches Archäologisches Institut, Rome: pp. 142 top, 159 top, 175 top, 176 bottom, 194, 197 top, 207 center; Giraudon, Paris: pp. 140 bottom, 147 bottom, 284 top, 303 top, 307 top, 332, 482, 550; Österreichische Nationalbibliothek, Vienna: p. 384 bottom; B. Ortolani, Tokyo: p. 108; G. Pagenstecher, Bremen: p. 679; E. Rapsilber, Krailling: p. 130; Staatliche Museen zu Berlin, Bodestrase: pp. 152 top, 158 top right, 192 top; H. Steinmetz, Munich: p. 639 bottom; Theatermuseum, Munich: pp. 104 top and bottom, 110 top, 118 bottom left, 123 top, 324, 388 top, 454 top, 446 top, 510 top, 545 bottom, 560 top, 600 top and bottom, 609, 598, 617; S. Toepffer, Munich: p. 671.

Contents

Foreword

In one of the traditional scenes from the *Commedia dell'arte,* a buffoon appears on stage and attempts to sell a house. He praises it highly, describes it glowingly, and to prove his point produces a single stone from the building.

Similarly, to speak of world theater is to produce a single stone and expect the reader to visualize the whole structure from it. The success of such an attempt depends upon the persuasiveness of the buffoon, the expressive force of the stone, and the imagination of the reader.

Writing a book about world theater is a daring undertaking. The effort to discover within the heterogeneous panorama those common denominators that characterize the phenomenon of "theater" throughout the ages present a great challenge. Such a study's necessarily narrow framework dictates selectiveness, omissions, brevity, thereby bringing subjective factors into play. The very nature of the subject makes objectivity difficult. Problems arise as soon as an attempt is made to reach beyond the purely factual and grasp at those features that characterize an epoch. Nevertheless, it is precisely at that point that fascination with the artistic process of theater begins; the reader is then faced with the unspoken demand to pursue on his own those matters merely touched upon.

Theater is a living thing. Whether it enthralls, appalls, depresses, amuses, confuses, or enlightens the spectator, it thrives on strong reaction.

The mystery of theater lies in a seeming contradiction. Like a candle, theater consumes itself in the very act of creating light. Whereas a painting or statue has concrete existence once the act of creation is over, a completed theatrical performance immediately vanishes into the past.

Though theater is not a museum, the manifold contemporary theatrical forms make up something of a *musée imaginaire: a musée imaginaire* capable of being transformed into immediate experience. Every evening modern man is offered dramas, staging, and methods of direction that have developed over the centuries. These elements are adapted to contemporary taste; they are stylized, objectified, shattered, reworked. Directors and actors recreate them; authors reshape traditional themes into modern adaptations. Determined reformers all but do away with the text of certain plays, introducing aggressive effects and creating improvised, total theater. A successful effort brings the spectator under its spell, creates resistance, gets discussed, and makes one think.

No theatrical form, no anti-theater, is so new that it has no analogy in the past. The theater as an irritant? The theater in crisis? None of these questions and problems are specifically modern; all have arisen in the past. The theater pulsates with life itself and has always been vulnerable to life's infirmities. But there is no reason for concern or for Cassandra-like predictions. As long as theater is talked about, fought over—critical minds have always done just that—it will retain its significance. A non-controversial theater would be a museum, a complacent, repetitive institution. But a theater that stirs the mind is a sensitive, fever-prone membrane, a living organism. And that is the way it should be.

The Primitive Theater

Theater is as old as mankind. There have been primitive forms of it since man's beginnings. The transformation into another self is one of the archetypal forms of human expression. Theater's range therefore includes the hunting pantomime of the ice-age peoples and the differentiated dramatic categories of modern times.

The magic spell of all theater, in the broadest sense, rests on man's inexhaustible capacity for presenting himself to public view without disclosing his personal secret. The shaman who is the god's mouthpiece, the masked dancer who averts the demons, the actor who brings the poet's work to life—they all obey the same command, which is the conjuration of another, truer reality. To turn this conjuration into "theater" presupposes two things: the elevation of the performer above the laws that govern everyday life, his transformation into the mediator of higher insight; and the presence of spectators prepared to receive the message of this higher insight.

From the point of view of cultural evolution, the essential difference between primitive and highly advanced forms of theater is the number of stage properties the actor is allowed to use in expressing his message. The performer of primitive and primary cultures makes do with a gourd rattle and an animal's skin; the baroque opera mobilizes all the scenic paraphernalia of its age. Ionesco clutters up the stage with chairs and makes a deaf-mute proclaim the sad nullity of human incapacity. The twentieth century practices the art of reduction. Anything more than a helpless gesture or a spotlight tends to seem excessive.

The solo performances of the mime Marcel Marceau are a superb example of timeless theater. They provide us with insights into peoples of all times and places, into the dance drama of early cultures, the pantomime of the highly developed cultures of Asia, the mime of antiquity, the *Commedia dell'arte*. In a work entitled "Youth, Maturity, Old Age, Death," a few minutes are all Marceau needs for a high-speed portrayal of man's life, and in them he achieves a compelling intensity of elemental dramatic expressiveness. As Marceau himself says, pantomime is "the art of identifying man with nature and the elements close to us." He goes on to note that the mime can "create the illusion of time." The actor's body becomes an instrument that substitutes for a whole orchestra, a modality for expressing the most personal and, at the same time, most universal message.

The performer who needs only his body to evoke whole worlds and run the full gamut of the emotions is representative of the primitive theater's art of expression. The prehistoric and modern are manifest in his person. Discussing the theater of primitive tribes in his book *Cenalora,* Oskar Eberle says, "Real primitive theater is art incorporated in the human form and encompassing all the possibilities of the body informed by spirit; it is simultaneously the most primitive and the most protean, and in any event the oldest, art of mankind. For this reason it is still the most human, the most moving art. Immortal art."

We can learn about primitive theater from three sources: from aboriginal tribes that have little contact with the rest of the world and whose ways of life and magic pantomimes must therefore be close to what we assume to be mankind's primordial stage; from prehistoric cave paintings and carvings on rock and bone; and from the inexhaustible wealth of mimic dances and popular customs that have survived everywhere in the world.

The theater of primitive peoples rests on the broad foundation of primary, vital impulses. From them it draws its mysterious powers of magic, conjuration, metamorphosis—from the hunting spell of the stone-age nomads, from the harvest and fertility dances of the first tillers of the fields, from initiation rites, totemism, and shamanism, and from various divine cults.

The form and content of theatrical expression are conditioned by the needs of life and by religious conceptions. It is from the latter that an individual derives the elemental forces which transform man into a medium and enable him to transcend himself and his fellows.

Rock painting in the Cogul area south of Lerida, Spain: ritual dance scene. Old Stone Age. After H. Breuil.

Man has personified the powers of nature. He has turned sun and moon, wind and sea, into living creatures that wrangle, quarrel, and fight with each other, and that can be influenced in man's favor by sacrifice, prayer, ceremony, and dance.

Not only the Dionysian festivals of ancient Athens, but prehistory, the history of religion, ethnology, and folklore furnish a wealth of material on ritual dances and festivals of the most diverse forms that bear in themselves the seeds of the theater. But the development and harmony of drama and theater demand creative forces that foster the growth of both; they also require an urbane self-assertion on the part of the individual along with a metaphysical superstructure. Whenever these conditions were fulfilled, a flowering of the theater ensued. Where primitive theater is concerned, the reverse of this development meant that the satisfaction of higher insight was, at each stage, gained at the expense of some part of the original force.

It is fascinating to trace this development in the various parts of the world and to see how, when, and under what omens it took place. There is clear evidence that the process always followed the same course. Today it is completed nearly everywhere, and the results are contradictory. In the few untouched areas where aboriginal tribes have yet to go through the process, modern civilization provokes erratic leaps rather than a steady development.

To the theater historian, a study of prehistoric forms reveals synoptic parallels that tempt him to trace the development of mankind through the phenomenon of the "theater." While no other form of art can make this claim with more justification, it is also true that no other form of art is so vulnerable to having this claim contested.

The art form begins with the god's epiphany and, in quite utilitarian terms, with man's effort to enlist the god's favor and help. The fertility rites that to this day are common among the Cherokee Indians when they sow and harvest their corn have their counterpart in the musically and mimically more sophisticated Japanese court festivities in honor of rice; they also resemble the ancient festival of the golden ear of wheat celebrated each year at Eleusis by the women of Greece.

The mysteries of Eleusis are a significant borderline case. They are the expression of a highly developed end phase, which, though potentially theatrical, did not lead to theater. Like the secret male initiation rites, they lack theater's second component—the spectators. The drama of antiquity was born in the vast ring of the Theater of Dionysus at Athens, in full view of the assembled citizens, not in the mystic twilight of the Demeter sanctuary at Eleusis.

Primitive theater used extraneous accessories just as its highly developed successor does. Masks and costumes, stage properties, decor, and orchestras were common, albeit in the simplest conceivable form. The

Cave painting in southern France: the "Sorcerer" of Trois Frères. Old Stone Age. After H. Breuil.

ice-age hunters who gathered in the Montespan cave around a bearskin-clad clay figure of a bear were themselves masked as bears. In a magic miming ritual they killed the bear figure, to insure their success on the hunt.

The stone-age bear dance in the French rock caves at Montespan or Lascaux has its parallel in the Ainu tribe's bear trophy feast in prehistoric Japan. In our own time, it is found among some Indian tribes of North America and also in the African and Australian bush, e.g., in the buffalo dances of the Mandan Indians, the Australian corroboree dances, and the kangaroo, emu, or seal pantomime rituals of various native tribes.

In ever new versions and changing mythological garb, the primitive hunting ritual lived on in Central Europe; for example, in the ritual Germanic war dances, in Odin's dance fight with the Fenris-wolf (as seen on the sixth-century Torslunda plaque), and in all the early medieval personifications of the "wild chase," ranging from the French *"mesnie Hellequin"* to Arlecchino in the *Commedia dell'arte.*

There is a close connection between the anticipatory hunting magic —in which the quarry was animistically killed—or the subsequent expiation rite, and the ecstatic practices of the shamans. Meditation, drugs, dance, song and ear-splitting noise bring about the state of trance in which the shaman enters into a dialogue with gods and demons. His visionary contact with the other world gives him the magic power to heal sickness, call down rain, destroy the enemy, and arouse love. The shaman's conviction that he can make the spirits come to his aid, induced him to play with them. "In addition to the trance, the shaman makes use of all sorts of play-acting and artistic means; he is often very much an artist, and must have been even more so in early times" (Andreas Lommel).

The roots of shamanism as a particular psychological "technique" of early hunting cultures can be traced to the Magdalenian period of southern France, that is, roughly between 15,000 and 800 B.C., and hence to the examples of hunting-magic pantomimes depicted in the cave paintings.

Conceived and represented in zoomorphic terms, the hunting civilizations' pantheon of spirits survives in the mask: in that of the "ministering spirit" in animal guise, in totemism, and in the beast-demon masks of the peoples of northern and central Asia, of the Indonesian, Micronesian, and Polynesian tribes, of the Lapps and the North-American Indians.

The mask wearer loses his identity. He is gripped—literally "possessed"—by the spirit of what he personifies, and the spectators participate in this transfiguration. The Javanese dancer of the *Djaran-képang,* who dons the mask of a horse and leaps about grotesquely astride a bamboo pole, is fed chaff.

Intoxicating scents and stimulating rhythms reinforce the effects of primitive theater, an art in which both the performer and the spectators escape from their selves. Oskar Eberle writes: "Primitive theater is a great opera." A great open-air opera, we should add, which in many cases is intensified by the unreal nocturnal scene in which the light of the flaming wood pyre flickers across the faces of the dancing "demons." The primitive theater's stage is an open area of hard-packed, trodden ground. Its stage properties may include a totem pole planted in the center, a bundle of spears driven into the ground, a slaughtered animal, a heap of wheat, corn, rice, or sugar cane.

In the same way the nine women of the palaeolithic wall painting at Cogul dance around the figure of a man; or the people of Israel danced around the golden calf; or the aboriginal inhabitants of Mexico sacrificed, played games, and danced, invoking their gods; or to this day the Australian totem dancers assemble when the ancestor spirit makes its presence felt as the bullroarers sound. Thus, too, vestiges of primitive theater survive in popular customs, in the dance around the maypole or the St. John's fire. And thus Western theater began, on the dance floor of the Dionysus temple at the foot of the Acropolis.

In addition to the round dance and the theater arena, primitive theater also made use of processions for its celebrations of magic rituals. The visits of the Egyptian gods involved pageant—the priests who performed the sacrifice led processions that included singers, dancing girls, and musicians; the statute of Osiris was conveyed to Abydos in a bark.

Wall painting from a Theban tomb: girl musicians with double shawm, long lute, and harp. From the time of Amenhotep II, ca. 1430 B.C.

Maya "bird"-dancer with rattle and banner. Wall painting in the temple of Bonampak, Mexico. Ca. 800 A.D.

Persian Shiites began the Husain passion play with exorcising processions. Every year in March the Hopi Indians of North America perform their dance play of the Great Serpent in a procession carefully arranged according to a prescribed pattern. From logs and brushwood they construct six or seven ceremonial rooms (*kivas*) for the separate phases of the dance. There is even a "master of lighting," who extinguishes the glimmering pile of wood in each *kiva* as soon as the procession of dancers and spectators has moved on.

Various mystical and magic ceremonies are involved in the initiation rites of many primitive peoples, in the customs, that is, surrounding a boy's entry into the company of adults. Ancestor masks are worn in mimic play. With his first participation in the ceremonial, the neophyte learns the significance of the masks, the costumes, the ritual texts, and the musical instruments. He is told that to neglect even the slightest detail may bring incalculable disaster to the whole tribe. On the island of Gaua in the New Hebrides the elders critically watch the first dance play of young boys about to be initiated. If one of them makes a mistake, he is punished by being shot with an arrow.

On the other hand, in all places and periods the theater encompassed grotesque buffoonery as well as ritual severity. Farcical elements can be found in its most primitive forms. Animal dances and animal pantomimes have an *a priori* tendency to the grotesque. As soon as the cultic tie relaxes, the instinct of mimicry turns to provoking laughter. Situations and subject matter are taken from everyday life. When the honey seeker of the homonymous Philippine play runs into all sorts of minor misfortunes, he is rewarded with sustained laughter, as are, say, the performers of the parodistic pantomime "Encounter with the White Man" in the Australian bush. The native paints his face with light-colored ocher, puts on a yellow straw hat, wraps rushes round his legs—and the image of the gaitered white colonial master is complete. The costume sets the key for improvisation—a remote, but perhaps not so very remote prefiguration of the *Commedia dell'arte.*

As tribal societies became increasingly organized, some sort of professional acting developed among various primitive peoples. Among the Areoi of Polynesia and the natives of New Pomerania there were itinerant troupes that traveled from village to village and from island to island. The theater as a compensation for life's routine can be found wherever people gather in expectation of some magic that will transport them to a higher reality. This is true regardless of whether the magic takes place on a plot of bare earth, in a bamboo hut, on a platform of boards, or in a modern multipurpose glass and exposed concrete palace. It is true even if the end effect is brutal disillusion.

The proudest mask and the most imposing pomp cannot save

O'Neill's Emperor Jones from the nightmare of self-destruction. Ancient shamanistic powers overwhelm him in an eerie moonlit night to the sound of African jungle drums. In this expressionist play, O'Neill heightens the "little, formless fears," turning them into the menacing frenzy of the Congo witch doctor, whose bone rattle clicks the time for the fierce boom of the drums. A strident echo of primitive sacrificial rites haunts the twentieth-century stage. As though sprung from the trunk of the tree, the witch doctor, according to O'Neill's stage directions, stamps his foot and begins a monotonous croon.

> Gradually his dance becomes one of a narrative in pantomime, his croon is an incantation, a charm to allay the fierceness of some implacable deity demanding sacrifice. He flees, he is pursued by devils, he hides . . . springs to the river bank. He stretches out his arms and calls to some God within its depth. Then he starts backward slowly, his arms remaining out. A huge head of a crocodile appears over the bank and its eyes, glittering greenly, fasten upon Jones.

For a 1933 production, the American stage designer Jo Mielziner used an enormous Olmec head for the primitive stone altar called for in the script. African, Caribbean, and pre-Columbian fantasies combine in a nightmare out of the past. The primitive theater reappears and works on our modern existential fears.

Egypt and the Ancient East

INTRODUCTION

The history of Egypt and the ancient Near East provides us with a record of the peoples who, in the three millennia before Christ, laid the foundations of Western civilization. They were active in the regions extending from the Nile to the Tigris and Euphrates rivers and to the high plateau of Iran, from the Bosporus to the Persian Gulf. In those creative ages of mankind Egypt founded the plastic arts, Mesopotamia, science, and Israel, a world religion.

West and east of the Red Sea, Egypt's god-king was the sole, all-powerful ruler, the highest earthly judge and authority. To him homage was paid in manifold forms of music, dance, and dramatic dialogue. In festival celebrations, in glorification of life in this world or in the hereafter, he was the central figure, and all pomp was lavished on his person. This was the exalted position of the dynasts of Egypt, the great rulers of Sumer, the emperors of Akkad, the god-kings of Ur, the rulers of the Hittite empire, and the kings of Syria and Palestine.

In Egypt and all through the ancient Near East, all religion and mysteries, all thought and action, were determined by kingship, the sole principle of order. Alexander, wisely respectful, submitted to it in his triumphant progress. He visited the tomb of Cyrus and paid homage, as Cyrus himself had paid homage at the tombs of the great kings of Babylon.

For many centuries, the sources from which the image of the ancient Near East emerged were limited to a few documents: the Old Testament, which speaks of the wisdom and the fleshpots of Egypt, and the accounts of a few writers of antiquity, who blamed one another for their "remarkably poor orientation." Even Herodotus, the "father of history," who visited Egypt and Mesopotamia in the fifth century B.C., is often vague. The fact that he was silent about the "hanging gardens of Semiramis" diminishes our knowledge of this one of the Seven Wonders of the World, and that Nebuchadnezzar's New Year's festival pavilion remained unknown to him deprives theater researchers of valuable clues.

In the meantime, archaeologists have excavated the ruins of vast palaces, of mosaic-encrusted New Year's festival buildings, and even the sites of whole cities. Historians of law and of religion have deciphered the ingenious code of cuneiform tablets, which have also yielded some indications about ancient theatrical performances.

We know of the magico-mythical ritual of the Mesopotamians' "sacred marriage," and we have uncovered fragments of the Sumerians' divine disputations; we are now able to reconstruct the origin of dialogue in the Egyptian Hathor dance and the arrangements of the Osiris passion play of Abydos. We know that mime and farce, too, came into their own. There was Pharaoh's dwarf, who delivered his puns before the throne and also represented the gnome-god Bes in religious ceremonies. There were the masked performers who provided amusement at the princely courts of the ancient Near East, parodying enemy generals and, in the late periods of the twilight of the gods, even mocked the supernatural beings.

Besides the surviving texts, the plastic arts provide us with some evidence—to be interpreted, however, with caution—on the beginnings of the theater. The ornamental "masks" on the Parthian palace at Hatra, the grotesque masks on the houses of Phoenician settlers at

Dramatic Hathor dance. Painting in the tomb of Intef at Thebes. 3rd millennium B.C.

Mosaic standard from Ur: victory banquet with singers and harpists, probably a sequence of scenes from the "Sacred Marriage." Figures of shells and limestone fragments, on a background of lapis lazuli. Ca. 2700 B.C. (London, British Museum.)

Masks on the palace of Hatra, in the plain of northern Mesopotamia. Hatra was founded by the Parthians, whose last king, the Arsacid Artabanus, was vanquished in 226 A.D. by the Sassanid ruler Artaxerxes.

Tharros, or the masklike representations of the slain enemies' heads dangling from gold brooches and stone reliefs—all these give testimony to closely related conceptions: the primal power of the mask is intended to go on exerting its effect even when it becomes decoration. The ancient mask motifs—despite some contradictory interpretations—do not fundamentally preclude speculations about "theatrical" connections. But much necessarily remains supposition in the enigmatic panorama of the three millennia B.C.

The meager, sun-scorched soil of Egypt and the Near East, erratically watered by its rivers, has seen many civilizations rise and fall. It knew the power of the pharaohs and witnessed the cultic invocations of Marduk and Mithras. It shook under the tramping of Assyrian archers in ceremonial procession and under the marching feet of Macedonian warriors. It saw the Achaemenid princess Roxana, adorned in bridal attire and escorted by thirty young dancing girls, at the side of Alexander, and it heard the drums, the flutes and bells of Parthian and Sassanian musicians. It supported the wooden poles of tightrope dancers and acrobats, and it kept silent about the arts the hetaera practiced when the king summoned her from the dance to his inner rooms.

EGYPT

In the history of mankind, nothing has given rise to more lasting monuments than the demonstration of man's transience—the cult of the dead. It is manifested as much in the prehistoric burial mounds as it is in the pyramids and tomb chambers of Egypt. The musicians and dancing girls, banquets and processions, and the sacrificial offerings portrayed in the murals of the temples dedicated to the dead testify to the Egyptians' solicitude for a hereafter where no earthly pleasure was to be lacking.

To the powerful petition to the gods expressed in the painted and sculpted image was added the magic of the word: invocations to Re, the god of heaven, or to Osiris, lord of the dead, pleading that the departed be received in their kingdom, that the gods lift him up as their peer.

The dialoguelike form of these sepulchral inscriptions, the so-called Pyramid texts, has given rise to exciting speculations. Do the five-thousand-year-old hieroglyphs, with their fascinating pictographs, also permit us to make inferences about the state of the theater in ancient Egypt? The question has been answered affirmatively ever since the brilliant Egyptologist Gaston Maspero, in 1882, called attention to the

Limestone relief from the tomb of Patenemhab: a priest offering sacrifice, blind harpist, lute-player, and two flutists. Ca. 1350 B.C. (Leiden, Rijksmuseum.)

Girl musicians and dancers. Wall painting from Shekh abd el Kurna, Thebes. XVIIIth dynasty, ca. 1400 B.C. (London, British Museum.)

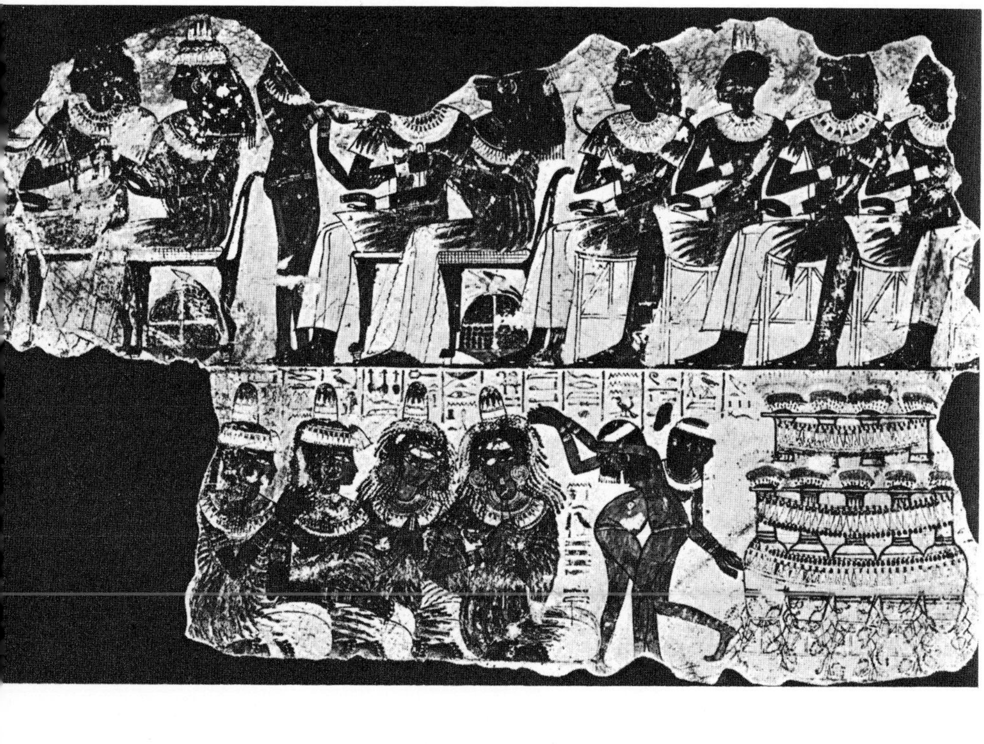

"dramatic" character of the Pyramid texts. It seems certain that the recitations at Egypt's coronation ceremonies and jubilees (*Heb seds*) were couched in dramatic form. Even the presentation of the goddess Isis in the process of casting a magic spell to protect her little son Horus from the fatal effects of a scorpion sting seems to have been dramatically presented.

An incantation of a different character was deciphered on the Metternich stele (named for Metternich Castle in Bohemia where it is preserved). This is a simple folk incantation, such as Egyptian mothers pronounce to this day when their child is stung by a scorpion: "Poison of Tefen, flow out on to the ground, do not advance into the body. . . ." Findings such as this and inscriptions of funeral chants and recitations give no clues to Egypt's theater arts but, rather, have led to some confusion.

The mix-up between first-person presentation and the invocative form in early translations has misleadingly suggested a supposed "dialogue" in no way supported by more recent research. Furthermore, the priestly offerings and appeals to the gods in the tomb chambers lack the decisive component of the theater: its indispensable creative partner, the public.

This does exist in the dramatic ceremonial dances, in the weeping and wailing and mimed lamentations, and in the presentations of the mysteries of Osiris at Abydos, which are reminiscent of the passion play. Every year, tens of thousands of pilgrims journeyed to Abydos, to attend the great religious festivals. Here the head of Osiris was said to be buried; Abydos was the Mecca of the Egyptians. In the mystery play about the god who has become man—about the entry of human emotion into the realm of the supernatural, or the god's descent into the regions of earthly suffering—there is dramatic conflict, and so the root of the theater.

Osiris is the most human of all the gods in the Egyptian pantheon. Legend eventually transformed the fertility god into a being of flesh and blood. Like Christ in the medieval mystery plays, Osiris suffers betrayal

Ecstatic acrobatic dance. Painting in the tomb of Ankhmahor at Sakkara. 3rd millennium B.C.

and death—a human destiny. After his martyrdom has ended, the tears and laments of the mourners are his justification before the gods. Osiris rises and becomes the ruler of the realm of the dead.

The stages of Osiris's destiny constitute the stations of the great mystery play of Abydos. The priests organized the play and acted in it. The clergy realized what vast possibilities for mass suggestion the mystery play offered. It is a testimony to their farsightedness that, with all the growing popularity of the Osiris cult, with the increasing funds of princely foundations, with their wealth of tombs and chapels, they still took into account the little man. Anyone who left a memorial stone or stele at Abydos was certain of the blessing of Osiris. And, after his death, through all eternity he would attend, "transfigured," the sacred ceremonies and rites in the temple, he and his family, just as they had done in life.

There is a stone stele of the court official Ikhernofret, who lived during the reign of King Sesostris III, in the days of the twelfth dynasty. The stele records the tasks of its donor Ikhernofret as they concerned the temple at Abydos. The upper part of the commemorative stone speaks of the restoration and reorganization work at the temple that was carried out by Ikhernofret; the lower part (lines 17–23) refers to the celebration of the Osiris mysteries. It is not clear from the inscription whether the separate phases of the mystery play, portraying the life, death, and resurrection of the god, were performed in immediate succession, at intervals of several days, or possibly even of weeks. Heinrich Schäfer, the first to interpret the hieroglyphs of the stone, conjectured that the Osiris mysteries "extended over a part of the religious year, as our festivals do, lasting over the period from the beginning of Advent to Whitsun, constituting one great drama."

The stone does, however, make clear the main features of the Osiris mysteries at the time of the Middle Kingdom (2000–1700 B.C.). The report begins with the words: "I organized the departure of Wepwawet as he goes to the rescue of his father." It seems clear, therefore, that the god Wepwawet, in the form of a jackal, opened the ceremonies. Immediately after the figure of Wepwawet "there appeared the god Osiris, in his full majesty, and after him, his ennead—the nine gods of his entourage. Wepwawet was in front, clearing the way for him. . . ." In triumph Osiris travels along in his ship, the Neshmet bark, escorted by the participants in the mystery ceremonies. They are his comrades-in-arms in his fight against his enemy Seth.

If the Osiris ship is to be conceived of as a bark carried overland, then the warriors presumably marched alongside it. If the journey was presented with a real boat on the Nile, a number of privileged persons will have gone on board to "fight" alongside Osiris. Ikhernofret, as a

Limestone relief from Sakkara: left, girls dancing and playing music; right, men walking with upraised arms. XIXth dynasty, ca. 1300 B.C. (Cairo, Museum.)

Ostracon with scene from Egyptian procession: the bark of Amon, carried by priests. Ca. 1200 B.C.; found at Der el-Medîne. (Berlin, Staatliche Museen.)

Dramatic scene from the Horus myth: the falcon-god Horus, portrayed in the bark, as victor over his brother Seth. Limestone relief at Edfu. Time of the Ptolemies, ca. 200 B.C.

high government official and favorite of the king, no doubt was among those privileged persons, for his inscription reads: "I repulsed those who had rebelled against the bark Neshmet, and struck down the enemies of Osiris."

After this prelude, there followed the "great departure" of the god, ending with his death. The death scene probably did not take place in full view of the general public, like the Crucifixion on Golgotha, but in secret. But all the louder did the participants join in the lamentations of Osiris's wife Isis. Herodotus reports of the Osiris ceremony at Busiris that "many tens of thousands of people raised their voices in lamentation"; at Abydos there must have been far more.

In the next scene the god Thoth comes by ship to fetch the corpse. Then, preparations for the burial are made. The dead Osiris is buried at Peker, a little over a mile from the Osiris temple, against the background of the wide, crescent-shaped plain of Abydos. In a great battle the enemies of Osiris are slain by his son Horus, who now has grown into a young man. Osiris, risen to a new existence in the realm of death, reenters the temple as ruler of the dead.

Nothing is known about the concluding part of the mysteries, which took place among "initiates," in the inner part of the temple of Abydos. Like the mysteries of Eleusis, these rites remained concealed from the public.

Osiris-cult festivals also took place in the great temple cities of Busiris, Heliopolis, Letopolis, and Sais. The festival of Upuaut, god of the dead, at Siut must have had a similar processional character. Here, too, the richly decked-out image of the god was escorted in a solemn procession to his tomb.

The ceremony of the erection of the Ded column, instituted by Amenophis III and always solemnly observed on coronation anniversaries, also had definite theatrical elements. Kheriuf's tomb at Assasif in Thebes gives a graphic picture of the scene: Amenophis and his wife are seated upon thrones at the site of the erection of the column. Their daughters, the sixteen princesses, are playing music with rattle and sistrum, while six singers are praising Ptah, the guardian god of the kingdom. The lower part of the Kheriuf relief depicts the festival's concluding ceremony: participants beating one another with clubs, in a symbolic scene of ritual combat in which inhabitants of the city also took part.

Herodotus, in the second book of his history, describes a similar ceremony, observed in honor of the god Ares though, to judge by the context, the god in question must have been Horus. This observance, held at Papremis, also involves ritual combat:

> At Papremis they carry out the sacrifices as elsewhere, but when the sun begins to set, a few of the priests are busy about the image of the god; all the other priests, armed with wooden clubs, stand at the temple door. Opposite them is a crowd of men, more than a thousand in number, also armed with clubs, who have a vow to keep. The image of the god stands in a small, gilded wooden shrine, and on the eve of the festival it is, they say, to be conveyed to another temple. The few priests still attending the image put it, together with the shrine, on a four-wheeled cart and take it to the temple. The other priests who are standing at the door stop them from coming in, but the votaries fight on the god's side and set upon the resisters. There is a fierce struggle, in which heads get broken, and not a few, I believe, die of their wounds. The Egyptians, however, denied that there were any deaths.

The ritual fanaticism which this scene suggests recalls the self-inflicted wounds of the Shiite Husain plays of Persia and the flagellants of medieval Europe.

All through the ages of the pharaohs' splendor and decline the Egyptian remained a docile liege. He accepted the laws imposed by the king and the king's priesthood as divine commandments. This patient adherence to tradition stifled the seeds of drama. For a flowering of the dramatic arts would have required the development of a more freely responsible individual who would have a share in the life of the community, as was encouraged in democratic Athens. The citizen of the Greek *polis,* who had a say in its rule, also had the possibility of a personal confrontation with the state, with history, with the gods.

The Egyptian lacked the impulse to rebellion; he did not know the conflict between the will of man and the will of the gods, from which arises the seed of drama. And therefore, in ancient Egypt, dance, music, and the beginnings of theater remained bound to the traditions of religious and courtly ceremonial. For more than three thousand years Egypt's plastic art flourished, but the full power of drama was never aroused. (The shadow play, which appeared in Egypt during the twelfth century A.D., provided the stimulus for the representation of folk legends and historical events. Its form and technique were inspired by the Orient.)

It was this inherited compulsion to obedience that finally subdued Sinuhe, a government official of Sesostris I who had dared to flee to the Near East. "A funeral procession will be held for you on the day of your burial," the pharaoh informed him; "the sky is above you when you are placed upon the bier and the oxen draw you along, and the singers go before you when the *muu* dance is performed at your tomb. . . ." Sinuhe

Egyptian shadow-play puppets of the 14th century. (Offenbach am Main, Deutsches Ledermuseum.)

returned. The law that had governed the performance of his office was stronger than his rebellion: the power of tradition crushed the will of the individual.

> Thus there is no indication, and indeed it is against all probability, that from this point a path could have been followed even approximately similar to that in Hellas which, from similar beginnings in religion, led to the development of Attic tragedy. To achieve this the first step would have needed to be an extension of myth to encompass man and then a particular way of being human, neither of which was found in Egypt. [S. Morenz.]

MESOPOTAMIA

In the second millennium B.C., while Egypt's faithful were making pilgrimages to Abydos and assuring themselves of divine grace by erecting commemorative stones, the people of Mesopotamia found that the contours of their harsh, despotic gods were growing milder. Men were beginning to credit them with justice and themselves with the capacity to obtain the god's benevolence. The gods were coming down to earth, becoming partners in the rituals. And with the descent of the god comes the beginning of theater.

One of the oldest mystery plays of Mesopotamia is based on the ritual legend of the "sacred marriage"—the union of god and man. In the temples of Sumer, pantomime, incantation, and music served to create a great religious drama out of the traditional representation of the banquet for the divine and human pair. The rulers of Ur and Isin derived their divine kingship from the "sacred marriage," which the king and queen (or a high priestess deputized by divine command) solemnized after a symbolic ritual banquet.

According to recent research, the celebrated mosaic standard of Ur from the third millennium B.C. is one of the earliest representations of the "sacred marriage." This magnificent work, with its figures composed of shells and limestone fragments inlaid in a background of lapis lazuli, dates from about 2700 B.C. and probably was part of the sound chamber of a musical instrument rather than of an army standard.

From the second millennium onward, the "sacred marriage" most likely was celebrated once a year in all the major temples of the Sumerian empire. Priests and priestesses acted the parts of king and queen, of city god and goddess. We do not know where the line was drawn between ritual and reality; but it is certain that King Hammurabi (1728–1686 B.C.), the great reformer of Sumerian law, struck the "sacred marriage" festival from his court calendar. Hammurabi set up a new ideal of kingship: he described himself as a "humble, god-fearing prince," as a "shepherd of the people," and "king of justice." Hammurabi designated Marduk, until then the god of the city of Babylon, the universal god of the empire. A Sumerian dialogue, believed to have been a play and entitled "Hammurabi's conversation with a woman," is devoted to the originator of the Codex Hammurabi and is considered by Orientalists to be a court play. It portrays feminine artfulness triumphing over a brilliant, enamored man, though he wears the splendid robes of the king. It is possible that the dialogue was performed at a rival royal court or, after Hammurabi's death, even at the palace in Babylon. Another famous Sumerian document, the epic in dialogue form, entitled "Enmerkar and the Lord of Aratta," may also have been a secular drama, performed possibly at a royal court of the Isin-Larsa period.

It is certain that in Mesopotamia the court musicians, both male and female, enjoyed the sovereigns' special favor. In the temples, priestly vocalists, young female singers, and instrumentalists of both sexes performed the ritual music at the ceremonies, and they were treated with great respect. A daughter of the Akkad emperor Naramsin is referred to as "harpist of the moon-goddess." Mesopotamia's plastic arts give testimony to the musical richness that served to extol "the majesty of the gods" on the great festivals. That the temple performers were invested with special mythological significance is suggested by the animal-headed musicians often seen on reliefs, cylinder seals, and in inlaid work. The Mesopotamians possessed a developed sense of humor. An Akkadian dialogue, entitled "Master and Slave," resembles the mime plays and

Atellan farces, Plautus, and the *Commedia dell'arte.* The servant's puns expose the hollowness of the allegedly good advice and the relativity of all "well-considered" decisions. Recently, further examples of Mesopotamian secular theater have come to light. The German scholar Hartmut Schmökel, for instance, has interpreted a so-called *Letter of a God* as a scribe's hoax, another religious-sounding text as a kind of clowning satire, and a heroic poem as a grotesque parody.

Sumer's divine disputations have a definitely theatrical character. So far, seven such dialogues have been uncovered. They all were composed during the period when the image of the Sumerian gods became humanized, not so much in their outward appearance as in their supposed emotions. This criterion is crucial in a civilization: it is the fork in the road where the way to the theater branches off. For the drama develops from the conflict symbolized in the concept of gods transposed into human psychology.

In form and content, the Sumerian dialogues consist of each partner in turn extolling his own merits and belittling those of the other.

In one of the dialogues the grain-goddess Ashnan and her brother the sheep-god Lahar argue which of the two is of more use to mankind. In another, the burning-hot Mesopotamian summer tries to outdo the milder winter of Babylon. In a third, the god Enki falls out with the mother-goddess Ninmah, but proves a savior in the great fundamental subject of all mythology, the return from the underworld. In a fourth dialogue, Inanna, the fertility goddess, banished to the world of shadows, will be permitted to return to the earth if she can provide a substitute. She selects for this purpose her lover, the royal shepherd Dumuzi, who is appointed prince of the underworld. With the legend of Inanna and Dumuzi the cycle closes and ends in the "sacred marriage." Inanna and Dumuzi are the original sacred pair.

Even the well-instructed priests of the period were not able to form a conspectus of the vast pantheon of the ancient East, with its innumerable major and subsidiary gods of the many separate city-states. The mythological relationships are even more complex than, for instance, are those between the mythological concepts of antiquity and those of early Christianity.

At the beginning of the twentieth century, the scholar Peter Jensen sought to establish a connection between Marduk and Christ, but he did not succeed. The so-called Bible-Babel controversy rested on the presumed existence of a ritual drama celebrating the death and resurrection of Marduk. But the latest research has proved that the textual interpretation on which this presumption rested is untenable.

In the reign of Nebuchadnezzar, the famous New Year's festivals, in honor of Babylon's city god Marduk, were celebrated with spectacular pomp. The climax of the twelve-day sacrificial ceremony was the great procession. There was Marduk's colorful retinue, followed by the much-honored cult images from the country's great temples, symbolizing "a visit of the gods," and in their train the long file of priests and faithful. At predetermined points on the red-and-white-paved processional way to the New Year's festival house, the column was halted for the recitations of the epic of creation and for pantomime performances. This great ceremonial spectacle honored the gods and the sovereign, and it amazed and thrilled the populace. "It was theater in the setting and garb of religious cult and demonstrates that the ancient Mesopotamians had, at least, a sense of dramatic poetry; further research on the cult remains to be done" (H. Schmökel).

During the third and second millennia B.C., other divinities of the Near East were honored in similar ways at Ur, Uruk and Nippur; at Assur, Dilbat and Harran; at Mari, Umma and Lagash. Persepolis, the old Persian necropolis and palace city, was founded specifically for the celebration of the New Year's festival. Here, at the end of the sixth century B.C., Darius erected the most splendid of Persia's royal palaces. And here Alexander sacrificed the Western idea of *humanitas* to his intoxication with victory: after the battle of Arbela, he allowed the palace of Darius to go up in flames.

The Islamic Civilizations

INTRODUCTION

No other region on earth has experienced as many political, spiritual, and intellectual metamorphoses in the course of the rise and fall of mighty empires as has the Near East. It was in turn the center or bridge of civilizations, seedbed or battleground of great historical conflicts. On the day in 610 A.D. when Mohammed, trader on behalf of the rich merchant's widow Khadija, received the revelation of Islam on Mount Hira, near Mecca, a new epoch again dawned for the Near East.

The common religious faith of Islam gave the peoples throughout the Near East for the first time a feeling of solidarity. Islam reshaped the history of the peoples of the Near East, North Africa, and even of the Iberian Peninsula. Islam shaped a new cultural style, following the precepts of the Koran.

The development of theater and drama was stifled under the Mohammedan prohibition of any personification of God; for this meant that all postantique beginnings of drama were stifled in the Near East. Yet excavations of Greco-Roman theaters, for instance in Aspendus, point to restorations under the Seljuks—an indication that the followers of Islam revived and enjoyed the circus, and the combat of gladiators. It is evident that they preserved and restored theatrical buildings of antiquity, and that such shows must have been tolerated.

The division of Islam into Sunnites and Shiites, as a result of the contested succession to Mohammed, gave rise to the Persian *taziya* passion play, one of the world's most impressive theatrical manifestations. The *taziya* passion play never traveled beyond Iran. It did not follow the victorious march of Islam along the North African coast to Spain, nor did it, along with mosques and minarets, spread across Anatolia to the Bosporus and the Balkans.

Contrary to the commands of the Prophet, however, there developed beyond Mount Ararat both popular plays and shadow plays of a folklore type, based on mime. Through the use of the Turkish puppet heroes

Karagöz and Hadjeivat in the shadow plays, the Islamic prohibition on images of human beings was slyly outwitted. These heroes, embodied by marvelous puppets, were cut out of camel leather. They were moved by means of rods, and had holes in their joints through which the light shone—who could accuse them of being images of human beings? Karagöz and Hadjeivat exploited their privilege so as to make their drolleries all the spicier and to let their shadows swindle their way all the more brazenly across the cloth screen into the hearts of their audience.

The passion play and the farce, joined in contradictory union in European mystery plays, remained hostile brothers under the law of the Koran. Yet both found their way to the people's heart. Both became theater: they both found an audience in the common folk.

PERSIA

Sir Lewis Pelly, who accompanied the British diplomatic mission to Persia and who was Political Resident from 1862 to 1873, was not given to exaggeration. Yet he wrote of the *taziya* passion play that "if the success of a drama is to be measured by the effect which it produces upon the people for whom it is composed, or upon the audiences before whom it is presented, no play has ever surpassed the tragedy known in the Mussulman world as that of Hasan and Husain." The annual performances of the *taziya* became of enduring interest to Pelly; through the agency of a former teacher and prompter of the performers, he collected fifty-two of the plays and, in 1878, published thirty-seven of them.

The plot of the *taziya* is historical fact embroidered with legend. When Mohammed died in 632, he left a harem of twelve wives, but no son. According to an alleged testament left by the Prophet, the succession was to pass to his daughter Fatima, wife of Ali. A blood-thirsty struggle flared up around her sons Hasan and Husain. In 680, the Imam Husain received from the inhabitants of Kufa in Mesopotamia, who supposedly were devoted to him, a call to join them and to assume with their help the leadership of Islam as the legitimate successor to the Prophet. Husain, accompanied by his family and seventy followers, journeyed to Mesopotamia. But, instead of enthronement, he was ordered to submit unconditionally to the Caliph Yazid and to renounce all claims. Husain tried to resist this treachery; but, cut off from all help and without access to the waters of the Euphrates, he and his faithful followers perished in the plain of Kerbela. Weakened by thirst, they fell

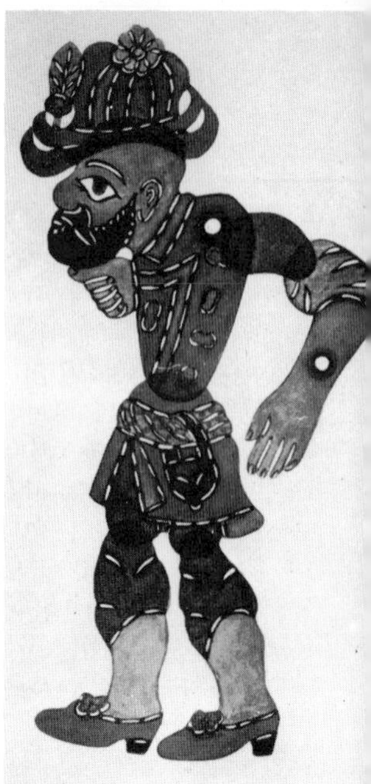

Turkish shadow-play puppets: the singer Hasan (left), and the two main characters Karagöz and Hadjeivat who do most of the talking in the coarsely grotesque dialogue. (Offenbach am Main, Deutsches Ledermuseum, and private collection.)

Group of Turkish shadow-play figures. To the left, a dialogue scene; to the right, a tradesman behind his counter. (Istanbul, Private collection.)

victim to the troops of Caliph Yazid. The women were led away captive. The only survivor of the massacre at Kerbela was Husain's son Zain al-Abidin, who is acknowledged by the Shiites (in contrast to the Sunnite rejection of the Fatima-Ali succession) as fourth Imam and legitimate successor to the Prophet Mohammed.

Dramatizations of this event, much embroidered with legends, are still performed on the last day of the Muharram festival. They last from midday until late at night and are the climax and termination of ten days of religious processions (*desté*) which begin at dawn on the first day of the Mohammedan month of Muharram. The faithful, dressed in white like the flagellants of medieval Europe, proceed through the streets with loud cries of lamentation. Two days earlier, on the eighth day of the festival, straw puppets, representing the corpses of the martyrs of Kerbela, are laid out on wooden biers and carried about amid unceasing, ecstatic lamentations. The men flagellate themselves with their fists and jab themselves with swords, bloodying their chests and heads. Those who value their skin more than the fervor of faith doubtless make do with some deceptive make-believe. In 1812 the French traveler Ouseley, who journeyed through Persia, observed both, wounds self-inflicted out of genuine fanaticism—and others, skillfully painted on the skin.

Early in the morning of the tenth day of Muharram, spectators hasten to the courtyard of the mosque or to the *tekie* (monastery) where an outdoor stage is arranged for the *taziya* play. If it rains or the sun is too hot, an awning is erected. The *sekkon*, a round or square platform, serves as stage. A water tub represents the Euphrates, a tent the camp at Kerbela, a footstool the heavens from which the angel Gabriel descends.

The performers are amateurs. They read their lines from a script, though for the most part they perform in pantomime, while the priest (*mollah*), who is the producer and stage director, comments on the action. He is placed on a stand, high above the players, and also recites the introductory and connecting texts.

Female roles are played by men. Costumes are made of whatever is available. In 1860, when the Prussian legation undertook to defray the cost of a *taziya* performance, Prussian uniforms and weapons were provided. Nowadays the angel may well descend from the roof of an undisguised automobile and be driven up to the stage, but none of the participants are disturbed by such anachronisms. What matters is the symbolic content. To walk around the stage signifies a long journey. A horse or camel led in, laden with bales of luggage and cooking utensils, indicates the arrival of Husain in the plain of Kerbela. An actor, once he has been killed, thereupon silently gets up and goes to one side of the stage. Each of the participants keeps a handful of chaff ready which, at moments of great sadness and despair, he pours on his head. (In accordance with the ancient Achaemenid usage the parents of Darius poured sand upon their heads when the news of the death of the "King of Kings" was brought to them.) The Husain passion play is often preceded by a performance of the story of Joseph and his brethren, which was introduced into the Koran by Mohammed as the "*sura* (chapter) of Joseph."

In Zefer Jinn, another *taziya* play, the king of the Jinn appears and offers Husain the help of his army. However, the Imam, ready to suffer martyrdom, refuses the proffered assistance and dismisses the king of the Jinn with the adjuration "to weep." The king of the Jinn and his warriors wear masks; this is the only case where the mask is used in the Persian *taziya* tradition.

The *taziya* passion play is an intrinsic part of the Shiite tradition. It developed out of the epic and lyrical lamentations of the mourning assemblies following upon the death of Husain. These songs of lamentation were first presented in dramatic form in the ninth century, when a Shiite sultan of the Buyid dynasty took over the caliphate. From movable stages, set on carts, resounded the call to do penance: "Tear out your hair, wring your hands, rend your clothes to tatters, beat your breast!"

It is probable that the later designation *taziya* is derived from the word for the awning (*ta'kieh*), erected over mosque courtyards and marketplaces. Eyewitnesses of the *taziya*—from Olearius, Tavernier, and Thévenot to Gobineau and Pelly—speak of the oppressive fanaticism of the performances, not about philology.

While the *taziya* performances in the remote highlands of the Islamic world and in the Caucasus have remained to this day a primitive affair—sometimes provided by a dervish functioning as a sort of ecstatic one-man show—in the cities a more and more costly popular festival has developed out of the *taziya*. Baghdad, Teheran, and Isfahan vied with one another in the getup and narrative richness of their plays. Until 1904, the *taziya* performances in the great arena theater Tekie-i Dalauti in Teheran were subsidized by the government. "After the revolution, however," writes Medjid Rezvani, "this theater faced a crisis, because the necessary funds that had previously come from private sources were no longer obtainable." And he quotes the remark of his Russian colleague Smirnoff: "The Persian mysteries are no less deserving of interest than the passion play at Oberammergau in Bavaria, which is visited by tourists from all over Europe and from America. It is the greatest pity that at a time when rail connections will be available not only for businessmen but also for tourists, Persia should lose this unique curiosity."

Today Teheran has a modern state theater, with every kind of

Taziya *in the open air, performed by wandering dervishes, 19th century.*

A performance of the Persian Husain play taziya, *in the court of the mosque at Rustemabad, 1860. (From H. Brugsch,* Reise der königlichen Preussischen Gesandtschaft nach Persien, *Leipzig, 1863.)*

technical equipment. Its program includes classical and avant-garde works of the international repertoire. The merit of having brought Shakespeare to the Persian stage for the first time belongs to the Zoroastrian Theater in Teheran, which was founded in 1927 and seats some four hundred spectators.

The rural people, however, cling as always to the traditional dance plays, to performances of an acrobatic, mythological, warlike, and folklore character. They confirm that what Herodotus has said still holds true, when he remarked that the Iranians have "at all times displayed a noticeable predilection for the dance." That predilection can be traced from the representations on the Sassanian silver bowls of antiquity down to the dancing dervishes of the twentieth century.

TURKEY

For the scholar of cultural history it would be both adventurous and revealing to draw a parallel between Alexander the Great and Genghis Khan. The immediacy and directness with which Alexander conveyed the spirit of the West to the East is balanced by the indirect influence of Genghis Khan upon the map of Europe. It was owing to the onslaught of the Mongols in the Far East and their harsh rule that the chieftain Suleiman in 1219 led his people from Turkestan to the region of the Euphrates. Suleiman's grandson Osman became the friend of the sultan of Konya and, succeeding to his throne in 1288, Osman became the founder of the Osmanli (Ottoman) dynasty. He created the expanding empire of the Turkish peoples whose warriors conquered the Balkans and drove on through North Africa to Spain, bringing with them their culture of minaret and mosques. Europe exhausted itself in its struggle against an avalanche that had begun with Genghis Khan. In 1922, with the abolition of the sultanate, the Ottoman empire officially came to an end, and a year later the Republic of Turkey was proclaimed.

Four major factors influenced the historical and cultural development of Turkey and, therefore, also Turkey's theater. These were: first, the shamanistic and vegetation rituals brought from Central Asia, which were to some extent blended with the Phrygian Dionysus cult and are still alive in Anatolian dances and games; second, the influence of antiquity more often denied than openly admitted; third, the rivalry with Byzantium; and, fourth, beginning with the tenth century, the decisive influence of Islam.

Konya, Bursa, and after 1453 the conquered city of Byzantium which is now Istanbul, were the capitals of the Ottoman empire and thus the centers of the Islamic world west and east of the Bosporus. At the Seljuk court in Konya parodies were performed and much enjoyed. Anna Comnena, daughter of a Byzantine emperor, gives proof of this in her historical work on Alexius Comnenus I (1069–1118). When the emperor Alexius in his old age was tormented by gout and thereby impeded in his campaigns against the Turks, farces were performed at the sultan's court in Konya, as his daughter Anna frankly relates, in which Alexius was satirized as a cowardly old man and a crybaby.

This is valuable information. It indicates the topicality and thematic orientation of Turkish farce. Impersonation and ridicule were the inexhaustible, vital sources of motif and inspiration in the Turkish improvisational comedy.

Along with the dancers and musicians, the traveling mimes, who were often called "impersonators," were never absent from festive occasions. They were prominent at the court and at market centers, in the baggage train of military campaigns and among diplomatic missions. When the Byzantine emperor Manuel Palaeologus II visited the Ottoman sultan Bayezid, he admired the sultan's versatile troupe of musicians, dancers, and actors.

The major characters of the Turkish comedy, Pishekar and Kavuklu, and the two shadow-play characters Karagöz and Hadjeivat traveled with Ottoman diplomatic missions through Greece, and on as far as Hungary and Austria. Along the Moldau and in Wallachia they became the ancestors of a new, independent, native form of theater. There were Turkish, Jewish, Armenian, and Greek mimes in the traveling troupes, but predominant were the Gypsies, who were well versed in every kind of juggling and conjury, dance and acrobatic entertainment.

Those who did not get to court played before the simple folk. And so developed the *orta oyunu*, a characteristically Turkish theater form, which still can be found in remote parts of Anatolia. *Orta oyunu* means "game of the middle," or "play the circle," or "play of the ring." It requires no particular equipment, and neither decor nor costume. (The Turkish theater historian Metin And points out that in Central Asia the word *oyun* also means the shaman's ritual of exorcism.)

An oval marked out on level ground is the acting area for the *orta oyunu*. The props required are no more than a three-cornered footstool and a double screen, to which sometimes are added a barrel, a market basket, and a few colorful umbrellas. The musicians, with oboe and kettledrum, squat at the edge of the acting area, and the audience stands

Theatrical reception ceremony at a Turkish palace. To the left, musicians with traditional instruments; in the center, a veiled woman. Miniature of the Ottoman period. (Istanbul, Topkapi Palace Museum.)

Scene from Turkish folk theater. Old hunchback, wearing pattens and dancing on a landing stage before a group of five people. To the left, musicians with wind and percussion instruments. Miniature of the Ottoman period (Istanbul, Topkapi Palace Museum.)

round about. The manager, director, extempore author, and protagonist is the character Pishekar. With flowery eloquence and a clacking wooden flail he opens the proceedings. The action and the comic element of the play are based on the variety of ethnic types represented, each of whom speaks broken Turkish in his own peculiar way—the Persian trader, the Armenian goldsmith, the Arab beggar, the Kurdish night watchman, the swaggering colonel of Janissaries, the Europeanized Levantine throwing his weight about, the quarrelsome market woman (impersonated by a man), the drunkard, and the unmistakable darling of the peasant audience, the clown Kavuklu with his jokes and tomfoolery, a close relative of Karagöz.

The origin and age of the *orta oyunu* are disputed. Its relationship to the antique mime is as obvious as a certain similarity to the *Commedia dell'arte.* Most striking of all, both in regard to the types of characters and to the resulting grotesque humor, is the parallel with Karagöz. In a 1675 manuscript it is asserted that a group of actors, dressed like the shadow-play characters, gave a performance at court.

Down to the nineteenth century the center of the *orta oyunu* was Kadiköy, a small town on the eastern shore of the Sea of Marmara, opposite Istanbul. Here also was the famous *tekke* (dervish monastery) where, on certain days of the week, the "howling dervishes" performed their ecstatic ritual. Their cousins, the dancing dervishes, preferred to go wandering through the country; it was always easy to gather a small circle of the curious and, after the prayer dance, to collect a few coins as reward. Today the dancing dervishes have become businesslike and appear as a tourist attraction at night clubs in Istanbul, Cairo, Aden, or Teheran.

The earliest Turkish theater with a pit for the orchestra and mechanically operated scenery appeared in the first half of the nineteenth century. Organized on the French and Italian pattern, it presented plays by Molière and Goldoni, and also Goethe's *Faust* and Lessing's *Nathan the Wise.* Jugglers, conjurers, and circus people, however, continued to get together their audience in wooden sheds and in tents. But in coffee and tea houses the centuries-old art of the *meddha,* the storyteller, continued in his old popularity. During the month of Ramadan, however, he retired and left the field clear for Karagöz.

In November 1867, during Ramadan, an Armenian by the name of Güllü Agop opened a Turkish theater in the Gedik Pasha quarter of Istanbul and called it "*orta oyunu* with a curtain." The circle play that had begun as an improvisation had arrived at a theater with a stage and an auditorium. Güllü Agop attracted talented native actors and writers.

The Gedik Pasha *orta oyunu* theater became a center of a national Turkish theater movement. In April 1873 it presented the first performance of the drama *Vatan* ("Homeland") by Namik Kemal. The play had a most enthusiastic tempestuous reception. The Sultan, sensing danger, banished the author. But, after the revolution of July 1908, Namik Kemal's star shone all the brighter: *Vatan* ran for weeks in all the theaters of the country.

Today, in the major cities and especially in Ankara, theaters offer a repertoire that, in addition to Turkish dramatists and composers, is truly international in its presentation of opera, musical comedy, ballet, and drama.

The Karagöz Shadow Play

Karagöz is the hero of the Turkish and Arab shadow-play theater, and for him the shadow play is named. The witty Karagöz, with his quick repartee, coarse puns, and earthy word play, has traveled far beyond his native land; he is at home in Greece and the Balkans, and in faraway places in Asia. A whole cluster of legends surrounds his origin. One of the most popular asserts that Karagöz—the name means "black eye"—and his companion Hadjeivat actually lived in the fourteenth century, at the time when the great mosque at Bursa was being erected. Their lively and grotesque verbal duels brought the building of the mosque to a standstill. Instead of working, the masons put down their trowels and listened to the long, amazing discourses of Karagöz and Hadjeivat. The sultan heard of their exploits—and ordered that both be hanged. Afterward, when he bitterly reproached himself, one of his courtiers had the idea of bringing Karagöz and Hadjeivat back to life in the shape of brightly colored, translucent leather figures and shadows on a linen screen: Karagöz with his beaky nose, black beard, cunning boot-button eyes, and violently gesticulating right hand; Hadjeivat in the dress of a merchant, cautious and meditative, good-natured and always being taken in. A range of picturesque types completed the ensemble of the shadow play: Celebi, the young dandy; the beautiful Messalina Zenne; Beberuhi, ingenuous dwarf; the Persian with his water pipe, the Albanian, and other regional characters; the opium addict; the drunkard.

An alleged tomb inscription for Karagöz at Bursa is attributed by Georg Jacob, a collector and expert on the Oriental shadow play, to the puppet master Mustafa Tevfik, who is supposed to have been active in this early period.

The shadow play was the favorite entertainment, both of the com-

Karagöz in women's clothes. As elsewhere, scenes in disguise were popular in the Turkish shadow-play theater. (From G. Jacob, Das Schattentheater in seiner Wanderung vom Morgenland zum Abendland, *Berlin, 1901.)*

mon folk and at the sultan's court. It was performed at marriages and circumcisions. But the greatest moment for Karagöz comes with the opening of Ramadan, the sacred month of fasting when, in the evening, everyone flocks to the coffeehouses. The Italian traveler Pietro della Valle, who arrived in Istanbul in 1614, has given a detailed account of the Turkish shadow play. "Indeed, at these inns, where they drink this drink," says della Valle in his *Viaggi,* published in 1650–58,

> there are, even during the time of their great fast, certain mountebanks and zanies who amuse the guests with all sorts of drollery and tomfoolery. Among the things they do, as I have seen myself, is that behind a cloth or painted paper, by the light of some torches, they give representations of ghosts and spirits who move, walk, and make all sorts of gestures in the very same way as is done in certain shows in our country. But these figures or puppets are not dumb as ours are; they make them talk just as the mountebanks do theirs at the castle in Naples or on the Piazza Navona in Rome. . . .
>
> Those who make these puppet plays also make them vocal or, rather, speak through them, by hiding themselves and then making their voice imitate various languages with all kinds of foolishness. Their performances are nothing but indecent farces and improper goings-on between man and woman with such gross gestures as they imitate the occasions of lust, that they could not be worse during a Shrove Tuesday carnival at a public whorehouse than they are during their fast.

Despite his crude jokes and hearty obscenities Karagöz eluded the shackles of the religious authorities. The puppets, which were moved by rods and were cut out of leather or parchment into which holes were punched here and there to let the light shine through, could not easily be described as images of human beings and thus got around the Koran prohibition. The use of stock types offered scope for satire and polemics in a seemingly harmless disguise. There was no human frailty, no arrogance of rank, no topical abuse that Karagöz did not hold up to laughter.

From the Bosporus, Karagöz wandered northward; he was at home throughout the Islamic world. He always called a spade a spade and was applauded even when people could barely understand the words, for they could not miss the meaning of the grotesque humor of the action.

When Karagöz once all too plainly aimed at the corruption of the court, in 1870, under Sultan Abdülaziz he was forbidden to engage in any further political satire; but then the journalists imitated his aggressive spirit. And even today a popular political weekly in Turkey is called *Karagöz.*

The Indo-Pacific Civilizations

INTRODUCTION

In classical India the dance and the drama were two equally important components of one great creed; they both served to express homage to the gods. Shiva, the ruler over earthly death and rebirth, was represented as the King of Dancers. In India's tradition, Brahma himself, the creator of the universe, also created the art of drama, and its close ties with religion for many centuries were expressed in the initial benediction and purification ceremony that preceded every theatrical performance.

India's three great religions—Brahmanism, Jainism, and Buddhism—all imparted their specific forms to cult and sacrifice, to the dance, and to demon-averting pantomime and dramatic recitation alike.

Neither the victorious campaigns of Alexander the Great nor Mohammed's teaching succeeded in undermining the vigorous inner strength of Hinduism. Its gods and heroes dominate the stage of the celestial pantheon just as much as the stage of earthly reality.

The anthropomorphic conceptualization of the gods provided the first impulse to drama. Its origin and principles are recorded in utmost detail and with painstaking scholarship by the sage Bharata in his *Natyasastra,* a manual of the arts of dancing and acting. But tradition gives us no facts concerning the practices of performance. It is characteristic of the ahistoric mentality of the Indians that the precision of the mythological aspects of the drama has no equivalent in its practice of acting. What was preserved was not the earth-bound reality, but the spirit. And therefore, the theatrical researcher must look for clues by working laboriously through the thicket of the Vedic sacrificial rites and invocation of the gods, through the ritual chants of the Brahmans, and through the rites of the Jainist and Buddhist religions, offsprings of Brahmanism which developed during the first millennium B.C.

Since the turn of the millennium, the old Vedic gods had been overshadowed by Shiva, the prince of dancers, mummers, and musicians, and by Vishnu and his wife Lakshmi whose beauty resembles that of the lotus flower. Religious activity was determined by the cult of the temples and idols. The *Ramayana,* which relates the adventures of the royal prince Rama and his wife Sita, and the second great Indian epic, the *Mahabharata,* with its wealth of mythological and moral wisdom, became the great common heritage of all Indo-Pacific civilizations. The monkey-god Hanuman establishes the connection with Buddhism in China and eventually with the *wayang* plays of the Indonesian islands.

Under the Gupta dynasty, in the fourth century A.D., Northern India enjoyed a brief period of political unity, which resulted in a flowering of the arts. In this period Kalidasa wrote his drama *Shakuntala.* (The literary world of Europe became acquainted with *Shakuntala* in 1789 in an English version and two years later in a German translation.)

During the reign of Harsha, who ruled the great Hindu empire from 606 to 647, the culture of India and the Buddhist doctrine spread throughout East Asia and the Indonesian islands, influencing temple and palace architecture, epic and drama.

The irruption of Islam and, in the sixteenth century, the rise of the Mogul empire with its strong Islamic central power, changed only the outward appearance of India, not its conservative spirit. The Hindus held fast to their beliefs, character, and way of thinking. There was always a contrast between the Indian's political passivity and his strong inner bond with religious tradition. He held fast to his religious convictions. Shiva, Vishnu, Krishna, and Rama were never dethroned in India's drama. When, on January 30, 1948, Gandhi was hit by the bullet of his assassin Naturam Godse, he fell to the ground calling to the God: "Hè, Rama."

INDIA

The origin of India's theater lies in the close link between dance and temple cult. The art of dance pleases the gods; it is a visible expression of men's homage to the gods and of their power over men. No other religion has so magnificently glorified the ritual (and erotic) dance. Stone images of gods and goddesses in a dancing embrace, celestial musicians, nymphs and girl tambourinists in provocative poses adorn the walls, columns, gables, and gateways of Indian temples. Representations of the dance can be found through three-and-a-half thousand years of Indian sculpture, ranging from the famous bronze statuette of the "Dancing Girl" at the ruined city of Mohenjo-Daro on the lower Indus to the reliefs on the columns of the Hindu temple at Cidambaram, display all the 108 positions of classical Indian dance according to Bharata's *Natyasastra.*

The dancing girls were under the authority of the temple priests and exercised their art, to the extent that it had to do with the cult, within the temple precincts. The temple grounds, often enormous and laid out in terraces over whole hillsides, included traditional places for religious dances and music. There was a special assembly and dance hall (*natamandira*) and, for more general purposes, a "celebration hall" (*mandapa*) where dancing girls, musicians, and reciters gave performances in honor of the gods. At some temples in southern India, such as the Jagannath temple at Puri, it is still the custom today for the *devadasis,* the temple's dancing girls, to dance at the ceremonial evening service.

Historians of the Indian theater have coined the concept "temple theater," which can be traced architecturally through the centuries. Among the eighth-century rock-cut temples in the Ellora caves there stands the beautiful theater hall of the Kailasa temple. And there are elaborate festival and theater halls in the eleventh-century Ghantai temple grounds near Khajuraho. Others can be found in the twelfth-century temple complex of Girnar and at the Vitthala Temple of the fourteenth-century Vijayanagar rulers.

Alongside the "temple theater," the theater had another precursor in India's highly developed form of popular folk entertainment, with its dancing and acrobatics. The dancer always was also a mime and an actor, all in one. He is still called *nata,* which is the vernacular, *Prakrit,* word for actor (from the Sanskrit root *nrt*). While the *natas* are, on the one hand, akin to the ritual dancers and dancing girls (*nrtu*), who are mentioned as far back as the *Rig Veda,* the Prakrit vernacular form *nata* indicates their popular character.

For while ritual dancers honored the gods, there were at all times itinerant singers, dancers, and mimes who entertained the people with their performances for a modest fee. The *Ramayana* mentions *nata, nartaka, nataka*—that is, dances and theatrical performances—in towns and palaces. It tells of feasts and gatherings at which entertainment was provided by actors and dancing girls.

The *nati,* the dancing girl of old Indian literature, was there for everyone. She was the *bayadère,* whom Goethe described in a ballad, the "lost, lovely child" who hospitably invited the stranger: "Ask for rest, diversion, pleasure, /All your bidding I will do."

Young female Indian dancer and musicians. Stone relief from the Temple of Purana Mahadeo, Harshagiri. Rajasthan 961–73.

Dance and theater hall of the Temple of Vitthala, Vijayanagar dynasty, 1350–65. The "celebration hall" (mandapa) *stands apart from the temple and is richly decorated with sculptures.*

Troupe of popular entertainers in an Indian town. Men and women acrobats, jugglers, and tightrope walkers. To the left, musicians; to the right, spectators. Mogul style, 18th century. (Berlin, Staatliche Museen.)

Patanjali, the Indian grammarian of the second century B.C., tells of a dancing girl (*nati*) performing on the stage who, on being asked, "To whom do you belong?" answered, "I belong to you."

The *Dharmasastras*, the metrical lawbooks, explicitly state that a dancing girl's husband need not pay her debts, because she has "earnings" of her own, and that she need not be treated with the respect owed to another man's wife. In *Kamasutra*, the "book of love," the dancing girl (*nati*) has to accept the lowest position among the courtesans.

But eventually she entered classical drama through a back door—as a deputy of Vidusaka, the Indian harlequin. In the introductory trialogue the female dancer, usually the manager's wife, may occasionally stand in for Vidusaka. Nevertheless, the art of the dance developed independently of the drama, and has survived to this day in its four characteristic forms of *bharata natyam, kathakali, kathak,* and *manipuri*.

The *bharata natyam* is a direct descendant of the supple graceful art of the temple dancing girls. It is practiced especially in southern India, in Madras, and derives both its dancing positions and its name from Bharata's manual of the art of dancing and acting, the *Natyasastra*. The pantomime dance drama *kathakali*, which developed into its present form at Malabar, is decidedly masculine in character. Its characteristic features are masks of heavy makeup, sumptuous and billowing costumes, and the grotesque dancing style of its characters—gods, heroes, monkeys, and monsters. The *kathak* is a less severe, more variable form of dancing, in which masculine strength and feminine grace intermingle; it developed in northern India, under the influence of the Mogul rulers. The *manipuri*, which is popular mainly in the mountains of Assam, is a dance of slow, almost serpentine movements. It has its origin in the mythical world of the gods; for *manipuri*, says the legend, was the dance the shepherdesses danced to Krishna's flute.

Bharata's "Natyasastra"

All our knowledge of the classical Indian theater derives from the one fundamental work: Bharata's *Natyasastra*. All the threads of the past converge in it, all that came later is built upon it. Sanskrit scholars believe that the author Bharata, a half-legendary, half-historical figure, lived some time between 200 B.C. and 200 A.D. It is characteristic of the Indians' lack of a sense of history that Bharata, one of their greatest and most influential sages, cannot be dated. His mythological relationship with the gods is beyond doubt, but so far, scholars can merely conjecture

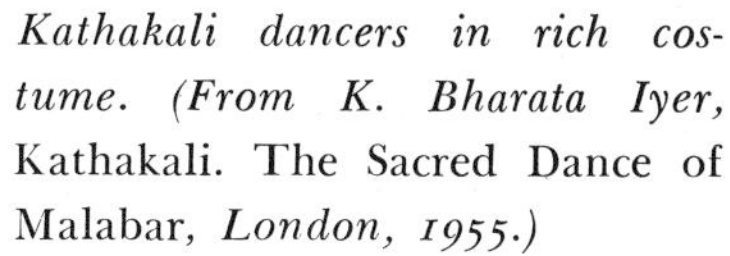

Kathakali dancers in rich costume. (From K. Bharata Iyer, Kathakali. The Sacred Dance of Malabar, *London, 1955.)*

Dance of Krishna and the shepherdesses (gopis). *Top left, two musicians in animal masks. Miniature from the second half of the 18th century. (New Delhi, Lalit Kala Academy.)*

about the facts of his life. Scholars now generally accept that Bharata wrote at a time when the early forms of ritual dance, mime, and popular entertainment began to merge in the new art form of the drama. Bharata laid the cornerstone of India's theater art; he laid down all its artistic rules, its language and stage techniques.

As he tells the story in the first chapter of *Natyasastra,* drama owes its origin to the god Brahma, the creator of the universe. Bharata relates that one day the god Indra asked Brahma to invent an art form that would be both visible and audible and could be understood by men in all conditions and of all walks of life. So Brahma considered the content of the four Vedas, the sacred books of Indian wisdom, and took one component from each—the spoken word from the *Rig Veda,* song from the *Sama Veda,* mime from the *Yajur Veda,* and emotion from the *Atharva Veda.* All these he combined in a fifth Veda, the *Natya Veda,* which he communicated to the human sage Bharata. And Bharata, to the benefit of all mankind, wrote down the divine rules of dramaturgical art in the *Natyasastra,* the manual of dancing and acting.

The first drama, according to Bharata, was performed at a celestial celebration in honor of the god Indra. When the play was approaching its climax, the victory of the gods over the demons, unbidden evil spirits suddenly paralyzed the performers' gestures, miming, speech, and memory. Angrily the god Indra raised the jeweled staff of his banner (*jarjara*) and smote the demons. The actors came to life again. And the god Brahma promised their art eternal validity that would endure beyond all strife: "For there is no learning, no skill, no science, and none of the fine arts, no religious meditation, and no pious deed which cannot be found in the drama." Ever since, Indian actors have carried Indra's staff in their baggage as a talisman. It has accompanied them through the ages in the form of a modest bamboo stick decorated with colored ribbons. But the god Indra, the daring tamer of demons and killer of dragons, was debased into a well-fed, sanguine fellow, the Indian equivalent of Offenbach's *Orpheus in the Underworld.*

The overriding importance attached in all Far Eastern theater to external form, to the rigidly defined expressive art of the human body, is amply documented in the *Natyasastra.* Dancing and acting are conceptually one. Bharata demands from both the dancer and the actor extreme concentration, down to the very fingertips, according to a precisely detailed schedule. His manual lists 24 variants of finger signs, 13 movements of the head, 7 of the eyebrows, 6 of the nose, 6 of the cheeks, 9 of the neck, 7 of the chin, 5 of the chest, and 36 of the eyes. Bharata leaves no room for intuitive spontaneity in this art; its rules resemble a sum of mathematical values. For the actor's feet, he lists 16 positions on the ground and 16 in the air—and numberless stock modes of walking designed to portray various types of characters: striding, mincing, limping, shuffling. A courtesan moves with a swaying gait, a court lady with mincing steps; a fool walks with his toes pointed upward, a courtier with solemn steps, and a beggar with a shuffle.

Here the pen of the erudite theoretician Bharata was clearly guided by the mime standing behind him—unnamed and unrecognized, but timelessly present and sure of his art of mimicry without the need of learned dogmatics. The mime, always and everywhere, has learned his tricks from life itself; he has used them unadorned, without literary sophistication and, especially in the Karagöz of the Near East, with delighted obscenity.

Bharata's strict code of gestures is matched by corresponding rules for language—Sanskrit for the educated class, Prakrit for the uneducated—by the definition of the various stock roles, costumes and masks, as well as rules for the tonality of the spoken word and for the musical accompaniment. And so his code culminates in the scientific classification of the species of drama.

In the second and third chapters of the *Natyasastra* Bharata discusses the problems of theater technique. He takes up the question of theater buildings, their dimensions and arrangements. Bharata declares that while performances usually take place in temples and palaces, the following rules should nevertheless be followed in planning a theater. A rectangular site is to be divided into two squares: an auditorium and a

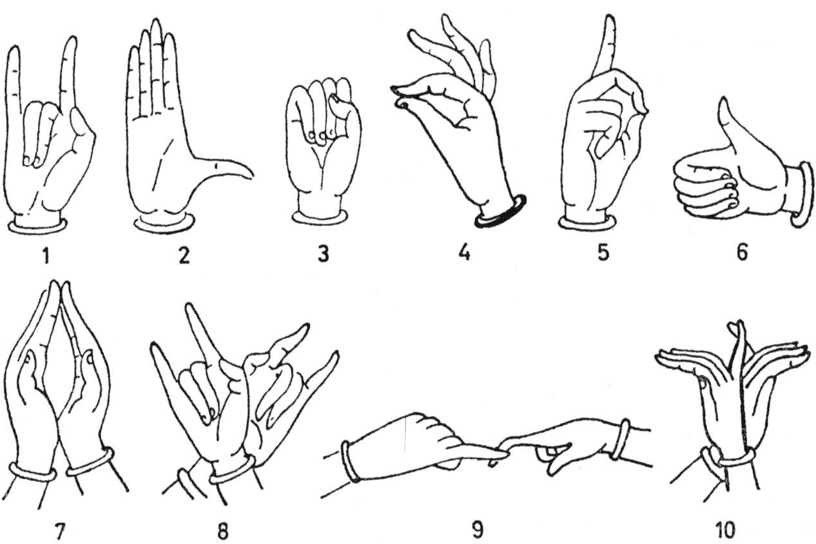

Finger language (mudras) *of the Indian art of dancing and acting: 1–separation, death; 2–meditation; 3–determination; 4–joy; 5–concentration; 6–rejection; 7–veneration; 8–proposal; 9–vexation; 10–love.*

stage. Four columns are to hold up the roof beams. The color scheme must strictly follow traditional symbolism: the white column stands for the Brahmans; the red for the king and the nobility; the yellow for the citizenry; blue-black for the caste of artisans thieves, and day laborers. (And all these are the colors of Indra's staff.)

At the eastern end of the terraced auditorium the king sits on his throne, surrounded by ministers, poets, and sages, with the ladies of the court to his left. The stage, as the entire building, is richly decorated with wood carvings and pottery reliefs. It is divided by a curtain into a fore and a backstage. The actors and dancers appear on the forestage, while their dressing rooms are backstage, hidden by a dividing curtain. The sources of acoustic effects, representing divine voices, the noise of crowds and battle, are also kept backstage and invisible to the public.

Bharata calls the dividing curtain *yavanika* and this term has unleashed a flood of theories about Greek influence on the Indian theater. Philologically, it certainly is tempting to establish a connection with the word *javanika,* meaning "Greek," or "Doric," but with reference to the stage curtain it is purely hypothetical. From the point of view of cultural history, it would be interesting to investigate to what extent Greek theaters in Asia Minor, as in Pergamon, Priene, or Aspendus, were used by non-Hellenic troupes of actors and to look for possible influences from this source of India.

The famous Sitabenga cave in Sirguja, in the northeastern part of Madhya Pradesh, suggests another explanation for Bharata's curtain; it may derive from a different kind of theater art: the shadow play. The Sitabenga cave has its place in the history of India's theater. The assumption that it was a sort of playhouse "in the form of a mountain cave" seems to be supported by passages in *Natyasastra.* The cave's internal dimensions are 44 × 10 feet, and it had room for about thirty spectators. Grooves and notches have been found at the entrance which may have served to secure a cloth screen. This would mean that the audience—a small number of initiates rather than a princely court in Bharata's sense—sat inside the densely crowded cave, while the shadow player made use of the daylight outside in projecting the mythological world of his flat, leather puppets. However, the cave of Sirguja was not a theater according to Bharata's prescriptions.

Although Bharata's erudite verse treatise does not expressly deal with the shadow play, this does not preclude his knowledge and use of it—for its importance for the whole Far Eastern culture is a proved fact. It is quite conceivable that it may have been used as a stage effect in classical Indian theater.

The second-century (B.C.) grammarian Patanjali, in his commentary on Panini, tells of people who gave recitals of stories in front of pictures "showing the events." Presumably he means the sort of shadow play that was to become characteristic of Siam, Java, Bali, and China. In a later commentary on Patanjali's term for the player, the tenth-century writer Somadevasuri explains, in his *Nitivakyamrta*, that a *saubhika* was a man who "at night makes various personages visible with the help of a cloth curtain." Beginning with the second half of the first millennium we also find the term *chayanataka* for shadow play; it first occurs in the seventh century in a Sakian didactic poem, presumably based on older sources.

Which came first, the Indian or the Chinese shadow play? This is still a controversial question, as there are so few sources. India's claim is supported by the evidence of the early shadow-play theater in the Sitabenga cave and by the fact that the shadow play's cultural influence spread throughout the Far East. It is quite conceivable that it followed the advance of Buddhism through Central Asia or Indochina to China. China's Middle Kingdom, on the other hand, claims in one of its most beautiful and wistful legends that the conjuration of spirits upon the linen screen is its very own invention.

Classical Drama

Classical Indian drama encompasses the whole range of life, both in heaven and on earth. As the fifth-century poet Kalidasa once said, it should "simultaneously satisfy the most diverse people with the most diverse tastes."

The spiritual ancestry of the classical Indian drama can be traced to the dialogues of the *Rig Veda,* which were couched in the form of balladlike poems and were recited antiphonically at sacred sacrificial rites. Their dramatic content, the love of the human king Pururavas for the celestial nymph Urvasi and the conflict with their opponents, the dark, mythical powers, provided endless material for theatrical treatment, indeed for grand opera. The *Rig Veda* dialogues became the most popular themes of the whole of Indian and Indian-influenced drama, though they themselves were not yet drama. In the form handed down to us they represent a highly developed stage of sophisticated poetry, but not ceremonial texts aiming at theatrical effect.

Starting from epic recitation at the time of the Vedas, from the early puppet or shadow players who were credited with magic powers, and from the mimes who provided a vivifying element, there was a long way to go to a drama fit to be staged.

The jester Vidusaka had played his pranks already among the itinerant mummers. With his big belly and bald head, he is a relation of the

Greek mime—a good-natured but sly dolt—an Indian harlequin who likes his comfort and eats a lot with obvious relish. In later dramatic works he turns into an obliging servant and reliable friend, who applies the right amount of cheek and horse sense in extricating his master from a scrape whenever the helper can do himself some good at the same time.

Classical Indian drama draws Vidusaka into the action. He is no longer a mere improvising clown but a character in the play, and as such is precisely defined by the author. He first comes upon the stage in the introductory scene, the traditional *purvaranga.* He participates in the subsequent trialogue (*trigata*) together with the manager and his principal assistant. (The manager, who is also the producer, director, and leading actor, is called *sutradhara,* that is, literally, "the string-holder." It is tempting to trace this, too, back to the puppet or shadow play.)

India's classical drama is contemplative. The author places his characters in an atmosphere of emotion, not in an arena of the passions as, say, Euripides or Racine do. The Indian dramatist does not push spiritual conflicts to the point of self-destruction. Nor is his aim catharsis in the Aristotelian sense. He is concerned with the stylized refinement of sentiments, with the aesthetics of suffering. On this plane the two aspects of old Indian poetry come into play: *rasa,* the mood or ambiance, which the work as pure aesthetic enjoyment is to arouse in the spectator; and *bhava,* the affective state and emotion—be it sympathy or antipathy—created and conveyed by the competent actor. We find a similar definition in the work of Seami, the great fifteenth-century Japanese playwright, actor, and theoretician of the *nō* theater. Seami defines *yūgen,* a concept derived from Buddhist doctrine, as the secret power that gives birth to beauty, the beauty of happiness as well as the beauty of despair.

Both in India and in Japan the actor's art culminates in the perfection of the dance. In Bharata's *Natyasastra* the concept of *nataka* (dance representation, or representation by dance) applies equally to the literary drama.

In the introductory scene (*purvaranga*) which, with its religious solemnity, harks back to ritual origins, the theater manager throws a bridge back to the world of myth, when, followed by two companions bearing a jug of water and the Indra staff, he makes his entry on the stage, strews it with flowers, plants the staff to one side and washes himself with water from the jug.

In the following trialogue, Vidusaka leaps upon the stage. He reminds the manager and his assistant that folly must have its place in life and also on the stage, which means to be life's mirror.

The introductory scene and the trialogue are followed by the action, which is interspersed with contemporary scenes from common or courtly life at the author's time (*prakarana*), portraying the goings-on among the doings of Brahmans, merchants, court officials, priests, ministers, or caravan owners in a freely devised plot. Vidusaka makes his appearance here, too—in the garb of a Brahman who, however, does not speak the literary Sanskrit as he should, but the vernacular Prakrit. He has sunk from his high station and become a poor, much-abused parasite, and is the butt of irony and allusions. As the spiritual role of the Brahmans deteriorated and withered in convention, they had to endure much mockery. But to Vidusaka the part of a down-at-the-heels Brahman gave much scope for clowning in a parody of self-pity.

Indian classical theater derives its realistic effects from the variations of speech—as between high and low, Sanskrit and Prakrit, persons of rank and members of the lower castes. But this is a highly stylized realism. Real life is reflected only in the pattern, not in its application on the stage.

The earliest fragments of Indian Sanskrit dramas were found in Turkestan. They were written by the great Buddhist poet Asvaghosha (around A.D. 100), who was also the author of the famous epic poem *Buddhacharita,* which is the story of Buddha's life. Asvaghosha's stage directions are characteristic of the more liberal approach of early Mahayana Buddhism. He actually puts Buddha on the stage, "surrounded by a radiant circle of light," and in one of the surviving fragments even

Indian theater stage for classical drama, according to Bharata's Natyasastra.

gives him lines to speak—in Sanskrit, naturally. This kind of personification would have been inconceivable in an earlier period of Buddhism. In the early centuries of Indian plastic art, a symbol only—the Wheel of the Law or the Tree of Enlightenment—indicated the presence of Buddha.

The medium of the shadow play comes to mind when we consider the works of Bhasa, which probably dates from the second to third century. In two of his plays, *Dutavakya* and *Balacarita,* the author requires that Vishnu's miracle-working weapons, his mount and even the mythological giant bird Garuda, appear in the play as speaking actors. Under India's religious prohibitions, how could that possibly have been done except on the cloth screen? It is tempting to think of shadow-play fade-ins.

Bhasa's most famous drama is *Charudatta,* a play in what we would call a middle-class setting. It tells of Charudatta, a merchant who has become impoverished because of his own generosity and his love for the noble-minded courtesan Vasantasena. Both characters recur in the better-known *Little Clay Cart (Mrichhakatika),* a later play based on the same theme. Its manuscript was found in Travancore, a remote corner of southwest India. With its effective gradations of Sanskrit and Prakrit, its careful characterizations and emotional exuberance—Vasantasena piles all her jewels into the toy clay cart of Charudatta's little son—the drama gives a colorful picture of life and manners from India's past. The play has been attributed to King Sudraka, who reigned in the third and fourth centuries. If the assumption is correct, *The Little Clay Cart* would testify not only to its author's genius, but also to the high quality of dramatic art at the royal court—regardless of whether it was written by the king himself or merely dedicated to him.

Kalidasa, India's best-known dramatist and author of *Shakuntala,* also was a court poet. He lived in the fifth century, at the time of the Gupta dynasty. His plays hark back to the sacred myths; they tell of mysterious powers, of how Urvasi is rescued by heroic valor and how Shakuntala is saved, recognized because of a ring. But ultimately Kalidasa conceives the characters of the Vedic legends in terms of his own time's courtly way of life. Shakuntala is presented as a refined, aristocratic lady rather than as an uninhibited child of nature; the legend's companion of gazelles and watchful sister of trees and flowers becomes the sensitive creature of an "artificial naturalness," resembling the characters in the pastoral plays of eighteenth-century Europe.

The enthusiastic response aroused by Kalidasa's lyrical love story in Herder, Goethe, and the Romantics is explained by the presumed naive innocence of the hermit's life, an innocence which Shakuntala was believed to incarnate—an ideal state long lost to Europe, and assumed by

Herder to survive only in the Orient. The Romantics hailed Kalidasa as their spiritual brother, who "charmingly draped the truth with poetry's magic veil." Herder compared Kalidasa's dramatic style with the Aristotelian rules. Goethe extolled the Indian shepherdess in an enraptured distich in *Der Westöstliche Divan*: "Heaven together with earth in a single word to encompass: Think of Shakuntala's name; nothing remains to be said."

When, toward the end of the nineteenth century, the symbolists retired into their symbolic woods, when Maeterlinck wrote his lyrical love drama *Pelléas et Mélisande, Shakuntala* made a brief comeback on the Western stage. Kalidasa's play was produced in Berlin, Paris, and New York. But, together with symbolist poetry, it soon disappeared once more into the treasure-house of the literature of the ages.

We do not know in what external setting and with what theatrical means Kalidasa's dramas were produced in India during his lifetime. The intensive poetic imagery of the dialogue suggests a décor relying mainly on the spoken word, and that, as in the Elizabethan English and the classical Spanish drama, it was the word that created the scenery. The dramatic text itself prescribes the stage properties to be used, such as the cloak that is to be held in readiness when Shakuntala's two girl companions urge upon her that it is time to depart: "Cover yourself now with the double cloak, Shakuntala, for we are ready." The same plastic diction is used by Shakespeare, when Cleopatra in her great death scene says: "Give me my robe, put on my crown; I have/immortal longings in me."

There are also suggestions of shadow-play fade-ins in *Shakuntala*, for instance in the fourth act, when the nymph Sanumati appears in a carriage of clouds. Although the director must have relied heavily on the audience's imagination, he may well have used visual aids as well. Such interludes, most likely, were not unusual. The play within the play was very popular in classical drama, not least with the author himself. In the play *Priyadarsika*, for instance, it is a central motif. This play is ascribed to Emperor Harsha, who in the first half of the seventh century helped the united Hindu empire to a brief period of glory.

Indian theater directors were most conscientious in the production of their plays, as we can deduce from a fragment of accounts relating to the production of *Ratnavali*, another of Harsha's plays. These accounts date from the reign of Jayapida of Kashmir in the eighth century. Their cost estimates for a performance of *Ratnavali* list all the items needed to execute the author's stage directions.

In the Buddhist monasteries of Tibet the classical Indian drama developed into didactic plays, conveying moral lessons. Alongside the shamanistic bards, who glorified the great deeds of Kesar, the hero of a

Tibetan epic, we find Tibetan dramas closely following the Indian model. The drama *Zugiñima* will serve as an example. It conveys the story of Queen Zugiñima, who is driven from the palace because of false accusations and delivered into the hands of her executioners. Eventually, she is saved by her faith from the torments of body and soul. *Zugiñima* reflects the influence of Buddhist missionaries in Tibet. The drama was written in the eleventh century, but its roots seem to reach back to *Shakuntala*. Traditions and themes of the Indian theater, long faded and overtaken in India itself, survived in Tibet, where dramas like *Zugiñima* were performed at Lhasa well into the twentieth century.

Around 700 A.D., the Indian dramatist Bhavabhuti resurrected the old Rama legends and brought them to new glory. The wealth and intensity of his range of characterization, "up to the uttermost bounds of love," put him on a par with Kalidasa, whom indeed he surpassed in emotional spontaneity, even though he could not match Kalidasa's sublime diction. Bhavabhuti put the force of destiny before grace of expression. To judge from the ceremonial of his introductory scenes, Bhavabhuti's dramas were intended for performances on specific religious feast days.

A Brahman from an orthodox family, Bhavabhuti banished the jester from his plays. But ultimately his reforming zeal came to naught. For in the meantime Vidusaka had set off on his own. In the *Bhana*, a humorous one-act monologue especially popular in southern India, he appears on the stage as a solo performer. He found a second domain in the *vithis* (from *vita*, "man of the world"), which were a sort of one-man cabaret, dealing with indiscretions among courtiers and courtesans, with cockfights and with the most timeless of all vices, venal love. Vidusaka took on the complexion of his Turkish brother Karagöz and yielded nothing to him in *double entendre*.

Farce and burlesque (*prahasana*), too, came into their own on the Indian stage. They probably developed quite early, alongside the classical drama. While in *Charudatta* and in *The Little Clay Cart* the Brahmans came in for a good deal of mockery, the authors of the farcical plays satirized the many sham Sivaite and Buddhist ascetics, who covered up their dissolute life with the mantle of piety. The oldest known work of this kind is *Mattavilasa-prahasana*, which is attributed to the seventh-century king Mahendra-Vikramavarman. With grotesque and cutting satire it attacks the excesses of debased asceticism and exposes, as the title promises, "the pranks of the drunkards." A few other farces survived from the period of the twelfth to sixteenth centuries; they satirize the goings-on in brothels, the affairs between ascetics and their disciples, and cliquishness at the princely courts. The later Sanskrit dramas, however, were pale and bloodless academic exercises in style,

Scene from Shakuntala, *by Kalidasa: first encounter between King Dushyanta and Shakuntala. Miniature from a Hindi manuscript, 1789. (New Delhi, National Museum.)*

Clay figurine of Cham da[...] Hoshang, the potbellied Bu[...] was a favorite comic figure o[...] Tibetan dance drama. Accordi[...] legend, Hoshang, with his her[...] doctrines, endangered the wor[...] conversion, but was exiled [...] being defeated in religious dis[...]tion. (Vienna, Museum für V[...]kunde.)

The great carriage of Mahendranath in the procession of the religious theatrical festival at Katmandu, 1953. (From: Toni Hagen, Nepal—Königreich im Himalaya, *1960. By courtesy of the publishers, Kümmerly & Frey, Berne.)*

without relation to the stage or any literary merit, of value only to the philologist.

It was not until the early twentieth century that, thanks to Rabindranath Tagore, Indian drama once more gained world renown. The poet Tagore was also a vigorous dramatist, actor, and producer. He drew both on the old Sanskrit tradition and on the modern drama of ideas to develop a new, specifically Indian style, which may be described as a loosely woven plot heavily fraught with symbolism and garbed in lyrical, romantic language. He revived the role of rhapsodist who gives a running commentary on the action, which is presented in pantomime. Tagore's work invites comparison with the epic theater of Bertolt Brecht and Thornton Wilder. Tagore's figures often remain shadowy and unreal, creatures of the borderland between fantasy and reality, made even more intangible by their melancholy songs. His plays, he once said, can be understood only if one listens to them as one would to the music of a flute.

They need no external display, hardly a prop, a minimum of décor. Like ferrymen from another world, they appeal to the imagination of the audience, both the Indian public of Tagore's native Bengal and European audiences at the International Theatre Festival in New Delhi. At the beginning of his play *The Cycle of Spring* Tagore says with poetic self-sufficiency: "We need no scenery. The only backcloth we need is the backcloth of the imagination, upon which we shall paint a picture with the brush of music."

INDONESIA

When Hinduism, coming from India in the wake of Indian seafarers, merchants, and priests, extended its domination over the Indonesian island empires, there developed in Java the most beautiful and famous of Southeast Asia's theater forms, the shadow play or *wayang* play. To this day, its four characteristic variants can be found all over the islands. Its graceful actors—the flat figures, cut out of transparent leather, and the wooden dolls, carved in the round or half-round, with their enigmatic, narrow eyes—now are highly prized by museum curators and private collectors.

The origins of the *wayang* plays no doubt go back to the pre-Hindu time of Javanese ancestor worship. Certain ceremonial rules, such as the initial exclusion of women from the audience and, later and still often to this day, their segregation from male spectators, suggest a close con-

Terracotta heads from Indian comedy: male and female types, as customary in the Bhana, a cabaretlike satirical one-act play. 19th century. (Poona, Archaeological Museum of the Deccan College.)

nection with initiation rites—a connection, incidentally, that also exists in the Turkish shadow play. The *wayang* play acquired its distinctive features during the high period of Hindu-Javanese civilization. It absorbed the old Vedic myths of the gods, the *Ramayana* and the *Mahabharata,* and draws on the wealth of these two great Indian epics' characters and their conflicts in war and peace. The *wayang* play is as rich in descriptive representation as are the figure friezes of Hindu-Javanese temples, the wall and gateway reliefs of Prambanan, Lara Janggrang, Borobodur, or Panataran.

The term *wayang purwa* testifies to the great age of the play. *Wayang* means shadow (later also spectacle in the wider sense); *purba,* or *purwa,* means old, belonging to remote antiquity. The *wayang purwa* has never become a mere profane entertainment; to this day it has not lost its magic function of mediator between man and the metaphysical world.

Early in the eleventh century, Javanese literature first mentions the *wayang purwa* as a widespread form of art. By the middle of the eleventh century, it was popular at the courts of Kediri, Shingasari, and Majapahit. After the political upheavals of the fifteenth and sixteenth centuries, it found a new home in the famous Kraton, the palace at Mataram, which developed into the cultural center of the island of Java.

The first records of Indonesian *wayang* figures made of leather date from the period of Sultan Demak (about 1430). Here, too, is the origin of the term *wayang kulit* (*kulit* means leather). The artfully cut and perforated figures are usually made of buffalo hide. The face is always shown in profile, the body usually half-frontal; the feet point sideways, following the direction of the face. The figure is firmly mounted on rods of buffalo horn; its shoulders and elbows are movable and can be guided with the aid of two thin rods. Since ancient times, the outline and design of the *wayang* figures have been strictly codified. Every line, every decorative feature, every characteristic of the body, every ornamental variation has its definite, symbolic meaning. Indeed, the puppet-maker has to be both master of the iconographic rules and of his knife and chisel. First, his character has to conform to iconographic specifications. Then, with knife and chisel, the puppet-maker produces the fine lattice work of the costume and coiffure, the helmet or crown. The strange, unearthy beauty of the figures is heightened by the ornamental use of gold leaf, glowing turquoise, deep-red, and black.

The *wayang kulit* is usually performed at night (except for the *ngruwat lakon,* a special ceremony symbolizing the exorcism of demons). It is projected onto a screen made of canvas stretched on a wooden frame and lit up by the mild glow of an oil lamp. The play is produced by the *dalang* (narrator), who skillfully brings to life his numerous cast.

In a box to his left the representatives of evil await their curtain call: the demons, traitors, spies, and wild animals, and in another box to his right queens and noble ladies, the hero's faithful helpers and companions-in-arms await their appearance. There are the five Pandavas, the warlike heirs of the kingdom of Astinapura; their well-meaning adviser Kresna and the tyrannical Werkudara with his characteristic claw thumb; there is the king's beautiful son Arjuna and his heir Abimanyu, both often shown a-courting and often accompanied by fat, old Semar and his sons, the "clowns" of the *wayang kulit*. But there are also King Pandu's bastard son, Adipati Karna, and the dangerous schemer, the Prime Minister Patih Sengkuni, both waiting for the moment of vengeance.

How the *dalang* manages to move this throng of figures with only two hands is his own secret. In addition, he also conducts the musicians, giving them their cues by tapping them out with a little mallet made of wood or horn. If need be, the *dalang* himself can accompany his narrative with sound effects produced with the help of little disks made of wood and metal and attached to the boxes in which he stores his puppets. If his hands are not free, he kicks the disks with his feet.

The play's action is determined by the *lakon*, a sort of exposé, laying down a specific plot based on traditional, structural models. After the introductory *gamelan* music the *dalang* pronounces the traditional incantation: "Be silent and depart, devilish beings—*suruh rep data pitana*!"

Before the play begins, the *dalang* gives a detailed description of the place and characters, and he introduces the action of the play as such; the successive phases will last all night long. From nine in the

The clowns of the Javanese wayang *play: (from left to right) Semar, Gareng, Petruk, and Bagong. From R. L. Mellema,* Wayang Puppets, *Amsterdam, 1954.*

evening until midnight the plot takes shape; from midnight to three o'clock in the morning it thickens; between three and six o'clock it is resolved. The play ends at dawn.

Usually, a *wayang* performance is devoted to one *lakon* from the whole cycle of the legend. Sometimes, however, at great festivals lasting several days, a whole cycle is performed. But the Javanese public is so familiar with the characters and episodes of the *Ramayana* and the *Mahabharata,* that a part can easily take the place of the whole.

The *dalang*'s task of actor, narrator, and commentator all-in-one demands the highest degree of concentration. For hours on end he remains devotedly absorbed in the play's purpose and atmosphere. The necessary technical skill requires many years' training. The *dalang* must bring to life dozens of different figures, each individually characterized in cadence and intonation. In the play about the *Bharatayuddha* legend of the Pāndavas and Kauravas, for instance, there are thirty-seven principal parts, not to mention the secondary figures, the animals, and the *gunungan,* the leaf-shaped or (on Bali) umbrella-shaped tree of heaven. An old rule says that the *dalang* will be most successful if he uses exactly one hundred forty-four figures for his productions; this number is held by Javanese mystics to correspond to the one hundred forty-four human characters and passions.

The *wayang* plays are performed in the palaces of Javanese nobles. Between the front porch and the inner rooms runs a covered passage (*peringgitan,* place of shade), and it is there that the often richly adorned, artfully carved frame for the shadow play's canvas screen is set up. Since *wayang* traditionally has always been the business of men, men still sit on the "good" side of the screen—that is, behind the *dalang,* so that they can see the puppets themselves. The shadow-play side is regarded as second-best and, traditionally, throughout Java, this is where the women are seated.

In Bali the artistic and, even more so, the social protocol of the *wayang* play is less strict. The *dalang* puts up his canvas screen in the open air, and the audience sits informally on the ground. Nevertheless, it is in Bali that the ritual character has remained strongest. Bali, the "Island of the Thousand Temples," has remained more faithful to Hinduism than Java, where Islam gained ground when it invaded the island, advancing from Sumatra during the fifteenth century. To this day, the *dalangs* of Bali perform in the temple precincts, and especially in the entrance to the first temple courtyard, the so-called *tjandi-bentar,* or "divided gateway." (In the first of these three courtyards Bali's very popular cock fights took place.)

Other forms of the *wayang* play developed later, alongside the *wayang kulit.* One subspecies, the *wayang gedok,* also made use of used leather puppets, but it is more recent than the *wayang kulit* and is thought to have originated at the time of the invasion of Java by Islam. Its themes are based on that period, and its origin is attributed to the Moslem saint Sunan ing Giri.

The *wayang* form most usual today, and widespread especially in central and western Java, is the *wayang golek* (*golek* means round, plastic), with its three-dimensional doll puppets, skillfully carved of wood and richly painted. Its repertory draws mainly on the story of Prince Menak, a precursor of the Prophet Mohammed. Menak's victorious armies prepared the world for the coming of the Prophet, according to a legend that goes back to Persian sources but, strangely enough, was never a theme for drama in Persia. In its Shiite form in Persia, Islam glorified not the triumphs of those who came before the Prophet, but the martyrdom of his successors, dramatically re-enacted each year as a renewed testimony of the faith.

The *wayang golek* puppets are carved short-waisted and clad in sumptuous costumes, richly embroidered or embellished with batik ornaments. The costumes artfully hide the handle by which the puppeteer holds his dolls. The arms are articulated at the shoulders and elbows and, as those of all *wayang* puppets, are moved with the help of thin wooden sticks. In 1931, the mysterious grace of the *wayang golek* dolls inspired the Viennese puppeteer R. Teschner to establish his *Figurenspiegel Theater*, which brought the *wayang golek*, and the concepts of the Indonesian shadow play, to puppet-theater fans throughout Europe.

Yet another form of *wayang* is the *wayang kruchil* or *klittik* (*kerutjil, klitik* means small, thin). Its figures are also made of wood, but flatter and fitted with leather arms. It takes its themes from the period between the decline of Majapahit (1520) and the rise of the Islamic Demak empire. Today it is almost extinct. Only the name, *wayang bèbèr*, has survived. It made use of a large picture scroll, made of bast paper or cotton fabric, on which the characters were painted. The *dalang* drew the scroll across the cloth screen, much like a film strip. The Ethnological Museum of Leiden and the Pahemon Radyapustaka Museum at Surakarta each possess a well-preserved *wayang bèbèr* picture roll.

Today, in the towns of Indonesia, the *wayang* play is as commercialized as are the indigenous dances, such as the mask dances of *wayang topeng*, the famous Dance of the Nymphs (*bedaja*), the acrobatic solo dance *kiprah*, or the *djaran-kèpang*, danced in pairs with plaited bamboos serving as horses—and all the numerous forms of *wayang wong* (*wong* means human), the human theater.

Gamelan music is an essential ingredient in all Indonesian *wayang*

Wayang golek *puppet of the Indonesian shadow play. Java, late 19th century. (Munich, Stadtmuseum, Puppet Theater Collection.)*

The god Indra. Javanese shadow-play puppet made of painted parchment, with three rods for manipulation. (Offenbach am Main, Deutsches Ledermuseum.)

Demon's mask for the Indonesian barong *dance. The* barong, *a mythical animal, is carried by two dancers. The mask is carved in wood and decorated with ornamental elements made of gilt buffalo parchment. From the island of Bali. (Offenbach am Main, Deutsches Ledermuseum.)*

Relief frieze with dancing nymphs (Apsaras), *at the temple-monastery of Preah-Khan in Cambodia. Built by Jayavarman VII, the last of the great Khmer kings, ca. 1190.*

performances. The orchestra consists predominately of percussion instruments (*gamel* is the word for hammer), gongs, drums, and xylophone, together with a few string and wind instruments. The *gamelan* scale system is built on intervals; its melodies are based either on the five-note scale (*slendro*) or on the seven-note scale (*pelog*), reminiscent of the major and minor keys in Western music. It may be taken as a rule of thumb that *gamelan slendro* is generally associated with *wayang purwa* —and *gamelan pelog*, with its minor key, *wayang gedok*.

A *gamelan* orchestra also accompanied the ceremonial dances performed at court. These court dances, which were introduced by the *dalang* with recitations and accompanied both the *gamelan* orchestra and by male and female choirs, attained their highest development at the courts of central Java.

These ceremonial dances were strictly reserved for performance at court. Well into the nineteenth century the *bedaja* dance, with its accompaniment of melancholy songs, was allowed to be danced only at the courts of Java's Sultans, before a selected public. It is performed by nine young girls who are dressed in precious, gold-brocaded robes and move with the perfect grace of the Oriental dance tradition. Every gesture has a ritual, magic meaning, according to the Hindu *mudras*. Today the *bedaja* is danced in the ceremony celebrating Garebeg, a Moslem festival of sacrifice.

How strongly Indonesians still respond to the magic spell of the *wayang* play can be judged from a poem written in the 1920's by the Javanese writer Noto Suroto:

> Lord, let me be a *wayang* in your hands. I can be a hero or a demon, a king or a lowly man, a tree, a plant, an animal . . . but let me be a *wayang* in your hands. . . . My battle is not yet fought to its end. And soon you will take me away; I shall lie with the others whose play is done. I shall be in the darkness with the myriads. . . . Then, after a hundred years or thousands, your hand will again give me the gift of life and movement . . . and I shall once more speak and fight the good fight.

China

INTRODUCTION

Five thousand years of history lie between us and the sources of the Chinese theater. Empires and dynasties have come and gone since the early days of the ritual fertility dances and the shamans' exorcism of evil spirits, since the beginnings of court pantomime and jesters' puns. Millennia, whole empires and dynasties, separate the days of the first imperial conservatory of music from those that witnessed, eventually, the legitimization of China's theater drama. This maturation was brought about by the collapse of an empire's solid edifice of power, under the shadow of Genghis Khan.

The inner mainspring of this drama was protest, camouflaged rebellion against Mongol rule. And so in the thirteenth and fourteenth centuries, China's drama celebrated its triumphs not on the stage, but in the columns of printed books. The playwrights were scholars, physicians, literati, whose disciples gathered around the master in the shelter of private recital halls. Their seditious message was passed from hand to hand in daintily stitched block-printed books.

The acclaim of the people, meanwhile, belonged to the jugglers, the acrobats, and mimes. By the precarious balance of tightrope walkers, equilibrists, and jugglers China's theatrical heritage was carried through the millennia. Today, still, at the Peking Opera, in one of the world's most highly accomplished theater forms, the art of acrobatics has its honored place. In China's theater, acrobatics, in nobility of tradition, ranks as the peer of music.

The mathematical logic of musical notes represents the world order, the laws that govern the course of the stars and life on this earth. The interplay between custom and music culminates in the strong ceremonial tradition upon which the power and absolute authority of the world's greatest state was built for thousands of years. Just as the common people were subject to the feudal lords and the feudal lords to the emperor, so the emperor in his turn was subject to the Lord of Heaven, whom he worshiped in his capacity as the Son of Heaven. This worship was expressed in sacred pantomimes and sacrificial rites, and in the sounds of music that was rooted in cosmic powers, music that through its laws laid upon the supernatural a duty to this world. "Whosoever understands the meaning of the great sacrifices," Confucius said, "understands the world order as though he were holding it in the palm of his hand."

The consequence of this world order is that virtue is rewarded and evil punished. Art and life move within these two postulates. Their religious foundations were always bound to ancestor and hero worship—notwithstanding the invervening Taoist nature mysticism of Lao-tzu, the moral philosophy of Confucius, the advent of Buddhism, and of Nestorian Christianity.

Heroism is the highest perfection of human life, and on the stage it celebrated its most striking triumphs either in the form of mighty valor or in that of humble endurance.

Modern poets and playwrights owe much to the Chinese tradition. Bertolt Brecht took over for his new form epic drama what he called the "exhibition aspect of the ancient Asian theater." Thornton Wilder, who spent his early years in Hong Kong and Shanghai, derived the technique for his illusionless primary theater from the Chinese art of acting. Paul Claudel, who spent fifteen years in China as a French diplomat, gathered the spiritual harvest of his Far Eastern experiences in *Le Soulier de satin* (*The Satin Slipper*). He had studied the theater, the character and the philosophy of China, and had come to the conclusion that the enigma of the strength and power of this populous giant state could be solved in five words: "The individual is never alone."

ORIGINS AND THE "HUNDRED PLAYS"

It is natural to the innate sense of order of the Chinese to subordinate all things, of this world and the next, to the utilitarian principle, whether it lies in the realm of ideas or of practice. Thus music, the conciliating mediator between heaven and earth, also has a legitimate educational mission. This insight into the usefulness of music is said to have led the mythical Yellow Emperor Huang Ti, the founder of the Chinese nation (about 2700 B.C.), to press the magic of sounds into the purposes of high politics. Believing that music serves to maintain peace and order, he welcomed his official visitors with instrumental performances.

Magicians and exorcisers were responsible for the safe course of rural life, for good harvests and good fortune in war. Shamanism was most highly developed in North and Central Asia, where its practitioners formed a distinct professional group. Ritual dances (*wu wu*) were performed in a state of ecstasy to counter natural disasters, floods, eclipses of the sun, the gods of rain and wind, illness and misfortune.

These shamanistic *wu* dances, about which the philosopher Mo Ti wrote around 400 B.C., were of vital relevance during the Shang period (until about 1000 B.C.). In the following Chou period, the first profane elements appeared. Pantomimes and jesters provided entertainment at imperial banquets. Ballads and folk-songs were performed in a pantomime "dance of praise" (*sung wu*).

Confucius is said to have been so angered once by the disrespectful antics of the court dwarfs that he ordered the ruler of Lu to execute half a dozen of the worse offenders. Centuries later, this was still held against him by the chronicler Ssu-ma Ch'ien, whose famous *Historical Record* (*Shih Chi*) contains a whole chapter on the actor's profession. In contrast with the Confucian teaching and its strict command of moderation and self-discipline, Ssu-ma Ch'ien declares: "But I say the following: the ways of the highest heaven are too incomprehensibly sublime; contrary to expectations, it is possible even by talking about trifling things to find one's way through the chaos of human entanglements."

By virtue of this veto, Ssu-ma Ch'ien made himself the advocate of all those court jesters and actors, explicitly named by him, who were among the vanguard of the Chinese theater.

Foremost among them was Yu-Meng, a musician, jester, and mime at the court of King Chuang (613–601 B.C.) in the Chou Kingdom. This

Scene from The Strategy of the Unguarded City, *a play of the Chou period.*

witty dwarf did not hesitate to castigate not only the excesses of court life, but also the injustices of his ruler. One day he appeared before the king in the robes of a recently deceased minister and reminded him of his debt of gratitude toward the minister's impoverished family: "Loyal unto death was the minister Sun Shu-ao in Chou. Now his destitute family have to cart wood for their living. Ah, it does not pay to be a minister in Chou!" Yu-Meng's mimic appeal was a complete success. The son of the deceased was summoned to court and invested with high office.

This may seem a trifling episode to tell of the early history of the Chinese theater, but its moral line is significant. Virtue prevails, whatever or whoever is responsible for its victory. Ssu-ma Ch'ien, the worldly-wise champion of the art of miming, lived at the court of the Emperor Wu-ti (140–87 B.C.) and enjoyed, together with numerous scholars and poets, the favors of this art-loving ruler. It was he who in 104 founded what is known as the Imperial Office of Music. He took over the new musical instruments which had been brought into the country by builders' teams from Central Asia who had come to China to help with the construction of the Great Wall, and he commissioned the composition of new melodies for these instruments. Since then the four-string lute (*pi-pa*) with its range of three octaves, and the *didze,* a flute with six holes and a stop, have been well-established components of the Chinese stage orchestra.

According to Ssu-ma Ch'ien, the beginnings of the Chinese shadow play also can be traced back to the period of Emperor Wu-ti. But this information still does not settle the controversy going on among twentieth-century scholars as to the origin of the shadow play: did it travel from China via India and Indonesia to Turkey—or the other way around? Ssu-ma Ch'ien is an important witness for its existence, but no arbiter in this matter.

As Ssu-ma Ch'ien tells the story, a man called Shao Wong, from the state of T'si, appeared before the emperor Wu-ti in 121 B.C. to display his skill in connection with ghosts and the spirits of the departed. The Emperor's favorite consort Wang had just died. With the help of his art Shao Wong caused the figures of the departed and of the god of the domestic hearth to appear at night. The emperor saw her from afar, behind a curtain. He bestowed upon Shao Wong the title of "Marshal of the Perfection of Learning," showered presents upon him, and accorded him the rites due guests of the court. When, ultimately, Shao Wong became too ambitious and failed several times to evoke the wanted spirits, the emperor became sceptical, and two years later Shao Wong himself was secretly despatched to the world of the spirits.

Chinese shadow-play puppets for the legendary "Journey to India," which the pilgrim monk Hüan-Tsang undertook in order to acquire Buddhist writings. He leads with bundles of books, and is followed by his white horse, the monkey-king Sun Wu-k'ung, the pig-headed Chu Pa-tsie, and the monk Sha Wu-tsing. (Chicago, Field Museum of Natural History.)

Shadow-play figures from Szechwan: princess on horseback has the young man whom she wants to marry taken prisoner. 18th century. (Offenbach am Main, Deutsches Ledermuseum.)

Shadow-play scene: Princess Kuan Yin on the lotus throne at a reception. (Munich, Stadtmuseum, Puppet Theater Collection.)

Shadow-play scene: encounter in the zoo, at the pagoda. (Munich, Stadtmuseum, Puppet Theater Collection.)

The shadow play, however—which, in some form, Shao Wong seems to have used—remained a favorite form of the Chinese theater. The Peking and Szechwan puppets, out of transparent donkey or buffalo hide, convey an impression of the imaginative wealth of action and characters of the mythical folk-lore epics.

The visual evocation of the "spirit of the departed" in Emperor Wu-ti's time is to this day reflected in the terminology of the Chinese theater where the two entry and exit doors, to the right and the left of the stage, have always been known as the "doors of the shadows," or "doors of the souls."

Besides court music, shamanistic and animal-mask dances, the theatrical entertainments at the time of Emperor Wu-ti included also the merry market-fair entertainment of the "Hundred Plays." Outside the western gate of the capital Lo-yang there was a fairground, where conjurers and jugglers, sword and fire swallowers displayed their skill.

Throughout the Suy period (220–618 A.D.) Western elements arrived in the wake of commercial travelers across central Asia and as far as the Caspian Sea. Persian and Indian merchants and ambassadors came into the country and, in 610, Emperor Yan-ti built the first theater for the specific purpose of entertaining ambassadors from Western countries. We know that the theater was outside the southern gate of Lo-

Siamese shadow-play puppet: the monkey Angkut.

yang; but we can only guess what it may have been like. Since the "Hundred Plays" involved mostly pantomimes, and dance, and acrobatic performances, we are perhaps right in imagining a simple, raised platform, possibly sheltered by a roof and backed by a wall. The guests probably watched from their palanquins, as was still the custom for the seventh-century audiences of the originally Korean *gigaku* dances of Japan.

THE STUDENTS OF THE PEAR GARDEN

The period of the T'ang dynasty (618–906) saw the beginnings of book printing and porcelain manufacture, a great flowering of lyric poetry and painting, and the intensification of trade with Arabia and Persia. It was during that period, too, that the most famous event in China's theatrical history took place—the founding of that so-called Pear Garden, the imperial theater academy, from which today's actors still derive their poetic designation of "students of the Pear Garden."

Ming Huang, known to history as Emperor Hsuan-tsung (712–755), was China's *roi soleil.* He loved splendor and fame, beautiful women, thoroughbred horses, hunting and polo playing, ballet and music. It is reported that he was the first who "collected the scattered blossoms of poetry, music, and dance, and wove them into the garland of drama." In 714, Ming Huang set up an imperial office for the promotion of instrumental music and composition (*Chiao-Fang*) and organized the so-called Pear Garden, China's first school of dramatic art. In the emperor's Pear Garden 300 young men received careful training in dance, instrumental music, and singing. The most talented could look forward to a brilliant career at court. Every day Ming Huang went to see for himself what progress the young men were making; he took a personal interest in judging their performance.

In the "Garden of Perpetual Spring," a school parallel to the Pear Garden, a group of 300 girls, hand-picked by His Majesty, were training to attain the perfect grace and elegance of dance movement. It is reported that, to please his beautiful concubine Yang Kuei-fei, the Emperor himself occasionally donned a fool's robe and improvised little scenes with the actors. The "stage" was either an open veranda in one of the palace buildings, a pavilion, or some fitting spot in the palace garden. For a picturesque setting, a group of trees might have been chosen, or a lily pond, a bridge, or a teahouse. There was song, dance, and music wherever and whenever the Emperor so commanded—at meals, at receptions given for guests of honor, as a diversion during a game of chess, or during ceremonial court occasions that often lasted for hours.

The story of Ming Huang and his "Madame Pompadour," Yang Kuei-fei, became one of the favorite subjects of Chinese art, music, poetry, and drama. One of the most impressive stage versions of it is the late-seventeenth-century drama *The Palace of Eternal Life.* The lines from this play, immortalizing the oath exchanged by the emperor and his beloved—"always to fly side-by-side, like the birds in heaven and above the earth, and to be united as a branch is united to the tree"—are as well-known in China as are in Europe the words of Shakespeare's Juliet: "It was the nightingale, and not the lark. . . ."

It is attested in chronicles, novels, and plays that Ming Huang kept his oath. When Yang Kuei-fei fell victim to a revolutionary coup, her imperial Romeo hastened to follow her to the Palace of the Moon where the blessed dwell. It is said that in happier days Ming Huang once had jilted his beautiful concubine. This episode is the subject of the play *The Drunken Beauty,* a masterpiece of histrionic virtuosity, which for many years was part of the internationally acclaimed repertoire of the Peking Opera.

The play might be described as a musical one-acter. Its plot tells how one evening the Emperor Ming Huang has invited his beloved to a glass of wine in the Pavilion of the Hundred Blossoms. She is awaiting him, dressed in her most gorgeous robes, when she learns that the Emperor has gone to another woman. She gets drunk to drown her sadness, shame, and jealousy.

In the direction laid down for this scene—handled most artfully and with awareness of the aesthetic problems the portrayal of drunkenness presents for the actor—scholars of Chinese culture find a bridge from the past to the present. In the theme and style of this virtuoso scene of the T'ang period, and in its blended-in vocal music and choreography, scholars see a parallel to the style of today's Peking Opera. Style here connotes the conceptual and artistic sense of presentation, the "inner" action, rather than the specific techniques of performance. The Chinese theater historian Huang-hung explains that "to gain a correct appreciation of the Chinese theater, the European must be aware that the major concern is not so much to underscore the action as such, but to let the public experience the story. The stress is on the spiritual rather than on the physical possibilities."

This circumstance also explains why over the course of very long periods no major stage innovations were introduced in the Chinese theater; all that happened was an enlargement of theatrical means, of the musical range of expression, of the number of actors taking part in the play.

During the period of the Five Dynasties (907–960), with its political unrest and instability, the theater found no propitious conditions for further development. The students of the Pear Garden had to wait for the Sung dynasty (960–1276) to restore peace and prosperity before they, too, could enter a new golden age.

Under the emperor Chen-tsung (998–1022) the traditional, though already variously scored and choreographed, songs and dances were for the first time interspersed with representations of historic events, such as court scenes, battles and sieges from the history of the famous third-century A.D. "Three Kingdoms" period. These "variety shows" (*tsa chü*), with their loosely knit but increasingly rich sequences of action, eventually became the direct precursors of Chinese drama.

In a description of an imperial banquet in the early eleventh century we find nineteen numbers listed in the program, including two "variety shows." Each of these usually had three characters: a venerable, bearded man, a robustly stout "painted-face," clownish type, and a commanding ruler figure. These variety shows included dances, poetry, and music, and scenes of farce and recitations. The "variety shows" were performed in the imperial palace or park, in the reception and ceremonial halls of the feudal lords, and, on the great popular festivals, on the fairground.

Scene from a historical play of the Three Kingdoms period. 3rd century A.D.

The most famous for the variety of its attractions was the annual spring festival (*Ch'ing Ming*) at Kaifeng, the capital of the Northern Sung dynasty. Thousands upon thousands of people came to the fairground at the banks of the river Pien, north of Kaifeng. Crowds would gather at the long rows of stalls, around the tightrope artists, fortunetellers, and jugglers, or visit the festively decorated boats. Close to the river, in an open field, the theater would be set up. Its wooden roof, decorated with colorful banners, could be seen from far away, for the stage platform, supported by two dozen sturdy poles, stood more than a man's height above the crowd. The stage floor was covered with grass mats. An adjacent wooden shed served as the actors' dressing room. During the performance, the audience stood around the stage in a semicircle.

The emperor Hwei-tsung (1101–25) commissioned the most famous painter of his time, Chang Tse-tuan, to depict the Ch'ing Ming festival in a magnificent picture scroll, which has come down to us, the precious legacy of a dynasty doomed to ruin. Shortly thereafter, Genghis Khan and his Mongols invaded the country. They took the emperor and his son prisoner and burned the capital Kaifeng to the ground. But the picture scroll, twelve yards long and twelve inches wide, was saved and taken to Hang-chow, a few hundred miles south of Kaifeng. During the eighteenth century, Chinese artists often copied it with endless, new, individual variations. In 1736, for instance, the emperor Ch'ien Lung had five of his court painters working on such copies.

The Southern Sung dynasty, in exile at Hang-chow, survived for another century and made every effort to give the people a feeling of prosperity and security, notwithstanding the loss of the North. At Hang-chow, as in the past at the Ch'ing Ming festival at Kaifeng, the show-stalls mushroomed again, more numerous perhaps than ever.

When Marco Polo reached China in the last quarter of the thirteenth century, he gave the country the name by which it was known to the Turks and the Mongol rulers: Cathay. Marco Polo's descriptions of Cambalu, the "Khan's city," caused it to be regarded in Europe for a long time as the quintessence of princely splendor—indeed, not least because of its theatrical court ceremonial.

APPROACHES TO THE DRAMA

In dealing with the emergence of the Chinese drama as a literary form, we have to ask, why the Mongols' breaking into this millennia-old

Chinese theater stage in the 12th century. Detail from a painted silk picture scroll, depicting the Ch'ing-Ming Festival at Kaifeng, the capital of the Northern Sung dynasty (960–1126). A 1736 copy, made by five court painters of the Emperor Ch'ien Lung, from the original of Chang Tse-tuan. (Taipei, Museum.)

civilization brought about the fundamental cultural crisis that was to lead to entirely new cultural and artistic forms? There is a plausible enough explanation: the abolition of the great state examinations, without which no scholar had previously been admitted to imperial office, released intellectual forces that were now applied to an attempt to foment internal resistance to the Mongol rule, in the apparently harmless guise of poetry.

In the atmosphere of intellectual freedom under Genghis Khan, protests were voiced against the corruption and venality of the Chinese themselves, against the opportunists and turncoats who agreed to serve the music-loving Mongols.

Genghis Khan fostered the arts; for he hoped that contact with China's leading artists and intellectuals would gain him an insight into the mind and mentality of the conquered people. But, as so often in its history, in China under Mongol rule the drama became a center of underground resistance.

In the thirteenth and fourteenth centuries, both in the North, which was under Mongol rule, and in the South, which still enjoyed an unfettered cultural life, China's two characteristic forms of drama more or less simultaneously developed: the Northern drama and the Southern drama.

The Chinese have compared the Northern drama with the splendor of the peony, and the Southern drama with the hushed glow of the plum blossom. These enchanting metaphors, with their implied range between blazing strength and shimmering bloom, characterize both the choice of dramatic subjects and the type of theme. The Northern School writes of valor and duty, in battle as in matters of love—themes dictated by the Confucian ethic with its insistence on public duty and filial piety as the "origin of all virtue."

The Southern School is more easygoing. It indulges in sentiments and in such little indiscretions as a peep into the women's quarters or even of a perfumed décolleté. In the Southern School, more flexible morals are matched by a more flexible informal style.

In the Northern drama, everything—from the strict four-act rule to the meticulously followed nomenclature of rhyme and music—makes for limpid clarity of style. In the Southern drama, with its gaily boisterous life and noisier music, poetic effect predominates.

It was in Hang-chow, the capital of the Southern Sung dynasty, that, in contrast to the "strict" Northern drama of the Mongol period, an operatic form of drama (*nan ch'u*) was developed. This was an important advance in the Chinese theater.

NORTHERN AND SOUTHERN DRAMA

Chronologically, the Northern drama was about two generations ahead of the Southern theater. It can claim to be descended from Kuan Han-ch'ing (b. 1214 at Tatu), the "Father of Chinese drama." Kuan Han-ch'ing was a high state official under the Kin dynasty before it was overthrown and later, in Peking, a physician and experienced specialist in the psychology of women. He wrote sixty-five plays—love comedies, court plays, and heroic dramas. Fourteen of his works have come down to us. Today, the Chinese like to put him on a par with the Greek tragic dramatist Aeschylus and the modern American psychoanalytical playwright Tennessee Williams—a perfect demonstration of how futile such comparisons can be. How little Kuan Han-ch'ing is in need of comparison is demonstrated by one of his saddest romances, a play called *The Exchange of Wind and Moon*—the story of a young slave girl who has to dress her mistress, who is about to be wed to the man she herself loves. Kuan Han-ch'ing's fame matches that of his contemporary Wang Shih-fu, for whose famous *Romance of the Western Chamber* he wrote a fifth act after the author's death. This play, incidentally, not only charms us by the lyricism with which it presents the romance between the student Chang Chün-jui and Ying-ying, the daughter of a minister under the T'ang dynasty; it also gives us an insight into the importance of the state examinations, which clearly were not only the key to the privileged status of public service, but, as in the *Western Chamber*, also a requisite for obtaining the hand of the lady of one's heart.

Another play, written a few generations later by Chi Chün-hsiang of Peking, found its way to the Western stage through Voltaire's free adaptation. This is *L'Orphelin de la Chine*, which was first performed in 1755 in Paris with the actress Clairon as Idamé in a performance that was enthusiastically acclaimed by Diderot. Goethe took up the same theme in 1781, with this fragment *Elpenor*, but the Far East defeated him: in this case, unlike his experience with *Iphigenie*, he was unable to refashion the ancient model in the spirit of *humanitas* and thus to absorb it into classical German drama.

It is not known whether, and how, the dramatic masterpieces of the Yuan period—in the time of Mongol rule under Genghis Khan and Kublai Khan—were ever performed on the stage. When Kao Ming, an influential official of wealthy parentage, published his famous play *The Tale of the Lute* in 1367, the South, too, was threatened by the Mongols. Like most members of the educated class of his time, Kao Ming was a follower of Confucius. He was against corruption and against social

Illustration for the drama The Romance of the Western Chamber, *by Wang Shih-fu. Late 13th century. Color print from a 1640 set of woodcuts by Min Ch'i-chi. (Cologne, Museum für ostasiatische Kunst.)*

inequality, and he deplored it when human feelings were disregarded by letting the differences between rich and poor prevail against the voice of the heart. Apart from *The Tale of the Lute,* the best-known works of the Yuan and Ming dynasties that have come down to us are *The Pavilion of Moon Worship, The Hairpin, The White Rabbit,* and *The Trick with the Dead Dogs.* Presumably, their dissemination rested largely on the printed book.

While the crowds of the common folk applauded the song-play with historical content, performed by strolling troupes on an improvised stage, the drama developed into a separate art form and became the subject of literary criticism. Some of these critical essays have been handed down by the scholars and considered worth handing down. But, although they speak of the literary value of a given play, these critics tell us nothing of the theater as a place where the drama is brought to life. This fact was pointed out by the critic Ku Ch'u-lu 200 years later, at the time of the renowned dramatist T'ang Hsien-tsu. Ku Ch'u-lu wrote the following remarkable sentence in a review of the famous *Peony Arbor* by T'ang Hsien-tsu: "As soon as the *Peony Arbor* appeared, everybody rushed to read it and talked about it, which made it possible to reduce the price of the *Western Chamber.*"

The *Peony Arbor,* it would seem, was not a theatrical sensation, but a literary one. T'ang Hsien-tsu, a contemporary of Shakespeare, was a scholar, not an actor. His residence, known as the Yu-Ming Hall, where his pupils assembled, does indeed suggest a connection with the theater by its inclusion of the old word *yu,* for actor; but, to judge from the historical records, the ambitions of master and pupils alike were of a purely literary kind. The "students of the Yu-Ming Hall" were interested in the criticism of the drama, not of the performance. When it was proposed to T'ang Hsien-tsu that he should give play readings, he replied with the inscrutability of the Chinese sage: "You are talking of the mind, but I am talking of love."

THE SONG-PLAY OF THE MING PERIOD

While the literary-minded students gathered around the dramatist T'ang Hsien-tsu in the Yu-Ming Hall, the musician Wei Liang-fu developed, from the elements of Northern and Southern music, a new musical style based on fixed tone systems and rhythms. He created a new theatrical form, the song-play (*k'un-ch'ü*). Wei Liang-fu was a music teacher in the town of Soochow, which became the cultural capital of the Ming period and attracted a host of poets, musicians, scholars, and theater troupes.

The musical reforms of Wei Liang-fu and the lyrical and poetic dramas of the Yu-Ming master, four of whose most famous plays are known by the joint title of *Four Dreams of the Yu-Ming Hall,* laid the foundation for the high perfection of the modern Peking Opera style. Its sumptuous costumes, its stylish ceremonial, its fascinating precision of the language of gesture, and its artistic control of the body—all these essentially go back to the Ming dynasty's golden age of opera.

On a bare stage devoid of scenery or decoration, the actor—who was singer, reciter, and dancer all in one—brought to life a magic world, scented with peonies, peach blossoms, and rose trees; a world where unhappy lovers unite like butterflies, but where the flaming sword of vengeance also takes its toll. The expressive language of gesture, the graceful movement of arms and hands under flowing white silk—all these were perfected in the Ming period.

One of the moral prescriptions of Confucius is that the body must be covered as far as is possible. This was one of his moral precepts, which he meant to be obeyed especially by the upper classes. Long ago, in the early T'ang period, the dancing girls had brought the language of the sleeve movements to the perfection of transcendent beauty. As a means of theatrical expression, the "sleeve language" ranges from the happy granting of a wish to the depths of despair.

"White sleeves can seem as light as butterflies and as downcast as bats; hands can appear to be of alabaster. Palms may be painted pink for women and young heroes, supple and lithe as though they had no joints. They make their effect even at a distance. They can thrill you, fill you with fear, conciliate . . ." (Kalvodová-Sís-Vaniš). Sleeve movements are the making of the great mad scene of the girl Yen-jung in *Beauty Withstands the Tyrant.* To evade the imperial command, she feigns sudden madness (this is also a favorite theme of the Japanese *nō* plays). She flings up her long, white sleeves in a distraught and hectic movement and drops them abruptly, vibrates in terror, tears off her precious coral diadem, laughs insanely behind a veil of long, black hair—and thus Yen-jung destroys the image of her beauty and with it the emperor's desire. The Peking Opera's great actor of female roles, Mei Lan-fang, used to play this scene with compelling, expressive force well into his old age (he died in 1961).

Scene from the Chinese song drama Fang-mien-ho. *Red chalk drawing by A. Jacovlev. (From:* Le Théâtre Chinois, *Paris, 1922.)*

Terracotta figure of a Chinese dancer from the T'ang dynasty (618–906): an early example of the "sleeve language." (Frankfurt am Main, Liebighaus.)

THE ARTISTIC CONCEPTION OF THE PEKING OPERA

Around the middle of the eighteenth century, during the Ching dynasty, the lyrical, poetic song-play began to develop toward a new style, stressing a sense of reality and demanding a large, "public" stage. The emperor Ch'ien Lung (1736–95) took a great interest in China's theatrical troupes and found time on his travels to visit the theaters in the provinces. He closely watched the performers' acting, singing, and dancing. The best of them he then called to Peking, to participate in his newly founded, beloved venture. He personally was the initiator of that unique, sovereign art form which today still enjoys world fame: the Peking Opera.

The name, incidentally, refers merely to the origin of the new style, not to its subsequent location. The Peking Opera style combines the two dominant elements of Chinese theater: the smooth perfection of ensemble play and, also, the uniquely individual performance of the star actor. Mei Lan-fang, a small delicate man of ageless grace, who for many years portrayed female beauty and charm, became the internationally acclaimed idol of the Chinese theater. His mentor Ch'i Ju-shan wrote or adapted some forty plays for him. Mei Lan-fang starred in each of them, displaying his individual, subtle art. The literary text was the canvas that Mei Lan-fang embroidered with the intricate and subtle ornaments of his histrionic variations.

Supposing the same play were given in Peking, Szechwan, Canton, or Shanghai, it would convey four quite different impressions not only as regards the production as such, but because the text is treated very freely and may be altered at will, sometimes even to the point of turning the whole action inside out to suit the star of the performance. Similarly, the composition of the orchestra varies greatly, for the musicians adhere closely to local musical tradition.

The actor performs on an empty stage. He has no external accessories to help him. He has to create everything by his movements alone, the symbolic action as well as the illusion of space. It is he who suggests the scenery, makes visible the nonexistent prop.

The Chinese stage is the same as it was centuries ago, a simple platform with a neutral background behind it. No wings, no revolving stage, no grid or trapdoor assists the actor; he himself must create the whole setting.

The only stage properties are a table, a chair, a couch covered with

Duel scene on the stage. Vietnam. From a Sino-Vietnamese manuscript.

precious brocade or with a grey cloth. But these objects can represent anything: a throne, a mountain, a cave, a court of justice, a fountain, a pavilion. If the actor steps on the table or chair and covers his head, it means that he has become invisible, has escaped his pursuers. If he takes a riding whip that is handed to him, it means that he is mounting a horse; he dismounts by handing the whip back to a servant, and when the servant goes offstage with the whip, he is leading the horse away. A suitably painted canvas screen held high represents a city wall with a gate. A banner with horizontal black lines signifies a storm, a warrior waving flags, a whole army. Two flags with painted wheels, held up either by the hero himself or by two attendants, indicate a journey by carriage. An actor holding an oar is a ferryman—he helps his lady into the boat, casts off, rows against the current, jumps ahead with a big leap on to the other shore. The illusion is complete, thanks to the expressive range of the actor's body and movements. His hands and gestures, the rhythm of his movements, tell whole stories, create a reality that others can experience.

Just as Marcel Marceau walks up a ship's ladder on the level stage, just as his Monsieur Bip traverses all the heavens of bliss and all the infernos of despair with nothing but a yellow straw hat and a red carnation, so the Chinese actor can move mountains, fathom the distances of time and space with a single step. He opens doors that are not there, crosses invisible thresholds; he clasps his beloved to his heart when he stands in front of her with outstretched arms.

To help him, he has only his mask, his costume. Both speak the inherited language of symbols; every color is anchored in ceremonial tradition. Red symbolizes valor, loyalty and uprightness; black signifies passion; blue facial make-up betrays brutality and cruelty; chalky white is the color of the swindler and cheat. A white smudge on the tip of the nose, together with, maybe, a butterfly pattern on the cheeks, makes the clown, the jester, the buffoon. He might just as well be named Grock, Oleg Popov, or Charlie Rivel—the clown's mask, his laughter and his tears, know no frontiers.

According to Chinese legend, it was in the T'ang period that masks were first used to alter, disguise, or transmogrify the human face. The king of Lan-ling, so the story goes, was a hero in the art of war, but his face was soft and feminine. For this reason he used, during his campaigns, to tie over his face a martial mask, to frighten the enemy. His subjects, the people of Ch'i, were not slow in turning this military bogey to good account in a very popular burlesque pantomime about their ruler's "false face," called *The King of Lan-ling Goes to Battle.*

But whether a role was that of a warrior or a beautiful young concubine—down to the twentieth century, it was always played by a male actor. Although there was no categoric exclusion of the actress in China, as there was in Japan, until nearly the end of the Ch'ing dynasty at the beginning of the twentieth century, it was thought unbefitting for women to appear on the stage together with men.

The prerogative of acting female roles, of highly stylized, masculine "femininity," had to be acquired by years of rigorous training, and it was more highly prized than nature itself. During the Mongol rule and under the emperor Ming Huang, women were temporarily admitted to the stage as equal partners. But Kublai Khan, equating art and venality in a decree dated 1263 relegated actresses indiscriminately to the ranks of the courtesans. This put them into the fifth and lowest class of the population, together with slaves, paid servants, jugglers, and beggars.

Neither the Imperial Music Office nor the aestheticizing ladies who wrote dramas in the Yuan period had this ruling changed. Yang Kuei-fei felt secure enough of her charms and her imperial master's favors not to worry about social problems, and the lesser members of her profession knew how to get back their own—on the stage or in the bedroom—for the humiliation of being called "greenbelts." They wore the green belt

General Ma-Sou, a character from the historical play The Retreat from Kai-Ting. *Costume, mask, and gesture correspond to the style of the Peking Opera (see illustration p. 91 top). Color print by A. Jacovlev. (From* Le Théâtre Chinois, *Paris, 1922.)*

Chinese theater in Shanghai. The stage is set in a halllike room, with galleries for spectators at the sides, and tables occupying the floor space in front of the stage—the Far Eastern equivalent to the music hall. Drawing by M. Koenig. (From L'Illustration *of November 21, 1874, Paris.)*

Picture of two-faced East Asian mask. (Cologne, Museum für ostasiatische Kunst.)

of the courtesans, which gave them their nickname, with no less assurance than the emancipated literary ladies of Europe were later to wear their blue stockings.

THE CHINESE THEATER TODAY

Compared with the primacy of the indigenous artistic tradition, Western theater styles made little impact in China. The music halls and variety theaters of the great ports were no yardstick for China's theatrical culture. The style of the Peking Opera reveals more of the essence of the Chinese art of acting than does any of the spectacular revues in Hongkong.

Western-style spoken drama first made its appearance during the revolution of 1907, when political propagandists got hold of the stage. The martyrs of the revolution, the uprising of the people, and national pride were the topical themes of the new, spoken drama (*hua chü*). Improvised dialogue in everyday language and equally improvised realistic acting filled in the sketched outline of the plot—in glaring contrast with the artfully stylized Peking Opera. After 1919 a "literary renaissance" originated in student circles. People studied Western dramaturgy, direction, scenery, lighting and acting styles. Zola's *Nana* and Ibsen's *An Enemy of the People,* both translated into colloquial Chinese, were given at the Nankai University in Tientsin and in Peking. Alexandre Dumas' *Lady of the Camelias* and Oscar Wilde's *Lady Windermere's Fan* were appreciated for their treatment of human and social problems. New theater clubs and agencies sprang up and arranged for visits from foreign companies, and a national theater academy was founded. The country's young authors were inspired by the political and literary revolution that began in the early 1930's and, through the incident at the Marco Polo Bridge on 7 July 1937, led to the war with Japan. Enthusiastic young patriots founded a host of theater groups with propagandistic repertoires.

After 1945, the tradition of the Peking Opera was kept up alongside the modern, topical, spoken drama. Mei Lan-fang, who had evaded Japanese offers of female parts by growing a beard, returned to the stage in the role of the lady of ageless beauty. Notwithstanding political conflicts, the Peking Opera had preserved its specifically Chinese and world-famous style. Today, some 400 students are undergoing intensive training at the National School in Peking, though lately there has been a clear tendency to revamp the traditional style.

Chinese New Year's pictures with theatrical scenes. Color prints of this type are sold in vast quantities on the Flower Market Street in Peking before the holiday; they are as popular in China as, for instance, the images d'Épinal *are in France. Both prints, ca. 1920.*

A Peking Opera production in 1956: The actor Wang Cheng-pin in the historical play The Fortress of Yentanshan, *based on a theme from the Suy dynasty.*

Kuen Su-shuang in the legend play The Theft of the Miraculous Herb. *Peking Opera, 1956.*

In Taiwan, in the meantime, the government of Nationalist China also is fostering the old Peking Opera tradition together with modern, spoken drama. Two theater schools and a theater-and-film division at the National Academy of Art at Panchiao, near the capital Taipei, offer courses in the history and practice of the theater. Since 1962, the then newly founded Taipei Committee of Dramatic Productions for Appreciation has been endeavoring to develop the spoken drama beyond its entertainment function into a form of art.

Japan

INTRODUCTION

"It is poetry that without effort moves heaven and earth, and arouses the compassion of invisible gods and demons, and it is in the dance that poetry assumes visible shape." These words are from the introduction to the first Japanese collection of poems, *Kokinshu,* published in 922 A.D. The Japanese theater may be described as a solemn, strictly formalized celebration of emotions and sentiments, ranging from the pantomime invocation of the powers of nature to the most subtle differentiations of aristocratic dramatic form. Its mainspring lies in the suggestive power of movement, gesture, and the spoken word. Within these means of expressions, the Japanese have developed a theatrical art so original and unique that it defies comparison, for any comparison will invariably be relevant only to one of its many aspects.

At first sight, the coexistence of several strictly distinct kinds and forms of theater seems confusing. The theatrical art of modern Japan is not the result of a synthesis; it is the result of a many-faceted pluralism, of centuries of development. Its history is not a chain of developmental stages that supersede each other; it resembles, rather, an instrument to which new strings are added at intervals, each parallel to the others. The length of each string (to evoke an allusion to history) determines its sound. But between the strings there lies silence, silence as a party to pathos and its ultimate culmination. "I regard pathos wholly as a matter of restraint," the Japanese dramatist Chikamatsu wrote around 1720: "when all the components of art are dominated by restraint, the result is very moving. . . ."

The separate styles of the Japanese theater at the same time constitute a milestone. Each reflects the historical, sociological, and artistic circumstances of its origin. The *kagura* dances of the first millennium testify to the exorcising power of primordial magic rites. The *gigaku* and *bugaku* mask plays reflect the influence of Buddhist religious concepts, taken over from China in the seventh and eighth centuries. The *nō* plays of the fourteenth and fifteenth centuries glorify the ethos of the

Samurai. The *kyōgen* farces, presented as grotesque and comic interludes between *nō* plays, are approaches to popular social criticism. The *kabuki* of the early seventeenth century was backed by the rising power of the merchants. In the late nineteenth century, the *shimpa,* under Western influence, first brought topical themes with a markedly sentimental bent onto the stage. In the twentieth-century *shingeki,* finally, Japan's young intellectuals took the floor.

All these basic forms of Japanese theater—including also the *bunraku* puppet play of Osaka—are still alive today, simultaneously and side-by-side. Each has its own, specific public, its own theater, its timeless validity.

KAGURA

In the Japanese island world, as everywhere else, the theater began with the gods, with the conflict of the supernatural powers. The two great myths of the divinities of sea and sun contain not only the germ of Japan's early sacred dance but, beyond that, the first elements of dramatic transformation, which is the essence of theatrical form. Japan's two oldest chronicles, the *Kojiki* and *Nihongi,* were both written in Chinese ideographs in the early eighth century for Japan's imperial court. They tell of pantomime representations of the two myths which to this day are a major source of East Asian dance plays. They survive in Vietnam, Cambodia and Laos, in Thailand, Assam, Burma, and in Southern China.

The first of these myths is based on the cult of the sun and relates the story of the sun goddess Amaterasu. After a quarrel with her brother, Amaterasu hides in a rocky cave, impervious to all entreaties. Heaven and earth lie in nocturnal darkness—one of mankind's great nightmare fears, which in Japan grew out of the historical occurrence of a solar eclipse. The "eight hundred myriads of gods" in the Japanese pantheon agree to lure the angry goddess out of her hiding place by means of a dance play. The virgin goddess Ama no Uzume

> steadied her hand with a wrist strap of heavenly club-moss from the heavenly Kagu mountain, crowned her head with a head-dress of the leaves from the heavenly spindle-tree and tied bamboo leaves from the heavenly Kagu mountain into a posy. Then she put down a sounding-board outside the entrance of the goddess's rocky abode and stamped on it with her feet to make a great noise, simulating the ecstasy of divine inspiration. . . .

Woodcut by Utashige: Bunraku Theater of Osaka, ca. 1880. Each of the three puppets on the stage is handled by two puppeteers; one in each pair is clothed in black. To the right, the reciter; next to him, the samisen *player whose presence is indicated merely by his hand and the instrument. (Munich, Stadtmuseum, Puppet Theater Collection.)*

And so Uzume arouses the curiosity of the sun goddess. Amaterasu steps out of her cave, and in a mirror the gods hold up to her she sees her own radiant image. The cocks crow. Light is restored to the world. The mythological significance of Uzume's dance that brings about return of the sun survives to this day in the custom of performing *kagura* plays throughout the night and until dawn, until the first cock's crow.

The second myth concerns the feud between two brothers and the intervention of the sea god. The ruler of the tides gives the younger brother Yamahiko, who at first is defeated, power over ebb and flood. The elder brother Umihiko realizes what danger this spells for him. He decides to propitiate Yamahiko. To this end he smears red earth on his face and hands and dances a pantomime of drowning: how at first the waves lap only his feet, how the water rises higher and higher until it reaches up to his neck. With the words, "Henceforth and until the end of time I will be your jester and servant," Umihiko submits to his brother's rule. And thus the Japanese theater found its first "professional actor" though admittedly in the realm of mythology, and as a matter of fiction rather than of fact. This myth, incidentally, which has wide ramifications throughout the Far East, underlies the legend of the descendance of Jimmu, the first Japanese emperor, from a dragon. The dragon mask, which is a symbol of the sea divinity, still has a prominent part in the *kagura* dances.

These two mythological pantomimes are important for the history of the theater for yet another reason. They initiate two major symbolic stage props which have remained characteristic of the Japanese theater: the bamboo branch, head ornament, and mirror in Uzume's dance, and the red earth on the face and hands of Umihiko foreshadowing the greasepaint mask that throughout East Asia is still an essential means of theatrical transformation.

All the different dance plays and sacrificial rites performed with the intention of gaining the favor of supernatural powers by the magic of pantomime and mask traditionally fall into the category of *kagura*. The etymological meaning of the word is controversial—it is variously interpreted as "seat of the gods" or "entertainment of the gods"—but the concept certainly predates the Chinese ideographs still used in writing it down. For the scholar, this constitutes proof that *kagura* dates back to the original inhabitants of Japan, and certainly predates the introduction of the Chinese language and writing in Japan.

The term *kagura* describes not only the mythological ritual dances, but also the originally prehistoric, shamanistic invocation of demons and animals, such as the incantations of hunting magic that is expressed in stag and wild-boar dances and survives in the lion dance (*shishimai*). The court ceremonies celebrating *Mikagura*, a winter festival (dating back to 1002), and derived from the dance of the goddess Uzume all the informally improvised pro- and anti-mythological folk farces performed by jesters, mimes, and acrobats in honor of the Shintoistic deities—all these fall into the category of *kagura.*

The modern concept of village *kagura* (*sato-kagura*) originated in the seventeenth century. Its connection with mythology and the shamanistic ritual, the invocation of benevolent spirits and the exorcism of evil ones, survived until the twentieth century in superstitious rites. In 1916, during a devastating cholera epidemic in Japan, *kagura* plays were organized in the belief that they might banish the plague.

GIGAKU

When Buddhism reached the islands of Japan, coming from China in the middle of the sixth century, it brought with it from the mainland the first Buddhist song and dance plays. A Korean immigrant, Mimashi from Kudara, is credited with their introduction. He arrived with a strolling troupe in the ancient capital of Nara in 612. Prince-regent Shotoku Taishi (572–621), a patron of the arts and zealous pioneer of Buddhism in Japan, took pleasure in the dances and plays of the foreign performers. He induced Mimashi to settle at Sakurai, not far from Nara, and there to instruct selected young pupils in the art of the new dance play. The emperor himself is said to have chosen the name for the dance play; he called it *gigaku*—"artful music." And the *gigaku* soon became part of the state ceremonial. It was performed in front of the temples all through the country every year on the two great religious holidays, Buddha's birthday and the day of the dead. There was as yet no stage; the dancers moved on the level ground, to the accompaniment of side drums, cymbals, and flutes.

A description of the *gigaku,* which soon was absorbed by a new form of courtly dance play, the *bugaku,* may be gathered from a much later treatise called the *Kyokunsho,* written retrospectively in 1233 by the dancer Koma no Chikazane. The initial procession of dancers and musicians was followed by pantomime plays, performed in grotesque helmet masks with long beak noses, powerful jaws, and bulging eyeballs.

The fact that the dance plays performed by Mimashi and his group originally contained phallic scenes, has led to the assumption of a connection with the late Roman *mimus.* Much more convincing, however, is the assumption that the phallic ritual did not originate in Greece, but in the highlands of Central Asia and that its influence flowed in the reverse direction.

The *gigaku* masks demonstrate that strong currents of ancient shamanistic concepts reached Japan from Tibet and North China via Korea. The surviving *gigaku* masks (there are about 200 extant) are among the oldest and most valuable records of early East Asian cults. Most of these masks are in Nara, in the treasure-house (*shoso-in*) of the emperor Tenji, some others in a few temples.

BUGAKU

In the course of the eighth century, the new dance play called *bugaku* gained predominance. Music was the bridge between the *bugaku* and the earlier *gigaku*—the instrumental court music known as *gagaku,* which was closely akin to the Chinese music of the T'ang period. The name *bugaku,* "dance and music," gives an idea of its character. *Bugaku* required two groups of dancers: "The dancers of the Music on the Right" and "the Dancers of the Music on the Left." The Dancers of the Music on the Right entered the stage from the right, and their musicians were stationed on the right side of the stage. Correspondingly, the Dancers of the Music on the Left made their entrance from the left, and their musicians were stationed on the left.

The *bugaku* stage was a raised, square platform, surrounded by railings, with stairs leading up to it on the right and on the left. The musical ensemble on the left consisted predominantly of wind instruments. In the ensemble on the right, percussion instruments dominated and marked the rhythmic pattern for the Dancers on the Right. The performance was preceded by the *embu,* a dance ceremony of purification of cultic origin. (The introductory scene of classical Indian drama, the *purvaranga,* begins with a rite closely related to the *embu.*) Then the left and the right groups begin to dance, in part in stately and in part in lively rhythms. The two groups are as rigorously distinct as are those of the "Blues" and "Greens" in the enigmatic Christmas play of the "Goths" that was performed at the imperial court of Byzantium. The dancers come onstage alternately from left and right, and always in pairs; those who dance to the music on the left which is inspired by Chinese and Indian sources, wear costumes in which red predominates, while green distinguishes the Dancers of the Music on the Right. This music is of Korean and Manchurian origin and adapted to the Japanese taste. The *bugaku* ends, now as it has always done, with the *chogeishi* composition by Minamoto no Hiromasa (919–80).

During the Heian period (about 820), the *bugaku* was the exclusive official ceremonial dance play at the imperial court. To this day, *bugaku*

Gigaku *mask, Nara era, 7th century. (Tokyo.)*

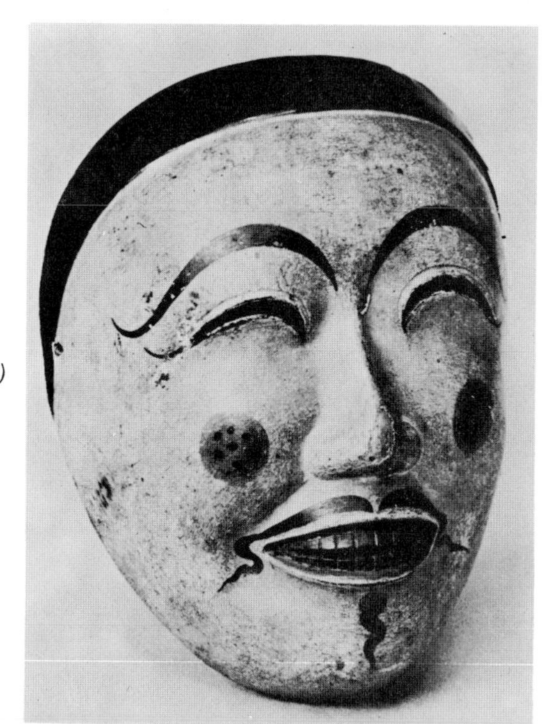

Bugaku *mask, Heian era, 1185. (Nara.)*

is performed at court, and the privilege of performing in it is passed on from generation to generation in the *bugaku* artists' families. Once or twice a year, usually in honor of some important state visitor, *bugaku* dance plays are performed at the imperial court before an exclusive audience. The traditional character of *bugaku* has been preserved unaltered in the dance and music, though the costumes and masks have changed. Popular, folk versions of *bugaku,* which are independent of the court ceremonial, have survived in many small Shinto temples, together with elements of *gagaku* music, in a great variety of Japanese folk dances.

SARUGAKU AND DENGAKU, PRECURSORS OF NŌ

The stately and controlled dance movement; the ceremonial steps; the significant raising and lowering of the head; the sudden, immobile, silent pose after a violent sally—all these basic elements of classical Japanese theater art can be traced back to the two forms of dance play from which eventually the great art of *nō* developed: the *sarugaku* and *dengaku.*

In the great temple cities of Nara, Kyōto, and Yedo (later Tokyo) the arts of miming, dancing, acrobatics, and chanting had always prospered. The *ennen-mai,* dance plays originally performed by Buddhist monks, came to be diversified by secular attractions. Acrobats, jugglers, stilt walkers, and puppet players would flock to the temples, and the people would acclaim them, grateful for the opportunity of combining the solemn ceremonial in honor of the gods with a spectacle gratifying to eye and ear. In the Heian period (794–1185), the word *sarugaku* had been used to define the whole, rich variety of popular entertainments. The term derived from the older art form *sangaku,* (probably meaning "scattered music"), which had a long and active history in China before it ever reached Japan, at about the same time as the courtly *bugaku.* The Chinese script character (symbol) "monkey," used for *saru,* has led scholars to define *sarugaku* as "monkey music," in contrast to the indigenous *dengaku,* "rice-field music." The derivation from *saru* would have interesting implications for the cultural historian. In China, the "monkey with the official's cap" had found his way onto the stage as a critic of contemporary affairs in clown's garb, and in the Indian *Ramayana* and the Indonesian shadow play the monkey-king Hanuman helps Rama, the son of the gods, to victory over the demon king of

Ceylon. Cult, legend, folk tale, moral theory, and the theater alike ascribe important functions to the monkey, ranging from the judgment of the dead in Egypt to Hans Werner Henze's opera *The Young Lord.*

Both *sarugaku* and *dengaku* resemble the popular carnival entertainments of the West. In the chronicle *Rakuyo dengaku-ki,* by Oe-no-Masafusa (1096), we find mention of riotous dances and processions in which the whole population of the capital took part—the old and the young, the rich and the poor; even high state officials participated, wearing masks and comic costumes and carrying enormous fans.

The *dengaku* had its origins in rural harvest dances, and in the course of the fourteenth century it developed into something going well beyond mere popular entertainment. It absorbed courtly elements from *gigaku* and, at the *dengaku* schools of Nara and Kyōto, was elaborated into the sophisticated form of art known as *dengaku-no-nō.*

There were in Japan actors' families or guilds, called the *za,* which dated back to the beginning of the Muromachi period (1392–1568). (*Za* still is the Japanese word for theater.) The *za* enjoyed the protection of the Buddhist temples. Their members were exempt from the severe tax and labor obligations and had a monopoly on performance in their specific temple district.

The general anonymity of Japan's professional actors came to an end early in the fourteenth century, when the names of individual actors were first recorded. Among these were the names of the *sarugaku* actor Kwanami and his son Seami, to whom the Japanese theater owes its most fascinating and profound art form. Kwanami and Seami both initiated and interpreted the new style they created.

NŌ

While in Europe the age of chivalry—when emperor and princes rallied to the Crusades—was coming to an end, there flourished in Japan the courtly civilization of the Samurai.

The atmosphere of splendor at the imperial residence, the palaces of the nobles, and the aesthetically refined temple cult bred an aristocratic class whose patronage was to make of the *nō* play the artistic epitome and the mirror of its age. The aristocratic warrior caste of the Samurai took pride in its descendance from the great heroic families, bearing such names as Genji, Heike, or Ise. The power of the leading feudal chiefs, the Daimyos, crystallized in the office of the Shōgun, by title general-in-chief and imperial administrator but in fact sole ruler of Japan. And just as the European ideal of chivalry was exalted in the courtly poetry of the Middle Ages, in the *Song of Roland,* the Arthurian cycle, and the *Cid,* so the Japanese epics exalted the world of the Samurai. Their unwritten code of honor demanded of them the virtues of heroism, magnanimity, loyalty unto death to the feudal lord, selfless championship of the rights of the weak, and contempt of cowardice, of avarice and treason. These ideals derived from the doctrines of Zen Buddhism, the striving for "enlightenment" and for the intuitive spiritual experience of the absolute. The strength for mastering the tasks of this world grew out of the observance of daily periods of intense meditation which, outside the purely religious sphere, became the mainspring of the whole of creative art. "Nothing is real," says the chorus speaking for the poetess Komachi, the protagonist of *Sotoba Komachi* ("Komachi at the Grave"), one of the major *nō* plays inspired by Zen Buddhism; "Between Buddha and Man/ Is no distinction, but a seeming of difference planned/ For the welfare of the humble, the ill-instructed,/ Whom he has vowed to save."*

Like the sensitive intensity of watercolor painting or the controlled imagery of the *haiku* verse, the whole art of *nō* is informed by the mystic chiaroscuro of Zen Buddhism.

With the refined *dengaku* and *sarugaku* the actors and the temple officials responsible for the performances had satisfied the high standards and won the favor of the exacting nobility; but now, with the rise of the *nō* plays, the convergence of art and patronage ushered in the golden age of Japanese theater. In 1374 the Shōgun Yoshimitsu saw a performance by the *sarugaku* actor Kwanami and his son Seami. The young ruler was so struck by the performance of the father and the beauty of the eleven-year-old Seami, that he attached them both to his court.

Kwanami Kiyotsugu set a high standard for his son Seami. He constantly enriched his own range of dramatic expression, and so refashioned the dramatic pattern in the *nō* play. Seami's work was greatly influenced by his father Kwanami's famous play about the fate of the poetess Sotoba Komachi. And Seami Motokiyo knew how to take advantage of the Shōgun's protection in advancing the cause of the theater. His aim was twofold; he wanted to gain recognition both for the art of acting and for the drama as such. He developed into a most accomplished actor, playwright, and director. With his unerring sense of what will move an audience, he watched the great actors of his day. He studied the techniques of the famous *dengaku* actors Itchū and Zōami, of the *kuse-mai* dancer Otsuro, the *omi-sarugaku* actor Keno, and the actor Kotaro of the *Komparu* School. Thus Seami perfected his own style. He

* English version from Arthur Waley, *The Nō Plays of Japan* (London: Allen & Unwin, 1921).

wrote both the text and the music for about 100 *nō* plays in which he himself acted the leading part. One of the highlights of his career was his famous performance of *The Star of Seami* before the emperor Go-Komatsu in 1408.

After the death of his patron Yoshimitsu and the loss of his son Motomasa, Seami retired from the court. He endeavored to expound in writing the spirit and significance of *nō,* which means, literally, "talent." Thanks to his three great theoretical treatises, *Hanakagami, Kwadensho,* and *Kyui,* Seami became the Aristotle of the Japanese theater. But this artistic testament remained unknown to his own age. It was written not for publication, but exclusively for the secret transmission of his art within his own family.

In 1434, Seami was exiled for reasons we do not know—perhaps because he refused to pass on his secret code of *nō* art to his nephew Onami, who was the favorite of the new Shōgun. History is silent on this point. Eventually, after the death of this Shōgun, Seami returned from exile. He then transmitted his artistic heritage not to his nephew Onami, but to his son-in-law Zenchiku, with whom he spent the last years of his life.

The *nō* play, because of its dramatic construction and set pattern, has often been compared with Greek tragedy. There are in fact certain analogies in such matters as cultic origin, participation of a chorus, and the sharp distinction between the protagonist and secondary characters. But these count for nothing against the entirely different spirit and approach of the two dramatic species. While Antigone defies Creon's command and challenges destiny and the gods, Komachi practices silent endurance, and the priests, "bending their heads to the ground, three times did homage before her" with the words, "A saint, a saint is this decrepit, outcast soul."*

The profound significance of the content of *nō* is not rebellion but acceptance, acceptance of a beauty culminating in sorrow. Seami sought to illustrate this "beauty so fascinating and surprising in its contradiction" by poetic comparison, as in his treatise *Kyui:* "In Shiragi the sun is bright at midnight." It is, perhaps, in terms of this example that we may best explain the meaning of the term *yūgen* which, according to Seami, constitutes the culmination of the aesthetic appreciation of the *nō* play. *Yūgen,* originally the hidden content of the Buddhist doctrine, is a secret power in which beauty is enfolded like a seed from which the flower (*hana*) is to blossom forth.

The firm spiritual foundation of the *nō* plays has its counterpart in their set dramaturgical pattern. There are five categories of *nō* plays,

* English version from Waley, *The Nō Plays of Japan.*

Woman with fishnet, clos
madness because of the d
of her only daughter, wh
pears to the right in the b
ground, sitting to the
of a bonze in a hooded c
Scene from nō *play.*
Color print, ca. 1900.

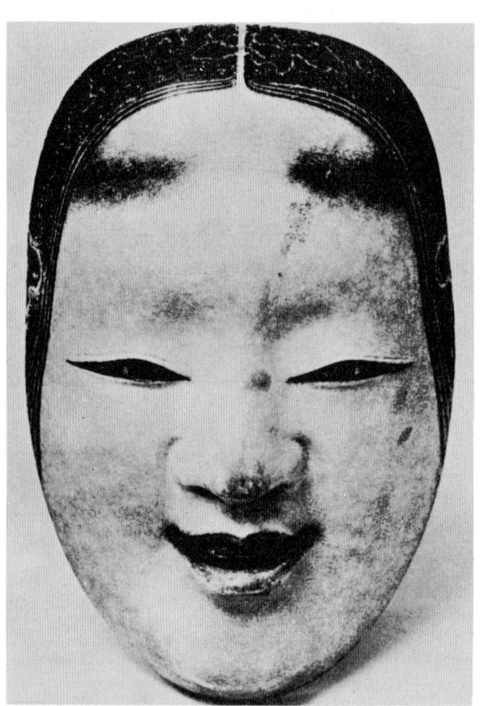

Nō *mask of a young woman, Muromachi era,*
century. (Tokyo.)

Old woman kneeling
reading from a scroll; p
ably the poetess Komachi
Scene from nō *play.*
Color print, ca. 1900.

all of which are to this day represented in the program of any *nō* performance. The first group deals with the subject of the gods; the second with that of battle (most often the glorification of some heroic Samurai); the third group is known as "wig plays," or "women's plays," because the leading actor wears a wig and plays the role of a woman; the fourth and dramatically strongest category portrays the fate of a broken-hearted woman, often driven to madness by the loss of her lover or son; the fifth category, which ends the program, tells a legend.

The protagonist and leader (*iemoto*) of a *nō* troupe is the *shite;* his partner and principal secondary actor is the *waki.* Each of them is accompanied by a following—actors representing servants or companions—and there is a chorus, normally of eight men who do the chanting. The members of the chorus all wear dark clothes and sit down on the ground at the beginning of the play. They comment on the action, but they do not intervene in it, as does the chorus of Greek tragedy. The *shite* wears a mask which, according to his part, may represent a valiant hero, a bearded old man, a young bride, or a careworn old woman.

The Japanese see nothing unnatural in a male actor expressing the feelings of a woman, her happiness or despair. On the contrary, they regard the mask as literally the expression of a higher truth. The mask confers on the actor a higher and more quintessential form of life. The carved masks of the *nō* actors are themselves works of art of high quality; they symbolize the character in its purest form, cleansed of all imperfections. The poet Yeats observed that "A mask . . . no matter how close you go, is yet a work of art." When, in 1915, in his search for "a form of drama, distinguished, indirect, and symbolic," he encountered the *nō* plays, he believed he had found a way of breathing new life into the Irish legends; he felt that nothing was lost "by stilling the movement of the features, for deep feeling is expressed by a movement of the whole body."

The art of *nō* requires the utmost concentration. For hours on end the actor, in his costume of gorgeous brocades, must so conduct himself that his gestures and movements never contradict his mask. His range of action is paced out precisely; every step he takes forward or sideways has its prescribed measure.

The traditional *nō* stage is a highly polished cedarwood platform about eighteen feet square, open on three sides. It has a temple roof, supported by four posts. The background is always the same; a large, knotty pine tree painted on the boards of the back wall as a symbol of eternal life. Three steps lead up to the stage, which is raised about three feet above the ground; it usually stands in the courtyard of a temple. The *nō* play is still closely connected with religious ceremony and the feasts of the temple saints. One of the oldest *nō* stages in existence stands in the temple district of Kyōto. It is dedicated to Shinran shōnin, the founder of the Shin sect. According to an inscription, it dates from the year 1591. Every year, on May 21, on Shinran's birthday, it is the scene of solemn *nō* performances.

Because of its creative vitality and intrinsic harmony with the fundamental traits of the Japanese character the *nō* play has survived intact since the fourteenth century. Occasional shifts of emphasis have merely caused minor changes in its dramatic structure, but none of its substance. There are, for instance, some *nō* plays—like *Rashōmon* or *Funa-Benkei*—in which the dominating figure is not the *shite* but the *waki*; the explanation is that around 1500 their author, the actor and poet Kwanze Kojirō Nobumitsu for years played the *waki* in a *nō* ensemble. Understandably enough, he wrote the best part for the second-ranking actor, himself.

Today's somewhat more stately pace of the *nō* plays, the instrumental subleties in their accompanying music (flute, drums, tambourines), and the splendor of the gold-brocade costumes all date back to the middle of the eighteenth century. But nothing has impaired the validity of what Zenchiku, Seami's son-in-law and artistic heir, said about the dramatic technique and ambiance of *nō*:

> Everything redundant has been pruned, the beauty of the essential is wholly and fully cleansed. It is the inexpressible beauty of doing nothing. . . . It is like the music of gentle rain in the few remaining branches of the famous old cherry trees of Yoshino, Chara, and Oshio: overgrown with moss, with a few blossoms here and there. . . .

Scene from the nō *play* Funa-Benkei. *Drawing by Toyoshi Kawanabe. Tokyo, 1899.*

Nō *stage in the temple district of Kyōto, erected in 1591 and dedicated to the founder of the Shin sect, Shinran Shonin, whose birthday on May 21, is celebrated annually with* nō *performances. The cedarwood floor is kept carefully polished to mirrorlike gloss.*

Empty nō *stage and auditorium: the Kwanze-kai-nō Theater in Tokyo, 1960.*

KYŌGEN

Kyōgen are a traditional component of the *nō* plays, and presumably as old, if not older. They are farce plays, providing interludes of comic relief in the solemn, formal conventions of *nō*. They make kindly and indulgent fun of human weakness and once served to introduce the first aspects of social criticism into the self-assured world of the Samurai.

Sly servants hoodwink their mean master, impostors are caught in their own trap, hypocritical monks are exposed, a droll little monkey saves its own life and, in his own person, the most cherished property of his weeping owner. Some of the buffoonery and jokes of the *kyōgen* are reminiscent of the European *Commedia dell'arte*; there is indeed one example of striking coincidence. In the *kyōgen* interlude *Bōshibari,* two servants are tied together by their hands to prevent them from doing mischief. But, despite this precaution, they manage to get hold of the rice wine. There is a similar *Commedia dell'arte* scene in which two similarly restricted *servitori* help themselves to the macaroni withheld from them.

Kyōgen farces are not bitter, but gay. They practice social criticism without making heavy weather of it. Anything immodest or vulgar is strictly excluded; for, as Seami says, on no account should vulgar words or gestures be introduced, however comic they may be.

Hardly anything is known about the authors of the 200 or so *kyōgen* scripts still in use. One of the oldest of the traditional texts dates from the fourteenth century and is attributed to the priest Kitabatake Gene Hōni of the Hieizan monastery. But thereafter it is hard to find clues to authorship. One thing seems certain: a jealously guarded succession must have been the rule in *kyōgen* as in all of *nō,* the scripts were kept strictly secret and were bequeathed from father to son—exactly as in the harlequin and *Hanswurst* tradition of the European theater.

Kyōgen actors generally wear no masks, except when portraying a few special types such as the little monkey in *Utsubozaru*. Like *nō, kyōgen* has its traditional hierarchy of actors, that is, a protagonist and principal (*omo*), and a second-ranking actor (*ado*). The *kyōgen* rallied the scattered remnants of popular theatrical forms that were cast off as *sarugaku* was being refined into *nō*. Several generations later, these became the source for the realistic elements of the early *kabuki*.

Scene with dancing monkey, reminiscent of the still popular kyōgen *play* Utsubozaru, *which the Kwanze-kai-nō ensemble of Tokyo took on a European tour in 1966.*
Color print, ca. 1900.

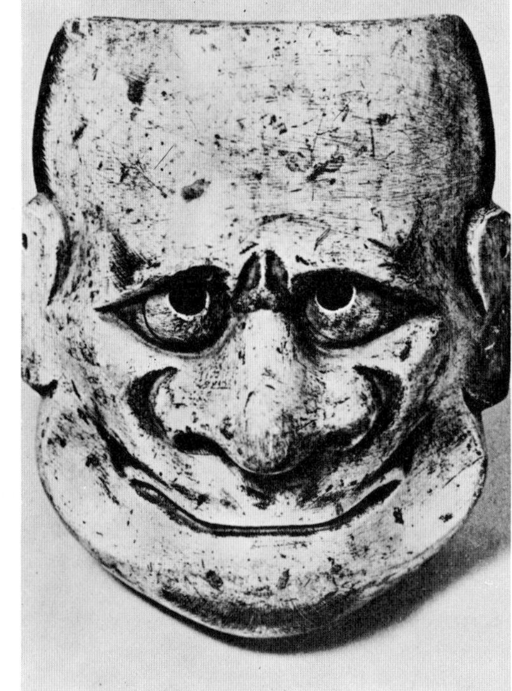

Kyōgen *mask of an old man, Muromachi era 15th century. (Tokyo.)*

THE PUPPET THEATER

The art of the puppet play can be traced all through the theater of the Far East. The marionette manipulated by strings or wires; the sumptuously clothed Javanese *wayang* doll; the rustic, carved hand puppet of the island of Awaji—all these, along with the ballad singer and the storyteller, have always found their public in high and low circles alike.

The first mention of puppets in Japan dates from the eighth century. It is recorded that some ancillary use was made of puppets in the *sangaku* (a form of musical play that had come from China).

During the Heian period (794–1185) puppet shows traveled throughout the land with the strolling troupes. The puppet "stage" was a rectangular box, open at the front. The puppeteer carried it by a strap slung around the back of his neck. During the performance, he moved his puppets, which were put together from bits of wood and cloth, through openings cut into the back and the sides of the box. This primitive and timeless form of puppet show is still common today in some remote regions of Japan.

But the highly stylized art of the animated puppets of Osaka owes its inspiration and development to the fusion of puppetry with the recitations of singers and storytellers. At the time when Europe's wandering scholars were singing of the deeds of Charlemagne in the *Chansons de geste,* blind Japanese monks sat before the temple gates and recited scenes from the Samurai epics to the accompaniment of the *samisen,* a three- to five-stringed lute. One of the best-known ballads tells the sad story of the girl Jōruri, who forever searches for her beloved, and finds him only to lose him once more. Toward the end of the sixteenth century, the much-recited ballad of Jōruri gave its name to a newly emerging form of art, the play of hand-manipulated puppets (*ningyo,* which means "hand puppet"); it came to be known as *ningyo jōruri.* It owes its origins to two itinerant performers, the puppet master Hikita Awaji-no-jō and the *jōruri* ballad singer and *samisen* player Menukiya Chōzaburō, who one day decided to give a joint show. Hikita made the dolls act out the story told by his partner, and the two of them were widely acclaimed. The emperor called them to his court, and soon their example was followed by other teams of singers and puppet players.

In no time, *ningyo jōruri* became widely popular, especially in the great trade center Osaka. Rich merchants financed a puppet theater, and under their influence the thematic accents shifted from the courtly world of the Samurai to the trading offices and the emotional range of the merchant class.

The puppet play was raised to artistic heights by its access to the masterpieces of the greatest Japanese dramatist, Chikamatsu Monzaemon (1653–1725). For "Japan's Shakespeare" wrote his finest works not for human actors, but for the carved wooden doll. When Chikamatsu's works are skillfully performed, the puppet, animated in some mysterious way, becomes the vehicle of emotions and passions that know no bounds. The puppet is never in danger of running off the rails, its pathetic gesture is always aesthetically beautiful and never embarrassing.

Kleist's brilliant remark in his study "Über das Marionettentheater," "that there can be more grace in a mechanical manikin than in the human body," applies as much to the Osaka puppets as to any. Even by Chikamatsu's time, the original dolls, which had been manipulated by hand, were developed into elaborately constructed figures and possessed remarkable dexterity in walking, dancing, and even in rolling their eyes and wrinkling their forehead. It is believed that as early as 1727 there existed devices for giving the puppets ingenious exits. First, there were small trapdoors for individual figures or for parts of the décor, later, devices for bigger platforms that could also be used to build up the stage floor on three different levels. In working with these stage devices of the puppet theater, Namiki Shōzō, the inventor of the Japanese revolving stage for the *kabuki* theater, acquired his first technical experience. In Japan, the revolving stage is reported to have been used first at the Kado-za puppet theater in Osaka.

The stage for *ningyo jōruri* consists of a wooden bridge on which the puppets act, while the puppet master who manipulates them stands in a sort of pit. He remains in view of the spectators without destroying their illusion in the least; if the puppets are large, he may even sit or stand on the stage itself. He wears dark clothes and a hood, and so melts into the background while he imparts the puppets in their sumptuous shimmering robes, with the capacity to love and hate, suffer and endure, fight and die.

The narrator sits to the right of the stage, behind a richly decorated lacquer stand that holds his script; next to him sits the *samisen* player. The number of speakers and musicians depends on the kind and intricacy of the play.

The difficulties of providing the technical requirements—as many as three puppeteers may be required to work a single puppet—together with competition of the *kabuki* theatre caused the gradual decline of *jōruri* in the course of the eighteenth century. Between 1780 and 1870 there was not a single artistically competent *jōruri* theater in the whole of Japan.

A hundred years later, *jōruri* was revived by a puppet master from the island of Awaji, the traditional home of popular folk puppet shows.

In 1871 Uemura Bunrakuken founded Osaka's Bunraku Theater (named after him), and it was there that the art of the *ningyo jōruri* revived in new glory. The building, which stood in a temple district outside the town, burned down in 1926. Today the famous Osaka puppets have their home in the modern Asahi-za, which is part of the great theater concern belonging to the Shōchiku corporation. For the last hundred years, the name Bunraku has been part of the international vocabulary; it evokes everywhere the accomplished art of the Japanese marionette theater of Osaka.

KABUKI

The early seventeenth century, marked in Europe by the splendor of the baroque, at last brought peace to Japan after a series of family feuds and civil wars. But it was also a time of new conflicts, generated by the first intrusion of a distant, alien, outside world. Portuguese merchants were bringing to Japan the goods of their lands, and Xavier's Jesuit missionaries were propagating their faith. Commoners began to have a decisive voice in governing their own affairs and the affairs of the state.

While the solemn *bugaku* dances had found their place in the ceremonial of the imperial court and *nō* had been entirely geared to the Samurai aesthetics based on Zen Buddhism, a new theater form now addressed itself to the full range of the social reality. This was *kabuki*. The three Chinese script characters which today express the word *kabuki* mean song, dance, and artistic skill.

The origin of *kabuki* is attributed to the dancer O-kuni, a former priestess of the Shintō shrine at Izumo. Around 1600, O-kuni was giving dance and song recitals at various places in the capital Kyōto, in order to collect donations for rebuilding her shrine at Izumo which had burned down. No doubt, she danced the *nembutsu-odori,* a prayer dance honoring Buddha, known since the tenth century and spread by wandering monks.

The success of her fund-raising campaign led O-kuni, either on her own initiative or at the instance of businesslike advisers, to change the originally religious character of her art to a more businesslike one. She trained a few young girls, rehearsed little dance and dialogue scenes with them, and proceeded to appear with her ensemble and an orchestra of flutes, drums, and tambourines at the summer amusement park of Kyōto, in the dry river bed of the Kamo, where numerous little restaur-

Women's kabuki *theater at the time of the dancer O-kuni in Kyōto. Ca. 1620.*

ants, teahouses, and dance troupes put up their stalls every year in the dry season.

In 1607 O-kuni took her girls to Yedo, today's Tokyo, where she again attracted large audiences. Shrewd teahouse owners began to attach a *kabuki* theater garden to their establishments. The young dancers were most attractive in every respect; but, as their morals grew more lax, their reputation rapidly waned. Twenty years later, an imperial edict prohibited the *onna-kabuki,* and the appearance of women (*onna*) on the stage.

A document from the early days of the *O-kuni kabuki,* the *Kunijo kabuki ekotoba,* which was written sometime between 1604 and 1630 and is today preserved in the university library of Kyōto, gives a vivid picture of this period. Its illustrations show how the old traditional features of the prayer dance combined with elements of *nō* and *kyōgen.* It records the following plot of one of O-kuni's dance plays.

O-kuni is mourning for her lover and, conjured up by the fervor of her dance, the dead man's ghost appears to her. The ghost is impersonated by a young actress and enters the stage from among the public. This device heralded a development that became a principle of *kabuki* stage technique. Ghosts, gods, and heroes make their entrance through the stalls along a wooden bridge called *hanamichi,* that is, the flower path. It is said that the public here laid flowers at their feet—a pretty, but unsupported interpretation.

In 1624 the founder of the line of actors called Nakamura, one of the most renowned of the *kabuki* actors' dynasties, built the first permanent *kabuki* theater in Yedo. Five years later, *onna-kabuki* was prohibited. No woman was henceforth allowed to appear in *kabuki*. Boy actors took over the parts of the banished ladies, together with their other duties. They soon inspired rivalries no less violent than had the ladies of the profession, for the pleasures of the stage and backstage were equally sought by the wealthy merchants, the Shōnins, and members of the Samurai class. In 1652 the authorities put an end also to the *wakashu-kabuki,* played by boys.

But two years later came the decisive turn, when permission was obtained to go on playing, provided that all performers had their head shaved as was the custom for men, and that no erotic scenes or provocative dances were included.

From then on, the development of *kabuki* bears the mark of the native Japanese bent for stylization and star performers. Soon there developed four distinct categories of plays, which still make up the *kabuki* programs today. The first is the historical drama, *jidaimono,* which glorifies the Samurai and their traditional virtues—loyalty and filial affection. The second is *sewamono,* a domestic drama set in the world of the merchants, traders, and artisans. The third category, *aragoto,* the strong-man drama, presents some superman in heavy makeup and with melodramatic speech. The fourth, *shosagoto,* is a sort of dance drama accompanied by hand drums, a big drum, flutes, and the *samisen,* as well

Boys' kabuki *theater in Kyōto. Ca. 1640.*

as by a chorus chanting the ballad story and lyrical incidents of the plot.

Four famous names are closely associated with the *kabuki* theater of the second half of the seventeenth century, those of the three actors Tōjūrō, Danjūrō, and Ayame, and of the great dramatist Chikamatsu, who had been so closely connected with the puppet theater. Their art and their life mirror the social situation of their time.

Sakata Tōjūrō (1647–1709), famous for the part of the affectionate lover in courtesan plays, dominated the stage at Kyōto and Osaka. As a boy, on his father's *nō* stage, kneeling in the background he had beaten the drum. Later, as a popular *kabuki* star and author of successful plays, he led the life of a prince. Tōjūrō is a typical representative of the *genroku* world where the merchants have waxed rich and the Samurai are impoverished, where the red-light districts flourish and the citizens are pushed by their ambitions.

With sound understanding of what made his contemporaries run, Tōjūrō declared that life itself was the great teacher of his art. "The art of the mime," he once said, "is like a beggar's sack. It has to contain everything, important and unimportant. If one finds something that does not look as though it can be used at once, the thing to do is to take it along and to keep it for some future occasion. A true actor should learn the trade of a pickpocket."

Tōjūrō's great rival of the stages of Yedo was Ichikawa Danjūrō (1660–1704). In his teens he was a member of a strolling troupe. When he appeared for the first time in Yedo, in 1673, he covered his face thickly with red and white paint for the part of an *aragoto* hero. This was the birth of the *kabuki* theater's makeup mask. Danjūrō took over the declamatory style of the puppet theater, whose rhapsodist Izumidayū, in Yedo, he greatly admired and took as his model. Danjūrō was a short and stocky man of astonishing physical strength and vocal power, which, as the chroniclers relate, caused not only the stage to shake but the porcelain in the nearby stores as well. When he opened all the stops of emotion in some *aragoto* part, his thundering voice could be heard miles away. Danjūrō's ideal was the hero of the Samurai world. Like Tōjūrō, he wrote at least some of his plays himself or adapted them from *nō* scripts, like the famous *Kajincho*. By an irony of history this invincible hero was killed by the sword of a rival actor during a dispute in the dressing room of the Ichimura-za Theater in Yedo.

The third of the stars of early *kabuki* was Yoshizawa Ayame (b. 1673). He was an impersonator of female roles and took his style so seriously that he ended up with an almost hermaphroditic narcissism. He always wore women's clothes, even outside the theater, as well as an elaborate towering wig, used cosmetics, and transposed his stage image into the whole of his private life. An actor of female roles, he claimed, must never—even after the performance, in the dressing room, or in the street—be "out of character." Ayame's absurd fixation of turning the *onnagata* into a courtesan, even in everyday life, introduced a conventional rigidity into *kabuki* which did not help its subsequent artistic development.

The man to which the *kabuki* theater owes its most powerful boost was Japan's greatest dramatist, Chikamatsu Monzaemon (1653–1725). His original name was Sugimori Nobumori, but it was common practice in Japanese theater life for a performer to take as his stage name the name of a performer he acknowledged as his model. In this way generations of Tōjūrōs and Danjūrōs succeeded each other (an 1858 woodcut by Kunisada shows Danjūrō VII) without having anything other than their artistic ambitions in common with their ancestor.

But no one ever dared take on Chikamatsu Monzaemon's stage name after him. From the age of nineteen he lived in Kyōto. He was in the service of a court noble called Ogimachi, who wrote *jōruri* plays. This is where Chikamatsu first came in contact with the puppet theater, to which he was to devote his finest works. About twenty of Chikamatsu's plays have come down to us; they all draw their strength from two sources, namely, the close connection with the *ningyo jōruri* and the influence of the actor Tōjūrō in Osaka. Both Tōjūrō's and Chikamatsu's art was rooted in the domestic melodrama (*sewamono*), in the hopelessly tragic conflict between the promptings of the heart and the rigid laws of the feudal social order.

There is an old theater maxim in Japan that says: "Theater expresses the people's wisdom. It must demonstrate the path of duty by examples and models." Chikamatsu sets his heroes and heroines in the conflict between human nature and the moral law. He makes them resist all temptations in exemplary fashion and lets them find the best possible and ethically justified way out.

During the first half of the eighteenth century, *kabuki* and the puppet theater competed for the people's favor with almost even odds. Thanks to adaptations of the great epic themes and with the help of Chikamatsu's masterly plays, *kabuki* outdistanced its rival. It also had the benefit of the star cult. Every city had its idols. The masters of the colored woodcut rendered their portraits or depicted them in some stirring posture of a stage part. The actor series by Sharaku, who himself had once been a *nō* actor in the service of the Prince of Awa, show the favorites of Yedo in impressive magnificence. And Hokusai's theater sketches captured the fleeting grace of the dancing movement. When, in 1794, the theater manager Miyako Dennai took over the bankrupt Nakamura-za in Yedo, he circulated a woodcut portrait of himself by Sharaku showing him in a decorative pose on the stage, holding a scroll—a somewhat expensive proof of his commercial soundness. At the same time, Sharaku was commissioned to make drawings of the actors at

Two color woodcuts by Sharaku, ca. 1790. Left, the Kabuki *actors Sawamura Yodogoro and Bando Zenji; right, Segawa Tomisaburo II and Nakamura Mamyo, as mistress and servant.*

Color woodcut by Shigeharu: two actors as dueling Samurai.

Color woodcut by Torii Kiyonaga: theater s[e] *with reciters and* samisen *player.*

Yedo's three main theaters. His large colored woodcuts of heads on a silvery grey mica background, all done between 1793 and 1796, are among the most precious pictorial records of the Japanese theater.

One of the most famous of the *kabuki* dramas, *Kanahedon Chū-shingura,* by Takeda Izumo and Namiki Sosuke, is still regularly performed every year, either in abbreviated form or in its entirety. It tells the tale of the forty-seven nobles (*ronin*) who exact cruel vengeance for a murder committed out of loyalty to the feudal lord. They obey the Samurai code of ethics at the cost of their own life. The historical episode underlying this play, the story of the forty-seven ronin, is one of the most popular subjects in Japanese literature.

The *kabuki* stage, originally taken over from *nō,* was a square platform without decoration. At first it was set up wherever convenient and in the open air, later in a circumscribed district and, finally, it moved into a permanent theater building. The audience sat on wooden benches. The bigger theaters had galleries and tiers along the side walls, often—like the seating arrangement on the ground floor—divided into boxes. The entrance fee was paid at the gate and depended on the seat category the theatergoer desired.

To this day, the flower path (*hanamichi*) is one of the most characteristic ingredients of *kabuki.* It runs, at the height of the heads of the ground-floor audience, from a little door in the back wall of the auditorium to one side of the stage. Large theaters often have a second, smaller entrance bridge, which runs parallel to the *hanamichi* to the other side of the stage. (When Max Reinhardt produced—in 1910 for the Berliner Kammerspiele—the pantomime *Sumurun,* which was inspired by Oriental motives, he also used a flower path.)

As the number of players grew and the program expanded, the *kabuki* theater began to need a sort of inner picture-frame stage, equipped with a draw curtain and variable background draperies. On the expanded *kabuki* stage certain characteristic props indicate the scene of the action; gold-painted screens, for instance, are part of the palace setting of the *jidaimono* plays, which, for this reason, are sometimes called gold-screen plays.

As early as 1753 the dramatist and stage technician Namiki Shōzō had constructed a device for raising and lowering the stage floor. In 1758, he had invented a revolving stage, operated by a system of rollers. This revolving stage was further improved in 1793 by Jūkichi at the Nakamura-za of Yedo. Japan was thus a full century ahead of Europe, which did not have its first practical experience of the revolving stage until 1896, when Karl Lautenschläger used it at the Nationaltheater in Munich. (This leaves aside, however, Leonardo da Vinci's sketches for an allegory to be presented in Milan in 1490, and the double revolving

Color woodcut by Kunisada: overall view of the Shintomi-za in Tokyo, 1881. On the left, the big flower path (hanamichi) *that leads to the* kabuki *stage; on the right, the small flower path. (Munich, Theater Museum.)*

Color woodcut by Kunisada: View of a kabuki *theater. On the stage, a battle scene; to the left, on the flower path, Danjūrō VII with partner. Single print, 1858.*

Color woodcut by Hokusai, from the series Famous Places of Yedo, *Tokyo, 1800. Stage and auditorium as seen by the musicians, who sit—unnamed—in the background of the set.*

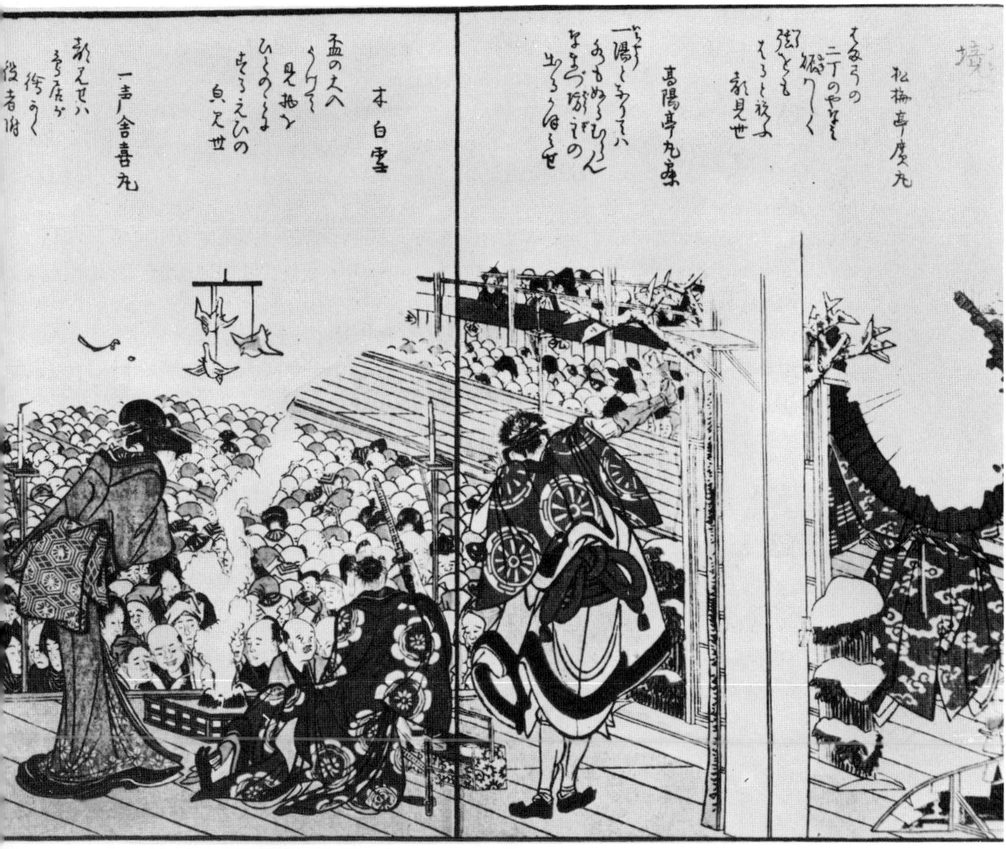

Kabuki *revolving stage, operated by coolies, as used from 1793 in the Nakamura-za of Yedo.*

stage Inigo Jones designed in 1608 for the "Masque of Beauty" in London.)

Twice, in 1841 and in 1855, great fires ravaged the city of Yedo and destroyed all its theaters. They were rebuilt, and the new theaters were larger and more spacious versions of their predecessors. No matter how many internal and external crises beset *kabuki,* it is still the most popular form of theater in Japan. Ultramodern lighting and stage techniques, fauteuils and folding seats, a foyer and multilingual playbills have in the meantime given *kabuki* an international gloss.

Today Japan has some 350 *kabuki* actors. They are employed by the great theater corporation Shōchiku-Kaisha, which owns a rich store of historical costumes and properties. The splendor of a *kabuki* performance depends today, as it always did, on the gorgeous costumes—heavy brocades lavishly embroidered and shot through with gold thread. "The effects are purely external," writes the theater scholar Benito Ortolani, "and this leads many critics to doubt the vitality of the species, and yet anyone who looks for the sources of the mysterious fascination of a remote, great civilization will find in *kabuki* the indispensable key to a profound confrontation and understanding."

SHIMPA

The political and social upheavals of the nineteenth century had their impact on the theater as well. The restoration of the Meiji in 1868 and the trade treaty with the United States ended Japan's centuries-old

Kabuki *scene: fisherwoman and bonze, near willow tree. Colored drawing by Saburo Kaneko, Tokyo, 1917.*

r representing a Samurai, in the drama ai Genji Mitsugi nō Furisode, *1782.*

Woodcut from the series Actors on the Stage *by Toyokuni: Masatsuya.*

isolation. Numerous domestic restrictions were abrogated at the same time, and the theater was one of the beneficiaries. Any number of theaters could be set up again anywhere on private initiative. The strict regulations regarding actors' costumes were relaxed and, for the first time since 1629, women were allowed to appear on the stage. But this new, liberal trend had questionable consequences from the artistic point of view. The loosening-up of the *kabuki* style as conceived by the actor Ichikawa Danjūrō IX (1838–1903) proved deleterious rather than enriching. Under European influence, groups of theater enthusiasts sprang up, which, under the name of *shimpa* ("New School Movement"), wanted to reshape the Japanese theater on European models. One of their initiators, Sudō Sadanori, introduced the portrayal of political commitment on the stage and created a sensation in 1888 with his debut at the Shintomiza in Osaka. Kawakami Otojirō, who appeared together with his wife Sadayakko at the Paris World's Fair in 1900, came to epitomize Japanese dramatic art in Europe. After his return to Japan, he made his major contribution to the Japanese stage. He introduced European plays, in Japanese translation, and staged them according to Western concepts. His fertile imagination eventually led him to have Hamlet enter the stage on a bicycle along a flower path (*hanamichi*).

The *shimpa* tendency to counteract the excessive formal rigidity of the traditional theatrical categories had an important influence on the development of the Japanese theater. It resulted in a trend toward a drama of romantic situations, a sort of *Madame Butterfly* surrogate tailored to bourgeois tastes. But this was a dead end. The success of the *shimpa* was short-lived and localized in Osaka and Tokyo, where it lasted from about 1904 to 1909.

After the Second World War, says Benito Ortolani, who was then teaching at the Sophia University of Tokyo,

> attempts were made to turn *shimpa* into a popular drama similar to *kabuki,* and to gain a wider audience by a more careful selection of plays and by the inclusion of talented young actors. This clever change of direction has secured a place in the modern Japanese theater for a species that has long outlived its function as a bridge from the *kabuki* tradition to the modern theater. But this also explains why theater and film people today, when they speak of the *shimpa* style, or of tragedies of the *shimpa* kind, have in mind sentimental, romantic, or melodramatic performances, and why most experts see no basis in *shimpa* for the future of the Japanese theater.

SHINGEKI

Another reform movement, whose influence lasted into the 1930s, was started by the dramatist and theater scholar Tsubouchi Shōyō (1859–1935). Apart from his own plays, as, for instance, the popular *Kiri Hito Ha* ("A Leaf from the Kiri Tree"), Tsubouchi Shōyō introduced Shakespeare to the Japanese stage. He spent decades translating virtually all of Shakespeare's plays. As a first sample, he produced the court scene from *The Merchant of Venice* at the Kabuki-za in Tokyo, as an interlude between two *kabuki* acts. This was subsequently followed by whole Shakespeare plays, as well as plays by Ibsen, Strindberg, Gerhart Hauptmann, and others of the European naturalist school. Tsubouchi Shōyō founded a society for literature and art, *Bungei Kyokai,* as well as the theater museum at the Waseda University of Tokyo, which became one of the centers of modern Japanese theater research. The same purposes are served by the Theater Institute of the Sophia University of Tokyo, whose publications, lectures, and exhibitions have done much to further an understanding of Japan's theater art in the West.

The *Teigeki,* or Imperial Theater Society, which was founded in 1911, was short-lived. It was taken over a few years later by the Shōchiku corporation, which has a monopoly of the whole Japanese theater industry, including opera, film, dance, and revue ensembles of international style. Today the Imperial Theater is a movie house showing foreign films.

The last offspring of the *shingeki* was the "Little Theater," founded in 1924 and named *Tsukiji-Shogekijo,* for Tokyo's Tsukiji district.

A splinter group of the *Tsukiji-Shogekijo,* finally, the *shingeki* ("New Theater"), is entirely international in conception. It became the rallying point of the young Japanese intellectuals' social aspirations. After decades of exclusive adherence to the Stanislavsky method, it has now gone over to other individual production methods of stage direction.

Today the *shingeki* of the modern Japanese ensemble is a place of experiment, of committed social criticism, of the performance of international hits—and of coming to grips with the great currents of world theater.

Greece

INTRODUCTION

The history of European theater begins at the foot of the Acropolis in Athens, under the luminous violet-blue skies of Greece. Attica is the birthplace of a form of dramatic art whose creative and aesthetic values have lost none of their effectiveness over a span of two-and-a-half thousand years. Its origins lie in the interplay of giving and receiving that at all times and in all places bound men to their gods and the gods to man. They lie in the rituals of sacrifice, dance, and worship. For Homeric Greece this meant the maenadic, bacchic, sacred festivals in honor of Dionysus, the god of wine, of vegetation and growth, of procreation and exuberant life. His retinue consists of Silenus, of satyrs and maenads. The rural festivals of the winepress in December were sacred to him, and so were the floral festivals of Athens in February and March. The unbridled revelries of Attic vintners honored him, as did the alternate voices of Athenian drinking songs and dithyrambs. When the Dionysiac rites developed into tragedy and comedy, he became the god of the theater.

Many influences from Mesopotamia, Crete, and Mycenae had converged in the sea-washed peninsula of Attica, and there found their

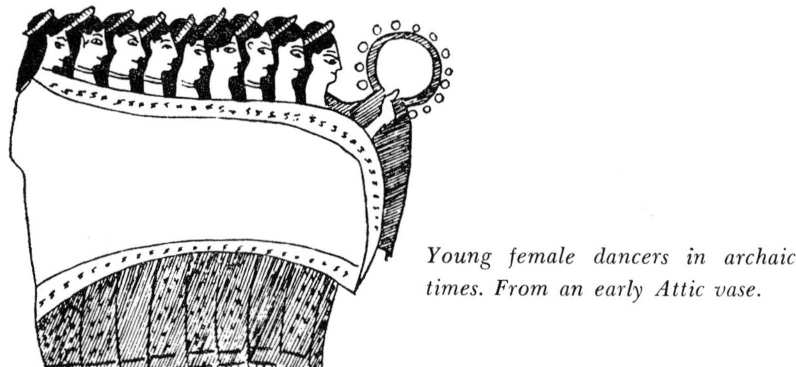

Young female dancers in archaic times. From an early Attic vase.

historic culmination in the *polis,* the city-state of Athens. Power politics and a deliberate and sagaciously guided intensification of religious life led to the pomp and ceremony of the Panathenaea, the festival of the city's goddess Pallas Athene. From the sixth century B.C. on, Athens also honored Dionysus in the great City Dionysia, which lasted several days and included dramatic representations.

The theater is a social and communal work of art; this was never more true than in ancient Greece. Nowhere else, therefore, could it have achieved the far-reaching importance it had in Greece. The crowd gathered in the *theatron* were not mere spectators, but participants in the most literal sense. The public was an active partner in the religious, theatrical ritual, was drawn into the sphere of the gods, and partook of the knowledge of the great mythological connections. Out of the common conceptual world of religion, and out of the commemorated heritage of Homeric heroes, grew the Olympian, the Isthmian, and the Nemean games, as well as the cultic celebrations of the Apollo sanctuary at Delphi—all of them events that preserved an overriding solidarity beyond political factions.

Despite this inherent solidarity, there were the perennial conflicts—between Sparta and Athens, and among all the ambitious little power centers of the mainland, the Peloponnese, and the Aegean islands—conflicts that may be regarded, in Jacob Burckhardt's words, as "an inner fever of this highly privileged national organism." Heraclitus's much-quoted words that "strife is the father of all things" are valid not only for the political unrest of the late sixth century B.C., when he wrote them in Ephesus, but also for the somber emotions of the drama, the passions of hatred born of "the heart's radical fury." When Thassilo von Scheffer says that "humanitas" is a word hardly applicable to the ancient Greeks, he does not thereby destroy our ideal conception of them, but adds the all-important reverse side, without which its theater—like other aspects of Greek antiquity—would evade our comprehension.

TRAGEDY

From Cult to Theater

To honor the gods, "in whose merciless hands lie heaven and hell," the people assembled in the great semicircle of the theater. With rhythmic chants, the chorus walked around the *orchestra*: "Come, O

Muse, and join the sacred chorus! Let our song please you and see the hosts of thousands of people sitting here!" These hymnic verses are from the *Frogs* by Aristophanes. Of all people he, the "incorrigible scoffer," in his late comedy once more invoked the power of classic Greek tragedy. Its golden age lasted about a hundred years. Its precursor was Homer's blind bard Demodocus, who sang his lay of the favor and anger of the Gods to the feasting heroes, for "when they had satisfied their appetite and thirst, the bard was inspired by the Muse to sing of famous men."*

Two currents combined to give birth to tragedy; one had come down from the legendary minstrel of remote antiquity, the other from the fertility rites of the dancing satyrs. Choruses of goat singers, according to Herodotus, existed as far back as the sixth century B.C. These choruses originally sang in honor of the hero Adrastus, that much-sung king of Argos and Sicyon, the instigator of the expedition of the Seven against Thebes. Cleisthenes, from 596 B.C. tyrant of Sicyon, for political reasons transferred these goat choruses to Dionysus, the Attic people's favorite god.

Dionysus, the incarnation of drunkenness and frenzy, is the wild spirit of contrast, the ecstatic contradiction of bliss and horror. He is the source of sensuality and cruelty, of procreative life and lethal destruction. This double nature of the god, a mythological attribute, found elementary expression in Greek tragedy.

The path from the Homeric bard Demodocus to tragedy leads to one of his successors, Arion of Lesbos, who lived around 600 B.C. at the court of the tyrant Periander of Corinth. With the support and friendship of this art-loving ruler, Arion undertook to guide the rural population's vegetative cults into poetic channels. He organized the goat dancers of the satyr choruses for a mimetic accompaniment to his dithyrambs. Thus he founded a form of art which, originating in poetry, incorporated song and dance, and two generations later culminated in Athens in the theater of tragedy.

Pisistratus, the wise tyrant of Athens who fostered trade and the arts and was the founder of the Panathenaea and the great City Dionysia, did his best to lend splendor to these public festivities. In March 534 B.C. he brought the actor Thespis to Athens from Icaria, and ordered him to participate in the City Dionysia. Thespis had an imaginative, new idea that was to make history. He set himself apart from the chorus as a single player, and so created the role of the response-giving *hypokrites* ("answerer" and, later, actor), who introduced the spectacle and engaged in a dialogue with the chorus leader. This innovation, at first

* From *Odyssey*, VIII, in the translation by E. V. Rieu, Harmondsworth, England: Penguin Classics, 1945.

Corinthian dancers at the time of Arion. Painting on a Corinthian phial. 6th century B.C.

no more than a germ cell within the sacrificial rite, was to develop into tragedy, which had its origin, etymologically, in *tragos,* "goat," and *ode,* "song."

No one present at the Dionysia in 534 B.C. could have dreamed what far-reaching implications for the history of civilization this new dialogue amplification of the rite was to have; least of all Thespis himself. He had until then roamed the countryside with a small troupe of dancers and singers and, at rural Dionysian festivals, had treated the Attic peasants to performances of dithyrambs and satyr dances in the style of Arion. He is supposed to have driven about in a four-wheeled wagon, the "cart of Thespis," but this is just one of those ineradicable, pretty illusions that linguistic usage has perpetuated. The culprit in this case was Horace, who tells us that Thespis was said to have "carried his poems around on wagons." But this information applies solely to Thespis's part in the Dionysia, and not to anything like a wandering stage-cart. The ritual of choral dance at the theater was preceded by a solemn procession, which came from the city and ended at the *orchestra* within the holy precinct of Dionysus. The climax of the processions was the god's festival car drawn by two satyrs, a sort of bark on wheels (*carrus navalis*), which carried the god's image or, in its stead, a vine-crowned actor. The boatlike car recalls the god's maritime adventures, for according to the myth the infant Dionysus was washed up on the shore in an ark. As the procreating element which harbors the ultimate mystery of life, water has always been an important ingredient of the cults of all peoples everywhere; witness the Osiris cult of ancient Egypt, the Biblical Moses, and the divine fisherman of the Japanese *kagura* dance play.

The god—or the actor—on the boatlike car sits between two flute-playing satyrs and holds vines in his hand, as shown in several variants by the vase painters of the early sixth century B.C. This, no doubt, is how Thespis appeared at the Athenian Dionysia. He wore a linen mask

Dionysus in his boatlike car. Attic vase painting on skypos, *ca. 500* B.C. *(Bologna.)*

Chorus dance: Hephaestus with the blacksmith's hammer, Dionysus and Muse of Comedy with thyrsus and cantharus, Marsyas with double-pipe. Drawing by A. L. Millin (1808), after a red-figured vase in the Louvre in Paris.

painted in the likeness of a human face, visible from afar as set apart from the chorus of satyrs with their shaggy loincloth and horse's tail.

The site of the Athenian Dionysia was the hill slope of the Dionysus sanctuary south of the Acropolis. There stood the temple with the old wooden image of the god brought from Eleuthera; there, a little lower down, was the dancing circle, then, on a level terrace, the *orchestra*. At its center on a low pedestal stood the sacrificial altar (*thymele*). The god's presence became real to the onlookers; Dionysus was there with them, the center and invigorator of a solemn, religious, theatrical ceremonial. Like all the world's great cultic plays, it began with a sacrifice of purification.

Tragedians before Aeschylus

Sixty years went by between the first appearance of Thespis and the first theatrical triumph of Aeschylus. They were years of violent political strife which put an end to the rule of the tyrants, led to the intervention of the Marathon warriors in the organization of public affairs and, through Cleisthenes, to the founding of the Athenian Republic. But regardless of the political upheavals, the new art form of the *tragodia* gained ground, developed, and became the subject of a theatrical contest (*agon*) at the City Dionysia.

Along parallel lines, but possibly going back earlier in its origins, the satyr play developed as an independent species. It came from the Peloponnese, and its literary pioneer was Pratinas of Phlius. The satyr play, this "problem child of propriety," combined with the tragedy, made bold to mock the lofty sentiments and give them a grotesque turn. As part of the Dionysia it represented the anticlimax, the relaxing return to the all too human lowlands. Just how abrupt the descent was to be was a matter for the discretion and self-irony of the tragic poet, for he himself wrote the satyr play as an endpiece to the tragic trilogy he entered in the contest.

Phrynichus of Athens, who was a pupil of Thespis, enlarged the function of the "answerer" (*hypokrites*) by giving him a double role and making him appear alternately with a male and female mask. This meant the actor had to make several entries and exits, and the change of costume and mask underscored the elementary scenic pattern so introduced into the choral sequence. Another step forward had been taken from declamation toward "action."

Maenad and satyr. Cup by the Brygus painter, ca. 480 B.C. *(Munich, Staatliche Antikensammlung.)*

Tanagra figurine from Hellenistic times: an actor in a satyr play. (Paris, Louvre.)

Aeschylus

It is to Aeschylus that ancient Greek tragedy owes the artistic and formal perfection, which was to remain a standard for all future times. As his father belonged to the land-owning nobility of Eleusis, Aeschylus had direct access to the cultural life of Athens. In 490 B.C. he took part in the battle of Marathon, and he was one of those who passionately embraced the democratic concept of the *polis*. His gravestone praises his bravery in battle, but says nothing about his merits as a dramatist.

Aeschylus won the victor's laurels at the theatrical *agon* only after several attempts. It is known that he began to compete at the City Dionysia in 500 B.C. with tetralogies, the obligatory unit of three tragedies and a concluding satyr play. The records do not tell us what works he entered to be defeated in the contest by Pratinas and Choerilus. All his work prior to 472 B.C., when the *Persians* was first performed, is lost. According to ancient chroniclers, Aeschylus wrote in all ninety tragedies; of these, seventy-nine titles have come down to us, but among them are only seven plays.

In the *Persians*, Aeschylus took up a topical subject that had been treated four years earlier by Phrynichus in his famous *Phoenician Women*. He deliberately invited comparison with the earlier work by starting the *Persians* with the first verse of the *Phoenician Women*. With this trilogy, followed by the satyr play *Prometheus the Fire-bringer*, Aeschylus won the first prize. Pericles, then twenty-five years old, performed the honored task of paying for the chorus.

The dramatic components of the archaic tragedy were a prologue that explained the antecedents, the entrance song of the chorus, the report of the messengers on the tragic turn of destiny, and the lament of the victims. Aeschylus followed this structure. At first he confronted the chorus with two individual actors, later, like Sophocles, with three.

The intellectual background for the *Persians* is conveyed in the glorification of the young city-state of Athens, as seen from the royal court

Choral dance in archaic times. From an early Attic vase.

Scene from Aeschylus' Persians: *the ghost of Darius appears to Atossa while she is sacrificing to him. Attic vase painting. (Rome, Museo Vaticano.)*

of Persia after its defeat at Salamis. When Atossa asks the chorus leader: "Who rules the Greeks, who governs them?" the answer expresses the author's pride in the Athenian *polis*: "They are not slaves, they know no ruler."

What Atossa, Antigone, Orestes, or Prometheus suffers is not an individual destiny. Their fate represents an exceptional situation, the conflict between the power of the gods and the will of man, man's impotence against the gods magnified in the monstrous event. This is seen in its most elementary force in *Prometheus Bound*. The son of the Titans, who stole fire from heaven and brought it to the mortals, cries out his lament into the "shining vault" over the ring of the theater: "I call to you, Mother Earth, and to you I call, all-seeing circle of flames: see what I, a god myself, suffer at the hand of the gods!"

The cry of torment uttered by Aeschylus' Prometheus rises above the primordial forces of the ancient nature religion: "I, who pitied the mortals, have been shown no pity." Two-and-a-half thousand years later, Carl Orff chose him for the hero of an exotic quasi-archaic musical drama, which sets divine against human passion. Historians of religion have drawn a connection from the Titan's primordial suffering through the revolt of Lucifer to the Christian Redeemer—an example that again demonstrates what so often has been expressed in the theater: that "pagan presentiments often penetrate with astonishing depth and certainty into later historical reality" (Joseph Bernhart).

Sophocles

Four years after winning the prize with the *Persians*, Aeschylus first came up, in the annual tragedy contest, against a rival whose fame was rising meteorically: Sophocles, then twenty-nine years old, the son of a wealthy Athenian family who, when still a boy, had led the chorus of youths in the victory celebrations after the battle of Salamis.

Both rivals entered their tetralogies for the Dionysia of 468 B.C. Both tetralogies were accepted and performed. Aeschylus scored a *succès d'estime*, but the prize went to Sophocles, thirty years his junior. The two poets were friends and until the time when Aeschylus left Athens, shared the laurels of tragedy as equals. Sophocles won eighteen dramatic prizes. Of the one hundred twenty-three dramas he wrote, which are known to have been kept in the library of Alexandria as late as the second century B.C., we know one hundred eleven titles; but only seven tragedies and the remnants of a satyr play have come down to us.

Sophocles was an admirer of Phidias, who, at the same time, shaped the image of godlike man in marble, bronze, and ivory. As Phidias gave

Orestes committing the murder of Aegisthus. Campanian vase, ca. 420 B.C. *(Berlin.)*

Purification of Orestes. Southern Italian crater in the style of Euripidean tragedy. (Paris, Louvre.)

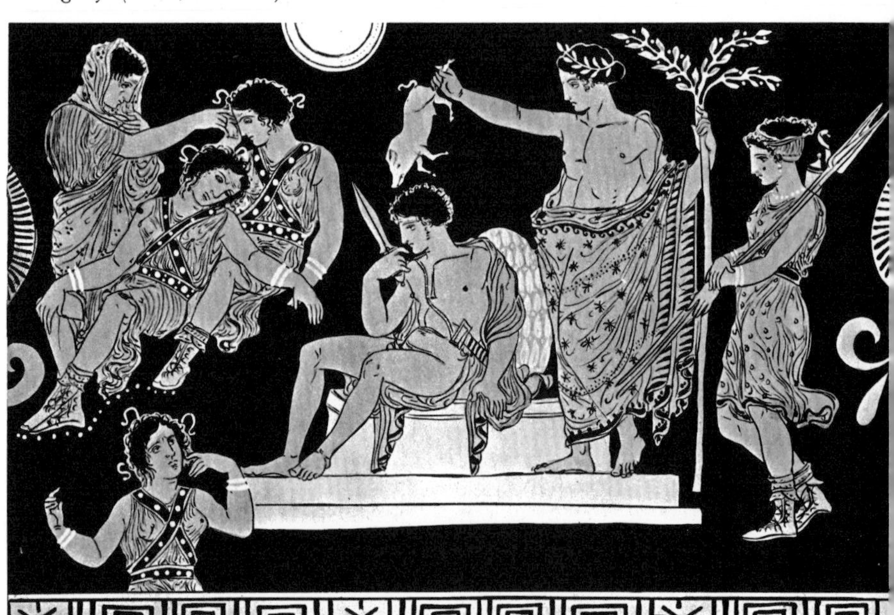

a soul to the archaic statue, so Sophocles humanized the characters in his tragedies. He stripped them of the typifying archaic garb and penetrated the shell of their individual capacity for suffering. He put on the stage personalities, like little Antigone rising to the heights of her self-imposed task, who had the courage to defy the command of superior power: "I have not come to join you in hate, but in love."

The gods subject the rebel to "suffering without issue." They heap upon him such burdens that he can preserve his dignity only in torment. Man is aware of this menace. But by his actions he forces the gods to go to extremes. For Sophoclean man, suffering is the hard but ennobling school of self-knowledge. Misled by cruel oracles, at the mercy of enigmatic destinies, plunged into fatal madness, driven to unintended evil deeds, he delivers himself by his own hands to the Erinyes, the avengers from the underworld, and to correcting "Justice," the arm of the law. Ajax dies by his own sword; King Oedipus blinds himself; Electra, Deianeira, Jocasta, Eurydice, and Antigone seek death.

Sophocles, the pious sceptic, gives the gods their victory, their unabridged triumph; they rule above earthly destiny, above all the chasms of hatred, frenzy, vengeance, violence, and sacrifice. The meaning of suffering lies in its apparent meaninglessness. For "in all this there is nothing that does not come from Zeus," he says at the end of the *Trachinian Maidens*.

It was from the unalterable nature of the Sophoclean concept of destiny that Aristotle derived his famous definition of tragedy, the interpretation of which has been debated for centuries; the German writer and dramatist Lessing took it to mean the purification of the passions by terror and pity, while in our day the contemporary classical scholar and cultural critic Wolfgang Schadewaldt explains it as the "pleasurable relief from horror and affliction." Every genuine tragedy, Schadewaldt says, is a cultic play and, like the cult, it is not meant to improve, purify, or educate. Schadewaldt writes,

> Tragedy deeply moves the heart. It proceeds from the primordial pleasure in the horror . . . , and from the pleasure in lament, to lead up eventually to the cathartic pleasure in liberating relief; but, just because it is essentially oriented to quite other purposes, it does carry within itself all the more possibility of now and then so striking a man's heart that he will, perhaps, emerge a different person from this encounter with the truth of reality.

Euripides

With Euripides the psychological theater of the West begins. "I represent men as they should be, Euripides represents them as they are," Sophocles once said. The third of the great tragic poets of antiquity moved on to an entirely new level of conflict. He exemplified the saying of Protagoras about "man as the measure of all things."

While Aeschylus saw the tragic hero's temptation to hubris as a delusion condemning itself by its own excesses, and while Sophocles had superimposed the destiny of divine malevolence upon the human willingness to suffer, Euripides debased divine dispensation into the blind power of chance. "For under cover of night our destiny impends," we read in his *Iphigenia in Tauris.*

Euripides, the son of a landowner, was born at Salamis and was taught by the Sophists of Athens. He was a sceptic who doubted the existence of absolute truth, and as such was opposed to any palliative idealism. He was interested in contradictions and ambiguities, in the principle of deception, the relativization of ethical values. The divine pronouncement was no absolute truth for him, and it offered him no ultimately conciliating solution. "Natural necessity and the human mind are not representational forms of one and the same mode of existence, but alternative possibilities: nothing is beyond comparison any more; the unique point of reference for everything has long become invisible; change rules the hour" (Walter Jens).

In contradiction to the Socratic doctrine that knowledge passes directly into action, Euripides concedes his characters the right to hesitate, to doubt. He unfolds the whole range of instincts and passions, of scheming and plotting. His searching exploration of the weak spots in the mythical tradition earned him sharp criticism from his contemporaries. He was accused of atheism and of the sophistic perversion of moral and ethical concepts—" 'Twas the tongue forswore itself, not the heart," says his Hippolytus. Of his seventy-eight tragedies (of which seventeen and one satyr play are extant) only four gained him a prize during his lifetime, the first of them being the *Peliades,* in 455 B.C.

When, in 408 B.C., the Macedonian king Archelaus invited him to his court at Pella, Euripides turned his back on Athens without regret. At Pella, he wrote a court drama called *Archelaus,* in honor of his royal patron, of which we know no more than the title, as well as two works that were helped to posthumous victory by his son: *The Bacchae,* a return to archaic, mystical sensuality under the sign of Dionysus's sacred wand, the *thyrsus;* and *Iphigenia in Aulis,* the paean of humanism. (Racine and Gerhart Hauptmann, in their plays of the same title, similarly glorified serene humanism.) Euripides died at Pella in March of the year 406 B.C.

When the news reached Sophocles in Athens, he went into mourning and caused the chorus to appear without the customary wreaths at the City Dionysia which were just then in full swing. A few months later, Sophocles in his turn died. Now the throne of the great tragic poets stood empty.

Aristophanes' comedy the *Frogs*, written in this period, might have served as the obsequies of Attic tragedy. At the Lenaean festival in 405 B.C. the judges awarded the prize to this biting play, though they themselves came in for some sarcastic thrusts. In the *Frogs* Aristophanes bears witness to the artistic and political tensions of the late fifth century, to the inner conflicts of the crumbling *polis,* and to the recognition that the classic period of the art of tragedy had passed on into history.

In the *Frogs,* Dionysus, the god of the theater, is to assess the relative merits of Aeschylus and Euripides; but he proves just as undecided, wavering, and susceptible as the public and the judges are in the contest. Seen in the crass, distorting mirror of comedy, the god grudgingly forces himself to make a decision: "And that's how I end up weighing out like cheese the art of great poets. . . ."

The golden age of antique tragedy was irrevocably gone. The art of tragedy disintegrated as did the city-state's way of life and the unifying power of the cult. The Athenian nobleman Critias, an unbending enemy of democracy and in 404 B.C. one of the most ruthless of the Thirty Tyrants, wrote a satyr play in which Sisyphus describes religion as the "invention of a pedagogic smart-aleck." The spirit of tragedy and Athenian democracy had perished together.

The City Dionysia

Beginning with the time of Pericles, the Great or City Dionysia constituted a festive highlight in the religious, intellectual, and artistic life of the city-state of Athens. While the much more modest, rural Dionysia held in December had a purely local character and were sponsored by the separate counties of Attica, Athens deployed all the glamour representative of the capital in its six-day City Dionysia. Especially after the foundation of the Attic naval confederacy, ambassadors, traders, and envoys bearing tribute flocked together at this time in Athens from the whole of Asia Minor and the Aegean Islands.

The arrangements for the dramatic contests were the responsibility of the *archon,* who, as the highest state official, decided on both artistic and organizational questions. The tragedies entered for the contest were

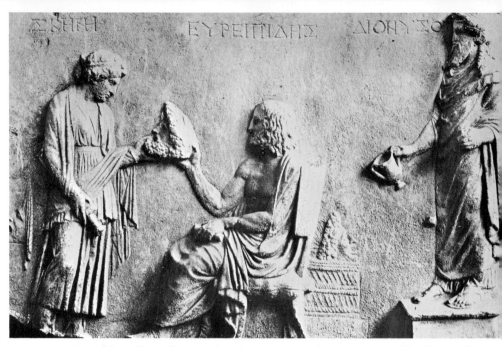

Euripides relief: the poet hands a tragic mask to the personification of skene *at his left; to the right, a statue of Dionysus. (Istanbul.)*

Tragic actor in the role of Clytemnestra. Late Roman ivory statuette from Rieti. (Paris, Louvre.)

submitted to him and he selected the three tetralogies that were to compete at any one contest (*agon*). The *archon,* finally, assigned to each poet a *choregus,* some wealthy Athenian citizen who would finance a performance, covering not only the costs of training and equipping the chorus, but also the fee for the chorus director (*choro didascalus*) and the costs for victuals for all concerned.

To have helped some tragic tetralogy to victory as its *choregus* was one of the highest merits a man could attain in the contest of the arts. The prize to be gained was a laurel wreath, a far from negligible sum of money (as compensation for the prior expense), and immortality in the state archives. These records (*didascalia*), which the *archon* caused to be prepared after each dramatic *agon,* list the names of the prize-winning *choregi* and dramatists, together with the names of the three tetralogies performed at any one contest. These records represent the most valuable documentation of a glory of which only a few rays have fallen on us—few, at any rate, compared with the creative abundance of the theater of antiquity.

Initially the poet himself was his own *choregus,* chorus director, and leading actor. Both Aeschylus and Euripides often appeared on the stage. Sophocles acted in his own plays only twice as a young man, once as Nausicaa and once as Thamyras.

While later, in Hellenistic times, it was perfectly possible to revive a play previously performed, the dramatic contests of the fifth century demanded new works for each festival. The City Dionysia in March were originally reserved exclusively for tragedy, while comedy writers competed at the Lenaean festival in January. But by the time of Aristophanes both types of plays were eligible for both festivals.

On entering the auditorium, each spectator was handed a small metal token (*symbolon*), which had the number of his seat engraved on it. He did not have to pay anything. Pericles had secured the favor of the people by paying out of state funds not only for the people's participation in courts of justice and public assemblies, but also for their visits to the theater. In the lowest tiers, right at the front, seats of honor (*proedria*) were waiting for the priest of Dionysus and for the authorities and privileged guests. Here, too, were placed the judges, the *choregi,* and the authors. A separate section was set aside for young men (*ephebi*), and women sat in the uppermost tiers.

Clad in festive white, the public would arrive in large numbers early in the morning and begin to fill the semicircular, terraced tiers of the theater. "A swarm of white," Aeschylus calls it. Besides free citizens, slaves also were allowed to attend, provided their masters gave them time off. Approval was indicated by loud hand clapping, disapproval by stamping or whistling. The freedom to express his opinion was one of

Vase painting on voluted crater: Dionysus and Ariadne (top, center), surrounded by satyr-play actors. Ca. 420 B.C. (Naples, Museo Nazionale.)

Mosaic from Pompeii: satyr chorus rehearsing. (Naples, Museo Nazionale.)

which the ancient theatergoer made ample and uninhibited use. From the very outset he considered himself as one of the theater's creative elements.

"Let us not forget that the Greek tragedy in Athens was a ritual action," Ortega y Gasset reminds us, "and therefore took place not so much on the stage as in the spectator's mind. Theater and public were encompassed in an extra-poetic atmosphere, religion."

The necessary condition for this community experience was the magnificent acoustics of the ancient open-air theater. The merest whisper carried to the farthest seat. In its turn, the mask—usually made of stuccoed linen pressed in terracotta molds—amplified the power of the voice. It gave both the face and the words their effect at a distance. Thanks to the power of the words it did not matter how small the scenery—for example, the rocks to which Prometheus was chained—might appear. The visual background was less important than the human framework for the hero's torments: the chorus, which took part in the events as commentator, warner, adviser, and observer.

Aeschylus still had very modest requirements for scenery. Low, roughly carpentered wooden structures hung with painted cloth panels served as mountains, houses, palaces, encampments, or city walls. These timber constructions, which also housed a dressing room for the actors, are the origin of the term *skene* (hut or tent), which was passed on from these early makeshifts to the sumptuous *skene* architecture of the Hellenistic and Roman theater and ultimately to the scene as we know it today.

But no matter how primitive these beginnings were, the scene painter was a man worth mentioning, even at the time of Aeschylus, with whom a "skenograph" named Agatharchos is reported to have collaborated. He was no doubt responsible for the design and painting of the timber sheds and their painted cloth decorations. Vitruvius, the Roman authority on architecture, even attributed to Agatharchos a treatise about the *skene,* which is supposed to have appeared in 430 B.C. but to have been lost later. Other scene painters of the ancient Greek theater whose names have come down to us are the Athenian Apollodorus and his contemporary Themocretus.

Aristotle credits Sophocles with having invented scene painting. The friendship between Aeschylus and Sophocles during the years 468 to 456 B.C. explains the overlapping both of scenic and histrionic innovations. Apart from the possibilities of "masking" the *skene* and of introducing such movable properties as battle or display chariots, the skenographs had at their disposal the so-called Charonian steps, a subterranean staircase leading up to the *skene* to facilitate apparitions from Charon's underworld. In the *Persians,* for instance, Darius is conjured up by the smoke of the sacrifice and appears to his wife Atossa and the chorus of Persian old men. The *mechanopoioi,* or technicians, were responsible for thunder, uproar, or earthquake noises produced by rolling stones in metal or wooden drums.

A change of mask and costume gave the three individual speakers the chance of taking several parts in one play. They could be a general, a messenger, a goddess, queen, or an ocean nymph—and these they were, thanks to the magic of the mask.

It was Aeschylus who introduced large, dignified masks. The heroic impression was intensified by the three-cornered high coiffure (*onkos*), built up over the brow. The tragic actor's costume usually consisted of chiton and mantle, and of the characteristic *cothurnus,* a thick-soled, laced, high boot.

With Sophocles, the archaic, linear quality of the mask began to soften. The eyes and mouth and the color and structure of the wig were used to indicate the age and the type of character represented. As masks became more individualized, Euripides required in addition striking contrasts of costume and milieu. "His kings go in rags," just to tear at the people's heartstrings, mocked Aristophanes, his implacable adversary.

What seemed particularly derisive to Aristophanes, and came in for gleeful parody in his comedies, was Euripides' predilection for a stage device of the antique theater that has become part of the vocabulary all through the Western world: *deus ex machina,* the god springing from the machine.

This "flying machine" was a scenic element of surprise, a mechanical device that came to the rescue of the poet when he needed to solve an apparently insoluble human conflict by divine pronouncement "from above." It consisted of a crane that swung a basket down from behind the roof of the playhouse. In this basket sat the god or the hero whose command got the dramatic action moving again in the obligatory mythological tracks when it had got stuck. That Euripides could not help relying on the *deus ex machina* is explained by the spirit of his tragedies. His characters act with individual determination, and thereby transgress the limits traced by a mythology that now no longer was accepted without question; Electra, Antigone, and Medea follow the commands of their own love or hate, and all this headstrong passion eventually is tamed by the *deus ex machina.*

But before this point is reached, another of the ancient technicians' stage devices essential to tragedy comes into action, namely, the *eccyclema,* a small, rolling, and most often raised platform, on which a setting is moved out from the doors of a house or palace. The *eccyclema* serves to bring into sight all the atrocities that have been perpetrated backstage: the murder of a mother, a brother, or children. It displays the

Earliest structure of the theater of Eretria, Island of Euboea. 5th century B.C. *Reconstruction by E. Fiechter.*

blood, terror, and despair of a torn world, as in the *Oresteia,* in *Agamemnon, Hippolytus,* and *Medea.*

Occasionally, the roof of the *skene* itself was pressed into service, as in the *Weighting of Souls,* by Aeschylus, or in *Peace,* by Aristophanes. As, naturally enough, it was the gods who usually appeared on these airy heights, this roof platform became known in Greece as *theologeion,* the place from where the gods speak.

The "flying machine," the *eccyclema,* and the *theologeion* presupposed a firmly constructed stage building, such as developed in Athens toward the end of the fifth century B.C. on the basis of plans going back to Pericles. When work began around 450 B.C. on the embellishment of the whole Acropolis, the Dionysus theater was not forgotten. The wooden benches of the auditorium are said to have been replaced by stone terraces as early as 500 B.C., when the overcrowded wooden stands broke down under the weight of the people. This dating, however, is contradicted by biographers of Aeschylus, who maintain that a second collapse of the stands had caused him to leave Athens in disgust and to settle at the court of Hieron at Syracuse, where he died in 456 B.C.

The Periclean *skene* plans provide for a monumental stage building

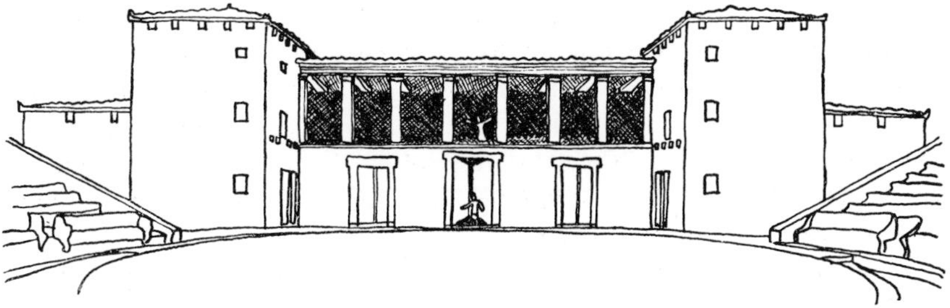

Theater of Dionysus in Athens. Skene, *according to the Pericles plans. Construction began ca. 400* B.C. *Reconstruction by E. Fiechter.*

with two large side wings, or *paraskenia*. These must have been executed between 420 and 400 B.C., at the time when the auditorium was enlarged and the *orchestra* reduced in size. The reason for this change was an intended shift of the action from the *orchestra* to the *skene*. This innovation proved all the more justified later on, when the chorus located on the *orchestra*, still numbering twelve to fifteen persons in classical tragedy, was steadily reduced in the course of Athenian economy measures and eventually disappeared completely toward the end of the fourth century.

None of the three great tragedians, nor Aristophanes, lived to see the completion of the new theater building. In the second half of the fourth century, when Lycurgus was in charge of the finances of Athens (338–326 B.C.), the new, magnificent setting finally was ready; but by that time the great, creative era of ancient tragedy had already passed into history.

COMEDY

The Origins of Comedy

Greek comedy, unlike Greek tragedy, had not one peak, but two. The first was due to Aristophanes, and it accompanied the peak of tragedy in the last decades of the great tragedians Sophocles and Euripides; the second peak of Greek comedy occurred in the Hellenistic era with Menander, who once more gave it historical importance. It always was a spiritually and formally independent form of theater art. Leaving aside the satyr plays, none of the Greek tragic poets tried his hand at comedy, nor did any of the comic poets write a tragedy.

Plato, in his *Symposium*, vainly pleaded for a union of the two great branches of dramatic art. He concluded with the information that Socrates tried until late one night to persuade Agathon and Aristophanes that "the same man should be capable of writing comedy and tragedy," and that a "true tragic poet is also a comic poet." The two others admitted it, but "they did not follow with much attention, for they became sleepy, and Aristophanes went to sleep first, and later, when day was breaking, also Agathon."

It stands to reason that not even the famed persuasive powers of Socrates could have succeeded in making a personal union of the two arts palatable to Aristophanes, the waspish *advocatus diaboli* of tragedy.

mask of a tragic heroine. (*Naples*, *Nazionale.*)

Mask of a youth, found at Samsun (Amisus). 3rd century B.C. *(Munich, Staatliche Antikensammlung.)*

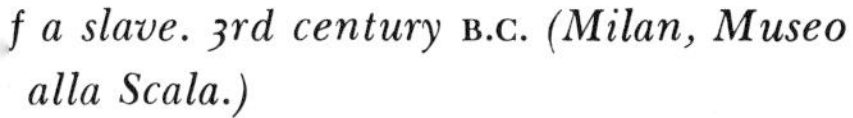

f a slave. 3rd century B.C. *(Milan, Museo alla Scala.)*

Mask in the hand of a statue thought to represent Ceres. (Paris, Louvre.)

Had he agreed with Socrates at night, in broad daylight, he would certainly have changed his mind; such a union would have taken all the wind out of his sails. For Aristophanes liked to turn his artistic craft on current politics; he adored crossing swords with the great men of his time in a cabaretlike show of malicious banter as he planted his poisoned arrow into their Achilles' heels. The bawdy obscenities with which the "impudent darling of the Graces" made it his business to "castigate the people and men of power," the crude phallic jokes, the choruses of birds and frogs and clouds—all draw on the cultic heritage of the riotous satyr revelries, of animal dances and fertility festivals.

The origins of comedy, according to Aristotle's *Poetics,* lie in the phallic ceremonies and songs that in his day were still common in many cities. The word comedy derives from *komos,* the nocturnal revels in which the gentlemen of Attic society for a few days shed all their dignity in the name of Dionysus and indulged their proclivities to drink, dance, and love. The great festival of the *komasts* was celebrated in January (later the date of the comedy contest) at the Lenaea, a riotous sort of carnival which lacked neither rough slapstick nor licentious wit.

The Attic *komos* was joined in the fifth century by the Doric mimes and jesters, complete with phalluses and sham fat bellies, who were masters of improvised farce. They had received literary backing around 500 B.C. by Epicharmus of Megara, in Sicily. His good-natured, coarse comic scenes and travesties of myths were the source of the Doric-Sicilian comedy. Epicharmus established the motley range of stock characters—the boasters and flatterers, parasites and procurers, drunkards and cuckolds—who survived to the time of the *Commedia dell'arte* and even to that of Molière. Epicharmus was particularly fond of debunking the gods and heroes: Hercules as a gourmand, attracted no longer by heroic deeds but only by the smell of roasting meat; Ares and Hephaestus, haggling with spite and malice over the release of Hera from the throne from which she cannot rise; or the seven Muses, appearing as the "buxom, well-fed" daughters of Father Pot-belly and Mother Fat-paunch.

It is a disputed question whether the comedy actually came from Megara Hyblaia in Sicily, or from Megara, the ancient Doric town between Athens and Corinth, which was famous for its jesters. Aristophanes says in the *Wasps,* "You must not expect too much of us, nor jests stolen from Megara." Aristotle cuts the Gordian knot by mentioning both with Solomonic wisdom: "Comedy is claimed by the Megarians, both by those of the mainland who contend that it took its rise in their democracy, and by those of Sicily, because this is where Epicharmus came from, long before Chionides and Magnes."

Old Comedy

The writer Chionides, mentioned by Aristotle, won a comedy prize in Athens in 486 B.C. Magnes, who is mentioned with him, is known to have won the first prize eleven times, the first time in 472 B.C., probably at the Athenian Lenaea, the year when Aeschylus' *Persians* was performed in Syracuse. None of Magnes' plays survived even to Alexandrian times.

The comedy contest, which took place partly at the Lenaean festival and partly at the City Dionysia of Athens, was not, like the tragedy contest, a peaceable trial of strength. It was a crossing of swords, and each author sharpened his blade on the whetstone of the other's success. Actors changed into authors, authors hid behind actors. When Aristophanes entered his *Banqueters* in 427 B.C., he did so under the pseudonym Philonides, the name of an actor who was his friend (possibly because he was too young to compete at the *agon*), and Philonides again let him borrow his name twenty-five years later for the *Frogs*.

The "old" Attic comedy is a brilliant precursor of what was to become, thousands of years later, political caricature, burlesque and cabaret. No statesman, no official, no fellow author was safe from its attacks. Even the splendid new buildings of Pericles came in for derision. In an extant fragment by Cratinus an actor enters the stage wearing a model of the Odeion on his head as a grotesque mask. The other actors acclaim him: "Here comes Pericles, the Zeus of Athens! Wherever did he get his cap? A new headdress in the Odeion style, terribly tousled by the critics' storm!"

The four great rivals-in-abuse and masters of the Old Comedy were all Athenians: Crates, Cratinus, Eupolis and, towering above the others in frame, genius, wit and malice, Aristophanes.

Crates, originally the leading actor in the plays of Cratinus, began to write his own plays in 449 B.C. His works are entertaining comedies, suitable for family consumption and dealing with such relatively harmless things as exposing duped braggarts, jilted lovers, and oracular drunkards. When his teacher Cratinus, then ninety-six years old, and twenty-one-year-old Aristophanes first engaged in open theatrical battle, Crates was already dead.

Aristophanes, in his *Knights* (the Greek title is *Hippes* which is, rather, "horsemen"), performed in 424 B.C., thought fit to tease the aged Cratinus by accusing him publicly of senility and praising the merits of the entertaining Crates. Cratinus had provoked this insult; he had described Aristophanes on the stage as an imitator of Eupolis.

Eupolis, who won first prize seven times, was of the same age as

Aristophanes and originally his close friend. In the period of their friendship, the two often collaborated, but later they mutually accused each other of plagiarism. Quarrel, in the realm of the comedy, was the source of much vitality; speaking of the *Knights*, Eupolis declared later in one of his comedies that he had "helped the bald-pate Aristophanes write it and had made him a present of it."

In his turn, Cratinus, a man notorious for his thirst and his copious sacrificial drinking in the service of Dionysus, also got back his own. At the age of ninety-nine he had the laughers on his side. In his comedy *The Bottle,* he describes how two ladies compete for his favors—his lawful wife, Madame Muse, and his mistress, Mademoiselle Flask; with a twinkle in his eye, he extricates himself with the motto of the Dionysian artists: "He who drinks water, gets nowhere."

Aristophanes had to swallow the bitter pill; the "old drunk" indeed still enjoyed the favors of the public and the judges. In 423 B.C. Cratinus won the first prize with *The Bottle* over Aristophanes' *Clouds,* which took third place. Of this selfsame *Clouds*—famous, or infamous, for its ferocious attacks on Socrates (which were subsequently toned down)—Plato relates that in the opinion of Socrates this play had prejudiced the jury when he had to face the tribunal.

The theater was the forum in which the most vehement controversies were fought out. Aristophanes regarded himself as the defender of the gods—"because they are the gods of our fathers who gave them their fame"—and as the accuser of the subversive, demagogic tendencies in Athens' politics and philosophy. He accused the philosophers of "arrogant contempt of the people" and denounced them as obscurantist atheists—all of them, and especially Socrates.

Little is known of Aristophanes' background and life. He is said to have been born around 445 B.C. and to have come from the Attic deme Cydathene. He lived in Athens during the whole span of his creative life, from the time he wrote his first play, *Banqueters* (427), to the year he wrote his last, *Plutus* (388). Of the forty comedies he is known to have written, only eleven are extant. Each of his plays is the mouthpiece for a passionate idea, for which he battles with hot-blooded militancy. In Aristophanes' work, passages of naked aggressiveness alternate with choral strophes of the highest lyrical beauty. Underlying his mordant irony and stinging scorn was an urgent concern with democracy. He argued that its fate can be entrusted only to persons of superior intelligence and moral integrity. Similarly, he pressed the case for terminating the fratricidal war between Athens and Sparta. In *Peace,* the peasant Trygaeus soars to the heavens on the back of an enormous dung beetle, to ask the gods to release the goddess of peace held prisoner in a cave. In the *Birds'* "cloud-cuckoo-land" he parodies the weaknesses of democracy and of a utilitarian popular religion. In *Lysistrata*, he has his women of Athens and Sparta resolve to deny themselves to their warring husbands until the latter are ready to make peace at last.

The audience could be directly addressed not only by an individual actor, but also by the chorus. To this end, Old Comedy had developed the *parabasis,* a specific formal expedient of which Aristophanes made masterly use. At the end of the first act, the chorus would take off their masks and step forward to the front, to the edge of the *orchestra,* to address the audience. "But you, fastidious judges of all the gifts of the Muses, lend a gracious ear to our festive anapestic song!" Then followed a polemic version of the author's opinions on topical events, political and personal controversies and, not least, an attempt to curry favor for his play. The *parabasis* could also be used for justification, denial, or retraction of some recent event that had gone before. After Cleon had taken his revenge for being lampooned in the *Knights* by having Aristophanes beaten up in a stage part, the poet referred to the incident in the *parabasis* of the *Wasps*: "When the blows fell upon me, they laughed out there, the spectators"; he then admitted to having tried to ingratiate himself a little with Cleon, for diplomatic reasons, but asserted that he had done so only in order to attack him all the more sharply in the future.

The performances of Old Comedy were given in the stage building, with its painted wooden walls and cloth panels, while the chorus, as in classical tragedy, was placed on the *orchestra.* For "airborne" scenes, the roof of the *skene* was pressed into service, as, for instance, in the *Acharnians,* the *Clouds,* and *Peace.* When Trygaeus flies to the heavens on his dung beetle with the aid of the crane, he anxiously asks the mechanic: "Please, do be careful with me." The following scene with Hermes in front of the palace of Zeus took place on the *theologeion,* while the subsequent liberation of the goddess of peace from her cave was shifted back to the customary stage of the *proskenion.*

The masks of Old Comedy range from grotesque animal heads to caricature portraits. When a portrait mask of Cleon was needed for the *Knights,* it is said that no mask-maker was willing to make one. For the first time, it would seem, fear of the victim's anger cast its shadow on the democratic freedom of the theater. The actor who played Cleon appeared without a mask, merely with his face painted red. It is thought that Aristophanes himself took the part—possibly one more reason for the thrashing he received soon thereafter.

Grotesque animal figures had already been used on the stage by the older contemporaries of Aristophanes. He himself mentions, in the *Knights,* a bird comedy by Magnes. Beaks, crests, tufts of hair and wattles, claws and birds' tails together with feather-covered tights produced

Flute player and costumed chorus, portraying knights and their horses, another motif that recurs later in Aristophanes' Knights. *Black-figured vase. (Berlin, Staatliche Museen.)*

Actors costumed as birds, painted on a black-figured vase; about seventy years earlier than the premiere in 414 B.C. *of Aristophanes'* Birds. *(London, British Museum.)*

a grotesque effect, as can be seen on vase paintings from the fifth century onward, and still amuses the twentieth-century audiences in modern productions of the *Birds.* It was difficult, of course, to come by enough plumage to costume the actors for the *Birds,* as Aristophanes knew only too well; the birds were molting, he explained in the play.

Like the animal masks, the dances of Old Comedy were of cultic origin. "Unbolt the gates, for now the dance begins," Philocleon exclaims in the *Wasps,* whereupon follows the *kordax,* a riotous phallic dance whose origins possibly go back to the ancient East. Even ancient sources describe this dance as so licentiously obscene that it was regarded as shameless to dance it without masks. This may have been one of the reasons why women were so long excluded from comedy performances.

In the *Ecclesiazousae,* Aristophanes has the actors, who are playing the women of Athens marching up to the Council meeting, "disguised" as men with tied-on beards and stout, Spartan boots to claim the state power for women; this was regarded as the acme of coarsely grotesque ambiguity. Transvestite effects, complete lack of restraint in gesture, costume and imitation, and, finally, the exposed phallus, are characteristic features of the acting style of Old Comedy.

In Cleon's time there was a very real, political reason why comedies were given primarily at the Lenaean festival. Few ships braved the stormy winter season, and it was not until March that they brought an influx of foreign guests to Athens for the Great Dionysia. Understandably enough, Cleon was anxious to keep the revealing comedy contest in the family, as it were. Aristophanes, in his turn, thought this was a splendid stick with which to beat "the son of a tanner and the misleader of the people"; witness the following passage from the *Acharnians*:

> Not even Cleon shall reproach me now
> That I malign the state in front of strangers.
> We are among ourselves on this occasion.
> The strangers have not come as yet, the tributes
> Have not arrived, our allies are not here.
> We're nothing but the purest Attic corn,
> No chaff among us and no unfree settlers.

With these lines Aristophanes was also rubbing in a personal triumph. A year earlier Cleon had brought an action against him for insult to the authorities and denigration of the state in front of strangers; this charge had been based on the content of the *Babylonians.* But the Athenian democracy did justice to the *demos,* the people's decision: Cleon's complaint was rejected, and the art of comedy prevailed.

Middle Comedy

With the death of Aristophanes, the golden age of the ancient political comedy came to an end. The literary historians of antiquity themselves were well aware of the steep drop from Aristophanes' comedies to those of his successors, and they drew a sharp dividing line and assigned everything that came after Aristophanes, up to the reign of Alexander the Great, to a new category, "Middle Comedy" (*mese*).

We have evidence of about forty authors' names as well as a large number of titles and fragments. Antiphanes, the most industrious of those pen-happy play manufacturers, is said to have written 280 comedies, and his contemporary Anaxandrides of Rhodes wrote sixty-five; other writers whose names have come down to us are Aubulus, Alexis, and Timocles.

Anaxandrides, who won first prize at the Dionysia in 367 B.C., was called by King Philip to the court of Macedonia, where he contributed one of his comedies to the celebrations of the victory of Olynthus. His departure from Athens is a straw indicating which way the political wind was blowing: Macedonia was aspiring to hegemony in Greece, and the glory of Athens was dimming.

Comedy now withdrew from the high wire of political satire into the less perilous realm of everyday life. Instead of gods, generals, philosophers, and heads of government, it lampooned boastful officers, comfortable citizens, fishmongers, notorious courtesans, and the cavaliers of

The Madness of Hercules. *Scene in the style of the hilarotragedy. Vase by Assteas, 4th century* B.C. *(Madrid.)*

"active" love. It fell back on the repertoire of Epicharmus, whose harmless travesties of myths now served as a model to yet another species of epigones. Around 350 B.C., at Tarentum, in the Greek colony of Taras in southern Italy, Rhinthon developed a form of comedy that parodied tragedy. This is the so-called hilarious tragedy (*hilaros,* which means gay, funny), but all our knowledge of it is based merely on fragments and vase paintings. Neither Middle Comedy nor *hilarotragodia* introduced any innovations as regards stage technique and decoration. Both seem to have used the upper story of the scene building (*episkenion*) for their sets; their masks are less grotesque than those of Old Comedy; they make concessions to propriety and give a first hint of sentimentality.

New Comedy

Toward the end of the fourth century B.C., a new master rose from the artistic lowlands of Middle Comedy. This was Menander, who led the comedy of antiquity to its second summit, the New (*nea*) Comedy. Its strength lies in characterization, in the motivation of inner change, the careful weighing of good and evil, right and wrong. Menander was born into a wealthy Athenian family about 343 B.C. His characters are individuals, and his action is carried by individuals. Character, as he says in his comedy *The Arbitrants,* is the essential factor in human development and hence also for the course of the action.

Of his 105 plays, only eight gained him prizes—three at the Lenaean festival and five at the City Dionysia of Athens. But this small number of victories diminished neither his contemporary renown nor his later fame. Menander was to have great influence on the Roman comedy writers Plautus and Terence who were to draw heavily on the substance of his work. Apart from a wealth of fragments, these two Roman poets were until the early twentieth century the only testimony to Menander's writings. In 1907, finally, his comedy *The Arbitrants* was reconstructed from papyri, and in 1959 the *Sullen Man* (*Dyskolos*). With the latter play the twenty-four-year-old Menander had won his first theatrical victory in 317 B.C.; its subtitle, *misanthropos,* foreshadows the later plays by the same title, the first by Terence and, ultimately, Molière's *Misanthrope.*

Even in this early work, Menander demonstrated his human and artistic mettle. All the characters are carefully drawn; the suspense is heightened in successive stages, and the action unfolds with plausible consistency.

The second-century B.C. grammarian Aristophanes of Byzantium, who was chief librarian at Alexandria and has handed down to us numerous quotations from Menander's plays, expressed his profound admiration for the poet: "O Menander and life, which of you two has imitated the other?"

Despite many tempting offers, Menander never left Athens and his villa at the Piraeus, where lived with his mistress Glykera. He refused an invitation to Egypt by King Ptolemy, though not without showing how flattered he was and not without playing with the idea of accepting, in the name of "Dionysus and his bacchic ivy leaves, with which I would sooner be crowned than with the diadems of Ptolemy, in full view of my Glykera as she sits in the theater." A famous relief of Menander shows the poet sitting on a low stool with the mask of a youth in his hand, and on a table in front of him the masks of a courtesan and of an old man. Somewhat disrespectfully, the Roman Manilius once described Menander's range of characters as consisting of "young men in the fervor of love, maidens abducted for love, derided old men, and slaves who can cope with any situation." Menander was self-confident enough not to care when the fickle judges at the comedy contest gave preference to his rival Philemon of Syracuse. According to an anecdote he once greeted Philemon, when he met him in the street, with these words: "Pardon me, Philemon, but tell me, when you gain the victory over me, does it not make you blush?"

The chorus, which already in Middle Comedy had been pushed to the sidelines, disappeared completely in Menander's works. As the actors no longer made their entrance from the *orchestra,* the shape of the stage building was altered. The major scenes now were performed on the *logeion,* a platform in front of the two-storied *skene.* Character comedy, with its intrigue and individual nuances of dialogue, demanded the concentrated interplay of actors, as well as closer contact between stage and the auditorium.

Menander was the only one of the great dramatists of antiquity who lived to see the Dionysus theater completed. For in Athens, as again three hundred years later in Rome, history played a strange trick on the theater: the external, architectural frame achieved its most sumptuous splendor only at a time when a great, creative flowering of the dramatic arts was coming to an end. The glory of antiquity's theatrical architecture was achieved in the time of the epigones; the magnificent theaters would serve to catch only a reflection of the former radiance.

Menander relief: the poet holding a mask. To the right, Glykera or perhaps a personification of skene, *as in the Euripides relief. 3rd century* B.C. *(Rome, Museo Laterano.)*

Phlyakes vase with scene from comedy: servants helping Cheiron up to the stage. To the right, Achilles, two old nymphs at the top. 4th century B.C.*, found in Apulia. (London, British Museum.)*

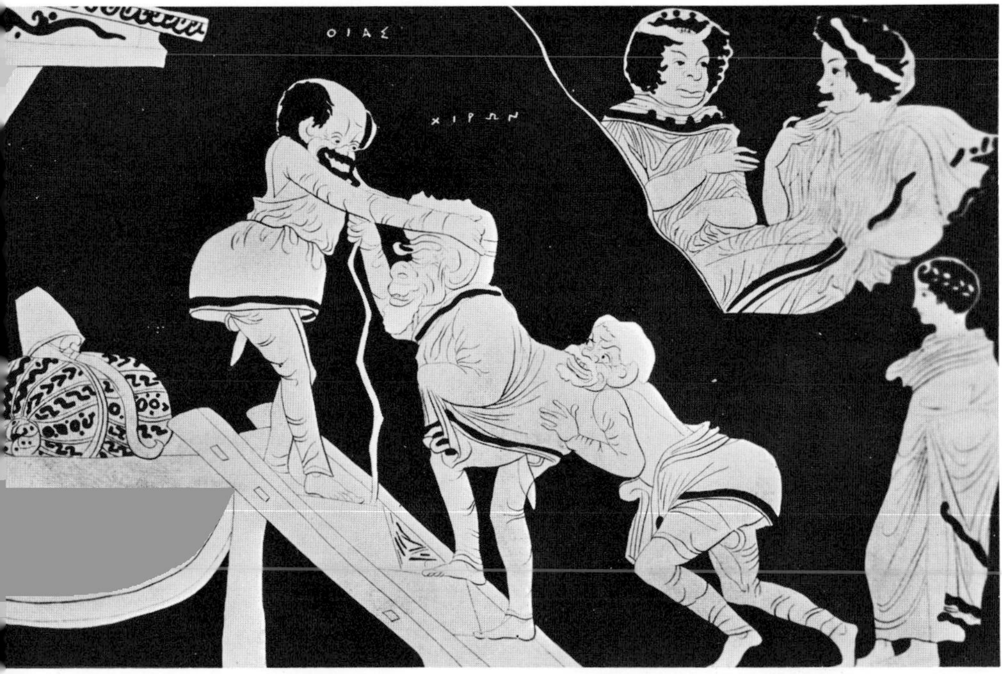

A peddler resembling the character of Xanthias in Aristophanes' Frogs. *(Munich, Staatliche Antikensammlung.)*

Two old drunks. (Berlin, Staatliche Mu

Terracotta statuettes representing Greek comedy characters. 4th century B.C.

Procuress, a typical character of New Comedy. (Munich, Staatliche Antikensammlung.)

Man and woman in conversation, as, p Praxagora and Blepyros in Aristophan sembly Women. *(Würzburg, Martin-vo ner Museum.)*

Phlyakes vase with Amphitryon travesty, possibly inspired by Rhinthon's Amphitruo: *Hermes holds up the light for Zeus below the window of Alcmene. Ca. 350* B.C. *(Rome, Museo Vaticano.)*

Vase painting by Assteas: the old miser Charinus, lying on his money chest, is threatened by two thieves. 4th century B.C. *(Berlin, Staatliche Museen.)*

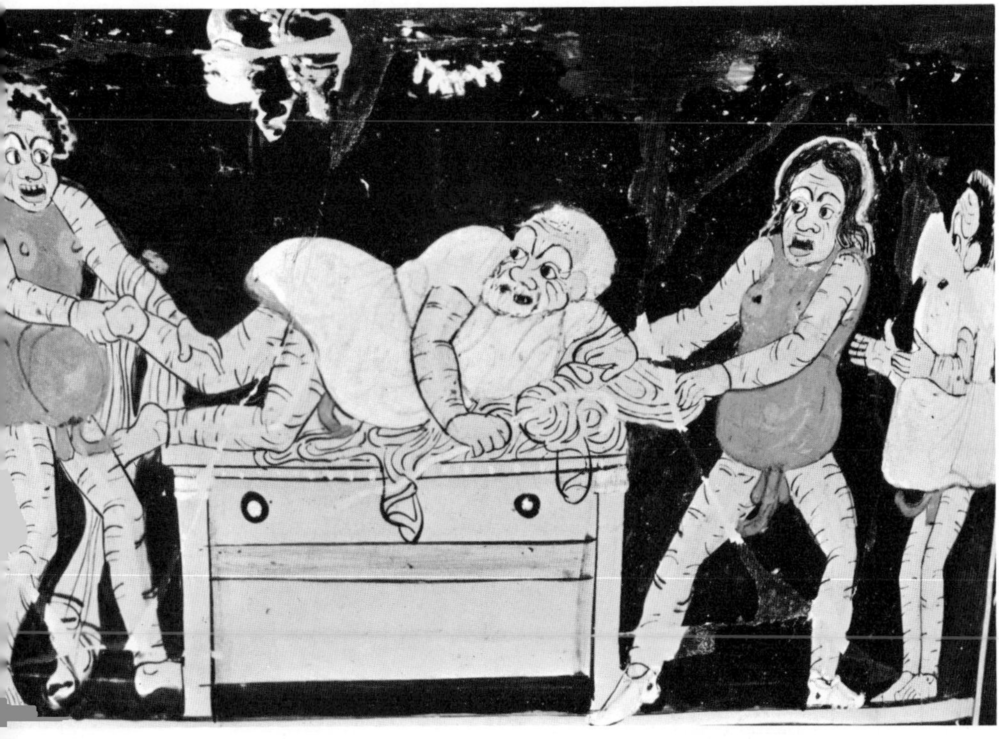

THE HELLENISTIC THEATER

When Lycurgus brought to its completion the new stone buildings of the theater of Dionysus, while he was in charge of Athens' finances (338–327 B.C.), he was conscious of his duty as an epigone. He not only caused the works of the classical tragic poets to be collected, but also had splendid marble statues made of them and placed then in the foyer of the new theater, in an open colonnade along the rear wall of the *skene* building. The theater itself consisted of a spacious stage building with three entrances and wings (*paraskenia*) projecting to the right and the left, providing two additional entrances from the dressing rooms to the stage. Holes along the back wall of the *skene* suggest that they may have been used to hold the posts, securing a temporary upper story (*episkenion*) on top of the *proskenion*, which the stage directions for comedies often required.

The auditorium rose in terraces, and its three tiers could hold as many as 15,000 or even 20,000 spectators, a number roughly corresponding to the population of Athens in the Hellenistic era. Some of the seats for the guests of honor (*proedria*), made of Pentelic marble, survive to this day. In their midst still stands the priest's special chair; it is decorated with reliefs and bears the inscription: "Property of the priest of Dionysus Eleuthereus." The other official seats are simpler, but also have a curved back; two or three of them are hewn out of a single block of marble.

At about the same time when Lycurgus completed the new Dionysus theater in Athens, another theater was erected in Epidaurus. It was built by the architect Polycleites the Younger, around 350 B.C., in the sacred precinct of Asclepios and soon gained fame for its beauty and harmony. Today it is the best-preserved theater of Greek antiquity. Its auditorium resembles a giant shell set into the hillside. From the height of the sixtieth row one has an unimpeded view of the remnants of the *skene* building and of the wooded plain beyond. Epidaurus conveys an experience of the ancient theater; even without a performance, Aeschylus, Sophocles, and Euripides come to life. It is hard to imagine that none of them saw his tragedies performed in one of the magnificent later settings; none of them lived to make use of the great theaters in Epidaurus, Athens, Delos, Priene, Pergamon, or Ephesus. By the time the spectators assembled in front of the colonnaded *skene* of the Hellenistic theater, the contest of the dramatists had long turned into a competition of actors. Even Aristotle already complained in the *Poetics* that virtuosity ruled the stage and actors had more power than poets.

Performance of Aristophanes' Frogs *in the Theater of Dionysus, 405* B.C. *On the* orchestra *Dionysus is being rowed across the swamp, with croaking frogs all around him. Reconstruction by H. Bulle and H. Wirsing, 1950.*

Theater of Epidaurus. Built by Polycleitus the Younger ca. 350 B.C. *View from the uppermost seats across the circular* orchestra. *In the background, the Arachnaeon mountains; at the far end of the* orchestra, *remnants of the* skene; *to the left, the reerected* parodos *gate.*

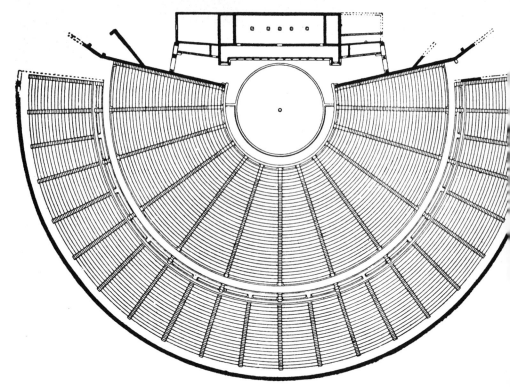

Plan of the theater of Epidaurus, which could seat about 14,000 spectators.

Theater of Delphi, built during the 2nd century B.C. *At the bottom, the remnants of the temple of Apollo.*

Vase fragment from Tarentum. Left, paraskenion *with richly ornamented entablature supported by slender columns. 4th century* B.C. *(Würzburg, Martin-von-Wagner Museum.)*

While in the fifth century, in the great age of classical drama, the poets had been the declared favorites and familiars of kings, princes, and heads of state, in the fourth century they were replaced by actors. It is true that Philip of Macedonia called the comedy poet Anaxandrides to his court; but he accorded greater honors to the actor Aristodemus. His son Alexander the Great, a pupil of Aristotle, entrusted the actor Thessalos with a diplomatic mission; as actors were not only exempt from military service but, as the servants of Dionysus, enjoyed safe-conduct in enemy territory even in wartime, they were eminently suitable political agents.

During the fourth century, the actors joined together in guilds of "Dionysiac artists," headed by a protagonist (leading actor) or musician, who was at the same time a priest of Dionysus. These artists' unions also organized performances, which usually were revivals of classical tragedies and comedies, in the smaller theaters of Attica and the Peloponnese.

The most popular works at this time were those of Euripides. Plutarch relates that Athenians taken prisoner and enslaved during the disastrous Sicilian expedition in 413 B.C. were given their freedom by the Syracusans—if they could recite by heart passages from Euripides' dramas. For, in his warning prophecy in the *Trojan Women,* Euripides

Theater of Oropus, Attica. 2nd-century B.C. skene. *Reconstruction by E. Fiechter.*

had predicted that the Athenians would be destroyed and that the fortunes of war would smile upon Syracuse. This may also explain the Roman dramatists' later predilection for Euripides. In the prologue to the *Trojan Women,* which was performed together with the satyr play *Sisyphus* at the Athens Dionysia of 415 B.C., Poseidon makes his exit with these ominous words:

> Oh, foolish is the man who town and temple ruins,
> Lays waste the sacred habitation of the dead,
> Their graves, for he is doomed to perish in the end.

Rome always looked to the Greek theater as its great paragon, even after the Roman world had irrupted into Greece after the latter's decline. The Roman conquerors' love of sensational, real "spectacles" led them to remodel and restructure the Greek theaters. *Proscenia,* decorated with reliefs and statues, now jutted out in front of the stage building; the *orchestra* was enclosed by parapets and turned into a *conistra,* an arena for the combat of gladiators and the baiting and slaughter of animals. In Athens' theater of Dionysus, in addition to these indignities, the emperor Nero desecrated the sanctuary of Dionysus, dedicating it "jointly to the God and the emperor"—as an inscription on the architrave testifies to this day.

The ruins of Athens' theater of Dionysus reflect "the development not only of dramatic poetry, but of the whole culture of antiquity: there are the dances of the chorus; alongside them, covering the large *orchestra,* enfold scenes from the great dramas and, on a smaller *orchestra,* those from a variety of plays. There is the *proskenion,* with its representations of typical, permanent scenery; finally, on the parapet-encircled conistra, there are the brutalizing games of the circus" (Margarete Bieber).

The words of the great poets who gave birth to Europe's theater can be heard every year in classical Greek in Athens' Herodes Atticus Theater at a summer festival of classical tragedy and comedy—an echo of the celebrations at the foot of the Acropolis at which, two-and-a-half thousand years ago, the ancient Greeks honored their god Dionysus.

THE MIME

From time immemorial in Greece as in the Orient, strolling players have traveled through the lands. Dancers, acrobats and jugglers, flute players and storytellers have performed at marketplaces and courts, for

Theater of Dionysus in Athens, as it was ca. 1900, showing the excavated Roman channel and the marble parapet put up by the Romans for animal games. The pedestal on the left also dates from Roman times. The tiered stone seats of the auditorium are of Greek origin. 4th century B.C.

peasants and princes, among the wartime tents and the banqueting tables. Pure art was joined by the grotesque, the typed imitation and caricature of men and animals, of their movements and gestures.

Verbal wit, added to these wordless, physical feats, led to the first, brief, improvised scenes. It was the beginning of primitive mime. Its aim was lifelike imitation of real types, or, in a higher sense, the art of self-transformation, of mimesis.

While the Homeric epic and the classical drama had glorified the gods and heroes, the mime (*mimus*) paid attention to the nameless, common folk who lived in the shadow of the great—and to the crooks, knaves and thieves, innkeepers, procurers and courtesans. Every region provided the mime with its own, characteristic figures and local concepts. In Sparta, the mime, traveling and performing alone, was seen as a representative of Dionysiac drunkenness and was called *deikelos* (drunkard), and thus Sparta's primitive, rustic farce was named *deikelon.* In Thebes, the players of mimes and farces, whose favorite theme was a travesty of the Boeotian Kabeiric cult, were called "volunteers."

The mime play originally developed in Sicily. It was a rustic burlesque, first given literary form by Sophron around 430 B.C. His characters are ordinary people and, in the broadest sense of mimesis, anthropomorphized animals. Sophron created the ancestor of Shakespeare's Bottom of *Midsummer Night's Dream.* In one of Sophron's plays (of which only fragments survive), an actor who is playing the part of a donkey talks about "munching thistles."

Among the animals, as among men, the lots are not distributed according to merit, and so a sizable portion of good-natured mockery was meted out in antiquity to the mountain people's frugal and faithful companion. Donkey dances and donkey grotesques, with their indestructible jests and jokes, survived, beyond the Roman farce in the Feast of the Ass (*festum asinorum*), with which the French clergy of the

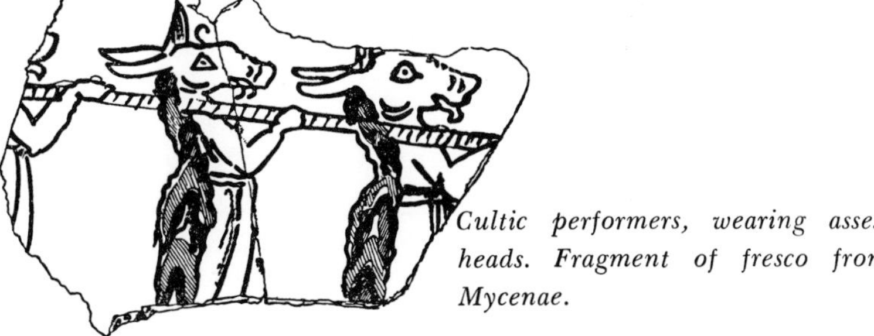

Cultic performers, wearing asses' heads. Fragment of fresco from Mycenae.

twelfth century commemorated the Flight into Egypt in a somewhat pagan and antique, and rather broad manner.

The art of the mime was not impeded by geographical barriers. From southern Italy it went northward with the strolling players, and wherever it went, it assimilated all sorts of popular, farcical, more or less improvised histrionic acts.

The classical stage of antiquity had excluded women, but the mime gave ample opportunity for the display of female charms and talent. The fourth-century B.C. Athenian writer, farmer, and sportsman Xenophon tells in his *Symposium* of a Syracusan mime who, with his troupe consisting of a boy and of two girls (one a flute player, the other a dancer), performed at a banquet in the house of the wealthy Callias, in Athens.

At the request of Socrates, who was among the guests, the mimes presented the story of Dionysus and Ariadne, in which the young god saves the daughter of Minos, who is abandoned on Naxos, and marries her. That Socrates' request could so easily be fulfilled, without special preparations, demonstrates that the Greek mimes were as familiar with the heritage of mythical themes as their earlier counterparts had been on the banks of the Euphrates and the Nile, and as their successors were to be in the future on the banks of the Tiber and at the Bosporus.

Numerous Attic vase paintings show a variety of young female entertainers—acrobats, jesters, and tumblers; girls doing the handstand, juggling with plates and drinking cups; dancers with musical instruments. The arts of these young female mimes were obviously widely popular with the Greeks, especially at private entertainments. On a fourth-century *hydria* from Nola (now at the Museo Nazionale in Naples) we see four groups training for various acrobatic feats. A naked young girl has arched her body into a bridge and supports herself on her elbows, at the same time pushing a *kylix* with her foot toward her mouth (around her calf she has tied a ribbon, the customary *apotropeion* of girl mimes); another girl is shown dancing between swords planted vertically in the ground, while a third one practices the *pyrrhic*, a mythological war dance, wearing a helmet and holding a shield and a lance.

According to an Attic legend, the goddess Athena invented the *pyrrhic* and danced it to celebrate her victory over the giants, though in Sparta the Dioscuri were credited with this invention. The dance turns up again in the second century A.D., when Apuleius, in *The Golden Ass*, described a mythological ballet that the Romans produced at Corinth. After the ballet, Apuleius said, people tried to make Lucius, who was dressed up as an ass, take part in an "obscene mime"; but Lucius ran away.

Most of the texts for mimes were in prose, but some, called the *mimeidoi,* were sung. These are the precursors of the music-hall song. Their stock characters were the same as Philogelus once used for his jokes, and apart from doctors, charlatans, fortune-tellers, and beggars, the favorite butt was the dolt from Abdera, or Sidon, or some other ancient Gotham.

Special poetic variants of the Greek mime are the *mimeiambics* by the poet Herondas of Cos (about 250 B.C.). The plots of these are short mime texts, which are written in iambics, and concern the secret revelations of lovelorn girls, the punishment of naughty pupils, the persuasive arts of shrewd matchmakers, and all sorts of not always edifying intimacies.

Like the much more decent bucolic mime lyrics of Theocritus, these *mimeiambics* of Herondas were, most probably, meant to be read or recited by an individual mime with a great range of voice.

The Greek mime play did not gain access to the stage of the great public theater until the Hellenistic era. Greece never conceded it the importance it was to gain under the Roman emperors in Rome and Byzantium.

Rome

INTRODUCTION

The Roman empire was a military state. Before Augustus the Romans were warriors; after Augustus they ruled the world. The road from the legendary foundation of the City of the Seven Hills in 753 B.C. to the worldwide *imperium romanum* is a succession of wars of conquest, and at the same time the legitimization of a nationalism that rested from the very beginning on the power of authority.

Even the gods were subject to the fiat of the state. The location of their principal sanctuaries was determined not by tradition, but by the *res publica.* Before the Roman legions captured an enemy town, its gods were requested in a religious ceremony, the *evocatio* ("calling away"), to leave the besieged citizens and move to Rome, where they could expect more magnificent temples and greater respect. In this way the sanctuary of Diana was moved from Aricia, in Latium, to the Aventine, and the Etruscans' Juno Regina was "relocated" from Veii to the Capitoline. In the same way Minerva, a successor of the Greek Pallas Athene worshipped at the Etruscan city of Falerii, came to Rome and there joined Jupiter and Juno as the third member of the Romans' highest triad of gods on the Capitoline Hill. Rome still remembers her today in the Church of S. Maria sopra Minerva, founded in the eighth century.

The Ludi Romani, the earliest of the official religious festivities at which plays were presented, also were sacred to the triad of Jupiter, Juno, and Minerva. The very name indicates that worship of the gods had to share the honors with the glorification of the rising city, the *urbs romana.* As Cicero said, the secret of Rome's domination rested on "our piety, our religious customs, and our wise belief that the spirit of the gods rules everything."

The state religion had taken over the hierarchy of the Olympic gods from Greece, with a few changes of names, but no major change of character. On the banks of the Tiber as in the shadow of the Acropolis in Athens, Thalia, the muse of comedy, and Euterpe, the muse of the flute and the tragic chorus, were the tutelary goddesses of the theater.

This rational, technically and organizationally so highly gifted people must have found it quite natural to apply to the arrangements of its religious ceremonies the same purposive determination that distinguished its military expeditions. The theater of Rome was based on the political slogan *panem et circenses*—bread and circuses—which clever statesmen have always tried to follow.

As regards both its dramatic and its architectural features, the Roman theater was the heir of the Greek. Livy and Horace declared that the origins of the Roman theater were to be sought in the Fescennine songs—the satyrical and suggestive carnival dialogues of the Etruscan city of Fescennium—with their obvious intent to take their bearings from the origins of the Hellenic theater. The comparison is all the more valid for the era of the greatest flowering of the Roman theater. As earlier, in Athens, this era is divided into a period of literary dramatic activity and another in which succeeding generations endeavored to create a worthy architectural setting. For Rome's literary dramatic flowering this means the third and second centuries B.C., when the historical plays and comedies prospered (on temporary wooden stages), and for its high period of theater architecture, the first and second centuries A.D.

The amphitheater did not belong to the poets. It served as the showplace for gladiatorial games and animal fights, for naval combats, acrobatic performances, and variety shows. When the persecution of Christians began under Domitian, human blood was shed in the Colosseum, at the selfsame place where crowds of 50,000 people cheered the winning athletes, or the actors of mime and pantomime performances. Its theater was the mirror of the *imperium romanum*—for better or for worse. And it was organized show business rather than a place dedicated to the arts.

LUDI ROMANI, THE THEATER OF THE RES PUBLICA

During the same decade when Aristotle described the by then fully developed Greek tragedy, Rome saw its first *ludi scaenici* ("stage games"). These were modest mime performances by a troupe from Etruria. The show included dances and songs, accompanied by flute-playing, and also religious invocations of the gods in the spirit of the mysterious, other-worldly faith of the Etruscans, who had once been the rulers of Rome. At this time, the concern of players and audience was to placate the powers of life and death, for it was the year 364 B.C. and pestilence was raging in the country.

From the very outset, Rome's art of statesmanship expressed itself in offering the vanquished peoples a chance to develop their talents and to maintain good relations with their own gods. The Romans annexed the spiritual no less than the terrestrial property of those they conquered, together with the right of displaying it in public to the pleasure of all and to the greater glory of the *res publica*. And so Rome's theater, too, was an instrument of state power, directed by the authorities. As in Athens the art of tragedy and comedy had developed out of the program of the festivities at the Dionysia and the Lenaea, so Rome now set out to organize the art of drama on the basis of the program for its festivities.

The external occasion was the Ludi Romani, instituted in 387 B.C. and from then on celebrated annually in September, with four days of theatrical presentations. Other festive games offered to the gods (*ludi*) were instituted later, such as the Ludi Plebeii in November, the Ludi Cereales and Megalenses (in honor of the mother of the gods) in April, and the Ludi Apollinares in July.

These festival celebrations owed much to the family of the Scipios, who helped strengthen Rome's world renown not only in military, but also in cultural affairs. In the third and second centuries B.C., the Scipios practiced the sort of patronage of the arts that later, at the time of Augustus, would be associated with and named for the nobleman Maecenas.

The ambitious metropolis on the Tiber took pains to foster the talents especially of those of its conquered areas that were the home of Greek intelligence and education. The Romans indeed owed their first dramatist—Livius Andronicus—to the town of Tarentum, one of the greatest and wealthiest of the old Greek colonies in Southern Italy. Livius Andronicus was brought to Rome as a slave of the wealthy house of Livius. Thanks to his gift of language, the young Greek was soon promoted from private tutor to educational and cultural adviser. He translated Homer's *Odyssey* into Latin Saturnian verse for the use of Roman schools, and composed Latin hymns at the behest of the Senate.

In 240 B.C., for the victory celebrations following the first Punic War, Livius Andronicus, probably again on official orders, wrote his first adaptations of Greek plays. One tragedy and one comedy were performed, in which Livius Andronicus himself took part as actor, singer, and producer, all in the best Athenian tradition.

The example of Livius Andronicus soon brought the first Latin dramatist upon the scene, Gnaeus Naevius from Campania, a witty writer with a sharp critical faculty, who first presented some of his own works at the Ludi Romani five years later. In the view of Theodor Mommsen, the great nineteenth-century German classical historian, he was "the first Roman who deserved to be called a poet, and to all appearances was one of the most notable and outstanding talents in Roman literature."

Naevius was a soldier. He had fought in the first Punic War, and had first-hand experience not only of the victory of the Roman legions but also of the shortcomings of military leadership. His writings reflected his enthusiastic faith in the Republic yet also his sharp criticism of its corrupt elements. Naevius was the founder of the Roman drama, the *fabula praetexta,* named for the official garb of the praetors, the highest officials and servants of the Republic, who were its central characters and heroes. In Rome's comedy, a distinction was made between the *fabula palliata,* modeled on Greek comedy and performed by actors wearing the Greek mantle (called in Latin *pallium*), and the *fabula togata,* home-grown in Rome, as it were, and performed in the native *toga.*

Naevius's dramatic glorification of Roman history, especially in his most famous play *Romulus,* which portrays the legendary foundation of Rome, brought the author rich honors. But he risked them all with his comedies, in which he ventured into the field of topical polemics and, true to the example of Aristophanes, attacked the politicians and noblemen of his time.

But Rome was not Athens. The men of the Senate were not like Cleon, who had been content to retaliate with a good thrashing for Aristophanes' disrespectful candor. Naevius had to pay dearly for the militancy he expressed in his comedies. He was imprisoned and then exiled. He died (around 201 B.C.) in Utica, the old Phoenician commercial center Scipio Africanus the Elder had unsuccessfully besieged three years earlier.

In 204 B.C., presumably in the wake of Scipio's returning army, the third pioneer of the Roman theater appeared in the capital: Quintus Ennius of Rudiae in Calabria, then thirty-five years old. As a soldier in the second Punic War, in their defeat by Hannibal, he had admired the good conduct of the legionnaires and their generals, the absence of which in victory Naevius had so critically deplored. What Ennius saw, instead, was "the unshakable faith of the Romans in their state as well as their profound understanding of the real balance of power," which in defeat merely strengthened their faith in their military mission.

Quintus Ennius, who also had been raised and educated in the Greek cultural tradition, had the good fortune to gain the friendship of the most respected men in Rome. He gained fame for his major work, a national epic entitled *Annales,* and also for his adaptations of Greek tragedies and comedies for the Roman public. He modeled his work after that of Euripides, and wrote such plays as *Achilles* and *Alexander,* and another on the theme of the Eumenides. He also wrote *Sabinae*, a dramatization of the Roman legend of the Rape of the Sabines, in which the theater was involved in a double sense, for it was at a festival in Rome that Romulus was to have organized the rape of the Sabine woman, because the power-hungry city of warriors was short of women. When subsequently the Sabine army advanced on the Seven Hills, the contested beauties, under the leadership of Romulus's own wife, employed themselves for a peaceful settlement. A treaty was arranged by which Romulus and Titus Tatius, the Sabine king, were to be joint rulers of rome.

Ennius, the "spokesman of well-born, Hellenized gentlemen," was careful all his life to keep away from controversial subjects. He was popular with both the people and the aristocrats. His choice of dramatic themes shows how carefully he maintained his position in the tug-of-war of a favorite's existence. He always chose subjects which, usually with some didactic aspect, could be smoothly transposed into the rational Roman view of the world.

The second century B.C. yielded a rich harvest of dramatic productions along the pre-established line of the *fabula praetexta* and the adaptation of Greek themes. In tragedy, there was a succession of writers from Quintus Ennius through his nephew and pupil M. Pacuvius of Brundisium (Brindisi) and Lucius Accius, the favorite of Brutus, to Asinius Pollio, the "cothurn-worthy" [the Greek tragedian's high boot, now possibly with a sole that was elevated by a few inches] orator of the time of Augustus, and eventually, in the Christian era, to Annaeus Seneca—of whose nine extant tragedies, however, none was ever performed on the ancient Roman stage.

ROMAN COMEDY

While tragedy and comedy had entered jointly upon their Roman stage career and had originally been written by the same authors, Thalia soon began to emancipate herself. Rome's first great comic poet imbued Roman comedy not only with his own work but also with the invigorating influence of popular folk mime.

Plautus (ca. 254–184 B.C.), born in Sarsina, was not a man of the study or burner of midnight oil, but, in the course of an adventurous youth, is said to have roamed the country with an Atellan troupe. His middle name, Maccius, seems to confirm this background, for "Maccus" was one of the fixed types of the Atellan farce—the greedy yet sly block-

asks of a young female flute ayer (a courtesan) and of a slave earing a garland of leaves. osaic found on the Aventine, ome. (Rome, Museo Capitolino.)

Wall painting from Herculaneum: victorious tragic actor after the agon. *To the right, the mask he has removed; the kneeling woman is writing a dedicatory inscription. (Naples, Museo Nazionale.)*

Roman wall painting: scene from Medea. *(Naples, Museo Nazionale.)*

Roman terracotta relief with scene of tragedy. From the tomb monument of Numitorius Hilarus. 1st century A.D. *(Rome, Museo Nazionale Romano.)*

head who in the end always managed to make the other characters bear the insult and injury.

Leaving behind the unpretentious stock repertoire of his early theatrical experience, Plautus landed with a leap in world literature. The dramatic models of his comedies were the works of Attic New Comedy, especially those of Menander. Anyone in Rome who took himself seriously knew not only the famous Athenian's name, but could quote at least some of his polished epigrams. How much more rewarding, then, must it have appeared to deploy the whole abundance of his works on the stage!

Plautus knew enough about stage practice to pick out the most effective scenes from his models. In so doing he did not hesitate to interlock the themes of several plays, if only this helped to enhance the effect. He worked with as much skill as good luck on the principle of "blending," in which he was to be matched a generation later by Terence, Rome's second great comic poet.

But where did the Umbrian actor Plautus acquire all this knowledge of Greek literature and all the other qualifications, apart from his own native intelligence, for achieving world status as an author? With the savings from his career as a mime in his baggage, he is said to have become a traveling merchant and eventually to have lost everything in some mercantile speculation. No doubt, his commercial Odyssey helped him to a sovereign knowledge of all classes of people in the lower,

Boastful officer and parasite. Wall painting (now destroyed) in the Casa della Fontana Grande, Pompeii, 1st century A.D.

middle, and upper strata, to his art of unerring characterization and his skill in coordinating characters and situations.

Plautus transposed the refined urbanity of his model Menander into robust situational comedy, in which farcical elements and burlesque pranks gained the upper hand. Comic characters, mistaken identity, intrigue and middle-class sentimentality provide the mechanism that drives his comedies smoothly along. Inserts of songs with musical accompaniment (*cantica*) give them a touch of operetta. Plautus scored a hit with his first three comedies, which were staged when he was about fifty years old. The recorded dates of first performance are 204 B.C. for *Miles gloriosus,* 201 for *Cistellaria,* 200 for *Stichus,* and 191 for *Pseudolus.*

In all, twenty of Plautus's plays are extant in full. Significantly, they reflect not only the Attic New Comedy's stock of plots and characters, but, in their effective theatrical coarsening, the mentality of their author and of the public for which he wrote. They also became the inexhaustible storehouse of European comedy. The Plautine *Amphitruo* survives in Molière's and Kleist's *Amphitryon,* not to speak of the modern versions by Jean Anouilh and Peter Hacks; the *Menaechmi* ("Twins") gained a second immortality in Shakespeare's *Comedy of Errors.* The hero of *Miles gloriosus,* Bramarbas, became the epitome of vainglorious pseudo-heroism. In *Aulularia* ("The Hidden Pot of Gold") Plautus created a prototype of duped avarice, which Molière, in *L'Avare,* later clothed with the glittering mantle of French *haute comédie.*

Publius Terentius Afer, now better known as Terence (ca. 190–159 B.C.), the second of Rome's great comic poets, came to the capital from Carthage, the proud, defeated city. A Berber by birth, he was, like Livius Andronicus, brought to Rome as a slave. His master recognized the young man's gifts and emancipated him. In the circle of the younger Scipio Africanus he found friendly recognition and support.

His six comedies reveal by their very titles what Terence was after, namely, character studies: of a self-tormentor in *Heautontimorumenos,* of a parasite in *Phormio,* a mother-in-law in *Hecyra,* and of a eunuch in *Eunuchus.* All Terence's six plays belong to the period between 166 B.C., when he made his debut with *Andria* at the Ludi Megalenses, and 159 B.C., the presumed year of his death.

While Plautus had an ear for the speech of the people and relied heavily on the contrast between rich and poor for his comic situations, Terence set out to imitate the cultivated talk of the Roman nobility. "In this play the speech is pure," he says in the prologue to the *Self-tormentor,* and he adds expressly that it is a "character play without a lot of noise."

Terence was terribly upset about the unlucky accident which befell

Marble relief, showing a typical scene from New Comedy: an angry father confronts his son who is returning from a banquet supported by a slave. (Naples, Museo Nazionale.)

Scene from New Comedy: women seated around a table. Mosaic, from the Villa of Cicero, Pompeii; signed, Dioscurides of Samos. (Naples, Museo Nazionale.)

Street musicians. Mosaic, from the Villa of Cicero at Pompeii; signed, Dioscurides of Samos. (Naples, Museo Nazionale.)

Wall painting from Pompeii: a slave, mocking a pair of lovers. House of Casca Longus.

his *Hecyra.* When the play was first performed, a troupe of ropedancers nearby was noisily trying to claim the public's attention—and Terence's comedy was a flop, because, as the poet bitterly complained, "no one could see it, let alone get to know it."

The urbane refinement and formal perfection of his dialogues, the carefully drawn characters and their development in the course of the action—these were the things that Terence wished to see appreciated with due attention. He meticulously followed the Greek models and did his best not to overstrain the plausibility of the fable. But that was not all that easy to do. For Terence, like Plautus, often "blended" two or even three existing plays. The artful crisscross of people recognized or mistaken, lost and found again, made it hard for the spectator to keep track of the intricate structure of the action. *Eunuchus,* for instance, is based on two comedies by Menander, and *Adelphi* on one by Menander and one by Diphilus.

Adelphi was first performed, together with a revival of *Hecyra,* on the occasion of the funeral games honoring Lucius Aemilius Paulus, which were organized by the younger Scipio Africanus, the dead man's son and adopted son of the Scipio family. Quite possibly, there is a connection between the content of the play and the personal history of Scipio Africanus. It is even said that the latter collaborated in the writing of Terence's comedies—a reproach with which the poet dealt most diplomatically in the prologue to *Adelphi*:

> But what ill-wishers say, the noblemen
> Were helping him to write his plays, which they
> Pronounce a terrible disgrace, he counts
> The highest praise. . . .

Shortly after the performance of *Adelphi,* Terence left for a journey to Greece and Asia Minor, from which he never returned. He died an unknown death while retracing the footsteps of the Greek dramatists whom he so greatly admired.

Terence's comedies, however, survive in the world's theater. His dramatic devices, eavesdropping scenes, asides, the tactics of revealing and concealing characters and motives, all set an example. Hrotsvitha von Gandersheim, Shakespeare, Tirso de Molina and Lope de Vega, and the French and the German classic playwrights adopted Terence's techniques. The eighteenth-century German dramatist Lessing in his *Hamburgische Dramaturgie* discussed at some length the merits of Terence and his influence on the later theater.

The French humanist Anne Lefèvre Dacier, translator and adaptor of the classics, enthusiastically declared toward the end of the seven-

Shelves (scrinium) *with masks from Terence's comedy* Phormio. *From a 9th-century Terence manuscript.* Codex Vaticanus latinus, *3868.*

Scene from Terence's comedy Andria: *Simo summons the cook Sosias and sends two other servants into the house.* Codex latinus, *7899. (Paris, Bibliothèque Nationale.)*

teenth century in her edition of Terence: "It may be said that in the whole Latin world there is nothing of such nobility and simplicity, such grace and polish as in Terence, and nothing comparable to his dialogue."

FROM WOODEN PLATFORM TO STAGE BUILDING

The Roman theater's first home was the wooden platform of the wandering players of popular farce. For two centuries the stage was nothing but a temporary structure, erected for a short-lived occasion and then dismantled again. However quickly the Roman dramatists caught up with their Greek models as regards at least the quantity of their output, the external conditions of the theater lagged far behind—not, to be sure, in matters of organization, of which the Romans always were masters, but in providing the play with an architectural background.

Responsibility for the theater in Rome belonged to the *curule aediles*, two top-ranking officials, who were at first always patricians, though later the office was open to plebeians. They were in charge of the police, of architecture and construction works, of the supervision of public buildings and streets, and were responsible for the orderly course of the games, the *ludi* and *circenses*.

The aediles paid out a public subsidy to the theater director (*dominus gregis*) to cover the expenses for actors and costumes. The stage itself initially occasioned least expense. It consisted of a rectangular wooden platform, raised about three feet above ground level and accessible by wooden steps at the side, with a plain curtain to close it off at the back. It was the same improvised sort of scaffolding as the *phlyakes* of southern Italy, and the mimes and players of Atellan farce set up shop wherever they hoped to attract enough spectators to earn a few pennies.

Livius Andronicus and his contemporaries and successors had to make do with these primitive arrangements. But the actors had to be all the more resourceful and versatile. They wore no masks and were distinguished only by wigs, especially in female roles. It was important that their voices be clear and carry well. Livius Andronicus is said to have once had his part spoken by a hidden speaker, he himself doing just the "acting."

The public stood in a semicircle around the platform. In 150 B.C., at least, it was still forbidden to sit down at a theater performance, when

Scipio Africanus the Younger suggested that seats might be provided for senators and state officials, this proposed privilege angered the people.

Gradually, the primitive stage became better adapted to the needs of dramatic art. First, the background curtain (*siparium*) gave way to a wooden shed, which served as a dressing room for the actors. At the front of the stage, where eventually the Roman *scaenae frons* was to take the place of the Greek *skene,* a roofed wooden structure with side walls had been developed in the time of Plautus to meet scenic requirements. Three doors gave access to the front stage through the timber wall, one central (*porta regia*) and two lower ones on either side of it (*portae hospitaliae*); later, another two side entrances were added. This arrangement permitted the actors to come onstage from five "houses," an essential arrangement for the street scenes of Plautus and Terence. The smaller the stage was, the closer the doors were to each other. (Eventually, in the sixteenth century, it reached extreme compression in the "bathing-box" stage, which was a reconstruction built by German humanists for school use.)

Plautus, with his Atellan experience behind him, presumably took a personal part in staging his comedies; but Terence was lucky enough to find an influential principal who produced all his plays. This was the theater director Lucius Ambivius Turpio. Turpio's troupe had a good reputation with the *curule aediles,* for he was skillful in securing success for the comedies he recommended. The musical accompaniments for Turpio's productions, scored for several flutes, were composed by the slave Flaccius.

Since the stage was put up near the circus and the plays therefore had to compete with chariot races, boxers, dancing girls, and gladiatorial games, the poets had many a sad disappointment, as happened to Terence with *Hecyra.* Even when this play was produced for a second time, Terence figured on the risk of a similar mishap, for he wrote some lines for Turpio to speak in the prologue to the effect that "when there's a rumor that the gladiators are about, the crowd comes running. They shout and bustle and fight for a seat."

Contrary to the custom of the time, it seems that when Turpio produced the *Adelphi* in 160 B.C., he gave the actors masks to wear, to judge from a report by the grammarian Donatus. The medieval imitators of Terence had no doubt on this point; they had a full set of masks made for each play, probably on some common model now lost, and kept them neatly arranged on shelves in the exact order of their wearers' appearances onstage. In the case of *Adelphi,* there were thirteen masks corresponding to the number of the cast, but presumably any one actor took several minor parts.

Five years after the death of Terence, in 155 B.C. the censor Cassius

Longinus built the first stage house with columns to decorate the *scaenae frons,* but after the *ludi* were over, it was pulled down on Senate orders. The same happened with the expensive wooden structure put up in 145 B.C. by Lucius Mummius, the conqueror of Corinth, for his triumphal plays; this complete theater building was the first to include seats for the spectators, but, as Tacitus relates in his *Annals* (XIV:21), it was torn down after the end of the games.

As late as 58 B.C., the aedile Aemilius Scaurus had to bow to the law that forbade permanent theater buildings. He had erected a grandiose building with a plastically organized *scaenae frons,* with 360 columns and an auditorium that allegedly held 80,000 people; but like those built by his predecessors it had to be torn down again.

Obviously, there was a limit even to the power of the aedile with his curule seat of honor. Even the powerful aediles, for a span of two centuries, could not change the fairground character of the old Roman theater.

It is not certain whether and in what ways painted decorations were used. According to Livy, the aedile Caius Claudius Pulcher was the first, in 99 B.C., to have the wall of the stage decorated with naturalistic paintings. They are reported to have been painted on movable wooden panels divided in the center so that they could be pulled away to both sides of the stage. Vitruvius, the famous theoretician of architecture, says that painted side decorations were introduced in 79 B.C. by the brothers Lucius and Marcus Lucullus. These subsequently developed into the system of *periaktoi,* a set of three-sided devices arranged in perspective sequence and revolving around a pivot, so that any one-third turn adapted them to the changeable background. (The same system was used again in the seventeenth century by the German theater architect Joseph Furttenbach on his *telari* stage, a further development of the reconstruction designs of the antique *periaktoi* stage by Vignola and Danti published in 1583.)

Virgil has described how on one occasion the *scaena* walls divided and at the same moment the *periaktoi* turned. The doors by the side of the *periaktoi* had an invariable meaning with which all spectators were familiar; people entering the stage from the left were coming from abroad, those entering from the right were coming from town. In the early days, an altar was erected on the left side of the stage with the statue of the god in whose honor the play was performed; at funeral games, there stood a statue of the departed instead.

The use of the crane as a flying apparatus—which had gone out of use in Greece by the time of Middle Comedy—as well as of other similar machines, was reserved in Rome for the circus games in the arena and the amphitheater. One new device, which has since become part and parcel of every theater in the world, was unobtrusively introduced in 56 B.C., on the very margin of the Roman theater's literary and technical development: the drop curtain.

Its predecessor in Roman lands was the white *siparium*, which the mimes used to hang up to conceal the *scaenae frons* in the intervals of tragedies and comedies, and in front of which they produced their dialogue farces and jests.

As the decorations grew richer, there was a natural tendency to present them to the public as a surprise. Contrary to modern usage, the curtain fell at the beginning of the play. The movable cloth panels were fixed at the front edge of the roof of the *scaenae frons* and were lowered into a narrow trench in front of the stage. This trench can still be seen quite clearly in Roman stone theaters, as for instance in Orange in southern France. The European theater adopted this system of the drop curtain (*aulaeum*) at the time of the Renaissance.

THE THEATER IN IMPERIAL ROME

Rome's first stone-built theater owes its survival to a ruse. It was built by Pompey, first the ally and later the adversary of Julius Caesar. Pompey had been much impressed with Greek theaters in the course of his various sea and land campaigns. He was thinking of Lesbos as a model when, as a consul in 55 B.C., he obtained permission from the authorities in Rome to build a theater of stone. By a clever stratagem he forestalled the danger of the theater being pulled down again after the games; above the top tier of the semicircular amphitheater, he erected a temple of Venus Victrix, the goddess of victory. The terraced stone seats, he then argued, were a flight of steps leading up to the sanctuary.

Pompey prevailed, and Rome got its first permanent theater building. It was situated at the southern end of the Campus Martius. (Remnants of it can still be seen at the Palazzo Pio.) Reconstructions show that its layout was subsequently to become characteristic of Roman theater construction. The wall of the stage building is decorated with columns and the auditorium is of semicircular shape, divided into tiers by two broad passageways and into wedge-shaped sections by radially ascending stairs. At the top, the auditorium was closed off by a colonnaded gallery containing statues.

Towering aloft over the whole theater like a medieval fortress church there rose, opposite the *scaenae frons*, the steep gables of the temple of Venus Victrix. The presence of the gods, which at the theater of Dionysus in Athens had been the condition of a religious cult, became a diplomatic pretense at Pompey's theater in Rome. For Pompey, it had been a question of prestige to outwit the *curule aediles* and the Senate; seven years later, he himself was eclipsed by a stronger man, whom the populace had booed shortly before when he appeared at the gladiatorial games–Julius Caesar.

At that time the celebrations of the Ludi Romani extended over fifteen or sixteen days. At Caesar's behest, Brutus traveled to Naples to recruit "Dionysiac artists" for the Greco-Roman theater performances planned for all the urban quarters of Rome. Before his assassination at the foot of Pompey's statue on March 15, 44 B.C., Julius Caesar had commissioned the construction of a new stone theater, below the Capitoline Hill, near the Tiber.

The building was completed under Augustus, and in 13 B.C. it was dedicated to the memory of his young nephew Marcellus. Shortly before, the Romans had witnessed the inauguration of yet another stone theater, built by Lucius Cornelius Balbus, a friend of Pompey; of this, only a few scattered remnants are preserved in the Via del Pianto, near the Palazzo Cenci.

By contrast, the outer walls of the Theater of Marcellus–able to seat about 20,000 spectators and therefore the biggest of the three–still stand. Although this theater has not been used for its original purpose for centuries now, the building still conveys an impression of the majestic splendor of its architecture. The dominance of Augustan classicism is reflected in the didactic sequence of stylistic forms taken over from Greece, a pattern to be repeated on an even grander scale eighty years later in the Colosseum. Here the high, vaulted arcades are articulated by engaged columns of the Doric order in the lowest story, of the Ionic order in the second story, whereas those of the Corinthian order in the third story are not preserved. The Colosseum's inner layout corresponded to the pattern of the facade. First, there was the lower semicircle of seating tiers, subdivided into six wedges; then, the upper semicircle subdivided proportionately into twelve wedges; and above the uppermost tier of seats, there was a covered gallery supported by Corinthian columns.

This basic pattern recurs, with many variants, in all Roman theater buildings, such as the much smaller ones of Herculaneum, Aosta, Falerii, and Ferentum, which all show direct Roman influence. The same principles are applied, on a small scale, in the theaters of the North African coast, e.g., at Djemila (El Djem), Leptis Magna, or at Timgad, a town Trajan built for war veterans. Nearly all of these theaters were built during the second century A.D. and were used largely for the entertainment of Roman occupation forces.

The first permanent theater in Rome, which was built 55 B.C. *by Pompey as a multi-purpose edifice and included a temple of Venus. (Reconstruction by Limongelli.)*

Etching by Piranesi (ca. 1750): exterior view of the Theater of Marcellus in Rome, completed in 13 B.C. *under Augustus.*

Roman theater in Asia Minor: Gerasa (Jerash, Jordan), built in the 2nd century A.D. under Hadrian.

Roman theater built into the rocks at Petra, the former capital of the Nabataeans, in the 2nd century A.D. Above the rows of seats hewn out of the cliff are the remnants of rock-cut tombs.

With the expansion of the Roman empire, it was always the principle of the conquerors to extend to the new lands not only a system of central government, but also the achievements of their imperial civilization. The theater of Dionysus in Athens was enriched, under Nero, by a *scaenae frons* in the Roman style, decorated with reliefs. A few hundred yards further along, on the south-west slope of the Acropolis, the wealthy orator Herodes Atticus built an *odeum* in the Roman style in 161 A.D., in memory of his deceased wife Regilla. The auditorium (*cavea*) is of the typical semicircular shape, and equally typical are the pilasters on the wall of the stage building with its projecting side wings, which form a connection with the *cavea* and thus create a closed, harmonious unit. The theater was originally called an *odeum* because it was mainly used for musical performances; in recent times it has housed the Athens Summer Festival.

One of the best-preserved Roman theaters outside Europe is that of Aspendus, in Asia Minor, which was designed by the architect Zeno during the reign of Marcus Aurelius (161–180 A.D.). The auditorium, part of which is built onto the sloping hillside, forms a closed unit with the stage building. Behind the stage is a narrow corridor from which five doors lead onto the stage (*pulpitum*); two other entrances lead onstage from the *paraskenia* at the sides. The sumptuous facade of the *scaenae frons* was protected by a pent roof, such as existed also at the *odeum* of Herodes Atticus and at the first-century theater of Orange.

To many of the Greek theaters in Asia Minor—e.g., at Pergamon, Priene, Ephesus, Termessus, Sagalassus, Patara, Myra and Iasus—the Romans gave new, sumptuous facades, or at least *proskenion* pedestals with relief decorations. This also served to lower the position of the stage, in accordance with Roman practice. The theater of Miletus was rebuilt toward the end of the first century and completed by the time of Hadrian's reign. The buildings of Miletus must have been magnificent, to judge from the imposing market gate now re-erected at the Pergamon Museum in Berlin. The new *scaenae frons* of the theater was no doubt built on the same majestic scale. In imperial days, painted, wooden or cloth coulisses were probably no longer in use, but the combination of several stories supported on columns arranged in relief and graduated recession provided the comedy stage with a rich choice of ledges, windows, and balconies for the appearance of actors.

The fusion of Hellenistic and Roman elements both in southern Italy and Greece for a long time left the theaters at widely distant places using both scenery systems: either painted decorations or purely architectural ones. While at the great theater of Pompey in Rome the ornate, sculptured, architectural background most probably ruled supreme even before the beginning of the Christian era, Roman theater directors at

Corinth, in the second century A.D., were still working with practicable wooden decorations and lowering devices.

Apuleius, the author of *The Golden Ass* and a man as fond of traveling as of mockery, has left us a description of a performance of the ballet *Pyrrhiche* at Corinth: the scenery, made of wood, showed the whole of Mount Ida, complete with animals, plants, and springs—and these were real springs, with flowing water. Live trees and shrubs were part of the scenery, too. Against this background, the Judgment of Paris was danced by a beautiful young man and "divine" women. Venus appeared naked, save for a thin silk cloth around her hips. She was surrounded by dancing Cupids, Horae, and Graces. Minerva was accompanied by the demons of horror, Juno by Castor and Pollux, and Paris by his flock. At the end of the ballet a fountain rose from the summit of Mount Ida and perfumed the air, and after that scene, the mountain was lowered with the aid of a sinking machine. It all sounds like a period description of the Baroque theater with its mechanical devices.

Exploding mountains, volcanic eruptions, and collapsing palaces always were popular stage effects. (When the Paris Opera in 1952 revived Rameau's *Indes Galantes* with all the scenic paraphernalia of the Baroque, with Wakhevitch, Carcov, Moulène and Fost, Chapelain-Midy each contributing one setting, it ran for years to full houses.) In a *fabula togata* by Lucius Afranius, called *House on Fire,* a house was actually shown burning on the stage. The show received enthusiastic applause and, ironically, the Emperor Nero watched it from his seat of honor—just as a few years later he watched the burning city from the roof of his palace.

THE AMPHITHEATER: BREAD AND CIRCUSES

The two characteristic features of the Roman empire, both in matters of art and of organization, were synthesis and exaggeration, and these can also be found in the specific forms of the Roman theater. The drama alone did not give enough scope for the display of power and splendor. The theater of imperial Rome was out to impress. Indeed it had to be impressive in an empire reaching from the far North of Germania to the coasts of Africa and to Asia Minor. Wherever the Roman legions set foot, they were followed by "games" to provide diversions and sensations of all kinds, to keep up morale in the ranks of the Romans and among the conquered peoples.

Market gate from Miletus, probably an example of the architectural style of the stage house of the theater at Miletus, whose reconstruction was completed under Hadrian. (Berlin, Staatliche Museen, Pergamonmuseum.)

Etching by Piranesi (ca. 1750): the Colosseum in Rome, built under the Flavian emperor Vespasian and completed in 80 A.D.

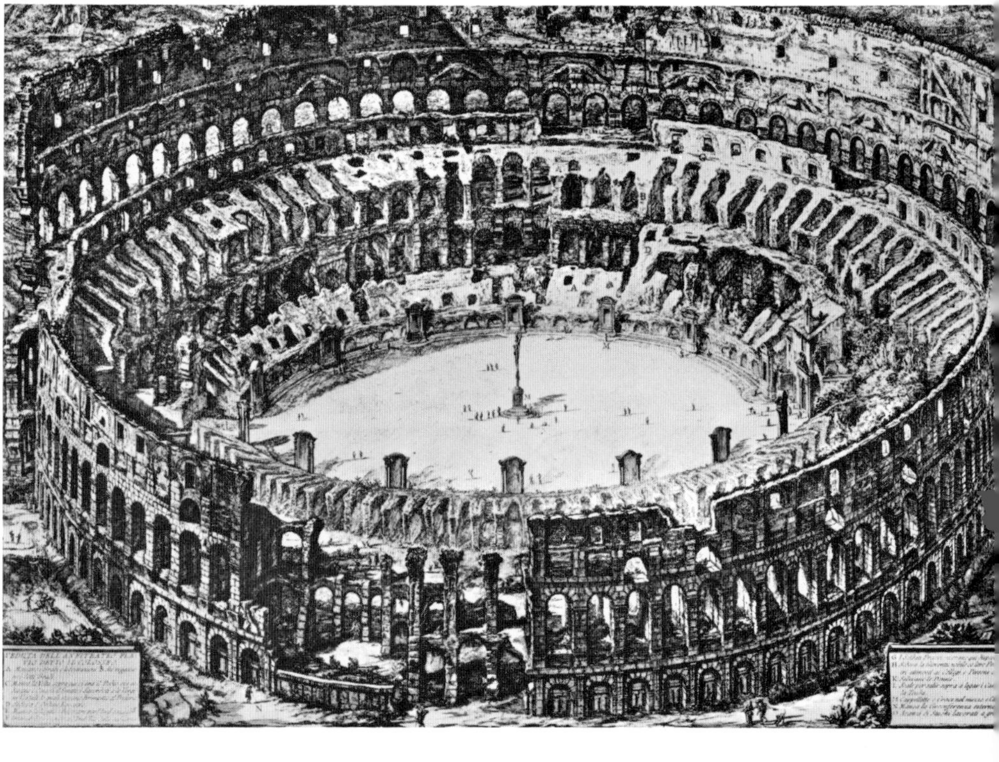

Within the peripheral territories of the Hellenistic civilization, the Romans kept to the tradition of the *skene*-theater, merely adapting it for the requirements of animal baitings, gladiatorial games, and *naumachiai* (naval battles); at the heart of the empire, by contrast, they built the specifically Roman amphitheater, which was designed for mass spectacles. This combined the requirements of the circus arena with the principle of the self-contained theater unit in a solution of impressive grandeur.

The partiality for *circenses* which the Roman satirist and poet Juvenal so contemptuously ascribed to his contemporaries in that sink of iniquity, Rome, actually went back to the first settlers on the banks of the Tiber. The enormous arena of the Circus Maximus is said to date from Tarquinian times. The Etruscans, in their funeral games, had developed gladiatorial fights and contests long before the Romans introduced them. The Circus Maximus was repeatedly enlarged and improved under Julius Caesar, Augustus, Vespasian, Titus, Trajan, and Constantine, from which we may conclude that it never lost its importance in all these centuries, not even at the time when the citizens of the *res publica* flocked, on more than a hundred days of the year, to the most grandiose theater building of the Flavian emperors, the Colosseum.

The Colosseum had two very unequal predecessors. One of them was the amphitheater of Pompeii, which was built around 80 B.C. quite close to the *palaestra*, but did not as yet have any subterranean rooms in which to keep the cages of animals or the machinery needed to lift beasts, scenery, and props. The second was a theatrical curiosity, built by Scribonius Curio in Rome in 52 B.C. for his father's funeral and allegedly at Caesar's bidding; it consisted of two semicircular wooden theaters, placed back to back. In the morning a separate play was performed on each stage; in the afternoon, the two theaters were turned around so that together they formed an amphitheater; in its closed arena gladiatorial fights were presented as the second part of the show. This technical miracle, it is said, was accomplished without the spectators in the two auditoria having to leave their seats.

The Colosseum, first known as the Flavian Amphitheater, was erected on the site Nero had ravaged by burning, in the shallow hollow he had flooded to form the lake on the edge of which he had built his palace, the Golden House. The construction of the Colosseum was begun in 72 A.D. by Nero's successor, the Flavian emperor Vespasian, and completed in 80 A.D. At the inauguration ceremonies of the new Flavian Amphitheater, which lasted for one hundred days, some 50,000 people filled the auditorium for the gladiatorial fights and the baiting and slaughter of animals. Five thousand wild beasts lost their lives on this occasion.

Wall painting from Pompeii: the amphitheater (built in 80 B.C.*), presenting a contest in 59* B.C. *(Naples, Museo Nazionale.)*

Nero's memory, indirectly, survives in the popular name by which the majestic building has been known since the Middle Ages. It is called Colosseum after the 80-foot-high colossal statue of Nero cast by Zenodorus, which showed the emperor in gilt bronze as the sun god.

The external construction rises in four mighty stories, with columns of the Doric, Ionic, and Corinthian orders in turn; inside, four galleries accommodated the spectators. Apart from the imperial box on its raised podium, the first gallery contained the seats of honor for the senators and officials, the priests and the vestal virgins. The second gallery accommodated the nobility and officers, the third Rome's patricians, and the fourth gallery the plebians. There also seems to have been a colonnade reserved for women.

The auditorium could be covered by linen canopies, to protect it against sun and rain. Pierced brackets for the 240 poles holding the velum were placed at regular, short intervals along the upper cornice of the external wall, and the awnings were hoisted by sailors of the imperial fleet. Below the arena were the tunnels containing the cells for animal cages, machinery for handling stage decorations and transformation of scenery, as well as the plumbing needed to flood the arena when naval battle shows (*naumachiae*) were on the program.

In all probability, no drama of any literary merit was ever performed at the Colosseum. Its walls sheltered everything that was a "show" and a spectacle in the broadest sense. By the time of Augustus the emphasis in theater programming had already so decisively shifted from the spoken drama to the variety show that Atellan players, mimes, and pantomimes had little to fear in competition with dramatic actors. Short sketches, clown acts, music-hall songs, revues, acrobatics, water intermezzi, dressage turns and animal shows were put on to amuse a public coming to the theater with no other qualification than that of being consumers.

Under Domitian, Christian blood flowed in the amphitheater. His attempt to institute the *Capitolia* as a counterpart to the Greek's Olympic games does not exonerate him. Domitian's national contests in sports and intellectual achievement trickled away in the sand of the arena.

By this time, the Romans had no use for an intellectual trial of strength in the theater. They wanted a "show." They cheered those who sought to gain popularity in the amphitheater by spectacular arrays of artistes, fine animals, witty soloists, musicians, and buffoons. The popularity of a new consul rose and fell with the theatrical spectacles he organized upon taking office at the time of the New Year. Numerianus and Carinus, in 284 A.D., still had been content to pit a bear against the mime players—or possibly a man with a bear-mask, since the Roman

New Year was celebrated by all the people with animal masquerades, even outside the arena. Manlius Theodorus, however, in 399 A.D., arranged a far more ambitious program for the games he financed to celebrate the inauguration of his term of office. The greater part of the spectacle on this occasion consisted of fights between men and wild beasts, which either suffered or caused bloodshed. The scene of the spectacle was the Colosseum.

There was no longer any common language for the heterogeneous mosaic of the empire. The Roman drama had exhausted its effectiveness with Plautus and Terence. The comedies and tragedies of their successors were of no lasting value at all, or, as in the works of Seneca, stood miles apart from a public taste wholly attuned to chariot races, the games of the arena, animal baitings, and buffoons.

What the Roman theater of the imperial period gained in geographical extension had to be paid for with the total loss of national character. It became an instrument to be used with any score and with any partner. When Theodoric the Great became ruler of Italy, at the beginning of the sixth century, he thought the proud Romans could best be reconciled to a Germanic king by offering them the richest possible choice of circus games and mime plays.

But the decline of Rome's imperial power had dimmed the glitter of its theater. However much the Christian Church repeatedly reproached the people with "neglecting the altars and worshiping the theater," by the fifth century Salvian, writing from Marseilles, could rightly add a reservation:

> But the answer to this is perhaps that it does not happen in all Roman cities. This is true. I would even go further and say it does not now happen where it always used to in the past. It does not happen any more at Mainz, because the city is ruined and destroyed. It does not happen any more at Cologne, for the city is full of enemies. It does not happen any more in the famous city of Trier, for it lies in ruins after fourfold destruction. It does not happen any more in most of the cities of Gaul and Spain.

Salvian, probably himself a native of Trier, accused his countrymen that "as the best remedy for the ruined city" they had petitioned the emperor to reestablish the circus games: "I thought that in your defeat you had lost merely your goods and chattels, but I did not know that you had also lost your mind and good sense. Is it theater, is it circus, that you want from the government?" How gratifying these words would have been to Juvenal!

Relief from a marble sarcophagus: chariot race at the Circus Maximus in Rome. Late 3rd century A.D. *(Foligno, Museo Civico.)*

Ivory relief: animal baiting in the arena. From a diptych of the consul Anastasius, 517 A.D. *(Paris, Cabinet des Médailles, Bibliothèque Nationale.)*

Terracotta relief: gladiators and lions. To the left, spectators in their boxes; to the right, statue of a god. (Rome, collection of the former Museo Kircheriano.)

Mask of late Roman Atellan farce, with crooked nose and the typical wart on the forehead, here exaggerated. Terracotta. (Taranto, Museo Nazionale.)

THE ATELLAN FABLE

The decline of the Roman drama and the extinction of comedy opened the doors of the Roman state theater to an artless species of farce known as the Atellan fable. As early as the second century B.C., the popular farce players of the Oscan town of Atella in the Campania had flocked northward to Rome along the Via Appia. Their coarsely grotesque masks were matched by the robust ribaldry of their improvised dialogues. Their modest repertory relied on half a dozen stock types, like the sly dolt Maccus, who made up by his ready wit for his fumbling clumsiness; the chubby-faced simpleton Bucco, who was always worsted; good-natured Daddy Pappus, whose senility was the butt of the crudest allusions; and the gluttonous hunchback philosopher Dossenus, a favorite target for the mockery of illiterate peasants.

The Atellan players, who were later joined also by professional Roman actors, had their own function at the state theater festivals. Like the satyr plays of Greece, they provided a grotesque, comic endpiece (*exodium*) to the performances of serious historical plays and tragedies at the Ludi Romani, a gay rearguard, as one of Juvenal's scholiasts puts it, "to help the spectators dry their tears." The Atellanae had their high period in the first century B.C., when the Roman dramatists Pomponius and Novius undertook to give metrical form to rustic and richly obscene farce. Yet they retained the dialect of the Latin peasantry, together with its earthy expressiveness—as, for instance, when someone asks: "What is money?" he gets the picturesque answer: "A brief happiness, a Sardinian [that is, quickly melting] cheese."

Although it had outlived both tragedy and comedy, the Atellan farce lost ground to the *mimus* at the time of the later emperors.

> But it penetrated to all the provinces of the Roman Empire and probably retained the main stock types of the Campanian farce. This is suggested, in the first place, by the circumstances that the masks from all parts of the world, from Crete, say, and Tarentum and Germania, are strikingly similar. Second, there is the detail that a wart on the forehead recurs on these masks. Such an excrescence became known in antiquity as the Campanian illness. . . . The fact that the Roman farcical masks reproduce this abnormity regarded as comic, proves at the same time that the late Roman farce was influenced by the universally popular mime (M. Bieber).

MIME AND PANTOMIME

Contrary to the Atellan players, the Roman mimes did not wear masks. The mime needed nothing but his own person, his versality and art of imitation, in short, his mimesis. Even speech was only an accessory. *"Sanniones,"* face-makers, are what the Roman called the mimes, a nickname that seems to have survived in Zanni, the merrymaker in the *Commedia dell'arte.* "Can there be anything more ridiculous than Sannio," Cicero remarked disparagingly, "who laughs with his mouth, face, mocking gesture, with his voice, and indeed with his whole body?"

It was to this art of laughing and arousing laughter that the mime owed his popularity in Rome. At the Ludi Romani, he was allowed to draw his white curtain (*siparium*) across the scene in the intervals between tragedies and comedies and to present his jests. At the Floralia, indeed, he had an unchallenged monopoly of theatrical performance. From 173 B.C. on the Ludi Florales, a spring festival lasting several days, were an occasion for "intimate" theatrical art. While at the Circus Maximus, in the close vicinity of the Flora temple, goats and hares were baited in honor of the goddess instead of wild beasts, the mime served her after his own fashion with coarse phallic grotesques and attractive female charms. The *mimus* was indeed from the very outset the only form of theatrical entertainment where the appearances of women was not taboo. The girl mime and dancer who displayed her acrobatic suppleness at the Floralia, who could—and had to—make bold to throw off her gown in paying tribute to the goddess of flowering nature, is a sister of all those who engage in the timeless craft of pleasing men. She is a

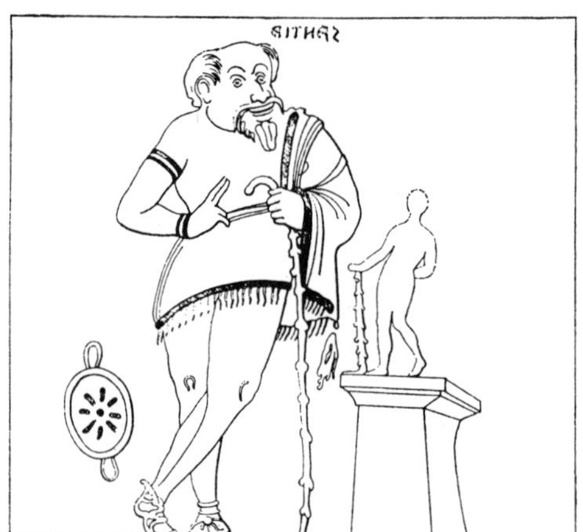

Xanthias (in Oscan, Santia) beside a statuette of Hercules. Oscan vase from the time of the Atellan farce, 2nd century B.C.

sister of the Indian dancer who answers the stranger's question: "To whom do you belong?" with a straightforward: "I belong to you." And she is a sister of the mime actress of Byzantium with whom the Emperor Justinian shared his throne and whom he made *imperatrix* of the Roman world empire.

Mimes played by the side of the highway, in the arena, on a platform of boards or the theater's *scaenae frons.* They wore the ordinary clothes of men and women on the road—rags, like the people they represented, which they themselves were—or silk and brocade, when they had gained the favor of some rich patron. The fool wore a motley dress of patchwork (*centunculus*), such as Harlequin still wears today, and a pointed hat (*apex*; hence the later expression *apiciosus*). The mime wore only a light sole for footwear, and this sandal, which differed from the *cothurnus* of the tragic actor and the *soccus* of the comedian, earned him the nickname *planipedes* in Rome. The grammarian Donatus, however, has a less charitable explanation; the *mimus,* according to him, was called *planipedia* because its subjects were so flat and its players so low that it pleased only libertines and adulterers.

Caesar thought otherwise. In his time mime and pantomime, secure in imperial protection, outweighed all other theater forms. Two men of entirely different rank and origin were prominent in Rome as "text" writers for the mime, namely, the nobleman Decimus Laberius and the actor Publilius Syrus.

A tragicomic incident that happened to Laberius exemplifies both the glory and the misery of the mime. He was a man of wit and education, and had amused himself by writing texts for mime players; he would never have dreamed of appearing on the stage himself. But he lived under Caesar. And Caesar saw fit one day to force the then sixty-year-old Laberius to partake in an acting contest on the stage with Publilius Syrus. For the old man this was a public disgrace, but Caesar had his fun, watching the worthy nobleman having to put up with coarse jokes as was the mimes' way.

It was of no avail to Laberius that, in the part of a whipped slave, he exclaimed reproachfully: "Alas, Romans, our freedom is gone!" and, even more pointedly aiming at Caesar: "Who is feared by many, must fear many!"—Caesar laughed and awarded the prize to Publilius Syrus.

When Laberius, after the bitter spectacle, wanted to take his place again among the nobles, none of them moved over to make room for him; not even Cicero. "I'd be happy to have you sit by my side, if only I weren't so cramped myself," he tried to excuse himself. But if Laberius's honor had suffered, his wit had not; he replied: "Strange that you should be sitting in so cramped a position, since you usually manage to sit on two stools."

Late Roman pantomime actor, holding three-faced mask. Ivory relief from Trier, 4th century A.D. *(Berlin, Staatliche Museen.)*

Mime as snake charmer, with bells on his dress. Late Roman ivory.

Detail from a mosaic representing gladiatorial games: Libyan prisoner attacked by a panther. Ca. 200 A.D.; *found in Zlitan, Libya. (Tripoli Museum.)*

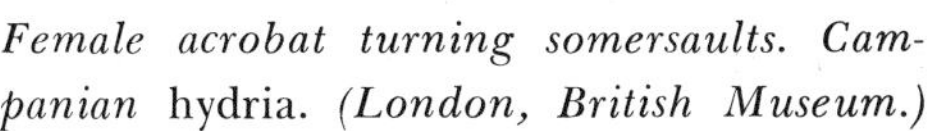

Female acrobat turning somersaults. Campanian hydria. *(London, British Museum.)*

The incident is indicative of the social distinctions within the theater. Actors may have been honored by effigies and statues erected in public squares, in the circus and in the amphitheater, but to put oneself on a par with them could, at best, be forgiven an emperor, but not a nobleman.

The director and leading player of a troupe of mime actors and actresses was called the *archimimus.* It was he who supervised the play and determined how it was to go, whether it followed a literary text or was improvised. As late as the sixth century A.D. Choricius of Gaza wrote that the mime needed a good memory so as not to forget his part and get stuck on the stage. Improvisation demanded a very sure balance on the knife-edge of the word, especially at the time of the emperors and the competition for their favor.

The archimime Favor knew he would have the public with him when, at the funeral of the Emperor Vespasian in 79 A.D., he risked a joke parodying one of the most well-known traits of the departed: the prudent and calculating thrift that had gained him the reputation of a miser. As was the Roman custom at funeral ceremonies, Favor appeared in the part of the dead man. What was the cost of the funeral, he wanted to know. The answer was: "Ten million sesterces." Thereupon Favor, as the late Vespasian, quipped that it would be better to save all this expense, to give him 100,000 sesterces and throw him in the Tiber.

The art of the theater had turned into the artfulness of the interpreter. Divorced from the dramatic work of the poet, it was left to the discretion of the individual actor. The great age of the pantomimes was at hand, which always flourishes where language frontiers and wastelands of verbal communication have to be crossed and native elements reconciled with foreign ones. The pantomime was the theatrical star at the glittering festivities of Egypt under the Ptolemies, and the darling of the Caesars and the Roman people.

When the Emperor Augustus once banished the pantomime Pylades from Rome, there was such a popular outcry that he soon had to repeal the sentence and call him back from exile. Pylades was a Greek from Cilicia in Asia Minor. He specialized in tragic pantomime, and was praised by his contemporaries as "sublime, moving, and a man of many parts." His most brilliant role was that of Agamemnon. It was thanks to Pylades that, from 22 B.C. on, pantomimes were regularly given musical accompaniment by an orchestra of many instruments. He founded a school for dancers and pantomimes and is said to have written down the principles of his art in a theoretical treatise, which, however, has been lost.

No less popular than Pylades was his contemporary Bathyllus, who owed his access to pantomimic fame to Maecenas, the Roman patron of the arts. Bathyllus, too, was a Greek, born in Alexandria, and came to the house of Maecenas as a slave. He became the idol of the Roman ladies—a sensitive youth of feminine grace, whose solo turn "Leda with the Swan" was enthusiastically acclaimed by his enraptured female audience.

Seneca—who watched the pantomime prosper under the three emperors Augustus, Tiberius, and Caligula, and who once had some spectators flogged for disturbing a performance by the pantomime Mnester—scornfully described the young noblemen of Rome as personal slaves of the pantomimes. The general situation of the theater in Rome at that time is perhaps the best explanation for the perennially puzzling circumstance that Seneca, famed in posterity as the classic writer of Roman tragedy, never saw any of his works performed. As a learned moralist, Seneca could have no truck with the crude, cheap, and artificial show business that the Roman theater was to him. But in the same city of Rome, where the theater disdained—or, according to latest research, was disdained by—Seneca in his lifetime, he was resurrected to great glory toward the end of the fifteenth century through the efforts of the humanist Pomponius Laetus (Giulio Pomponio Leto).

A pantomime star could, however, lose his popularity overnight. The gamble for applause and fame could bring triumph or extinction. When Nero realized that the pantomime dancer Paris the Elder, his favorite and close confidant, was more popular with the public than he was himself, he had him beheaded without further ado. The son of Nero's victim, Paris the Younger, fared no better. He, "the splendid ornament of the Roman theater," had to pay for the favors of the young empress with his life, when the jealous emperor Domitian one day challenged him in the street and stabbed him with his own hands.

Quintilian, the great orator of Domitian's time, wrote the artistic apologia of the pantomime. The pantomimes, Quintilian said, could speak with their arms and hands:

> They can speak, entreat, promise, call, dismiss, threaten, and implore; they express revulsion, fear, question, refusal, joy, grief, hesitation, confession, remorse, moderation and excess, number and time. Are they not capable of exciting, calming, beseeching, approving, admiring, showing shame? Do they not, like adverbs and pronouns, serve to designate places and persons?

These sentences might equally well have been culled from the *Natyasastra,* the Indian didactic manual on dancing and acting, from an appreciation of Mei Lan-fang, the star of the Peking Opera, or from a review of the modern French pantomime Marcel Marceau. The pantomime's art is universal. Its laws are the same everywhere and at all times. Its wordless language speaks to the eye. And this is why the art of pantomime spread from Rome to all the regions of the empire.

One form of entertainment that enjoyed particular popularity with the Romans both of the Western and, later, the Eastern Byzantine empire, was that of the water ballets and water games. Such shows were held in pools, or performed in Greek theaters in the East, were suitably remodeled and made watertight. Martial (ca. 40–102 A.D.) mentions such an aquacade in his *Libellus spectaculorum,* and describes it as a water ballet with nereids and a mime, in which Leander literally swam across the water to Hero.

The famous mosaic floor of the late Roman villa at Piazza Armerina in Sicily gives an often-quoted impression of the charms of the water nymphs. This mosaic, probably made around 300 A.D. for the Emperor Maximinianus Herculius, shows ten young girls in red-and-blue bikinis, jumping, running, and playing the tambourine in the style of the variety shows customary throughout the Roman empire. The Guildhall Museum in London in 1956 exhibited a part of such an antique miniature bikini; it was made of leather, cut all in one piece, and furnished with narrow leather strips right and left for tying up at the hips. It was found in a Roman well shaft discovered during excavations in London, in today's Queen Street. However, other objects found at the same site, such as a cup of sigillate ware, a large iron key, a spoon, and a wooden spindle, suggest that this exciting bit of leather underwear from the first century A.D. probably belonged to a slave girl rather than to a courtesan.

Mime actors and actresses were feted and courted. But, later, they also incurred the anathema of the rising Christian Church. The Carthaginian presbyter Tertullian, that militant opponent "of all the pagan devilry of the iniquitous world," in his book *De spectaculis* denied both the mime and the pantomime any claim to Christian redemption. And in 305 A.D., ten years before Christianity was an officially accepted religion, the provincial synod of Illiberis (Elvira) in Granada declared: "If mimes and pantomimes want to become Christians, they must first give up their profession."

CHRISTOLOGICAL MIME

The severity with which the Christian Church opposed all forms of *spectaculum* for a thousand years—until it inaugurated a new form of

Young female aquatic acrobats. Mosaic at Piazza Armerina, Sicily, ca. 300 A.D.

Street scene with popular entertainers. Columbarium (destroyed) of the Villa Doria Pamphili, Rome.

l games. From the diptych of the consul Areo-
, 506 A.D. *(Leningrad, Hermitage.)*

theater itself—was based on very real historical circumstances. From its earliest days, Christianity had been not only persecuted by the Roman emperors, but mocked on the stage by the mimes.

A religion whose Redeemer uncomplainingly suffered the most ignominious death of common criminals was bound to be scorned by the populace, at any rate so long as that religion was not protected by the state. The mime curried favor with rulers and people alike. What could be more tempting than to incorporate the figure of the "Christian" into the stock of traditional types? The mime made no difference between travesty of the ancient gods and exposing to ridicule the followers of a new faith. Baptism with the ceremonial it soon developed as a visible expression of conversion to Christianity was a welcome subject for effective mockery on the stage. Actors made a caricature of what they failed to understand. The public derided what in other ways was beyond its reach.

Hermann Reich, the expert on the *mimus,* even suggests a direct derivation of Christ's martyrdom, the flagellation and *Ecce homo,* from the *mimus.* The soldiers who placed the crown of thorns on the head of the King of the Jews, he says, were performing a typical derisive scene from the mime repertoire, such as was popular among the Roman armies and included both the king and the vanquished subjects as a fixed type. This argument seems to be supported by an Egyptian papyrus. Here, too, the mime, the itinerant *ioculator* and *maleficus,* has the function of contributing coarse and burlesque elements, and above all of taking on the soldiers' parts which were brought to a pitch of harsh realism.

Under the Flavian Emperor Domitian, who was the first to cause Christian blood to be spilled in the Colosseum, the following incident happened. The emperor thought the customary mime representation of the robber chief Laureolus, who is crucified at the end, was rather feeble. He gave orders that the title role should be given to a convicted criminal. The play ended in dreadful earnest. Domitian let the crucified man be torn to pieces by wild beasts.

A strange pictorial record, found on the walls of a house on the Palatine Hill gives evidence of the currents connecting mime and martyrdom, mockery and faith. This primitive scribble, dating from the second or third century, represents the parody of a crucifixion. A figure with an ass's mask stands leaning on the cross, to the left a man raises his arm in greeting, and underneath there is an inscription: "Alexamenos worships God."

Alexamenos, we may conjecture, was a slave whom the others mocked for being a Christian. The mask of the ass, a symbol of comic satire since the early days of antiquity, suggests that the *graffito* is based on a christological mime, in which the performer of Christ had been

Mock crucifixion. Graffito from the wall of a house on the Palatine Hill, 2nd or 3rd century A.D. *(Drawing after the original in Rome, Museo Nazionale Romano.)*

made to wear an ass's mask as an obvious sign of mockery.

This primitive drawing is the first extant representation of the Crucifixion. There are good grounds for believing that it was occasioned by the *mimus*. Passionate worship and the loud voice crying, "Crucify him!" have always been close neighbors. This is how it came to pass that the theatrical effect of the christological mime suddenly turned into martyrdom freely chosen. Mocking mime players confessed to the new faith. In 275, the mime Porphyrius became a convert to Christianity in Caesarea in Cappadocia, and the same is reported of the mime Ardalio a year later, also in some town of Asia Minor. The most famous case among such conversions was that of the actor Genesius, who was converted in Rome in the year 303, under the reign of Diocletian and at the time of the most severe and cruel persecution of Christians. Genesius fell victim to the persecution. The Church made him the patron saint of actors.

But mimes stubbornly stuck to christological themes, as is proved by the decisions of Church Councils which, well into the second millennium after the spread of Christianity in the Western world, forbade mimes to appear on the stage in the dress of priests, monks, or nuns.

The *mimus* is like a thread leading from early antiquity through Rome and Byzantium to the Middle Ages. It was as familiar to the man in the street as to the scholar at his desk. The Latin Christian writer Lactantius paid it the tribute of a lofty comparison: the doctrine of Pythagoras, according to which human souls are put into the bodies of animals, he wrote, was ridiculous and reminiscent of the inventions of mime.

Byzantium

INTRODUCTION

In 330 A.D., when Constantine the Great made the city of Byzantium on the Bosporus the new capital of the Roman empire and gave it his name, the splendor of Rome was fading. The continual frontier battles had sapped the strength of the *urbs romana*. At this time came the triumph of Christianity. The Edict of Milan assured the new religion freedom of worship. With the transfer of the imperial residence to Byzantium a second center of Christendom was to arise, as fascinating as it was exotic.

It was no longer the Capitol but the Church of Hagia Sophia which was the symbol of divine and earthly power, shedding its radiance over the coming centuries. For its reconstruction the Emperor Justinian caused the most precious materials to be procured from all the provinces of the Byzantine empire. Columns and other architectural elements were gathered together from Ephesus, Baalbek, Egypt, Athens, and the island of Delos to the glory of the "Divine Wisdom."

The emperor and the church were the two pillars of the East Roman empire. They were the subject and the vehicle of everything in the way of theater that developed in Byzantium. As Franz Dölger wrote: "The theatrical needs of the population of the capital were satisfied by the gorgeous ceremonies of the imperial court and by the rich and elaborate liturgy in the Hagia Sophia with its processions, splendid vestments, its acclamations, and antiphonal anthems."

The radiating waves of imperial magnificence, which in the following centuries were transmitted to the West, bore the mark of Byzantium. The hieratic severity, the purple splendor, the solemn stylization, which were the hallmarks of the court ceremonial and religious art of Byzantium, became a model for the Western world. Throughout the West, Byzantine artists were in demand, Byzantine luxury was the standard of taste and culture, Byzantine princesses were taken by princely suitors to the courts of the West.

The patriarch of Constantinople had the temerity to call the pope in Rome a heretic, and thereby began the fateful schism that was to lead to a tragic conflict between the Eastern and Western churches. The Crusades ended with the sack of Constantinople. The "Latins," led by the aged Doge Dandolo, had demanded recognition of the papacy as the central force in Christianity. Byzantium refused. On May 9, 1204, Count Baldwin of Flanders was crowned by the papal Legate as Latin emperor of Byzantium.

The unbroken sequence of military conflicts, to which the succeeding Greek emperors of the Palaeologue dynasty were exposed, broke the city's internal and external powers of resistance. In 1391 the Ottoman sultan Bayzeid compelled the city to pay tribute. Sixty years later, on May 29, 1453, it fell to the armies of Sultan Mohammed II. The Byzantine empire had ceased to exist. Its last emperor, the eleventh to bear the famed name of Constantine, lost his life in the fighting. Out of the ruins of the devastated capital of Constantine arose Istanbul, the capital of the Ottoman empire.

For a thousand years Byzantium had been the center of cultural exchanges between East and West, the bridge, in matters of belief, between antiquity and the Middle Ages, and in matters of the theater the bridge between the Dionysian heart of Attic drama and the Te Deum of the Christian play in the church.

THEATER WITHOUT DRAMA

One of the first official imperial acts by which Constantine endeared himself to the Byzantines was the dedication of the Hippodrome. The edifice dated back to Septimius Severus who built it in 124 A.D. on the model of the Circus Maximus in Rome. It was a long, narrow racecourse with a low dividing wall (*spina*) between the two tracks; on it were placed statues, obelisks, memorial tablets, and monuments to race winners.

The Hippodrome, with its marble seats for 80,000 spectators, was decorated with rich carvings and the most celebrated works of art from all over the world. For a millennium it was to be as much the scene of bitter historical conflicts as the splendid setting of the theatrical and circus shows for which it was intended. Here the chariot races and the gladiatorial combats took place, here the Empress Eudoxia had her own silver statue set up, accompanied by such provocative festivities that Chrysostom, preaching in the nearby Hagia Sophia, blanched with fury. Here the passions of the two chariot-racing factions, the "Greens" and the "Blues," were discharged, as well as the enthusiasm of the people.

Here the blood of 30,000 people stained the sand when Belisarius, in 532 A.D., crushed the Nika revolt and burned to the ground large parts of the city.

Constantine the Great is said to have built other theaters. One of them is believed to have stood close to the imperial palace near the Church of St. Irene (today part of the Saray precinct). In Byzantium, as in all other important cities of the East Roman empire, there were capacious theater buildings, dating back partly to Hellenistic and partly to early Roman times. The city of Antioch—seat of the Roman governor of Syria, residence of the patriarch, and the home of a theological university—possessed four large theaters built of stone. According to Palladius, the comedies of Menander were still being performed there in the fifth century A.D., until the Persian king Chosroes destroyed the ancient city in 538 A.D.

The great puzzle of the Byzantine theater lies in the fact that it never produced any drama of its own. It was content with the colorful kaleidoscope of variety, revue, and solo performances, which it took over ready-made, with dialogue extracts and lyrical pieces that were delivered from the stage by individual reciters in a "tragic pose."

Byzantinists have gone thoroughly into this remarkable situation. Franz Dölger says:

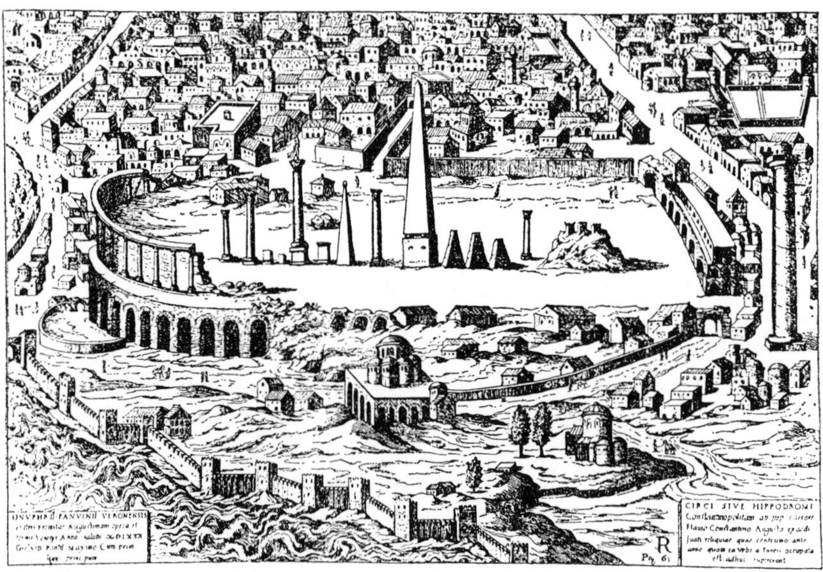

The Hippodrome of Constantinople. Woodcut by Onupl.rius Panvivius, Verona, 1450.

A valid comparison with the plastic arts has often been made, namely that Byzantine art also has never produced sculpture in any way notable, that one "dimension" was missing in both the plastic art of the Byzantines and in their literature. The reasons for this are quite clear. By the third century A.D., complete performances of tragedies or comedies were seldom given in the Roman empire. Pantomimes still performed separate lyrical, and chiefly choral, parts. For the rest the *mimus,* a sort of operetta like sketch, with a great deal of spectacular display and usually a rather "blue" content, had long captured the taste of the broad masses, and despite the prohibitions of the emperors Anastasius I and Justinian (in 526 A.D.) must have continued clandestinely throughout the whole Byzantine period.

The often cited passion play *Christos Paschon,* which for a long time was incorrectly attributed to the Bishop St. Gregory of Nazianzus, does not date from the fourth century, but from the eleventh or twelfth. It is what is called a cento, an erudite assemblage of quotations without any demonstrable connection with the living theater—an intellectual pendant to the gay patchwork *centunculus* of the mime players.

One component of those put together to striking effect in the *Christos Paschon* is an imitation of a Good Friday hymn by the Greek religious poet Romanus who lived in Constantinople in the sixth century, whereas Gregory of Nazianzus, the alleged author of the *Paschon,* died in 390 A.D.

What is fascinating in the strange agglomeration of the *Christos Paschon* is the superimposition of Greek drama on the Christian Passion. A good third of the 2,640 lines, which begin with the walk to Golgotha and end with the resurrection of Christ, are paraphrases of lines from Euripides. Both the *Christos Paschon* and the 325 quotations from Euripides' tragedies to be found in the work of Archbishop Eustathius of Salonika (died 1194) show what intense interest was devoted in Byzantium to the dramatists of antiquity—in the study.

In contrast to the erudite cultivation of the Greek cultural inheritance, theatrical practice was so naive as to recall the early period of the Roman Atellan troupes. St. John Chrysostom (347–407 A.D.), patriarch of Constantinople, on one occasion spoke at length about this sort of performance, which provided theatrical entertainment not merely at official state festivals:

> In bright daylight, curtains are hung up and a number of actors with masks appear. One plays the philosopher, though he is nothing of the kind himself; another plays the king; a third the physician, though really only recognizable as such by his costume; an illiterate plays the schoolmaster. They represent the opposite of what they are. . . . The philosopher is only

Comic poet, and masked muse representing Thalia. Fragment of a sarcophagus from the northeast of the Byzantine empire, ca. 250 A.D.

> one because of the long hair of his mask; so, too, the soldier is not a real soldier, but everything is pretense and masks.

The very tenor of this oversimplified description indicates the sharp decline. The highly developed art of the antique drama had become this primitive dialogue version of "an old story." Its degradation is not to be attributed to malicious disparagement by a belligerent Chrysostom who elsewhere thundered violently enough against the "immorality" of the theater—it is a historical fact.

A description of "what goes on in the theater," which agrees almost literally with Chrysostom, was given toward the end of the fourth century by the former teacher of rhetoric, St. Gregory of Nyssa:

> A myth or an old legend serves as the subject of the representation, and it is reproduced in imitation before our eyes. What corresponded to the story is performed in the following way. The actors put on costumes and masks. In the *orchestra* curtains are hung up which represent a city, and the whole thing is so true to nature that the public thinks it is a miracle.

On this level the classical drama of antiquity could not be a source of inspiration to Byzantium in the way Greek tragedy was for the national drama of the Romans, or Menander was for Plautus and Terence. Moreover, how could the government and the church have served up the Olympian deities for the people, how could Zeus or Jupiter, Athena or Juno and, above all, how could Dionysus, whom the church fathers considered an abomination, the devil incarnate, be reconciled with the Christian doctrine of salvation? It was considered that the general public could not be expected to display the wisdom with which the men of the church themselves appreciated the spirit and wit of ancient literature.

The consistency of this point of view came home plainly enough to the mimes and pantomimes, "the last priests of paganism," as Hermann Reich calls them. They paid for their loyalty to the well-tried repertoire, handed down from generation to generation, by being excluded from salvation under the new faith. For in the Byzantine theater, *mimus* and *pantomimus* drew on the spirit and "antispirit" of antiquity. The stock-in-trade of their theatrical program was made up of themes from Greek and Roman mythology, of fragments handed down from Phoenician, Assyrian, and Egyptian sources—in fact, of everything that had been treated by tragic poets since Homer and Hesiod.

In all this, the mime and pantomime were accompanied, even in the early Byzantine period, by the tragedian, a solo artist strutting on high, elevated wooden platform clogs, who attempted to capture the reflected glory of antique dramatic art in ranting one-man shows. The fourth-century sophist and orator Libanius, whose various occupations took him about the cities of the East Roman empire, encountered such tragedians in Antioch, Athens, Constantinople and Nicomedia.

The figure and costume of the tragedian contained features that evoked the Far East and others that foreshadowed the high Middle Ages of the West. Chrysostom speaks of the exaggeratedly long sleeves of the tragedians by means of which they emphasized their arm and hand movements, and he criticizes the vanity of the ladies, who went so far as to adopt this style as a fashion.

Remote, but related images glimmer behind the "dramatic" sleeve of the Byzantine tragedian—the Sassanian dancing girl, the aristocratic Chinese lady of the T'ang period, the young female students of the Pear Garden and, in the sphere of Christian art, the dancing Salome, the epitome of worldly vice. All these images have their "play" in the expressive power of the long sleeves that hang down over the actor's skillfully moving hands.

The medieval monks' scriptoria owed one thing to the furious scorn the Fathers of the Byzantine church poured upon the seductive arts of the female mimes and dancers: the vividness with which they were able to portray the sinful Salome.

"They come with uncovered head and do not care what they reveal. They dress their hair as extravagantly as possible, they paint their cheeks, their eyes glitter with voluptuousness. . . ." Thus the female mimes of the Byzantine theater are described, and thus Salome dances in the Aachen Ottonian codex of the tenth century, with naked breasts and bare arms, her blonde hair falling to her knees.

"They glitter with gold and pearls. And they wear the most sumptuous costumes. They dance, laugh, and sing with sweet, seductive voices." Thus the description of the women mimes continues. This picture, too, has been preserved in Salome's dance in the Gospel book of Otto III, which is among the treasures of the cathedral at Bamberg.

Chrysostom did not forget to drive home to his congregation, with ever renewed insistence, the fact that he had once succeeded in wresting away from the devil one of these "corrupt daughters of men," one of those mimes who had paraded in exciting costume before all the world and had made many a rich man poor and many a wise one foolish. That liking for dancers and mimes, which Chrysostom in his fury held against the Empress Eudoxia, would lead Justinian 150 years later to take his imperial consort from the arena. The charms Theodora, in her days as a mime, had displayed so liberally were metamorphosed, once she was enthroned as empress, into no less amazing imperial qualities. But even Theodora could not change the general disdain for her former occupa-

Miniature representing the dance of Salome. Picture of a Byzantine mime actress, her hair unbound and the upper part of her body nude. Gospel book of Emperor Otto, 10th century. (Aachen, Cathedral Treasury.)

Salome's Dance. Gospel book of Otto III. (Munich, Staatsbibliothek.)

tion. As the Codex Theodosianus lays down, actors were classed among the *personae inhonestae,* those who had neither honor nor rights, who were excluded both from civil rights and the salvation of the church. Anyone who ventured to marry a mime, actor, or *ioculator* was expelled from the Christian community. Only an emperor could dare to ignore this commandment.

THEATER IN THE ARENA

Mimes, pantomimes, singers, dancers, and tragedians were all performers in the "shows" of the Byzantine theater, but they were not its chief representatives. The main attraction in the "delights to eye and ear" that were offered in the Hippodrome and amphitheaters of the empire consisted of animal combats and gladiatorial games, especially at the New Year's state festivities which lasted several days. These were provided by the newly elected consuls, who had to celebrate their entry into office in this expensive way. This was already the custom in Rome, but in Byzantium, the citadel of court ceremonial, these games were developed into a splendid pageant, the course of which was minutely laid down by imperial command.

A novel of Justinian's, written in the year 536, set down the precise sequence of the ceremonies with which the new consul was to present himself to the emperor and the people. They range from the ceremonial procession (*processus*) at court to the various *ludi circenses* in the arena. The overture was the "tame *venatio*" (animal baiting), games of skill featuring comical, not necessarily dangerous animals, such as performers and bears chasing each other on a bar, behind movable gratings, in merry-go-round baskets moved from below ground. These games stirred up the excitement of the audience. The following "wild *venatio*," fights with wild beasts such as lions and panthers, satisfied the public's desire for blood.

Pictorial documentation of these arena games is provided by the ivory consular diptychs, numbers of which have been preserved. The earliest specimen dates from 406 A.D. and the last from 541. They were an obligatory New Year's present from the consul to his friends, individually signed, like the annual gifts of modern industrialists. The front relief shows the donor in all the glory of his new dignity, for instance, as the patron of the games. He sits on a richly carved throne, with the scepter in his left hand and in his right the white cloth (*mappa*), which gives the starting signal of the contests. Below this relief often is carved a theater scene with performers and animals. Actors in the costume of tragedy with mask and high headdress (*onkos*), groups of comedy players and bald-headed mimes testify that the descendants of the ancient theater had their share in the circus program.

The convenient, little ivory diptychs, the interior surface of which was covered with wax and served as a writing tablet, traveled as far as the mimes did. A diptych of the consul Areobindus reached Spain. There, a stone carver of the ninth century took it as his model for the door frame of the village church San Miguel de Lillo. And thus a scene from the Byzantine circus has ever since caught the eye of the faithful as they enter the church. Below the primitively stylized consul on his throne who has just raised his hand for the games to begin, an acrobat is balanced on his hands on a pole toward which a lion leaps but is held back by a man wielding a whip.

What could have impelled the carver to choose this motif of such remote origin? And what considerations could have led the founder of the church to let him do it? Was it a last admonition to the congregation to leave all worldly thoughts behind, to think of their entrance into the church as a release from earthly play? Romanesque art is notable for the fact that its many images in stone of dancing and music, of mimes and performers resulted from the church portal being considered as a partition between earth and heaven.

THE THEATER IN THE CHURCH

Regardless of the decision of the Emperor Theodosius II at the Council of Carthage that all theatrical entertainments were to cease on church holidays, the dramatic instrumentation of the liturgy within the Byzantine church itself gained more and more resonance.

The splendor of the liturgy in the Hagia Sophia, the dramatic acclamations, evocations of the prophets, and antiphonal singing, the colorful wealth of ecclesiastical vestments, the festival processions—all these sought by thoroughly theatrical means to satisfy the people's need for spectacle.

The Easter ceremony, which five centuries later became the embryo of the Christian church play, was in Byzantium the occasion of a pageant that wound from one church to the next through the streets of the city in a solemn procession. The Easter troparion *Christus aneste*, begun by the singers on the ambon of the Hagia Sophia, was repeated in the other churches, and the procession through the streets was headed by the imperial master of ceremonies who led the singing.

Ivory relief representing arena and theater scenes. Above, horses led by amazons; below, mimus *scene, obviously a mock healing of the blind, and tragic group. Detail from a consular diptych of Anastasius, Constantinople, 517* A.D. *(Paris, Cabinet des Médailles.)*

Stone relief on the portal of San Miguel del Lillo, Spain, 9th century.

Relief on the Theodosius obelisk in the Hippodrome, Constantinople: Emperor Theodosius, patron of the circus games, between his two sons, Honorius and Arcadius, in the royal box. Ca. 390 A.D.

Ivory relief from a consular diptych: tragic actor with doffed mask, probably after reciting a Medea *monologue. Ca. 500* A.D. *(Leningrad, Hermitage.)*

From the beginning, the liturgy of the Eastern church assumed a dramatic character with its alternating recitations, hymns with solo parts and responding choirs, and feast-day sermons with inserted dialogues. As early as the fourth century the great orators made their sermons an exercise in rhetorical art. They applied the rules of the Greek orators and dramatists and developed their exegesis of the Bible by the use of dialogue and an intensified dialectic of pro and contra in their interpretations.

The tradition of Byzantium does not signify merely the concentrated tranquility of the icons. It also means a wealth of stories from the inexhaustible treasurehouse of legend, the copiousness of which was only remotely approached in the late medieval passion play, which would last several days.

The texts of sermons in dialogue (homilies), which have been preserved in many manuscripts, mainly from Syrian sources, contain a vast efflorescence of episodic detail, above all in relation to the Virgin Mary. One of these surviving manuscripts, a "Glorification of the Virgin Mary," was written by one of the last significant neo-Platonists, Bishop Proclus, who was born in Constantinople in 410 and brought up in Athens. The fragments of this manuscript, taken together, constitute the outline of a complete play. A hymn glorifying the virginity of the Mother of God is followed by a conversation between the Angel Gabriel and Mary, which is interrupted by a questioning monologue of the Virgin, and terminated by the voice of God proclaiming the mystery of the Incarnation.

After this presentation of the supernatural comes a dialogue as crudely natural as could be. Joseph accuses Mary of having behaved like a whore and of "having deceived him with a lover." Mary explains that she is not in a position to justify herself. She proposes to Joseph that he should read the prophets, then he would understand that she had received her child from God. This contrast between the decree of Heaven and earthly reality could not have been more theatrical.

The jealous, white-haired husband and the alleged unfaithfulness of his young wife are a well-tried recipe for success, taken from the stock-in-trade of the *mimus,* which maintained its popularity for centuries, down to the mystery plays of the late Middle Ages. The theme recurs in a dialogue fragment that is attributed to the patriarch Germanus of Constantinople (ca. 634–733 A.D.). It is found again in the illuminated manuscript of a collection of homilies by the monk James of Kokkinobaphos, from the first half of the twelfth century. The pictures in this collection were admitted even by so sceptical a critic as Cardinal Giovanni Mercati, the Vatican librarian who died in 1957, as evidence of religious theater in Byzantium. The theme occurs again, in form almost identical with the Germanus fragment, in a scene of the fifteenth-century English Coventry plays, the *Ludus Coventriae* ("Joseph's Return"). For all its rhetorical vividness, the theatrical dialogue included in the Byzantine church service was not without the appropriate dignity. The freely treated episodes were contained within the contemporary, measured style of representation, as indicated by the manuscript by James of Kokkinobaphos, of which two copies survive.

It is due to the iconoclasts that pictorial evidence is lacking for the early period of Byzantine theater. Thousands of icons and illuminated manuscripts were lost as a result of the official destruction of images under the Emperor Leo III, who sympathized with the Arabic civilization and the religion of Islam.

It is not known to what extent the iconoclastic movement (726–843) affected the dramatization of the Gospel within the framework of the church service. During this period of crisis the church itself was divided, particularly at the Council of Nicaea in 787, between iconodules and iconoclasts. Both groups drew their arguments from the Bible and from tradition. As long ago as 370 A.D., St. Basil the Great, the clever preacher and bishop of Caesarea, had affirmed that the respect the faithful showed to the image referred not to the work of human hands, but to the subject it represents—the primal image (*eikon,* the icon). And St. Theodore the Studite declared that "if the supernatural cannot also be made visible to the eye of the senses, by pictorial representation, then it remains hidden to the spiritual eye."

Along with the painted image, this declaration justified the *living* image, that is, the theatrical reproduction of the sacred story. It indicates what the church in Byzantium already considered to be the task of Christian theater: to be a living *Biblia Pauperum* ("Bible of the Poor"), just like the great medieval cycles of frescoes and miniatures were to be.

But to Western Christendom in the tenth century this feeling for the living image of theatrical performance was still alien, to judge by one of the liveliest observers of the Byzantine theater, Archbishop Liudprand of Cremona, who came to Constantinople as envoy of Otto I and recorded his impressions in two reports. In 949 he witnessed with amazement and displeasure two performances in the Hagia Sophia which culminated in the prophet Elijah's ascension to heaven.

The ascension of Elijah in the fiery chariot is a common subject in Byzantine wall painting, executed with great imagination and richness of coloring. The fact that Liudprand saw this subject theatrically enacted proves the persistence of the early Byzantine dramatic prophet-sermons; it also suggests that the technical devices of the antique theater, such as the cranes and so-called flying machines, had not been entirely forgotten in Byzantium.

THE THEATER AT COURT

Nineteen years later, in the year 968, Liudprand of Cremona reported on his second visit to Constantinople. This second report takes us to the theatrical shows given at court on a festive occasion. On June 7, 968, the emperor gave a great state banquet. The meal was followed by dance and acrobatic performances, and by a show that was anticipated with special excitement: men wearing terrifying masks and clad in animal skins performed the so-called *gothikon,* a kind of cultic pantomime, accompanied by wild gestures and barbaric yelling.

Liudprand's description corresponds with the puzzling "Gothic Christmas Play," which is included by the emperor Constantine Porphyrogenitus (912–59) in the *Book of Ceremonies* among the performances to be organized in honor of the birth of Christ. Only the date of the performance differs: Liudprand saw the *gothikon* in June. As the banquet was attended by a number of other envoys of countries friendly with Byzantium—in fact, Liudprand complains about his seating at the table—it is likely that the emperor wanted to honor a special occasion with a special entertainment.

The actors in the *gothikon* were soldiers from among the 7,000 Gothic Guards in Constantinople who were in the personal service of the emperor. These actors were chosen, two each, by delegations of the "Greens" and the "Blues," the two celebrated and notorious circus factions. Wearing masks and animal skins, the men came onstage in pairs and at a run. Shouting "Tull! Tull!" they struck their shields with their lances. After alternating anthems were sung to celebrate the day, for which the "Blues" on the left and the "Greens" on the right assembled in a semicircle, and after the extolling of Hezekiah, who in the struggle against the Assyrians put all his trust in God and thus overcame the heathen, homage was paid to the emperor, the benefactor of mankind and defender of the empire. At the end, the two parties of the "Greens" and of the "Blues," each with its two shaggy Goths, danced out of the hall through opposite doors.

This curious play seems to owe much to Germanic Yuletide observances and cultic weapons' dances and to the New Year's customs of the Varangians. If the explanation is correct and the text was of Gothic origin, subsequently Latinized, and then given Greco-Christian additions in the style of the Byzantine court ceremonies, the *gothikon* would be one more proof of the intermingling of pagan and Christian elements, which can repeatedly be observed in the early theater of the West.

Thus no one could consider as unseemly profanation the association of religious and circuslike festival custom in a sacred place. In the stairway of the Hagia Sophia at Kiev, which Jaroslav the Wise began to build in 1037, there is a cycle of frescoes that gives a pictorial demonstration of the essence of the Byzantine theater. The emperor and empress are shown as spectators of the *circenses* at the Hippodrome. Acrobats display their skill; an orchestra, including a female musician, accompanies the dance of some short-skirted figures; mimes, standing in a group, await their cue.

In the vaulted ceiling of the Kiev stairway, armed warriors are portrayed facing each other. Some of them wear birdlike masks. One of the men holds a shield and an axe, the weapons of the Varangians, of whom it is said in the *Book of Ceremonies* that "in their native tongue they wish one another long life, and strike their axes together as they do so." There is an obvious parallel with the *gothikon*; it makes for a very tempting hypothesis for the history of the theater, though it is questioned by some scholars. There is, however, no doubt that the Kiev frescoes give significant evidence of theatrical performances in the Eastern church.

The court ceremonial itself was a theatrical display of the emperor's power and exclusiveness: a red curtain parted to reveal him seated upon a throne as though in a scene on the stage, and the course of the ceremonial giving him homage was no less strictly regulated than the liturgical ceremonies devised in honor of God. The tradition of divine kingship, derived from Egypt and the ancient East, found its last great glorification in the court ceremonial of Byzantium. The raised throne of the secular ruler set the pattern for the Christian altar, which "in its spatial location, its significance in the cult and its canopy shielding the ciborium corresponded to the imperial throne" (O. Treitinger).

The fact that mimes and actors who displayed their arts before the emperor should have been one and all condemned by the church shows a lack of logical consistency. The writer Zonaras endeavored to correct this inconsistency. In his interpretation of the forty-fifth canon of the Council of Carthage, which had condemned alike all performers and "theater fans," he explained that a distinction must be drawn between actors who performed before imperial personages and enjoyed full civil rights and the "disreputable jokesters who engage in fisticuffs at country festivals."

In his native city of Constantinople, Zonaras was an important court and state official under the emperor Alexius I Comnenus. When he wrote his vindication of the court actors he was unaware that his imperial master himself was to become the butt of court comedians—at the Seljuk court of Konya. Perhaps he would have revoked his commenda-

Wall painting in the staircase of the Hagia Sophia, Kiev: mimes, musicians, and acrobats. Middle of the 11th century.

Detail from the ceiling in the staircase of the Hagia Sophia, Kiev: man with lance, wearing duck's head mask, and warrior with shield and axe. Middle of the 11th century.

tion. But when the *Alexiad* was written, in which the emperor's daughter Anna Comnena reports the incident, Zonaras was busy with the composition of his own *Chronicon*.

At an early period in Byzantium, pictures and statues of mimes were set up in public squares and buildings. As a result of this custom a passage was included in the Codex Theodosianus, providing that statues to mimes were permitted solely in the theater and not in places where statues of statesmen were erected. Despite this prohibition, however, marble tablets and fragments that have been found suggest that the monuments of emperors, consuls, and comedians often enough harmoniously kept company.

The Middle Ages

INTRODUCTION

The theater of the Middle Ages is as colorful and varied, as full of life and contrast as the centuries to which it belongs. It holds discourse with God and the devil, builds its paradise upon four plain posts, and moves the whole universe with a windlass. It carries the heritage of antiquity in its baggage as an "iron ration," keeps company with the mime, and is shod with a glimmer of Byzantine gold. It provoked and ignored the interdicts of the church, and beneath the vaulted arches of this selfsame church reached its flowering.

Just as the Middle Ages were no "darker" than any other age, so their theater was not grey and monotonous. But its forms of expression were not those of antiquity and, by the latter's standards, were "unclassical"; its dynamics defied the discipline of harmonious proportions and preferred rank exuberance. This is why the medieval theater is so difficult to survey, and why it is often given a low rating amid the world's rival theater forms.

The Christianization of Western Europe had reclaimed forests and souls. Elements of the "primitive theater" surviving in popular customs, the native instinct of play and the unsecularized force of the new faith combined around the turn of the millennium to gather together the stray vestiges of the European theater in a new form of art, the play in the church. Its point of departure was the divine service on the two most important Christian feast days, Easter and Christmas. The altar became the scene of drama. The choir, the transept and the crossing framed the expanding liturgical play and returned the echo of the solemn antiphonies from the imaginary heights to which they were addressed.

It took five centuries for the Easter adoration of the cross to develop into the mysteries of the Passion, spanning several days, and for the "good tidings" announced to the shepherds to grow into the Christmas and Prophet cycles with their numerous casts. During these centuries the Church Triumphant extended its authority beyond the house of God to the cities and guilds, and analogously the liturgical play was brought out of the church and before the portal, to the church square and the marketplace. The theater could not but gain in color and originality from thus being placed in the very center of everyday life.

Wooden platforms and scaffolds were erected on sites specially staked out, *tableaux vivants* were carried along in procession and went into scenic action at predetermined stations. While once upon a time wealthy Athenian citizens and ambitious Roman consuls had vied for the honor of financing theatrical spectacles, their place was taken in the late medieval community by the guilds and corporations. Alongside the Gospel, they discovered and explored the inexhaustible store of mime, of the actor's art in all its potentialities—the Shrovetide play (*Fastnachtsspiel*) and peasant play, the farce, *sottie,* allegory, and morality play.

The artistic problem of the medieval theater, the German philologist and historian Karl Vossler once said, was not the tragic conflict between God and the world, but, rather, the world's subjection to God.

> Thereafter, once the world was secure in the church, it shifted more and more to the question of the formal compatibility between the main action's ecclesiastical, ritual, and liturgical character and the mundane accretions and interludes. Throughout the Western world, the history of the religious play is one of progressive theatrical dramatization of the Sacrament. Thus, eventually, the stage was divorced from the divine element and became entirely of this world—whether this trend led, as in Italy, to a lyrical and melodramatic result, or, as in Spain, to a nationalistic and military one, or, as in France, to didactic allegory or entertaining anecdote. Everywhere the evolution ends with a broad spectacle, roomy and far-ranging enough to encompass the world's affairs in all their richness.

RELIGIOUS PLAYS

Scenic Celebrations at the Altar

On any Saturday afternoon, the Church of the Holy Sepulcher in Jerusalem is the scene of a unique, unforgettable spectacle—the worship of the Lord in many spiritual tongues. The visitor encounters in turn High Mass, Divine Liturgy, and procession; he sees the Franciscans in their dark-brown cowls walking from the Chapel of the Apparition to the Catholicon, hears the crescendo of the Armenians' "Kyrie" as they proceed through the Rotunda until their chant dies away in the depths of the Helena Chapel. The air is heavy with incense rising from the vaults and alive with the prayers chanted in the raised Calvary Chapel by the Greek Orthodox and Roman Catholic faithful.

The Church of the Holy Sepulcher, the Christian's most holy spot in the Holy Land, testifies to the range and variety of Christendom, but also to its division. Conflict and wars have raged for 1500 years around the edifice built over Golgotha. Here, in the Church of the Holy Sepulcher in Jerusalem, the roots of the Christian faith reach down to the historical events under Pontius Pilate. Here, in the fourth century, the *Adoratio crucis* was celebrated for the first time, the Easter adoration of the cross, which six centuries later became the germ of the Christian play in the church.

Under the dome of this church, originally erected by Constantine, the evening hour seems to bring two millennia tangibly within the beholder's reach through the common foundation of the faith and the variety of its ritual. The schism between the Eastern church and Latin church, which sealed the doom of Byzantium and which still, in spite of many an effort at reconciliation, complicates the legal situation in the Church of the Holy Sepulcher, also caused the church plays of the early Middle Ages to develop along two distinct lines.

From about the middle of the first millennium, there was a perceptible impulse in the Byzantine church to encourage dramatizations of liturgical antiphonies, but it found no meaningful response in the Balkan countries. It did, however, have a definite influence on the development of the church play that was to grow out of the purely ritual ceremony—but in the Roman church this development took place, almost simultaneously, throughout the Roman Catholic Christian world during the ninth and tenth centuries.

The motivating subject was the Easter celebration, the reenactment of the death on the cross and the Resurrection and, in the border terms of the timeless significance of all religious cult, the victory of divine light over the powers of darkness. The more prominence the cross gained in the canon of religious symbols, the more emphatically the act of redemption, of which it was the instrument, had to be made visible to the faithful.

The sequence of the paschal adoration of the cross followed the phases of the Passion. The *Adoratio crucis* on the morning of Good Friday is followed in the afternoon by the *Depositio crucis,* the placing of the veiled cross on the altar. The bells are silent until Easter morning. The *Elevatio crucis,* the raising of the cross, announces the resurrection to one and all.

The customs connected with the symbolism of the cross can be traced back to the eighth century. During the ninth century, they became widely established and provided the first graphic interpretation of the Gospel story. At almost the same time, the liturgy expanded. Additional Latin sequences were inserted into the poetic and musical score of the Eastern matins. These can be attributed with certainty to the St. Gall monk Notker Balbulus, the Stammerer (840–912). His fellow monk Tutilo (ca. 850–915) went a step further and inserted into the liturgy of the Mass prose texts in dialogue. These, called tropes, are antiphonal chants that lead up to the hymn of the Resurrection.

The first biblical witnesses of the Resurrection are the three Marys on Easter morning (*Visitatio sepulchri*). They set out on their way with an anxious question: "Who shall roll us away the stone from the door of the sepulcher?" But the sepulcher is open. An angel sits on the empty sarcophagus, which contains only the white grave cloths, and the following dialogue ensues between the angel and the alarmed women:

"Quem quaeritis in sepulchro, o christicolae?"
"Jesum Nazarenum crucifixum, o caelicolae."
"Non est hic, surrexit, sicut praedixerat.
 Ite, nuntiate, quia surrexit de sepulchro."

This oldest form of the Easter trope is contained in a St. Gall manuscript of 950. It links up directly with the tropes of Tutilo and with the Limoges version of the Easter service.

While it would be easy enough to trace a connecting line from St. Gall, a monastery of international cast engaged in lively cultural exchanges, to the liturgical dialogue of the Eastern church, say, to the "Christus aneste" of the Byzantine Easter Monday procession, there are nevertheless unmistakable northern influences, especially in the Easter liturgy. The *Regularis Concordia,* drawn up around 970 by Ethelwold, Bishop of Winchester, demonstrates these influences. This work contains exact instructions on the dramatic representation of the *Visitatio sepulchri* and shows that it was precisely amid the gloomy, misty nights of England and Ireland that there was a strong missionary emphasis on light and salvation.

The *Regularis Concordia* of Winchester, which reaches back to the seventh century and is one of the earliest foundations of the Anglo-Saxon church, is also—in the narrower sense of theatrical history, the first example of a "stage direction" for the medieval play in the church, even though it does not go beyond the ceremonial solemnity of liturgical celebration. Time and place are matins on Easter Sunday, celebrated at the altar, which is to represent the Holy Sepulcher.

"Dum tertia recitatur lectio, quatuor fratres induant se. . . ."—this is how the Latin stage directions of Winchester begin. The whole text, translated into English, reads as follows:

The Women at the Sepulcher on Easter Sunday. In the center, the angel; to the left, the sleeping guards. Miniature from the Benedictional of St. Ethelwold, Winchester School, ca. 970. (Collection of the Duke of Devonshire.)

Outdoor visitatio *scene with Sepulcher, surrounded by a wall. Miniature, School of St. Gall, 10th century. (Basel, University Library.)*

Easter dialogue between the three Marys and the angel. Miniature from a Silesian Psalterium Nocturnum, *ca. 1240. (Breslau, Staatsbibliothek.)*

> While the third lection is being recited, let four brothers costume themselves, of whom one shall be clothed in an alb, and as if for a purpose let him proceed to go secretly to the place of the sepulchre, and there let him sit quietly holding a palm in his hand. While the third responsion is being sung, let the remaining three advance, all indeed clad in copes, holding thuribles with incense in their hands, step by step in likeness of persons seeking something, to the place of the sepulchre. These things are, you see, done in imitation of the angel sitting at the monument and of the women coming with spices to anoint the body of Jesus. When therefore he who is sitting there shall see the three come near him, as it were wandering about and seeking something, let him begin in a modulated voice, but sweet, to sing, *Quem quaeritis.* This having been sung to the end, let the three respond in unison, *Ihesum Nazarenum.* The angel says to them, *Non est hic: surrexit sicut praedixerat. Ite nuntiate quia surrexit a mortuis.* At this voice of command let the three turn to the choir saying, *Alleluia: resurrexit dominus.* This having been said, let the one remaining at the tomb, as if calling them back, sing the anthem *Venite et videte locum*: and while saying these words, let him arise, remove the veil and show them the place now bare of the crucifix but yet containing the cloths in which the cross was wrapped. Having seen this, let them lay down the censers which they have used to cense the sepulchre, take up the cloths, extend them towards the choir to show that the Lord is risen and that he is not wrapped in them, and let them begin the antiphon *Surrexit dominus de sepulchro,* and let the grave clothes be placed on the linen cloths of the altar. The antiphon finished, let the Prior, rejoicing in the triumph of our king because, death being conquered, he has achieved resurrection, begin the hymn *Te Deum laudamus.* When this has begun, let all the bells be struck.*

This is how the *Regularis Concordia* established the basic pattern of the Latin dramatization of the Easter celebration throughout the Western world. The *Te Deum Laudamus,* one of the oldest choral hymns, is still sung in all Christian churches today. It was originally called an "Ambrosian hymn" and attributed to St. Ambrose, but probably was written by Nicetas of Trier about 535. Across all countries and all ages, the jointly sung *Te Deum* formed the conclusion of all the Easter celebrations and Easter plays that proliferated from the original *Visitatio.*

Subsequent additions to the scenic representation closely followed the text of the Gospels. Peter and John, having learned the news from the returning women, hurry to the sepulcher. The symbolic force of the ac-

* From Hardin Craig, *English Religious Drama of the Middle Ages* (Oxford: 1955), p. 115.

Peter and John at the Sepulcher: Mary Magdalene looks on from behind the hill. Miniature from the Gospel book of Emperor Otto, 10th century. (Aachen, Cathedral Treasury.)

Race of the disciples to the Sepulcher, Peter in the lead. Miniature from a Book of Pericopes. Clm. 15713. School of Regensburg. Ca. 1130. (Munich, Staatsbibliothek.)

tion is in no way diminished by this "race to the tomb," heralding the first grotesque elements of theatrical performance. Peter, the older of the two disciples, limps and puffs behind John. But John, of course, lets him step up to the sepulcher first. Extensive gesturing, understandable to all, interprets the solemnly chanted text. Here we have the first pantomime scene in the church—especially when, in the twelfth-century Brunswick Codex St. Blasii, the antiphons are sung by the choir and the two apostles do not intone "Ecce linteamina" until they are shown the linen cloths.

The three women, meanwhile, have left the scene, except when, as shown in a tenth-century miniature of an Ottonian manuscript of Aachen, they are allowed to remain nearby and watch the race from behind the sepulcher.

Much greater scope for theatrical embellishment was offered by the *Mercator* scene, which was first introduced around 1100. According to St. Mark, Mary Magdalene, Mary Salome the mother of James, and Mary Cleophas had bought sweet spices on their way to the sepulcher—and this statement opened the door to one of the traditional stock characters of the popular theater—the *Mercator*—apothecary, quacksalver, medicaster, and pillroller of the burlesque and mime. He did not have to be invented, but simply to be brought into the play. He accosts the women on their way to the sepulcher and offers them his wares with much gesticulation. A low sales table, a pair of scales, spice boxes and ointment pots mark the scene of this first "worldly" interlude.

At the beginning of the eleventh century, the artist of the Uta Gospel book of illuminations from Regensburg considered the spice-buying scene important enough to depict it in an ornamental medallion of the Gospel of St. Mark. In French cathedral sculptures at Beaucaire and St. Gilles, the apothecary is shown with a wife. But there was still a long way to go to the coarse jesting that surrounded the purchase of spices in the later Passion plays. The *Mercator* of the Easter Sepulcher at Constance suggests nothing of the kind. Wearing the scholar's cap and holding his magnifying glass, he casts his eyes downward and silently pounds the ingredients of his ointment in the apothecary's mortar. Should this dignified Hippocrates speak at all, it could only be in solemn, measured Latin. A thirteenth-century text from Prague does indeed give him some lines:

Dabo vobis unguenta optima,	The best unguents I shall give you,
salvatoris unguere vulnera,	to anoint the Redeemer's wounds,
sepulturae eius ad memoriam	in memory of His burial
et nomini eius ad gloriam.	and to the glory of His name.

The three Marys buying spices. To the left, the apothecary with his wife. Frieze sculptures in the northern transept of Notre-Dame-des-Pommiers at Beaucaire, 12th century.

The ointment vendor as scholar, with apothecary's mortar and magnifying glass. Stone sculpture inside the Holy Sepulcher in the Chapel of St. Maurice, Constance Cathedral, ca. 1280.

Two Marys buying spices. Earliest extant depiction of this play scene in book illustration. In a medallion on an ornamental page of the Gospel according to St. Mark, Gospel book of the Abbess Uta of Regensburg, ca. 1020. (Munich, Staatsbibliothek.)

This is a far cry from the fifteenth-century Erlau merchant scene, where Medicus still holds forth in broken Latin, but, supported by his wife Medica and his assistants Rubin and Pusterbalk, lets loose a flood of invective which reduces the three Marys to helpless silence. Nothing could be more outspoken than his threat that they should stop weeping and pull themselves together, or else "I'll give you one on the nose." In the end, Medicus himself begins to wonder whether he and his companions have not gone too far, and he turns apologetically to the public; we may have fooled you with our blustering, he suggests, and announces that he will withdraw and let the Marys go their way.

The angels call out their "silete" and the first of the three Marys intones the Latin "Heu nobis." The rough *Mercator* interlude recedes as the laments are solemnly recited, partly in German and partly in Latin.

But the *Mercator,* together with his wife and assistants, has forfeited salvation. Berthold of Regensburg roundly condemned them in his sermons in the thirteenth century; the very names of his assistants, Pusterbalk and Lasterbalk, were treacherous and repulsive enough, two devils' names that good Christians were wont to attach to the players. This sharp criticism rests on a fact of theatrical history. The nostrum peddler and his voluble and abusive kin were the first to speak again with the voice of the immortal mime. When the mime thus came to life again he had, of necessity, to do so in Latin, but this links him all the more closely to his ancient predecessors.

The 224 Latin dramatizations pertaining to Easter services, collected from all over Europe and which Carl Lange published in 1887, prove how universal throughout the Western countries was the development of the liturgy in the sense of dramatic representation.

The dialogue of "quem quaeritis" between the angel and the Marys could be heard on Easter Day at St. Gallen and in Vienna, in Strasbourg and in Prague, at the Italian monastery of Sutri and in Padua, at Litchfield Cathedral in England, at the Spanish monastery of Silos, at Linköping in Sweden, and under the Gothic arches of Cracow Cathedral.

The apostles' race to the sepulcher is known to have been part of the proceedings at the monastery of St. Martial at Limoges, in Zurich and at St. Gallen, at the monastery of St. Florian in Austria, in Helmstedt in northern Germany, and also in Dublin. From Dublin, we even have a description of the costumes the two apostles are to wear: they are barefoot, clad in "albis sine paruris cum tunicis"; John wears a white tunic and Peter a red one, John carries a palm and Peter the keys of heaven.

The scene itself corresponds exactly to the rules laid down in the painters' manuals of the Byzantine church as guidelines for icon painters. The most famous of them, the book of the painter-monk Dionysios of Mount Athos, gives the following prescription for the "race to the tomb": "Peter stands stooping within the tomb and touches the sudary with his hands. John is outside and looks on in astonishment. Mary Magdalene stands by his side, weeping." This describes the stage scene. Byzantium had codified the representation, which the miniaturist of the Aachen Ottonian codex had anticipated five centuries earlier (see page 235).

The question of the relationship between the visual arts and the theater in the Middle Ages is as fascinating as it is controversial. Ever since Emile Mâle in 1904 advanced the bold hypothesis that there had been a renewal of art through the mystery plays, there has ensued an uninterrupted series of partly disagreeing, partly agreeing comments. Scholars specializing in the Byzantine period have provided some firm points. They have demonstrated a definite concordance of narrative exuberance in textual and pictorial evidence, and they have taken theatrical influences into account. Similar relationships can be observed in Central Europe, for instance, in the Epiphany cycle of Lambach, in the St. Albans Psalter of Hildesheim, or in the Uta Gospel Book of Regensburg.

Every conjectured relationship constitutes a temptation to read into the past images that, notwithstanding every care and caution in interpretation, may have been meant quite differently from what we now believe. Subject to this reservation, we may draw for the theater on pictorial evidence not concerned with the theater, yet reflecting the spirit of an age in which early theatrical elements were present. Otto Paecht, who pursued the fascinating traces of theatrical influences without throwing his cool skepticism overboard, concluded in 1962 that what in the Middle Ages "stimulated the artist's imagination in the first place was not visual experience," but that "the primary creative impulse seems to have come from the talking world," in accordance with a saying attributed by Plutarch to Simonides, that poetry is a speaking picture, and painting a silent poem.

All these early dramatic Easter celebrations were observing the time laid down in the *Regularis Concordia,* namely, during Matins on Easter Day, after the third responsory. This timing for the dramatic representations of the liturgy was retained even when the steadily expanding Passion and mystery plays had long emancipated themselves from the church, had shifted their locale to the marketplace and the theater auditorium, and were performed in the summer months. In the fifteenth century, it was still one of the duties of the supervisor of the Chapter School at Utrecht to rehearse "de vertoonigen van de opstanding des Heeren" for the Easter morning service in Utrecht Cathedral. At the Cathedral of Gerona, a 14th-century liturgical codex informs us, the duty of performing the play of the three Marys fell to the "young canons."

For the Good Friday service, the famous Latin lament "planctus ante nescia" had developed early in the Middle Ages into the Marian lament, which was later expanded into a dialogue between Mary and John. This is the first occasion on which Christ himself is heard—though only in the recitative—and not actually seen.

In a Zurich manuscript of the late twelfth century there is a dialogue deeply moving in its terseness. It is a choking cry of woe from the mother to her son who for men's sins hangs upon the cross: "*Mater:* fili! *Christus:* mater! *Mater:* deus es! *Christus:* sum! *Mater:* cur ita pendes? *Christus:* ne genus humanum tendat ad interitum." Exactly the same words were found on a chandelier which had been installed at the Regensburg monastery of St. Emmeram in 1250, during the conflict between the papal faction and that of the Hohenstaufen. It had been donated by the Bishop of Regensburg in expiation of an attempt on the life of King Conrad IV, an incident of which he did not feel innocent.

The extent to which the altar was transformed into the holy sepulcher for the Easter ceremony was left to the discretion of each monastery. The *Regularis Concordia* rests content with an "assimilatio sepulchri velamque." But as early as in the twelfth century, special tomb structures were erected in churches in an attempt to create a worthy scene for the annual Easter celebration. One of the finest examples is the Holy Sepulcher in the Chapel of St. Maurice in Constance Cathedral. This chapel was built by Bishop Conrad of Constance (934–75), and it is reported that in it "he adorned the Lord's tomb with marvelous works." He had made three visits to Palestine in order to see the "earthly Jerusalem." In its present form, the Holy Sepulcher of Constance—which in type follows the Jerusalem model—and its interesting sculptures date from 1280. It throws a bridge from the Crusades to the scenery of the Easter ceremony. The Crusaders not only returned with a personal knowledge of the Jerusalem model and with the desire to reproduce it at home as faithfully as possible; those who were fortunate enough to get home safely also had every reason to celebrate their return with generous donations.

Walbrun, provost of Eichstätt Cathedral, returned from the Crusades in 1147 with a splinter of the Holy Cross in his baggage, together with the exact measurements of the Holy Sepulcher. He founded a small monastery outside the town and gave it to a group of Irish and Scottish friars of friendly disposition toward pilgrimage. The church he dedicated to "the Holy Cross and the Holy Sepulcher," and in 1160 he erected in it a copy matching the Jerusalem original in all measurements. Today the Romanesque monument is in the Capuchin church of Eichstätt. Similar examples are the crypt of the Holy Sepulcher at

Gernrode in the Harz mountains, San Sepolcro at Bologna, St. Michael at Fulda, and St. Benigne at Dijon.

All these more or less faithful copies of the Holy Sepulcher became the spiritual and scenic center of the Easter ceremony. The text of the service was the same in Jerusalem as it was in the West. The Vatican Library possesses a unique document, "Ordin. ad usum Hierosolymitanum anni 1160" (MS. Barberini lat. 659), which contains the text of a dramatic Easter ceremony performed in 1160 in Latin at the original Holy Sepulcher in Jerusalem. The text corresponds literally with the Easter tropes from Ripoll and Silos, with the playbooks of Besançon, Châlons-sur-Marne and Fleury, and with liturgical dramatic texts from Sicily to Scandinavia, with texts from the Atlantic coast to the Vistula.

The thirteenth century was still the Age of Chivalry, of knights, of nobles, and princes who all pride themselves on giving their special patronage to the art of dramatic ceremony. The role of patron of the arts, pleasing in the sight of God, always held out the promise of reward in this world and the next. Thus in 1230 Lippold, the *advocatus* (protector) of the Abbey of St. Moritz in Hildesheim, endowed the church there with a prebend to pay the costs of a dramatic representation of the "Assumptio Christi" every year on Ascension Day. Similarly, in 1268 Count Heinrich der Bogener of Wildeshausen made over a sizable sum to the local *Alexanderstift*, to be used "for a solemn celebration of Our Lord's burial on Good Friday."

In its turn, the Easter play of Muri, which is the earliest play extant in the German language—and in very refined language at that, clearly modeled on the epic verse of the courts—seems to suggest a princely patron. But this play was probably not performed in the church. Eduard Hartl, who was responsible for a new edition of it in 1937, suggests that in "one of the larger Swiss castles, around 1250 the play may have been produced under the direction of the private chaplain, a man of courtly education, for the Christian edification of the residents." The omission of all Latin anthems, the recognizable emphasis on the knight's pride in his status, and the introduction of servants, all suggest an effort at presenting the Easter story to the lord of the castle and his guests at an adequate social setting. Thus, out of the ecclesiastical oratorio developed the first spoken drama in the northern lands of the West, and it owed its production to a noble patron.

The Easter Play in the Church

The thirteenth century brought with it two innovations of great importance for the development of the Western theater. Christ, who so far had been only symbolically present, now appeared as a speaking and

A Spanish Passion cycle, whose narrative wealth matches that of scenes in the Passion plays. Above, Judas' kiss and the soldiers taking Jesus. Center, Golgotha with crucifixion and the thieves; below, the descent from the cross; to the left, Judas has hanged himself from a tree. Miniature page, Biblia Sacra *from Avila, ca. 1100. (Madrid, Biblioteca Nacional.)*

acting participant, and the vernacular lent animation to the rigid liturgical texts. The dramatic ceremony broadened out into the freely adaptable play.

Now scenes portraying Pilate and scenes involving the soldiers of the watch preceded those of the *Visitatio* and the three Marys' purchase of spices. The Roman soldiers keeping watch at the sepulcher now haggle about their pay. The resurrection, originally merely indicated by the guards' jumping up in alarm, now leads to an aftermath in which Pilate accuses the men of neglecting their duty, and here the vivid language of gesture interrupts the staid solemnity of the representation.

The introduction of the role of Christ opens the way to the representation of the occurrences after Easter: His appearance to Mary Magdalene as a gardener ("Noli me tangere"), to the doubting Thomas, to the disciples on the road to Emmaus (*Peregrinus* play), to the apostolic group in Jerusalem and, finally, with its endless further possibilities, the descent into hell and the deliverance of Adam and Eve from limbo that is Christ's first act of redemption.

With this addition of new scenes, the space allotted for the dramatization had to be extended accordingly. While the encounter of Jesus and Mary Magdalene could still conceivably take place near the altar or the Holy Sepulcher, the journey to Emmaus necessarily demanded some spatial interval. In the thirteenth-century Easter play from St. Bénoit-sur-Loire (Fleury), Emmaus is situated in the Western part of the church, and the table for the supper in the center of the nave; Jerusalem is in the choir. The scene under the roof at Emmaus is marked by a table with wine, an uncut loaf of bread, and three thin wafers. Before the beginning of the supper scene, water is brought for the washing of the hands.

Each playing space needed for the action was specified from the beginning and identified by appropriate decorations and properties. This simultaneity of the action and the areas to be used for it determined the future stage of the entire medieval theater—whether in the form of spatial disposition over an entire area set aside for the play or of juxtaposition along a narrow strip of stage. The religious play makes the biblical occurrences visible to the spectator in the same simultaneous juxtaposition as does a painted panel. The two great paintings by Hans Memling, *The Seven Joys of Mary* and *The Seven Griefs of Mary*, with their abundance of scenes extending far and wide across the landscape, are rooted in the same approach as the simultaneous settings of the medieval stage.

Heaven and hell, Gethsemane and Golgotha, Satan and the Blessed are as didactically confronted in the play as in the sermon. The medieval religious play always had a pedagogic function, even when it had long shifted to the marketplace and had become the concern of the citizenry. The Latin word *pulpitum* still encompasses the divergent forms of representation, for it can mean either pulpit or stage scaffolding.

Christ's descent into hell throws a bridge from the Redemption of the New Testament back to the story of the Creation in the Old Testament. For the initiators of the play in the church it meant an effective displacement of the scene of action. The performers walk in procession around the outside of the church to the portal, which symbolizes the gates of limbo. Christ, impersonated by a selected canon, knocks vigorously several times. Inside, Satan, impersonated by a deacon costumed for the part, seeks to prevent the entry of the Redeemer, but in the end he has to open the "gates of hell" and release the poor, imprisoned souls of Adam and Eve and the Patriarchs. At this moment the church portal reverts to its role that is so richly documented in sculptural decoration: it is the crossroad where the parting takes place between the sinful world and eternal salvation. Now all who have participated in the performance enter the church together, followed by the congregation.

No other biblical conception fascinated medieval artists as much as that of hell, the contrast between damnation and salvation. Theatrical dramatizations competed with the imagination of sculptors, painters, wood carvers, and engravers. Soon the symbolization of hell went far beyond the mere wing of the church door. It was symbolized by the wide-open jaws of a beast, belching smoke and fire—or interpreted literally as the gaping mouth of hell, showing between its fangs a host of gruesome, grotesque devils belaboring the poor souls with pitchforks and iron chains.

The Easter play of the thirteenth and fourteenth centuries was still a modest, imaginative ritual action, fitted into the physical surroundings of the church scenery. In the fifteenth- and sixteenth-century Passion cycles, however, which often lasted several days, hell assumed a more important, provocative role often verging on coarse violence. In the portrayal of hell the theater tried to outdo the pictorial art. The sinful world was to be shown plainly what abyss it was approaching. It was to be made to recognize the power of hell, which awaits emperors and kings, just as it does disreputable priests, misers, whores, cut-throats, and procuresses. Once the Doomsday play had become independent of the locale of the church, only one further step was needed toward the development of the secular guild satires and the secular presentation of the Dance of Death. In line with old popular beliefs about the nocturnal revels of the dead, in the Banquet of the Dead and the Dance of the Dead, Death personified forces the living into his retinue, irrespective of

Hell-mouth with Adam, Eve, and the Patriarchs. Decoration, choir stall at Valenciennes, 14th century.

Last Judgment with hell-mouth. From the tympanum on the southeast portal of the Ulm Cathedral, ca. 1360–70.

Hell-mouth from a Baroque mythological play, presented on a pageant cart in a Procession of Gods, held in Dresden, in 1695, with courtiers participating. Sketch for a copper engraving. (Dresden, Kupferstichkabinett.)

their age and sex and station—the pope as much as the aged beggar, the respectable townswoman as much as the wanton minstrel. The Spanish "Danza de muerte," the French "Dance macabre," the English, Slav, and German fifteenth-century dances of Death with their conscience-stirring didacticism found effective expression in sculpture and painting. But, strangely enough, they had little impact on the theater. (Hugo von Hofmannsthal took up this theme in his lyrical drama *Der Tor und der Tod*—"Death and the Fool.")

While the earlier religious plays were written, arranged, and organized exclusively by regular and secular clergy, later Latin-school teachers in their turn undertook such productions and directed their pupils in Easter, Pentecost, or Christmas plays. The transition period produced manuscripts in touchingly faulty Latin, which still tried to survive as an erudite vestige, side by side with vernacular passages. From the fourteenth century on, finally, the wandering scholars took a hand in the religious play—and who should have grudged them an occasional insertion of a plea in their own cause? In the Innsbruck Easter play, the apostle John, while giving Peter precedence in entering the sepulcher, recites a sort of epilogue, in which the quintessence of the play's theme is linked with a request to the spectators to think of the "poor scholars" and show their gratitude to them by treating them to a good meal:

Ouch hatte ich mich vorgessen: dy armen schuler haben nicht czu essen! wer yn gebit ire braten, den wil got hute und ummirmehr beraten, wer yn gebit ire vladen, den wil got in daz hymmelriche laden.	Besides, I had forgotten: the poor scholars have nothing to eat! If you give them some roast meat, God will shield you and counsel you always; If you give them some bread, God will take you to Heaven.

The prospect of gaining a place in heaven, thanks to a piece of roast meat and a loaf of bread, must have made the public feel it was worth giving the priests and scholars a meal.

Well into the fifteenth century, the roles of women, even that in Mary's lament at the cross, were played by clerics or scholars. In the Middle Ages, as in antiquity, in the ancient Near East, and in the Far Eastern theater, the audience saw no incongruity in the male actor's impersonation of the female character. It would seem that even in nunneries clerics took the female roles. In the Prague Easter play produced at the nuns' convent of St. George, only the singer (the *cantrix*) is specified as a female participant; she represents the choir of the apostles.

Peter and John are described as "duo presbyteri." It is not clear from the text whether the parts of the three Marys were taken by nuns. The abbess had the privilege of kissing the prayer book at the beginning and at the end of the *Te Deum*.

A surviving carving from Gandersheim, the convent of the dramatist Hrotsvitha, may perhaps best be interpreted in terms of the Prague Easter play. It represents an Annunciation. Mary is depicted as a canoness of Hrotsvitha's time, in the choir of the convent church of Gandersheim. The exquisite little carving dates from the second half of the tenth century. The question is whether or not it is based on a dramatic representation. If it is, it anticipates far later developments. It might also help to illuminate the "theatrical twilight" surrounding the inventive and prolific writer Hrotsvitha, whose Latin dramas, written in the manner of Terence, are alternatively thought highly significant or totally insignificant for the history of the theater. It may well be that the Gandersheim ivory means no more than that the artist intended to pay special tribute to his patronesses by showing Mary in the robes of a venerable canoness.

However uniform the mainstream of the medieval theater appears in an overall view as regards its roots, in its aspirations, its representational possibilities and, above all, in its origins in the Christian faith, it split up into multiple currents in the delta of its subsequent development. It became increasingly more lifelike, thanks to the use not only of different vernacular languages, but also of different costumes and stage properties. In the *Noli-me-tangere* scene, Christ is a gardener with a large hat and a spade, so as to make it quite plain to the spectators why Mary Magdalene could not recognize the resurrected Lord "in specie hortulani." Moreover, Jesus addresses her with harsh, critical words:

Ist daz guter frawen recht,	Is it right for decent women
daz sy umlauffen alz dy knecht	to wander about light-heartedly
so fro yn desem Garten?	in this garden like servants?
wez hastu hy czu warten?	Who are you waiting for?

Mary Magdalene has every reason for her astonished question: "What are you shouting at me for?" She informs the gruff gardener that she is looking for "the holy man" and asks whether he can tell her something about him. Later, in the Innsbruck Easter play (and in the much cruder one from Erlau which is textually often similar), the recognition culminates in the old Latin *planctus*, "Dolor crescit." Mary Magdalene's monologue takes up the time the actor who plays Christ needs for changing his costume.

For the journey to Emmaus, Christ is equipped with a felt cap, a pilgrim's satchel, and a staff. The play, in fact, shows him as the same *Peregrinus* who appears as early as the twelfth century in the stained-glass windows of Chartres, in the English St. Albans Psalter, and in a bas-relief from the Spanish monastery at Silos. The same motif is embroidered with many details in panel paintings.

The mildly farcical aspect that had made its first appearance in the "Currebant duo simul" of the "race to the sepulcher" is developed into a hearty parody of old men, in which Peter is addicted to the bottle and fortifies himself with a good swig from it before approaching the miracle of the Resurrection. Even earlier, in the tenth century, the minstrels had made good-natured fun of the figure of the old man with the white beard, who had so many understandable, all too human personal characteristics, yet was indeed the legendary rock upon which "I will build my church." They saddled him with the role of cook for the meals of the blessed, argued to and fro whether and to what extent this was compatible with his office as the doorkeeper of heaven, and led the way to that warm-hearted and humoristic treatment of the saints which was later reflected in such manifold forms both in the theater and in the visual arts.

The minstrels have their say, and the mime, too, when the *Mercator* and ointment vendor are required to be bald. The *mimus calvus* of antiquity had bluffed his way into religious drama, and had brought in his wake all his kin—the mummers, jugglers, and fools. A fresco of the Danish church of Fyn shows a fool with his cap of bells heading the procession in which Christ bears the cross. In the frescoes in the Church of St. George at Staro Nagoričino, Yugoslavia, mimes and minstrels perform a blasphemously boisterous dance at the foot of the crucifix. Two of them wear a garment with the characteristic long, wide sleeves reaching down below the hands which play such a large part in the gesture language of many civilizations—underscoring parody as well as the expression of grief. For better or for worse, they had long been a symbol of the actor's estate in China, the ancient East and Byzantium.

For all its heterogeneity, the medieval theater public must have had reactions of such uniformity as was hardly ever to recur in the Western world. In France, Spain, Italy, and in the German-speaking lands, in the Scandinavian and Slav countries alike, the organizers of plays met with a response which, if it did not encourage their efforts, at least did not discourage them either.

The organizational aspects of the medieval theater developed in step with its theological and didactic superstructure. Though the clergy lost its hold on the increasingly secular plays, the flagellants and the religious guilds were drawn to them.

In Italy, beginning with 1261, a splendidly staged, typically Italian form of the religious play, the *sacra rappresentazione,* was produced by the Confraternità dei Battuti at Treviso and, in Rome, by the Confraternità del Gonfalone, which was founded in 1264. Local and national saints were pressed into the service of theatrical religious propaganda. The actors' fraternities, as the initiators of the dialogue plays called *laudes dramaticae,* proudly bore the designation *ioculatores Domini* ("the Lord's minstrels") on their coat of arms.

In the realm of the French language, the religious plays were the responsibility of the *confréries* (Passion fraternities), specially founded for this purpose. Such fraternities existed in Limoges (the place where the earliest Easter celebrations were held), at Rouen, Nantes, Amiens, Arras, Angers, Bourges, Valenciennes and, of course, in Paris. The Paris Confrérie de la Passion was famous by 1400, and in 1402 outdid all similar European acting companies: it was given an absolute monopoly for Paris, which it kept until well into the sixteenth century. The clergy no longer merely initiated and produced the plays, but participated in them, wrote the script, or, in some special cases, financed them.

The store of stage properties and costumes, for two hundred years carefully guarded by churches and monasteries from one play season to the next, now passed into the ownership of the burghers and craftsmen. For, from the moment the guilds and corporations took over the financing of the plays, they also claimed the right to make their own arrangements, to spend the money as they saw fit, and to choose the cast. The development of liturgical celebration into theatrical play, which the church had initiated and fostered, now merged with that of the civilization of the rising European townsfolk who, in the succeeding centuries, would determine the course of history, and so also the complexion of the Western theater.

Dissociation from the Church: The Legend Plays

The texts of the Gospels indeed had provided an important source material for the religious plays, but not the only one. The "bursting-in of the world" manifested itself not merely in a more realistic style of representation, but in costuming and the rise of farcical and grotesque elements within the church play. It also showed itself in topical references and criticism of contemporary affairs, which became an element in Europe's theater in the twelfth century.

The Crusades were the era's chief preoccupation. The idea of Jerusalem and the current notions about the millennium, which greatly influenced church politics, also inspired one of the most magnificent twelfth-century plays extant, the Tegernsee "Antichrist." Its author is unknown, though it is presumed that he may have been a member of the Bavarian monastery of Tegernsee, which adhered to the emperor's party. At that time, this picturesquely situated Benedictine abbey was experiencing a period of great cultural flowering. The reputation of its scribes and miniature painters was matched by the political influence of its abbots. The "Antichrist" of 1160 proclaimed their allegiance to the emperor.

According to available sources, the *Ludus de Antichristo* was performed by clerics. Its text is written in Latin and, notwithstanding its obviously current political concerns, fully preserves the oratorical character of the play within the church.

The literary model for the Tegernsee *Ludus* is the *Libellus de Antichristo,* written in the tenth century by the Lotharingian abbot Adso of Toul, which in turn rests on an early Christian notion that, shortly before Christ's Second Coming, a false Messiah sent by Satan would appear and rally all the powers of evil in the world for battle against the Christian church; but in the end, he would be overcome by the true Messiah.

In the text of the Tegernsee play, the scenes portraying the events immediately concerned with the Antichrist are preceded by scenes dealing with the decline of the Roman empire and the triumph of the German emperor. The Rex Teutonicus subjugates all the kings of the West. The rulers of Greece and France and, in the end, Rex Babiloniae, the prince of the heathens, are routed in battle. Then the German emperor deposits his imperial insignia before the altar in the Temple of

Antichrist, seducing the Three Kings with gifts. Miniature from the Hortus deliciarium *of Herrad of Landsberg, 12th century.*

Jerusalem. Crown and scepter give way to a higher power. The play reflects the apogee of the spirit of the Crusades at the time of Barbarossa. It has been suggested that it was written in connection with the Diet of Mainz in 1184, when Barbarossa declined to occupy the throne, saying that it belonged to Christ alone.

This would invalidate the dating to around 1160. On the other hand, Gerhoh of Reichersberg clearly refers to the Tegernsee *Ludus de Antichristo* in 1162.

The highly patriotic, topical first part of the play is followed by the Antichrist play itself. As soon as the German emperor lays down his crown and scepter, the false Messiah appears. Supported by Hypocrisy and Heresy, he seizes power, partly through terror and partly through gifts. "Rex Teutonicus" resists, but even he is finally convinced by faked miraculous healings. Synagoga, too, submits to Antichrist.

But when Antichrist is bold enough, at the height of his power, to proclaim "pax et securitas," God annihilates him with a crash of thunder. Ecclesia regains the honors due to her. At the head of all the participants, who included even the Prophets, she enters the wide-open doors of the church to the sound of bells and the common singing of the *Te Deum.*

No stage plan of the Tegernsee "Antichrist" is extant, but the play was presumably performed on the half-oval, open space to the west of the abbey, toward the lake. Its apex—where the altar of the play stood, flanked by Ecclesia and Synagoga—was the church portal, a logical arrangement that corresponds to the religious content of the play. If, then, the north side was occupied by the *loca* of the Western kings and the south side by the platform of the King of Babylon, the whole center was left free as a neutral playing space to be used and interpreted as required. It could be the Mediterranean Sea, which had to be crossed on the journey to the Holy Land, or it could be a battlefield upon which the adversaries crossed swords. The portrayal of battles was a popular ingredient of medieval plays, which the Tegernsee actors certainly could not have neglected.

A performance of the "Antichrist" play in German by students of the Delphische Institut at Mainz in 1954, in front of the northern side portal of Eichstätt Cathedral, demonstrated the play's timeless dramatic and artistic force. Low, unadorned wooden platforms were used as "loca" for the separate performers. The only stage decoration was a wooden altar with the cross. The actors were identified by costumes, beards, crown, and sword. All the rest was left to the text and the actors' art of projection. At the end of the play, when Ecclesia makes her exit, disappearing into the cathedral at the head of the cast, the public remained standing motionless for several minutes.

The themes of the Tegernsee "Antichrist" were taken up by successors, from the battle scenes in the Prophet play "in media Riga" (1204), which so frightened the heathens assembled for conversion that they ran away, to the Swiss Shrovetide play *Entkrist* (1445). Whole passages of dialogue were taken over into the Benediktbeuren Christmas play—one more proof of the esteem in which even immediate posterity held the literary value of the *Ludus de Antichristo* and its stage effectiveness. At the time of the Reformation, the figure of the Antichrist still supplied Protestants with a useful image in their struggle against the papacy. The fiery Lutheran and anti-Rome polemicist Naogeorgus, otherwise Thomas Kirchmayer of Straubing, declared in his drama *Pammachius* (1538) that Antichrist was none other than the pope. Naogeorgus dedicated his play to Archbishop Cranmer of Cambridge. There it was performed in 1545 by students at Christ's College—giving much offense to Bishop Gardiner, Chancellor of the University, and leading to a correspondence that has come down to us.

The public of the thirteenth and fourteenth centuries was, for the time being, more ready to be impressed by the crossing of swords than by subtleties of argument. The religious wars at home were, by good fortune, still far in the future. The more the fencing skill of secular heroes constituted the climax of the performance—as, for instance, in 1208 and 1224 at the "Ludus cum gigantibus" in Padua—the more the effect of the tournament scene overshadowed the play's religious content. Motifs from cultic sword dances, peasant customs, and the legends of chivalry intermingled. In the Magdeburg Pentecost play of *Rolandsreiten,* or in the *Round Table* of 1235, the pagan tradition is more strongly evident than the Christian gloss. But the knights and minstrels had an important function in the outdoor play of the thirteenth century: they brought color into the fable and into the performance. They gave the language their imprint and were seen—or saw themselves—in the mirror of glorification as well as in the mirror of parody. The *Carmina burana,* written down at Benediktbeuren around 1230, is one of the best-known testimonies to unadulterated medieval sensual pleasure. Some of its wandering scholars' songs owe as much to the poetic art of Ovid and Catullus as to these poets' enjoyment of love and wine. The political and religious poems display the sort of ironical attitude toward authority that no doubt was expressed even in the Middle Ages, and more frequently and strongly than is commonly assumed. The rhythmic and theatrical elements in some of its Latin songs inspired Carl Orff's choral works *Carmina burana* (1937) and *Catulli Carmina* (1943).

Jean Bodel, a Crusader, town official at Arras, member of the *Confrérie des jongleurs,* and author of a St. Nicholas play (around 1200), gives a vivid and colorful picture of the knights, citizens, and peasants of his time. An older contemporary of Bodel's, the English wandering scholar Hilarius who had come to France in 1125, also had devoted a miracle play to St. Nicholas. Jean Bodel's *Jeu de Saint Nicolas* is built around the saint's pious deeds. He helps a pagan king to recover his treasures and thereby saves a Christian's life. But for Jean Bodel the legend is merely the framework on which to hang the gay pennants of his genre scenes—the battle of the Crusaders against the heathen in the Near East, "la vie joyeuse" in tavern and brothel, with lines that give a first foretaste of French argot.

The legend, parable, and miracle plays very early moved out of the interior of the church. They aimed at and achieved effects that needed an uncircumscribed area that would allow the noise of battle and—as with Jean Bodel—loud laughter. When the spectators viewing the Riga Prophet play took flight in terror, the chronicler could excuse that with their "ignorance." But when Frederick the Undaunted, margrave of Thuringia, in 1321 turned his back in distress on a play about the Wise and the Foolish Virgins, performed in Eisenadi, the entire Christian teaching of redemption was shaken.

Banquet of Archbishop Balduin of Trier. Miniature, Rhineland, 14th century.

"What is the Christian faith if the sinner is not to receive mercy upon the intercession of the Virgin and the Saints?" Thus the margrave exclaimed in consternation and went away. He left behind him bewildered courtiers, a stunned audience, and a no less stunned band of secondary-school boys, not to speak of their teacher, who had done his best with his play to draw due attention to an Indulgence scheduled by the church. The margrave's sudden revulsion demonstrates how deep an impression the medieval theater could make with its themes and representation, even though their artistic level may not have been above that of earnest amateur theatricals. Legend has it that after the shock of the merciless parable, Margrave Frederick suffered a stroke and died two years later. The parable of the Wise and the Foolish Virgins—depicted by the artists of early medieval manuscripts, the *Codex Rossanensis*, the Vienna *Genesis*, and on the church portals of Strasbourg, Magdeburg, Trier, and Nuremberg—elicited an entirely new and striking impression in the theater.

Not only the great mystery and Last Judgment plays, but all the legend and miracle plays throughout the Western world drew heavily upon the contrast between damnation and redemption. Worldliness, ambition, pride, and mundane pursuits are confronted with eternal damnation, but also with the redemption that awaits the repenting sinner. But the devil, the tempter who is the most frequent personification of evil in the medieval theater, must be cheated in the end.

Thus Theophilus, who sells himself to the devil for the sake of worldly honors, obtains divine grace through Mary's intercession. *Le Miracle de Théophile,* written by the Parisian *trouvère* Rutebeuf, anticipates, in the garb of Christian legend, the quintessence of Goethe's *Faust*: "Eternal Womanhead leads us on high."

Spiel von Frau Jutten ends with the same solution of forgiveness. This play, written around 1480 by the priest Dietrich Schernberg of Mühlhausen, in Thuringia, is based on the legend of "Pope Joan," a woman who is supposed to have acceded to the papal throne in 855 as John VIII. Disguised in man's clothing, she goes to study with the great scholars in Paris, together with her lover Clericus. Later, in the midst of a papal procession, Death steps up to her and strikes her. Soon thereafter, she gives birth to a child and is exposed—no longer Pope John, but "Pope Joan"—as Frau Jutta now, in shame and dishonor. She dies and the devils take her soul to hell. Frau Jutta prays to St. Nicholas for his intercession, and God dispatches St. Michael to fetch the repentant sinner to heaven. The scene of devils, saints, and archangels symbolically enacting the Christian doctrine of redemption is made vivid by the rich imagery of the language.

In these last two plays, we find the first beginnings of dramatic

The wise and the foolish virgins. Wall painting in the choir of the castle chapel, Hocheppan, South Tirol, 12th century.

Scene from the legend of Theophilus, the medieval Faust who makes a pact with the devil. Miniature from the Liber matutinalis *of Conrad von Scheyern, early 13th century. (Munich, Staatsbibliothek.)*

Peregrinus *scene: Christ with pilgrim's satchel and apostles on the road to Emmaus. Miniature from the English St. Albans Psalter, 12th century. (Hildesheim, Germany.)*

character and action. Both the characters of Theophilus and Frau Jutta have a chance of free, individual decision—and both do not repent until they are faced with eternal damnation. Thus they provide the theater with a splendid opportunity of deploying the effective apparatus of hell and devils, not to speak of winged angelic messengers, God the Father in His glory, white-bearded saints, and the poor soul in a state of utter despondency.

The first play within a play occurs in the Dutch miracle play *Marieken von Nieumeghen,* written between 1485 and 1510 by an anonymous author. The heroine, who is as beautiful as she is fond of the pleasures of life, sells herself to the devil for seven years. The performance of a religious play—performed on a separate stage that is set on a wagon—causes her to repent. She begs the pope for forgiveness of her sins and—a medieval parallel to antiquity's feminine mime Pelagia—ends her life in a Maastricht nunnery.

Stations, Processions, and Stage Wagons

No doubt, the Dutch *Marieken von Nieumeghen,* like so many plays of this period, was performed on an open space in the town; but the device of the play within the play presupposes another, typically medieval form of staging, namely, the wagon stage or stage cart, customary in processions in Spain, Italy, England, Germany, the Tirol, and the Netherlands.

The origins of the wagon stage go back to 1264, when Pope Urban IV instituted the feast of Corpus Christi, which was subsequently celebrated with solemn processions throughout Western Europe. The play often had developed out of the theatrical procession. Along with its roots in religious ceremonial occasion, the play had secular roots in the tournaments and in the street pageants that were arranged in honor of the sovereign and were the precursors of the great allegorical *trionfi* of the Renaissance.

The development of the processional and the wagon stage was quite independent of dramatic literature. Its mobile nature offered two alternatives. Either the spectators moved from one acting locale to the next and thus saw the sequence of scenes by changing their own position, or else the scenes themselves, their sets in readiness on the wagon, were moved through the streets and went into action at predetermined stations.

In Spain the ceremonial Corpus Christi procession developed into the *auto sacramental* and the *fiesta del Corpus,* the Feast of Corpus Christi, both occasions for the display of religious fervor. It is revealing of the full violence of the religious struggle, first against the infiltration of Islam and later against the Reformation, that the *auto sacramental* eventually found its counterpart in the *auto-da-fé,* the spectacle of the execution of heretics under the Inquisition.

The scenes were presented on the so-called *roca,* which was carried along in the procession from station to station. In the cathedral archives of Seville the *roca* is described as a platform that was carried by twelve men and on which the scenery was arranged as a *tableau.* When the procession reached the appropriate place, the *tableau* came to life in a theatrical performance. On both sides of the Pyrenees, as the decorations became more elaborate and the cast larger, the little stage for the procession play was constructed on a wagon or cart. The idea of the Spanish cart stage survives to this day in the general expression *fiesta de los carros.*

Originally, the "performances" were associated strictly with the occasion of the Corpus Christi celebration, with the mere recital of fairly short texts relating to the mystery of the Sacrament; but soon, this movable playing platform was used in many countries and in the celebration of other festivities as well. The Dominican monks of Milan, in 1336, adapted the wagon-stage procession for a play about the Magi. The City of Florence, in 1439 and 1454, used in festivities honoring John the Baptist twenty-two settings that were taken through the town

Great procession at Strasbourg (earliest pictorial representation of the Cathedral). Woodcut from Geschichte Peter Hagenbachs, *by Conradus Pfettisheim, Strasbourg, 1477.*

on movable scaffolds (*edifizi*)—a foretaste of the sumptuous pageants that were to take place under the Medici princes.

As records testify, in the Netherlands, especially in Flanders, the religious *Wagenspel* was performed in 1450 and 1483. The *Gesellen von de Spele,* craftsmen's acting associations, in Brussels and Bruges counseled their audiences from the platforms of their movable miniature stages to heed their conscience and examine their way of life. In the little town of Nymwegen their "well-meant epigram" found its way into the heart of the play's Marieken and made her repent. On Corpus Christi day, a stage cart rolled into the market square, and a trial was performed, in which the Virgin Mary interceded for sinful mankind and wrestled from the devil the poor souls that had fallen into his power. The play within the play in *Marieken von Nieumeghen* ends with the pious wish, "May it lead you to Heaven."

The dominating feature of all these plays was that of being part of a pageant procession—whether, as in Innsbruck in 1391, they were devoted to the Prophets; or, as in Bolzano and Freiburg im Breisgau, to the Passion; or whether, as at Künzelsau (1479), they ranged from the Creation to the Last Judgment. They made their impression on the public, even as they rolled by as mere dumb shows. Dürer's description of the great procession he witnessed at Antwerp on August 19, 1520—"when the whole city was assembled, all crafts and all trades, each in his best clothes according to his estate"—leaves open the question whether "wagon" and "play" were simply taken along or were the scene of dramatic representations. Dürer reports in the diary of his journey to the Netherlands:

> Twenty persons carried the Virgin Mary with Our Lord Jesus, in the most sumptuous finery in honor of God. And in this procession there were many pleasurable things done and most splendidly arranged. For there were many wagons, plays in ships, and other bulwarks. Among them was the host of the Prophets in their proper order, and after that the New Testament, such as the angels' salutation, the Three Kings riding on big camels and other strange, miraculous animals, most prettily decked out, and how Our Lady flees into Egypt, very devout, and many other things here omitted for lack of space. At the end came a large dragon; he was led by St. Margaret and her maids on a leash, that was particularly pretty. She was followed by St. George with his knights, a very handsome cuirassier. And in all this crowd there also rode boys and girls, dressed most prettily and splendidly, according to various local customs, to take the place of many saints. This procession from beginning to end, before it was past our house, took more than two hours. . . .

Marieken von Nieumeghen. *From an edition of woodcuts, ca. 1518.*

Wheel of Fortune, and reception of the archbishops by Emperor Charles V in Brussels, 1515.

In England there emerged a specific style of the processional and wagon stage. The Corpus Christi celebrations, which developed from 1311 on with increasingly lavish scenery, found a formal counterpart in the stations of the mystery cycles. While multiple settings became usual elsewhere, on the open-space stage in German lands and on the platform stage in France, English producers worked within the narrow setting of the wagon stage—which, however, was not as narrow as has hitherto been assumed. Unlike the characters of the later theater, those of the pageant theater were not "imprisoned in their drawing room," as Wickham points out, but their stage was the world.

The term pageant, usually associated with the English wagon stage, originally meant the places arranged throughout the town for festivals or festival plays. The occasion could just as well be a worldly event as a church feast. John Lydgate's allegory that welcomed young Henry VI to London was performed in six separate pageants, at key points of the city. This took place in 1432, and was an early example of the Renaissance *trionfi.*

The first pageant awaited the young ruler at the south bank gate of London Bridge. There he was told in well-chosen words what the city expected of its new king and "Cristis champioun." Subsequent pageants reminded him of the loyalty appropriate to his high office. In the tower of the drawbridge, richly hung with silk, velvet, and cloth of gold, the allegorical figures of Fortune, Nature, and Grace represented the attributes of which a glorious king had need. Seven attendant maidens personified the gifts of the Holy Ghost and seven others the worldly gifts that were to be his. At Cornhill the procession was met by Dame Sapience, attended by Aristotle, Euclid, and Boethius. At the sixth and last of the pageant stages, on the Conduit in Cornhill, Clemency summoned David and Solomon as witnesses to the proper use of authority:

> Honour off kyngys, in every mannys siht,
> Of comyn custum lovith equyte and riht.

The whole thing was more a cleverly devised panegyric than a theatrical show, and it was as such indeed that Lydgate had planned it; but it does demonstrate how variously the procession principle was applied from the outset. It offered scope for worldly and religious purposes alike. The external setting of the station play could be filled just as well by allegories of homage as by an *auto sacramental.* It could serve the glorification of the Virgin Mary or of the Egyptian god Osiris. Beyond all its dependence on time, the theater is timeless, and shows itself so not least by the consistency with which it preserves its basic models across millennia and different latitudes.

The Passion Play with Open-Space Multiple Settings

With the ascendancy of the vernacular, even the Easter play broke its close link with the liturgy. The solemnity of timeless events gave way to the multiplicity of the present, and current language, costumes, and gestures splashed their colors on the biblical story.

When the church opened its doors and let the play escape into the busy bustle of the town, this meant more than mere spatial enlargement. The rising citizenry seized with dedicated enthusiasm upon the play, that new form of self-expression, pleasing in the sight of God and growing ever more exuberant. Patricians, burghers, and craftsmen took the liberty of presenting the truths of the faith in the garb fitting their own view of life. The proud citizens of Limburg, who had a luscious blonde symbolizing Luxuria painted on the wall of the nave in their cathedral, in one of their outdoor plays turned Mary Magdalene into a beautiful courtesan. She was allowed to lead the gayest of worldly lives, to sing a profane song clearly inspired by courtly poems, sit down to a game of chess with Jesse, and to play the lute. After that, the selfsame Mary Magdalene sang one of the most moving of the Easter sequences, the *Victimae paschali*. Contrasts did not clash, but heightened each other. Sophisticated forms of expression could be followed by the coarsest rudeness, passages of poetic tenderness by whole cannonades of obscenities. Farmhands, servants, devils, and underdevils outdid each other in inventing a wealth of invectives and blasphemous words.

"This goes to show," the Dominican Franz von Retz of Vienna wrote reprovingly around 1400 in his *Lectura super Salve Regina*, "that these theatrical shows about Pusterbalk and his unruly neighbors, which are performed by certain clerics at Easter, are godless and should be banned from sacred places. Such shows gave offense even in the old days in the theaters and public spectacles of the pagans."

But behind the severe stricture we perceive the admission that even under the wings of the clergy all sorts of impious goings-on had long since crept into the religious plays.

The Passion plays of Frankfurt am Main, in the wine market of Lucerne, in late medieval Vienna, in the marketplace of Antwerp or at Valenciennes—all of which stretched over several days—are examples of a colorful, inventive, unbridled, and unrestrainedly exuberant development.

The prosperous free city and emporium Frankfurt am Main was able to afford a two-day Passion play as early as 1350. Its content ranged from Christ's baptism in the river Jordan to His ascension. The didactic framework was provided by disputations between Ecclesia and Synagoga

Passion play, presented in the marketplace of Antwerp: ecce homo *scene Painting by Gillis Mostaert, ca. 1550. (Antwerp, Koninklijk Museum voor schone Kunsten.)*

The great ecce homo. *Copper engraving by Lucas van Leyden, 1510.*

Ecce homo *scene. Central panel of an altar in Brunswick Cathedral, Lower Saxon master, 1506. (Brunswick, Herzog-Anton-Ulrich Museum.)*

and between prophets and Jews. There were also topical allusions, e.g., to the plague that had afflicted the city in 1349 and to the fanaticism of the flagellant movement. The spokesman of the true faith was St. Augustine from whom, in an impressive final lesson, ten Jews received baptism.

The Frankfurt document relating to this play is a characteristic example of medieval stage directions. It is known as the Frankfurt *Dirigierrolle* (Director's Scroll). It is a scroll more than 14½ feet long, bearing script in the place of the music usually written down on the scrolls ("rotuli") and used by singers and minstrels. Dialogues are recorded only by key words, with clear indications of the actors' cues. All the more explicit, however, are the stage directions. They were specially entered in red ink by the scribe of the Frankfurt *Dirigierrolle,* Baldemar von Peterweil, canon at Frankfurt's Abbey of St. Bartholomew. From this scroll Julius Petersen, in a painstaking study, has reconstructed the scene and sequence of the performance.

As can be gathered from a contemporary description of the town written by Baldemar himself, the play was performed on the Samydagisberg Sancti Nicolai, today called the Römerberg. The sloping square is closed off at the southern end by a church, the Nikolaikirche, which was subject to the cathedral chapter and hence also to the attached Abbey of St. Bartholomew. Thus Baldemar was on "home ground" with his staging and the construction of the individual settings. It was here that a year earlier the citizens had rendered homage to Emperor Charles IV.

Optically, there was an advantage in the slope of the square where the Passion was to be reenacted, for the three crosses could be set up at the highest part and thus made visible afar. To the east of them the throne of heaven was raised, leaning securely against the fine old patrician houses that have survived into the twentieth century, and at its foot lay the Garden of Gethsemane. The angel with the cup of bitterness thus had to take only one step forward to appear above the kneeling impersonator of Christ. Medieval directors indeed were skilled in the tricks of their trade.

In an oval space about 120 feet long, the *loca* of the different players and scenes followed each other: the house of Mary, Martha, and Lazarus, the house of Symonis, Herod's *Carcer* and *Castrum,* Pilate's *Palatium* and *Pretorium;* at the lower, western end of the square was the gate of hell (making it possible for Satan to enter by rising from the Wassergraben, the old moat); here also stood the half-covered fountain used for the baptismal scenes. The table used for the Last Supper (*mensa*), the Temple, and the column with the cock whose crowing proclaimed Peter's betrayal—all these were placed in the middle of the open space. The public watched either from street level or from the windows of adjacent houses. As in all open-space multiple settings, therefore, the individual *loca* could be nothing but low platforms, if necessary roofed over by a light baldachin resting on wooden posts and leaving the view open on all sides.

Petersen assumes that the actors made their entrances from the Nikolai Church, where they could also change their costumes. The play's ties with the church were by no means disrupted by moving it outside the actual walls. Often the performance of a Passion play opened or closed with divine service. To be sure, the Latin chants, the music and choral passages soon gave way to an unbridled delight in language and acting, unconstrained by pious awe. The crude realism seen in late medieval panel paintings gained ground in the plays as well. The executioners who nailed Christ to the cross had by their very appearance to be ugly, brutal fellows, fiends with vile, distorted faces.

In the Passion play from Alsfeld, with its 8095 lines the longest from the Frankish-Hessian region, the Crucifixion is shown as a horrible torture scene. The executioners call to each other: "An hende und an fusz byndet em strenge und recket en nach des cruezes lenge" (Tie him up tight by hands and feet, and stretch him out to the length of the cross). And they demonstrate the effort they have to make to stretch Christ's body to fit the length of the cross so that they can hammer in the nails at the holes previously drilled into the beams of the cross.

Tremendous physical exertions were demanded of the actor playing Christ. He had to allow himself to be pulled and pushed, dragged along and beaten, and to suffer violence that did not fall short of what was common at an execution in his own fourteenth or fifteenth century. The little stoop of wood he was given on the cross itself to support his feet (*suppedaneum*) was scant compensation for the earlier mishandling, and just about made sure that the actor's role did not kill him. (The footrest on the cross often found in Crucifixions of the visual arts derives not from the Passion play, but from iconographic principles. It is a last reminder of the fact that early Christian art tried to preserve the image of the king enthroned even in the figure of the suffering Son of God. *Terra,* the earth, or Adam, kneels and holds up the crucified Christ raised on a footstool.)

"Robust, sensual pleasure, combined with sturdy piety"—these were the characteristics of the great civic Passion plays in German lands. Apart from the places in the Rhine-Hesse region, where such plays were presented very early, they were common especially around Vienna, in South Tirol (Bozen) in the Alemannic areas, St. Gall and Lucerne.

The Vienna Easter play "von der besuchunge des grabis und von dir ofirstendunge gotis" (of the Visit to the Grave and the Resurrection of God), which can be dated to 1472 and originated in the monastery of

The Lucerne wine market, view to the west, on the first day of the 1583 Easter play. The row of houses on the left is shown only in ground plan with indications of their owners' names at the time. In the background, to the right, the hell-mouth. Reconstruction and sketch by A. am Rhyn. (From Oskar Eberle, Theatergeschichte der innern Schweiz, *Königsberg, 1929.)*

the Augustinian Hermits, begins only after the Crucifixion. It shows "wy Christ ist erstanden von des todes bandin, und hat dy heiligyn veter irlost von der bittern hellin rost" (how Christ arose from the bonds of death and released the holy fathers from the bitter fires of hell), that is, the Resurrection and the Harrowing of Hell. The personages include Abraham and Isaac, the archangel Gabriel, and Adam and Eve begging to be saved. Language and sentiments are imbued with the heartiness of simple folk, and in the *Mercator* scenes turn to riotous farce closely akin to the Shrovetide plays. In Bohemian lands, the same trends turned the ointment vendor, the *Mastičkar,* into the earthy and grotesque hero of separate little farces.

The development of the Vienna Passion performances culminates in the name of a master famous both as a sculptor and organizer of plays, Wilhelm Rollinger. It was he who, in the period 1486–1495, created the relief panels of the so-called "old choir stalls" in the Cathedral of St. Stephen in Vienna. (They were destroyed in the fire of 1945.) Of a total of forty-six scenes, thirty-eight were concerned with the Easter story, beginning with Palm Sunday and ending with Christ's descent into hell. While not depicting actual scenes as performed in the play, they reflected its spirit. Wilhelm Rollinger was a member of the Vienna Corpus Christi fraternity, which was responsible for the annual Passion and Corpus Christi plays. In 1505 Rollinger supervised the entire production and artistic direction of a performance which, with its cast of more than 200, was the climax and—in the light of the imminent Reformation and Turkish siege—also the swan song of the medieval play tradition of Vienna. By the middle of the fifteenth century, Lucerne, in the region of Alemannic dialects, developed into a center of sumptuous plays. Here, too, the plays were produced by the citizens' religious fraternities. Performances of the Lucerne Passion continued well into the sixteenth century. At a time when the spirit of the Renaissance had long since broken with the old traditions, the citizens of Lucerne still forgathered in their town's wine market to devote two whole days, from dawn to nightfall, to a reenactment of Christ's Passion, with all its antecedents and subsequent acts of redemption. The city clerk Renward Cysat prepared and edited the playbooks, rehearsed the cast, directed the performance, negotiated with the craftsmen entrusted with the construction of the stage scaffolds, and played the part of the Virgin. He also drew up two stage plans in meticulous detail; to these we owe our knowledge of the setting of the great 1583 Lucerne Passion. On the first day the river Jordan, scene of the baptism of Jesus, ran diagonally across the playing area; the "Haus zur Sonne," situated at the upper, narrow end of the square, represented heaven, and before it on the second day the three crosses of Golgotha were erected; the *loca* of

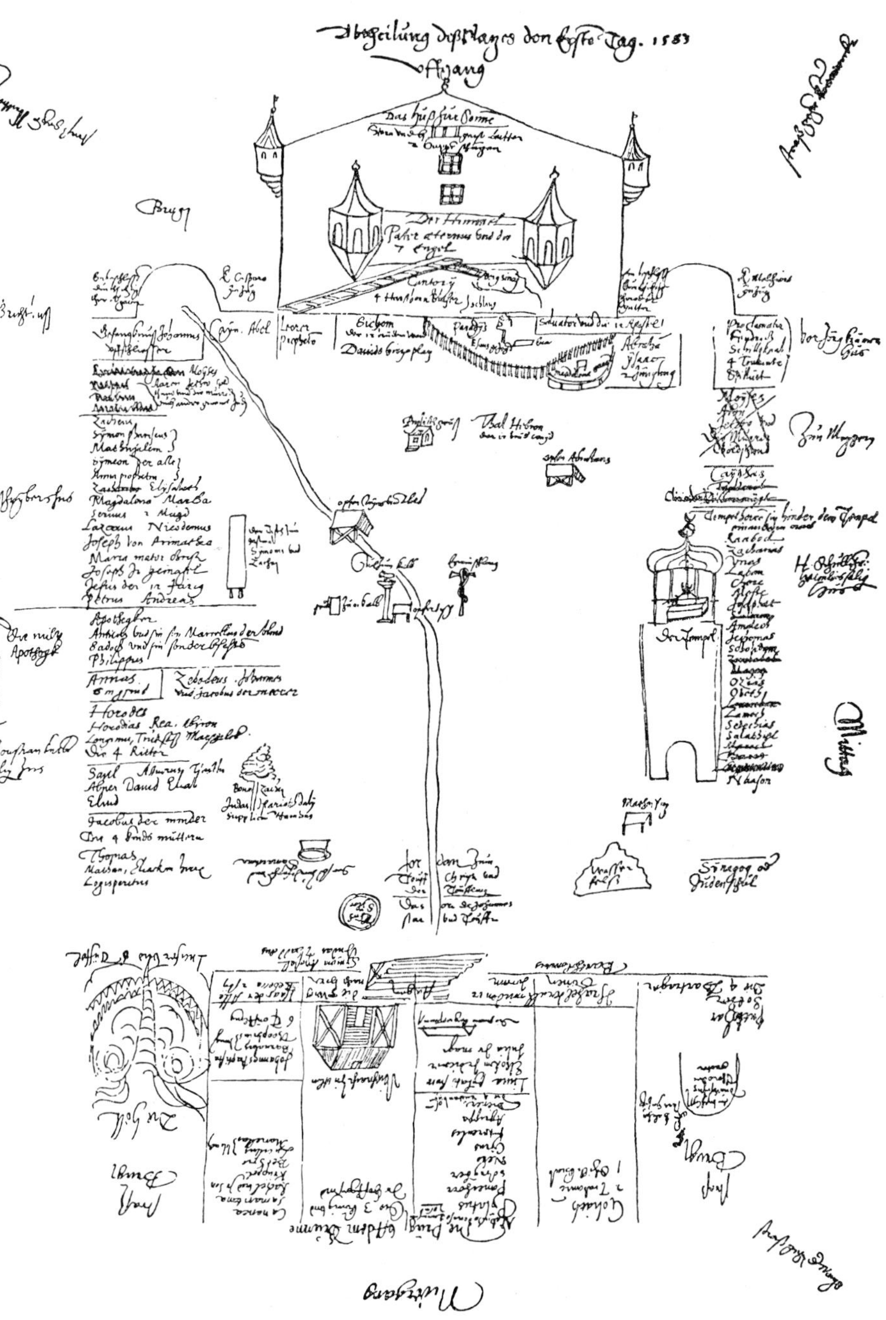

Renward Cysat's stage plan for the Passion play of Lucerne (first day), as performed in 1583.

the disciples, the holy women, Joseph of Arimathea, and Herod were to the north, those of the Temple of Jerusalem and Synagoga to the south. Lucifer and the "eight devils" have their gaping mouth of hell in the west, alongside the Nativity shed on the first day and alongside the column of the scourging on the second.

Similar arrangements are evident in the so-called Donaueschingen stage plan. Heaven, Gethsemane, and Golgotha are at the eastern end of the playing area, while the representatives of evil and darkness are in the west, toward sunset. However, recent research has convincingly proved that contrary to its usual designation, the plan as we know it refers not to the Donaueschingen Passion of 1485 but, as regards both its overall layout and its scenic details, to the second day of the Passion play, which was performed on March 21 and 29, 1646, at Villingen in the Black Forest. This correction, which we owe to A. M. Nagler, does not exclude that an analogous layout was used for the wealth of crudely grotesque scenes of the Donaueschingen play, in which before the scourging the chair is pulled from under Christ and, after his inevitable fall, he is pulled up again by his hair. We can assume that similar stage arrangements existed for the great Easter and Passion plays, lasting several days, at Erlau in Hungary, on the market square of Eger, or in the Hansa town of Lübeck (which most probably was also the scene of the Low German Easter play of Redentin).

A fair amount is known about the Passion-play tradition in South Tirol (now the Italian Province of Bolzano), which was developed by both the region's ambitious peasants and townspeople. The large-scale play cycles, presented by such prosperous trading towns as Bozen (Bolzano) and Brixen (Brescia), and Sterzing, profited by a native bent for play-acting and pride in civic display. More and more scenes were added to the play cycle until, as a climax, in 1514 the Bozen (Bolzano) Passion stretched over no less than seven days. It began with a prologue on Palm Sunday (Christ's entry into Jerusalem), continued on the Thursday be-

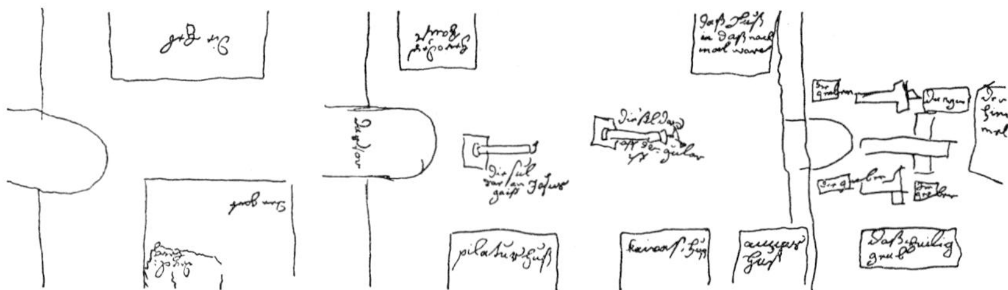

Stage plan of the Donaueschingen Passion play (second day), presumably for the 1646 performance at Villingen.

The 1583 Easter play presented in the wine market of Lucerne. Reconstruction model by Albert Köster, after stage designs by the Lucerne city clerk Renward Cysat. At the upper narrow end, the "Haus zur Sonne," with Heaven between its two bay windows, accessible by a ladder; in front of it, the three crosses of Golgotha. In the center, to the left, the tree from which Judas hangs himself, and to the right of it, the Temple represented by a baldachin supported by four columns. On the raised platform in the foreground, the fountain whose column was used for the scourging. (Munich, Theater Museum.)

fore Easter with the Last Supper and the scenes on the Mount of Olives, and presented the Scourging and the Crucifixion on Good Friday. The Lament of the Marys and a Prophet play were performed on Saturday, the Resurrection on Easter Sunday, and on that Monday the journey to Emmaus. The cycle ended with Christ's glorification on Ascension Day.

The seven-day play was directed by the painter Vigil Raber from Sterzing, who was much in demand throughout the Tirol as a text writer, stage and costume designer, director, and actor. We possess a sketch by Vigil Raber for the prologue of the Bozen Passion. This was performed not on the market square, but in the Gothic setting of the parish church. The players entered in solemn procession through the main portal, the *porta magna.* On the left, distributed through the nave and the transept, were the *loca* of Caiaphas and Annas, and the house of Simon Leprosus; to the right, the Mount of Olives and, toward the choir, the stand of the Synagogue; opposite the Infernum and in the round of the choir, Heaven and the *angeli cum silete.*

It had been a long road across the centuries, from the beginnings of the Passion play to the Bozen Passion. In terms of theater history, the development was as consistent in intellectual as in scenic aspects. The church and the market square were the playing space for the play, the clergy and townsfolk its protagonists. The principle of multiple settings was differentiated in elaborate arrangements, governed by practical

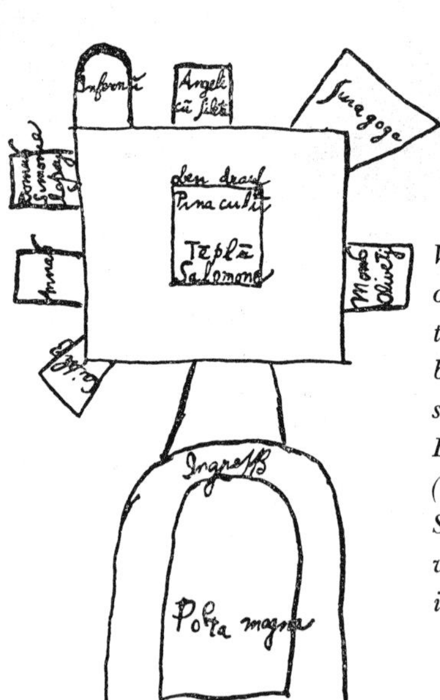

Vigil Raber's stage plan for the Passion play of Bozen (Bolzano), as performed in 1514 in the town's parish church. The players entered by the porta magna, *the main portal. The stands for Caiaphas, Annas, and Simon Leprosus were on the left; Hell, Heaven (*Angeli cum silete*), and the stand of the Synagoga were at the far end; Mount Olivet was on the right, and Solomon's temple was in the center.*

necessities and optical effects. Every participant had his predetermined position, his place, which was variously described as *locus,* mansion, *sedes,* house, or *stellinge.* He stepped down from his platform into the open center of the playing space when his part required it; he received the other players at his own "place" when their part led them to him.

The arrangement of the playing stands might be topographical, as in the wine market at Lucerne; or it might follow the chronological sequence of events, as in the Donaueschingen/Villingen Passion; it might be derived from stylistic considerations, as at Alsfeld, or from local necessities, as in the Bozen church.

The settings were governed by the ineluctable rule of the open-space stage that a free view from all sides must not be impeded by walls. The houses of Pilate, Caiaphas, and Annas, as well as the temple of Jerusalem had to make do with a roof held up by four posts. A modest element of surprise was sometimes introduced by curtains, which the actor, (for example, if portraying Herod on his throne) pulled back when it was his turn to come onstage.

The performance was announced and commented upon by the *praecursor,* who spoke the introductory lines, often gave didactic explanations during the play, and summed up the events. "Hut und tret mir aus dem wege, das ich meyne zache vor lege!"—thus he opens the Vienna Easter play with an appeal to custom and propriety and to a good hearing. He urges silence on the "alden flattertaschin," for "wir wellin haben eyn osterspiel, das ist frolich und kost nicht vil"—let the old chatterboxes keep their silence, for we are about to have a joyful Easter play, which doesn't cost much, though the "joy" is clearly not meant to be of a worldly but of a salutary spiritual kind.

The spectators would stand all around the playing space or sit on folding chairs they had brought along and, if the crowd was not too dense, they would follow the action as it moved from place to place. There was not much chance of doing this, of course, at plays within the church and in the late medieval marketplace settings. But anyone fortunate enough to be the town's guest of honor or to inhabit one of the houses overlooking the market square could get a view of the whole playing space from a window.

Whenever a performance was announced, people from neighboring villages would flock in to join the townsfolk, and traders, minstrels, and wandering scholars would come from afar. The craftsmen bolted their workshops and the gatekeepers barred further entry into the town by closing the heavy gates. All work came to a standstill as soon as the call to order was heard: "Nu swiget alle still!" (Silence, everyone). The Latin formula "Silete, silete, silentium habete" survived as a last vestige well into the vernacular plainness of the late medieval Passion play. The term "silete" came to be used both to separate and connect the individual scenes. It introduced the next phase of the action and hushed the disturbance thereby occasioned among the public, especially insofar as they still moved about with the action. In the case of performances stretching over several days, "silete" marks the place for a possible interruption until the next appointed time. Often, however, each day's performance ended on a deliberately didactic or utilitarian note, as when the faint-hearted and the doubters were urged to be converted from their *compassio* to a new *promissio*; or, on an altogether worldly level, they were asked to reward the "poor scholars" with food and drink for their exertions in the play; or, indeed, the highly satisfactory announcement was made that now it was time to go "for a good beer."

Once the plays had shifted from within the church itself, their direction and organization passed increasingly to the townsfolk. City clerks, Latin teachers, and eventually "free artists" did much to secularize the plays more and more. This development began as soon as the acting parts went to seminarists, Latin students, wandering scholars and, ultimately, to mimes who were offering their services everywhere. The successors of the ancient *joculatores* gladly and expertly took on the parts of devils, of Judas and the executioners—all the representatives of evil who offered much scope for comedy, but with whom a respectable, established burgher would have been loath to identify himself.

It was to the inclusion of the mime that the late medieval Passion plays owed much of their exuberant and down-to-earth approach, as well as a realistic animation of the acting style, which lay circles alone could never have developed.

The Mystery Play with Platform-Stage Multiple Settings

The great Passion mystery of the French dramatist and theologian Arnoul Gréban contains a very significant scene. As a background to the Agony in the Garden, there is a discussion between God the Father and Justitia, in which they argue about the necessity of Christ's suffering. The eschatological idea begins to reach beyond Christ's human life, the premises of the act of Redemption.

It was a natural thing for the French rational mind to take the Gospel story, the here and now of the Passion, as the center of world history, not only in the erudite disputations of theologians, but also on the stage of the religious spectacle. This led increasingly to the inclusion of parts of the Old Testament, the predictions of the Prophets, and eventually of the whole story of the Creation. The Passion as such was displaced by *Le mystère de la Passion*, the mystery of the Passion—a spectacle originating in divine service and at the same time firmly anchored in theological interpretation, with heaven and hell constantly present in every word and image.

This did not mean, however, that the actual location of the plays was tied to the interior of the church. On the contrary, the very oldest of the religious dramas extant in the French language, the *Mystère d'Adam* of the middle of the twelfth century, already took place outside the doors of the cathedral. In three great thematic cycles it treats of sin and the promised redemption of mankind: the Fall, Cain's murder of Abel, and the prophets. The stage directions suggest the use of a wooden scaffold with decorative props, supported by the church facade, rather as in today's performance of *Jedermann* in front of Salzburg Cathedral. The portal was the gate of heaven. To one side of it there was paradise, on a raised platform, and on the other side, situated lower down, the hell-mouth.

The spoken word, solemn chants (with the chorus parts still in Latin), and vivid pantomime in the action (Eve and the serpent) were combined in a theatrical experience that must have made a profound and lasting impression on the spectators. A modern counterpart is the *Misterio de Elche* performed every year on August 15 in Spain, at Elche, the city famous for its date palms. The climax of the play, which is a combination of chorus and pantomime, is the moment when a host of children, costumed as angels with wings—just as they were long ago in the fourteenth century—is lowered from the dome of the Church of Santa Maria into the choir, right into a place radiantly illuminated by thousands of flickering candles. This is the same cumulation of decorative and psychological elements that finds such bewildering expression in the art of Spanish cathedrals.

The French mystery plays, paralleled for a while but never surpassed in theatrical perfection by the English ones, had their greatest flowering in the fifteenth and sixteenth centuries. Arnoul Gréban's *Mystère de la Passion* ran to very nearly 35,000 lines and required four days for its performance. Alternating effectively between serious, and pathetic and coarsely grotesque scenes, it tells the story of Adam, the story of the life of Jesus on earth and of His Passion and Resurrection, and ends with the miracle of Pentecost. Mary's motherly love for her son is confronted with Christ's divine love for mankind. The manuscript includes miniatures that give an impression of the wealth of scenes and characters and their theatrically highly effective arrangement.

A younger contemporary and successor of Gréban, the physician and dramatist Jean Michel, enlarged and altered Gréban's existing text and produced a new version in his hometown of Angers in 1486 under the title *Mistère de la Passion de nostre Saulveur Jhesucrist*.

Relief panels from late Gothic choirstalls (destroyed by fire in 1945) of St. Stephen's Cathedral, Vienna, made by the sculptor and play producer Wilhelm Rollinger, between 1486 and 1495.

Jesus is taken to town as a prisoner.

Jesus is sent by Pilate to Herod.

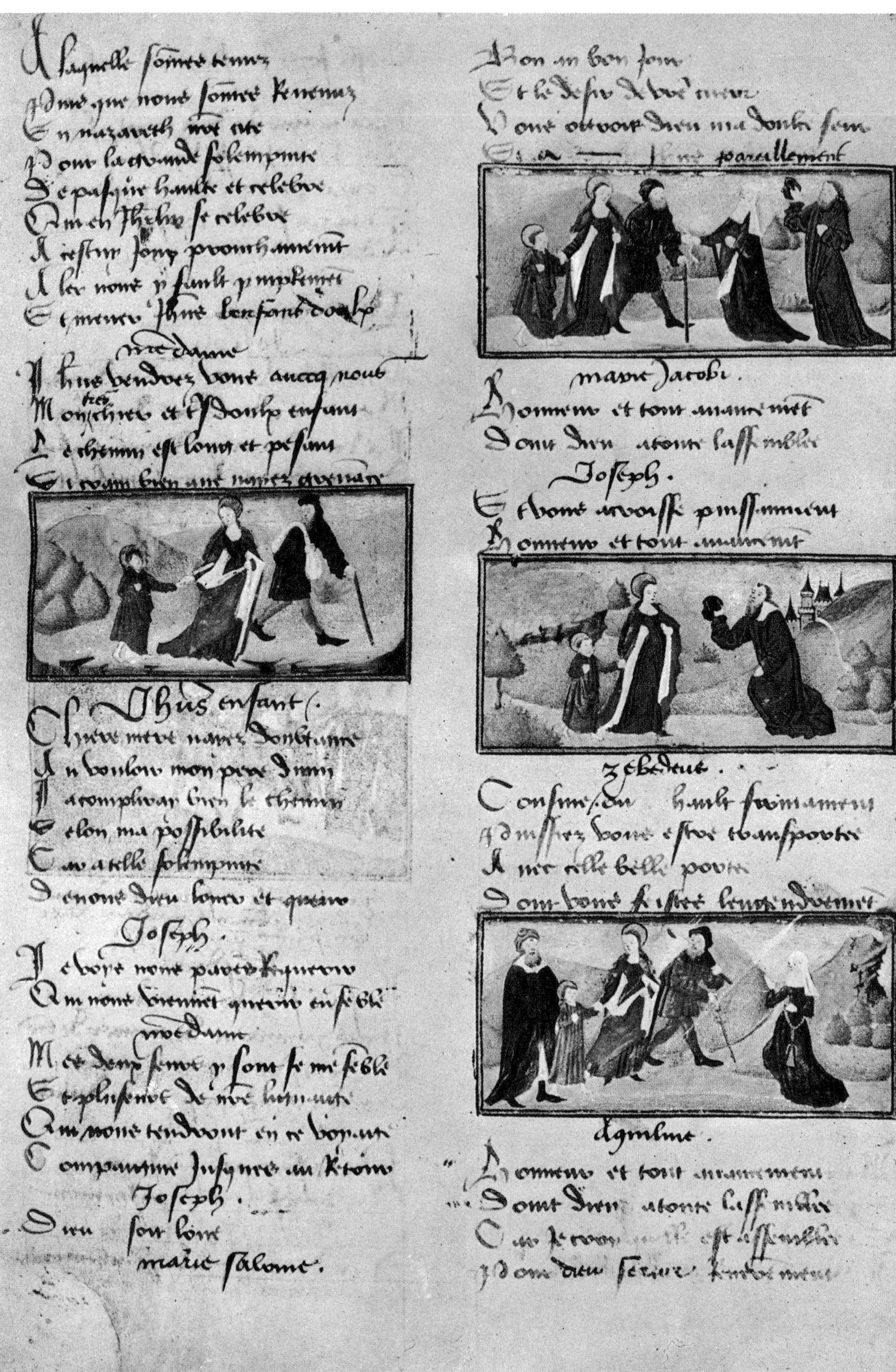

Page of text and miniatures from Arnoul Gréban's Mystère de la Passion. *The performance took four days; the play runs to almost 35,000 lines. Shown here are scenes from Christ's childhood. Ca. 1450. (Paris, Bibliothèque de l'Arsenal.)*

That play contains a scene that is highly relevant to the much-debated question of the reciprocal influence of painting and the theater in the Middle Ages. A woman, the "fèvresse Hédroit," forges the nails for the Crucifixion. The play director and miniaturist Jean Fouquet depicted her around 1460 in the *Heures d'Estienne Chevalier,* and so did the illuminator of a somewhat earlier manuscript of a Passion by Mercadé. Jean Michel designates the woman Hédroit as "canaille de Jerusalem"; but the Bible does not mention her. According to a legend, obviously widely known in the early Middle Ages, this "fèvresse Hédroit," a servant in the house of the High Priest Annas and sister-in-law of Malchus, carried the lantern on the occasion of the betrayal at Gethsemane. She is depicted on fourteenth-century ivory reliefs. But how did she come to be forging nails in the Angers Passion play? It would seem that we must look to the mummers, the *joculatores,* for an explanation. The figure of Hédroit turns up in a *Passion des Jongleurs* dating back to the twelfth century, and also in the English narrative poem *The Story of the Holy Rood* (Harleian Library, Ms. 4196). The following is said to have happened on the eve of the Crucifixion in Jerusalem. Three men came to the blacksmith and asked him to supply the nails. But the man was a secret adherent of the Nazarene and shammed an injured hand, so as to get out of the ignominious deal. In his place, however, the mistress blacksmith, Hédroit, took hammer, tongs, and iron and stepped to the anvil.

Jean Michel incorporated this scene into his Passion play. There are interesting parallels in sculpture, book illumination, and wall paintings. On the tympanum of the central west portal at Strasbourg Cathedral (1280–90) a young woman holding three long nails in her hand grasps Christ's cross; in an English manuscript of 1300 she is seen at the anvil, an old woman swinging her arm vigorously; and in a fresco at the Zemen monastery in Macedonia a whole group of persons is gathered around the forge.

The mummer with his inexhaustible store of tales, much-loved and much-abused as he was, managed to find a narrow back door for his stimulating entry even where the authorities were sure they had barred him. Hidden between the lines of the commonly accepted tradition, he lies in wait with all his kind to disprove the hackneyed clichés about the dark Middle Ages.

In 1547 the inhabitants of Valenciennes forgathered in order to give themselves over to the great *Mystère de la Passion* for twenty-five days. Spread out before their eyes lay the scenes, each added to the next, along one longitudinal axis, as on the *scenae frons* of antiquity. Stage principles of the Renaissance link up with the multiple-setting platform stage of the late medieval French plays. Yesterday's modes of thought and representation are assimilated into the renewed forms of tomorrow.

Speaker of the prologue.

Miniatures from the Passion d'Arras *by Eustache Mercadé. First half of 15th century.*

The woman Hédroit forging the nails. (Arras, Bibliothèque Municipale.)

For all its wealth of scenery and length of performance, Valenciennes had rivals in the gigantically swollen cycles of Apostle and Old Testament plays of Paris (1541 and 1542) and in the forty-day Apostle plays of Bourges—unsurpassed accumulations in the history of world theater. Whether and to what extent such monster cycles still allowed of coherent effect and concentration in performance remains doubtful. A miniature by Hubert Cailleau depicts the platform stage of Valenciennes with its multiple settings, its *loca,* baldachins, thrones, podiums and curtained interiors. At the extreme left is God the Father enthroned in a gloriole as the symbol of paradise, and at the extreme right is hell, surrounded by flames and crowded with wildly gesticulating devils. Beside the traditional animal's jaws, hell here has a specifically French feature, a fortified tower supplemented by a well, into which Satan is hurled after Christ has opened the gates of hell.

The dramatists and producers of the late medieval French mystery plays were clearly able to count upon high standards of stage techniques. The *conducteurs de secret,* the magicians of theatrical production, could easily do as much as the *mechanopoioi* of antiquity. They caused cloud-brimmed platforms to float down, to bring God the Father to earth or take Christ to heaven. They even worked out a trick by which to make visible the Holy Ghost coming upon the apostles, by tongues of flame lit "artificially, with the help of brandy" above their heads. Jean Michel had specially insisted on this optical representation of the miracle of Pentecost for the 1491 performance of his *Mystère de la Résurrection.*

For the hell-mouth, it was not good enough simply to have maneuverable wooden doors; the monstrous jaws themselves had to open and close as required. "Enfer fait en manière d'une grande gueule se clouant et ouvrant quand besoin en est," we read in the stage directions for the *Mystère de l'Incarnation* performed in 1474 at Rouen.

This display of technical ingenuity was matched by the realistic style of the performance. The gross realism displayed in the tortures of Saint Apollonia matched that of the executioners in the Alsfeld Passion play. The scene is represented in a miniature by Jean Fouquet, dating from between 1452 and 1460. Behind the open playing area in the foreground, the stage scaffolds are arranged in a shallow semicircle—above on the left, God the Father enthroned and flanked by angels and musicians, below on the right the hell-mouth. The spectators, densely packed, sit below the stage platforms, though some privileged personages evidently occupied raised seats among the actors.

This miniature, which has often been reproduced, is possibly responsible for the mistaken notion of the "three-tier mystery-play stage." Otto Devrient concluded from the stage directions of the French mystery play, which prescribe a paradise "en hauteur," that hell, earth, and heaven were arranged on three different tiers or stories, and in 1876 he

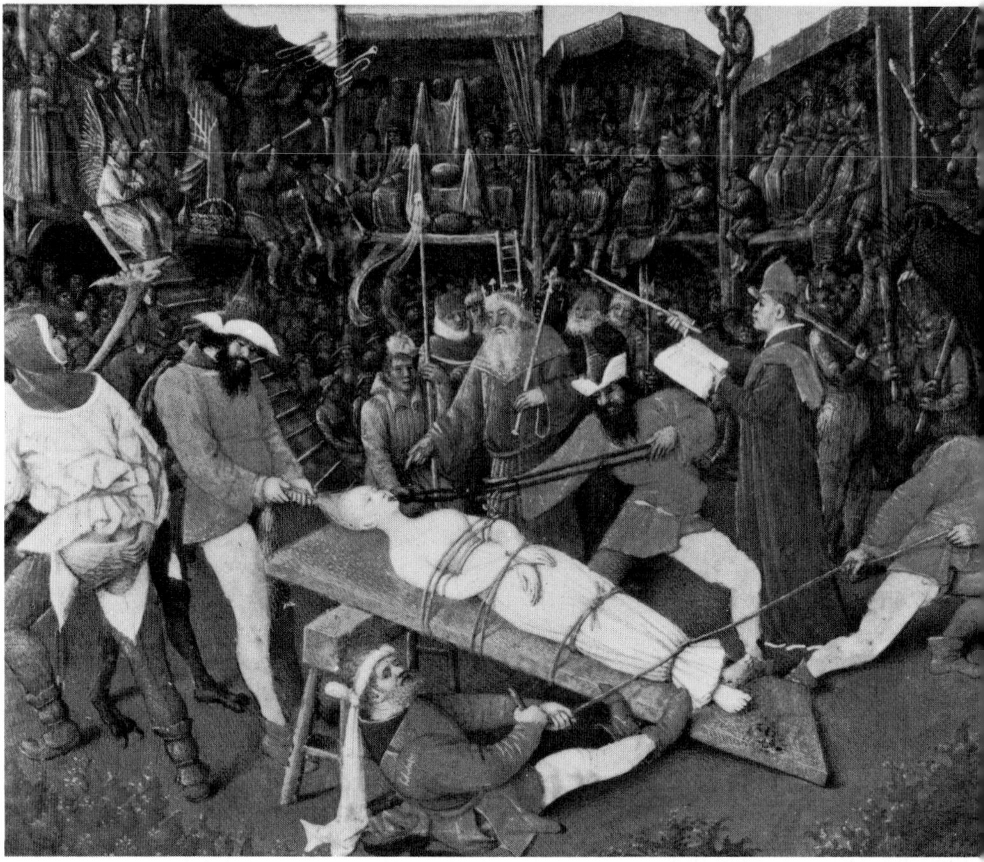

Mystery play, representing the martyrdom of St. Apollonia. To the right, the magister ludens *wearing a long cassock and holding in his left hand the open playbook. In the background, heaven with a ladder, two angels sitting on its top rungs; to the right, the hell-mouth with devils. Miniature by Jean Fouquet, ca. 1460, for the* Book of Hours *of Étienne Chevalier. (Chantilly, Musée Condé.)*

Stage plan for the Valenciennes Mystère de la Passion, *1547. The individual play stations are strung out in a line: on the left, Heaven with God the Father in gloriole; on the right, in the background, inferno with hell-mouth and fortress tower, and in the foreground, a water basin ("la mer") for Peter's draught of fishes. (Paris, Bibliothèque Nationale.)*

produced *Faust* on such a stage, which he supposed to be that of the medieval mystery plays. Four years later, scholars proved this conclusion to be wrong, but the inappropriate notion of the "three-tier mystery-play stage" still persists stubbornly.

The mere length of the performances and the wealth of scenery demanded an open space of fair dimensions—at Rouen, the stage was 180 feet long, and at Mons in Belgium 120 feet long and 24 feet deep. But in addition and very early, there was a tendency to move the play into an indoor theater hall. The principle of the platform stage with multiple settings was comparatively easy to transpose into an appropriately large and long room, and rising rows of seats had already been constructed outdoors.

The Paris Confrérie de la Passion played indoors since the year 1411, at first at the Hôpital de la Trinité, later at the Hôtel de Flandre, and eventually at the Hôtel de Bourgogne, where the French theater later set out on its brilliant career with Molière and the Comédie Italienne.

The expenses for the play and the responsibility for its production were shared by the *confrérie,* the town council, and the participants. The actual production was the business of the *meneur de jeu* who, as in all medieval theater, usually also spoke the prologue and the connecting or explanatory passages holding the action together. Until well into the fifteenth century, the difficult task of "directing" the motley group of craftsmen, students, scholars, and strollers who worked in a play was usually undertaken by clerics and sometimes by academics or ambitious patricians.

Jean Fouquet's Apollonia miniature shows a cleric as *magister ludens,* wearing a tall, red hat and a long, blue cassock edged with white. In his raised right hand he holds a baton, in his left the open playbook. Cailleau's play director wears a flat cap and a purple gown over short, wide breeches, and he holds the *rollet,* or script roll. This is how we may imagine Jean Bouchet—public prosecutor by profession, and by inclination a producer of mystery plays and author of aggressive *sotties*—to have appeared as *meneur de jeu.* When he faced the public as prologue speaker, Jean Bouchet made the highest demands on himself as to clarity of diction, and he made the same high demands on his lay cast. Dialect was ruled out, and so were improper or barbarous expressions. A cultivated diction has always been a rule of the great theatrical school of Paris and its citizens with their proud national consciousness.

Pageant Cart and Theater in the Round Present the Story of the Creation

In England, the formal pattern of the mystery plays was much less strict than it was in France. The stations customary in Corpus Christi celebrations were taken over for the great mystery cycles of the fifteenth century. This meant dividing the text into a series of short dramatic sequences, or one-acters of equal length.

The cycle of the York mystery plays, which is extant in a manuscript dating from about 1430, contains more than thirty separate plays, each staged on its own wagon and arranged like a row of dominoes. While each individual play had to be dramatically concise, there is a certain amount of repetition to keep the thread of the action from being interrupted. The York cycle, which shows clear signs of revisions and additions by several hands, takes 160 lines to cover the creation of the universe, Lucifer's revolt and fall, the confirmation of divine omnipotence, and the creation of Adam and Eve. Lucifer's determination to get his revenge, so the text explicitly specifies, is to leap like a spark onto the next stage wagon as it draws up. Adam and Eve, tempted by the serpent, are his first victims.

The Chester and York mysteries, as well as the Towneley mysteries performed at Wakefield, display a bold and in part highly original sense of humor that is attributable to an early fifteenth-century revision by a monk from the neighboring monastery of Woodkirk. They contain a masterly scene of dialogue in the episode of Noah's Ark. Scolding like a fishwife, Noah's wife flatly refuses to set foot on the Ark; she should have been told of the whole plan beforehand, and in any case what about saving her gossips as well? It is only when the flood actually reaches her that she allows herself to be dragged into the Ark. To put across such a scene must have made great demands on the actors, but equally on the audience's ability to accept it.

How it was possible on a rectangular space of barely 10 by 20 feet to represent in anything like coherent fashion the history of the world and the Gospel story, divided into 20 or even 40 one-act plays and ranging from the Creation to the Resurrection of Christ, is a problem inexplicable to anyone who was not there to see it. The reports of eye witnesses, however, make it seem quite easy. A sixteenth-century description by Archdeacon Robert Rogers of Chester recapitulates the mechanics of a pageant performance as follows:

> They began first at the abbey gates, and when the first pageant was played it was wheeled to the high cross before the mayor, and so to every street; and so [the people in] every street had a pageant before them at some time,

> till all the pageants appointed for the day were played; . . . and all the streets have their pageants afore them, all at one time playing together.

Each play, then, had its own wagon. And so, at any one point in the city, a succession of wagons would draw up one after another to perform the separate plays in an unbroken sequence—which, however, presupposes that all the plays were of more or less equal length, so as to prevent any hold-up. During the move, the actors remained on their pageant wagons, in a mute pose, until at the next stop they went into action again. Each had his own assigned place, where he stood or sat. A few personal and stage properties indicated the scenery. The hell-mouth, presumably, was the lower part of the wagon, draped with cloths—at any rate, this is how David Rogers, Archdeacon Rogers' son, describes it. But then Glynne Wickham has proved that David Rogers was in several respects not a reliable chronicler. Wickham gave a good deal of thought to how the demands of the text for scenery could be reconciled with the limited size of a pageant wagon; he set his conclusions down in a reconstruction of the English pageant stage, and this model explains a lot.

Wickham's reconstructed wagon stage is open on three sides. Along the boarded back wall, he screens off a narrow "tiring house" (dressing room), which is concealed on the stage side by a curtain; in front of it are the *loca,* with the actors in appropriate groups during the move from one station to the next. At the place where the performance is to proceed, a second cart, the so-called scaffold cart, is moved directly alongside the first. This second cart simply carries an empty platform at the same level as that of the pageant cart. This is the playing stage, on which the players now step forward and have room to move and gesticulate, and to deploy their dramatic skill as they could not have done in the inevitably cramped pageant cart.

Wickham's ingenious combination of pageant cart and scaffold cart (the scaffolds had previously always been interpreted rather vaguely as additional stage constructions) even makes us understand how Noah could have argued with his recalcitrant wife on the front stage, and eventually pulled her to safety into the Ark on the main cart.

Ahead of the series of carts came an expositor, on horseback or afoot, who informed the public assembled at the different playing stations of the meaning and course of the performance to come. The performances themselves were managed by a so-called conveyor, who gave the sign for the play to start, acted as prompter and, when the play was over, had to get his cart to move on according to the program. Generally, the conveyor was a member of the guild that had financed the scenery and the actors for a particular pageant. It was a point of honor for every craft to take part in the mystery plays of the city concerned.

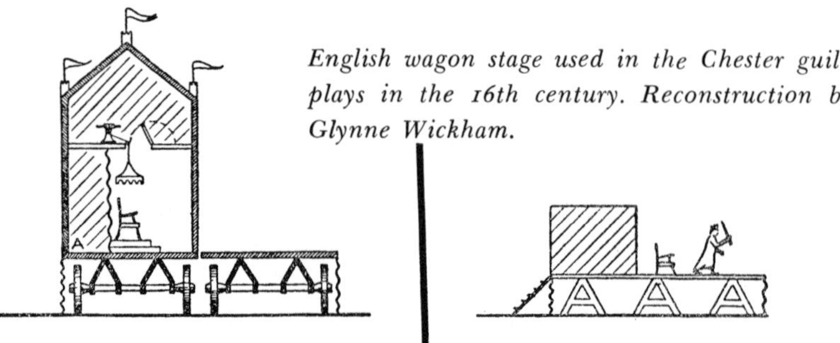

English wagon stage used in the Chester guild plays in the 16th century. Reconstruction by Glynne Wickham.

The purse-strings were loosened and no expense was spared. If the shipbuilders were responsible for Noah's Ark, the goldsmiths for the wagon of the Magi, and the drapers for the dignified appearance of the prophets, then the public could expect not only to hear, but also to see remarkable things. Inadequate provision for the pageant cart assigned to any guild could attract a severe reproof from the aldermen, and even a heavy fine. This is what happened to the painters of Beverley in 1520, "because their play . . . was badly and confusedly played, in contempt of the whole community, before many strangers."

Although the texts were by and large established, they always had to be revised and adapted for particular groups of performers. In addition to rivalry among the separate guilds, towns were often trying to outdo each other with their plays. Anyone who prepared a play for production was allowed to display his erudition and, better still, to add original, grotesque interludes of his own. Thus the Woodkirk monk who made additions to the Towneley cycle had the idea of inserting before the Adoration of the Shepherds a farce that may well stand comparison with the work of Hans Sachs. The shepherd Mak, a sly rascal, steals a ram from the others and takes it home to his wife. For all that she gives him a sound scolding, she tucks the—clearly stage-trained—animal into the cradle, lies down in bed herself and, when Mak's fellow shepherds arrive and suspiciously search the house, she asks them to keep quiet out of consideration for herself and the new baby. But when one of them lifts the baby's blanket the fraud is discovered, and Mak is beaten up. Exhausted, everyone then falls sound asleep, to be awakened by the angels' *Gloria in excelsis.*

The sources of the 1468 collection of plays called *Ludus Coventriae* —though there seems to be no connection with Coventry (Craig suggests Lincoln)—have been traced back to the Byzantines. One of the most effective scenes, "Joseph's Return," is almost word for word the same as a dialogue fragment attributed to Patriarch Germanus of Constantinople. The Eastern church and the cart stage meet across the centuries in the expression of Joseph's only too human feelings, of which the Syrian sources still had spoken openly and over which Western interpreters solicitously spread the cloak of the immaculate conception. Joseph accuses Mary of having made a cuckold of him and shamed his name:

JOSEPH: Sey me mary this childys fadyr ho is. . . .
MARY: this childe is goddys and your.
JOSEPH: Goddys childe thou lyist in fay
God dede nevyr jape so with may
And I cam nevyr ther I dare wel say
yitt so nyh thi boure
but yit I sey whoose childe is this.
MARY: Goddys and youre I sey i-wys.
JOSEPH: ya ya all olde men to me take tent
and weddyth no wyff in no kynnys wyse
that is a yonge wench be myn a-sent
ffor doute and drede and swych servyse
Alas alas my name is shent
all men may me now dyspyse
and seyn olde cokwold thi bow is bent
newly now after the frensche gyse.

While the cart or wagon stage was a highly characteristic medium used in the English mystery plays, it was not the only one. Multiple settings were used in Cornwall in the fifteenth century, either on a circular stage accommodating the *loca* at ground level, as in the morality play *The Castle of Perseverance,* or in a wider arch reminiscent of the amphitheater of antiquity. The text of the so-called Cornish Plays includes diagrams that mark, within two concentric circles, the *loca* of the players, ranging from the Creation to Christ's Ascension, and ending not with the solemn *Te Deum,* but with a direction to the minstrels to pipe for a dance, and an invitation to players and spectators to join it.

Two such stages or "Cornish rounds" still exist, one at St. Just in Penwith, the other at Perranzabuloe. Both are medieval open-air stages, about 126 to 143 feet in diameter—a stormy northern land's adaptations of the ancient amphitheater. William Borlase, an antiquary who published, in 1745, his *Observations on the Antiquities Historical and Monumental of Cornwall,* describes them as follows: "In these continued Rounds, or Amphitheatres of stone (not broken as the Cirques of Stones-erect) the Britons did usually assemble to hear plays acted," and he adds that "the most remarkable monument of this kind" which he has yet seen "is near the Church of St. Just, Penwith." The fascination of the site has continued to the present day—and now sets the scene for

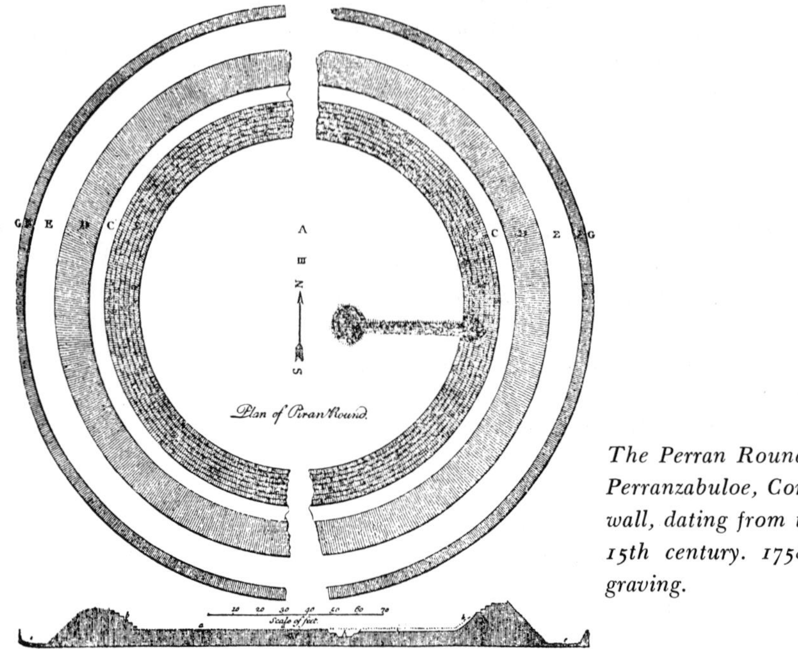

The Perran Round, Perranzabuloe, Cornwall, dating from the 15th century. 1758 engraving.

retrospective productions, far removed from festival stereotypes. Richard Southern quotes a twentieth-century spectator who had attended a performance at St. Just:

> "The bare granite plain of St. Just, in view of Cape Cornwall, and of the transparent sea which beats against that magnificent headland, would be a fit theatre for the exhibition . . . of the great History of the Creation, the Fall, and the Redemption of Man . . . The mighty gathering of people from many miles round, hardly showing like a crowd in that extended region, where nothing ever grows to limit the view on any side. . . .

Southern adds, with reference to "the mental influences of expectation and religion," that the original spectators were

> country people or from country towns, of an agricultural age, eager for any treat and now in crowd collected, among gay toys of costumes, hills and banners, with a moat and barrier crossed that cut them off from all the workaday world. . . . Whether each was devout or not was probably dependent upon the individual, but the crowd as a whole belonged to an age with a dominant religious shape; and so, I think, they would be prepared to listen to the long argument on a theological strain that runs through this performance.

The boundless vista of land and sea played its part as did the blue skies of Athens, even though here the Greek light was replaced by gray clouds and storms, vaulting the Last Judgment in this northern land.

The Christmas Play

All along, the Passion, mystery, and legend plays were accompanied on their path by the services and cycles connected with Christmas. They took their origin from the same oratoriolike *Quem quaeritis* that is the germ of the Easter plays. "Who are you looking for?" was the question addressed both to the three Marys on Easter Sunday and to the shepherds coming to the manger on Christmas Eve.

Tutilo of St. Gall was the first to include a dialogue passage in his Christmas trope *Hodie cantandus.* The scene lends itself readily to dramatization. The approaching shepherds are greeted by two deacons dressed in long, wide dalmatics. They portray the women who, according to the apocryphal Book of James, or Protevangelium, assisted Mary at the birth. They have the additional task of bearing witness to the immaculate conception and parthenogenesis, a double role that medieval art assigned to them very early, especially in Byzantine monuments. As *obstetrices* (midwives) they busy themselves around mother and child, and bathe the newborn babe in golden bowls and chalices.

In early versions of the liturgical *officium pastorum,* the *quasi obstetrices* act vicariously for the Holy Family. The earliest information about the "staging" of these Christmas celebrations is contained in the eleventh-century tropers; one is from St. Martial in Limoges, and the other, of unknown origin, is now at Oxford. The introductory question "Quem quaeritis in presepe, pastores, dicite?" ("Whom do you seek in the manger, oh shepherds?") and the subsequent adoration are followed, as a transition to the Alleluia of the Mass, by the command: "Et nunc euntes dicite quia natus est" ("Go and tell all the people that He is born"). The text of the *officium* is still very close to the Gospel text.

By the eleventh century, the scene was enriched by the inclusion of new characters. The returning shepherds meet the three Magi who, having heard the glad tidings, in their turn approach the child, respectfully proffering their gifts. In these early representations they do not kneel. In ancient as in early medieval art, the *genuflexio* was not an expression of veneration but an imploring of mercy. The first representation showing one of the Magi kneeling appears in the Klosterneuburg *Antependium* by Nicholas of Verdun (1181), which suggests, with the vivid impact of its wealth of scenes, a connection with the plays performed at Klosterneuburg, near Vienna. The Three Kings also are not shown wearing crowns before the middle of the twelfth century; earlier representations show the Kings as "wise men," wearing the Phrygian cap.

Until the thirteenth century, the Madonna herself appeared merely as an image, usually as the Virgin enthroned with the Child, on the altar decorated to represent the manger. The child Jesus, foreshadowing the future Pantocrator, lifts His right hand in blessing. Around Him crowds the numerous cast of epiphany cycles. The Romanesque wall paintings in the former west choir of the abbey church at Lambach on the Danube, which have been completely uncovered since 1967, are probably a visual reflection of the similarly extant *Officium Stellae* of Lambach, a Magi play written in Latin. The three women standing around the enthroned Madonna are the *obstetrices,* who were the first to greet the Magi as they arrived at the manger. Karl M. Swoboda, in 1927, was the first to point out that the fresco painter must have taken his lead from the personages of the Latin Magi play.

The scene was further enlarged by the inclusion of the angels, announcing the glad tidings "from on high" (as at Orléans). The arcaded galleries of Romanesque churches and the triforia of Gothic cathedrals provided ideal *loca* for this purpose.

The liturgical *officium* turned into theater from the moment an antagonist appears: King Herod, the personification of evil. Upon him and his court the medieval compilers of plays lavished all their unstinted wealth of invention. Sitting on his purple throne and surrounded by scribes, Herod receives the Magi, after a messenger has announced the oriental visitors. In the Christmas play of Orléans, Herod has his son Archelaus by his side. Angered by the disclosures of the

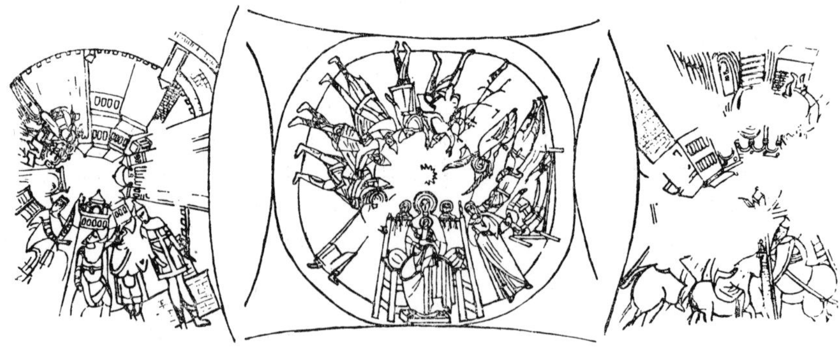

Epiphany cycle with the characters of the Magi play. After a wall painting in the former west choir of the abbey church at Lambach on the Danube, Upper Austria, 11th century.

scribes, Herod throws the Prophetic book to the ground. In pantomime the actors portray the wrath of father and son as they brandish their swords at the star, which is drawn on a strip through the church to announce the new-born King.

Fits of anger and the threat of violence, in contrast to credulity and innocent trust, always were an effective subject on the stage.

The Christmas plays are another case of early irruption of the mime into the solemnity of the church. Around 1170 the abbess Herrad of Landsberg complained about the buffoonery that had gained undue ground, especially in the Herod scenes, and just to show how things should be done properly, in her own *Hortus deliciarum* (which was destroyed by fire in Strasbourg in 1870), has Herod enthroned in dignity.

The plays, in the meantime, went their own ways, partly condemned by the church and partly promoted by the clergy. The basic scenes were embroidered with more and more episodic detail, though at the same time no effort was spared to adduce theological proof for the Christmas miracle.

The Benediktbeuren Christmas play included in the 13th-century *Carmina burana* begins with a disputation of the Prophets, with appearances of Balaam and his ass, Saint Augustine, and an *episcopus puerorum*. The Boy Bishop, who in the French Feast of Fools and *Festum asinorum* presides over a fair amount of clerical levity, in the Benediktbeuren play merely announces precociously that the question of the virgin birth can be adequately explained only by Augustine.

The Annunciation and Visitation then lead into the Christmas story as such. The star appears to the *tres Reges* in the orient. They call on Herod, who receives them in the presence of a messenger. The announcement of the Nativity to the shepherds contains a theatrically effective contrast in the person of *diabolus*, who does his best to demolish the credibility of the angels' message. The shepherds go to the manger, adore the Child, and on their return meet the Three Kings, who in their turn proceed to the manger and worship. Warned by an angel in a dream, they start on their homeward journey without going back to Herod. But Herod learns from the Archisynogogus and his high priests that the prophecy has come true. He commands the Massacre of the Innocents. The hillsides of Bethlehem resound with the lament of the mothers. Rachel, the representative Jewish mother, weeps for her sons: "O dulce sfilii. . . ." (Quite apart from the plays, the *ordo Rachelis* in any event formed part of the liturgy for December 28, the day of the Innocent Children.)

Herod feels his end approaching. He hands over his crown to his son Archelaus, drops dead from his chair "gnawed by worms," and is

Ecce homo *scene, presented on an English wagon stage: Pilate on his throne; on the left, the column of the scourging and a servant with the basin of water. Engraving by David Jee. (From Thomas Sharp,* A Dissertation on the Pageants or Dramatic Mysteries Anciently Performed at Coventry, *1825.)*

Birth of Christ. Christmas scene, with spectators in contemporary dress. Painting by Hans Multscher, 1473. (Berlin-Dahlem, Staatliche Museen, Gemäldegalerie.)

The woman Hédroit forging nails, while her husband displays his injured hand; to the left, two men drilling holes in the cross. From the manuscript Ms. 666 Holkam Hall, ca. 1300. (Library of Lord Leicester.)

Holy Family with angels. Panel painting by a Rhenish artist, ca. 1400. The popular realism, the wealth of detail, and the baldachinlike "Christmas hut" are akin to the narrative exuberance of the Christmas plays. (Berlin-Dahlem, Staatliche Museen, Gemäldegalerie.)

Christmas scene with "dumpling eater," a maidservant who prepares and tastes the local dish for Mary. Wall painting, in the castle chapel at Hocheppan, South Tirol, 12th century.

The Three Kings with Herod, three scribes seated at his feet. Miniature from the Codex Aureus *of Echternach, ca. 1020. (Nuremberg, Germanisches National-museum.)*

gathered up by the devils with wild jubilation. An angel appears to Joseph in a dream and tells him to flee to Egypt. He sets out with Mary and the Child. This is followed by a *Ludus de Rege Aegypti,* which deals with the arrival of the Holy Family in Egypt and the fall of the Nile empire's gods—and parts of this dialogue are borrowed from the Tegernsee "Antichrist" play.

And thus every dogmatic aspect of the Christmas story, with all its antecedents and ramifications, is covered in episodic breadth. Give and take some details here or there, parallels can be found in Nativity plays from Nevers (1060), Compiègne, Metz, Montpellier, and Orléans, to the monastery at Einsiedeln in Switzerland and the Belgian monastery at Bilsen, and to Toledo in Spain, with the cathedral's *Auto de los Reyes Magos.*

With the ascendancy of the vernacular, the dogmatic character of the plays gradually receded to give way to popular scenes centering on the manger and on the child in the cradle, as they survive to this day in songs and local customs. Joseph pokes up the fire, busies himself with bellows and candles, cooks a milk pudding for the infant (as in Gréban's *Mystère*), flirts with the maid servants and is the butt of much mockery.

In the chapel of the castle at Hocheppan a twelfth-century Tirolese fresco painter depicted a maid kneeling at the fire with a frying pan and tasting the locally customary dumplings before the new mother gets hers. Two hundred years later, in the Hesse Christmas play, a kindred soul deals with the scene in a similar manner. Yet, while at Hocheppan Joseph is allowed to think his own thoughts quietly, as Mary supervises the preparation of the dumplings from her Byzantine couch, in the Hesse play he has his hands full getting the recalcitrant maids to attend to the cooking. After the most lively altercations, the only result Joseph has to show for his labors is that the maids together with the two innkeepers gaily dance around the crib.

At about the time of the Hesse Christmas play, Konrad von Soest, who created the magnificent Niederwildung altar with its gold ground, makes his white-bearded Joseph squat by the fire and prudently cook the contested milk pudding. The altar can be dated to 1404, while the play was written down some time between 1450 and 1460, though it had probably been performed since the end of the fourteenth century. Hesse monasteries, and more particularly the Friedberg Franciscans, were notorious at that time for their "improper ribaldry." The aldermen of Friedberg were led in 1485 to require the two monasteries of the Augustines and Discalced friars in the strongest terms to conduct themselves properly.

In the Christmas plays, as in other religious plays, robust sensual pleasure and naive piety are close neighbors. The monk who wrote down the Hesse manuscript puts a strange lullaby into the mouth of the child Jesus in the crib: "Eya, eya, maria liebe mutter myn, sal ich von den joden liten grosse pin." (Ah me, ah me dear mother Mary mine, the Jews will make me suffer such great pain.) Mary soothes him: "Swige, libes kindelyn iesu christ, beweyn dein martel nicht zu dieser frist." (Hush, hush, dear child, dear Jesus Christ, bewail not now your martyr's death.) The crude tavern comedy is suddenly overshadowed by the child's premonition of the Passion to come.

In *Representación del nacimiento de Nuestro Señor,* a Nativity play written by the Spanish poet Gomez Manrique in the middle of the fifteenth century, the child in the manger is shown the instruments of the Passion; the scene ends with a cradlesong sung in psalmody, each stanza underscored by a double cry of pain: "Ay dolor!"

The Flemish painter Roger van der Weyden incorporated in his Magi altarpiece (Alte Pinakothek, Munich) the idea of the Crucifixion being foreshadowed in the manger. Inconspicuously, and hitherto unnoticed, a crucifix is attached to the central arch of the Nativity ruin. (A contemporary copy by the Master of St. Catherine does not reproduce this *Mene tekel,* though it faithfully corresponds to the original in all other details.)

The Christmas play hardly had any need of special technical stage arrangements. In German-speaking countries, and in those in which the Romance and Slav languages were spoken, it remained within the churches, even when Passion and legend plays were beginning to spread to monastery yards and marketplaces. Where it became a part of the great Passion cycles, the manger, of course, had its place, as in the great outdoor, open-stage, multiple settings at Lucerne in 1583, or in the mystery plays performed on the English pageant carts.

The prophet plays, which had originally been tied to the Christmas service, had become independent of the manger scene at the altar by the twelfth century. Instead of the theological and didactic interpretation of the Gospel, as practiced by the Church Fathers under the dome of the Hagia Sophia in Constantinople, the North preferred devils' dances and the clash of swords, sometimes of such crude realism that some unwary spectators were horror-struck. The chronicle of Bishop Albertus of Livonia records with questionable satisfaction that his by no means lily-livered compatriots were so terrified by the *Ludus prophetarum ornatissimus,* performed in 1204 by clerics at Riga, that they took to their heels.

A prophet play performed ten years earlier, in Regensburg in 1194, caused no panic, though it covered the creation of the angels, the fall of Lucifer and his kin, the creation of man and his fall. Perhaps the portrayals were on a smaller scale—or, perhaps, the inhabitants of this cosmopolitan city on the Danube were more familiar with the effects of the prophecies from the sermons they had heard. The people of Regensburg, after all, lived at a crossroad, at intersection between influences emanating from Byzantium and antiquity; they knew, perhaps, not only about Balaam and his ass, the three youths in the burning fiery furnace, and the sibylline prophecies, but also about how Virgil came to be a witness to pre-Christian world history.

The later development of the Christmas play was in no way influenced by erudite theological disputes. Having jettisoned all the ballast of the Old Testament, it has retained the magic of the manger to this day, enriched by the most manifold local folk customs.

SECULAR PLAYS

Joculatores, Minstrels and Vagantes

The same arguments with which around 1100 the Byzantine statesman Zonaras sought to vindicate the court actors were propounded later before a Western ruler by another sympathetic spokesman. At the court of the Spanish king Alfonso X of Castile (1252–84), the troubadour Guiraut Riquier petitioned to the king to lay down, by virtue of his royal authority, a precise nomenclature for minstrels, so that "noble" and "common" entertainers could be distinguished from each other. It was unjust, he argued, to treat the highest representatives of the art of recital, whose well-turned verses and songs beguiled the courts, on a par with all the tribe of jugglers, buffoons, jesters, mountebanks, and animal keepers who exercised their trade on the open marketplace in view of every Tom, Dick, and Harry.

The benevolent, rhymed edict, which Riquier claimed was the king's response to his plea, probably came from his own pen. The only official record we have is a justification of church plays contained in *Leyes de las partidas,* the code of law completed under Alfonso X. Having severely censured all the "wanton buffoonery" that diminished the dignity of the house of God, this goes on to say: "But there are performances that priests are permitted, for example the birth of our Lord Jesus Christ. . . ."

This was no satisfaction to the pride of the ambitious troubadour Riquier. Yet he had to be content with the personal favor he himself enjoyed. The same applied to all the hundreds of minstrels, singers, and musicians who were much in demand as court poets, organizers of festivities, advisers, and heralds of their prince's fame. Widely traveled and of proven worth in many a delicate mission as they were, they could often match the best of the nobility in diplomatic skill and general culture. "I live in the generous landgrave's household," Walther von der Vogelweide said of himself, "it is my way always to be found among the best."

Chronicles, tracts, and church edicts refer to the wandering singers—the *ministeriales*, minstrels, *ménestrels*, *ménétriers*—and report that they "served" their princes with lute and song. Eventually, this designation merged almost undistinguishably with that of the *joculator*, inherited from antiquity, with the French term *jongleur* and with the German *Spileman*.

Alfonso of Castile—the scholar, poet, and astronomer king—refused Riquier, the noblest of his troubadours, the legal recognition he so fervently desired. Yet King Alfonso's successors were all the more eager to have themselves depicted in the *Tratado de batallas* as rulers over orient and occident, adopting the prose of kindly princes surrounded by little Moors, jesters, and droll monkeys.

The jugglers, musicians, dancers, and animal keepers of the Middle Ages could certainly not complain that their existence was allowed to fall into oblivion. They survive—on church portals, tympanums, capitals, choir screens, and cornices, in manuscripts, in enamel and ivory objects—and are portrayed in the most loving detail and variety.

The monastery of St. Gall made it a point of honor, in the eighth and ninth centuries, to welcome the ruling prince not only with pious songs, but with music, and with performing dancers and acrobats. Its Christmas revels were so famous that in 911 King Conrad I decided to visit St. Gall to see them for himself. (Louis the Pious, on the other hand, had no desire to attend such shows; we are told by his chronicler Theganus that he never laughed even at the gayest feasts, when jesters and mimes, flute and zither plays gave great merriment to all others who were present.) To judge by Ruotger's biography of the learned archbishop Bruno of Cologne, the antique dramatic heritage was as much in evidence at this time as the Atellan comedy. His Eminence, Ruotger tells us, never had any but the most serious purposes in mind when he read farces and mime plays that caused others to roar with laughter. Although he thought little of the content of both comedies and tragedies, he valued them as models for figures of speech.

The *Comedia Bile* of the talking fishes, a popular ventriloquist farce of the *histriones* of late antiquity, also survived to the fifteenth century as a star act of the mimes. Animal dances, imitations of animal voices, and the stock-type farce as a means of social criticism were the

Entertainer with monkey. Romanesque bas-relief, Bayeux Cathedral.

Entertainer and St. John the Evangelist. Miniatures from a Beatus commentary on the Apocalypse. Spanish manuscript from the monastery Santo Domingo de Silos, ca. 1100. (London, British Museum.)

Tu ni morras humes se emes coupes non
De cele part delost ou lamiral tornoie
Anulas dabilac de ioster se desroie
fiert si licanor que sa lance pechoie
licanor feri lui que de mort le guertoie
es le coste li passe le gfanon de soie
ant ghanste li dure labat en une voie
damoisel le vit qui nen ot mie ioie
feri i greiois qui li pecha le foie
anclins fu abatus licanor li envoie
le destrier abilac au monter ni deloie
e chevalier sen torne qui le ceval ot pris

Comment ... alixandre
... lamiraut ...
Amiraut lesgarda
si dist a i lien dru
En moie foi amis
mal nous est avenu
maudit soit cist tornois
quant il gmenchies fu
Car ie ni gaingne riens ains i ai tout pd
es se mi dieu me sauuet ma force & ma vert
inchois que ie men aille mi auront gneu
l fait soner iii cors & i grelle menu

Entertainers wearing caps with bells, masked dancers, and dressage scenes. Decorated bottom margins from Li Romans d'Alixandre, *14th century. (Ms. Bodleian 265, Oxford.)*

inexhaustible sources of the mime. When the tenth-century *Ecbasis captivi* followed Aesop into a cozy allegory in making fun of monastic life and transposing it into the animal kingdom, its clerical author drew on the same source as the much-abused mime and *joculator*. When the Paris *trouvère* Rutebeuf, in his *Dit de l'Erberie*, has a medical charlatan boast of all the hundreds of medicaments he has tried out on the Sultan of Egypt, this character is just as much a survival of antiquity's quack as is the *Mercator* of the Easter play. This part always belongs to the *joculator*, as much in the *ménestrel* and *goliardi* song as in the religious play.

Singly or in pairs, these entertainers performed their scenes in costumes and makeup. Vivid gestures and the dancer's agility reveal the *joculator*, for all his literary ambitions, as an immediate successor to the art of recital of antiquity's mimes and pantomimes—although he borrowed the biblical story of the prodigal son in the French *Courtois d'Arras*, a "dramatic poem" written and recited by a *jongleur* around 1200. Beyond doubt, he took part in the *mystères mimés*. When Philip the Fair in 1313 entertained the King of England with a pantomime performance of the entire Passion, "professional actors" did their bit to enliven the dumb show. And when the author of the Kreuzenstein Passion (extant only in fragments), in the fourteenth century, provided for a formal ballet of Salome with four of her maidens, he could hardly have intended that this should be performed by gawky friars. For such purposes he could count on the wandering minstrel and his woman partner, the "spilwip." Early in the twelfth century, the recluse Frau Ava, who lived near Göttweig on the Danube and wrote a rhymed poem on John the Baptist, had Salome dancing just like a "spilwip" expert in all the arts of pantomime and dance: "vil wol spilt div maget. Si begunde wol singen, snaellichlichen springen mit herphin vnde mit gigen, mit orgenen vnde mit lyren." (This girl can perform very well. She knows how to sing, and to dance nimbly to sound of harp and fiddle, organ and lyre.)

Thus the Danubian Salome of 1120, whom Frau Ava means to appear in "chunichlichem gaerwe," in royal robes, is the spit and image of the Byzantine girl mime described by Chrysostomus around 400.

But in the monastic life of the thirteenth century, the gods smiled even upon the poor tumbler. The French legend *Le tombeur Notre-Dame* tells a moving tale. A tumbler, weary of his worldly life, gives away his money, his horse and clothes and is admitted to a monastery. Every night he secretly descends into the crypt where there is a statue of Our Lady in the chapel. He slips off his cowl, girds his thin shirt, and worships her not in prayer, but in acrobatic dances. He performs the French, the Spanish, and the Breton leap, "whirls his feet through the

Salome dances before Herod. Miniature from the Hortus deliciarium *of Herrad of Landsberg, 12th century.*

air," stands on his head—until, exhausted, he collapses. The abbot, warned of the man's strange behavior, secretly watches him and witnesses a miracle: Mary descends from heaven and fans the prostrate tumbler with cool air. Profoundly moved, the abbot takes him in his arms and admits him into the community of friars. But he commands him to go on doing "service" in front of the Virgin's image, until the "tumbeor Nostre Dame" dies in bliss. Massenet's opera *Le Jongleur de Notre Dame* (1902) is based on this old legend.

St. Uncumber of Lucca is reported to have rewarded a fiddler with her golden shoe, and the Madonna of Rocamadour to have lowered a burning altar light upon the instrument of a humbly worshipping *joculator*. And since ultimately the church itself cannot allow itself to be outdistanced by its own legends, all the interdicts did not prevent *vagantes* and "artful minstrels" being employed as church musicians.

Finally, not the least of the debts of gratitude we owe the *joculatores* is that they preserved one of the oldest and most popular forms of theater, the puppet and marionette play. Articulated figures moved by strings and rods, as depicted in her *Hortus deliciarum* by Herrad of Landsberg, enjoyed as much popularity as did the puppets of the immortal Punch-and-Judy show, in which the players remained hidden behind the draped booth. The puppet stage could on occasion be quite splendidly elaborate, as witness a miniature in the 14th-century Flemish manuscript of *Li romans du boin roi Alixandre,* where the stage is equipped with battlements and balconies, and the fighting warriors are decoratively flanked by two sentries, armed with clubs and maces. The play is obviously giving rise to lively discussion among the courtly spectators. A subject of such vast scope and so rich in historic and legendary associations as the Alexander romance clearly demanded of the medieval puppet player as much detailed familiarity with his exacting theme as

Conjurer. Painting by Hieronymus Bosch. (St.-Germain-en-Laye, Musée Municipal.)

Puppet players performing for the king. Miniature from the Hortus deliciarum *of Herrad of Landsberg, 12th century. (Original destroyed by fire in Strasbourg in 1870.)*

was required of the Indonesian *wayang* or the Japanese *bunraku* player. In one respect, however, the medieval puppeteer had an advantage; he did not have to make his host of heroes perform for hours without interruption, nor to go without a hearty meal in the servants' quarters or, if he was accepted as a peer, at the lord's table.

From Street Masque to Stage Play

Toward the end of the eleventh century, the Norman chronicler Ordericus Vitalis wrote of a priest's terrifying experience. One night early in spring, a wild and howling crowd of demons stormed past him through the air, led by a giant armed with a club. It was the wild chase of the harlequin folk, the "familia Herlechini."

Barely a hundred years later, Peter of Blois, in his Fourteenth Epistle to court officials of the English king (1175), mentioned the nefarious doings of the harlequin folk. They were sons of Satan, he said, the image of mankind addicted to the world's vanity; their leader, the chief devil, had no other aim than to assault the church and all its works and to lead even the cleverest and wisest men into temptation and sin.

The old French *mesnie Herlequin* is one of the innumerable versions of the wild chase, of the army of damned souls, the army of the dead—all deeply rooted in pagan demon cults. Their attributes are fear-inspiring animal masks, wolves and dogs as companions, loud tinkling of bells, roaring and raging, whistling and screaming. This is how they appear in many examples from the Germanic Odin's Host and its many derivatives in folk custom to the werewolves of Asia Minor and, later, in the silently approaching streak of mist in Goethe's *Erlkönig*. The chief devil Herlequin eventually gave his name to Arlecchino in the *Commedia dell'arte*.

Adam de la Halle, ex-theologian, passionate champion of justice, poet and musician, assigned an important role to Herlekin Croquesot in his *Jeu de la Feuillée*. In this play, which was performed at Arras in 1262, the character Croquesot appears with a shaggy, big-mouthed devil's mask. To the accompaniment of bells set atinkling as the harlequin folk rush past, he makes his entrance. And he addresses the audience: "Me sied-il bien, li hurepiaus?" ("Doesn't it suit me well, this mask, this devil's mug?") Presumably he also wore a bright-red cowled cloak, the common garb of devil and Herlekin alike.

Adam de la Halle's *Jeu de la Feuillée* may be considered the oldest French secular drama. It combines elements of cult, fairy tale, and superstition in an inspired manner. It was the author's witty and imaginative farewell to his native city Arras, before going off to Paris and its university, and he could be certain that his audience would understand all his open and hidden allusions. The riotous revels of the harlequins were aimed at the heart of his time and of his city, as was his satire, replete with logical allusions, rudeness and charm, malice and magic spells.

Twenty years later, in his musical play *Jeu de Robin et Marion,* graceful *pastourelle* with musical accompaniment, Adam de la Halle anticipated the Renaissance pastoral play.

In the course of the fourteenth century, the "familia Herlechini" emancipated itself in a most down-to-earth manner. In the Charivari the demythologized harlequins turned into brawling devils, creating mischief and unrest wherever they roamed through the streets. The Charivari was a sort of carnival fools' parade; its participants scared the honest burghers with pokers and the clanking of copper pots, with wooden rattles, tin bells and ringing cow-bells.

What was still a masquerade in the form of comic theater in the works of Adam de la Halle, now became, under the protection of animal skins and grotesque masks, an inartistic hooliganism for its own sake. Whether demon or fool, the wearer of the mask could be certain of immunity from punishment: for the fool's freedom is the only freedom mankind has preserved from prehistoric times to this day.

No rule of propriety and decency could keep the nocturnal revelries within bounds. No wonder that the church enjoined clerics and laymen alike "not to watch nor to take part in the gaieties called Charivari, in which people wear masks in the likeness of demons and dreadful things are perpetrated."

The Neidhart plays, developed in the Austrian Alps and in Tirol, are in the tradition of the customs connected with the winter solstice, carnival, and the rites of spring. They go back to such customs as the election of a May king and queen at Whitsuntide, resembling the Italian "sposa di maggio," and the "Lord and Lady of the May," the English equivalent of Adam de la Halle's *Robin et Marion.*

The German Neidhart plays take their name from the late Minnesinger Neidhart von Reuenthal, a knight and liege of the Bavarian Duke Otto II. Around 1230, Neidhart von Reuenthal fell into disfavor with Duke Otto. Thereafter he found refuge in Austria, where he broke away from the poetic conventions of the Minnesang, which had by that time become rigid, and became the outstanding representative of what is known as "höfische Dorfpoesie," that is, village poetry under court influence. Through this new form a bridge is built between the customs of the court and those of the villagers—expressed so well in the old, popu-

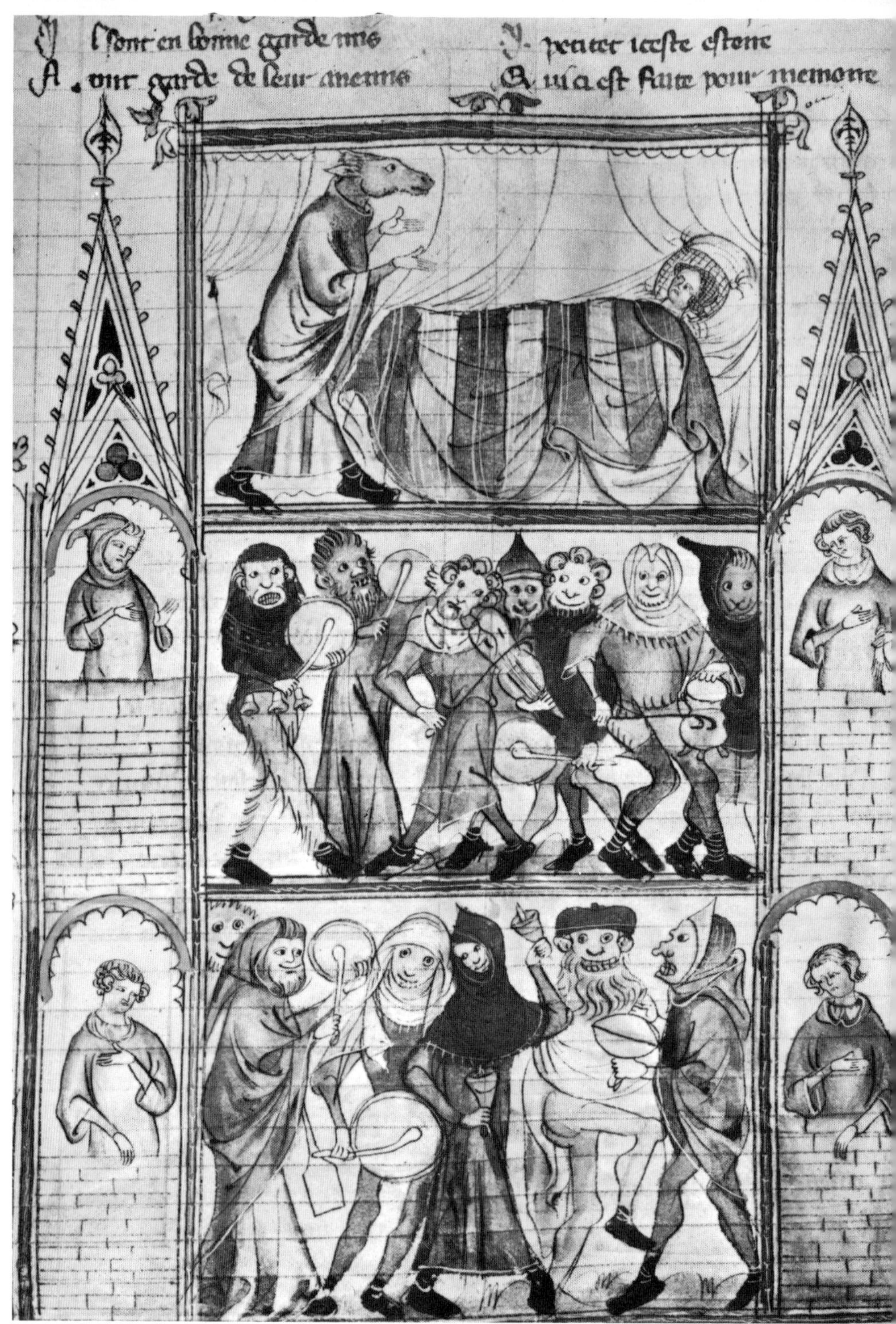

Minstrels. Miniature from the Roman de Fauvel, *a satirical poem, the hero of which is a horse. The serenade to a widow bent on marriage is akin to the Charivari, with musical and noise-making instruments, such as was customary in the mask processions of the French "mesnie Herlequin" and in performances of farce. Manuscript of Gervaise du Bus, before 1314. (Paris, Bibliothèque Nationale.)*

lar annual ceremony of violet picking, in which both the villagers and the court took part. In the early Neidhart play, the Duchess of Austria promises the Knight of Reuenthal to elect him her "May lover," if he leads her to the first violet.

With pipers in the vanguard, the lords and ladies of the court proceed in festive procession to the countryside along the Danube. Neidhart finds the flower that promises so much. He puts his hat down over it and hastens to apprise the Duchess of the "great joy." But the peasants, who have a bone to pick with Neidhart because of his mocking verses, spoil his triumph. When he arrives with the noble lady and with a flourish picks up the hat, there is under it something a good deal less sweetly scented than a violet.

This first version of the Neidhart play has come down to us in a fragment from the Benedictine monastery of St. Paul in Carinthia (dated around 1350). It was presumably meant to be recited by two minstrels and is theater in the sense that its subject is a spring festival on a bounded meadow; notwithstanding its rustic jokes it is still distinctive court poety. At the end, all join in a round dance to conclude the play in a general holiday mood.

In the larger, Tirolean version of the Neidhart play of the fifteenth century, the two-person recitation becomes a secular counterpart to the Passion play's wealth of scenes and cast. The setting has moved from the spring meadow into the city. No fewer than 103 performers participate in the play. Colorful stock-type costumes, vivid gestures, and coarse, humorous episodes acted with obvious relish in contrast to the courtly and elegant speech and dress of the knights turn the romance into a boisterous Shrovetide comedy. All hell is now let loose around the mishap with the violet; devils indulge in noisy argument, wooden-legged peasants trip it on the light fantastic toe, and old harridans get into a

Neidhart and the Violet. *Woodcut, presumed to be from an Augsburg edition. Before 1500.*

King David, followed by a fiddler and a lutist, dances in front of the Ark of the Covenant, which is drawn by a yoke of oxen. Miniature from the Bible of King Wenceslas IV, Codex Vindobon, 2960. *Ca. 1400. Bohemia's city and Court musicians were famous at that time. (Vienna, Österreichische Nationalbibliothek.)*

Title-page engraving for the Shrovetide play Der Ablasskrämer, *by Niklaus Manuel, 1525. (Berne, Stadtbibliothek.)*

row with the inn-keeper. It is like a preview of Hans Sachs who, in 1557, set his hand to rewriting the traditional Neidhart play into a Shrovetide *Schwank*.

Shrovetide Plays

The town councillors of the Free City of Nuremberg were men much concerned with propriety and public order. Since their spokesmen were intelligent men, they knew that the first thing to do was to guide entertainments into controllable channels. And so, on January 19, 1486, they signed and sealed a document stating that "Master Hans, the barber, and the rest of his kin" were to be allowed to perform a seemly Shrovetide play in verse, provided they observed the properties and took no money for it.

The Master Hans for whom this permit was intended was Hans Folz, a native of Worms, master surgeon and barber, who had come to Nuremberg in 1479 and soon became known as the producer and author of sturdy, comic Shrovetide plays. His activities found an ideal ground in Nuremberg, with its aristocratic constitution, its wealth, its civic and artisan pride, and its cultivation of the arts and sciences.

His predecessor, the Nuremberg brazier and gunsmith Hans Rosenplüt, had developed the old, traditional processional form, with its jokes of disguised identities discovered, into a new form of coarsely grotesque verse anecdote, the so-called *Schwank*. Hans Folz was known to his contemporaries and fellow craftsmen as the "Schnepperer." He not only struck mighty blows in the feud between the people of Nuremberg and the Margrave of Brandenburg, but also in his *Fastnachtsspiele*, or Shrovetide plays, in which he spoke out for the citizenry against the politically and morally declining knights. In one of the plays attributed to him, *Des Turken vasnachtspil*, he even went so far as to contrast the orient, "where the sun rises, and things are well and peaceful," with the corrupt state of affairs at home. To clinch the argument, the herald, who precedes and introduces the whole cortege of participants including the Turk's shield-bearer, makes the transparently critical announcement: "His country is called Grand Turkey, where no one has to pay interest." There ensue all sorts of brawls and violent threats between the knights and imperial and papal delegates, and the Grand Turk who reproaches the Christians with "arrogance, usury, and adultery." The Christians reply by warning the Mussulman that he is going to have his beard shorn off with sickles and his face washed with vinegar.

Two Nuremberg burghers have their work cut out to assure safe-conduct to the ill-treated guest. The Turk takes his leave of them with gratitude and blessings, and the herald announces a move on to another, better place. This is a frequent conclusion of Shrovetide plays, which suggests that, as in the original short scenes of the pageant, the whole thing started again a few streets further on.

A stage was easily provided without special preparation anywhere in a house or inn, where it was agreed in advance that the performance should take place. A flat boarding raised on barrels, a wall as background, and a door for the actors' entrances, perhaps a table or a chair serving as a courtroom bar, shop counter or throne—these were the simple props. The effect of these farces about knights, Jews and clerics, canon and procuress, of emperor and abbot, accusers and accused, physician and patient, peasant and noblewoman—they all owed everything to verbal wit. The townsfolk's vitality and buoyant enjoyment of life violated all the taboos, delighted in coarseness and plain speaking, in the realm of the sexual and the fecal, and in that of politics and morals.

When the fools have done with them, old women come out as young girls; sly justices of the peace take advantage of a grateful plaintiff if she happens to be a woman; a father promises his inheritance to the son who proves the most accomplished slanderer and loafer; lecherous peasants have to undergo punishments whose obscenity would have made a trooper blush.

A favorite subject of Shrovetide plays, and one used more than once by Hans Sachs, was the story of Aristotle and Phyllis. The triumph of female guile over erudition is a theme that had been exploited in the theater three thousand years earlier by the Sumerians. The resolute epigone Phyllis now managed to bring the mastermind to his knees and make him crawl on all fours, urging him on with the riding whip.

Another entertainment that was part and parcel of the Nuremberg Shrovetide merriments was the *Schembartlauf*, or *Schönbartlauf*, vestiges of which still survive in the popular customs of Bavaria, Austria, and the

The bold woman and the quiet woman. *Woodcut from a Shrovetide play, by Hans Folz. Nuremberg, ca. 1480.*

Storming the Schembart Hell, Nuremberg, 1539. Hell is represented by a ship on wheels, with people wearing devils' and birds' masks. (From the Schembart manuscript, Nor.K.444, Nuremberg, Stadtbibliothek.)

Festum asinorum *in a French cathedral, 15th century. (Paris, Bibliothèque de l'Arsenal.)*

"Aristotle and Phyllis," a theme that recurs in the Shrovetide plays by Hans Sachs, but can also be found in a Tuscan wall painting of the 14th century, at San Gimignano. Woodcut by Hans Burgkmair. (Berlin, Staatliche Museen, Kupferstichkabinett.)

Tirol. Etymologically, the word is rooted in the late middle-high German *schembart, schenebart,* which is a bearded mask. Goethe was familiar with it as an epitome of masquerade. "But tell me why," the Emperor asks in Part II of *Faust,* "in days so fair,/When we've withdrawn ourselves from care,/And beards of beauty masquerading wear. . . ."

The *Schembartlauf,* which from 1449 on was organized every year by Nuremberg's various guilds, occasionally entered into serious rivalry with the Shrovetide plays. The highly respectable merchants, especially those of a certain age, who were greatly addicted to this officially sanctioned entertainment, sometimes tried to steal the Shrovetide players' thunder. In 1516 the town council gave them a licence limited to only two days, "lest the *Schembart* discredit itself."

In the Alpine regions, the Shrovetide play and the *Schembartlauf* kept their close ties with popular customs. There was less, or at least less marked, controversy between city folk and peasants, and so the Tirolean *Schwank,* or comic anecdote, relied more on mother wit and good-natured humor. And since the South has always had a weakness for the North, the plays were shifted to King Arthur's court. The fame of the legendary Celtic king's heroic deeds had been spread during the eleventh and twelfth centuries by British and Breton minstrels and their lays, and was well-known in the Alemannic region. In Switzerland, King Arthur, the paragon of chivalrous rulers, had a companion in the Antichrist, turned into a figure of farce in the play *Des Entkrist Vasnacht.*

Shrovetide masque, 1484. Sketch from the armorial of Gerold Edlibach. (Staatsarchiv, Zurich.)

None of the improprieties of the Southern German, Austrian, Tirolean, and Swiss Shrovetide plays invaded the Lübeck clubs, the so-called *Zirkelgesellschaften.* The dignity of patrician manners ruled out any indecent jokes and obscenities. The tendency toward moral allegory was already in evidence in the Shrovetide plays. The administrative records of the Free Hansa City of Lübeck for the years 1430–1515 show that these clubs, which drew their members from patrician circles, organized performances of little comedies. Their stage was a scaffold set on a wagon—predestined by the very type of its cart stage to the same aspirations as the morality plays.

Farce and Sottie

"But let's get back to our sheep"—in other words, let us take the much-quoted *corpus delicti* as evidence that French esprit, too, did not despise the fool's garb. It is said that the words "Revenons à ces moutons" were first spoken on a stage near the Seine, at Rouen. They belong to a type of play the trenchant theatrical effect of which owes everything to Gallic wit: the farce.

Its origins can be traced back both to the fools' feasts and to dialogue recitations of wittily outspoken minstrels. It made a brilliant entrance into the history of literature and the theater with *Maistre Pierre Pathelin,* a play that deals with a swindler who has been swindled and with the aforesaid affair of the sheep. It was written by an unknown author and first performed around 1465. The undated first edition points to Rouen as its origin. The snappy dialogue, the polished phrases

Maistre Pierre Pathelin. *Woodcut from a 1490 edition.*

verging on coarse drollery betray inside knowledge of the contemporary lawyers' profession. Later fellow authors, from Rabelais through Grimmelshausen to Reuchlin's *Henno* and Kotzebue's *Kleinstädter,* have borrowed the trusty "muttons" quote.

Maistre Pierre Pathelin, after whom the farce is named, is a distinguished lawyer, an ornament of his profession. Nevertheless he not only has no scruples, but takes positive pleasure in swindling his neighbor, the draper Guillaume out of the price of a few yards of the best cloth. In addition, he undertakes to defend a shepherd whom Guillaume accuses of stealing sheep. After his client's acquittal, however, Pathelin is cheated of his own reward. He has drilled the shepherd to act the nitwit and to answer nothing but "Baa-baa" to every question in court; when it now comes to the payment of the lawyer's fee, all Pathelin gets instead of hard cash is—"Baa-baa."

The heart of the play, of course, is the trial, which gets hopelessly bogged down in a confusion of irrelevancies. In vain the judge keeps trying to bring the litigants back to the point with his "Revenons à ces moutons."

Social criticism and satire found a welcome outlet in the farce. Its originators were jurists and scribes, students and civic acting associations, wandering scholars, merchants, and craftsmen. Foremost in wit and originality were the law-clerks' associations known as *Basoches,* which had been established during the fourteenth century in Paris and in the provinces. These associations held annual meetings at which they organized pantomimes and short farcical dialogues. They had an inexhaustible fund of themes in trial scenes, fictitious law cases, and matters of jurisdiction seen in the distorting mirror of humorous self-irony. No doubt, the anonymous author of *Maistre Pierre Pathelin* came from a *Basoche* background. There is historical proof that the origins of the farce go back to an edict of the Prévot of Paris dated 1398; and these origins widen out with the performances of the Paris *Basoches du Palais,* documented from 1442 on. These were preferably scheduled for Shrove Tuesday and, reaching a public well beyond the circle of members, were widely acclaimed as entertaining "fools' plays."

The farce had no scruples. Its effectiveness depended on self-irony, on mockery of current abuses, on the impudence with which political polemics were camouflaged as seemingly harmless allegories. When Marshal Pierre de Rohan had to pay for his state trial against Anne of Brittany with defamation at court, Paris had a farce to laugh at. A farrier trying to shoe a she-ass is rewarded for his pains by a hefty kick of her hindleg. Everyone knew what the crude joke meant. The annexation of Brittany to France, the political shoeing, had been Rohan's misfired scheme.

However, too blunt a spirit of aggressiveness could mean an aftermath in court even in fifteenth-century France. In 1486 the Paris *Basoches* put on a farce in which the young king Charles VIII was allegorically represented by a clear spring "muddied by the courtiers, so that they could the better fish in troubled waters." This was poking one's finger into a hornets' nest. The victims of the insult caused the author and organizer of the play, Henri Baude, to be arrested together with the actors. But Parliament saw no reason to convict them and, almost in secret connivance, set them all free again.

The farce triumphed. Eventually, it even found its way into high society. When, in 1499, the archbishop's palace at Avignon was made ready for the visit of the notorious Cesare Borgia, no effort was spared to gain the goodwill of this unpredictable guest. And so the cobbler Jean Bellieti, an obscure forerunner of Hans Sachs, was instructed to oblige with a presentable farce. History is silent about the outcome of this enterprise. At any rate, Cesare departed from the palace in a friendly enough mood. And when Bellieti later fell into poverty, he was kept going by public funds, "for he deserved well of the city because of his plays and farces."

Like its first cousin, the Shrovetide play, the farce made no technical demands on the stage. A simple podium, a few means of entry from the sides or the back—rather as on the Terence stage—were amply sufficient. The farce lived on verbal wit, regardless of whether its stage was set up in a public hall, a university lecture room, a private house, or an archbishop's palace. Comic situations and comic characters, mistaken identities, and plots to dupe someone offered splendid opportunities for star turns and thus were an incentive for professional mimes to come to the aid of the amateurs and earn special applause.

What the cast lacked in acting routine, it made up in costumes and masks. The carefully combed beard of the pompous philistine, the lawyer striking attitudes in wig and gown, the bold headdress of the cocotte, the dandy costume of the courtiers, and the bell cap of the fool identified the persons and the milieu of the farce and of its twin, the *sottie.* Farce and *sottie* provided so much the same entertainment for performers and public alike that it is almost impossible to draw a precise distinction between them. The heroes of the farce are fools in common or court dress—the heroes of the *sottie,* common folk and courtiers in fools' dress.

The *sottie* is closely connected with the Paris *Enfants sans souci* and innumerable other groups of a similar kind that were set up throughout France in the fifteenth century. Each had its own statutes, its own fool's king, its *Prince des sots,* and its *Mère des sots.* In concept and image they were actually much older. Ever since the twelfth century, a bracket carving on the south tower of Chartres Cathedral had shown a fat and ugly fools' mother supporting a lyre-playing ass.

Fools' prince and the fools' mother are the title roles of the best-known play by Pierre Gringoire of Paris, author of satires and *sotties.* His *Jeu du prince des sots et de la mère sotte* was performed on Shrove Tuesday in 1512 in Paris; it was a sharp polemic against the church, a panorama of the age in fool's guise.

Gringoire was a member of the Paris *Enfants sans souci,* and it was not for naught that he was Louis XII's favorite. The king could not have wished for a better propagandist in his controversy with Pope Julius II. The *sottie,* acted in fool's costume, was the sixteenth century's political cabaret. Apart from writing *sotties,* Pierre Gringoire, just as his contemporary Jean Bochet, also acted as *magister ludi* at performances of mystery plays. In addition, he wrote a play extolling the exploits of Saint Louis, and was a successful theater manager, too. Gringoire is idealized and immortalized in Victor Hugo's novel *The Hunchback of Notre Dame.*

Sotternieën, Klucht Plays, and Peasant Plays

Falstaff, as we know him from *The Merry Wives of Windsor,* had many predecessors, as a boon companion, a merry sponger, and even in the basket affair. In the Dutch theater, he had an ancestor in Mijnheer Werrenbracht, though here the story was in reverse; he was a respectable burgher, plagued by destiny and his fellowmen. He had himself carried in a basket into his own home, in order to surprise his spouse while flirting with a priest.

Molière's Tartuffe was on the way. But for the time being, there

Title page of Jeu du prince des sots et de la mere sotte *by Pierre Gringoire, performed in Paris in 1512.*

Street stage in France, ca. 1540. Drawing. (Ms. 126, Cambrai, Bibliothèque Municipale.)

Performance of a French farce in Paris, around 1580. Engraving by Jean de Gourmont.

were the Dutch burlesques, the *Sotternieën* and *Klucht* plays, crude and robust, a bridge between the French farce and the German *Fastnachtsspiel.* Their colors are rich and fast, their humor hearty, and saturated with the same easy self-irony that is the mark of the peasant folk in the paintings of Pieter Brueghel the Elder. The *Klucht* play that is in progress in his painting of the "Kermess," among a happy crowd enjoying their food, drink, and dance, could well be about Mijnheer Werrenbracht. There is a woman at the table with an amorous swain, and a fellow with a heavy load in a basket on his back is entering the stage. The prospect is clearly not peaceful. From backstage, behind the curtain, someone is being handed a footstool. It is easy to imagine the brawl that will follow.

The *Sotternieën* and *Klucht* plays had been preceded by the fools' companies' *Vastenavondgrappen,* the Dutch version of the Shrovetide plays with their mummeries and mistaken identities. The municipal accounts of Dendermonde referred in 1413 to the old-established custom of offering the young folk "amusing plays" at Shrovetide, "goede solaselike spele," such as were performed on cart stages.

These pranks used the same theatrical forms as the Corpus Christi and the legend plays. The *Sotternieën* went beyond them to approach the function of the satyr plays of antiquity. They formed the lighthearted rearguard of a specifically Dutch form of drama that had sprung up in Brabant around 1350; these were the *Abelespele,* learned dramatic productions, which in the sixteenth century were to become the specialty of the *Rederijkers.* In fourteenth- and fifteenth-century Holland as elsewhere, notwithstanding the worthiest rules of poetry, the farce had its recognized place. At the end of the *Abelespele,* the spectators were enjoined to give their kind attention also to the concluding *Sotternie.*

At the time burlesques and peasant plays, which were on the same level as the *Sotternieën* and *Klucht* plays, were becoming popular throughout Europe. In Italy, the students of the University of Pavia performed *Ianus sacerdos* in 1427 and *Commedia del falso Ypocrito* in 1437, both of them plays that combined local satire with scholastic larks.

A Sienese group, the *Congrega dei Rozzi,* was so successful with its peasant plays that it was invited to perform in Rome and at the Vatican. One of its most active members was the author, actor, and manager Niccolò Campani, a man so talented as to rank closely to the famous "Ruzzante," Angelo Beolco of Padua: both were, in their work, on the very threshold of the *Commedia dell'arte.* Campani became the talk of the town in Rome under the name "Strascino," his favorite part in one of his own plays. Pope Leo X was not sparing with his favors, and in 1518 "Lo Strascino" appeared at an Orsini wedding where, after the

Street stage in Holland, ca. 1610. Detail from a copper engraving with fair-ground scenes. After a 1610 painting attributed to David Vinckboons, in the Koninklijk Museum voor schone Kunsten, Antwerp.

Klucht *play at a peasant fair in the 16th century. Detail from a painting of the Flemish school, after P. Brueghel the Elder. (Vienna, Kunsthistorisches Museum.)*

appearance of a few other comedians, he was acclaimed as a solo interpreter of his own texts.

But unlike his contemporary "Ruzzante," whose plays were still being printed in the sixteenth century, "Strascino" made as little mark upon the history of literature as did all the nameless burlesque and peasant actors who, in the tradition of antiquity's mimes, took up the popular themes of past and present—from the Bohemian ointment vendor *Mastičkar* to the Turkish *Karagöz.*

They all shared the common, simple stage—mere boards raised on barrels or wooden posts at the fair, no matter whether the dress of actors and public was that of Italian, Slav, or Dutch peasants and townsfolk. Theirs was the wisdom of jesters and fools, timeless and at home anywhere in the world. The Danish playwright Ludvig Holberg epitomized it at the end of his comedy *The Lying-in*: "Now you have seen, good folk, that it's no good worrying; you just end up as a fool and people laugh at you."

Allegories and Morality Plays

In late antiquity, around 400, the orator Prudentius wrote a work in praise of Christianity called *Psychomachia.* Its theme—the struggle of virtues and vices for the soul of man—was to become a favorite with the morality plays a thousand years later. Prudentius had been the first to personify the basic concepts of Christian ethics. He had talked of Ecclesia and Synagoga, of the Prince of this World and the Wheel of Fortune. Since then, the early medieval sculptors and miniaturists had long depicted them before the theater came to see how useful they could be on the stage.

Ecclesia and Synagoga, Hypocrisy and Heresy had indeed appeared earlier, in the Tegernsee *Antichrist,* and here and there in some Passion play; but it was not until the fifteenth century that they were given a direct function in the action. Georges Chastellain, chronicler and diplomat at the court of Philip the Good, duke of Burgundy, in 1431 wrote and produced a play called *Le concile de Bâle.* Its allegorical figures included not only Ecclesia and Heresy, but Peace, Justice, and eventually the Council of Basel itself. They are not, as in the legend and Passion plays, mere cornerstones of the spiritual-religious superstructure, but active protagonists of the play itself.

The personification of the conceptual world was in line with the fifteenth century's growing efforts to look behind things, to discover the essential relevance of "morals." For the theater this meant that the traditional abstractions ceased to be venerable figures relegated to the frame, the prelude or postlude, and became the very subject of the plays.

Thus the students of the Paris Collège de Navarre in 1426 made a morality play out of a sermon given by the University's chancellor and "doctor christianissimus" Jean de Gerson. Reason appeared as a "bona magistra," and her pupils were the human sense organs, whose task it was to resist the world's temptations and to uphold the Christian teaching of virtue. The heart of the play was the inevitable trial scene, an exercise in dialectical disputation, in this case a natural consequence of the theme itself, under the auspices of the "bona magistra."

The stage and scenery of the early morality plays were unpretentious. Since the theological and pedagogical elements were dominant and the performance served as a test of rhetoric, all that was needed was a podium. Clear diction was of the essence and, in the case of students' performances, well-rehearsed declamation. Nor was much fancy needed for the costumes. The "bona magistra" wore a long scholar's gown, Ecclesia a crown, Synagoga a bandage over her eyes, and the scholars were identified by their birettas.

On the other hand, the performance of the morality play *Bien avisé, mal avisé* at Rennes in 1439 made considerable claims both on the purse and the power of invention. The rivalry between "Well-advised" and "Ill-advised" was elaborated in 8,000 lines and required a cast of sixty. The Wheel of Fortune had to turn on the stage, and at the moment of his death "Well-advised" had to be carried off to heaven by angels. The morality stage availed itself of the technical achievements of the Passion play, and in the second half of the century became its equal also as regards length of performance and wealth of content.

Several days were needed in 1476 for the performance of *L'homme juste et l'homme mondain"* at Tarascon. The author of this play, Simon Bougoin, valet of Louis XII, deployed a "véritable carnaval d'allégories." Mondain, the worldly man, happily falls in with all the personified vices, whereas Juste, his counterpart, turns a deaf ear to them in Christian renunciation.

In this case the allegorical figures undoubtedly required some underscoring by means of originality of costume. The same applies to the 1494 performance at Tours of *L'homme pécheur,* the sinner whose soul "ascends" at the end while his corpse "rots" on the ground—and also to the famous *Condamnation de Banquet,* printed in Paris in 1507 and no doubt also staged around the same time.

The author and producer of this morality play, Nicolas de la Chesnaye, presents against a medical background a broad survey of physical and mental hygiene, written partly with Rabelaisian profanity and partly with would-be sophisticated *esprit.* Diner, Souper, and Banquet try to put each other in the wrong and—with the help of Bonne-Compagnie, Gourmandise, Passe-temps, and personified toasts—saddle each other with the whole pack of evils attendant upon good living, including Colic, Gout, Jaundice, Apoplexy and Dropsy. The entire medical compendium is passed in review. Souper and Banquet end up before the court. Hippocrates and Galen act as assessors. Souper is condemned henceforth to wear "manchettes de plomb" (lead cuffs) as a safeguard against any relapse into gluttony, but Banquet is sentenced to death by hanging. His hangman is Diet.

In this ambitious work Nicolas de la Chesnaye provides a wealth of information about table manners, the art of serving and dishing up, as well as about table music. He describes in detail in what costumes his characters are to appear. Moderation, Diet, and all other servants of Dame Expérience appear in men's dress and speak with men's voices, because they have executive functions at the court of law and "concern themselves with things to which men are more prone than women." The fool wears his traditional cap with asses' ears, a suit of many colors, bells on his doublet and on his shoes—no different from his brother in Jean Fouquet's miniature of the mystery of St. Apollonia, or from all his kin in manuscript miniatures, ivories, enamels, wall paintings, in the boundless wealth of medieval pictorial representations.

A century was holding a mirror up to itself and got its image back a thousandfold. The mirror reflected the caricatures of dissipation and gluttony against the background of jurisprudence, medicine, and philosophy, mobilizing the full forces of the parable, but it also showed, in the most modest setting, what difficulties honest lower-middle-class parents have "nowadays" with their children. These children, *Les enfants de Maintenant*, are the sons of a baker. One of them, Finet, ends on the gallows, whereas the other, Malduict, is only just disciplined into better ways by the cane. A clever pedagogue had written this unpretentious but instructive play for a students' performance. *La moralité* was an instrument as sensitively responsive in the humdrum setting of everyday life as on the richly furnished allegorical battlefield.

Throughout the continent of Europe, the morality plays were increasingly invaded by scepticism; truth is rejected everywhere in the world, faith is sought but never found and, eventually, in the Lübeck *Henselyn*, the fool's wisdom prevails once more, as it had done in the Shrovetide plays.

In England, meanwhile, the morality plays gained a firm footing. England indeed shares with France the honors of being the classical home of the genre. As early as 1378 John Wiclif refers to an allegorical "play of the Lord's Prayer," performed in his native Yorkshire. Again in 1399, a York document mentions a guild of the Lord's Prayer, which clearly performed Paternoster plays every year. Other, similar records from Lincoln and Beverley are extant.

Virtues and the Deadly Sins, Good Fame and Disgrace, Sloth and Avarice, Wit and Science were pitted against each other in the English morality play with no less didactic purpose and rhetoric than in the Continent's dramatized lectures on ethics. The English morality play reached its zenith with *The Castle of Perseverance,* performed in 1425. Three plays in all are contained in the manuscript of the so-called Macro Morals, which in addition includes a detailed stage plan—among the earliest, if not the first, theatrical designs in England.

The manuscript consists of four parts, "The Banns," an announcement of the play in the form of a prologue, the play itself, a list of characters and, on the last page, the stage plan. Richard Southern has published an exhaustive investigation of all aspects of the stage techniques involved in his book *The Medieval Theatre in the Round* (1957) and, with the help of the text and the plan, has reconstructed the whole performance.

Two flag bearers announced the play in nearby villages and towns a week before the performance. They took their leave with the hope of meeting their "fair friends" again as good listeners on the day of the performance. This proclamation corresponded to a general custom of actors' troupes (though we have no comparable other medieval texts), and circus people have preserved it to this day.

The setting of *The Castle of Perseverance,* which the public found upon arrival, was unique and without any parallel on the continent. It was a circular stage area, surrounded by a water ditch and a mound of earth (or palisades) as tall as a man. In the center stood the "Castle," a battlemented tower, and around its periphery the "scaffolds" for God, World, Satan, Flesh, and Covetousness. The scaffolds, according to Southern's reconstruction, were made on the same principles and looked the same as the "mansions" of Fouquet's Apollonia miniature. Each of the five scaffolds was closed off by a curtain. As the play begins, the curtain of the "World" scaffold is the first to be opened and World introduces himself and his kin, Voluptas, Stulticia, and a Boy. Next comes Satan (Belyal) and Flesh (Caro). They announce that they are busy night and day to destroy Mankind. The little soul of Mankind, "this night . . . of my mother born," which now begins to move under the central tower (which Southern places on four high legs, so that the bed below is visible to all), is invested by every possible sort of temptation. He withstands the siege well, but in old age, when the sorely tried poor soul already believes itself to be beyond good and evil, the powers of destruction mount the final attack. Satan spits fire and smoke. Salvation seems forfeited. But Mercy intervenes and conducts the poor soul of man to God's throne. "Pater sedens in trono" speaks the final words from his scaffold, addressing the assembled audience and actors: "So endeth our games. To save you from sinning,/Ever at the beginning/ Think on your last ending."

There is a striking analogy between the circular scene of *The Castle*

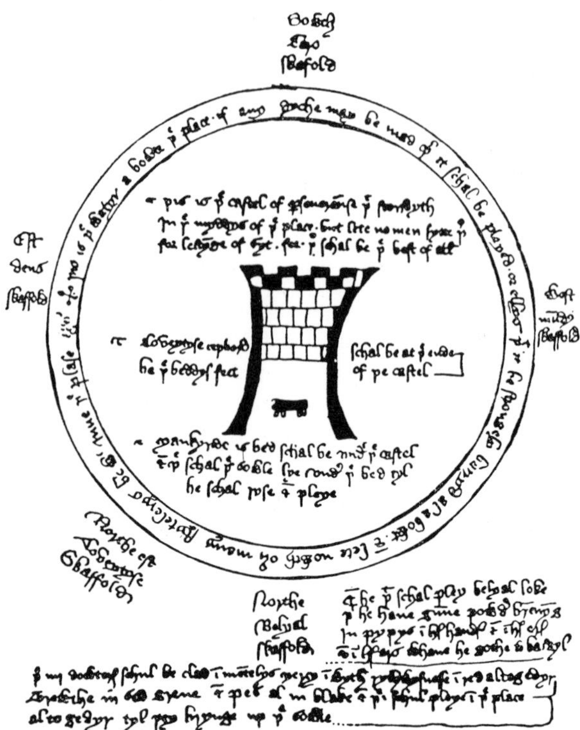

Plan of the theater for The Castle of Perseverance, *1425. From the Macro Morals manuscript.*

Plan of the theater for The Castle of Perseverance, *1425. Tentative reconstruction by Richard Southern.*

of Perseverance and that of the Cornish Rounds. To the best of our knowledge, the theater in the round was unknown on the continent as a distinct medieval theater form. The only approximate parallel is a theoretical one, to wit, the early Humanists' conception of staging Terence, as exemplified in the miniatures of *Térence des Ducs,* dated around 1400. The actors, designated as *joculatoirs,* wear clearly recognizable half-masks and are closer in style to the *Commedia dell'arte* than to the Middle Ages. In both cases, however, we find an almost total absence of decoration. Gesticulation and movement had to be highly artful to create the illusion, to make visible the invisible. In between, the medieval performer was allowed to act out of character, to return to ordinary life, like the "poor scholar" Johannes in the Innsbruck Easter play, and like the characters of the twentieth-century's epic theater—say, Thornton Wilder's Antrobus family in *The Skin of Our Teeth* or Pirandello's *Six Characters in Search of an Author.*

In the last play of the three English Macro Morals, called *Mankind* and written down about 1475, one of the actors steps forward at the most exciting moment of the performance and announces that the chief devil Titivillus can make his appearance as announced only on condition that a collection that has just started among the public brings in enough money. The jump from the theatrical plane to that of reality had a thoroughly substantial, definite aim. The small cast of *Mankind,* consisting of only five to seven performers, most probably put on the play not in connection with some guild event, but on their own account and for their own profit. They probably were a strolling troupe and had to do all they could to make sure of their money before the public dispersed at the end of the play.

Back in courtly society and under the auspices of an influential patron, the morality play *Nature* ("A goodly interlude of Nature") was performed in 1495 before Cardinal Morton of Canterbury. It was written by Morton's chaplain Henry Medwall, who was also the author of England's first known secular play, the interlude *Fulgens and Lucrece.* So far as the theater is concerned, he is forgotten.

But not forgotten to this day, and as alive as ever, is an unknown author's work: *Everyman.* While scholars worry whether to concede priority to the first English edition of 1509 or to the 1495 Delft publication of *Spyeghel der Salicheyt van Elckerlijk,* the theater has kept its faith with him for close on 500 years.

It was Hugo von Hofmannsthal who recast *Everyman* into the form of *Jedermann,* in which he is now also known the world over. And Salzburg has become the twentieth-century's Everyman's city, thanks to its performances in the cathedral square. The play preserves a reflection of the late medieval morality stage—the multiple settings, the colorful

Theater of antiquity, as conceived by the early Humanists. Representation of Calliopius as recitator *and, to the left in the lower half of the picture, of the playwright Terence. Miniature from* Térence des Ducs, *early 15th century. (Paris, Bibliothèque de l'Arsenal.)*

Everyman. *Title page from an edition by John Skot, ca. 1520.*

glow of allegory, the roots in a religious conception of the world—even when it has to be moved indoors because of rain. As the English *Everyman* of old, it grips theater pilgrims from the four corners of the world, even though some sceptical, contemporary critics wonder whether "this artfully naive simplification of the theme of guilt and atonement is still valid," and even though the majority of the spectators possibly give no thought to the question whether and to what extent this is a last offshoot of the medieval theater.

The Renaissance

INTRODUCTION

Jacob Burckhardt has said that the two mainsprings of the Renaissance were the freeing of the individual and the awakening of personality. Lonely on the summits of literature, Dante and Petrarch had dreamed of the rebirth of man in the spirit of antiquity. Among the painters, Giotto had initiated the departure from the formal Byzantine code. But it was not until the end of the fifteenth century that the new outlook spread and the medieval scholastic view of the world was finally left behind. Decisive influences emanated from the circles of Roman and Florentine humanists.

The fall of Constantinople had made the works of Greek writers accessible to the West. Thousands of Byzantine scholars took along on their flight to the West their most precious treasures, the ancient manuscripts. The monasteries that sheltered the exiles piled up spiritual riches awaiting exploration.

Pope Paul II established the first printing press in Rome in 1467, which issued works in Greek. It was followed in Venice by the press of Aldus Manutius and the long series of Aldine classics. The Renaissance became the great age of discovery in the realms of the intellect and of geography. The seafarers explored new lands and seas on this earth, to which at the same moment Copernicus denied its central position in the universe and assigned the rank of a star among stars. For the first time, Christianity was facing antiquity on a broad front.

Nicholas of Cusa had tried to apprehend God as the "unity of contrasts." The worldly popes of the Renaissance had no trouble at all reconciling the seemingly irreducible contradiction between the Christian faith in another world and antiquity's addiction to this one. Sixtus IV had his sumptuous banquets served with mythological garnish. Julius II commissioned the young Raphael to paint a life-size *School of Athens* for the Vatican apartments—a pictorial expression of the desire to achieve a harmonious synthesis of antiquity and Christianity in the ideal of the Platonic Academy. Walking in procession from the Vatican to the Lateran Church of St. John, Leo X passed pedestals bearing statues of Apollo, Ganymede, Minerva, and Venus. He allowed his servants the carnival entertainment of a battle of oranges in front of the Castel Sant'Angelo and, on the point of setting out for a deer hunt, signed the bull excommunicating the German Augustine monk Martin Luther.

The Spanish and German mercenaries of Emperor Charles V invaded the eternal city, and their sack and pillage put an abrupt end to the flowering of the arts and extravagances. But although the old St. Peter's fell victim to the sack of Rome in 1527, the vitality of the Vatican did not. Michelangelo was commissioned to design a mighty dome for the new cathedral.

In the waning Middle Ages, monasticism and chivalry had already ceded their leading role to the rising middle classes. Guilds, corporations, and what contemporary records call vernacular academies became vital forces in cultural life. The humanists' interest in the drama converged with the popular delight in playacting.

England broke loose from the papacy under Henry VIII. The rivalry for the throne between his daughter Elizabeth I and Mary Stuart, Queen of Scots, was a clash of power politics no less than of religious ones. Protestantism was spreading across the whole of northern Europe. Fostered by the self-confidence of England's rising world power, the Elizabethan theater flowered on the banks of the Thames under the star of Shakespeare. The imperial courts of Paris and Vienna began to unfold their own monarchic splendor. Paris and Madrid, under Francis I and Philip II, became new centers of European power politics. But it was from Italy that the world took its cue in matters of the sciences and arts, poetry and diplomacy, culture and education.

The proud dictum of the age of the Caesars, "all roads lead to Rome," proved true for the second time in world history. While in the past the victorious legions had carried the culture of the Roman imperium to three continents, Italy's spiritual forces now drew the whole of Europe into their magnetic field.

If a milestone were to be erected for the "renaissance" of the theater, it would have to bear the date 1486. This is when the first tragedy by Seneca was staged in Rome by the humanists, and the first comedy by Plautus by the Duke of Ferrara. It was also the year when Vitruvius's *Ten Books on Architecture* appeared in print, a work that did much to shape the stage and the theater after the model of antiquity.

THE THEATER OF THE HUMANISTS

When Nicholas of Cusa, a young graduate in law at Mainz, in 1429 discovered the texts of twelve comedies by Plautus, hitherto known only by name, he hailed his find as a gain for scholarly rhetoric rather than for the theater. Similarly, a Terence commentary by Donatus, found soon afterwards by Cardinal Giovanni Auspira at Mainz, only aroused the interest of scholars. A certain Magister Johann Mandel, a native of Amberg, gave a lecture at the University of Vienna in 1455 about Terence's *Adelphi*, which he regarded as a subject for the humanities and the practice of language—an aspect stressed earlier by scholasticism and still crucial for Erasmus of Rotterdam at the beginning of the sixteenth century. "Without Terence," he declared, "no one has yet become a good Latinist."

A philologist in Rome and a Renaissance prince at Ferrara were the first to rescue the drama of antiquity from its petrified state as a mere subject of learning. They returned it to the stage in tangible and visible form. In 1486 Pomponius Laetus staged a performance of Seneca's *Hippolytus* in Rome; at the same time, Plautus's *Menaechmi* was staged at the court of the Estes in Ferrara. What never happened in Seneca's lifetime was, fifteen hundred years later, now made up for on the highest academic level. The most famous humanists of Rome took part in the production; Sulpitius Verolanus wrote the prologue, and the part of Phaedra was taken by Tommaso Inghirami, a pupil of Pomponius and later favorite of Pope Alexander VI. The financial patron of the performance was the Spanish cardinal Riario, its director was Pomponius Laetus, and it was first staged in the Forum. This was followed by a repeat performance before Pope Innocence VIII in the Castle Sant'-Angelo, and another in the Palazzo Riario.

The dramatic event was combined with a deliberate reconstruction of the antique stage. Sulpitius Verolanus, who was preparing Vitruvius's *Ten Books on Architecture* for print, furnished his friend Pomponius Laetus with reliable information about the old Roman *scenae frons,* which is described in detail in the fifth book of the great work on architecture.

Here was final refutation of all the vague and misleading concepts of the theater in the round of antiquity, found in medieval manuscripts. Even the medieval scholastics had still assumed that a learned reader recited the text, while masked *joculatores* represented it in pantomime. The last and most splendid testimonial to this view, based partly on errors of translation and partly on sheer imagination, is the *Térence des*

Ducs, a French manuscript dating from the beginning of the fifteenth century. Its full-page miniatures surrounded by luxuriant ornamentation show, instead of the spacious round of the ancient theater, a closely packed, narrow cylinder. In the center, flanked by musicians, stands the *recitator* in a curtained booth designated as "scena"; in front of him the "joculatoirs" are acting, surrounded by the public, "populus romanus." The speaker is named Calliopius, by a completely unfounded reference to the third-century Latin grammarian Calliopius, who is not known to have engaged in any theatrical activity. He was assigned this strange part of a tacit, posthumous convention whose origins have disappeared.

The "authentic," Vitruvius-inspired stage for *Hippolytus* looked quite different. It adopted the principle of the Roman *scaenae frons* with the row of access doors, only transposed from the old pillared splendors to a wooden, makeshift stage. This latter, as Sulpitius Verolanus explained in his introduction to the Vitruvius edition published in 1486, immediately after the performance, had a height of five feet and was fitted out with a "great variety of color effects." Presumably, this refers to the painted back wall of a standard setting.

Compared with the rich scenery of the late medieval multiple settings—to recall only the rotating spheres of the microcosm constructed in 1438 by Brunelleschi for the *sacra rappresentazione* at the Feast of the Annunciation in Florence—the early humanist theater looked very modest indeed. The text mattered more than any efforts at artistry in stage effect. Seneca, Terence, and Plautus were dominant as masters of language and fluent speech, as prototypes of a cultivated way of life (with Plautus being the model for robust, quick repartee and Terence for urbane and polished wit), as a standard for everything that the drama had to contribute to the new image of man.

In 1513, in the Capitoline Square (now the Piazza del Campodoglio), Terence's *Poenulus* was performed. For this famous gala production the whole square (between the palace of the Senatori and that of the Conservatori) was transformed into a huge *theatrum* that was covered by an awning. The action took place on an open forestage with five access doors. Tommaso Inghirami, who had in the meantime advanced to the post of Vatican librarian and had been crowned with the poet's laurel by Maximilian I, supervised the production, entirely in the spirit of his teacher Pomponius Laetus. Special praise was bestowed on the cultivated Latin pronunciation of his actors, the "handsomest young men of Roman nobility."

During the thirty years Pomponius Laetus devoted to theatrical applications of his teaching of rhetoric, his lecture room was the meeting place of Europe's young scholars. While the aspiring jurists went to Bologna and the world-be physicians to Padua, the students of philosophy and rhetoric flocked to Rome, to the Platonic academy of Pomponius Laetus.

Konrad Celtes, the German humanist and roving teacher, became acquainted in Ferrara and Rome with the practical revival of the ancient theater. Jodocus Badius, classical philologist and an important collaborator in the 1493 Lyons edition of Terence, also called on the Pomponians during his study tour of Italy. In 1497, when the Pforzheim humanist Johann Reuchlin staged his *Henno,* a play in the tradition of the French Pathelin farce, he made use of what he had seen and learned while visiting Rome in 1482 and 1490. The Freiburg university professor Jacob Locher took advantage of the theatrical impressions he had gained in 1492 and 1493 in Italy and more especially at Ferrara when, in 1497, he wrote *Tragedia de Thurcis et Suldano,* a play in the manner of Celtes.

The theater of the humanists grew out of their activity of teaching and was developed by academic societies specially founded for the purpose. It enjoyed high esteem both south and north of the Alps. Universities and Latin schools put up improvised stage scaffolds in their yards. Cardinals and princes liked to be patrons of the theater; emperors, kings, and popes called to their courts poets, actors, and painters to organize festivities.

The art of dramatic speech, domesticated by the school theater for pedagogical and didactic applications, was combined in the courtly program of festivities with the patterns of procession and homage. In the pastoral play it took on a sentimental grace; in tragedy it submitted to the newly rediscovered Aristotelian rule of the unities and, eventually, helped the first topically relevant historical themes to gain the stage.

While painters and sculptors glorified the here and now, the stage answered with the historical drama, offered in the great manner of tragedy—which alone, as Jean de la Taille put it, was "worthy of serious men." The medieval theater, he wrote in his treatise *L'art de la tragédie,* had descended to the level of servants and low persons—a harsh judgment, explained both by the arrogance of the French intellectual aristocracy of the sixteenth century and by the often coarsened tone of the late mystery plays. For his own dramas, which he meant to be exemplary, Jean de la Taille nonetheless chose biblical themes. He introduced the book version of his *Saul furieux* (1560) with an interpretation of the Aristotelian three unities, brought the multiple settings together in a single set, and specifically directed in the text that Mount Gilboa and the Cave of Endor should be close together (*icy pres*). Unavowedly, he took over the late medieval platform stage with multiple settings in order to give his drama the required unity of place "selon l'art et la mode des vieux Autheurs tragiques." As Jean de la Taille put it, the dramatist's task was so to mix good and evil, passion and sentiment, that they combined in a clearly defined action—in the sense of the Renaissance—to convey "a true imitation of human life, in which sorrow and joy follow each other and vice versa."

In Aristotle the humanists found the necessary ancient authority for the drama, in harmony with the Vitruvian rules for the form of the stage. The playwright's problem of form and time was the counterpart of the artist's problem of space. The theater of the humanists tried to do justice to both. It did its best to face up to the medieval heritage of the past with a new, contrasting theory of art modeled on antiquity, and so to prepare an intellectual and theatrical foundation for the new Renaissance spirit.

Humanist Tragedy

The Spanish cardinal Riario, generous patron of the first Roman performances of Seneca, in 1492 handed Pomponius Laetus a historical drama that he was particularly anxious to see produced—Carlo Verardi's *Historia Baetica*. Its subject was taken from contemporary history: the Spanish city of Granada's recent liberation from Moorish rule. The play was performed in the Palazzo Riario, in honor of the Cardinal, who was understandably involved. It was acted by students of the Pomponian academy, no doubt with the authorization, but without the artistic participation of Pomponius Laetus himself (as Max Herrmann has proved in *Entstehung der berufsmäßigen Schauspielkunst im Altertum und in der Neuzeit*). The topicality of the play could not disguise its literarly inadequacy from the great Roman humanist: for Pomponius Laetus remained unmoved—faithful to the peerless models of antique tragedy. The novel creations of the day fell far short of the standards acceptable to this exacting scholar.

The humanist tragedy took to dark paths. In its attempt to mete out to its heroes a destiny of antique doom, it wallowed in blood and horror.

While Trissino took his lead fairly objectively from ancient tragedy, both in his *Arte poetica,* based on Aristotle, and in his model drama *Sofonisba,* written in 1515, the Ferrarese professor of philosophy and rhetoric Giovanni Battista "Cinthio" Giraldi had the ambition of outdoing the horrors of the legend of Atreus. In 1541 he arranged a performance in his own house of his tragedy *Orbecche,* in which horror was piled upon horror. Incest, the murder of husband and grandchildren, patricide, and eventually the suicide of the unfortunate princess Orbecche led in a mounting crescendo to a pandemonium of Nemesis and the Furies. Fear and terror dominated the stage and gripped the spectators. "Horrible" was the watchword Giraldi chose for himself in his *Discorso delle commedie e delle tragedie* (1543), involving Aristotle. He became a forerunner of the French baroque classics and of Lessing in his interpretation of the Aristotelian catharsis as purification of the passions by fear and terror.

In the dramatic construction of his horror tragedies, which later he mitigated somewhat, Giraldi retained the antique unity of place and action. In *Orbecche,* the scene is set in front of the palace; the murders perpetrated inside the building are reported by messengers and the chorus.

Giraldi unleashed a whole flood of learned dramas, and his prose tales were used by the greatest writers in world literature. His *Moro di Venezia* was the source for Shakespeare's *Othello.* The theme of incest appeared so seductive to Sperone Speroni, professor of literature and philosophy at Padua, that he wrote a tragedy called *Canace* modelled on *Orbecche.* He managed to arouse the interest of his gifted compatriot, the manager of an actors' troupe Angelo Beolco, who was to provide a connecting link between the learned *Commedia erudita* and the professional *Commedia dell'arte.*

The theater itself, however, took no part in the violent controversy among the academies, which Speroni sparked off with the publication of his work in 1542 and which continued beyond his death. Court society and the Curia were more amused by the wit of comedy than by the grim fury of tragedy, and left the literary circles to fall out among themselves about the pros and cons of artistic principles.

At the French court, meanwhile, the "tragédie à l'antique" aroused great interest. In Paris, the Pléiade, the group of writers led by Pierre de Ronsard, also set out to refashion the stage after the classical model. This reform movement was strengthened by the 1548 prohibition of the performance of mystery plays. Étienne Jodelle was unanimously acclaimed in 1552 by the Paris aristocracy for his tragedy *Cléopatre captive,* which took its subject from Plutarch. The twenty-year old author himself took the part of Cleopatra. King Henri II honored this performance at the Hôtel de Reims with his presence and caused a royal souvenir to be presented to Jodelle—though we cannot be sure whether this was in recognition of the ambitious Alexandrine verses of *Cléopatre captive,* or a reward for the comedy *Eugène* which followed. In any event, Jodelle's character Abbé Eugène, who is presented with many critical allusions to contemporary affairs, may claim to be the immediate precursor of Molière's Tartuffe.

The play was performed with a single setting on a ballroom stage, with a "magnifique appareil de la scène antique" which greatly satisfied Jodelle. Strictly following Aristotelian rules of unity of time and place, the tragic end of Cleopatra was portrayed in front of a palace facade, with the tomb of Antony annexed at its side—for in it, in order to escape captivity, the queen must take her life. At a repeat performance shortly afterward at the Collège de Boncourt, Jodelle complained about the disappointingly meager state decorations. But more important than this unavoidable deficiency was the influence Jodelle's five-act Alexandrine tragedy acquired in academic circles concerned with the theater. Jodelle's fellow writers of the Pléiade hailed him as a young man of great promise who pointed the way to the future of the *tragédie classique.* He satisfied alike Du Bellay's demands for cultivation of the language and the poetical ideals of Ronsard, Baïf, and Péruse.

Jodelle's success and the growing prestige of the Pléiade motivated the royal court librarian Mellin de Saint-Gelais to translate Trissino's model tragedy *Sofonisba* into French prose. Henri II granted Mellin a gala performance at court. The king's daughters took part, "in sumptuous costumes"; in their company was the Dauphin's betrothed, Mary Stuart. The performance at the Château de Blois in 1556 was produced with "grande pompe," enlivened by musical interludes. It was merely one among many entertainments in a series of festive days arranged in honor of the young Scottish princess. But what could *Sofonisba* be to her? What meaning could she find in the tragedy of the unhappy Numidian queen, who has to drink the cup of poison sent by her own husband? After the play, Mary Stuart danced like all others and with all others, unsuspecting how soon she herself was to give her name to a European tragedy.

Less than fifty years later, in 1601, Antoine de Montchrestien wrote his play *L'Ecossaise.* This first drama about Mary Stuart, written from a Huguenot's point of view, appeared fourteen years after her execution and still in the lifetime of Queen Elizabeth I. It was Montchrestien's second play; his first had a classical theme: *Sophonisbe.*

The nemesis of tragedy willed that in England, too, the strands of Renaissance drama should be interwoven with the fate of Mary Stuart. George Buchanan, translator of Euripides and author of the tragedies *Baptistes* and *Jephtes,* was Mary Stuart's tutor until 1567, but after Darnley's murder became her enemy and in 1572 published an indictment of her, *Detectio Mariae Reginae.*

In contrast to the French predilection for Alexandrines, the English humanists preferred to write their tragedies in blank verse. The first authoritative example of this style was *Gorboduc, or Ferrex and Porrex,* a speechifying, didactic play in the manner of Seneca; its plot relates the struggle of two hostile brothers for the throne and the harm caused to their country. It was written in 1561, and its joint authors were Thomas Sackville and Thomas Norton, both members of Parliament and the

Inner Temple. That same year Mary Stuart returned to Scotland. It is tempting to see in *Gorboduc* a premonition of the coming struggle between the two unequal queens. Thomas Sackville, Baron of Buckhurst and first Earl of Dorset, was despatched to Fotheringay in 1568 to convey the sentence of death to Mary, Queen of Scots.

After this prelude in the style of Seneca, the English Renaissance drama emancipated itself from strict formal rules. Shakespeare, like the Spaniards, preferred to take a free hand with time and place. He presented a mosaic of concentrated snapshots which, by continuous change of scene and contrast of the tragic and the comic, eventually made up the whole, great picture. He resolved in action what the French Renaissance tragedy piled up in imposing, solo declamations. The report of the death of Hippolytus in Robert Garnier's *Hippolyte, fils de Thésée* (1573) takes up more than 170 lines—which not only taxed the actor's powers of concentration but also required a closed theater hall. The oratorical flights of Garnier, the immediate precursor of Corneille and Racine, demanded close contact with the audience and as little distraction as possible. The paradoxical result for the *tragédie classique* was the noxious custom of seating certain privileged spectators on the stage.

During the second half of the sixteenth century, the Renaissance drama of antique complexion began to spread throughout Europe. The Polish poet and dramatist Jan Kochanowski chose a subject from the Iliad in order to appeal to his king's conscience. His patriotic single-set drama *The Dismissal of the Greek Envoys* was an unmistakable allusion to the danger threatening Poland from Ivan the Terrible. When, on the stage, the Trojan Antenor called the timorous Priam to resolute action, there was an answering clangor of arms in the hall. The performance, which took place in January 1578, on the occasion of the betrothal of the Polish Chancellor Jan Zamoyski to the Lithuanian princess Christine Radziwill at Jazdowo Castle near Warsaw, fulfilled its double purpose. It earned the young academicians on the stage their hoped-for acclaim; it also brought the impatient patriots in the audience King Stephen Bathory's approval of the defensive measures they so fervently advocated —measures which this Transylvanian vaivode, elected king of Poland barely two years earlier, would only too gladly have done without.

Humanist Comedy

The princes of the house of Este in Ferrara knew how to hold on to their lead as patrons of the literary Renaissance comedy. The initial revival of classical drama in 1486 with Plautus's *Menaechmi* was fol-

Initial with theater scenes for Hercules furens, *by Seneca. On the right, top and bottom, spectators. From* Codex Urbin, *14th century. (Lat. 355, Rome, Biblioteca Vaticana.)*

Humanist stage around 1550: probably a monologue scene from Il Pellegrino *by Girolamo Parabosco. First edition in Venice, 1552.*

lowed by further performances in Italian translation. Terence's *Andria* was presented in 1491, and his *Eunuchus* in 1499. The ducal court of Ferrara attracted humanists and poets. While Isabella d'Este, who meanwhile had married and moved to Mantua, was arranging in 1501 for a production of Terence's *Adelphi* and thus helped the dukes of Gonzaga, in their turn, to early fame in the history of the theater, a new star was rising at Ferrara: Lodovico Ariosto.

At first, to be sure, the lean poet gifted with luxuriant fancy found himself in straitened circumstances. All the more readily was he inspired to enrich the court's festivities with his own comedies. Thus he wrote *La Cassaria* in 1508, and in 1509 followed it with *I Suppositi,* his most famous work for the stage, closely modeled on Plautus as regards the range of characters and scenic techniques. The stage form used at Ferrara, ever since the first performance of 1486, was a flat street facade with five pinnacled houses, each with one door and one window.

The principle of the raised platform stage with a row of several "houses," a reduced adaptation of the ancient Roman *scaenae frons,* became characteristic of the theater of the humanists. It recurs in the woodcuts of many Terence editions and was not beyond the modest means of the school theater, if need be in the most primitive form of a wooden shed, partitioned into curtained booths—"rather like the bathing cubicles at a swimming pool" (Creizenach). Therefore, early in the twentieth century the apt term "bathing-box" stage was coined to describe this sort of scenery.

I Suppositi introduced Ariosto to Rome, where the play had a gala performance in 1519 at the Castel Sant'Angelo, before Pope Leo X. The décor was designed by Raphael; it depicted, "true to nature in perspective art," the city of Ferrara as the scene of the comedy. To secure the necessary surprise effect for his masterpiece of scenery, Raphael con-

Scene from Terence's comedy Andria. *Woodcut from a Terence edition, Venice, 1497.*

Overall illustration for Terence's Andria, *printed in Strasbourg, 1496. The engraver has designed imaginary scenery for events merely related in the text, and has indicated the relationship between the characters by connecting lines.*

A performance of Terence's Phormio. *Woodcut by Albrecht Dürer, intended as title page for an unpublished illustrated edition of Terence comedies. Ca. 1492. (Basel, Kupferstichkabinett.)*

Woodcut for Terence's comedy Phormio. *From the Lyons edition of 1493.*

cealed it behind a curtain which, in ancient Roman fashion, was lowered into a cavity in front of the stage at the beginning of the performance.

Ariosto and Raphael shared equally in the acclaim. The Ferrarese envoy Paolucci, however, did not mention Ariosto's name when he reported to his prince on the Roman carnival festivities of 1519: ". . . the talk of the town was nothing but the masquerades and the comedies . . . and Raphael of Urbino's apparatus for them." But *I Suppositi* was launched on its stage career; it was performed at court parties, the *Commedia dell'arte,* and the school theater. Antonio Vignali, a member of the Sienese Accademia degli Intronati, staged the play at Valladolid in 1548, as the theater's contribution to the celebrations in honor of the marriage of Maximilian of Austria to the Infanta Maria, daughter of Emperor Charles V. The character of the Saracen Rodomonte in Ariosto's *Orlando Furioso* was adopted by the *Commedia dell'arte,* and the boasting, bombastic speeches in which the *Capitano*—joined by other braggarts—puffs up his fame became known as rodomontades.

In the years 1518–21, the most distinguished men rivaled each other as authors of comedy, eagerly encouraged by Pope Leo X, whose enjoyment of the papacy encompassed the theater as well. A fashionable man of intellect and culture could do no less than prove his mastery of polished speech as a dramatist. A good deal earlier, Aeneas Sylvius Piccolomini, subsequently Pope Pius II, had based his comedy *Chrysis* (written in 1444) on Terence. whom he had read in his youth. The painter and architect Leon Battista Alberti wrote a Latin comedy called *Philodoxeos,* and as late as 1582 Giordano Bruno tried his hand at a regular humanist comedy, in his satire of alchemy, *Il Candelaio.* In Rome, in 1518, before departing for France as papal envoy the Roman

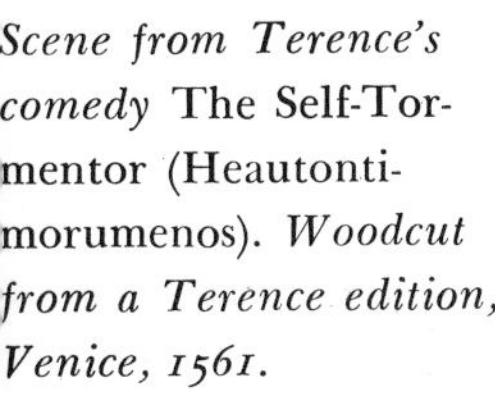
Scene from Terence's comedy The Self-Tormentor (Heautontimorumenos). *Woodcut from a Terence edition, Venice, 1561.*

cardinal Casentino Bibbiena arranged—in honor of Pope Leo X—a costly gala performance reviving his *Calandria,* a Plautine comedy on the theme of twins, which had had a successful debut in Urbino in 1513. (Thirty years later, in 1548, the Florentine colony at Lyon chose *Calandria* as its contribution for the reception honoring King Henri II and his young bride Catherine de' Medici.)

The cardinal-author was joined in 1520 by the politician-author, in the person of Niccolò Machiavelli, another adaptor of Terence. But Machiavelli's comedy *Mandragola,* first performed in Florence and shortly afterward in Rome, surpassed all predecessors in originality, boldness, and wit. Modern Italian literary critics go so far as to regard *Mandragola* as the "dramatic masterpiece not only of the *Cinquecento,* but of the entire Italian theater" (G. Toffanin). Nothing was fit to hold a candle to it, except, with reservations, the comedy *La Cortigiana* by Pietro Aretino, friend of Titian and master of the Venetian style of *chronique scandaleuse.* But Aretino's acerbity cost him the good graces of the Curia. *La Cortigiana* yielded her stage rights to the Courtesan of the *Commedia dell'arte,* while that character's knowledge of the tricks of her trade found a place in Aretino's *I Ragionamenti.*

In the days of the Renaissance the authors of comedy could not complain of a general lack of magnanimity. Polished wit earned Pope Leo X's forgiveness even for overt attacks on his court. Torres Naharro, forerunner of the Spanish cloak-and-dagger plays, had become acquainted at his Roman master's house with the intrigue and tug-of-war for power and influence, plums and sinecures. He worked off his displeasure in a comedy called *Tinelaria,* a sharp attack on the machinations in the servants' and officials' hall (*tinelo*) of a cardinal. In the very prologue the author warns, "What makes you laugh here, you may punish at home," and in the closing lines he once more points out that these abuses were no credit to Their Eminences.

The daring play was performed in 1517 in the presence of Leo X and Cardinal Giulio de' Medici, subsequently Pope Clement VII. The eminent gentlemen did not feel that the cap fitted them and were amused by the grotesque gibberish of language with which the author let fly. To them this was a record—a tape-recording, as it were—of a household assembled from the four corners of the earth. Here, on the stage, was the same babel of Spanish, French, German, and scraps of Italian dialect—intensified in the drinking scenes to the point of a veritable witches' sabbath. Leo X was so taken with the play that he granted Torres Naharro a ten-year privilege for printing his comedies. Even Cardinal Bernardino Carvajal, to whose house the *Tinelaria* referred, took no offense and graciously accepted the edition of the play dedicated to him by Torres Naharro. The author had made his meaning as plain as could be by including the play among his *comedias a noticia,*

Scenes from the comedy Gli inganni *by Curzio Gonzaga. Woodcuts from an edition printed in Venice, 1592.*

comedies of observation, as distinct from the *comedias a fantasia,* fictitious events with the mere semblance of reality.

Soon, two of the most famous Renaissance comedies began to sweep across the whole of Europe without benefit of an author's name: the Spanish *La Celestina* and the Sienese *Gli Ingannati.* The namesake heroine of *La Celestina* (today ascribed to Fernando de Rojas) is a high-grade bawd, well-versed in all the problems her trade is faced with. The first edition that was circulated appeared in Burgos in 1499; twenty years later, the play had been translated into Italian, French, English, and German. *Gli Ingannati* was first performed in 1531 by the Accademia degli Intronati and was printed anonymously in 1537. Soon thereafter, Lope de Rueda, Spanish dramatist and leader of an actors' company, performed it in streets and yards as *Comedia de los Enganados.*

The versatile brother-and-sister theme with its disguises and plot possibilities was taken over by Shakespeare in *Twelfth Night.* A French translation by Charles Estienne, published in 1540 and dedicated to the Dauphin, conscientiously notes the origin of the play: "*Ingannati*: comedy in the manner and after themes of the ancients, called 'The Abused.' First composed in the Tuscan language by the professors of the Sienese vernacular academy by name of Intronati, and translated into our French language by Charles Estienne."

Notwithstanding this careful reference to the source, Estienne regarded himself as the creator of a new, original French comedy. In the preface he claims to have superseded the primitive, medieval farce, and urgently recommends that the new art should be given a "new house," with "comfortably constructed seats arranged in an amphitheater, which should make even a fastidious audience feel at ease."

But several decades were to pass before this was to happen. With

Scene from the comedy La Celestina. *Frontispiece of the Spanish edition, Toledo, 1538.*

the advent of opera, theater audiences were to enjoy both the magical transformations of settings wrought by stage machinery, and also sumptuous, comfortable playhouses. The *Commedia erudita,* the scholarly theater of the Renaissance, made do for decades with single sets according to the rules, though these were presented with increasing skill in perspective and ornamented with stucco. When the comedy *Le Brave* by Jean Antoine de Baïf, a French version of Plautus's *Miles gloriosus,* was performed in 1567 at the Hôtel de Guise in Paris, contemporary chroniclers talked of a "sumptuous courtly production." The thanks for this, perhaps, should go to Ronsard and a few other Pléiade poets who had contributed a number of interludes with verses in honor of the guests of honor, King Charles IX and Catherine de' Medici.

The direct influence of Roman comedy is evident in the dramatist Martin Drzič of Dubrovnik, the widely traveled, adventurous ancestor of the Yugoslav theater. In his *Dundo Maroje* he created the character of a miser, who—fitting in somewhere between Plautus and Molière—goes beyond the crude comic situation and in the direction of the comedy of character. The scene of *Dundo Maroje* (1551) is Rome, whither the father follows his frivolous son—only to meet nothing but compatriots from the author's native Ragusa (Dubrovnik). The play is a mirror of the morals of its time, quite on the level of Torres Naharro's *Tinelaria.*

This category of plays includes also the comedy *Mother Bombie* (1594), by the English court dramatist John Lyly. This comedy is based on Terentian themes and gives a realistic picture of Elizabethan everyday life. But in this decade the star of Shakespeare rose in London—and *Mother Bombie* was eclipsed by *Romeo and Juliet* and *A Midsummer Night's Dream.*

The Pastoral Play

"The golden age, whither has it fled?" ask's Goethe's Tasso, and conjured up the vision of the same elysium that the historical Tasso extolled: the "realm of beauty, free of error" in which hero and poet lived together in concord, and fauns and nymphs, shepherds and shepherdesses woo each other with graceful verses. The cool air of humanist scholarship and the unscrupulous struggle for political power led, as formerly in the times of Theocritus and Virgil, to an escape into the other extreme—into an unreal, sentimentally idealized world of "pure humanity," a world "at nature's heart."

The new, tender note struck by Dante's unfulfilled love for Beatrice, by Petrarch's lyrical sonnets to Laura had lingered on. Painters, poets, and courtiers extrolled beauty and youth. Lorenzo de' Medici in his carnival songs urged enjoyment of the fleeting "bella giovinezza" and, in honor of the beautiful Simonetta Vespucci, organized a theatrical tournament lasting several days. Angelo Poliziano found in it an occasion for a long panegyrical poem, Botticelli for his allegorical painting "The Birth of Venus." Lorenzo Lotto depicted as "A Maiden's Dream" a romantic wooded landscape with a spring and satyrs. The poet's highest bliss beckoned to him when the lady of his heart amid lovely beds of flowers handed him the laurel wreath.

The literary cultivation of the city-dweller's longing for bucolic idylls had found a far-famed home at the Este court at Ferrara, an Arcady such as was sung by Boiardo in his eclogues, by Ariosto in his stanzas, by Tasso in the pastoral play *Aminta.* But in Ariosto there are already slight overtones of doubt as to whether all this heroic and noble spirit was still to be taken altogether seriously. During his time as organizer of plays and festivities at the court of Ferrara, a new, more earthy element began to invade the courtly play, brought along by Ruzzante's players with their Paduan peasants' dialogues. At first, in 1529 and 1531, they recited their madrigals and conversations as table entertainment. For 1532, however, a stage play seems to have been planned, for Ruzzante had asked in advance for the help of Ariosto, who was so thoroughly experienced in theater arrangements.

Tasso, too, took care himself of the rehearsals for his *Aminta.* Throughout Europe, this moving love story and its paean of the golden age became the quintessence and much-copied model for the pastoral play. At its first performance in 1573, on the little Po island of Belvedere, a summer residence of the Este family, the cast included not only members of court society, but also a few professional actors of the well-known Comici Gelosi company.

The action of *Aminta* contains all the elements of bucolic allegory. The prologue is spoken by Love, disguised as a shepherd. The shepherd Aminta, a grandson of Pan, vainly woos the cold nymph Silvia. The helpful intervention of Daphne—as well as that of animals, an uncouth satyr, and a providentially placed thorn bush—are marshaled in order to help the constant Aminta to his hard-earned happiness.

Giambattista Guarini, Tasso's successor at the court of Ferrara, tried to outdo the latter by every conceivable kind of poetic complication. The poor shepherd Mirtillo, hero and protagonist of Guarini's *Pastor fido,* had to battle through a vertible maze of jealousy and intrigue before he gained the hand of the beautiful Amarillis. *Pastor fido* was first performed at Crema in 1595, the year of Tasso's death. It was the last climax and the swan song of the Italian Renaissance pastoral play, which had begun, exactly one hundred years earlier under Lorenzo de' Medici, with Angelo Poliziano's pastoral *Favola d'Orfeo,* the first secular Italian drama, which still had been wholly indebted to the stylistic conceptions of the *sacra rappresentazione.*

F. Leclerc: scenes from Tasso's Aminta. *Engravings printed in Amsterdam, 1678.*

Copper engraving for the pastoral play Pastor fido *by Giambattista Guarini. Venice, 1602.*

In the hundred years spanning the period from Poliziano's *Orfeo* to Guarini's *Pastor fido,* pastoral idylls flourished throughout the Western world. Regardless of frontiers, they were unanimous in their lyrical praises of the groves of Arcady.

Juan del Encina, the gifted pioneer of the Spanish theater, preferred to stage his *representaciones* in rural settings, abounding with shepherds and mythological figures. His actors donned shepherds' costumes, even for the gala performance of his *Egloga del Amor* in 1497, at the celebration of the wedding of Juan of Castile and Emperor Maximilian's daughter, Margaret of Austria. In the staging of his *Egloga de Placida y Vitoriano,* at the house of Cardinal Arborea in Rome, sets of woods and arbors were used. Presumably, the author was present at this performance. Although he now was archdeacon at Malaga since 1508, he kept in close touch with Rome and repeatedly journeyed there.

Gil Vicente, organizer of Portugal's court festivities and his country's greatest dramatist, also preferred a pastoral milieu. The Goddess of Fame in his *Auto da Fama* (1510) appears as a playful shepherdess.

Beyond the Pyrenees, as elsewhere, pastoral plays were performed in

Woodcut of the old Urner Spiel *of Tell, 1545. The story of Wilhelm Tell of Uri was known in Switzerland from the middle of the 15th century. The old* Urner Spiel *was first performed at Altdorf in 1512.*

the theater halls of palaces and in noblemen's houses. By the middle of the sixteenth century, the bucolic idyll also became part of the repertory of strolling players. Lope de Rueda—the theater director and playwright who, in the years 1544–65 roamed with his troupe through the whole of Spain—often chose the shepherd's costume for scenes of folk life. His stage properties, so Cervantes records, consisted of

> four white shepherds' smocks edged with gilded leather, four beards and wigs, and four staves—more or less. The plays were colloquies or eclogues between two or three shepherds and a shepherdess; they were adorned and expanded with two or three interludes, about a Negro woman, a pimp, a fool, or a Basque: for all these four characters and many others were acted by the said Lope with the greatest skill and excellence that can be imagined.

Cervantes adds that the stage merely consisted of four benches with four or six planks laid across them, so that it was raised about four spans above ground; the only decoration was an old blanket drawn across the back, which served as a dressing room and behind which were the musicians.

Musical accompaniment was an indispensable accessory of the pastoral, for an unhappy, lovelorn shepherd and a young rustic beauty naturally needed song to express their feelings. There was only a short step to take from the pastoral play and the song-play to opera. But first, it would lead through the setting of courtly homage.

The English poet George Peele, a bohemian who combined a lyrical and panegyric gift with a university education, gained the Queen's favor in 1584 with *The Arraignment of Paris.*

Paris appears in shepherd's garb, playing the flute, and in artfully constructed verses praises the beauty of Venus, the majesty of Juno, the wisdom of Pallas Athene. The golden apple, however, is due to Queen Elizabeth I, "the noble Phoenix of our age, our fayre Eliza, our Zabeta fayre." Diana and her nymphs hand it to her, with Venus, Juno, and Pallas Athene all confirming the award:

> This prize from heaven and heavenly goddesses,
> Accept it then, thy due by Dians dome,
> Praise of the wisedome, beautie and the state,
> That best becomes thy peereless excellencie.

But the poetic pastoral was unworldly only in appearance; it never quite lost sight of its often very realistic intentions. The flowery homage was most often addressed to a very real recipient and pursued a very real purpose; it might be a woman, a queen, a town, and the object was to gain favor.

The Serbo-Croat poet Gjivo Franje Gundulić, a humanist of an old patrician family and admirer of Tasso, in 1628 glorified his native city Dubrovnik in the pastoral play *Dubravka*. The Nuremberg patrician George Philipp Harsdörffer praised the industrious folk of the city on the river Pegnitz in 1641 in his *Pegnesisches Schäfergedicht,* a pastoral of Anacreontic, allegorical exuberance, an artful conglomerate of dialogue, lyric, and song, which has nothing to do with the theater.

But the setting of the pastoral play, used likewise in the novel and lyrical poetry, lived on for centuries—still shaping Mozart's *Bastien und Bastienne,* and Goethe's *Die Fischerin* and *Die Laune des Verliebten.*

In 1545 Sebastiano Serlio established its basic type in his *L'Architettura* as the "Scena satirica," with groups of trees, grottoes, and arbors.

The Development of the Perspective Stage

Perspective had been the great passion of the *Quattrocento.* The counterpart to the humanist ideal of the harmony of the universe was the mathematically precise systematization of art and science, the harmonious balance of detail and overall construction. The proportions of a face or a beaker involved no less complicated calculations than the facade of a building, or the measurements of a monumental pictorial composition.

Brunelleschi, Alberti, and Bramante gave expression in architecture to the perspective illusion of space; Piero della Francesca, in painting; Ghiberti and Donatello, in sculpture. They all were both artists and scientists. Similarly, useful application of the chapter on the theater in the fifth book of Vitruvius's work on architecture presupposed an experienced builder. The shape of a theater, Vitruvius explained, is to be so designed that, according to the length of the diameter of the lower area and starting at its center, a circle is to be described and within it four equidistant, equilateral triangles. These triangles touch the circle, in the same manner as astronomers proceed in plotting the twelve signs of the zodiac, according to the musical laws of the stars.

Geometry, mathematics, astronomy, and music—Vitruvius was presenting distinguished credentials indeed for the modest here-and-now appearance of the theater. The 1486 edition of Vitruvius, prepared by Sulpitius Verolanus, served primarily for learned study and, so far as matters of the theater were concerned, hardly for application in practice. The prescripts of Vitruvius did not make their effect in broader circles until the new edition of 1521, which was furnished with drawings by Cesariano, and, more important still, the 1556 annotated edition in Italian by Daniele Barbaro, Patriarch of Aquileia.

In the early period of the Renaissance, the performances in Rome and Ferrara presumably still had relatively modest, flat street scenery—or so we must assume, for they were described as *picturatae scenae*. But by the time Cardinal Bibbiena's *Calandria* was staged at Urbino in 1513, the décor had gained some perspective depth. In this performance there had been shown on the stage, as Baldassare Castiglione wrote in a letter to Count Lodovico Canossa, "a city with streets, palaces, churches, and towers, all in relief."

For the repeat performance in Rome, arranged by Bibbiena in 1518 for Pope Leo X, Baldassare Peruzzi created scenery so well-made, as Vasari reports, that it seemed "not make-believe, but as true as could be, and the square not a painted and little thing, but real and very large." Peruzzi had transformed the painted back wall of the stage into a usable acting area projecting real depth. This was achieved by the arrangement of a stage proscenium with practicable décor and a back wall painted in full perspective.

In his *Architettura* (published in Venice in 1545), Sebastiano Serlio, the great theorist and architect who was a pupil of Peruzzi, described how, with the help of angled wings it was possible to build up a whole vista of streets with colonnades and loggias, towers, and gates. Bramante, the brothers Sangallo, and Peruzzi, too, before his innovation, had always fixed the major perspective and its vanishing point within the picture, both in their monumental frescoes and in their stage designs. Serlio now placed it in the distance, farther than the painted view—that is, *beyond* the back wall of the stage, with the result that the foreshortening was less abrupt. And through this illusory depth the stage also gained some real acting space.

In accordance with the three categories of the humanist theater, Serlio established three basic types of décor: a palace architecture for tragedy (*scena tragica*); a street scene for comedy (*scena comica*); a wooded landscape for the pastoral (*scena satirica*). He fashioned them as Vitruvius prescribed: "The tragic scenes are shown with columns, pediments, statues, and other royal appurtenances. The comic scenes show private houses with views of windows, after the manner of ordinary dwellings. The satyric scenes are decorated with trees, caves, mountains, and other rustic objects delineated in landscape style."

Giacomo Barozzi da Vignola, author of the treatise *Le due regole della prospettiva pratica,* published posthumously by Danti in 1583, aims at a built-up perspective stage practicable up to the third street, that is, with stage entrances as far back as the painted distant view. He

Scena Comica.

Sebastiano Serlio: scena comica. Fixed architectural scene for comedy, designed in 1545. Woodcut from Libro secondo di Perspettiva *of Serlio's* Architettura. *Venice, 1663.*

Baldassare Peruzzi: design for a setting in perspective, ca. 1530. (Florence, Uffizi.)

recommends that the angled wings should be replaced by periaktoi fashioned after the models of antiquity. The scene is to be formed by five equilateral triangular prisms of wood, which could turn on pivots, with two smaller prisms of wood on each side as lateral boundary and one three times larger in the back. The problem of how to cope with the technical difficulties resulting from the rake (slope) of the stage was investigated fifty years later with Swabian thoroughness by the German theoretician of architecture Joseph Furttenbach at Ulm.

The finest existing example of an Italian Renaissance theater is the Teatro Olimpico at Vicenza. It was built by Andrea Palladio, who, after collaborating with Barbaro on the latter's edition of Vitruvius, set himself the task of reconstructing an ancient Roman theater. He strictly adhered to Vitruvius as regards the shape of the auditorium and *scaenae frons*. Three doorways punctuate the elaborate architecture of the stage wall, built of wood and stucco, and there is one proscenium door on each side. The semielliptical auditorium, in thirteen tiers, is directly connected with the stage wall and crowned by a gallery and colonnade with statues. The whole is a proportionally reduced copy of the huge late Roman outdoor stone theaters, transposed into the closed space of a charming toy-box. Presumably, Palladio's original design provided for the doorways of the *scaenae frons* to be closed off by a painted perspective view. But he died shortly before the theater was completed, and his successor Vincenzo Scamozzi transformed the painted vistas into practicable alleys. Following Serlio, he placed his vanishing point for the perspective beyond the scene, in the painted backdrops seen through the three doorways, and thus intensified the illusion of depth.

The theater had been commissioned by the Accademia Olimpica of Vicenza, one of the numerous humanist theater academies, for whose performances Palladio had on several previous occasions put up temporary stages in the hall of the basilica at Vicenza. The new playhouse was inaugurated in 1584 with Sophocles' *Oedipus Tyrannus*. The theater is still used today for performances on special occasions.

By the beginning of the seventeenth century, no one who traveled in Italy and had an interest in architecture or the theater failed to visit the Teatro Olimpico. Joseph Furttenbach inspected it in 1619, on his way back from Florence to Germany, and appreciatively notes in his *Itinerarium Italiae* that, although "merely built of wood, the scene was constructed most beautifully according to the art of perspective." He conjectures that 5,400 spectators could watch the comedies in this theater without getting in each other's way, but this is a gross overestimate of the theater's capacity, which barely exceeds 2,000.

Three years after the completion of the Teatro Olimpico, Scamozzi built another theater at Sabbioneta. Vespasiano Gonzaga, the last de-

Interior of the Teatro Olimpico at Vicenza, built by Andrea Palladio and completed by Vincenzo Scamozzi. It opened in 1584 with Sophocles' Oedipus Tyrannus.

Joseph Furttenbach: palace stage. From his Architectura civilis, *Ulm, 1628. Copper engravings by Jacob Custodis.*

scendant of an ambitious branch of the Mantuan ruling house, was transforming the village of Sabbioneta south of Mantua into his seat of government. It took him thirty years to do so, and it emerged rather like one of the models of Ammanati's and Vasari's "ideal town," designed with ruler and compass, neatly enclosed in a fortresslike pentagon. A plain, unadorned building contains the theater. It is smaller than the Olimpico at Vicenza and has the character of an elegant private playhouse. Thanks to the organic disposition of its entries and side rooms it makes the impression of being all of a piece. Even the classicized busts in the wall niches and the paintings were designed by Scamozzi himself, while the Teatro Olimpico at Vicenza did not get its last statues until 1700. As regards the proportions, Scamozzi followed the rules of Vitruvius even more closely than his teacher Palladio had done. Duke Vespasiano's model city allowed no compromise. After the duke's death, it relapsed into its rural isolation; but Scamozzi's theater still stands, and is very carefully looked after.

From the sixteenth century on, theaters in palaces assumed importance both from the cultural and the architectural points of view. In Florence, Bernardo Buontalenti expressed the splendor of the Medici princes in the decorative and theatrical arrangement of festivities. In 1585, Buontalenti built the famous great court stage at the east side of the Uffizi, and there sumptuous performances of *intermedii* and comedies were performed during the winter 1585–86. The hall was over 150 feet long and 60 feet wide, and had a sufficient slope along its longitudinal axis to allow all spectators a good view. The stage was at the low end, and the thrones for the ruling family stood immediately in front of it on a dais. Four years later, in 1589, Buontalenti remodeled the auditorium into an amphitheater with five concentric tiers of seats, divided by stair passages in the style of the ancient Roman theater.

In Florence, at the beginning of the seventeenth century, (as the plans and sketches in Joseph Furttenbach's architectural works confirm), the great hall of the Palazzo Pitti was used expressly for tournaments, jousts, dances, and comedies. Buontalenti was familiar with every technical device; he was the first to provide such decorative and stage effects as the Baroque theater eventually adopted on a larger scale. It is not known how Buontalenti contrived transformations of scene. It is assumed that he still employed the revolving prisms made of wood developed by Sangallo, Barbaro, Vignola, and Danti—which, in the beginning of the seventeenth century, were replaced by a system of sliding flat wings.

In the course of one century, the Renaissance theater went through a quick-motion repetition of the development of the Roman theater. The more magnificent the stage became and the more attention was

Vincenzo Scamozzi: design for a street scene. (Florence, Uffizi.)

Interior of the Theater in Sabbioneta, built by Vincenzo Scamozzi for Vespasiano Gonzaga, 1587. New benches have been installed in the oval auditorium, but the original colonnade, statues, and wall decorations have been preserved.

Stage of the Teatro Olimpico in Vicenza, with Scamozzi's perspective views into practicable streets. The vanishing point is placed beyond the set. In the center, the porta regia, *subsequently further developed and widened into the peep-show stage at the Teatro Farnese in Parma.*

Longitudinal section of the Teatro Olimpico at Vicenza. On the left, the central street décor on the raked stage; on the right, the tiered seating arrangement in the manner of an amphitheater.

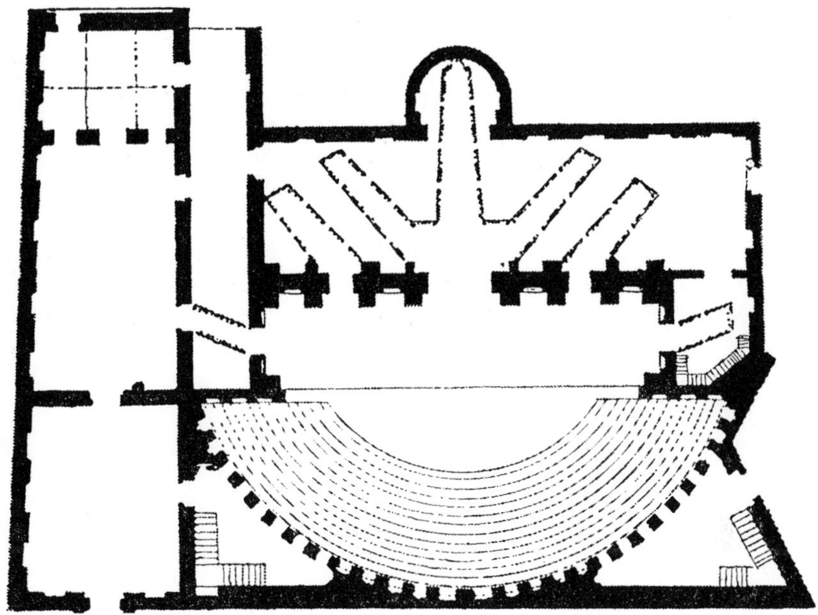

Ground plan of the Teatro Olimpico at Vicenza. Built by Andrea Palladio and completed in 1584 by Vincenzo Scamozzi.

claimed by its visual aspects, the more worthless became the literary content. For now, first and foremost, the actors had to subordinate their movement and grouping to the calculated optics of the scene. As once the monumental architecture to the late Roman *scaenae frons* had left no room for drama of matching quality, the increasingly elaborate decorations of the late Renaissance eventually relegated the word to a subordinate function.

The stage with its angle wings or rotating prisms of wood was, at best, available for acting only up to the second cross street, and rarely for entrances as far back as the painted view. The actors were to keep away from this area, for their full-size and real bodies clashed with the perspective illusion and destroyed the perfection of the scene, contrived by the mathematics of aesthetic principles. The paramount rule of Renaissance painting, that the eye was not to be offended by discordant overlapping, was applied also to the position of actors on the stage.

The type of play performed and the consequent type of décor also determined the choice of costume. When the Teatro Olimpico at Vicenza was opened in 1584 with Angelo Ingegnieri's production of *Oedipus*, he wrote:

> it needs to be considered in what country the action of the play to be performed is supposed to take place, and the actors should be dressed accord-

> ing to the customs of that country. And if the play be a tragedy, the costumes should be rich and sumptuous; if it be a comedy, common but neat; if, finally, it be a pastoral, humble but of good cut and graceful, which is worth as much as ostentation. In the latter case it has already become the immutable practice to dress the women in the manner of nymphs, even though they may be simple shepherdesses.

Ingegneri undertook this production with members of the Academy primarily as a choreographic exercise. "It was a marvel how they had mastered all their positions and movements and how accurately they placed themselves," he reported. The floor of the stage had been laid out in squares, like a chessboard, and

> every person knew according to what pattern of squares he was to come and go, and after how many floor tiles to stop. And when the number of persons on the scene increased and it became necessary to change positions, everyone proved well-instructed as to what other row or what other color of tiles he was to retreat to; so that all learned without difficulty to play their parts.

A hundred years had passed since the first performances offered by the Pomponian Academy in Rome, since its production of *Hippolytus* in 1486. The inauguration of the Teatro Olimpico at Vicenza was the end of a development that had begun as an illustration of texts, the transposition of classical subject matter from its presentation by words only into physical, palpable representation. Tommaso Inghirami, as an actor in *Phaedra,* had excelled through his mastery of Latin. A century later, it was no longer the word that predominated but the scenic arrangement. What mattered for Angelo Ingegneri was the perfection of aesthetic grouping.

COURT FESTIVALS

Machiavelli considered it more advantageous for a prince to be feared than loved. Nevertheless, his recommendations in *Il principe* include one to the effect that a prince, "at convenient seasons of the year, ought to keep the people occupied with festivals and shows." This practice abounded in the age of the Renaissance.

The princes played the power game as expertly through the splendor of court pageantry as in the web of conspiracy. When the ambitious Lodovico Sforza, "Il Moro," arranged a tremendous allegorical show at the court of Milan in 1490, his purpose was to win the favors of young Isabella of Aragon, the newly arrived bride of his nephew Gian Galeazzo Sforza. The marriage celebrations offered the best opportunity for flattering the "puppet duchess." Shortly thereafter, Lodovico married Beatrice d'Este, another occasion to be celebrated with great pomp and pageantry. The court poets were kept busy turning out panegyrical hyperboles in elegant rhyme.

Lodovico himself devised a great allegorical masque that culminated in homage to Isabella. He had it written by the Florentine court poet Bernardo Bellincioni and organized by Leonardo da Vinci, who at that time was employed at the Court of Milan as military engineer, inventor, canal builder, painter, and organizer of festivals. Leonardo designed a movable planetary system, picturesque costumes for gods and goddesses, masks representing savages and fantastic fabulous beasts. Bellincioni's verses wallowed in ecstatic compliments: Apollo welcomes Isabella as the new sun among the planets, the rulers of heaven and earth send messages honoring her, and even Venus bows to the splendor of the new duchess. Apollo presents the seven virtues to Isabella, and in conclusion hands her a book containing Bellincioni's text of the whole *Festa del Paradiso.* With this performance, Lodovico il Moro conquered a defensive position.

Leonardo's ingenious devices, as displayed at the glittering festival at Milan, secured him a place in the history of stage decoration. Bellincioni boasted long of his collaboration with Leonardo on this festive occasion; in the later printed edition of his *Rime,* he introduced the *Festa del Paradiso* by explaining:

> The following work by Messer Bernardo Bellincioni is a festival play or rather spectacle *(rappresentazione),* called Paradiso, which the Lord Lodovico caused to be organized in honor of the Duchess of Milan. It is called Paradiso because, by the great gift of invention and the art of Master Leonardo da Vinci of Florence, there was constructed Paradise with all the seven planets, and it turned in a circle, the planets being represented by men in the character and costume described by the poets.

The paradise turning in a circle was the famous first example of a revolving stage, of which, in addition to Bellincioni's description, we possess also some sketches by Leonardo. These give some indications as to how the device may have functioned. The Italian engineer Roberto Guatelli reconstructed it for a Leonardo exhibition in Los Angeles in 1952. George J. Altman, at whose instance this model was made, cites an eyewitness account of how the original worked: "The semicircle divided in the middle. The two quarter-circles rolled forward and closed up again, and the stage was suddenly transformed into a rugged mountain peak." Leonardo used his revolving stage for a second time in 1518, at the Château Cloux near Amboise, where he prepared another performance of *Paradiso* for the wedding of one of King Francis I's nieces and the Duke of Urbino. Galeazzo Visconti reports that it was organized in the same way as the one in the Castello Sforzesco.

But it would be to underestimate the motive forces of the great Renaissance festivals to interpret them merely as an expression of the courts' delight in representation. Behind the costly self-advertisement lurked the claim to political power, the expression of tactical moves and reasons of state. This can be traced further in the example of Lodovico Sforza. At the promotional festivities in Pavia in 1492, for instance, he elegantly dispelled the ill-feeling of Beatrice's family against him. On this occasion he had commissioned Bellincioni to write a poem proclaiming Beatrice the "new sun" and the courts of Ferrara and Mantua the

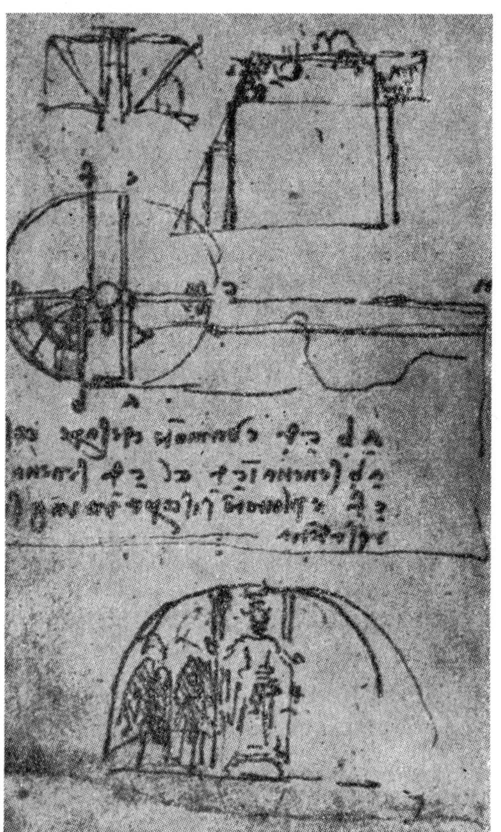

Leonardo da Vinci: design of a revolving stage for the Festa del Paradiso *at the Court of Milan, January 1490. Jupiter sits enthroned, surrounded by the seven planets; the setting is a kind of grotto, which could be closed by movable circular segments.*

Elysian fields of art and learning. The poem also reveled in verbose eulogies of Duke Ercole d'Este of Ferrara and of his second daughter Isabella, Duchess of Mantua, who was also present. Similar intentions can be detected in all the innumerable allegorical pageants and processions by which dukes and kings, usurpers and rulers paid tribute to, sought to win over, or to deceive one another.

As the specific form of these court festivals, the idea of the Roman triumphal procession was revived and transformed into the glittering splendor or the Renaissance *trionfi.* While the late medieval processional theater had on the whole been content with the single principle of sequence, that is, with a once-only drive past the spectators lined up to the side (of streets and squares), the new endeavor was "to enjoy the procession not only in its separate, individual sections, as will the spectators positioned at the periphery, but rather in its totality: from above and, if feasible, even in the axis of the processsion" (Joseph Gregor).

Palace courtyards with their archways and galleries, town squares with their arcades and balconies offered an opportunity for highly placed guests of honor to watch the *trionfi* literally highly placed, from above—as the pageant passed by in a circular course. In Florence, the Piazza Santa Croce, with its balconies and specially constructed grandstands, and the courtyard of the Palazzo Pitti were favorite localities for the famous Medici festivals, upon which Buontalenti brought to bear the full richness of his allegorical fancy. He designed costumes for the planets, for the virtues, for nymphs and gods; wheeled dolphin and triton floats—even gala boats, used when the courtyard or square was flooded to heighten the effect. He also devised costumes for winged genii, fire-spitting dragons, and dancing cherubs who dipped into gilded cornucopias to scatter perfumed flowers among the members of court society.

The common people marveled at the theatrical pomp of their rulers, or suspected it—in so far as they caught a glance of it. Not infrequently, the seemingly carefree magnificence was the last, euphoric flicker of a power long undermined.

When Henri III of France in 1581 celebrated the wedding of the Duc de Joyeuse with theatrical pomp, his whole court, politically in utmost danger as it was, was plunged into a festive frenzy. The program began, in the Italian fashion, with mythological and allegorical *trionfi,* or rather their French counterpart, the *entrées solenelles,* and culminated in the internationally famed *Ballet comique de la Royne,* a combination of dance figures, recitations, arias, and pantomimes in honor of the queen.

The great Bourbon ballroom of the Louvre in Paris glittered with gold and glowed with candlelight, while Versailles at the time was still a

Francesco del Cossa: Festive chariot portraying the Trionfo di Apollo. *From a mural painted in 1470, representing the month of May, in the Salone dei Mesi of the Palazzo Schifanoia, Ferrara.*

Bernardo Buontalenti: costume designs for the intermedii *at the great Medici theater festival organized in 1589 in the theater hall of the Uffizi, Florence. (London, Victoria and Albert Museum.)*

Scene at a tournament, watched by the king and his court. Decoration from a chest. Ca. 1480. Attributed to Domenico Morone. (London, National Gallery.)

Water pageant (Naumachia) in the park of Fontainebleau: warriors, arriving in ornate boats, are storming an island; in the foreground, right, King Henri III and his wife. 16th-century wall tapestry. (Florence, Uffizi.)

village in the woods and was given a hunting lodge only by Henri IV. All the more striking must have been the effect of the perspective garden scene as a setting for the entertainments, which the king had asked his closest collaborators to devise: his chamberlain Balthasar Beaujoyeulx acted as producer, his counsellor d'Aubigné as manager, and the court poet de la Chesnaye provided the text.

The *Ballet comique de la Royne,* expression of a deceptively self-confident monarchy, marked the decline of a dynasty, which was therefore all the less forgiven by the strife-torn country for this costly theatrical fata morgana. The Duc de Joyeuse was defeated in 1587, and in 1588 Henri III was unable either to storm the barricades or to suppress the riots. He fled, and died in 1589 of the wounds inflicted by a Dominican's poisoned knife. But the new genre of the dance-and-drama *ballet comique* survived, and eighty years later prospered again at court, thanks to Molière and Lully and their *comédie-ballet.*

The allegorical festival as an art form outlived catastrophes and dynasties. It was at home north and south of the Alps, and on both sides of the Pyrenees. When, in 1581, King Philip II united the crown of Portugal with that of Spain, the fathers of the Jesuit College of St. Anthony at Lisbon received him with a *Tragicomedia del descubimiente y conquista del Oriente,* performed on a three-story open-air stage of antique appearance. João Sardinha Mimoso described it in his *Relacion* (1620) as hung with colored damask and richly adorned with "pilasters, cornices, and architraves." To the right and to the left, entrance portals were built into the wings resembling the stage entrances of the Greek *paraskenia.* In this production, the Portugese king Emanuel and his retinue entered the stage from the right, and his Moorish opponents from the left. Two niches in the upper story represented the house of Aeolus, god of the winds, and the hell-mouth; high above, angels were enthroned. Here, vestiges of late medieval multiple settings were combined with architectural features of the ancient *scaenae frons* in a highly original style of courtly homage, anticipating the later forms of the Jesuit theater.

Similar scenic allegories and arrangements were common at the English Renaissance court revels, the Interludes. Together with the court masques, popular as entertainment during meals, they constituted an autonomous variant of the *trionfo.* One of John Heywood's most successful Interludes, *Play of the Weather,* was performed in 1533 for the royal court on a two-story stage, with Jupiter at the top listening to the complaints proffered against the dispensers of wind and rain, Aeolus and Phoibe. The sea-faring merchants request favorable winds, just like Vasco da Gama's navigators in the Portugese *Tragicomedia.* In the fateful year 1588, Aeolus was on the side of the English when he caused the remnants of the defeated Spanish Armada to sink amid storms in the Bay of Biscay. While the court poets of sea-faring nations preferred to take their themes and allegories from the realm of Neptune and Saturn, their land-locked colleagues preferred the imagery of vineyards and the hunt. Diana gave her name to many a court spectacle; one of the earliest to be devoted to her was written by the German humanist Konrad Celtes.

This German from the banks of the Main took his audience back in time and to Italy, to the origin of the court triumph and panegyric. He had become interested in the theater in Rome and Ferrara, and in March 1501 became responsible for the first famous example of the genre as it was to develop north of the Alps. Together with his friends of the Vienna humanist academy Sodalitas litteraria Danubiana, he organized a performance of his five-act *Ludus Dianae* at the castle of Linz on the Danube. The spectacle was organized in honor of Emperor Maximilian I, who had established his court at Linz for the carnival weeks, and had surrounded himself with the loyal Vienna humanists.

What could have been more apposite on such an occasion than to pay tribute to His Majesty with gods, nymphs, fauns, satyrs, and verbose panegyrics on the glory of the realm and Danube wine—which was being poured out in "golden cups and bowls" at the urging of a drunken Silenus and to the sound of drums and horns?

At the end, Diana took the floor. She promised the imperial couple all the good gifts of the gods, wished Maximilian and his Italian wife Bianca Sforza many splendid sons, assembled all the participants around herself and declared, in a final tableau with musical accompaniment, that she would now return to the woods of Wachau. The next day, as we learn from the printed edition of the play (May of the same year), the "divine Maximilian played host at a royal banquet to all the participants [they numbered twenty-four] and showered them with royal gifts."

The emperor was rewarded by Konrad Celtes and the Vienna humanists of the Danubiana academy by many more similar tokens of homage, ranging from a polyphonic ode to the Latin text of Maximilian's *Triumphal March*—ingeniously contrived, bombastic word constructions today buried in libraries and archives. It has long been forgotten that the abbott Benedictus Chelidonius (who used to organize Celtes performances at Vienna's Latin school called the Schottengymnasium) extolled *Maximilianus triumphator* in scholarly verses. Not forgotten, however, are the works of art that had inspired him: Albrecht Dürer's magnificent woodcut, the "Ehrenpforte des Kaisers Maximilian" of 1515, and his blocks of 1522 for "Triumphwagen"—a posthumous glorification of Maximilian, the "last of the knights," who had died in 1519.

Entertainments celebrating the wedding of the Bavarian hereditary prince Wilhelm and Renata of Lorraine, at Munich, 1568. Colored engravings by Nicolas Solis.

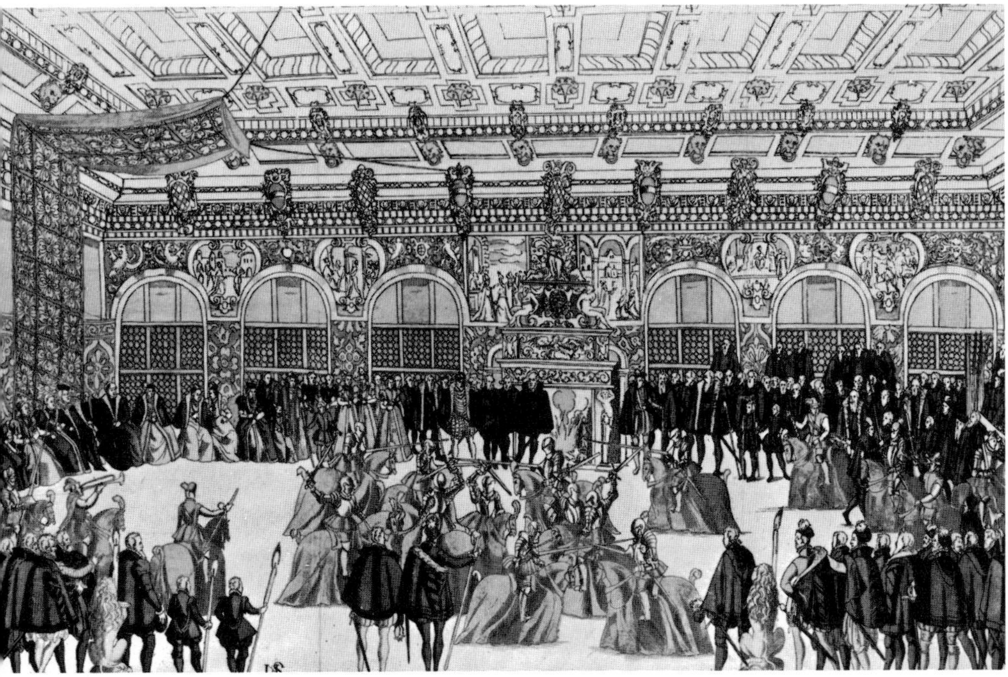

Horse tournament in the great hall of the Residenz (Alter Hof) *in Munich.*

Kübelstechen (joust) on the Marienplatz. The square's east-west axis is marked by two triumphal arches. (Munich, Stadtmuseum.)

The Baroque, with its inexhaustible scenic and decorative wealth, would pay the most sumptuous, final, tribute to the Holy Roman Empire, in the *Ludi Caesarei* performed at the courts of Prague and Vienna.

THE SCHOOL DRAMA

The philosophy and theology student Christoph Stummel of Frankfurt on the Oder was barely twenty years old when he was propelled into unexpected dramatic fame. In 1545 he was celebrated at Wittenberg as the author of a play that "greatly pleased" the learned scholars. It was called *Studentes,* no doubt after Ariosto's comedy of the same title, and was a cheerful, plain-spoken description of a contemporary student's life and all the pleasures and perils that lie in wait for the young scholar between severe Philosophia and seductive *filia hospitalis.* At the end of each act, the chorus pronounces good advice, as indeed it has ample occasion to do after the preceding carousings, brawls, and nocturnal adventures. In the end, the students' fathers hurry to the scene in alarm and decide to rescue their respective sons with a dip into the money bag and willy-nilly agreement to wedlock.

Stummel—who had studied dramatic technique with his professor, the Terence commentator Jodocus Willich—had both a gift for astute observation and enough good sense to realize that success on the school stage required proof of sound moral application.

Stummel's *Studentes* was performed twice at Wittenberg. Among the guests of honor was Melanchthon, who bestowed upon it the attribute "elegantissima," praise that referred both to the Latin dialogues fashioned after Terence and Plautus, and to the proof that the young author obviously was well-read. This indeed was apparent from the mere list of *dramatis personae.* One of the students was named Acolastus, the dissipated—a bow to the Dutch Protestant school dramatist Gnapheus, who in 1528 had written a play about the prodigal son, called *Acolastus.* Eubulos, the good counsellor, proved that Stummel was familiar with the Greek comedy writers. Eleutheria, the unprejudiced, bore witness to his knowledge of ancient mythology.

Historians of the theater are not agreed as to what sort of stage was used for these productions. Some, like F. R. Lachmann, visualize a décor made up of several sets of curtains, others a simple, neutral scene of the bathing-box type. The contrapuntal change of location from the university to the students' hometown, all on a single set, is still influenced by the late medieval morality play's principle of sequence. Transitions of this kind were frequent in the school drama, and were still used in the performance of the Laurentius play in Cologne in 1581.

Notwithstanding all attempts at scenic liveliness, the school stage was a podium for the art of recital. Professors, masters, and rectors took a hand as authors, adaptors, or translators of plays. Their names are legion, from the Alsatian Jakob Wimpheling and his comedy *Stylpho* (1494), to Johann Reuchlin and his *Henno,* performed in 1497 by students at Heidelberg, and Jacob Locher's *Tragedia de Thurcis et Suldano,* to Philipp N. Frischlin. To Frischlin the Protestant Latin school comedy of the late sixteenth century owes the fact that "it did not die of enfeeblement and boredom, but was absorbed in the new forms of dramatic art, as represented on the one hand by Frischlin's pupil Heinrich Julius von Braunschweig and Ayrer, and on the other by the Jesuit drama" (G. Roethe).

Philipp Melanchthon, the *Praeceptor Germaniae* and great reformer of the school and educational system, initiated intensive efforts to revive the drama of antiquity. In his private academy, in 1525, Euripides' *Hecuba,* Seneca's *Thyestes,* Plautus's *Miles gloriosus,* and several of Terence's comedies were performed, all with prologues by Melanchthon.

Martin Luther acknowledged that the theater could have a beneficial influence; witness the following passage in his *Tischreden*:

> Playing comedies should not be forbidden, but for the sake of the boys at school allowed and suffered. First, because it is good practice for them in the Latin language; second, because in comedies there are artfully invented, described and represented such persons as instruct people and remind each of his station and office, admonishing what is fit for a servant, a master, a young fellow, and an old man, and what he should do. Verily, they make plain and evident as in a mirror all dignitaries' rank, office, and due, and how each should behave and conduct his outward life in his station.

The reformation not only added depth to the content of the school theater, but also gave it a combative note. But by taking sides in the religious controversies it came into conflict with the pedagogic intent. When Agricola in 1537 wrote a bitter accusation in his *Tragedia Johannis Huss,* Luther censured him for excessive bias; this, Luther pointed out, was not rendering good service to the school play.

From Switzerland, too, came violent attacks against Rome. In 1539 Jakob Ruoff, stonecutter and town surgeon in Zurich, wrote the *Weingartenspiel,* a play accusing the vintners of murdering the Son of God, and presenting them as papists.

Thomas Naogeorgus, in his *Pammachius* (1538), took up the theme of the Antichrist and elaborated a complex intellectual structure covering a millennium of church history. The play takes its name from

Bishop Pammachius, a contemporary of the Roman emperor Julian the Apostate. In a grotesque scene in hell, he receives the tiara from Satan. The noisy banquet with which the Antichrist-pope Pammachius and Satanas celebrate their victory is interrupted by the news of Luther's nailing his Theses to the church door at Wittenberg. In the epilogue it is announced that the Antichrist's battle against Luther is still raging and that its issue would not be decided until Judgment Day.

Naogeorgus dedicated his drama to the "highest antipapist prince of the church in England," Archbishop Thomas Cranmer of Canterbury. Cranmer had made personal contacts with the reformers during a trip to Germany and had married a niece of the Nuremberg evangelical preacher Osiander. He had *Pammachius* performed, presumably at his own house in Canterbury. The first documented performance of it took place in March 1545 at Christ's College of the University of Cambridge.

Cranmer saw to it that the Protestant school drama got established in England as well. He encouraged John Bale, an English dramatist influenced by Naogeorgus, and helped his historical and allegorical drama *King John* to performances on college stages. Naogeorgus had made straight for the Antichrist as the spokesman of his polemics, but Bale went a roundabout way with allegorical figures taking on the character of real ones, so that Usurped Power became the Pope.

While the religious controversies grew more and more vehement, the French Queen Marguerite of Navarre tried to bridge the conflict with her *Miroir de l'âme pécheresse* (1531). But her religious poem was burned as "Protestant" in 1533 by the Catholic faculty at the University of Paris. As Calvin wrote in October 1533 to his friends in Orléans, the teachers and students of the Catholic Collège de Navarre were outraged by the Queen's pro-Protestant attitude. The attempts at mediation on the part of this intelligent, sensitive, and well-educated humanist, whose allegorical religious plays testify to profound piety, were hopelessly drowned in a wave of mutual hatred. The religious antagonists invoked the right of free and individual expression of opinion as understood in ancient democracy, but they forgot the second, crucial ingredient: tolerance.

While the leading representatives of the school drama were thus engaged in an aggressive crossing of swords, for home consumption its practitioners retreated to more neutral confessional ground. As by secret accord, and not infrequently even by direct mutual emulation, themes from the Old Testament cropped up as favorites throughout Europe, with Susanna, Jacob, and Tobias in the lead.

Sixt Birck of Augsburg in 1532 produced first a German, and five years later a Latin version of *Susanna*. At Strasbourg, in 1535, for the inauguration of the new *Gymnasium* (secondary school) that consisted of three Latin schools, Johannes Sturm chose a Lazarus theme for his play. In the little collegiate town of Steyr on the Enns, in Austria, the evangelical dramatist and producer Tobias Brunner put on a *Jakob* and a *Tobias.* In Prague, Matthias Collin, a pupil of Melanchthon's and professor of classical philology, gained the king's favors with *Susanna.* The first performance, given in 1543 at the Collegium Reček, had to be repeated at the express wish of Ferdinand I at the castle, in the presence of the entire court; Queen Anne and the two princes Maximilian and Ferdinand were seated in the royal box next to the king.

In Hungary, at the classical school of Bartfeld, Leonhard Stöckel produced a *Historia of Susanna,* as "an exercise in public speaking and moral behavior" for the young.

Another *Susanna* appeared in Denmark, written and produced by Peder Jensen Hegelund and based on the work of Sixt Birck. It had an interlude called *Calumnia,* in which the Vergilian symbolic figure of many-tongued slander, Fama mala, comes on the stage in a costume picturesquely sewn with tongues of cloth.

The choice of a subject from the Old Testament or antiquity kept teachers and pupils safely away from the slippery ground of confessional or political controversy. Any nonconformist had to pay dearly for his daring. The militant Swabian Philipp Nikodemus Frischlin—who had received the poet's crown from Emperor Ferdinand in 1576 and had benefited the school theater as rector of the Latin schools of Laibach (Ljubljana) and Braunschweig—went too far in his major work *Julius Redivivus.* In this play he combined praise of the Germans' technical achievements with blame for their national weaknesses. Frischlin died in 1590, a prisoner in the castle of Hohenurach for "continuous insult of the authorities."

In Sweden, in the period 1611–14, the much-traveled jurist Johannes Messenius, professor at the University of Uppsala, sought to awaken his students' historical interest with presentations of historical episodes in dialogue. But his theatrical projects aroused suspicion; he was accused of conspiracy with the Poles and brought to trial. Thus the offshoots of the school theater, whose origin lay in harmless Latin declamation, strayed into religious polemics and eventually ended in the crossfire of politics.

The school drama was performed in the courtyards of colleges, in school rooms, university lecture halls, town halls, on guild premises, dance floors, or in public squares when the size of the audience required it. At Eger, cantor Betulius sought permission from the town council in 1585 to have his comedy *De virtute et voluptate* played in the marketplace, after it had been given "several times before, in the school and the *Deutscher Hof,* and Sunday before last also at the town hall."

The simple single-set stage, erected on crossed beams or on barrels,

Woodcut for Tragedia de Thurcis et Suldano, *by Jacob Locher, representing the scene of the sultans: "Consultatio baiazeti et suldani." From* Libri Philomusi, *Strasbourg, 1497.*

Stage design for the Laurentius play, by Stephan Broelman, Cologne, 1581. The play was performed in the yard of the Laurentianer Burse; the stage is built around two standing trees. (Cologne, Stadtmuseum.)

needed no special equipment. A popular and helpful device for following the action, with its often numerous cast and complications was the practice of writing the characters' names on top of their "houses" in clearly legible letters. Who are the characters that are speaking? Where do they come from? Where are they going? These were questions on which the lay public, who knew no Latin, needed a few pointers. There were plenty of precedents to be found in the numerous editions of Terence, the woodcut illustrations of which had similarly stood godfather to the "bathing-box" stage. If any stage properties were needed, the local joiners helped out.

The school theater sought its effects through words rather than visual scenes. (The Baroque drama produced by the religious orders went about it the other way round.) It was by loud and audible declamation in Latin—later, in the national language—that the pedagogues proved their didactic intent to parents and public authorities. The public's attention was drawn to the fact that "what is not actually represented, is depicted in the verses," as schoolteacher Tobias Brunner of Steyr puts it in the prologue to his play *Jakob* (1566). Notwithstanding this self-denial, Brunner seems to have indulged in the luxury of a curtained stage. He talks of a "hanging," needed partly to conceal the scene, and partly for "drawing forward" in the course of the play.

The Alsatian *Meistersinger* and dramatist Jörg Wickram no doubt staged his *Tobias* in a similar manner, when it was performed by "respectable citizens" in 1551 on the market square of Kolmar, and the same applies to the 1573 performance of the pedagogue Johann Rasser's *Spiel von der Kinderzucht* in neighboring Ensisheim.

The stage possibilities of college quadrangles (Strasbourg already possessed a festival *theatrum* in 1565) are illustrated by a sketch of the Cologne Laurentius play. Its author, Stephan Broelman, was a teacher at the *Laurentianer Burse*. Between August 8 and 12, 1581, his students organized, in honor of their patron saint, four performances of the Latin

Two scenes from Johann Rasser's Spiel von der Kinderzucht. *Woodcuts from an edition printed in Ensisheim, 1574.*

drama in the schoolyard, where two of the yard's standing trees were skillfully incorporated into the scenery. The floor of the stage consisted of planks, joined end to end and resting on stout, square joists supported by wine barrels. Green canvas panels framed the stage like a peep show. The stage props to be used for the various scenes of action—inserted doors, an obelisk, an imperial throne and praetor's curule chair, a barred prison, and a pagan sacrificial altar—all these were simultaneously present, as in the late medieval legend play.

Broelman's manuscript, which was found by the Cologne theater scholar Carl Niessen, contains not only the text of his play and a colored stage design, but also numerous notes on costumes, gestures, and the course of the action. The hero-martyr wears a long, ample tunic and a yellow cloak ornamented with plant forms. Faustina appears in a black palla and with a high headdress; her name is affixed in silver letters to her shoulder.

On more modest occasions, a cloth thrown over one's shoulder had to do as a Roman toga, some obvious attribute identified the gods or allegorical figures, and a guild emblem served as indication of professional status. A plume of feathers on the hat signified a nobleman, a cudgel a trooper, a white beard an old man, a towel wound around the head a Turk.

What the professors of the high faculty expected of the school theater by way of expression and gesture can be learned from Jodocus Willich's *Liber de prononciatione rhetorica,* which is the text of the lectures he delivered at Basel and Frankfurt on the Oder. The head, forehead, lips, eyebrows, nape, neck, arms, hands, fingertips, knees, and feet—all are assigned a part in declamation "in theatro aut in theatralibus ludis." Jodocus Willich can hardly have been an Indic scholar. He would have been irritated had he known how literally close he came to the *Natyasastra,* the great Indian manual on dancing and acting. What he put down, without thought of the higher arts, just for the use of schools, was still to occupy Riccoboni in France, Goethe in Weimar, and Stanislavsky in Moscow many generations and centuries later.

THE REDERIJKERS

There exists a painting from the workshop of the Leiden painter Jan Steen, which shows a group of worthy craftsmen in a window. A bearded old man reads something from a piece of paper, with visible effort and seconded by the raised forefinger of his neighbor, a third one nonchalantly points with an empty beer mug to a tablet on the wall, with the inscription "in liefde bloeinde" (blossoming in love) over a flowerpot. They are members of the famous Amsterdam Rederijker-Kammer "Eglantine." This applied not only to their craft, but also to the art of theater, which the Dutch guilds practiced with growing devotion from the fifteenth century on.

Gripped by humanist cultural aspirations, they took up the late medieval morality plays and channeled them into the art of voluble rhetoric—in accordance with their name, which is derived from the French *rhétoriqueur.* They were the counterpart of the German *Meistersinger* as regards their guild origin, their aims, and also their proud hierarchy, ranging from patron to dean, standard bearer, and writer down to the simple member. In the sixteenth century, every town of any size in the area between Brussels and Amsterdam had its own chamber of rhetoric. The climax of their dramatic and theatrical activities was the annual *landjuweel,* a festival to which the chambers invited each other. These festivals lasted several days, included allegorical processions and *tableaux vivants* (*Vertooninge*), and culminated in a competition of moral and religious allegorical plays. The early ideas of the Reformation, too, made their appearance as, for instance, in 1539 at the Rederijker assembly in Ghent, when the motto chosen for the dramatic *Speel van Sinne* was "What gives a dying man most consolation."

When the Antwerp "Violets" were preparing their great *landjuweel* in 1561, they left the final choice of the subject to the regent, Margaret of Austria, Duchess of Parma. Of the twenty-four titles proposed to her, Margaret considered three: Is wisdom fostered more by experience or by learning? Why does a rich miser desire more riches? What can best

Allegorical group from a "Speel van Sinne." Woodcut on an invitation to the Landjuweel, *presented by the Camer van den Violieran, Antwerp, 1561.*

Group portrait of Amsterdam's Rederijker-Kammer with its motto "in liefde bloeinde." After a painting from the school of Jan Steen, 17th century.

Street stage in the horse market in Brussels. Painting by Adam Frans van der Meulen, ca. 1650. (Vaduz, Galerie Liechtenstein.)

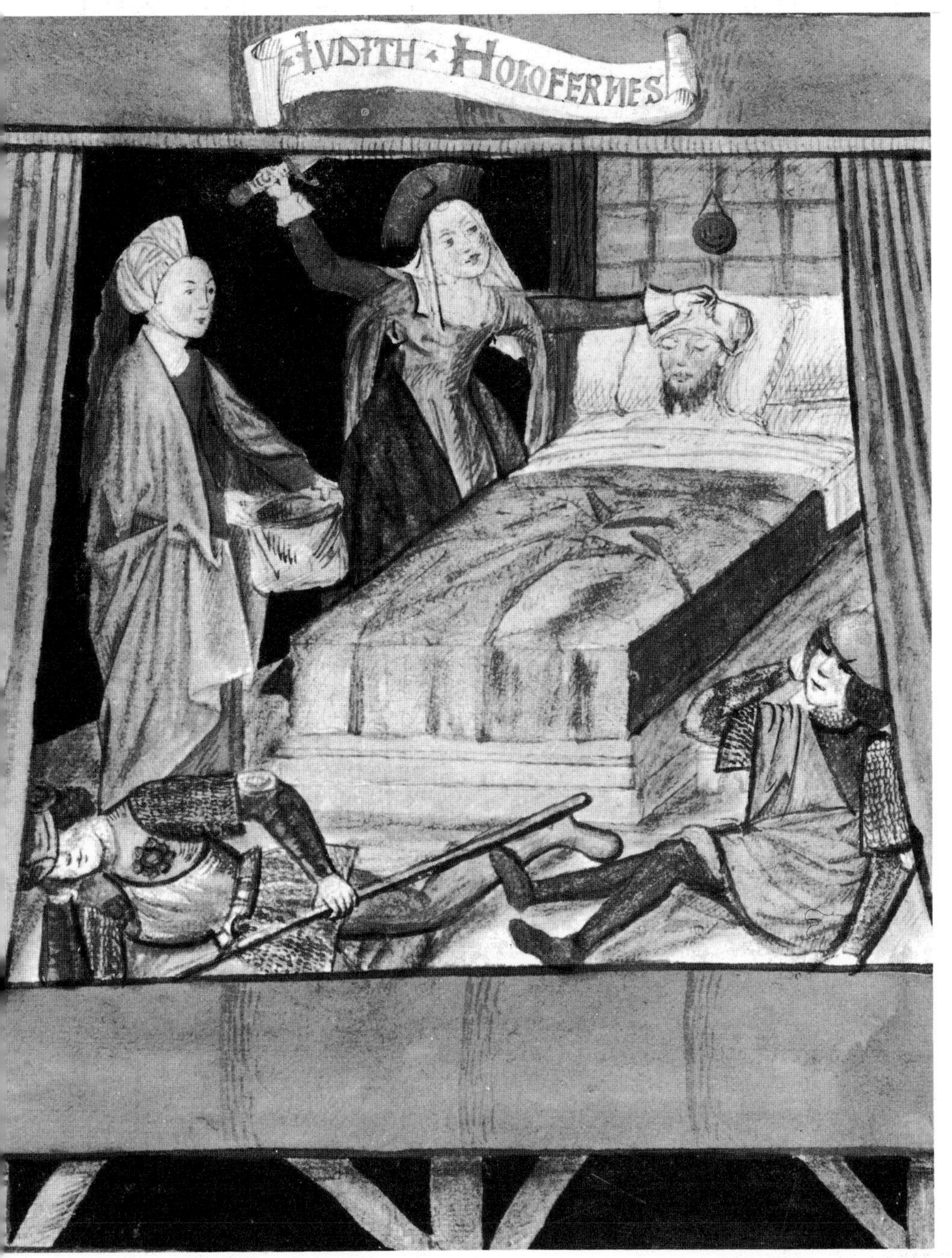

Tableau vivant *on a wagon stage: Judith and Holofernes. From the procession celebrating the arrival of Joan of Castile in Brussels in 1496. Colored drawing. (Berlin, Staatliche Museen, Kupferstichkabinett.)*

"Rhetorica," rhetoric personified, against the background of a street stage. Watercolor from the sketchbook of Hans Ludwig Pfinzing, Nuremberg, ca. 1590 (Msc. Hist. 176, Bamberg, Staatsbibliothek.)

Judgment of Solomon, *performed on the market square of Louvain, 1594. After a drawing by Guillaume Boonen, 1594; copied by L. van Peteghem, 1863. (Louvain, City Museum.)*

The great "Ommeganck" (Procession) in Brussels. Detail of the float of the Nativity. At the lower edge of the picture, the queen of the Amazons and her retinue on horseback. The procession of the guilds and corporations was made up of numerous floats and groups on Biblical and mythological themes. Painting by Denis van Alsloot, 1615. (London, Victoria and Albert Museum.)

Procession of the Rederijkers, *arriving in Malines to perform the* Landjuweel *in 1620: the "Maria Crans" Chamber of Brussels with its float and coat of arms* (Blasoen). *From the commemoration volume* De Schadt-Kiste der Philosophen ende Poeten, *printed in Malines, 1621.*

An actor. Pen drawing by Rembrandt. (Hamburg, Kunsthalle.)

awaken man to the liberal arts? The "Violets" finally chose the last question, one that offered wide scope for their traditional predilection for allegory in rhetoric and decoration. The invitation sent out by the Camer van den Violieren, in the form of a woodcut, anticipates the array of sunlit virtues on the one side, the disarray of vices on the other, with Rhetorica throning in the middle.

The Peoen-Camere at Malines printed the whole program of all the numbers spoken and sung at its festival of May 3, 1620. It appeared in 1621, illustrated with woodcuts, under the pretentious title "A Treasure Chest of Philosophers and Poets."

Scholars and artists flocked to the *Rederijkers.* Ruling princes graciously accepted honorary membership, and the Amsterdam chamber "Eglantine" could boast of having received its blazon personally from Emperor Charles V. From this background emerged the dramatist Pieter Corneliszoon Hooft, son of the mayor of Amsterdam. The performance of his *Achilles en Polyxena* in 1614 inaugurated the classical revival in the Netherlands. His pastoral play *Granida* was inspired by Guarini's *Pastor fido,* and his tragedy *Geeraerd van Velsen,* though formally in the Seneca tradition, took its subject from his own country's history and thus was the first Dutch stage work respecting the Aristotelian rule of unity of place and time. Hooft's contemporary G. A. Bredero, a member of the Amsterdam "Eglantines," is famous for his popular, realistic farces and comedies, rich in types reminiscent of Plautus and Brueghel. These were performed mainly on the peasant *Klucht* stages, but sometimes, as the *Spaanschen Brabander* in 1617, also by members of his own chamber of rhetoric.

By the beginning of the seventeenth century, the *Rederijker* stage had acquired imposing eminence. The combination of dramatic and rhetorical play and didactic and decorative *Vertooninge* demanded a setting that could do justice to both. And so an architectural rear stage was developed to close off the acting area in the back; this partition was ornamented with columns and arcades, sometimes two stories high, and thus provided the setting for the *tableaux vivants* of the *Vertooninge.* The late *Rederijker* theater, trained in humanist learning and influenced both by the indigenous craftsmen's theatrical tradition and by English strolling players, used a stage in which relics of the ancient *scenae frons* merged with elements of the Elizabethan stage.

THE MEISTERSINGER

The German *Meistersinger* share with the Dutch *Rederijkers* the merit of having preserved the continuity between the late medieval arts of acting and recitation and the world of the Renaissance. The origins of the *Meistersinger* go back to the civic culture of the fourteenth century, and their forerunners were the *Minnesänger*. The period of their greatest flowering in Nuremberg, at the time of Hans Sachs, has been immortalized in Richard Wagner's opera *The Meistersinger*.

While the "singing schools" of the *Meistersinger* taught the laws and rules of their art, strictly according to the *Tabulatur*, and while the Shrovetide plays indulged in the rhymed couplets known as *Knittelverse*, Hans Sachs, cobbler and poet, sought to familiarize his fellow craftsmen also with the higher heritage of humanism. He tried his hand at learned drama and, besides his farces, wrote voluminous dramas and tragedies for the *Meistersinger* stage. Its themes were classical and medieval, and also often biblical, which explains how performances came to be given at Nuremberg's Church of St. Martha, as became the practice in 1550, beginning with the *Enthauptung Johannis* ("Beheading of St. John"). A podium, almost 3 feet high, was put up below the Gothic choir vault, closed off in the back by a curtain, with entrances at the back and also from the door of the sacristy on the right. This is how Max Herrmann reconstructed the *Meistersinger* stage, in his *Forschungen zur deutschen Theatergeschichte des Mittelalters und der Renaissance* (1914). Albert Köster, on the other hand, maintained that the podium was constructed in the nave. The controversy was bitter and has remained unresolved. The archives of Nuremberg were of no help, but the Church of St. Martha still stands—and leaves conjectures on both possibilities open.

We can be certain that the feast-day performance of the *Meistersinger* on the whole made do with verbal decorations. On the other hand, Hans Sachs did not forgo having a ship rolled in, just as had been done at the court of Ferrara in the 1486 performance of *Menaechmi*. In the stage directions to his *Beritola*, performed in 1559, we read, "She kisses the boy and steps out of the ship. They depart in the ship." We may trust the Nuremberg guilds to have been no less inventive than the Italian *ingegnieri*.

THE ELIZABETHAN THEATER

London possessed three public playhouses when the young Shakespeare came to town in 1590. In the northern outskirts, close together, were "The Theater" and "The Curtain," and in the entertainments district south of the Thames, amid bear-baiting and bull-baiting arenas, "The Rose." The ferrymen were kept busy when the flag was flying from the roof to indicate that on this day a play was shown—a white flag for comedy, a black one for tragedy.

The theater had become an established part of city life. Like a burning glass it caught the literary radiations of the continent and focused them in vivid colors, flowing with the newly awakened national consciousness. The great theme of the Renaissance, the individual conscious of his own self, reached its zenith of artistic perfection in the Elizabethan theater. The powers of its playwrights were matched by the creative response of the audience. The theater gave expression to the confidence of an ascendant world power, whose fleet had defeated the invincible Armada. The players became, in Hamlet's words, "the abstract and brief chronicles of the time."

Under Elizabeth I—daughter of Henry VIII and Anne Boleyn, contemner of the papacy and antagonist of Mary Stuart—half a century was shaped. In this period the theater, too, found its artistic premises, its themes, its style. The new watchword of Elizabethan England was: free of France, free of the pope, a proud island realm "set in a silver sea."

In 1589 Richard Hakluyt published his great work *The Principall Navigations, Voiages and Discoveries of the English Nation.* Christopher Marlowe's Tamburlaine reveled in the newly discovered treasures of this earth, the "golden mimes, inestimable drugs and precious stones," and in the expectation of what else was to be conquered "from th' Antarctic Pole eastward."

The faraway beckoned, but at home meanwhile the heroes of national history claimed attention. John Bale had led off with his *King John* in 1548. Raphael Holinshed's *Chronicles* (1578) were an inexhaustible source of material. Shakespeare and his fellow playwrights found in them everything they needed for their historical dramas.

At the same time, classical influences still emanated from the continent. John Lyly chose mythological subjects for his comedies, Marlowe's poem *Hero and Leander,* which gave the cool sceptic Thomas Nashe occasion for mockery, is a free adaptation of *Musaeus.* Even Shakespeare's *Titus Andronicus* is still steeped in the passion of Senecan revenge and horror. The subject of Ariosto's *Suppositi* turns up once more in Shakespeare's *Taming of the Shrew*. Romeo and Juliet in their love dialogues do not deny their debt to Petrarch's *Canzoniere*, and with Rosalind's game of hide-and-seek in the Forest of Arden, *As You Like It* is still half in the pastoral tradition.

But in his historical plays, Shakespeare dipped into England's own history and took passionate issue with the problems of power and destiny. Sudden rise and abrupt fall, exultant power, crime, revenge, and murder unleash the full imagery of language, and in the rapid change of fragmentary scenes culminate in glowing synthesis. As the battle rages, a light is thrown on it now from the royal, now from the opponents' camp. The action leaps like a spark from scene to scene. Richard III's final retreat brings his end in silent combat.

The hot breath of events, which the French *tragédie classique* had captured in the great monologues of the unity-of-place drama, erupts with Shakespeare in short, powerfully contoured dialogues. Every occurrence is transposed into action. "A kingdom for a stage" he covets in the prologue to *Henry V*, instead of the "unworthy scaffold," and calls on the audience's "imaginary forces": "Suppose within the girdle of these walls/Are now confin'd two mighty monarchies. . . . For 'tis your thoughts that now must deck our kings,/Carry them here and there, jumping o'er times,/Turning the accomplishment of many years/Into an hour-glass."

Shakespeare's plays offered superabundant scope for the transforming capacity of the imagination, from the poetic magic of *A Midsummer Night's Dream* to King Lear's madness on the stormy heath. He rose above the classical rules by virtue of his poetic genius. He brought to life periods and places, tenderness and coarseness in the "cockpit" of the theater.

Shakespeare took no part in the dispute about theoretical rules, though it did flare up in London, too. Sir Philip Sidney, the lettered nobleman highly esteemed at the court as a nephew of the Earl of Leicester, had come down on the side of the Aristotelian unities in his *Apologie for Poetrie* (written around 1580, but printed, posthumously, in 1595), and had denounced his countrymen for not paying sufficient attention to them. But when, in 1603, Ben Jonson came forward with his strictly constructed Roman tragedy *Sejanus*, it was a flop. His strength lay in the field of realistic, contemporary, critical comedy, in which indeed he also respected the three classical unities, in protest against the dramatic indiscipline of many playwrights of the time.

Shakespeare had his fun in rolling off an ironic catalogue of the recognized types of drama. When Polonius announces the arrival of the players to Hamlet, he praises them as "the best actors in the world, either for tragedy, comedy, history, pastoral, pastoral-comical, historical-

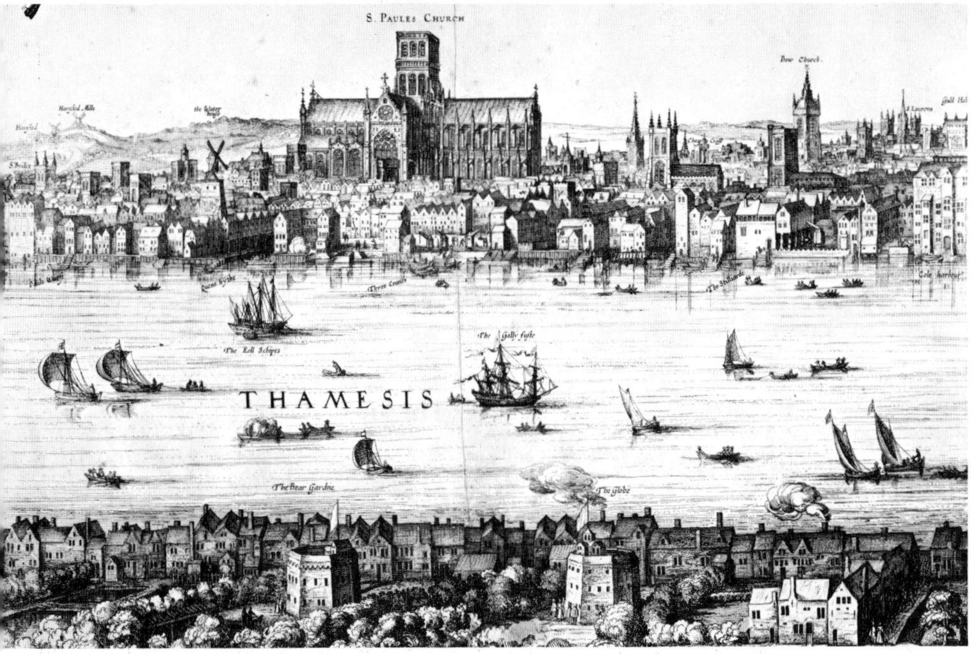

J. C. Visscher's map of London in 1616: part of the panorama, showing Bankside at Shakespeare's time; front center, the Globe and the Bear Garden.

Detail from Ralph Aga's map of London, 1569–90 (ed. 1631): Bankside entertainment quarter with bull-baiting and bear-baiting arenas, precursors of the Elizabethan theaters built after 1587 on the right bank of the Thames.

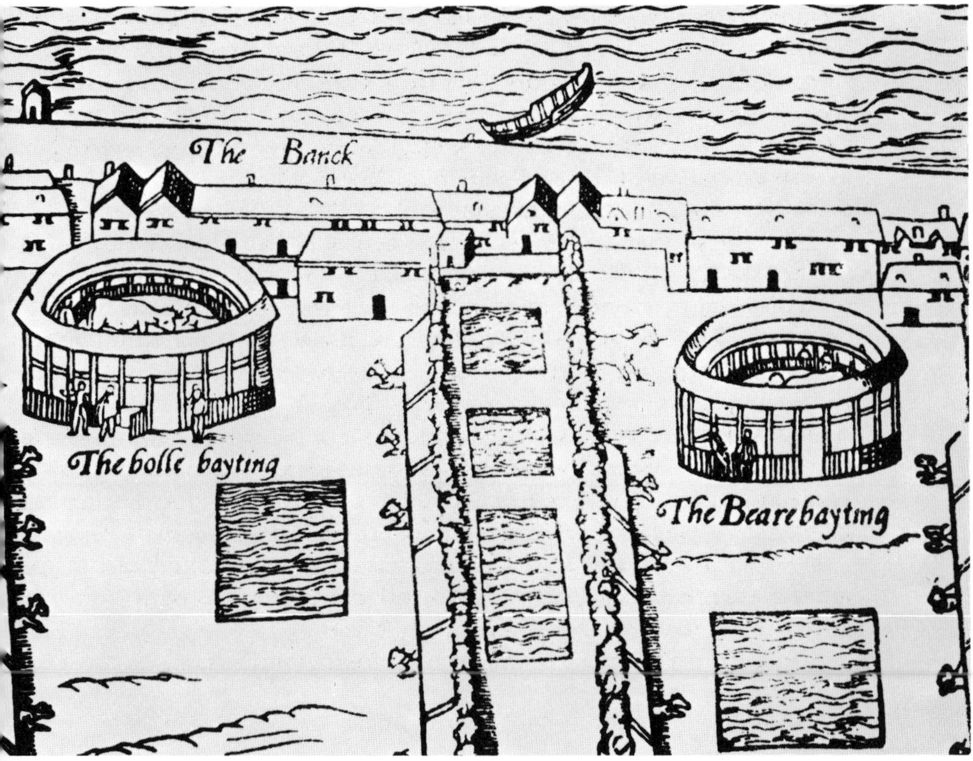

pastoral, tragical-historical, tragical-comical-historical-pastoral, scene individable, or poem unlimited: Seneca cannot be too heavy, nor Plautus too light. For the law of writ and the liberty, these are the only men."

The young Shakespeare burst upon the Elizabethan stage at a time when the professional actor already had his secure position in the structure of society. Nothing reliable is known of his personal qualities as an actor. He is supposed to have appeared in Ben Jonson's comedy *Every Man in His Humour* in 1598, and allegedly took the part of Adam in his own comedy *As You Like It.* His biographer Nicholas Rowe thought he was best in the part of the Ghost in *Hamlet.* It would seem that he no longer appeared on the stage after 1603, for his name is not included in any of the lists of actors printed with each play. Research into this matter, while plentiful, is not made easier by his company's repeated change of name, successively known as Lord Hunsdon's, the Lord Chamberlain's, and, ultimately, the King's Men.

The noble patrons conferred upon the actors' companies they sponsored not only a license to play, but most often their own name. They gave them legal protection, much needed by actors at that time, given the hostility of the Puritan clergy.

At court, however, they had always been welcome. Richard, Duke of Gloucester, had actors in his employment before he ascended the throne as Richard III. King Henry VIII kept a company, and from time to time released it for touring, which saved him the cost of their board and lodging and was good for public morale. Queen Elizabeth was rather less partial to the pretty art of make-believe. Nevertheless, Lord Leicester succeeded in 1574 in obtaining a patent from her, authorizing his own men "to use, exercise and occupie the arte and faculty of playenge Commedies, Tragedies, Enterludes, stage playes, and such other like . . . as well within oure Citie of London and liberties of the same, as also . . . thoroughte oure Realme of England."

But the plays to be performed first had to be submitted for licensing to the Master of the Revels, a functionary who superintended royal festivities. In 1581 another patent extended this censorship to the programs of all public stages. The Master of the Revels thus acquired all-powerful, centralized control, which was to govern the fate of theaters and their playwrights for four centuries. Even in the twentieth century, critical young dramatists were barred from the stage when the Lord Chamberlain's Office withheld its approval; John Osborne and Edward Bond at first had to be content with club performances—for the English club is sacrosanct and safe from the interference even of the Crown. It was not until 1968, and after vigorous representations on the part of the avant-garde, that Elizabeth II abolished the censorship of the theater originally exercised by the Master of the Revels.

The Crown's control authority was doubly burdensome to the Elizabethan theater of the late sixteenth century, for the Common Council of London felt that their rights of censorship were thereby infringed upon and so laid down restrictions of their own. No performances were to take place on Sundays, and none at all when there was a danger of the plague; they also took exception to the disorders ensuing from performances in "Innes, havinge chambers and secrete places adioyninge to their open stagies and gallyries."

The first to hold the absolute power of censorship was Edmund Tilney, who was Master of the Revels for thirty years, from 1579 until his death in 1610. Through his hands passed the dramatic masterpieces of the Elizabethan theater, as also the great mass of the ephemeral good, bad, and indifferent. None of Tilney's official records are extant, but we have the register of licenses issued by one of his successors. Sir Henry Herbert, who succeeded to the office in 1623 and carefully recorded not only the title and author of each play, but also all—often rather silly—objections and cuts required.

Tilney's ledgers, like the theater itself, might well have been described, in Shakespeare's words, as "the abstracts and brief chronicles of the time." His entries would be a living inventory. They would record the dialogues of Lyly, which were models of refined and elaborate flattery in polished verse, and surely as unexceptionable as were George Peele's allegorically decked-out pastorals; they would name Thomas Heywood's and Thomas Dekker's most successful plays—*A Woman Killed with Kindness* by the former, and *The Honest Whore* by the latter—both forerunners of the middle-class tragedy; they would tell about Robert Greene's satirical miracle plays and George Chapman's gory blank verse tragedies; and, finally, they would list, as the chief items on the assets' side, all the works of Shakespeare, which Tilney was the first to read. It speaks well for his tolerance and judgment that he let pass such caustic and brilliant satires as Ben Jonson's *Volpone* and *The Alchemist*. Master of the Revels Tilney was, perhaps, the most impartial figure in the tug of war for authority in questions of the theater. The city fathers were only too susceptible to such polemical treatises as Stephen Gosson's *Playes confuted in five Actions* (1582) and were apt to oppose the theater as a sink of iniquity that, in Thomas White's words (1577), "set a-gog: theft and whoredom; pride and prodigality; villainy and blasphemy. . . ." But no reprisals or restrictions could impair the importance and flowering of the Elizabethan Theater. The outlawed strollers had become men of a respectable profession, and sometimes men of considerable wealth. Actors' companies were organized like guilds; the owners of playhouses sometimes had several business enterprises, took a share of the box-office takings, and shrewdly increased their sources of income.

James Burbage, builder of the first permanent public playhouse in

Sir Henry Unton's Wedding Masque, ca. 1600: party at table, musicians, and round dance. Portion of an anonymous painting representing the principal events of Sir Henry Unton's life. (London, National Portrait Gallery.)

Scene from Titus Andronicus, *1595. Only extant contemporary drawing of a Shakespeare play, attributed to Henry Peacham. (Collection of the Marquess of Bath, Longleat.)*

Title-page woodcut for Thomas Kyd's Spanish Tragedy. *In the arbor, Horatio hanged by murderers; Hieronimo (Horatio's father), Bellimperia, and Lorenzo hurry to the scene. From a 1633 edition.*

Woodcut representing the Tragical History of Doctor Faustus, *by Christopher Marlowe. Ca. 1620.*

London, is known to have been a privileged member of the Earl of Leicester's company. When in 1576, he opened his playhouse in Shoreditch, outside the city limits and to the north beyond Bishopsgate, he proudly gave it the plainest of names: The Theatre. In choosing a site in the outskirts, he prudently removed himself from the immediate jurisdiction of the Lord Mayor. The Theatre was a circular timber construction with galleries and boxes, and it created a sensation. Even the severe preacher John Stockwood paid it the compliment of describing it as a "gorgeous playing place."

A year later, another playhouse was built in the immediate vicinity. It was named the Curtain. With its three tiers of balconies, the Curtain closely resembled the Theatre, as well as all the future unroofed round theaters of Elizabethan London. It was, of course, a matter of long experience that a theater in this district could draw large crowds. James Burbage himself had acted at the Cross Keys, an inn in Gracechurch Street, which in 1594 still served as winter quarters to the Lord Chamberlain's Men, of whom Shakespeare was a member. At the Bull near Bishopsgate, Richard Tarleton, the great clown and improvisor of the Queen's Men, had filled ten years earlier the inn premises with closely packed crowds.

Another good spot was Bankside, south of the Thames. Here the most popular places of entertainment were a bull-baiting arena, marked

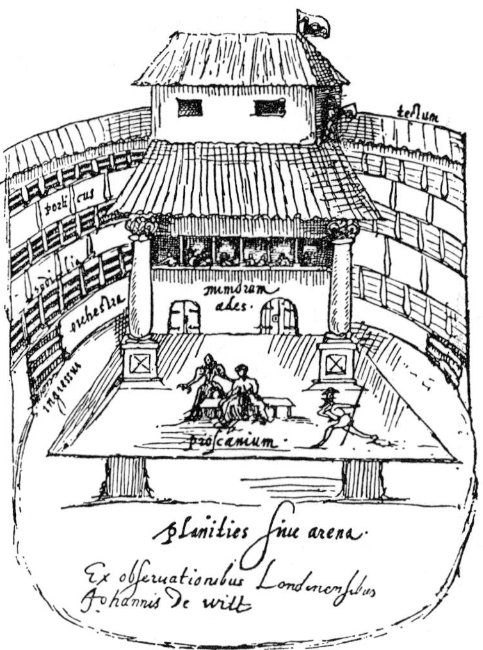

Inside view of the Swan playhouse in London. Drawing based on notes by Jan de Witt, 1596.

on London maps since 1542 as "Bull Ring," and a bear garden, not to speak of acrobats, tightrope walkers, jugglers, and strolling players.

Here Philip Henslowe, dyer and pawnbroker, built his first theater in 1587, the Rose. It proved a lucrative business, to judge by his diary and accounts, which have come down to us. Henslowe opened another two theaters, the Fortune (around 1600), in Finsbury, half a mile from the Curtain, and the Hope (in 1613). The Hope stood on the site of the demolished bear garden and was the last of the unroofed London playhouses. The profitable right bank of the Thames became the center of the Elizabethan theater world. The Swan, built in 1595 by Francis Langley, was followed in 1599 by the Globe, and in 1605 by the Red Bull.

The Dutchman Jan de Witt, who visited London in 1596, described the Rose and the Swan as the finest of the four London playhouses of that period. Of the Swan, as the largest, he had a drawing made, which shows the inside with the stage and is the only extant contemporary pictorial record of an Elizabethan theater, leaving aside maps.

The cylindrical frame accommodates three spectators' galleries, of which the topmost is protected by a roof sloping inward. The closed ring of the auditorium is accessible by two sets of stairs from outside, and inside it towers above the stage building. The spacious acting podium, labeled "proscaenium," juts out into the unroofed inner yard. Two doors lead to the "mimorum aedes," the actors' dressing and property room. Above it is a gallery covered by a canopy roof supported by pillars. This could be occupied by musicians, become part of the play as an upper stage, or serve as an audience chamber.

Above this gallery rises a narrow loft with two windows and a balcony on the right. From here the trumpeter announced the beginning of the performance (which de Witt, for convenience, shows already in full swing).

De Witt's sketch may be seen in conjunction with a map of London by Visscher, published in 1616. This shows the circular Swan as an equilateral dodecagon.

George Topham Forrest's reconstruction of the Globe is similar in form. The back screen of the acting podium can be used as a room, the central gallery as an upper stage. There are dressing rooms on both sides of the "inner stage." Above them, in the upper story, are the "Lords' Rooms," reserved for noblemen in the audience.

This basic pattern, give and take a few variants, probably was the same for all the unroofed round or polygonal theaters of the Elizabethan age. (After 1620, only indoor playhouses were built.) The spectators paid a penny at the outer gate, which gave admittance to the inner yard—the notorious pit—where the groundlings raised their voices in approval or disapproval, thus often enough irreversibly sealing the fate of a play. The origin of this use of "groundling" is not known. Perhaps the vicinity of the Thames suggested the transfer of the word for river-bottom fish to the occupants of the pit. Those who could afford a seat paid a supplement at the entrance to the appropriate gallery.

The box-office takings went into a common pool, out of which each actor was paid his contractual share. This distribution was not always a peaceful affair, yet this earliest of the theater's profit-sharing systems survived for centuries. As a rule, scant reward fell to the dramatist, unless he was a permanent member of the company and as such had a share in current takings. If he was not, he sold his play to a principal, who then made as much profit as he could from the performances. All Thomas Heywood is reported to have received for his most popular play, *A Woman Killed with Kindness,* is six pounds, while Henslowe paid no less than six pounds thirteen shillings for the leading lady's black velvet costume.

Generally, the dramatists' motives were pot-boiling and mutual rivalry. While Shakespeare was busy reshaping Thomas Kyd's—now lost—original Hamlet into a tragic hero of his own, Ben Jonson had a similar task in hand. He was adapting Kyd's major work, *The Spanish Tragedie,* which also involves a theme of revenge, the appearance of a ghost, and a play within the play. Shakespeare's *Hamlet* was staged at the Globe in the summer of 1600. It captured London and came to provide the most-acted hero of world theater. Jonson's effort was too late and fell into oblivion.

The popular appeal of a play far outweighed the question of its literary origin. What mattered in the Elizabethan theater, as in others, was not the invention of a plot, but its creative elaboration. Often several authors joined in writing a play. Francis Beaumont and John Fletcher wrote some fifty popular comedies together in the years 1606–16, to which Fletcher contributed frivolous wit and lively fantasy, and Beaumont dramatic flair.

There was plenty of money to be made in the theater. Philip Henslowe made a fortune from his three playhouses. Edward Alleyn, then the most famous member of the Lord Admiral's and the Lord Chamberlain's companies, leading actor and manager of Shakespeare's plays, retired from the stage at the age of thirty-nine, a wealthy man. He then followed his philanthropic inclinations and endowed a college.

Richard Burbage, of the best-known actors' family in Elizabethan England, was said to enjoy a substantial income from the properties he owned. By comparison, the house at Stratford-on-Avon to which Shakespeare retired in 1610—now a man of repute and comfortable circumstances—seems rather modest.

The boy actors, directed by enterprising choirmasters and schoolmasters, were regarded rather as a nuisance by the Elizabethan professional companies. Such groups as the Children of the Royal Chapel and the Children of St. Paul's consisted of choirboys originally trained to sing at divine service. In the course of the sixteenth century, they appeared before the public in theatrical performances. They played at the Convent of the Blackfriars in the city, and around 1600 in a theater hall of their own. Their public consisted of a circle of patrons and friends, and they enjoyed the good will of both the court and the magistrates. Christopher Marlowe, whose *Tamburlaine the Great* and *Doctor Faustus* were first performed by the Lord Admiral's and the Lord Chamberlain's men, fell out with the professional actors over a reference to the boys' companies, and at some point thought of entrusting his *Dido* to the children—not a very judicious idea, in view of the suicidal amorous passion of the heroine. But the children's companies could be used to good effect in the competitive struggle. Even Ben Jonson, at the time of his falling-out with Shakespeare, saw fit to supply "the nestlings" with texts containing mocking verses on Shakespeare's theater.

But Shakespeare hit back, in Hamlet: "but there is, sir, an eyrie of children, little eyases, that cry out on the top of question and are most tyranically clapped for't: these are now the fashion, and so berattle the common stages—so they call them—that many wearing rapiers are afraid of goose-quills, and dare scarce come hither."

The fear of "goose-quills" confirms how much importance the Elizabethan theater attached to the spoken word and clear diction, be it in poetical or polemic verse. The stage directions suggest a subtly refined art of acting. But loud ranting no doubt was there, too. The unroofed stage, the crowded galleries, and the multitude of groundlings in the pit inevitably demanded of the actor a penetrating voice and widely visible gestures.

James Burbage was famous for his powers of expression even in pantomime plays. But for him, as also for Edward Alleyn, the great moment came when they stepped forward from the group to the front edge of the platform and launched into a great soliloquy. To "drown the stage with tears and cleave the general ear with horrid speech," that was the ambition of the Elizabethan actor. Edward Alleyn, said Ben Jonson, had so perfectly mastered this art that nothing ever appeared overdone or artificial, and that he seemed wholly filled with the spirit of his part.

Shakespeare used the stage itself to criticize excess of bombast, when Hamlet instructs the players:

> Speak the speech, I pray you, as I pronounced it to you, trippingly on the tongue: but if you mouth it, as many of your players do, I had as lief the

Stage of the Red Bull playhouse in London. Frontispiece to The Wits, *by Francis Kirkman, 1672.*

> town-crier spoke my lines. Nor do not saw the air too much with your hand, thus, but use all gently; for in the very torrent, tempest, and, as I may say, the whirlwind of passion, you must acquire and beget a temperance that may give it smoothness. O, it offends me to the soul to hear a robustious periwig-pated fellow tear a passion to tatters, to very rags, to split the ears of the groundlings, who for the most part are capable of nothing but inexplicable dumb-shows and noise. . . . Be not too tame neither, but let your own discretion be your tutor: suit the action to the word, the word to the action; with this special observance, that you o'erstep not the modesty of nature: for anything so overdone is from the purpose of playing, whose end, both at the first and now, was and is, to hold, as 'twere, the mirror up to nature; to show virtue her own feature, scorn her own image, and the very age and body of the time his form and pressure. . . .

For outward effect, actors could rely on colorful and often sumptuous costumes, and on the necessary personal and stage properties, which could be carried to the front stage during the play and taken away again. Backstage, an inner room and balcony were provided. If need be, hoisting machines and traps were available. These were as indispensable to Shakespeare as to Calderón; they usually went into action to the accompaniment of a roll of thunder, which not only heightened the suspense, but also drowned out the creaking of the machinery. But the "mood" had to be created by the actor himself, by his interpretation of the playwright's words. He had to conjure up the time of day, the sun that tinges the evening sky with red, "the morn, in russet mantle clad" rising over the eastern hills, and the stars glittering in the heavens—notwithstanding the pale and misty London afternoon (plays were usually performed between three and six o'clock), notwithstanding the rain clouds blowing up and the noise that intruded from the Thames.

The "spoken décor" is a crucial stylistic feature of the Elizabethan stage. Shakespeare handled it with genius. So did the Spaniards Lope de Vega and Calderón. It is revealing that even a theoretician of the French *tragédie classique,* which obeyed wholly different laws, acknowledged the need for poetic conjuration of scenery. In his treatise *La pratique du théâtre,* Abbé d'Aubignac demanded that the scenery must be explained in the verses, "so as to connect the action with the place and the events with the objects, and thus to link all parts to form a well-ordered whole."

It would be startling if some producer should ever see fit to have bird song accompany Juliet's soothing words of love: "It was the nightingale and not the lark." Sometimes, Shakespeare does call on music, when he wants to sharpen a contrast in mood. In *Romeo and Juliet,* the musicians stop abruptly as "wedding cheer" is turned to a "sad burial feast." In *The Tempest,* Ariel enters, invisible, playing and singing, solemn and strange music surrounds Prospero, the banquet vanishes with thunder and lightning, and a strange, hollow and confused noise chases away the dancing nymphs. Shakespeare says farewell to the stage that was his world.

"Now my charms are all o'erthrown," says Prospero with melancholy wisdom, and commends himself to the audience's prayer, "which pierces so that it assaults/Mercy itself and free all faults./As you from crimes would pardon'd be,/Let your indulgence set me free."

These were the last verses Shakespeare ever wrote.

The Baroque

INTRODUCTION

The Swiss art historian Heinrich Wölfflin once characterized the Baroque as "the convolution of Renaissance forms." The remark is literally borne out by the great volute buttresses of the Church of S. Maria della Salute in Venice. In the Baroque age the clear, classic linearity of the Renaissance acquired emotional appeal, the straight line—in structure as well as in thought—dissolved in ornament, clarity gave way to abundance, self-confidence to hyperbole. Concepts assumed the garb of allegory, and reality lost itself in a realm of illusion. The world became a stage, life turned into playacting, into a sequence of transformations. The illusion of infinity sought to conjure away the bounds of man's brief earthly existence.

The Baroque revived the allegorical multifariousness of the late Middle Ages and enriched it with the sensuous worldliness of the Renaissance. But in the background the sand of time was running out, and the "memento mori" of the Dance of Death was heard again. Worldly pleasures and the shadow of death, things terrestial and things celestial, theatricality and spirituality flowed together in a great crescendo. An age was creating the setting for himself.

Neither before nor afterward did an era ever paint its own image in such lavish colors. And just as Baroque art unfolded in resplendent theatricality, as absolutism strove for an imposing apotheosis of sovereignty, as the Counter-Reformation called upon every optical and intellectual means of stagecraft—so, too, the theater rose to great heights.

Word, rhyme, image, representation, phantasmagoria and pedagogic applications were now joined by music, which rose from a merely accompanying element in the theater to an autonomous art. For the Baroque saw the birth of opera. From the courts of Italy, opera now set out on its triumphal progress, supported by the patronage of popes, princes, kings, and emperors. Painters and architects fell under its sway. Romain Rolland described the music theater at the time of Pope Clement IX as a *"passion maladive,"* displaying all the symptoms of collective folly:

> A pope composes operas and sends sonnets to prima donnas. The cardinals busy themselves as librettists or stage designers; they design costumes and organize theatrical performances. Salvator Rosa acts in comedies. Bernini writes operas, for which he paints decorations, sculpts statues, devises machinery, writes the text, composes the music and builds the theater.

In the late days of the Renaissance and the early days of the Baroque period the theater hall became one of the most important state rooms of any palace. Stages were erected in the Vatican in Rome, in the Uffizi in Florence, in the Palais Royal in Paris. Amid the splendor of the Château de Versailles, the measured grace of courtly dance gave birth to the art of ballet. Louis XIV appeared in a golden sun-ray costume as a young "roi soleil," long before history bestowed this name upon him. Queens took the parts of nymphs, princes and princesses were dressed up as cherubs—on the stage as well as on the painter's canvas. To please Queen Christina of Sweden, the philosopher René Descartes wrote a ballet called *The Birth of Peace,* which was performed at the Castle of Stockholm in 1649, following the end of the Thirty Years' War. Meanwhile, the strolling comedians and the *Commedia dell'arte* had provided a bridge between the enemy camps.

From the improvised theater hall of patrons of the arts the next step led to the independent, free-standing opera house, the architecturally ornate theater with its auditorium of tiers and galleries, equipped with a sovereign's box and articulated in accordance with the court hierarchy of the spectators. The stage assumed the peep-show form, framed by a splendid proscenium arch. Caryatids supported architraves, cherubs held back stucco curtains. The newly developed system of staggered side wings made possible the illusion of depth and frequent changes of scene.

Transformation is the magic word of the Baroque. Metamorphosis became its favorite theme, inexhaustible in its potentialities of glorification. Seeing Nature as the great manifestation of God, in Giordano Bruno's words, Man now emerged as the stage manager of himself. But, *Life's a Dream.* The universe is the great world theater in which the roles are distributed by the most powerful of all authors. Calderón laid bare the reverse side of Baroque hubris, in an appropriate symbol of his age: the image of the stage upon the stage. When his beggar complained that all he got was the duty of poverty, that he was given neither scepter nor crown, the answer came from the deepest convictions of Christian faith: "When finally the curtain falls, you [and the ruler] shall be equals."

OPERA AND SINGSPIEL

In 1581, when Galileo Galilei, at the age of seventeen, enrolled at the University of Pisa, his father Vincenzo published a highly erudite work on the theory of music, *Dialogo della musica antica e della moderna*. Vincenzo Galilei was a mathematician, but beyond that an *uomo universale* in the fullest sense of the classical ideal. It was he who took the bold step Vitruvius only explored, that is, from the logic of numbers to the calculable secret of musical notes.

Vincenzo belonged to the Florentine circle of Count Giovanni de' Bardi, an academic club. Its members spent long hours discussing the Aristotelian theory of music as an essential part of tragedy. While adducing practical examples to demonstrate the "dramatization of music," they certainly also had a high regard for comedy. Bardi's *Amico fido*, first performed in 1585 in a production by Buontalenti, had been acclaimed by the whole of Florence. This friend and patron was chosen by Vincenzo as his partner in the spirited discussion of contemporary polyphony and instrumental composition. Bardi took the more moderate line in this dialogue, for after all he was indebted to his friends, the Florentine musicians, for the song and dance numbers of his *Amico fido*. Vincenzo had harsh words to say about the courtly music of his time. He accused it of impropriety and called it a "depraved, impudent whore." He demanded the subordination of music to poetry and, as an example of what he meant by the "representative style" of future composition, set to music a few passages from Dante's *Divine Comedy* and the lamentations of Jeremiah.

In 1594, three years after Vincenzo Galilei's death, the first work in the new dramatic style was performed before a small, select circle in Florence. This was the world's famous first opera, *Dafne,* with music by Jacopo Peri to a text by Ottavio Rinuccini, and some songs by Guilio Caccini.

In 1597, at a repeat performance in the palace of the Florentine scholar Jacopo Corsi, the host, the composer, and the librettist were congratulated by a distinguished audience on their "revival of antique drama in the spirit of music."

But, apart from its laudable intentions, the learned artifice had little in common with the drama of antiquity. Rather, its lyrical and dramatic foundation was akin to the pastoral play, the *intermedii,* and the *trionfi*. With its graceful sound painting it transfigured the Elysian Fields of shepherds and nymphs and blended their originally independent choral songs into the new "stilo rappresentativo." Orpheus, the

Thracian bard who had cast his spell over trees, rocks, and wild animals, led in the new art form with his lyre.

Peri and Rinuccini cooperated once more in a joint "tragedia di musica" for the wedding of Maria de' Medici and Henri IV of France. They chose the Orpheus theme and named their second opera *Euridice.* It was performed with great splendor on February 9, 1600, in the ballroom of the Palazzo Pitti. Caccini again contributed some songs, as he had done for *Dafne.*

Jacopo Peri sang Orpheus, the part of Eurydice was taken by Vittoria Archilei, the celebrated coloratura soprano of her time. Shepherds, nymphs, and spirits of the underworld were represented in the chorus, which was headed by a chorus leader after the pattern of antiquity. Rinuccini closely followed Poliziano's pastoral play *Orfeo,* but since this "tragedy" was intended for a wedding celebration, he gave it a happy ending: Orpheus makes Pluto relent and is allowed to take Eurydice back from Hades to life.

The stage designer of this gala performance, presumably Buontalenti, had the challenging task of contrasting a pastoral setting of "wonderful woods" with the somber horrors of the underworld, which in the end are retransformed and changed into the pretty pastoral setting. "Si rivolge la scena, e torna come prima," as Rinuccini specifies in his stage directions. It may be assumed that Buontalenti worked with the revolving prisms made of wood already used in 1585 for *Amico fido.*

Three days after the performance of *Euridice,* another opera was given in the theater hall of the Uffizi. This was *Il Rapimento di Cefalo,* by Giulio Caccini, who this time was named as sole composer. Gabriele Chiabrera had written the libretto, and Buontalenti again had created the stage designs. The expenses were paid by the city of Florence. Close to four thousand guests, according to the generous count of the chroniclers, admired the scenic miracles revealed when the ornamented red silk curtain dropped: the gold chariot of Helios, the magnificent throne of Jupiter, mountains vanishing into the ground, whales popping up and down, frightening earthquakes, and lovely fields scented with perfume.

Opera was launched on its triumphal progress, with all the scenic extravagance of the early Baroque art of stage transformation. Its stage designers proved inexhaustible in their invention of ever-new pulling, flying, and gliding mechanisms to move the host of mythological and allegorical accessory figures that crowded out the opera's true theme.

Given the range of antique subjects, it is surprising how monotonously the early opera composers stuck to the same few themes. No doubt, the pioneers of the "stilo rappresentativo" sensed how questionable was their musical interpretation of the classical theater. For decades they stuck to the two subjects that could not be contested, because no one knew any better, that is, to Orpheus and Daphne. No dramatic texts on either character are extant from the Greek or ancient Roman dramatists.

Rinuccini's *Dafne* was again set to music in 1608, now by the Florentine chapel master Marco da Gagliano. The new work was performed at the instance of Duke Vincenzo Gonzaga at the court of Mantua, where a high standard prevailed in the cultivation of both the theater and music. As early as 1601 the prince had appointed to his court as *maestro di cappella* the viol player and singer Claudio Monteverdi of Cremona. At the carnival festivities in February 1607 Monteverdi first appeared as a composer. *Orfeo* was the theme and title of his work. The text, by Alessandro Striggio, retained the original ending. Orpheus looks back as he leaves Hades, Eurydice is lost to him. Apollo consoles him with the promise that they will meet again in the afterworld. The performance closed with a Moorish dance.

The first admirers of the work were the members of the Accademia degli Invaghiti, who used to hold their meetings at the ducal palace and had recommended the production. Upon the duke's wish, *Orfeo* was repeated at court on February 24, and March 1, of that year. The whole of Italy talked about Monteverdi. The master's admirers were enthusiastic; it was impossible, they maintained, to give better expression to the soul's sentiments in the harmony of poetry and music than had been done in *Orfeo*.

The great lament of Ariadne in Monteverdi's second opera, *Arianna*, became the most famous heroic-dramatic aria of its time. The part was created by Virginia Andreini, whose expressive acting, as the chroniclers record, contributed much to the success of the first performance in 1608. The era of the prima donna was at hand.

For five more years the star of Monteverdi's name shone over the court of Mantua. In 1613, after the death of Duke Vincenzo Gonzaga, Monteverdi accepted an invitation to Venice, where, as director of music at S. Marco, he witnessed in 1637 the opening of the world's first public opera house, the Teatro di S. Cassiano. Its initiator was the musician, composer, and librettist Benedetto Ferrari, who had written the text for the opening performance, an opera called *Andromeda*, with music by Manelli.

The new art of opera—a term first used by Monteverdi's pupil Francesco Cavalli—immediately conquered all of Venice. It became a lucrative business to build opera houses. Low admission charges attracted large audiences. Everybody who wanted to be anybody rented a box and played the patron. Within a few years, Venice possessed half a dozen opera houses, which were often open simultaneously during the main playing season, the carnival weeks.

Naples opened its first opera house in 1651, with a production of

Monteverdi's *L'Incoronazione di Poppea.* Florence, Rome, Bologna, Genoa, and Modena soon followed suit.

North of the Alps, Salzburg, Vienna, and Prague took up the new art form, initially in the setting of the court festival and with casts of predominantly Italian singers. In 1627, the poet Martin Opitz and the composer Heinrich Schütz produced the first opera in the German language—*Daphne,* modeled on the works of Rinuccini and Peri, and performed at Hartenfels Castle near Torgau, on the occasion of the wedding of the Saxon Princess Luise and the Landgrave Georg of Hesse-Darmstadt.

At the court of Vienna, close family ties with Italy assured opera of a hospitable reception. The Empress Eleonore, wife of Ferdinand II, who was of the ducal house of Gonzaga at Mantua, received news of the latest musical developments at first hand, so to speak. In 1627, she sponsored a performance of a "dramma per musica" with *Commedia dell'arte* characters, which was given in the great hall of the Hofburg in Vienna. Monteverdi was honored with a production of his *Arianna.* Francesco Cavalli dedicated his opera *Egisto* to the Habsburg dynasty. The Italian musician Antonio Bertoli was appointed director of the imperial court chapel.

But the scenic magnificence of Vienna's opera house originated with Giovanni Burnacini, an architect and designer who had proved his mettle in Venice and Mantua, and whom Ferdinand III called to his court in 1651. Burnacini made his debut in 1652, with a production of an opera called *Daphne,* presumably the Rinuccini-Peri version. A year later, he impressed the Diet of Regensburg with a construction improvised for the festival, "a theatrum built of mere boards, of the dimensions and height of a fair-sized church." He was helped by his son Ludovico, who soon afterward succeeded his father in Vienna and was to equal him both in ability and in fame.

Ludovico Burnacini designed decorations, stage machinery, pageant cars, and costumes for more than 150 operas, for water festival shows performed on the lake of the château Favorite, and for horseback ballets in the Florentine style.

The new Vienna opera house was opened in June 1668 with the reliable *trionfi* theme of Paris and his golden apple. On this occasion Burnacini outdid himself—and the musical work as well. He presented a gigantic display of picturesquely grouped choruses of gods; massed clouds receding into infinite depth and finally gliding out sideways to reveal Jupiter enthroned; wave upon foaming wave of sea plied by ships; fearful marine monsters and dainty nymphs—all these doubtless held the attention of the admiring gala audience more than did the comparatively modest efforts of singers and orchestra. The actor who

Interior of Munich's opera house on the Salvatorplatz, built by Francesco Santurini and opened in 1654. The royal box was added in 1685 by Domenico and Gasparo Mauro. Engraving by Michael Wening, 1686.

Open-air performance of the grand opera Angelica, vincitrice di Alcina, *by J. J. Fux, in the Favorite Park in Vienna, 1716. Stage design by Ferdinando and Giuseppe Galli-Bibiena; engraving by F. A. Dietel.*

Ludovico Burnacini: stage design for the opera Il pomo d'oro *by Cesti and Sbarra, Vienna, 1668. Hell-mouth with the ferryman Charon. Engraving by Mathäus Küsel.*

Gala performance of Il pomo d'oro *in the new opera house in Vienna, built by Ludovico Burnacini, 1668. On the dais in the stalls, the emperor Leopold I and Margareta, with their retinue. Engraving by Frans Geffels. (The building was destroyed in 1783.)*

Acis et Galathée, *opera by J. B. Lully, performed at Versailles, 1749, with Madame de Pompadour and Vicomte de Rohan in the title roles. Pen and wash drawing by C. N. Cochin the Younger.*

"L'Opera seria" in an 18th-century Venetian theater. Painting from the school of Pietro Longhi. (Milan, Museo teatrale alla Scala.)

took the part of Paris had the honor of descending from the stage in the final apotheosis and handing the golden apple to the young Empress Margareta. She accepted it with a smile, no less flattered than Queen Elizabeth of England had been a century earlier at the performance of George Peele's pastoral play.

Opera, meanwhile, had developed to the point where the theater itself, intended to be its servant, became its master. Opera was a means to an end, an occasion for the display of the Baroque magic of decoration and machinery. When *Il Pomo d'Oro* was given in Vienna in 1668, its music, by Marc Antonio Cesti, and its libretto, by the Jesuit Francesco Sbarra, took second place to the sumptuous scenery designed by Ludovico Burnacini, under whose name the performance found its place in the history of the theater.

THE COURT BALLET

Plutarch, who once described the dance as "poetry without words," was one of the chief authorities invoked by Baïf and his collaborators in their efforts at reviving the drama of antiquity. As they saw it, the combination of the four great forms of art—music, poetry, dance, and painting—offered the only legitimate possibility of "expressing everything, representing everything, and illustrating everything, down to the deepest secrets of the soul and nature."

In France, this Renaissance idea of the "fusion of the arts" gave rise to a theater form specifically suited to the court and high society. In this new theatrical form the dominating share fell to the dance: the *ballet de cour*. It answered the court's desire for pageantry and gave infinite scope for homage magnificently staged. At the same time, it gave the king an opportunity of showing himself off in his most lovable guise, as the addressee and sponsor of all the sumptuous pageants, masques, intermezzi, and dances arranged for the pleasure of the court and, ultimately, the people.

Absolutism in theatrical pageantry found a congenial form of expression. "It was a whirl and a frenzy—a great deal of beauty and culture, a great deal of wit and prodigality of wealth and character," wrote the historian Veit Valentin, "the whole magic of adventure, of improvised life, of carefree play with the most serious matters; the seductive attraction of evil envelop these courts ruled by absolutism, and that is why they were always berated by theologians, but admired and loved by artists."

When Ottavio Rinuccini and Giulio Caccini, the two pioneers of Italian opera, came to Paris in 1604, they had to start thinking along entirely different lines. King Henri IV did not want statuesque recitative, but the gracefulness of the dance. He loved the "ballets mascarades"; these were balls in fancy dress in which the whole court took part.

Neither Rinuccini nor Caccini could make any headway in French theatrical life with their "dramma per musica." Nevertheless, they succeeded in interpolating recitative in the Italian style into the court ballet—for the first time in the lines spoken by the sorceress Alcine in the Duc de Vendôme's ballet, performed in January 1610, an occasion recorded as a memorable theater and court event in the reign of Henri IV.

But the very name that appears in the title of this nocturnal revelry on the banks of the Seine suggests that the occasion was a testimony to royal favor rather than one of epoch-making art. The Duc de Vendôme—a legitimatized son of Henri IV and Gabrielle d'Estrées and an elegant, intelligent, and ambitious man—directed the ballet himself and was allowed three performances in one week. The first performance in the great ballroom of the Louvre on January 12, 1610, was followed by two others, on January 17, and 18, in the Arsenal. The Duc de Sully, superintendent of finances, did not wish to be reminded of his economy drive on this occasion and had the hall equipped with two spectators' stands and other arrangements for the ballet.

The king and his entire court honored "Monseigneur le Duc" with their presence:

> His Majesty on his throne, the Queen [Marie de' Medici] and the former Queen Marguerite by his side, the Dauphin at his feet, and across the whole width of the hall all the princes and princesses of the royal blood, and other princes and princesses of the realm, officers of the crown, dukes, marquesses, counts, barons, seigneurs, noblemen, the ladies of the court—all placed according to their rank and merit. The captains of the guard at the back of His Majesty, and behind them the armed archers; police officials with the masters of ceremonies near the barriers, to forestall any disturbance or confusion.

The Duc de Vendôme's ballet was one of the last great theater festivals arranged in the reign of Henri IV, who was assassinated on May 14, 1610.

His son Louis XIII at first left theatrical ambitions to his mother Marie de' Medici—who was his guardian and managed to get hold of the regency as well—and later to Cardinal Richelieu, who, in 1624, took over the reins of France's destiny.

Richelieu had the sumptuous *Ballet de la prospérité des armes de la France* staged in 1641, in honor of the royal couple. It was presented in the newly built theater hall of the Palais Cardinal, and for the first time the action took place exclusively on the stage, leaving the floor to the spectators. The scenery was built up of the side wings fashioned on the Italian pattern, and some of the machinery, used a month earlier for the opening with the drama *Mirame,* was now employed for the ballet. As a result, the court ballet acquired an entirely new form. From now on it took place on the stage alone and thus separated from the main floor of the hall, which meant a division between the dance on the stage and the dance of the courtiers. It was the first approach to professional dancing and to the "classical" ballet.

To be sure, Louis XIV, then aged fifteen, took part in 1653 in a court dance-play called *Ballet de la nuit,* appearing as "Roi Soleil," glittering with gold. In his reign, Jean Baptiste Lully and Molière developed a new art form, in which the dance was tied more closely to the word than before. This was the *comédie-ballet,* a successful attempt at merging the wit of comedy with the courtly grace of the *ballet de cour,* and for Molière and his company the key to the benevolence of their king. A great theater festival took place at Versailles in May 1664. Under the motto "Plaisirs de l'Isle enchantée," there was presented a two weeks' series of jousts, banquets, pageants, fireworks, ballets, and pastorals. Molière contributed to this occasion the *comédie-ballets Les Fâcheux, Le Mariage forcé,* and *La Princesse d'Elide.*

When, in October 1670, Louis XIV expressed the wish to see a "turquerie" on the stage—everything Turkish was highly fashionable at the time—Molière obliged with a *comédie-ballet, Le Bourgeois gentilhomme,* which, with its elements of the *Commedia dell'arte,* is a sparkling sequence of topical parody on the conceits of culture and fashion, on stupidity and vanity, on pastoral song and minuet in middle-class homes and, above all, on the aftereffects of the establishment of the Turkish embassy, whose entry into Paris a few years earlier had stirred up a wave of picturesque aberrations of taste.

"You know that the son of the Grand Turk is in town, don't you?" the servant Coviello asks Jourdain, the "bourgeois gentleman," whose daughter he wins for his own master by a piece of riotous dupery. "What, you don't know that? He's got an altogether splendid retinue with him, and all the world goes there and they all pay their respects, and he has been received hereabouts as befits so powerful and great a lord."

The king was greatly amused by this masterpiece of comedy and

Ballet comique de la Royne *in Paris. Presented 1581. Engraving from the play-book, Paris, 1582.*

Jacques Callot: "Le combat à la barrière," at the Court of Lorraine in Nancy, 1627.

Gala performance of the opera Alceste, *by Lully and Quinault, in the marble court of Versailles, celebrating the opening of the court festival arranged there by Louis XIV in July and August 1674. Engraving by Le Pautre, 1676.*

Theater in Prince Schwarzenberg's castle at Cesky Krumlov, equipped by J. Wetschel and L. Merkel (1766–67). Wing flats and painted backdrop representing town scenery.

Castle theater at Cesky Krumlov: View into the wing flats, to the left side of the stage.

took no offense at Molière's blunt allusions to his own pro-Turkish diplomacy. At the end came a reminder of the *ballet de cour*, a small ballet of Spanish canzone, Italian duets, with Arlecchino, Scaramuccia, and Trivellino. This provided a transition to the court ball and gave Molière's partner Lully his opportunity to contribute the musical and dance ingredients of the successful performance.

SLIDING WINGS AND STAGE MACHINERY

Flat, sliding wings were the great novelty of the Baroque theater. The new form of stage decoration came from Italy, and after about 1640 spread through the whole of Europe. Its invention is credited to Battista Aleotti, court architect at Ferrara, who developed a scenery changing system that differed from the angled wings and revolving wooden prisms then used and offered richer possibilities than the customary three standard settings of the Renaissance stage. This new scenery consisted of a series of flat batten frames, covered with painted canvas and sliding sideways in grooves. It is known to have been used at the Teatro Farnese at Parma, which Aleotti built in 1618. On July 25, it is recorded, "the *scena tragica* stood there, all ready." The flat wing had arrived. The public, however, did not get to see this innovation until ten years later, when the Teatro Farnese was belatedly opened in 1628.

Possibly, Aleotti installed a similar scene-changing system in the theater he built in 1606 for the Ferrara Accademia degli Intrepidi, which at the time was renowned as the most beautiful Baroque theater in Italy. It burned down in 1679, and the sketches that have come down to us give no certain indication of the mechanism of the stage decorations.

The magnificent timber edifice of the Teatro Farnese in Parma, consisted of a horseshoe auditorium facing a stage where the central *porta regia* widened to make a proscenium arch for an inner, or peep-show stage, furnished with six pairs of sliding wings. Thus Aleotti was the first to extend the acting area in depth as far as the back wall of the stage, a feature characteristic of the best period of Baroque theater and a decisive formal break with the transversal forestage acting space of the Renaissance.

Six years after Aleotti's death, Nicola Sabbattini, stage architect at Pesaro, published a pioneering work on stage machinery, called *Pratica di fabricar scene e machine ne' teatri* (1638). Drawing on his own experience, he demands as the foremost condition for a functional change of scenery a stage with plenty of room, so that "behind, alongside, above, and below the background and the scenery there is enough room for all the kinds of machinery that have to be used, for the appearance of heaven, earth, sea, and underworld, also for the necessary extensions and contractions." To match the changing wings, he also changed the background curtain with its perspective painting, by either raising it or dropping it into a pit behind the stage.

Giacomo Torelli, who had established the system of flat, sliding wings was celebrated in Venice, Paris, and Versailles as the "great magician" of Baroque stage decoration. Technically, Torelli's wizardry rested on the system invented by Aleotti and developed by Sabbattini's techniques. In Florence, Alfonso Parigi did outstanding work with picturesquely fantastic wing settings. His décor for *La Flora* (in 1628) and *Le Nozze degli Dei* (1637) introduced into the Baroque theater the visions in depth that Ludovico Burnacini later brought to artistic and technical perfection at the Vienna opera house.

Joseph Furteenbach at Ulm meanwhile continued to use the "right method of the transformation stage," the well-tried *telari* system of which he had learned in Florence (around 1620) from Giulio Parigi (Alfonso's father). The theater he built in 1641 in the Binderhof at Ulm and described in detail in his *Mannhaffter Kunstspiegel* (published 1663) had three pairs of prisms made of wood, one pair each for each of Serlio's three standard scenes. Notwithstanding this "backwardness," however, Furttenbach furnished his stage with ships and sea monsters, movable along a rear pit in typical Baroque fashion, and also with hanging soffits representing clouds, and also movable back shutters, lamps that could be dimmed for lighting effects, and flying machines. Another of Furttenbach's ideas, entirely in the spirit of the Baroque concept of the necessary illusion of depth, was his device of clearing the dressing rooms behind the back shutters in special cases and revealing them as part of the stage for spectacular scenic effects. Modest as the Ulm theater appeared from the outside, narrow as it was inside, and furnished only with plain chairs and rows of benches, Furttenbach's stage equipment was comparable to the later Baroque court theaters of Schwetzingen, Hannover, and Ludwigsburg.

Furttenbach's theater was indeed the first civic theater house in Germany (built in the precincts of the former Dominican monastery); it belonged to the citizens of the town. It served the school drama and the *Meistersinger,* as well as English and German strolling players. In 1652 Furttenbach sold all his stage equipment to a troupe from his native Leutkirch, "*telari,* rigging, machines, costumes, and in short everything belonging to it, at a cheap price," as we learn from his handwritten diary. The building was later used for other purposes and was destroyed in the Second World War.

While Furttenbach was so generously informative, other stage de-

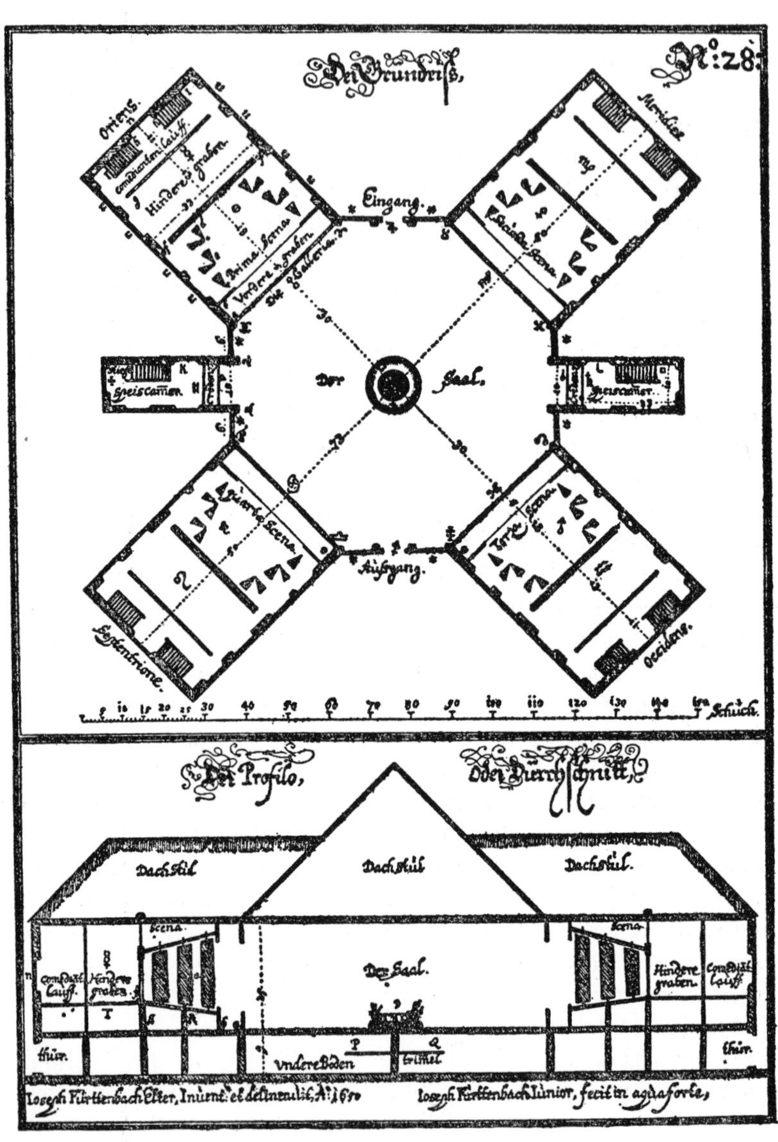

Design for a theater hall with four stages, by Joseph Furttenbach. Engraving from Mannhaffter Kunstspiegel, *Augsburg, 1663.*

signers guarded their secrets most jealously. This is well demonstrated in a letter Furttenbach received in 1653 from Regensburg, dated February 17, and signed by the Frankfurt engineer Georg Andreas Böckler. It refers to the famous theater construction put up by Giovanni Burnacini with the help of his son Ludovico at Regensburg. It had been ordered by Emperor Ferdinand III in honor of the Diet, and after the celebrations it was carefully dismantled, loaded on barges, and shipped downstream to Vienna, where it was later used for popular performances. This is what Böckler reported to the theater expert Furttenbach about Burnacini's "Teatro":

> On February 12, His Imperial Majesty caused to be performed an extremely beautiful comedy, in which more than 2,500 people participated. The teatro is rather spacious and equipped with five very pretty changes of scene, and allegedly cost 16,000 crowns. The master who made it is named Johann Burnacini, an Italian. Since the Italians are very secretive about their own precious concerns, I was unable to see the equipment. But since I know that you, Sir, are expert in these things, I would beg you to explain in what manner people get in a hurry from one place to another from the stage up into the clouds. I've made an invention by means of a swing. But I don't know whether yours is the same.

The miraculous tricks of stage technique passed the understanding even of fellow experts. This not only explains up to a point why Furttenbach stuck so conservatively to his *telari,* but has a parallel in the stage designs of the Englishman Inigo Jones. Jones had been in Florence at about the same time as Furttenbach and also had studied with Giulio Parigi. Rather like Furttenbach, Inigo Jones for decades kept to the Italian Renaissance theater's system of *periaktoi.* After 1640, however, he abandoned the rigid schematicism of the revolving wooden prisms with different scenes on each side. From then on he designed woodland stage decorations, which played their part, from the stage, in influencing the development of English landscape painting.

Another successful theater architect of this time was the Venetian Francesco Santurini. In 1650 he was called to the Bavarian court in Munich, where he began his career by building an opera house in the Italian style on the site of a granary in Salvator Square. It was inaugurated in 1654. Santurini also designed the stage decorations, though they were executed by Francesco Mauro, the "master of the machinery" of the new theater. Later, Francesco Mauro's sons Domenico and Gasparo in their turn put their knowledge of stage technique handed down to them by their father, to good use at the Munich theater. Francesco Mauro's grandson Alessandro went to Dresden, where Johann Oswald Harms, the "court and chief theater painter" born in Hamburg, had

Setting by Inigo Jones for the pastoral play Florimène, *ca. 1625. (Collection of the Duke of Devonshire, London, Courtauld Institute of Art.)*

Giuseppe Galli-Bibiena: gala performance of the grand opera Costanza e fortezza, *by J. J. Fux, at the imperial castle in Prague, 1723. The open-air stage —flanked by two towers and bounded by nine wing flats on each side—recedes into illusionist depth. The architectural constructions in the background can be altered to match the threefold change of scene. (Munich, Theater Museum.)*

gained fame for the Saxon Baroque theater with his sumptuous opera and ballet scenery. Alessandro Mauro enhanced Dresden's renown with his spectacular gala productions, giant fireworks, and water festivals. In the spirit of the High Baroque, the dominating feature of all these productions was the sensuous effect of shifting illuminations.

The art of Baroque perspective stage scenery—and its exposition in writing and illustration—reached its zenith in the works of the Italian Jesuit Andrea Pozzo. In his treatise *Perspectivæ pictorum atque architectorum,* published in Rome in 1693, he laid down his precepts for the artists of the Baroque and the nascent Rococo: the indefinite, extended perspective, which gives the illusion of endless expansion of space—to be achieved in the medium of painting. Andrea Pozzo put these precepts into effect in his ceiling frescoes, altars, and architectural designs, and, in Vienna, in his decorations for the Jesuits' celebrations of the great church festivals.

In theater and stage designs, this precept was realized by the gifted Italian family of the Galli-Bibienas. Past masters in the application of diagonal perspective and the use of complex ramps of stairs, arcades, and palace architecture, they created stage designs of limitless depth, superlatives in the tradition of the illusionist stage, which was carried on well into the nineteenth century, thanks to such designers as Quaglio, Gagliardi, and Fuentes.

Giuseppe Galli-Bibiena, the most famous member of the family, designed opera sets for Vienna, Dresden, Munich, Prague, Bayreuth, Venice, and Berlin. In his imposing open-air productions he remodeled the given garden or architectural setting into an apotheosis of perspective in which reality and illusion were harmoniously fused. There exists a series of engravings of his designs for the opera *Costanza e fortezza,* which was performed in 1723 at the park of the imperial castle in Prague, in honor of Emperor Charles VI. They form an optical polyphony so grandly self-sufficient that it seems almost paradoxical to expect an orchestra and singers to make any impact in such a setting.

In 1748 Giuseppe Galli-Bibiena was called to Bayreuth. There, together with his son Carlo, he executed the interior design, furnishings, and decoration of the Margrave's opera house. In the remodeling of the opera house in Dresden, in 1750, he put into effect his ideal of fusing auditorium and stage. In 1751 Frederick the Great called him to Berlin. There, in 1756, Giuseppe Galli-Bibiena died while working on an opera in collaboration with the composer Carl Heinrich Graun. His death marked the end of the great era of Baroque stage design.

Three years earlier, "the most precious jewel of the Rococo" was completed at Munich: François Cuvilliés's Residenztheater, glittering in white, gold, and red.

Giuseppe Galli-Bibiena: scenery in diagonal perspective for a gala performance celebrating the wedding of the electoral prince of Saxony (later King Augustus III) and the Austrian princess Maria Josepha, at Dresden, 1719. Engraving by J. A. Pfeffel.

Ferdinando Galli-Bibiena: drawing for a stage setting, with double staircase lined with statues and a coffered ceiling, projecting Baroque depth illusion. (London, Victoria and Albert Museum.)

THE JESUIT THEATER

The consecration of Munich's Church of St. Michael in 1597 culminated in a mass spectacle such as had never before been seen in Bavaria. To the sound of drums and trumpets, hundreds of participants, on foot and partly on horseback, were kept busy for hours in a gigantic display of allegorical groups: they represent the "Triumph of St. Michael." Envoys of heaven and dragons of the abyss, idolaters, apostates, heretics, and imperial despots were to be seen. The show concluded with a tumultuous scene, in which three hundred devils, complete with mask and tail, were plunged into hell. This remarkable consecration festivity in honor of the new Church of St. Michael was organized by the Jesuit college. This imposing church, inspired by Il Gesù in Rome, was the first early Baroque building north of the Alps. It gave effective expression to the power of the Society of Jesus (founded by Ignatius of Loyola in 1540) and became a stronghold of the Counter-Reformation. The theater, as readily used in the service of religion as it was condemned as a peril to faith whenever it got onto the wrong tracks, found purposeful sponsors in the Jesuits.

It was the general custom in all the secondary Latin schools of the Society to test the students' grasp of rhetoric and eloquent disputation on the stage. The Protestant school drama, in its modest way, had aided the defenders of the Reformation to sharpen the edge of their verbal weapons. The Jesuit theater now, on the other hand, quite deliberately sought scenic effects and summoned the arts that appeal to the eyes and ears, to the mind and the senses. The mere word from the pulpit was outdone by living representation on the stage. The power of gaiety, to which Baroque church architecture owed such decisive stimulus, proved "foremost in fruitful effect."

"It is known," so we read in the preface to the 1666 edition of the plays of Jakob Bidermann, a Jesuit and southern German dramatist,

> that *Cenodoxus,* which like hardly any other play caused so much merry laughter throughout the whole auditorium that the benches nearly collapsed, nevertheless caused a great movement of true piety in the spirit of the audience, so that the few hours devoted to this play did what a hundred sermons could hardly have done. For fourteen men from among the most eminent in the Bavarian court and the city of Munich were gripped by salutary fear of God, the severe judge of men's actions, and not long after the play had ended withdrew to us for the Ignatian exercises, as a result of which most of them underwent a miraculous conversion. . . .

> Among those who withdrew for the exercises, there was the man who had acted the part of Cenodoxus exceedingly well. He was received into our Society not long after, and lived in it for many years so guiltless and holy a life that he won eternal victory and now dwells among the blessed angels.

The pedagogic and propagandistic goal was achieved: fourteen courtiers renounced the world. Bidermann's "Comico-Tragoedia" of the vainglorious life, the damnation and conversion of the learned Cenodoxus, who as St. Bruno later founded the Carthusian order, has the appeal of sovereign, formal perfection. Elements of the ancient comedy are combined with Christian allegory in an effective whole. The play—first performed in Augsburg in 1602 and repeated in 1609 at the Jesuit College in Munich with the missionary success related above—set the example for the Baroque form of the martyrs' tragedy. Personages from the Bible, especially the Old Testament, from church history and the legends of the saints provided material that demonstrated the futility of all earthly pursuits in the face of the threat of eternal damnation; thus the spectator was dismissed, as in *Cenodoxus,* with the admonition: "Mundi disperite gaudia!"

The Bavarian Jakob Balde, a preacher and tutor to the princes, was the author of a tragedy called *Jephtias,* which was performed at Ingolstadt in 1637. Biblical narrative and the humanist cultural heritage are interwoven with the missionary ideas of the Counter-Reformation, and the Iphigenialike theme is made to point forward symbolically to Christ's sacrifice and death. The work's ingenious characterization and dramatic construction were such that even in Herder's time it earned his appreciative comment.

In Prague, the Jesuit students of the Clementinum performed a drama entitled *Maria Stuart* in 1644, which, with the help of a wealth of allegory, demonstrates how shameful this judgment was in the eyes of Catholics. In the *Argumentum,* a playbill in German that explained the meaning and story of the Latin Jesuit plays to the public, this was called a "Royal Tragedy," or "Maria Stuarta, Queen of Scots and Heir to the Kingdom of England, whom Elisabetha, the ruling queen of England, caused to be decapitated out of hatred for the Catholic religion and out of ambition." A. A. Haugwitz, the dramatist of the Silesian High Baroque, took up the same subject in 1683 in his tragedy *Maria Stuarda* but, modeling his treatment on Gryphius's and Lohenstein's hard-tried heroines of the faith, without discussing the question of guilt.

Far-reaching influence was exercised on the Jesuit drama of the second half of the seventeenth century by the theoretical treatise *Ars nova argutarum* (1649) by Masenius, a Jesuit teacher active in the Rhineland and Westphalia. Jakob Masen had joined the Society of

Jesus in 1629, and his own dramas contributed much to the flowering of the Jesuit theater in northern Germany. His tragicomedy *Androphilus* was accorded the honor of being performed at the peace negotiations at the end of the Thirty Years' War, in Münster, in Westphalia, in 1647 and 1648. His *Sarcotis* influenced Milton in writing his great religious epic *Paradise Lost*.

Apart from the Jesuits, the Piarists and Benedictines fostered the drama in a big way. The *Akademietheater* at Salzburg and the Benedictine monastery at Kremsmünster became great centers of monastic theater in the High Baroque under Simon Rettenbacher. He himself, as a secondary-school teacher, wrote and composed the music for some twenty Latin dramas, of which only a few were printed.

As the religious orders meant their dramas to appeal not so much through the word to the mind, but through the image to the sentiments, national and language boundaries were no obstacle. If the performance was in Latin, the spectator could follow the action with the help of the *Argumentum*, written in his own language. Adaptable as they were, furthermore, the Jesuits always tried to encourage local talent for their missionary purposes. This applies more particularly to the school drama. The Jesuit schools at Ljubljana, Krumlov, and Chomutov, in the Hungarian coronation city of Pressburg, now Bratislava in Czechoslovakia, and in Poland soon attracted local dramatists. By 1628, plays in Latin were performed in Bratislava, at first on a simple open-air podium and later indoors; in Tirnau (now Trnava), on the other hand, the Hungarian language was used on the stage of the Jesuit College as early as 1633. In Poland, the Jesuit Gregorious Cnapius produced his martyrological and moralizing *Exempla dramatica;* he initiated the development of a distinct, ethnic style of Polish drama, which spread as far as Pultusk, Vilna, and Poznan.

While in faraway lands the monastic drama made do for a long time with a neutral stage erected in the college yard, the lecture room, or sometimes even in a church, the Jesuit theater on the Society's own home ground soon availed itself of every existing means of illusionism.

In Vienna, Nikolaus of Avancini wrote allegories and miracles for which he required the whole bag of tricks of Baroque scenic decoration and transformations: illuminations and fire magic, gods, ghosts and devils, with interludes of music and ballet inserts, and other media of the Baroque. His play *Pietas Victrix* was presented before Emperor Leopold I in Vienna in 1659. This performance was the climax of the Jesuit order's contribution to the "heady splendor of Baroque Catholicism," of all those panegyrical emperor plays (*Ludi Caesarei*) which, from the middle of the seventeenth century on, extolled the Habsburg dynasty in the theater. Such projects took the Jesuit drama far beyond

PHASMA DIONYSIACVM PRAGENSE, EXHIBITVM S. CÆS. M.
Anno CIↃ. IↃ. CXVII, Febr. Menſe.
Nomina duodecim Heroum Illustr:. et Generos: Dnorum:
A. D. Gulielmus Baro Slauata.
B. D. Fridericus Baro de Dalemberg.
D. D. Henricus Baro de Colowrat.
E. D. Maximilianus Comes de Dietrichſtein.
G. D. Ferdinandus Baro de Nomi.
H. D. Ge. Achatz Baro de Loſenſtain.
K. D. Bucian Caplirz de Sule.
L. D. Iohan. Baro Wratislaw.

Phasma Dionysiacum, *festival ballet in the style of the Roman Ludi Caesarei, presented at the imperial court in Prague, 1617.*

the boundaries of the college and school theater. The glorification of the ruling dynasty had made sure of the latter's generous support. For *Pietas Victrix* the court provided the funds, part of the costumes, and—most important of all for Avancini's ambitious scenic fantasies—the services of the theater architect Giovanni Burnacini.

The subject of Avancini's *Pietas Victrix* is the victory of the Christian emperor Constantine over the Roman "pagan emperor" Maxentius. Both rulers are guided by dream visions; Peter and Paul fortify Constantine, the spirit of Pharaoh incites Maxentius against Jehovah's people. The battle of Rome in 312 is part of the plot. So is Constantine's dream, before the battle, in which, according to legend, he saw a fiery cross in the sky with the words "Hoc signo victor eris"—happens right on the stage. Angels rise from pillars of fire, the spirits of hell intervene in the fighting, flames flicker out of the Tiber. Constantine's soldiers form living stairs on which their companions climb to the top of the city walls, while on the other side of the stage a naval battle rages on the Tiber. Even for so experienced a stage technician as Giovanni Burnacini this was no mean task.

The *furioso* of Avancini's stage dynamics was stylistically significant in so far as it consistently worked with the typically Baroque shift from the front to the rear of the state. Constantine saw his dream vision on the rear stage, and on awaking stepped forward to deliver a great monologue, while a curtain was drawn to conceal the transformation to be arranged meanwhile on the rear stage. This astonishingly theatrical rhythm of forward and backward can be traced throughout the whole play.

Pietas Victrix ended with a Baroque apotheosis in the style of the *Ludi Caesarei,* showing the emperor Constantine enthroned as victor, surrounded by his subjects and blessed by an angel floating down on a cloud. The triple-portal triumphal arch behind the throne, decorated with the emblem of the Habsburg double eagle, made the quintessence of the play clear enough even to those who failed to understand much of the Latin text: the Christian empire of the Habsburgs rested on Constantine's victory. Nine engravings of scenes from *Pietas Victrix* are extant and show how close this drama, with its choral and ballet inserts, was to Baroque opera.

In France, the Jesuit theater from the outset fell into line with the court's cultivation of opera and ballet. The dense network of Jesuit schools and colleges guaranteed far-ranging influence on the development of the theater. Some of the fundamental theoretical works were produced in Jesuit circles. Father Ménéstrier wrote the first history and methodology of French ballet, and Father Jean Dubreuil's *Perspective pratique* was an important contribution to the development of stage perspective.

More than that, out of the schools of the influential Society of Jesus came the greatest French classical writers: Corneille, Molière, Voltaire, and Le Sage.

FRANCE: TRAGÉDIE CLASSIQUE AND CHARACTER COMEDY

Ever since Aldus Manutius had published the original Greek text of Aristotle's *Poetics* at his Venice printing press in 1508, the stream of erudite commentaries on this work had never ceased. In seventeenth-century France it assumed flood proportions. The most discussed and controversial problem was that presented by the rule of the three unities, which Aristotle had by no means laid down as unambiguously as his later interpreters had claimed. Everybody was agreed about the required unity of action—but not as to whether and to what extent unity of place and unity of time—"one revolution of the sun or a little over"—were to be regarded as equally obligatory. This last question was at the heart of the theoretical debates that shaped the intellectual climate out of which the French *tragédie classique* developed.

The question of the time the playwright is to allow for the dramatic action, and that of the place of the scene, is discussed in great detail in Abbé François Hédelin d'Aubignac's *Pratique du théâtre.* Cardinal Richelieu, no less purposeful a manager of intellectual capital as he was of economic assets, set up the famous Society of Five Authors to investigate and test the theoretical rules in joint work. Among Richelieu's appointees to this Society was a young lawyer from Rouen, who had achieved his first theatrical success in Paris in 1629—Pierre Corneille.

A year earlier, Corneille had met the actor and troupe manager Mondory at Rouen, where the latter was arranging performances under a provincial license granted by Richelieu. Mondory had begun his career as a member of Valleran-Lecomte's troupe and, like his former chief, formed a link between the late medieval and humanist theater and the impending great age of French classical drama. In Paris, Mondory at first shared with the *Comédiens italiens* the traditional theater hall of the Hôtel de Bourgogne, owned by the Confrérie de la Passion, but in 1634 he moved his troupe into a building of their own, in the Vieille Rue du Temple in the Marais quarter of Paris. This new Théâtre du Marais was destined to become one of the three mainstays of Parisian theater life.

Mondory's repertory consisted of pastorals and tragicomedies by that prolific manufacturer of plays, Alexandre Hardy, of Seneca-inspired tragedies by the criminal lawyer Robert Garnier, of Plautus and Terence adaptations and, finally, of allegorical biblical plays. This repertory covered the same range as the court and academic amateur theater. When, in 1628, the twenty-two-year-old lawyer Pierre Corneille in Rouen offered him a comedy he had written, Mondory agreed at once to produce it in Paris. It was called *Mélite ou les fausses lettres,* a clever and polished play in the Spanish fashion, geared to the mood of the time. Its success admitted the promising young author to the houses of the Paris aristocracy, and brought him the honor of an appointment to Richelieu's Society of Five Authors.

Richelieu commissioned this group to write joint plays on some given theme, each author one act, and strictly according to the Aristotelian rule of the three unities. Corneille dutifully supplied his contribution to the *Comédie des Tuileries,* which was manufactured by this method in 1635. He had every expectation of a seat in the Académie Française, which had been founded by Richelieu. His first tragedy, *Médée,* similarly followed the classical pattern. But a year later, Corneille forfeited the powerful cardinal's favor by a stroke of dramatic genius. He put on the stage a theme that transgressed all academic rules. Out of a Spanish source, *Mocedades del Cid,* Corneille created *Le Cid,* the ideal young hero ardent with love and passion, courage and fighting spirit. No French stage ever before had heard poetic language of such force.

Le Cid became the idol of the young generation. The theater burst from its shell of conservative aestheticism. Sparks were flying. Corneille's drama, which had its first performance in 1636 at the Théâtre du Marais, unleashed a wave of enthusiasm. The *jeunesse de France* saw its own glorification in Don Rodrigue's resolute stand in the fatal conflict between honor and love. The Spanish Cid became the French national hero.

But Corneille was sharply censured by his fellow dramatists. They accused him of unforgivable offenses against the laws of morality and probability. The bold changes of scene, the unity of place and action dictated not by principle but by poetic mood, contradicted all their painstaking theoretical endeavors. Friend and foe took sides in the dispute. A stream of polemic pamphlets kept the controversy going for months. In the name of Richelieu, the Académie Française condemned the dramatist and his work.

Disillusioned, Corneille withdrew to Rouen. And so he was not among the guests of honor at the most glittering of the Paris theatrical events of his time, the opening of the new ballroom theater at the Palais Cardinal in 1641. Richelieu had commissioned the architect Le Mercier to equip the stage of his town *palais* with all the transformation devices of Baroque stage machinery. A costly cloth curtain concealed echelons of

Theater in the Palais Cardinal in Paris: the guests of honor include Cardinal Richelieu, King Louis XIII, the Queen, and the Dauphin. Engraving by Lochon, before 1642, after a grisaille now in the Musée des Arts décoratifs in Paris.

perspective wings, and, when drawn, revealed George Buffequin's scenery in varying atmospheres, with lighting that varied according to the desired time of day. The play was *Mirame*, now forgotten as the group of dramatists who had been commissioned to write it. Richelieu himself is said to have signed as author. At the ballet performance following *Mirame*, the records say, the new theater showed off its astonishing and ingenious transformation devices.

Corneille had to wait for his due until 1647, when at last he was admitted to the Académie Française. In the interval, he wrote his historical dramas *Horace, Cinna,* and *Polyeucte,* in which he had followed the academic principles of form. His *Andromède* was staged in Paris at the Petit Bourbon during the carnival weeks of 1650, with the famous décors created by Torelli in 1647 for the Paris production of *Orfeo*. The privilege of being allowed the use of the existing opera décors suggests that even in Paris an occasional economy measure in the realm of the arts was not disdained. But there was a contradiction in style. The court opera of France bore the mark of Baroque Italian stagecraft. The *tragédie classique,* on the other hand, was Baroque tempered by language along classicist lines, rather like Poussin's paintings. Its emotional force was an expression not of overflowing feelings, but of carefully graded escalation. "Icy spectators of their own fury, professors of their passion," this is how Schiller once defined the characters of the French *tragédie classique.*

The rules of alexandrine verse (the twelve-syllable iambic line, named for those used in an old French romance about Alexander the Great) with its antithetical rigidity determined the rhythm of the verse. By a corresponding rule, the number of acts had to be five, with the third as their central axis. The linkage of scenes was obligatory; when a character left the stage, he had to establish a connection with the following scene, even if with such trite phrases as, "But whom do I see coming? The queen approaches. I must be quickly gone."

Corneille and, even more so, his younger contemporary and rival Jean Racine handled the alexandrine with sovereign elegance. For twenty years they vied with each other as to who should be master of the classical tragedy. When Racine made his debut in 1664 with the play *La Thébaïde,* Corneille had begun to learn from his earlier experiences. In his *Discours des trois unités* and in the self-critical *Examen* included in the 1660 edition of his collected works, he bowed to the reproach of having changed the scene too often and too arbitrarily in *Le Cid.* How far removed he was, then, from Lope de Vega, who mocked the pedantic pen-pushers and defied the Aristotelian rules—and how far removed, too, from Claudel's *The Satin Slipper,* which so imaginatively revels in the scenic wealth of the Spanish Baroque drama. Only the absolutely essential was to be shown on the stage, Racine declared in his preface to *Mithridate.*

The self-imposed compulsion of language and place of the *tragédie classique,* which even Voltaire still acknowledged as binding, had its counterpart in the deliberate stylization of the world and the human image, which alone seemed appropriate to the ethical aspiration. "Henceforward, the characters of the classical French stage are pressed like pieceworkers into the timetable of the action and, chained to the post of their inner crisis, have to lay bare their soul" (Karl Vossler).

In technical matters, Corneille had always submitted to the Baroque stage system. For all its bold irregularity, even *Le Cid* keeps to the Baroque principle of fore and back stage. The imperial palace in the background remains constant, while the free platform in front of it allows of all the required changes of scene. "The jurists admit certain fictions of the law," Corneille wrote in his discourse on Aristotle's three unities, "and I meant to follow their example and introduce certain fictions of the theater, in order to create a place on the stage that is neither the room of Cleopatra, nor that of Rodogune in the play of that title, nor yet that of Phokas, Leontine, or Pulcherius in *Héraclius,* but a hall onto which these different rooms open. . . ."

Both Corneille's and Racine's dramatic characters were overwhelmed by the sumptuousness of Baroque costumes. They appeared in crinoline and buckled shoes, Polyeucte removed his plumed hat for prayer, and it was not until Diderot that anyone took occasion to praise an actress—Mlle. Clairon, for her attempt at a realistic rendering of despair. At the time of French classical tragedy, furthermore, the noxious habit gained ground of giving well-heeled spectators privileged seats on the stage, an abuse that no one before Voltaire managed to get rid of.

Jean Racine, son of a lawyer and pupil of the Jansenists of Port-Royal, owed his first stage successes—with *La Thébaïde* in 1664 and with *Alexandre le Grand* in 1665—to a theater manager and fellow author whose name had risen meteorically like Racine's own: Molière. Personal controversies and rivalries for the favors of the actress du Parc led Racine to have his *Andromaque* and later dramas produced by Molière's competitors, the troupe at the Hôtel de Bourgogne. It was here, at the venerable ancestral seat of the Paris theater tradition, that the grand declamatory style of the *tragédie classique* developed. Here was the soil in which rooted the "sublime Alas!" that Racine demands of his characters in a metrically tempered outcry. Racine did not see the Aristotelian rule of the three unities as a dry, formal compulsion to be accepted grudgingly—but as the strict dramaturgical conception that is the necessary precondition for psychological intensity.

Bérénice's conflict of conscience, the heart-rending agony in *Mithridate,* both declaimed in great melodious monologues, hardly needed any décor. To this day they fascinate every theatergoer in Paris, timelessly preserved as they are in the grandiloquent style of the Comédie Française. No other language, no other dramatist, ever made the alexandrine meter yield more majestic power.

In seven prodigious tragedies, counting from *Andromaque* to *Phèdre,* Racine spanned the range of his moral and artistic experience. His public renown received confirmation by his admission to the Académie Française, but his inner certainty was undermined by violent quarrels with the Jansenists, who detested the theater. After a court intrigue that painfully dimmed the success of his *Phèdre* by the presentation of a rival play of the same title, and after his break with the actress Mlle. de Champmeslé, he withdrew from the theater for twelve years.

A new interest in religious questions reconciled Racine with the Port-Royal. Madame de Maintenon, the energetic morganatic wife of the now elderly *roi soleil,* eventually succeeded in making Racine break his silence. In 1689 he wrote the biblical tragedy *Esther* for the Maison de Saint Cyr, an institution for the education of poor girls of noble families founded by Madame de Maintenon, and two years later *Athalie,* a tragedy based on the Book of Kings, with a title role that was still coveted by the greatest tragic actresses at the time of Voltaire.

Within a few decades, the *tragédie classique* had raised the French Baroque theater to dazzling literary heights. It was held in such esteem that Molière, too, was led to try his hand at the genre. In 1661 he wrote a heroic drama called *Don Garcia de Navarre ou Le Prince jaloux.* It had a miserable run of seven performances and taught him that his strength lay in another field.

In the same year, 1661, the king gave Molière and his troupe the Palais Royal theater, formerly Richelieu's Palais Cardinal, in recognition of Molière's long and hard efforts in the service of the theater. It was here that the classical tragedy's counterpart and peer developed as the *haute comédie,* the classical French comedy. Its sovereign genius was Molière. Ever since 1643, Jean Baptiste Poquelin, son of an upholsterer and royal valet, pupil of the Jesuits and graduate law student, had dedicated himself to the theater. He had founded the Illustre Théâtre troupe together with the actress Madeleine Béjart and taken the stage name Molière. He had acted in a hall near the Porte de Nesle and in converted indoor tennis courts, had been thrown into debtor's prison for debt, and kept alive his passion for the theater through years of poverty while touring the provinces.

On October 24, 1658, came the great chance of which every company manager dreamed: Molière and his troupe performed at the Louvre before the king. The program consisted of Corneille's *Nicomède,* followed by a farce by Molière himself, *Le Dépit amoureux.* The main work was all but a failure, but the entertaining afterpiece and its author—and chief actor—were warmly applauded by Louis XIV and his court.

The happy occasion had a sequel. The young king, still under the tutelage of Mazarin in the affairs of state, asserted himself as a patron of the theater. Molière and his troupe became the official actors of Monsieur, the King's brother, and were assigned first to the stage of the Petit Bourbon and later, in 1661, to the Palais Royal. Under the sun of royal benevolence, Molière began to collaborate with Lully, and together they created the *comédie-ballet* for the diversion of court society. The "Gallic wit" contributed by Molière to these gay entertainments was the precursor of the accomplished character comedy.

In *École des maris,* in 1661, Molière took his theme from Terence's *Adelphi,* but a year later, in the companion piece *École des femmes,* he used to model and relied wholly on his own insights into contemporary foibles. For ten creative years, in one masterpiece after another, Molière declared war on the hypocrites, bigots and grudgers, or whoever else thought the cap fitted. Two years earlier, in 1659, the whole of Paris had perceived in *Les Précieuses ridicules* the underlying satire on the affected literary circle at the Hôtel de Rambouillet. Nor did he spare his rival actors at the Hôtel de Bourgogne, as they discovered in 1663 on the occasion of *L'Impromptu de Versailles.*

Competition was keen, and Molière's troupe had no easy time holding their own against the two established houses, the Hôtel de Bourgogne, where the great classical tragedy reigned supreme, and the Théâtre du Marais with its amusing comedies. In addition, there was the Comédie Italienne, the French adaptation of the *Commedia dell'arte,* which was authorized to play up to four times a week.

Molière incurred the enmity of clerical and literary circles. The most violent attacks were leveled at *Le Tartuffe.* Court intriguers and rivals, evil gossips and the testy reactions of the victims combined in preventing public performance; it took years of nerve-racking tug-of-war before Molière was allowed to show this piece in public.

The profound and vulnerable sadness behind Tartuffe, behind the Misanthrope, the Miser, and the Imaginary Invalid alike, reflects social and moral criticism, to be sure, but also Molière's personal disappointments. His brittle marriage with Armande Béjart, Madeleine's daughter, undermined his health. Nothing came of his proposed election to the Académie Française, because it would have meant giving up the stage, and that seemed to him too high a price for the honor. He was as

Scenes from Molière's Le Bourgeois gentilhomme *and* Les Précieuses ridicules. *Engravings by P. Brissart, after the Paris edition of 1682.*

passionate a comedian as he was a writer of comedies. As an author he wrote for the actor, as an actor he guided the author's pen.

Molière was deeply influenced by the Comédie Italienne. He modeled his acting on Tiberio Fiorilli, the famous Scaramuccia; his troupe and the Italians for a time shared the same theater, and the *Commedia dell'arte* stock types furnished him with the outlines, and sometimes even the names, of his own characters. But Molière, the creator of the character comedy, gave them a new, individual life. He put on the stage persons who were more than just pretexts for funny situations. His Scapin and his Sganarelle, the guardian Arnolphe in *The School for Wives* and the enema foolery at the end of *The Imaginary Invalid* do not disown their origin in the *Commedia dell'arte,* but they display a greater differentiation and sensitivity. Molière gave literary form to characters derived from the stock types of the improvised play.

At first Molière used the Italians' stock masks. In the role of Sganarelle he merely blackened his eyebrows and moustache, as shown in

Scene from Molière's Le Malade imaginaire. *Painting by Cornelius Troost, 1748. (Berlin, Staatliche Museen.)*

Molière's Le Malade imaginaire *at Versailles, 1674. Engraving by Le Pautre, 1676.*

Simonin's well-known engraving. Certain *Commedia* characters that he deliberately took over, such the two fathers in *The Tricks of Scapin,* or the philosophers in *The Forced Marriage,* continued in his troupe to appear with the traditional leather half-masks.

Molière acted more than thirty roles in his own plays, right up to that fateful February 17, 1673, when, in the role of Argan in *The Imaginary Invalid,* he collapsed on the stage and died.

His troupe, now without a master, joined up under the actor La Grange with the players of the Théâtre du Marais, and together this new *troupe unique* moved to the Hôtel Guénegaud. The play presented at the opening performance, on July 9, 1673, was Molière's most virulently attacked play, *Le Tartuffe.*

Seven years later, the Comédie Française was born by an edict of Louis XIV, dictated in the military camp at Charleville. This famous document, which bears the date August 18, 1680, and is countersigned by Colbert, declares:

> His Majesty has decided to unite the two troupes of actors established in the Hôtel de Bourgogne and in Rue de Guénegaud, and to have them carry on henceforth as one enterprise, with a view to achieving even more perfect performances.

La Grange was appointed director of the merged troupes. The new Comédie Française continued at first at the Hôtel Guénegaud, with comedy predominating in the summer, and tragedy in the winter. But the King's protection could not prevent the professors of the nearby Collège des Quatre-Nations, a foundation of Mazarin's, from complaining that the academic zeal of their students was jeopardized by the "loose morals of the comedians." La Grange moved his company to the empty Jeu de Paume de l'Étoile, an indoor tennis court with a hall spacious enough to house the stage and auditorium for 1,500 built by the architect François d'Orbay. The new theater opened in 1689 and soon became the center of the literary, artistic, and fashionable circles of Paris.

It is from about that time, too, that we have the first records of profit sharing at the Comédie Française. The author was entitled to one-ninth of the takings, while the group of actors had the right of discontinuing plays once they brought in less than a certain minimum quota. This latter was originally fixed at 300 *livres* for the summer and 500 for the winter, but was subsequently altered and raised more than once. The dramatists tried to improve their legal status. In 1775 Beaumarchais asked to see the box-office accounts when the Comédie Française proposed to take his *Barber of Seville* out of the repertory. He founded the Société des auteurs dramatiques, Europe's first association for the protec-

Les Comédiens Français. *Painting by Antoine Watteau, ca. 1720. (New York, Metropolitan Museum of Art.)*

tion of authors' rights. But it was swept away by the French Revolution, and again the author's only chance, both financially and artistically, was personal contact with the theater.

The death of Louis XIV in 1717 brought an era to its end. The Comédiens du Roi were established in Paris in their own playhouse, from which no evil slander could dislodge them, but shortage of space forced them to migrate two generations later.

The Salle Richelieu, which now houses the Comédie Française, owes this use to an order issued by Napoleon in 1812, at the gates of Moscow—a striking analogy with Louis XIV's constituent edict from Charleville. The Comédie Française still recalls with pride this "act which redounds to Napoleon's everlasting fame, that even on the battlefield, like Louis XIV before him, he had at heart the fate of his comedians." It could wish for no better motto than Napoleon's much-quoted words: "The French theater is the glory of France, the opera merely an expression of its vanity."

COMMEDIA DELL'ARTE AND POPULAR THEATER

Commedia dell'arte—comedy of skill. This means mimetic art on the spur of the moment, quick-witted improvisation, rough and comic, elemental playacting, such as in antiquity the Atellans had offered on their itinerant stages. It is the caricature of types based on human, all-too-human conflicts, the inexhaustible, endlessly changeable and ultimately always unchanged stock-in-trade of the comedian in the great theater of the world. But it also means artistic mastery of the body's means of expression, a ready pool of standard scenes and situations, resourceful combinations, spontaneous adaptation of wit to the situation of the hour.

When the concept of the *Commedia dell'arte* first emerged in Italy at the beginning of the sixteenth century, it initially meant merely a distinction as against the literary theater of the scholars, the *Commedia erudita*. The *dell'arte* players were craftsmen of their art, that of the theater, in the original sense of the word. As distinct from the academic amateur groups, they were the first professional actors.

Their ancestors were the wandering mimes, jugglers, and improvisers. Their immediate background was the carnival with its masked processions, the social satire of its fools' costumes, its acrobatic and mime shows. The *Commedia dell'arte* was rooted in the people's life, took its inspiration from it, lived by improvisation. It arose in contraposition to the humanists' literary theater. At its threshold stood Angelo Beolco of Padua, nicknamed *Il Ruzzante* after the shrewd peasant character he created and acted. He wrote plays based on observations of everyday life in the countryside, at first with echoes of the pastoral play, while his late work *La Piovana* and *La Vaccaria* are adaptations of Plautus, "tailored to fit the living."

Ruzzante first appeared with his small troupe in Venice, during the carnival of 1520. He played in private houses, gained access to scholarly circles through the wealthy patrician Alvise Cornaro, whom he knew from Padua, and in 1529 was invited to Ferrara by Duke Ercole d'Este. Ruzzante had one foot in the humanist theater, the other in the popular theater. With the five-act form of his comedies he still belonged to the *Commedia erudita;* but with his stock types, which he characterized by different dialects, he opened the door to the broad field of the *Commedia dell'arte.* His servants and country folk spoke the Paduan or Bergamask dialect; his masters, Venetian or Tuscan—a device further developed by Andrea Calmo.

Characterization by dialect became the distinguishing feature of the *Commedia dell'arte.* The contrast of language, status, and wit or foolishness of predetermined characters assured the comic effect. Typification led actors to specialize in one particular character, in one part that fitted them so perfectly and in which they moved so naturally that there was no need for a preestablished text. It was enough to agree before the performance on the "business" of the plot: intrigue, entanglement, and solution. The details were left to the moment's mood—all the earthy jokes and pranks, the puns, misunderstandings, sleights of hand, and buffoonery of gesture that had kept impromptu comedians going for centuries. These now entered into the *Commedia dell'arte* as *lazzi,* that is, ready-made tricks or stock business. The *lazzi* acquired a dramaturgic function and became the star turns of particular actors. The *lazzo* of the fly is, to this day, the pantomimic masterpiece of "Arlecchino, servitore di due padroni," Harlequin serving two masters, in Giorgio Strehler's Goldoni production at the Piccolo Teatro di Milano. And when Charlie Chaplin in mute self-oblivion eats shoelaces instead of macaroni, he salutes the *lazzi* bravura of the *Commedia dell'arte* just as much as does the actor who pretends he has a hair in his mouth—and is praised for it by Stanislavsky.

In the performance of any given play, actors followed the scenario, or *soggetto* (subject), of which two copies were hung up, one to the right and the other to the left behind the stage, to inform participants of the course of the action and the sequence of scenes.

Commedia dell'arte *characters: Pantalone, young hero (or Capitano), and Zanni. Etchings by Jacques Callot. Florence, 1619.*

Commedia dell'arte and carnival on the Piazza Navona, Rome. Strolling players' booths; to the right of the fountain, a singer of grizzly ballads with his broadsheets. Detail from an engraving by Petrus Schenk, Amsterdam, 1708.

Commedia dell'arte with simple peasant characters. Next to the masked servant girls, to the right, a Zanni and a Pantalone. Anonymous painting of the 18th century. (Milan, Museo teatrale alla Scala.)

The mainstay of the comic element are the *zanni*, servants who come from Bergamo. (The variants of their name, Zannoni, Zan or Sanni suggest a Venetian dialect form of Giovanni; another theory, which traces the etymology to antiquity, links up with the Greek word *sannos*, fool, and the Latin *sannio*, one who makes faces.) Zanni usually appears in duplicate. He is clever and malicious, or good-natured and stupid, and in both cases a glutton. He wears a half-mask made of leather, an unkempt beard, a wide-brimmed hat and, in the belt of his full and baggy trousers, a blunt wooden dagger. The successors of Zanni are legion—there are Brighella and Arlecchino, Truffaldino, Trivellino, Coviello, Mezzetino, Fritellino and Pedrolino; there are Hanswurst, Pickle-herring and Stockfish, and all the innumerable local country or city types of jesters. Pulcinella from Acerra has become Punch in England, Polichinelle in France, Petrushka in Russia, and some of his traits survive in the German Kasperl.

The butt and object of the comic tricks are the passive types, always fooled, who become caricatures of themselves. They are headed by the two father characters, Pantalone and Dottore. Pantalone, the senile, rich, suspicious Venetian merchant, the Signor Magnifico with the white goatee and the black cloak over his red jacket, either has a marriageable daughter or else attracts mockery by his own tardy courting. His servant Zanni plunges him into adventures in which Pantalone is worsted. Zanni at bests gets something to eat but more often reaps a sound thrashing.

The Dottore from Bologna, the erudite star of all faculties, wears a black gown with white ruff, a tight black cap under a black hat with a wide, upturned brim. He throws out Latin tags, creates a hopeless confusion, takes the Graces for the Fates, and produces the most disarming logic—for instance: "A ship that is not at sea, clearly is in port."

The third in the league of the fooled is Capitano, a *miles gloriosus* type, a lily-livered braggart and a coward when things turn serious. Originally a caricature of a Spanish officer, he subsequently became universally interchangeable as a swashbuckler and windbag. The best-known representative of this character was the actor Francesco Andreini of the Comici Gelosi troupe. He published his stage improvisations in 1624 in a book entitled *Le bravure del Capitan Spavento*. One of Capitano's successors was Scaramuccia, who became famous throughout Europe in the person of Tiberio Fiorilli, the star of the Comédie Italienne in Paris, Molière's teacher and celebrated as "the greatest of clowns" and "the great original of the comic theater."

The son and daughter of Dottore or Pantalone, the lovers (*innamorati*), courtesans, and bawds joined the cast as required. These types were less fixed—most defined, perhaps, the servant girl Colombina

Scenes from Comédie Italienne at the time of Henry III. Series of woodcuts, published by Fossard, Paris, ca. 1575. (From the collection Recueil Fossard, *Drottningholm Theater Museum.)*

or Smeraldina as the partner, mistress, or wife of Arlecchino—and generally wore no masks.

One of the most famous actresses of the *Commedia dell'arte* was Isabella Andreini, wife of the actor Francesco Andreini. She was, as is grandly stated on the title page of her husband's edition of her *Letters,* a member of the Accademia dei Signori Intenti, received sonnets from Tasso and replied to them in equally well-turned verses. Her star part was La Pazzia, a linguistic *tour de force. "Bella di nome, bella di corpo e bellissima d'animo"*—beautiful in name, beautiful in body, and most beautiful in spirit—thus was she praised in Italy. When, in the eighteenth century, Bustelli made his Nymphenburg porcelain figurines of the *Commedia dell'arte,* he named the most graceful of his female figures Isabella.

Commedia dell'arte scene by Alessandro Scalzi, called Padovano, from his murals in the fools' staircase at Castle Trausnitz in Landshut (1578): Pantalone and Zanni serenading; in the window, a cat instead of the courted lady.

In the middle of the sixteenth century, the *Commedia dell'arte* began to spread to the countries north of the Alps. Italian actors turned up in Nördlingen in 1549, and soon afterward in Nuremberg, Strasbourg, Stuttgart, throughout southern Germany and more particularly in Linz and Vienna. The Comici Gelosi, the Confidenti and the Fedeli troupes all were hospitably received at the Vienna court. In Munich, where Orlando di Lasso conducted the court orchestra, the *Commedia dell'arte* was very popular by 1568. That year the Bavarian Duke Albrecht V arranged a festival program lasting several weeks to celebrate the wedding of his son Wilhelm and Renata of Lorraine. The program included a series of tournaments and concerts, and theatrical presentations, and concluded on March 7 with a "Commedia all'improviso alla italiana." Orlando di Lasso was the producer and took the part of Pantalone. The action was made up of elements of Venetian carnival burlesque. It followed the customary scenarios and is described in detail in the festival book written by Massimo Troiano for the bridegroom and hereditary Prince Wilhelm.

The plot can be regarded as typical of the *Commedia dell'arte.* A rich Venetian enters and praises the joys of love. He receives a letter that calls him away instantaneously from the company of the beautiful courtesan. Pantalone and his servant Zanni court the forsaken beauty. A Spanish nobleman appears and emerges as a preferred rival. Scenes of mistaken identity and thrashings, misdirected serenades, and quixotic duels trip over each other. It all ends up in peaceful reconciliation, and players and spectators join in an Italian dance.

Prince Wilhelm and his bride took the comedians along to Trausnitz Castle at Landshut where, for ten years, "greatly addicted to amusing and foreign things," they enjoyed being the carefree patrons of the actors at this gaily festive court. Eventually, paternal orders from Munich commanded economy measures and so put an end to the comedians' heyday. Thus, Prince Wilhelm had to dismiss the *Commedia* players; but one thing he was able to keep: a life-size portrait of his players. This painting by Alessandro Scalzi, known as Padovano, furnished the whole of the "fools' staircase" at Trausnitz Castle, from the cellar up to the fourth floor, with illusionist frescoes showing variations on the basic types and situations of the *Commedia dell'arte.* Here are its first pictorial witnesses north of the Alps. They correspond to Massimo Troiano's descriptions, but are not a copy of the Munich performance.

Frescoes of *Commedia dell'arte* characters, painted by Lederer in 1748 and artistically richer and more festive, can be found at Krumlov Castle in Bohemia. Twenty years later the Schwarzenberg family, then living at Krumlov, engaged the painters Wetschel and Merkel to equip the castle's theater with ingenious new scenery of staggered wing decorations.

Paris gallicized the *Commedia dell'arte*; it became the Comédie Italienne, adopted the language of the host country, and adapted itself to the latter's taste for "more plausibility, regularity, and dignity," as J. B. Du Bos put it. However, to judge by the collection of scenes and dialogues published around 1700 by Evaristo Gherardi under the title *Le Théâtre italien,* the contrary was nearer the truth. The Comédie Italienne was adept not only at general moral criticism, but also at hilarious parody of its French rivals. Arlequin (a successor to the medieval Herlequin with the shaggy mask) makes his entrance as Vulcan, parodying opera in an allegoric costume; Pierrot, as Mercury; Colombine, as Venus; they drag Pegasus onstage in the shape of an ass—and proceed to present *Arlequin Protée,* a parody of Racine's great tragedy *Bérénice.*

The motto of the actors of the Comédie Italienne was "Castigat ridendo mores" (he castigates the mores through ridicule); they had learned as much from Molière as he from them.

The Comédie Italienne troupe played at the Petit Bourbon in the years 1658–73, then at the Hôtel Guénegaud and moved, after the fusion of French tragedy and comedy in the Comédie Française in 1680, to the theater hall of the Hôtel de Bourgogne. At the Hôtel de Bourgogne with its venerable traditions, the Comédie Italienne enjoyed its greatest glory. And here, in 1697, it committed suicide. An insufficiently camouflaged satire attacking Madame de Maintenon, the comedy *La Fausse Prude,* after Saint-Simon, provoked the instantaneous closure of the theater by Louis XIV. The Italian comedians had to leave Paris.

Watteau recorded the "Departure of the Italian Comedians" in a painting, from which the engraver Louis Jacob created a "souvenir" print: Mezzetin's last bow before leaving, a regretful farewell by the company's ladies, women watching from neighboring windows, a young fellow pasting the royal decree of prohibition onto the wall of the house.

Nineteen years later, in 1716, the Comédiens Italiens were back in Paris. Led by Luigi Riccoboni, they made the transition from the improvised to the written play. Riccoboni, who earlier, in Venice and in the cities of Lombardy, had been active as a reformer of the native Italian *Commedia* tradition, now took French dramas into his repertory.

Improvisation, as of old, withdrew to the fairground and, in Paris, to the Théâtre de la Foire. Improvisation now looked for an audience among the common folk. Its main centers were Saint-Germain and Saint-Laurent. According to the Danish writer L. Holberg, who was in Paris around 1720, "extremely felicitous and faithful" parodies of the gestures and voices of French actors could be seen on these stages. But, he continues, they suffered from their being too many, for "everywhere in town, in the suburbs, on all public squares and stages such parodies are performed."

Much as it had first appeared in Paris, without much specific artistic

Farçeurs françois et italiens, *at the Théâtre Royal in Paris, 1670. At the left, Molière; distributed across the stage, singly or in groups, the gallicized characters of the Commedia dell'arte. Anonymous oil painting. (Paris, Collection de la Comédie Française.)*

Philippin.
llaume.
Gaultier Garguille
LeDottor Grazian Balourd
polichinelle.
Pantalon.
Briguelle.
Trivelin.

Fairground stages in Paris: Théâtre de la Foire, on Place Vendôme. This, and even more so Saint-Germain and Saint-Laurent, provided a refuge for the Comédie Italienne, the gallicized Commedia dell'arte, after the royal interdict of 1697. Colored print, 17th century.

Arlequin Grand Visir, Comédie Nouvelle, *by Fuzelier, performed by the Ancienne Troupe de la Comédie Italienne on the stage of the Hôtel de Bourgogne in Paris, probably in 1687. In the title part, Domenico Biancolelli, the troupe's famous Dominique, who died in 1688. Engraving by Bonnart, from the Paris Almanach for 1688.*

Investiture of the new Harlequin of the Comédie Italienne at the Hôtel de Bourgogne after the death of Domenico Biancolelli (Dominique), whose sarcophagus and mourning widow are seen in the background. Paris Almanach for the year 1689. (From O. Klingler, Die Comédie-Italienne in Paris nach der Sammlung von Gherardi, *Strasbourg, 1902.)*

Les Comédiens Italiens. *Painting by Antoine Watteau, 1720. In the center of the troupe, Pierrot or Gilles; to his left, Harlequin in a black mask. (Washington, National Gallery, Kress Collection.)*

adaptation, the *Commedia dell'arte* now wandered eastward. In its original form, it traveled as far as Warsaw, Cracow, Vilna, and Gdansk. In 1592, at Cracow Castle, "True-to-the-original" Zanni, in triplicate, took part in the musical play *intermedii*, presented at the wedding celebration of Sigismund III and Anne of Austria. At festivities in Warsaw, at the court of Ladislaw IV, the *Commedia dell'arte* was a favorite entertainment, for the king had traveled in Italy and there had enjoyed the popular, improvised plays. Its stock types and improvisation could overcome the boundaries of language, rank, and convention. A few decades later, the *Commedia dell'arte* traveled across the ocean. In February 1739, the guests at Mr. Holt's Long Room in New York were able to admire the first pantomime-harlequinade known to have been shown on American soil. It was announced as "A new Pantomime Entertainment in Grotesque Characters call'd the Adventures of Harlequin and Scaramouch or the Spaniard Trick'd."

Vienna, at the time Central Europe's cultural collecting reservoir, had opened its doors to the *Commedia dell'arte* around 1570. The players of the "foreign *lazzi*," Zanni and his fellows, were enthusiastically welcomed; but soon they were faced with a home-grown Austrian rival in Hanswurst.

The puppet player Josef Anton Stranitzky dethroned Zanni, Arlecchino, and Brighella. He created the figure of Hanswurst, the ancestor of many generations of irrepressible popular stage types right up to Nestroy and Raimund.

Stage with Commedia dell'arte *characters. Etching, frontispiece for Jacques Callot's* Balli di Sfessania, *1622.*

Troupe of entertainers on a raised stage without decorations. A quack praises his wares; next to him a comedian in Zanni costume, a female singer with lute, and two musicians. Fairground buffoons were an early form of Commedia dell'arte. Anonymous watercolor, early 16th century. (Bamberg, Staatsbibliothek.)

Masked revelry with Pulcinella types of the Commedia dell'arte. Wall painting by Giovanni Domenico Tiepolo (1726–95), from the Villa Zianigo. (Venice, Museo Ca' Rezzonico.)

In 1707, the same year in which the dentistry student Stranitzky passed his "Examen dentifraguli dentiumque medicatoris" at the University of Vienna, the comedian Stranitzky, codirector of the "German Comedians," doffed his green pointed hat with grotesque obsequiousness on the stage of the Ballhaus in the Teinfaltstrasse. He was surrounded by the acclamations of a rapturous suburban audience to whom he had introduced the prototype of the simple, shrewd little man, in the person of Hanswurst, of the Salzburg peasant come to settle in Vienna.

Stranitzky's Hanswurst, born of individual theatrical inventiveness nurtured by native mother-wit, became the focal figure of the Austrian folk theater. The *Commedia dell'arte* was his godmother. His external characteristics were a short red jacket, yellow trousers, a green pointed hat, and a white fool's ruff. As his own specialty he developed crude sexual and fecal jokes, which soon surpassed their predecessors of Italian origin in vivid descriptiveness. When, for instance, the *Commedia dell'arte*'s Zanni was required by the displayed script to portray "fear," and whimpered: "Oh, my knees are shaking," Stranitzky's Hanswurst announced: "What the devil, my arse is wobbling like pig's jelly." And when the King in the play indulgently forgives him his loose tongue with the words: "One's got to make allowance for a fool's ignorance," Hanswurst retorts: "I think so too, pal."

But the more artless improvisation becomes, the more trite the jokes and the more obscene the subjects, the closer is the danger of decadence, of debasement into mere vulgarity. Neither the *Commedia dell'arte* nor the folk theater was able to avoid this danger. Whether it was Zanni, Harlequin or Hanswurst, Stockfish or Pickle Herring—none of them in the end had the power to put new life into stale jokes. In Vienna Stranitzky's successor, young Gottfried Prehauser, clung to the heights of sly cunning; in Leipzig Hanswurst was driven in dishonor off the stage of the lovely Karoline Neuber.

In Italy, Goldoni and Gozzi tried to move the improvised folk theater into the realm of literature. Goldoni reduced the number of *Commedia dell'arte*'s comic types to four or five, and fitted them into firmly constructed milieu or character comedies. He took his subjects from everyday Venetian life and wrote *The Servant of Two Masters* for the troupe of the famous Truffaldino player Antonio Sacchi. Goldoni's plays brought about the long-overdue renewal of the Italian theater. He repeated the melting-down process that, a century earlier, Molière had undertaken in Paris.

Gozzi rejected Goldoni's imitation of nature. He denied the necessity of character comedy and deployed the colorful magic of his *Fiabe*, his fairy-tale comedies, which he peopled with witches, fairies, and sorcerers. In his violent controversy with Goldoni, he defended the improvised theater, claiming that Goldoni abused it. But although Gozzi meant to breathe new life into improvisation, he required the actors to stick to the texts he wrote. For twenty-five years he worked in close collaboration with the Sacchi troupe. Admiration for the celebrated Truffaldino actor Sacchi, who traveled as far as Portugal with his troupe, was the only point on which Goldoni and Gozzi were in unanimous agreement. The force of the living theater reconciled—and incorporated—the opposite intentions of these two antagonists and reformers.

Goldoni's and Gozzi's heritage outlived the cool reason of the Enlightenment. In the nineteenth century, it became an influence on the popular folk theater of Vienna. It lives in Laroche's Kasperle figure, in the parodistic fairyland comedies of the *Bäuerle* (little peasant) period, in Raimund's great romantic realm of fantasy, and in Nestroy's skeptical, ironical Biedermeier world.

Goethe in his early works gave the floor to Scapino and the Dottore; Ludwig Tieck marshaled Scaramuz, Pierrot, Pantalone, and Truffaldino for bitterly ironic criticism of his age; Grillparzer took his melancholy and ready-witted servant characters from the pool of the *Commedia dell'arte*; E. T. A. Hoffmann wrote a ballet suite entitled *Arlequino* and the grotesque, theater-happy *Phantasiestücke in Callots Manier;* Richard Strauss framed his *Ariadne auf Naxos* in an improvised play in the Italian manner; Gorky, in exile in Capri, became interested in the improvisations of the Neapolitan *Commedia dell'arte*. Later, he tried to fire Stanislavsky's imagination with the idea of a stage of improvisation, where "the actors themselves create the plays."

The *Commedia dell'arte* is the leaven in the dough of the theater. It provides a timeless form of playacting whenever the theater needs a new breath of life and threatens to get stuck in the worn tracks of convention.

THE SPANISH BAROQUE THEATER

Cervantes has his Don Quixote meet a strange conveyance one day on the road. It looks "more like Charon's bark than an ordinary carriage," and is pulled by mules driven by a horrible devil.

> The first personage revealed to Don Quixote [on that strange conveyance] was Death with a human face; next to him was an angel with large wings of many colors; on one side was an emperor, on his head a crown of glittering gold; next to Death sat a god by name of Cupido, without a bandage over

> his eyes but carrying his bow, quiver and arrows. A knight was there, too, in full armor except that he wore no helmet, but a hat with many feathers in different colors.

Alarmed, Don Quixote bars the way of the carriage and asks the meaning of this strange assortment. He gets his answer.

> Sir, we are actors, of the company of Angulo the Wicked. We've played in the village beyond that hill today, after the octave of Corpus Christi that is, and it was the play of Death holding court. Now we mean to perform it again this evening in the other village over there, and because it is so near and we don't want to go to the trouble of undressing and then dressing again, we are traveling in the clothes we need for the performance.

The incident described by Cervantes, which of course leads up to a Quixotic battle with the "devil," characterizes the situation of the Spanish theater at the beginning of the Baroque age: the sturdy trouper spirit of the wandering players, the mixture of antiquity and Christianity in the allegory of their shows, the traditional tinsel of their costumes and, not least, the fact that they needed no great preparations to play at several places on one day, especially during the "acting season," centered around the Corpus Christi festival.

The contrast between the highest mysteries of the faith and the most primitive reality in no way impaired the intensity of the effect. The miracle of the Eucharist issues forth from the twilight of the cathedral onto the creaking boards of a makeshift stage. The wandering comedians, still ranking before the law with thieves and executioners, fulfill an important mission in the Corpus Christi play.

The exuberant allegory of the Spanish retable is repeated in the dense symbolism of the *auto sacramental,* which, unlike the mystery play, is concerned not with the representation of the Passion but with the symbolic transfiguration of the sacrament of the Eucharist. The fantastic, the metaphorical, and the spiritual combine, be it in the most modest stage play or in the costliest Baroque pageant. Both were to serve the twin purposes of religious edification and Counter-Reformational propaganda. Spain's theater, with its rhetoric sharpened by the spirit of centennial conflict with Islam, provided the image for the concept. It clothed the sacrament of the Eucharist in the colorful raiment of fable. Moralizing interpretations had largely removed "sin" from the spiritual heritage of the Renaissance. More than four centuries had passed since Bernard of Morlaix had denounced the inflow of antique ideas into theological literature as "indecent kisses exchanged by Christian scholars with Zeus."

Now, as Spanish generals were fighting for the gold and Jesuit missionaries for the souls of the Indians, the theater did its bit, too. Lope de Vega, in his Corpus Christi play *Araucana,* dressed the Son of God as a South American Indian chief and, obviously to impress the native audience, let Him display His muscular prowess in wrestling and the high jump.

Behind the spiritual hide-and-seek and its bewildering disguises, however, stood the inviolate power of the church and, as Karl Vossler once said, "the often almost playfully insolent certainty of the believer in his relations with God"—for instance, when in Lope de Vega's *El caballero de Olmedo* a grey-haired tart dons a nun's habit and teaches a young noble maiden the elementary facts of love, or when the same author mobilizes the famous miracle-working Madonna of Guadeloupe to perform a "cure" by which a beautiful widow covers up a most mundane lapse.

All these comedies were printed—together with the interludes (*entremesses*) and *loas* that were originally short prefatory and later independent plays—at the time of their performance and distributed in hundreds of copies. All of them had to pass the censorship of the Inquisition. Provided, however, that the writers did not fail to submit to official censorship, they were able to get away with malicious remarks about the clergy, state institutions and, indeed, about religious fanaticism.

Research has shown the influence of the Inquisition on literature, art, and the theater to have been astonishingly slight. At any rate, the luxuriance of the imagination remained as rich as ever. "Don't they hereabouts put on thousands of comedies, full of thousands of improprieties and absurdities, and nevertheless they all get along with the greatest success." Thus Don Pedro, the puppet master, defends the extravagant nonsense of his Moorish-Christian fairy-tale world; "for if only I fill my moneybag, I don't mind putting on more absurdities than there are specks of dust on the sun." (Manuel de Falla has commemorated this episode from *Don Quixote* in his charming ballet *Master Peter's Puppet Show.*)

The moneybag argument was eventually also what helped the Spanish itinerant troupes to permanent playing places in the second half of the sixteenth century. The religious fraternities appreciated the advantages of exploiting the influx of crowds for charitable purposes. They made the courtyards (*corrales*) of their hospitals available to the theater people, took care of the local license for the play and, either as organizers or lessors, shared the takings with the comedians and authors.

Thus the theater had its home, and the hospital till, its extra revenue. And the authorities had no trouble keeping control of the comedians thus guided into orderly tracks. In Madrid, the Cofradia de la

Spanish corral theater in the 17th century: performance at the Corral del Principe, Madrid. Reconstruction in a drawing by Juan Comba y Garcia (1888).

Corral of Almagro, Ciudad Real. The courtyard has been restored and is now used for performances in the style of the Golden Age.

Pasión kept such *corrales* going from 1565 on, one in Calle del Sol and one in Calle del Principe; in 1574 the Cofradia de la Soledad opened its Corral de Burguillos. Valencia had had a corral theater since 1583, and for Seville there are records of repeated performances in a Corral of Doña Elvira in 1579 and thereafter.

At about that time, the Elizabethan stage in London began to take shape; but the Spanish corral theater, by contrast, kept its makeshift character. The golden age of Spanish drama, the *Siglo de oro,* the period 1580–1680, had nothing but the modest setting of an open-air stage surrounded by the walls of houses, a stage that could be erected one day and torn down the next.

The stage scaffold was put up against the main side of the paved patio. A curtain concealed the actors' dressing rooms and at the same time served as back shutter for the stage. The balconies and galleries of the house facade formed *lo alto del teatro,* "the upper stage," which was as indispensable as the trapdoor.

The windows and galleries of the surrounding houses made splendid boxes for the ladies among the audience, whereas the gentlemen were seated on tiers of benches. In the seventeenth century, a special women's gallery (*cazuela*) was set aside.

But those who could, and did, really make or break a play, were the *mosqueteros,* the common men crowding the pit. They made their views known with the vocal power of musketeers, and were held in as much awe by Spanish dramatists as were the groundlings by Elizabethan ones.

As on the far side of the Pyrenees and across the Channel, or indeed as anywhere else where open-air stages without lighting installations were in use, plays were given in the afternoon, before it got dark. In the cities, Corpus Christi plays often still employed the stage wagons of the late medieval processional theater. These would draw up alongside the corral podium and serve as side stages, or be stationed behind it and serve as an inner stage. They could also be used as dressing rooms for the actors.

The most important stage property was a ladder, to connect the lower, main, and upper stages. Its unconcealed visibility in no way impaired the magic of the supernatural. As late as 1675, Marie-Catherine d'Aulnoy, a French traveler in Spain and author of one of the most important and entertaining descriptions of the corral theater, reported from Madrid: "In the scene where Aline conjures up the demons, the latter come up from hell quite comfortably on ladders."

But the Spanish Baroque theater was directly linked with the late medieval tradition not solely through its techniques. It was also indebted to that tradition for its themes. When Lope de Vega, at the age of

Three-part cart stage, presenting a performance of the comedy La adultera perdonada, *by Lope de Vega, in Madrid, 1608. Reconstruction by Richard Southern (1960).*

Procession with allegorical groups in Barcelona, at the reception of Archduke Charles of Habsburg, claimant to the Spanish throne (as Charles III). Contemporary print. (Paris, Bibliothèque de l'Arsenal.)

thirteen, began to write for the stage in 1575, he had, as it were, "merely to open the sluice gates." The pent-up wealth of epics and romances, national history, myths, and legends furnished him with his themes. He found, as Grillparzer put it in his beautiful poem,

> For all that mankind ever has encountered,
> A word, an image, path alike and end.

For forty years, Lope de Vega was the uncontested ruler of the Spanish stage. His contemporaries called him "Monstruo de la naturaleza," and "Fenix de los Ingenios." He produced no less than 1500 plays, of which close to 500 are still extant, including Corpus Christi plays, comedies, and cloak-and-dagger plays (*Comedias de capa y espada*). Behind the reckless facility, however, there is always Lope de Vega's awareness of his Spanish nationality. Already in his early work *Jorge Toledano* he extolled the Spaniard's daring and pride: "I find it strange that Alexander stems from Macedonia, not from Spain."

In the so-called honor plays, a brother or father avenges a maiden's injured virtue. The cloak-and-dagger plays abound in high-spirited verbal and armed duels, subtly woven intrigues, and disguises, and they hardly ever lack a shrewd servant and confidant (*gracioso*) for comic relief.

Outstanding among the followers of the radiant "phoenix" Lope de Vega was the Mercedarian monk Gabriel Téllez, who started writing plays in 1624 and published them under the pseudonym Tirso de Molina. He took over Lope de Vega's dramatic technique and triumphed by the careful psychological development of his characters. Tirso experts say the Confessional helped him to sharpen his knowledge of human nature. One of his most brilliant plays is *Don Gil de las calzas verdes*; Don Gil in the Green Breeches—really Doña Diana in disguise, a clever and loving girl who resolutely defies the conventional tutelage of women, and sets forth to recapture her unfaithful betrothed.

In *El Burlador de Sevilla*, a play based on themes from two old Spanish legends, Tirso de Molina was the first to put Don Juan Tenorio on the stage. Don Juan Tenorio was to be the prototype of many successors—from the scenario of the *Commedia dell'arte* to Molière's *Don Juan* and Mozart's *Don Giovanni*, to Max Frisch's *Don Juan, or The Love of Geometry*. And Tirso de Molina's fine saying that "God's mercy adapts itself to our nature and ennobles it without destroying it," has in its turn an echo in Claudel's epigraph to *The Satin Slipper*: "God writes straight even on crooked lines." With his subtitle "Spanish Drama in Four Days," Claudel harks back formally to the pattern of the Spanish Baroque theater. Plays were divided not into acts, but into *jornadas*, day's journeys, which gave limitless scope to any leap across time and space, and set the poetic imagination free in a flowering field luxuriantly overgrown with lyricism, adventure, burlesque, and mysticism.

The greatness of the Spanish Baroque drama lay in the force of poetic expression. Modest though it was, the corral stage was sufficient. A few stage properties, an upper stage, and a trap were all that was needed; all the rest—the mood otherwise created by lighting, scenic imagination and change of place was projected by the spoken word. How else would it have been possible to stage a play like *Las Mocedades del Cid*—Guillén de Castro's major work and model for Corneille's *Le Cid*—an epic drama with a wealth of different scenes? (The French classical theater managed with the system of the long and short stage. The rear stage showed the king's palace, the forestage was essentially neutral and accommodated the changes of scene.) A second contemporary of Tirso de Molina, Juan Ruiz de Alarcón, was the originator of the character comedy in Spain. His principal work, *La verdad sospechosa* (Truth Suspected) became a perennial stage success, thanks to Goldoni's adaptation and Corneille's earlier adoption of the subject in his *Le Menteur* (1644).

As the seventeenth century unfolded, the advanced techniques of the Baroque transformation stage, by then common to court theaters throughout Europe, made their appearance in Spain as well. The Florentine architect Cosimo Lotti installed a theater in the east wing of the royal summer residence Buen Retiro, east of Madrid, and its technical devices were comparable with those of Florence or Vienna. Its back wall could be opened up to free the view into the garden. Lope de Vega, however, took no pleasure in the arts of the wizard Lotti. When, in 1629, his *La selva sin amor* was staged before the court at the Zarzuela palace with a rich décor by Lotti, Lope de Vega was disappointed. "My verses were the least of it," he said. "Faced with the visual splendor of Lotti's scenery, the sense of hearing had to retreat." The aging Lope de Vega found it hard to take to the newfangled "frame for cloth and nails" in which the theater was disintegrating. His heart belonged to the unpretentious corral stage, where the imagery of language and verbal wit ruled supreme.

But, just as in Italy, in France, and throughout the Europe of the Baroque, court society enjoyed the elaborate mechanisms of the side wings. Lotti's successors Baccio del Bianco and Francesco Ricci made certain that the costumes onstage were no less sumptuous than the audience's garments of velvet and brocade, and that the words, whether spoken or sung, were set in a "framework" as apt to make the author feel flattered as outdone.

During this golden age more than 30,000 *comedias* were written on the Iberian Peninsula. Its climax and swan song are linked with the name of Spain's great writer Pedro Calderón de la Barca. Calderón's aristocratic origin gave its imprint to his life, his personality, and his dramatic works. He was not in need of stage mechanisms, but did not despise them. In the productions of his great *autos sacramentales*—with their ceremonial solemnity, their sublimation of matter on the one hand and their personification of abstract concepts on the other—he readily enough availed himself of the technical accessories of stage magic, without becoming dependent on them. "His plays are entirely stage-worthy," Goethe later said of him appreciatively, "there is not a trait in them that is not calculated for deliberate effect. Calderón was a man of genius who at the same time possessed a superior intelligence."

Calderón indeed had more than great intelligence: he had the power of a superb, creative imagination through which he captured the transcendental, and "from the platform of eternity reflected life as a dream before man's awakening in God. *La vida es sueño*—Life is a Dream." Calderón saw the meaning and purpose of his own life as a service of honor to the church, the nation, the king. In 1640, during the Catalan rebellion, when the Order of Santiago, of which Calderón was a member, called all its knights to arms, Philip IV tried to keep back his court poet by royal order: he insisted on celebrating the festival at Buen Retiro as had been previously arranged. Calderón finished the play in a week—and hastened to join the campaign.

Measured against Lope de Vega's profuse fecundity, Calderón's output of 120 comedies, 80 *autos sacramentales* and 20 minor pieces may appear as "limitation to a very narrow range of themes," as Adolf Friedrich von Schack once said. But Calderón was unmatched in the flawless precision with which the cog wheels of his plots mesh together. Their motive power is the inexhaustible device of disguises and mistaken identities that are the hallmark of the cloak-and-dagger comedy, together with the witty little interludes known as "lances de Calderón."

But beyond the fine net of intrigues in *The Fairy Lady*, the stiff code of honor of *The Mayor of Zalamea*, and the melancholy self-sacrifice of *The Constant Prince*, Calderón poured his full creative power into the *autos sacramentales*, the theatrical celebration of man's repatriation into the divine world order. He sublimates and stylizes emotions and reduces human destiny to the underlying conception of God and man.

El gran teatro del mundo is Calderón's great metaphor for the "maquina de los cielos," the divine dispensation that rules the orbits of the stars and the distribution of men's lots. It is also the title of one of his greatest plays. The work was performed in 1675 at the royal palace theater of Buen Retiro, with Calderón personally supervising the pro-

Scene design for a play by Calderón. From a stage-design series of 1690. (Madrid, National Library.)

duction. The words of the play itself occasionally suggest some of the Baroque sumptuousness lavished upon the scenery and costumes of this gala performance: "Fit adornments and array. . . ."

And when we are told that the creation is set in "a garden of the loveliest design with ingenious perspectives," we can readily imagine the Baroque stage machinery springing into action to open out the view into the green palace gardens of Buen Retiro.

In Calderón the Spanish royal court had an extremely versatile theater producer, who provided not only high drama fraught with philosophical thought, but also gay musical comedy. He originated the *zarzuela,* a seventeenth-century Spanish form of musical comedy. It was named for the royal hunting lodge Zarzuela near El Pardo, on the southern slopes of the Guadarrama mountains, where King Philip IV and the Infante Don Fernando liked to attend musical entertainments. Calderón was commissioned to write texts for two-act lyrical song-plays. (Their musical scores, written by anonymous composers, have been lost.)

By 1657, when Calderón's "fishermen's eclogue" *El golfo de las sirenas* was staged, in which "Lady Zarzuela" was one of the allegorical characters, the designation *zarzuela* became the common term designating this genre. The subject of the *zarzuela* is a variant of the popular Odysseus-Circe theme, drawn upon by the pastoral plays of the whole of Europe. In the comedy *El mayor encanto amor* (Love the Greatest Enchanter), Calderón himself had written an earlier version of the play in 1637. The production of *The Gulf of Sirens* at the Zarzuela palace in 1657 was one of the most expensive in Calderón's time. It is said to have cost 16,000 ducats. The *zarzuela,* in its original character and almost untouched by developments in Western music, survived into the twentieth century.

THE STROLLING PLAYERS

In the first half of the seventeenth century, while the Spanish Baroque drama was flourishing, while France was approaching the great era of the *tragédie classique* and the *Commedia dell'arte* was finding open doors everywhere, Central Europe was racked by the Thirty Years' War. As always and everywhere, jesters and strolling players followed the train of the armies. Wherever there was actual fighting or where the battle had stopped, they could be sure of a welcome, whether it was under the imperial, Catholic or the Swedish, Protestant flag, at court or in the cities, on the marketplace, in the fairground, or in village inns. The strolling players could build bridges between people whose rulers were at war.

Via Denmark and Holland, English comedians had roamed as far south as Saxony and Hesse by the end of the sixteenth century. Keen competition in their own country, and even more the fickle favors of Queen Elizabeth, who would now issue prohibitions and then hand out privileges, caused many English professional troupes to emigrate. Letters of recommendation from one court to the next smoothed their path through the continent. They were applauded everywhere. Soon they took local actors into their troupe, changed over to the local language and so exercised lasting influence on the theater in the Netherlands, Denmark, and especially Germany.

While the *Commedia dell'arte* relied on stock characters, the English players took pride in presenting their audience with "beautiful magnificent, joyful, and consoling comedies from historiis." And because in the Protestant northern countries the moral lesson counted as much as the art of accomplished acting, Robert Browne, when applying in 1606 to the Frankfurt town council for leave to play, took pains to stress that it had always been his earnest endeavor to give the honorable spectators "cause and occasion to pursue propriety and virtue."

But, in the end, the public wanted a little less edification and a little more amusement—which was provided by the jester and clown. He was the first to leap the language barrier with plain and crude verbal wit. It is reported that there was a troupe of English comedians in Munich as early as 1599 and that there was a clown among them "who makes much patter and foolery in German."

The rival claims of literary ambitions and Hanswurst buffoonery, which was so demonstratively to come to a head in 1737, in the days of Karoline Neuber, were competing already in the early period of the strolling players. One of the most popular jesters was Thomas Sackeville, the spiritual father and creator of a character variously named with derivatives of the words "clown" or "posset," and eventually known himself by the stage name Jan Bouschet. He was a member of one of the earliest English troupes to tour the continent and, coming from Copenhagen, arrived at the Court of Duke Heinrich Julius of Brunswick in 1592. The Duke was married to a Danish princess and had advance information from Copenhagen about the players. He liked Sackeville so much that he retained him at his court at Wolfenbüttel from 1593 to 1598 as the director of a company of his own. The Duke himself wrote some ten prose plays, stoutly moralizing but theatrically effective, and relying in part on Sackeville's artful clowning.

The principal Robert Browne, on the other hand, was one of those who made things difficult for themselves. His ambition was to offer literary theater, though tempered by the announcement that he and his *Actiones* would provide splendid *oblectamentum* fit for everyone, and for the *melancholicis* a most pleasant recreation. Some of his men were taken on by the Landgrave Moritz of Hesse, whose court organist was Heinrich Schütz. Browne himself returned to England, leaving his troupe under the management of his successful and ambitious clown John Green.

Some years later, in May 1618, Browne was back on the continent, with a new troupe and a new repertory. In Prague, he contributed several "well-turned comedies, tragedies, and histories" to the brief royal glory of the "winter king," the erstwhile Elector Palatine Frederick, and for his queen the English princess Elizabeth. Thereafter Browne's traces are lost in the confusion of the Thirty Years' War.

Another Englishman, John Spencer, a clever tactician and versatile practical man, had by 1605 made a name for himself in Leiden and The Hague, and then spent several years touring via Dresden as far as Stettin, Königsberg and Gdansk. In 1615 he was converted to Catholicism in Cologne, and thereby acquired the privilege of being allowed to perform "religious, respectable, and approved *actiones*," even in Lenten season.

It is in connection with Spencer's company that we have one of the few extant indications as to what the stage of the English comedians on the continent may have looked like. For the performance of a "Comedy about the Turkish Triumph," *Die Einnahme von Konstantinopel,* a costly wooden construction was erected at Regensburg, clearly inspired by the Elizabethan model but, in this particular form, probably the exception rather than the rule. It was "a theater in which musicians played in more than ten different ways on all kinds of instruments. And above the acting stage there was a second stage, raised 30 feet high on 6 great pillars; over it a roof had been made, and underneath, a square opening, whereby they achieved beautiful *actiones*."

Spencer was versatile not only in religious, but also in artistic matters. He offered his public a new clown character, introduced in 1617 in Dresden and in 1618 at the court of Brandenburg under the name of Stockfish—a counterpart to Thomas Sackeville's Jan Bouschet and to Pickle Herring created by Robert Reinolds, an actor who had originally belonged to Robert Browne's company and later become a principal on his own.

English origin remained until the middle of the seventeenth century a guarantee of quality in actors and was prized throughout Central Europe and as far east as Elbing, Warsaw and Graz. "The Landgrave's English Comedians at Cassel" was the title of honor bestowed by Moritz of Hesse upon his court theater troupe, which had the privilege of playing in the first stone theater building constructed in Germany, the Ottonium, built in Cassel in 1606. The Ottonium still stands. After several reconstructions, it now houses a museum of natural history and the exhibitions of the Kassel Art Society.

In 1651, when the Thirty Years' War had ended, a troupe of English comedians were the first to be authorized by the Ulm town council to play in the Theater in the Binderhof that had been built by Joseph Furttenbach. This had been opened in 1641 and was the first civic theater in Germany; in the ten years since—to the extent that the troubled times permitted—then, it had housed performances of strolling players and of the school drama.

In Ulm as elsewhere, theater managers who were playwrights, too, had made sure that the school drama continued to hold its own alongside the plays presented by the professional comedians. Eventually both came to share the same aspirations and the same authors. The works of the Silesian Andreas Gryphius and of the Dutchman Joost van den Vondel—who both had originally written for the school theater—moved up to be included with the repertory of "historiis" in the English manner. In Frankfurt, as early as 1649, "die Greene-Reinoldsche Truppe" proudly announced that it had "far outdistanced the art of the foreigners." That same year Joris Jolliphus, who had come to Cologne in 1648 from Holland, made it known that he had "a company speaking high German, easily understood," and could offer pastorals and musical plays in the Italian fashion as well as tragedies "the Historia of which has never before been put on the stage hereabouts."

Presumably, this referred to the first performances of Gryphius's plays, for we know that, in 1651, his martyrs' tragedies *Leo Armenius* and *Catharina von Georgien* were presented by strolling players in Cologne. Andreas Gryphius had become acquainted with the Dutch professional theater during his student days in Leiden. He had come to admire the Baroque humanist dramatist Joost van den Vondel, the greatest among the Dutch classical writers. Gryphius's work was much influenced by that of Vondel; although, as his *Horribilicribifax* demonstrates, he also had close ties to the *Commedia dell'arte.*

Vondel's *Gysbrecht van Aemstel* was the play chosen for the gala

Strolling players: stage design for heroic drama. Engraving, frontispiece for a German collection of plays presented by English and French comedians. Frankfurt am Main, 1670.

opening of the Amsterdam Schouwburg in 1638. (It is still performed every year on New Year's Day). Thanks to Vondel's plays the Dutch strolling players became the English comedians' successful competitors. The Brussels troupe of Archduke Leopold Wilhelm of Austria, on a tour, performed in Amsterdam. Afterwards they traveled on, and gained fame with their guest performances at Gottorp Castle in Holstein (September 1649), and at Flensburg, Copenhagen, and Hamburg. When they returned to Amsterdam in 1653, Vondel greeted then with a poem that expressed his gratitude and admiration. Their principal Jan Baptista Fornenbergh in 1666 earned the praise of the Hamburg-Wedel priest and poet Johann Rist, who said of him that he and his excellent troupe had risen far above the unfortunately widespread manner of "quacks, tooth-pullers, and jack-pudding poets." Rist had specially driven out to Altona to watch the guest performance. He was somewhat perplexed that the Dutchmen, in accordance with a habit surviving from *Rederijker* days, introduced their play by a *tableau vivant*. "When that display, which is commonly called *Vertooninge*, is finished," Rist reports, "every spectator knows already how many and what kind of

Scene from the Baroque martyr drama Catharina von Georgien, *by Andreas Gryphius. Engraving by J. Using, 1655.*

players, and in what costume, are to appear in the forthcoming comedies or tragedies."

It would be an inextricably confused and crisscrossed map indeed if one were to trace the itineraries of the English and Dutch comedians, of the *Commedia dell'arte* players and their colleagues, the *burattini* with their puppet booths, and, finally, of the innumerable subsequent Central European strolling troupes. The names of known principals span a whole century of European theater history, through the ages of the Baroque and Enlightenment until the foundation of indigenous, national theaters.

There was rivalry for the favors of princes and magistrates, for the best plays and the most auspicious dates, and for the services of the most successful actors. The theater was not to gather any moss. The strolling players opened up Europe for the world theater. The Hamburg principal Carl Andreas Paulsen and the troupe of Michael Daniel Treu acquainted northern and eastern Europe with Marlowe, Kyd, and Shakespeare, with Lope de Vega and Calderón, even if their efforts were often more well-intentioned than artistic and, on the literary side, separated from the originals as much as they were by geography. They also played Vondel and Gryphius, whose heroic political tragedy *Papinianus* had a successful performance in 1685 before the Bavarian court at Schleissheim Castle, where every available means of heightening the emotion was mobilized on an improvised ballroom stage.

Magister Johannes Velten and his "Chur-Sächsische Komödianten" provided Dresden with its theater. In this "famous band," says Eduard Devrient, "was rooted the family tree of later notable troupes." For fifteen years Velten and his company were on the road, gaining popularity and esteem everywhere. In Nuremberg, Breslau, and Hamburg he introduced the practice of the "Ratskomödie" (council comedy), a benefit performance expressing the players' gratitude for a hospitable reception. On these occasions, Devrient reports, "the magistrates appeared *in corpore*, occupied the most privileged seats, that is, on the stage itself on both sides of the proscenium, and allowed themselves to be feted by a solemn musical offering (Serenada) for the high favor and benevolence shown." At Dresden, Velten was invited by Johann Georg II to participate in the theatrical court festivals organized in 1678, and after 1684 was given permanent employment by Johann Georg III.

Vienna, Graz, and Klagenfurt were the domain of Andreas Elenson's troupe, whose succession leads through Johann Caspar Haacke down to the actor Karl Ludwig Hoffmann, who in 1724 presided over the début of a young actress whose star rose and sank in the firmament of the Enlightenment. This was Karoline Neuber, née Weissenborn, a lawyer's daughter from Zwickau, who, after a humanist education, eloped with and married the actor Johann Neuber.

Not the least of the world theater's pioneers, finally, was the troupe of Johann Christian Kunst, which made its way through East Prussia as far as Moscow. Thirty years earlier Paulsen, then at Danzig (Gdańsk), had been invited by the Tzar to play in the Kremlin; but the trip had not come off. Kunst and his men reached the Volga in 1702. Tzar Peter I arranged for the actors to play on the indoor stage at the Kremlin, which had been in use since 1673, and engaged them as his court players. In 1702 a special comedy theater was built on the square before the palace (now Red Square). Russian court society, usually diverted by the artistic-musical offerings of vagrant buffoons known as "Skomorokhi," now was introduced by Kunst's ensemble to a semblance of West European drama. Alongside Corneille and Molière, however, they also had to put up with an ample supply of heroic tragedies in the bombastic style of Lohenstein, which were Kunst's speciality.

The decorations and the costumes of the strolling players were initially modest enough. A great display of sumptuous clothes and feather hats depended entirely on the disposable cash and the generosity of whoever happened to employ the players. If the troupe was in the service of an open-handed prince, the court's wardrobe no doubt helped to replenish the stock of costumes. When the original play included roles that could not be cast or fitted out appropriately, these were either rewritten or, if need be, omitted altogether.

The stage was usually partitioned in the middle by a curtain. This left a neutral playing area in front, and the additional surprise element of a back stage already set up with its props. By the middle of the seventeenth century, front stage curtains (its "marvel-masking" function had already been discussed in detail by the Ulm theater architect Joseph Furttenbach) were generally used by the strolling troupes. Both types of curtains were drawn aside from right and left. In the course of the eighteenth century, the outward appearance of the stage itself benefited from the general trend toward consolidation, when big cities licensed specific troupes to play regularly for definite seasons in existing permanent theater halls.

Effects relying on disguise were always popular, especially the exchange of beggar's tatters and king's robes, with its many possibilities. Oriental costumes were much in vogue as can be seen in the engravings of scenes from *Catharina von Georgien* for the 1654 performance at Wohlau. Caesar was given a full-bottom wig to wear and Arminius a plume. Christian Weise's *Bäuerischer Macchiavellus* sat enthroned beneath a Baroque canopy, and the pomp and pose of the leading character in heroic tragedy matched those of the *roi soleil* in his most gorgeous portraits. "All that glitters is not gold," wrote the Augsburg engraver Martin Engelbrecht across the top of his sheets peopled with luxuriously dressed and scepter-bearing strolling comedians. The attempt to apply this motto to a reform of theatrical costume was to involve the critic and drama reformer Gottsched in a bitter and largely unsuccessful struggle, which put an end to his collaboration with Karoline Neuber, the famous actress and principal of a strolling troupe.

The Age of Gentility

INTRODUCTION

Everywhere in Europe, the eighteenth century was an era of change in the traditional social order and in modes of thought. The age of Enlightenment brought the new postulate of the supremacy of reason. Humanitarian ideas, enthusiasm for nature, notions of tolerance and various "philosophies" strengthened man's confidence in the possibility of mastering his fate on earth. In 1793, God was officially dethroned in the cathedral of Notre Dame in Paris, and the goddess of Reason was put in His place.

In spite of its fragmentation into small states, Europe had become more unified. During the first half of the century, it felt united in the optimism of the Enlightenment while at princely courts the Baroque fortissimo was dying away in the mirrors and shellwork of the Rococo. While the gallants of Watteau's court society embarked for the island of Cythera, Hogarth roamed the streets of London sketching whores and servants. The court and the city were the two centers of eighteenth-century society, and France and England were the two spheres of influence from which society received its ideas.

From Paris and London emanated the first endeavors to reconcile the new secular and scientific ideas with the middle-class way of life. Pierre Bayle's secularizing, skeptical *Dictionnaire* and John Locke's *Epistola de tolerantia* were eagerly read in public libraries. The third estate raised its claim to participation in the affairs of the world and the mind.

But the foundations upon which European society rested in the eighteenth century were still feudal. Under the label "ancien régime" its course was set toward the French Revolution, which fused all the century's great emotions in one tremendous explosion of the people, nature, sentiment, and reason, defining its own form of life and demanding its due human and civic rights.

The theater tried to make its contribution to the shaping of the century that was to be so full of contradictions. It became a platform of man's new knowledge of himself, a pulpit of moral philosophy, a school of ethics, a subject of learned controversies, and also a common possession consciously enjoyed. Diderot's *Le Père de famille,* the great textbook example of the new middle-class drama, so Lessing declared, was "neither French nor German, nor of any other nationality, but simply human." The play sought to express only "what everyone could express, who understood and felt it."

The era of the great public theaters was at hand. Within a few decades splendid opera- and play-houses were built everywhere in Europe, with three, four, or five tiers of seats in semicircular or horseshoe curves facing the high and magnificently framed peep-show stage. Some of them, to be sure, were commissioned by monarchs, but they were intended for the same purpose that inspired Augustus the Strong, Elector of Saxony, when he had the *Zwinger* built at Dresden: to provide a place for popular festivals in the grand style. The Théâtre de la Monnaie in Brussels was the first in the long series of the eighteenth century's imposing public theater buildings, from the Teatro Argentina in Rome to the Haymarket and Covent Garden Theatres in London, from the Grand-Théâtres in Lyons and Bordeaux to the Royal Opera House in Copenhagen, from San Carlo in Naples to the Gran Teatro del Liceo in Barcelona.

The watchword was: "What the eye sees, the heart believes," and the theater, a magnificent building and the scene of the middle-class drama, provided an appropriately lavish frame for tempered self-contemplation.

The age, begun under the cool breath of Reason, ended in sentimentality, at the same time being fired by the *Sturm und Drang* notions of genius, which, by then tamed, were central in the era of Weimar classicism. The reservoir of the closing century flowed over into the intellectual and political currents of the nineteenth century. Romanticism became the first cosmopolitan literary movement that was able to rally both to the Revolution and Restoration. The countries of Central, Northern, and Eastern Europe wanted a national theater of their own, and this was one of the theater's crucial impulses; the other was the idea of a worldwide repertory, as conceived by Goethe.

For Victor Hugo the romantic historical drama was a *"miroir de concentration—"* opera wrapped it in the glorious sound of great orchestras, and realism turned the stage into an occasion for archaeology or a fashionable drawing room. The diversity of simultaneous forms heralded the approach of a process of democratization, which found its first expression in the naturalism of the late nineteenth century.

THE ENLIGHTENMENT

Two Trends in European Theater: Between Pomp and Naturalness

Inasmuch as the Enlightenment saw the supreme task of human thought and action as the subordination of life and environment to the concept of rationality, the theater in its turn was called to assume a new function. The stage was to be the forum and bulwark of moral philosophy, and it dedicated itself to this duty with decorum and zeal, to the extent that it did not prefer to sidestep into the enchanted realm of fantasy or the laughter of the *Commedia dell'arte.* The lodestars of the new literary drama were the rule of *bon sens*—common sense—as developed by Boileau in his *L'Art poétique* (1674), and the moral principle.

The century of Enlightenment had a bent for reflection, sentimentality, and criticism. There was much moralizing and argumentation, authorized and inspired by the new goddess of Reason. The new weekly reviews catering to the middle classes devoted entire pages to the subject of the theater. But the raised forefinger of admonition caused respectability rather than genius to prosper. In the preface to his middle-class comedy *The Lying Lover* (1702), a sentimental remaking of Corneille's *Le Menteur,* the English dramatist Richard Steele looked forward to the prospect of wit recovering from its excesses and encouraging virtue, while vice was delivered over to shame.

In France Marivaux, the first specialist in the female psyche, wrote a series of brilliant comedies, in which elements of Luigi Riccoboni's Nouveau Théâtre Italien are refined to serve the purposes of subtle psychological studies. Marivaux was the author of thirty odd plays and created an art form known as *comédie gaie,* which was far superior to the sententious morality of the tearful middle-class drama, yet contributed much to its development.

Luigi Riccoboni in 1738 set himself up as the first champion of a type of comedy in which magnanimity and renunciation are compounded in a happy end, and which Chassiron mockingly described as *comédie larmoyante.* (Lessing, in his translation of Chassiron's *Réflexions sur le Comique-larmoyant,* chose the German term *weinerliches Lustspiel,* and its advocate on the German stage was the playwright Gellert.)

In England, the so-called sentimental comedy was equally successful and attracted authors ranging from Richard Steele to the actor-manager Colley Cibber, and to the contemporaries of Laurence Sterne's *Sentimental Journey through France and Italy.* Lessing rendered the English word "sentimental" as "empfindsam" and thereby coined a German term for middle-class idyllicism around 1730: "Empfindsamkeit." Voltaire's *L'Enfant prodigue* is not far removed from the *comédie larmoyante,* but it overdoes the preaching. Voltaire flattered the spirit of his age without submitting to it. "I regard tragedy and comedy as lectures in virtue and respectability," he, too, declared. But he preferred to test the magnanimity of his characters in the faraway lands ruled by Moslem and Tartar princes rather than in the cozy warmth of the middle-class dressing gown.

"I have been conquered by your virtue," Genghis Khan confesses at the end of the drama *L'Orphelin de la Chine* to Idamé, the mandarin's wife, who incorruptibly has withstood both his courting and his threats. Voltaire reinterpreted his four-hundred-year-old Chinese model in the spirit of Reason. He admired the wisdom of the East and the obstinate persistence of its traditions in defying violation of any kind. And so he allowed his Tartar emperor the merit of yielding to Idamé's virtue and being an intelligent victor. "This is a strange example of the natural superiority of reason and genius over blind and barbarian force," Voltaire wrote in his preface. His persecuted heroes suffer in verse, exactly as do those of Corneille and Racine. He admired Shakespeare, but felt incapable of taking advantage of his free treatment of dialogue.

"An English poet is a free man who lets his language serve as the spirit moves him," Voltaire wrote in 1730 when he sent his *Brutus* to Lord Bolingbroke, with whom he had remained in correspondence since his stay in England. "The Frenchman is a slave to rhyme and is obliged sometimes to turn out four lines in order to express an idea an Englishman can render in one single line." Voltaire invoked Corneille, Racine, and Boileau before he came to the following conclusion: "Anyone who wished to cast off the burden borne by the great Corneille would be regarded not as a bold spirit striking out on a new road, but as a weakling unable to survive in the old track."

Voltaire saw no future in attempts to write tragedy in prose. Diderot proved him wrong—the bold methodologist of *Paradoxe sur le comédien* and tenacious compiler of the great Encyclopedia accepted the middle-class sentimental drama, and wrote *Le Père de famille* in the artless prose of everyday language.

The French theater had its triumph of sentimentality. Even one of the "most hardened egoists of his age, King Louis XV," the chroniclers tell us, shed tears at the performance of *Le Père de famille* in March 1761. The consistency with which the Age of Gentility forged its own dramatic form outdistanced the stage. The actors of the Comédie Française were accustomed to the declamatory discipline of verse. When they were deprived of it, they felt lost in unknown country. After the per-

Mlle. Clairon as Idamé in Voltaire's L'Orphelin de la Chine. *Diderot, in 1758, praised her courage in wearing a fantasy costume in the Chinese style, without panniers. But in the* 26. Cahier de Costumes Français, *published in Paris, 1779, she is shown in a fashionable crinoline costume, designed by the court costumier Sarrazin.*

Stage setting with scene from Voltaire's middle-class drama L'Enfant prodigue *(1736): the prodigal son in the brothel. The painted garden vista of the backdrop accentuates the illusion of depth and distance.*

Performance of Voltaire's tragedy Irène *at the Comédie Française, Paris, March 30, 1778: on stage, a bust of Voltaire crowned with a laurel wreath. The eighty-four-year-old Voltaire looks on (from the dress-circle box on the left) as he is being honored.*

Final tableau of Diderot's Le Père de famille, *a production at the Nieuwe Schouwburg in Amsterdam, 1775.*

Scene from Le Glorieux, *by P. N. Destouches, at the Comédie Française, with Grandval as Valère, Quinault Dufresne as Comte de Tufière, and Mlle. Grandval as Isabelle. Engraving by N. Dupuis, after Nicolas Lancret, ca. 1738.*

formance, Diderot wrote to Voltaire: "Only Brizard, in the title part, and Madame de Préville as Cécile really answered the requirements of the play. For the others, the new genre was so alien that they assured me they were trembling all the time they were on the stage."

At that time, the Comédie Française had already inaugurated a reform that at first caused a shock, namely, to jettison the absurd ballast of the Baroque costume. The demand for *vraisemblance,* understood by Voltaire and Diderot as "embellished nature," had a hard time prevailing in stage practice. It was felt to be impudence when the actress Clairon in the part of Idamé in 1755 was so daring as to appear in a Chinese-style costume without panniers. But Diderot lavished enthusiastic praise upon her in his *Discours sur la poésie dramatique* (1758). He begged her: "Do not allow prejudice and fashion to have the better of you. Trust your taste and your genius. Show us nature and truth: for that is the duty of those whom we love and whose talents have made us inclined to accept gladly anything that they are willing to dare."

Just how much the French public must have resented being deprived of the customary period costumes can be guessed from what happened in opera and ballet. Louis René Boquet, the imaginative master of rococo costume, dressed his ballet dancers in crinolines of billowing silk with ruffled sleeves, lace veils, ostrich feathers, and garlands of flowers. The title heroes of Rameau's *Castor and Pollux* appeared with towering plumes, Phoebe wore a voluminous crinoline, the Furies were resplendent with plunging décolleté and appliqué snake decorations. Gluck's Iphigenie and Grétry's Zemire, in their respective operas, appeared in the same finery as ballet-master Jean Georges Noverre's mythological figures.

As always, opera claimed the privilege of being conservative. Financed by the courts, it defied all the commands of reason even in the age of rationality, and reveled in the magic of side wings and stage machinery, with erupting volcanoes, sinking ships, and Oriental ballets. (A retrospective production of *Les Indes Galantes* by Rameau at the Paris Opera was enthusiastically acclaimed in 1952 and ran to full houses for three years.)

London's opera life was dominated by Handel from 1720 on. As composer and conductor of the newly founded Royal Academy of Music, he helped Italian opera to a brilliance far beyond what it had achieved in Paris, Vienna, and even in Italy. Handel had gained the favor of the English court and nobility in 1710 with his opera *Rinaldo,* followed a few years later by *Pastor Fido* and *Teseo* and, in 1717, by the *Water Music* composed for a royal water party on the Thames. But then Jonathan Swift gave John Gay the idea of writing the century's most successful musical satire, *The Beggar's Opera,* which cleverly and brazenly

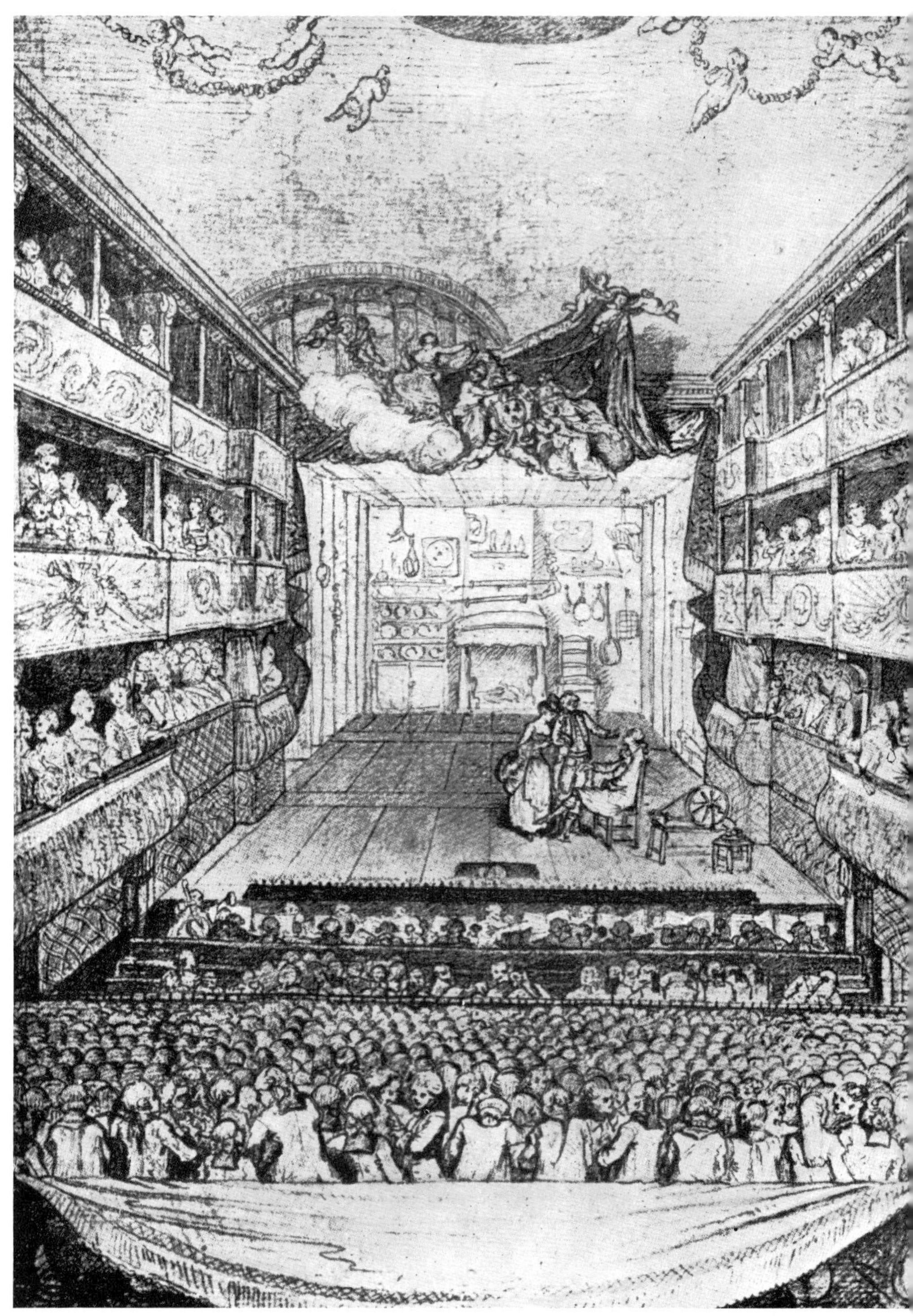

Performance of a middle-class opéra comique *at the Hôtel de Bourgogne, Paris, 1769. The wings in the back part of the stage, which has been extended forward and is equipped with footlights and prompter's box. Drawing by P. A. Wille the Younger. (Paris, Bibliothèque Nationale.)*

satirized the pathos of Handel's operatic style, and the contemporary musical theater's lofty and heroic sentiments that often enough sounded hollow, and, last not least, middle-class sentimentality.

When John Rich produced *The Beggar's Opera* in 1728 at the Lincolns Inn Fields Theatre, he risked his neck. Notwithstanding Defoe's opprobrious thunder, the piece was a hit and ran for sixty-three performances which, as Londoners quipped, made "Rich gay and Gay rich."

Gay's chosen form of alterating songs and dialogue had its parallel in comic opera. The German *Singspiel* developed along lines very close to the operetta; in Paris, the Théâtre de la Foire turned it into vaudeville with a touch of cabaret; thirty years later, Vienna's buffo arias parodying the *opera seria* were first cousins to *The Beggar's Opera.* A second development was the more closely knit melodramatic form, which had first been tried by the school theater and still showed its influence in Mozart's *Zaide,* and had its origin in the single-actor monodrama pioneered by Jean-Jacques Rousseau and Georges Benda.

The revival of antiquity's basic patterns in music and their application to middle-class sentimentality opened up a vast field of theatrical possibilities between the poles of pomp and naturalness, a field of contrasting currents and countercurrents.

The splendor of the absolute monarchies was celebrating its last triumphs. The middle classes proved a source of creative power. The puritanical and pietist spirit displayed a crabbed obstinacy in limiting the barely won fields of activity, but failed to stop the "journey toward good taste." "Oh grant the playful mind that it may own the field, the race track of our heart's desires, the tilt-yard of our loving dreams," thus Tieck, in his *Prinz Zerbino,* a century later mocked an age in which great thoughts and revolutionary ideas matured under full-bottomed wigs.

With *The Barber of Seville,* Beaumarchais broke through the drama's classical hierarchy of characters and the social order of his age. He elevated the confidant from his traditional secondary role and made him the play's hero, who dupes counts, doctors, and clerics, and disparages politics and privilege. And in The *Marriage of Figaro,* which censorship barred for six years, Beaumarchais disclosed chasms over which the guillotine was soon to be raised.

In *The Barber of Seville,* Figaro parodies the lofty art of antithetical verse, and at the same time Voltaire, who had been unable to break loose either from the alexandrine or from the "invention of seemly places." Together with Rameau, Voltaire had written the opera-ballet *La Princesse de Navarre,* which was performed at Versailles in February

William Hogarth's painting The Beggar's Opera *(1729): Polly and Lucy, pleading for Macheath's life. John Gay's opera was first presented in 1728, at the Lincoln's Inn Fields Playhouse in London, by John Rich.*

Satirical engraving by William Hogarth, on The Beggar's Opera*: in the background, a court company performs the work; in front of them, a folk troupe of strolling players has put up a stage and parodies the opera singers in grotesque animal masks.*

1745 and takes its place in the tradition of the *comédie-ballet* as derived from Molière and Lully.

But at Geneva, as the owner first of a country house called "Les Délices" and then of a property at nearby Ferney, Voltaire delighted to defy the Calvinist authorities' law forbidding theatrical performances. He summoned the stars of the Comédie Française, actresses Dumesnil and Clairon and actors Le Kain and Aufresne, and rehearsed his dramas with them. He himself played opposite Le Kain in *Mahomet* and caused "tears to gush from all Swiss eyes" within the very "precinct of the twenty-five wigs" of the Geneva town council.

Rousseau, in his *Lettre à d'Alembert sur les spectacles,* had opposed the predominance of the French classical drama in the Swiss theater and called the attention of his Confederate friends to their own tradition of popular theater. Voltaire thoroughly enjoyed himself playing the devil's advocate in the so-called Swiss theater war he had unleashed.

By the standards of Corneille and Racine, Voltaire's dramatic skill fell far short of his critical reason. But the actors loved him. They vied for the famous leading parts of Zaïre, Mahomet, Alzire, Brutus, Mérope. When Voltaire, at the age of eighty-four, once more returned to Paris in 1778 for a performance of his tragedy *Irène,* he was given a national hero's welcome, both on the stage and by the Académie Française, now, in Goethe's words, "itself advanced in years, like literature, which he had dominated for almost a century."

An author's success was measured by the tears his audience shed. Christoph Martin Wieland, then a young private tutor in Zurich, in June 1758 saw Sophie Ackermann, principal of the Ackermann Troupe, in the part of Voltaire's Alzire. He had begun to write a tragedy, *Lady Johanna Gray,* and now resumed work on it. A month later, on July 20, 1758, Madame Ackermann played Wieland's title role at Winterthur. She enraptured the public with "sweetest delight," alternating with "frequent tears." The author praised her acting for having expressed the whole dignity of the character, and also that which he himself could only feel but had not rendered in words.

The public wanted and was to have its fill of weeping and laughing, all in one evening. This was as true in London as elsewhere, and the eighteenth-century London theater obliged. The middle-class drama prospered in two rival theaters, the Drury Lane Theatre founded in 1663 and originally the home of the King's Company, and the Dorset Garden Theatre designed in 1666 by Christopher Wren. The Drury Lane Theatre produced Nicholas Rowe's successful *The Tragedy of Lady Jane Grey* (1715), the model of Wieland's German version. George Lillo was a pioneer of middle-class drama with *The London Merchant,* and his type of "sentimental comedy" attracted respectful attention on the continent as well. Diderot discussed it, and Lessing chose *The London Merchant* as a model for his own bourgeois tragedy *Miss Sara Sampson*.

George Farquhar's *The Recruiting Officer* is a coarse and licentious portrait of middle-class and army manners, yet stands out by its wit and humor well above the level of the contemporary "comedy of manners." In *The Beaux' Stratagem*, a comedy about the conversion of rascals first produced at the Haymarket Theatre in London in March 1707, Farquhar created a prototype of the dramatic confession of love in which he joined hands with Marivaux' heroines and exerted an influence still apparent sixty years later in Lessing's *Minna von Barnhelm*. The play's own middle-class heroine Dorinda obeys the principle of "matchless honesty," and considers her love rewarded best when it is proved disinterested: "Once I was proud, sir, of your wealth and title, but now I am prouder that you want it: now I can show my love was justly levelled, and had no aim but love."

There was a revival of Shakespeare in London's public theaters around the middle of the eighteenth century. The new approach at the time was to understand the writer's soul, and by doing just that David Garrick, manager and actor, fashioned the English theater for thirty years. He "banished ranting, bombast and grimace," as his biographer Thomas Davies writes, and "restored nature, ease, simplicity and genuine humour."

Garrick's Richard III became the standard of Shakespeare interpretation in eighteenth-century England. Samuel Johnson, who in 1765 published his great edition of Shakespeare, saw the dramatist's very soul embodied in Garrick and paid him the tribute of saying he was the first to have spread Shakespeare's fame throughout the whole world. From about 1730 on Shakespeare, Farquhar, Congreve, Otway, and Addison were played on the far side of the Atlantic as well. English professional actors appeared in New York, Philadelphia, Boston, and Charleston and acquainted the New World with the middle-class drama of the European Enlightenment. Garrick's own first play, the mythological burlesque *Lethe*, was first performed at the Drury Lane Theatre in 1740 and very soon thereafter was often on the program of North American theaters, usually as an afterpiece following a tragedy—a custom that had been taken over from a European tradition going back to antiquity's satyr play. (At the Comédie Française it is common to this day.)

Garrick at first acted in various London theaters, including the Covent Garden Theatre, which had been built in 1731. In 1747, he joined with James Lacy in purchasing the Drury Lane Theatre and shared its management with him until 1776. There was great rivalry between the two theaters as to which was putting on the best Shakespeare performances. In 1750, both simultaneously staged *Romeo and Juliet,* with Spranger Barry and Susannah Maria Cibber at the Covent Garden, and David Garrick opposite George Anne Bellamy at the Drury Lane. The public and the critics passionately took sides. The *Dramatic Censor,* however, mocked: "Romeo again? . . . A plague on both your houses."

Deliberately forgoing ostentation, Garrick used the current standard decorations in stock at the Drury Lane Theatre. In contrast to John Rich's showy sceneries at Lincoln's Inn Fields and later at Covent Garden, Garrick thought it more important to intensify the spoken word. But he conceded his guests the display of sumptuousness he denied himself. When, in the summer of 1754, he invited the celebrated French ballet master and choreographer Jean Georges Noverre to enter into an engagement at his Drury Lane Theatre for the ensuing winter season 1754–55, Noverre, as Thomas Davies reports, "composed that accumulation of multifarious figures, called the Chinese Festival; a spectacle, in which the dresses and customs of the Chinese were exhibited, in almost innumerable shapes and characters." As bad luck would have it, there were the frontier conflicts in America, and as hostilities broke out between England and France, the public protested against Garrick's employing such a large number of Frenchmen in an English theater. Seeing how much he had already spent on it, Garrick went through with the first night. The nobility in the boxes applauded, but the outraged pit discharged its anger in a free-for-all fight. Garrick only just got away safely under police escort.

Soon afterward, he made a longish trip to the continent. He was fêted in Italy and France, but gave no public performances anywhere. Sometimes he would consent to a sample recital in private circles, and on such an occasion Diderot heard him in Paris and praised him enthusiastically: "We saw him act the dagger scene from *Macbeth,* right in the room and in his ordinary clothes, without any aid of theatrical illusion. As he followed with his eyes the [invisible] dagger which hung in the air in front of him and moved away, his acting was so fine that he drew from the whole party a cry of admiration."

After his return from the continent, Garrick introduced a new lighting system at the Drury Lane, eliminating the candle hoops (chandeliers lighting the stage and often obstructing the view from the gallery). He intensified the lights from the wings by means of built-in reflectors and thereby achieved the advantage of bright and graduated lighting for the middle and rear stage as well. Throughout the romantic period, the Drury Lane Theatre maintained its lead in lighting techniques by being one of the first European theaters to introduce gas illumination.

Scene from Ben Jonson's The Alchemist, *with John Burton as Subtle, John Palmer as Face, and David Garrick in the title role. Mezzotint by John Dixon, after J. Zoffany, 1771. (London, British Museum, Somerset Maugham Collection.)*

The School for Scandal, *by Richard Brinsley Sheridan, as performed in 1777 at the Drury Lane Theatre, London.*

But Garrick's rejection of conventional pomp did not preclude his ambition to have his décor and costume "true to nature and in style." "The dresses were rich and magnificent," Thomas Davies reports with reference to the 1749 production of Samuel Johnson's tragedy *Irène,* "and the scenes splendid and gay, such as were well adapted to the inside of a Turkish Seraglio; the view of the gardens belonging to it was in the taste of eastern elegance."

In 1769, Garrick organized the jubilee celebrations at Stratford-on-Avon on a lavish scale, with a procession of Shakespearian characters, concerts, fireworks, and theatrical shows. Pouring rain and intrigues played havoc with this undertaking, and Garrick, as Davies says, "always joining the strictest economy to the most liberal expenditure," moved the jubilee show to Drury Lane, where "the public was so charmed with this uncommon pageant . . . that the representation of it was repeated near one hundred times." (By civic enterprise, the first Shakespeare Memorial Theatre was built at Stratford in 1879 and, after it burned down, a new one was erected in 1932 as the seat of an annual Shakespeare festival.)

In Germany, meanwhile, the natural style of acting found a champion in Konrad Ekhof, whose own stage characterizations continued into Lessing's time and indeed were responsible for the latter's confidence in the artistic claims of the theater. Ekhof's Odoardo in Lessing's *Emilia Galotti* was praised as an exemplary study in contained emotion. "His notes of smothered anger, gnashing rage, suppressed pain, his laughter of despair—who can describe that," wrote the critic Johann Friedrich Schink; ". . . his 'but, my daughter' . . . As the earth trembles under a thunderstorm at night, so the spectator's heart trembled when he spoke the words. Everyone felt the death-blow and cringed with the pain of it."

In addition to his personal powers of acting, Ekhof displayed a reformer's zeal. He founded an actors' academy at Schwerin in 1753, and laid down its aims in twenty-four articles. His idea of "concerted playing" was the first conceptual definition of future principles of stage direction.

Art must come so close to nature, Ekhof insisted, "that verisimilitude must be taken for truth, or things past be reproduced as naturally as though they were happening now. To attain proficiency in this art will demand vivid imagination, sincere judgment, indefatigable industry, and unceasing practice."

This professional code may sound somewhat pedantic. Voltaire expressed it more colorfully. "C'est le coeur seul qui fait le succès ou la chute," he wrote to the actress Quinault—success or failure comes from the heart alone. But Schwerin was not Paris. The more instructive there-

David Garrick as Richard III. Painting by William Hogarth.

Venice Preserved, *by Thomas Otway, as performed in 1762 at the Drury Lane Theatre, London, with David Garrick and S. M. Cibber. Mezzotint by J. McArdell, 1764.*

fore is the identity of views about stage direction. Again and again Voltaire, like Ekhof, insisted that careful allowance must be made for "verisimilitude" in the interplay of the ensemble and in the relationship of setting and plot.

Diderot went further still. He set up rules of stage direction such as recur in Goethe's Weimar style of staging. "The players must be combined, separated or distributed, isolated or grouped," Diderot demanded, "so as to make of them a series of paintings, all of great and true composition. How useful the painter could be to the actor, and the actor to the painter! It would be a means of improving two important talents at once."

Diderot's exacting conception presupposed actors who could be expected to respond to it—such style-creating protagonists, say, as the celebrated Voltaire interpreter Le Kain, who was renowned for his impressive play of gesture and, as a director, aimed at putting on the stage a "peinture animée." The great actor François Talma modeled his acting style on that of Le Kain. Talma acknowledged his debt in *Réflexions sur Le Kain et sur l'art théâtral* (1825); but even before then, around 1800, Talma served as a direct link between Paris and Weimar. Wilhelm von Humboldt had seen Talma in Paris and wrote about him in detail in a letter to Goethe.

However, at the Comédie Française in Le Kain's time any stage director's flights of fancy were tripped up by the notorious legs of the privileged seats on the stage, which were to be had for an extra price. These so-called *banquettes* provided a welcome fillip for the box office, but for the actors they were an imposition and enough to kill any mood. In a much-quoted phrase, a stage manager might have to ask: "Gentlemen, make room for Caesar's ghost!" In 1739, a performance of Racine's *Athalie* had to be broken off because the actors were in danger of being crushed by the occupiers of the *banquettes*. In the preface to his *Brutus*, Voltaire complained bitterly about this abuse that made "any action almost unfeasible." But it was not until 1759 that he finally succeeded in abolishing the nuisance. He persuaded the Count of Lauraguais to donate 60,000 francs in order to compensate the theater people for the loss of revenue liable to ensue.

In the case of the strolling players, the abuse of seats on the stage had been common elsewhere in Europe, too. There is a pictorial record of it from the Grönnegade Theater in Copenhagen. Lessing mentions in Section 10 of the *Hamburgische Dramaturgie* "the barbaric custom of allowing spectators on the stage." A guest performance of the great Lear actor Friedrich Ludwig Schröder in Hamburg, in 1784, attracted such a crowd that makeshift seats were put up eventually between the wings. But that was an exceptional expedient that presumably in no way dimmed Schröder's fire.

The Origins of National Theater in Northern and Eastern Europe

France sent out no strolling players, but its classics were performed throughout the whole of Europe. Europe learned graceful movement from French dancing masters, elegant conversation from French educators, culinary subtlety from French cooks. Everyone aspiring to culture read and wrote French. Paris set the fashion as far as Stockholm and Moscow.

The country in which the theater first bethought itself of its national potentialities was Denmark, once before the gateway through which new theatrical impulses came to Europe. Via Copenhagen the first English comedians had come to the continent at the end of the sixteenth century. And in Copenhagen, early in the eighteenth century, an indigenous theatrical art began to emerge, with the help of French actors. Its initiators were the puppet player Étienne Capion and René Magnon de Montaigu, who came with an introduction to the Danish court. When Capion was so deep in debt that it seemed he could not carry on, Montaigu wrote a petition to the Danish king Frederick IV, in whom, after the end of the great Northern Thirty Years' War, the people placed great hopes for the revival of the country's vital forces. Montaigu tried to interest the king in the theater. "The construction of a theater building," the petition reads, "in the history of nearly all peoples, has followed upon the realm's most prosperous period. The peace that Your Majesty recently gave to Your nation, after the victories of a long war, seems to me to mark the most appropriate moment for this undertaking."

The time was well chosen. Frederick IV signified his approval. But even more decisive was the "Yes" of history, which just then produced Denmark's first dramatist—Ludvig Holberg.

The new playhouse in Lille Grönnegade in Copenhagen was opened on September 23, 1722, with Molière's *The Miser* in a Danish adaptation. Two days later, an original Danish comedy was performed, *Den politiske Kandestöber* ("The Pewterer Turned Politician"). Its author, announced as "a new Danish master," was professor of metaphysics, rhetoric, and history at Copenhagen, but found the academic profession by which he earned his living utterly uncongenial. He wrote his early comedies under the pseudonym Hans Mikkelsen and did not reveal his authorship until a collected edition of his comedies was issued. His *Pewterer Turned Politician* soon became the epitome of everything he attacked in broad, popular satire, to wit, the political wiseacre of the lower-middle-class beer tavern.

Holberg had never paid much attention to the crowds that flocked to his lectures. But when his play, in its turn, drew the crowds, he proudly mentioned the fact in "News of my Life in Three Letters to a Distinguished Gentleman." At the first performance of *The Pewterer Turned Politician,* he said, the crush was so great "that many people who simply could not manage to get through at all had to remain standing in the outer yard." But Holberg resented any wrong or ill-comprehended interpretation: "There were nevertheless some who did not like this comedy," he noted with irritation, "for they did not grasp its meaning and imagined it was meant to mock the city fathers. But no one has ever written a comedy that more emphatically affirms the standing of the authorities."

However sharp Holberg liked to be in his criticism, he was not one to own up to it afterward. "I turn my pen only against vices and not against people," he protested. "For the rest, there is more jest than bitterness to be found in my works; for I do not seek to censure for the mere sake of censuring, but try to rectify men's faults."

Holberg's strong emphasis on the moral function of comedy was wholly in line with the utilitarian views of the Age of Enlightenment. He was concerned with the didactic and improving effect of the public stage. His efforts at clothing the action and characters in the garb of his own nation set the standard for Gottsched in Germany as well as for native theater reformers in Northern and Eastern Europe.

In the course of the five years 1722–1727, Holberg wrote twenty-six comedies. He drew his inspiration from his own observation of the world around him, from Plautus whom he greatly admired, and most of all from Molière's character comedies. He had encountered the *Commedia dell'arte* during a trip to Italy, and indeed had shared quarters with a troupe when in Rome. This association now bore its fruit. Gherardi's *Théâtre Italien,* the much-used, inexhaustible collection of themes used by the improvisors, was a source of quips and responses, sometimes of whole scenes and situations. In his comedy *Witchcraft,* Holberg has a scene in which two actors, unexpectedly asked for a merry afterpiece, quickly pull out a copy of Gherardi and look up a pattern.

Moliére had said: "Je prends mon bien partout où je le trouve." So, too, Holberg drew on the harvest of his reading to produce his entirely original, sharply defined and realistically depicted title roles: Jeppe of the Hill, the Voluble Barber, Jean de France, Ulysses, Jacob von Thyboe (a *miles gloriosus* type), Don Ranudo de Colibrados, the sly servants Henrik and Pernille (borrowed directly from the *Commedia dell'arte*). In other plays, such as *At the Spa, The Bacchus Feast, The Christmas Room,* and *The Lying-in Room,* he produced colorful pictures of the manners of his time.

Even in the Copenhagen Grönnegade theater, however, the first steps of the Danish national drama were overshadowed by the French *haute comédie.* Holberg himself judged his plays by the fact that "the performances alternated with those of Molière's famous comedies and were received with the same applause." In their case, he adds however, the actual performances were far more polished, for "Mr. Montaigu, a famous French actor," coached his people very carefully in how they should deliver their speeches, and "in manners, gestures, and other matters."

Holberg's plays are set in taverns, farm houses, and servants' rooms. The curses, thumps and kicks dealt out there kept the royal family away from the Lille Grönnegade; royal benevolence was extended, but the royal presence not. When, in January 1723, Frederick IV invited the Danish actors to play at court, he chose two comedies by French authors in preference to the native playwright's crude genre.

The era of the early Danish national theater lasted five years. On February 25, 1727, the venture that had begun with such high hopes was buried with Holberg's sadly grotesque *Funeral of Danish Comedy.* "What shall I do now, inasmuch as Comedy is dead," the actress Sophie Hjort lamented on the stage. "Where shall I find employment? We have fallen out with everyone, with officers, doctors, lawyers, pewterers, marquesses, barons, and barbers." In the end, only Thalia was left to describe the wretched state of Comedy between arrest and imprisonment for debt, before she "died of consumption."

A year later, the Grönnegade theater burned down in the great fire of Copenhagen. From then on and under the reign of Christian VI, the influence of the clergy held sway. There was no question of reviving the popular theater. When Frederick V became king in 1746 and offered the theater a new chance, Holberg, after an interval of twenty years, could only produce "pallid children of an aged father."

In a nineteenth-century drawing by R. Christiansen we have a reconstruction of the Grönnegade theater during a performance of *Jeppe of the Hill.* The stalls and two galleries are filled with spectators, two chandeliers with their many candles spread light and soot, a stage hand trims the wicks of the footlights, and on the side, between the wings, a few gentlemen occupy stage seats.

Johann Elias Schlegel, uncle of the German romantics Wilhelm and Friedrich Schlegel, was for some time secretary to the Saxon ambassador to the Danish court. In his treaties *Gedanken zur Aufnahme des dänischen Theaters* ("Considerations on the Reception of the Danish Theater"), written in 1747, used his experiences in Copenhagen as the basis of literary and social criticism. His considerations led him via the educational optimism of the Enlightenment to a discussion of the need for a national theater, and were further developed shortly afterward in *Zufäl-*

northern Germany and the Baltic countries. The Ackermann troupe, Konrad Ekhof and Friedrich Ludwig Schröder played his comedies. Of the 190 performances recorded at Hamburg in the years 1742 and 1743, 44 were of works by Holberg.

The national theater, as conceived by J. E. Schlegel, by Johann Georg Sulzer in Switzerland, by the promoters of the "Hamburger Enterprise," and also by Gellert and Klopstock, was to be "a mirror of self-knowledge." By awakening a country's own creative forces it was, at the same time, to do justice to the "specific manners and the temper of a nation." There was reason to hope, Sulzer declared in 1760 in his annual contribution to the Royal Prussian Academy of Sciences in Berlin, "that a number of favorable circumstances will restore to the theater the dignity it possessed in the heyday of the Republic of Athens."

As an example of what he meant by a German national drama, J. E. Schlegel wrote his *Hermann* which had a close patriotic affinity with Klopstock's *Hermanns Schlacht.* (Hermann is the Arminius mentioned by Tacitus. As chief of the Cherusci, he led the German tribes to victory against the Roman commander Quintilius Varus at the battle of the Teutoburg Forest.) Neither of them succeeded in winning stage success with these works born of patriotic feeling and cultural commitment. In 1809, when Kleist submitted for production in Vienna his own *Hermannsschlacht,* written with an eye to the times and the political situation, he said, "I am indifferent to the negotiations, I make the Germans a present of it." Nonetheless, it was refused. Counting also Grabbe's drama of the same name, that makes four versions of which none has been successful.

The champions of the national idea in the garb of the German victory in the Battle of the Teutoburg Forest failed where a century earlier the Dutch dramatist Joost van den Vondel had succeeded in Amsterdam. His tragedy *Gysbrecht van Aemstel,* a glorification of the city of Amsterdam based on historical sources, has survived to this day as a great national festival drama and is performed annually on New Year's Day at the Schouwburg. In Holland a vital national theater never was a problem, either in the eighteenth century or later. *Gysbrecht van Aemstel,* a work rooted in the country's past and in local traditions, "is looked upon almost as a national drama," as Frithjof van Thienen cautiously put it in 1963.

Thanks either to their great dramatists or to a native gift for acting, England, France, Spain, and Italy each have evolved their own indigenous theater forms in the sixteenth or seventeenth century, at a time when the north and east of the European continent were still groping their way toward self-expression in the theater.

Politically, the century of the Enlightenment was still under the

Strolling players on the Anger in Munich, ca. 1750. Painting by Joseph Stephan. (Munich, Theater Museum.)

Gysbrecht van Aemstel, *by Joost van den Vondel, at the Nieuwe Schouwburg, Amsterdam, 1775. Engraving after F. van Drecht.*

sway of absolute monarchy. Just as Louis XIV had made himself the patron of the Comédie Française, so the emerging national theaters of the eighteenth century often enough owed their creation to the artistic ambitions of some miniature *roi soleil.* As in Copenhagen, the theaters were often put into practical effect with the help of French actors. When Stockholm in 1737 received its first Royal Swedish Theater, its management was taken on by the French actor Langlois. Fifty years later, however, the Royal Drama Theater in Stockholm had its own ensemble of Swedish players and a marvelous baroque theater at Drottningholm, a building of the royal summer palace remodeled in 1766. (It has been preserved.) King Gustavus III, himself the author of the first plays written in the Swedish language, attracted poets and men of letters to his court. In his enchanting theater at Gripsholm Castle, he liked both to act in plays and to stage them. His stage designer was Louis-Jean Desprez, whom the king had called from Rome to Stockholm.

In Russia, the native drama owed much to Empress Catherine II. She wrote comedies and dramas on subjects from Russian history, and in so doing was inflenced by French models and anxious to draw her characters "faithfully true to nature." She discussed principles of dialogue composition in her correspondence with Voltaire and Diderot, and sent Voltaire her comedies, camouflaged as "works by an unknown young author," for his opinion. The master was chivalrous enough to express to the imperial authoress his "extrême admiration pour votre auteur inconnu, qui écrit des comédies dignes de Molière." Catherine II adhered to the philosophy of the French Enlightenment in regarding the theater as "the people's school." She saw the problem of a national theater in concrete, educational terms: "This school must remain under my control, for I am the highest educational authority and must therefore remain responsible before God for the morals of my people."

In Warsaw, the Polish capital, the tradition of the Jesuit theater had survived alongside those of the court opera and the *Singspiel.* The civic theater, built in 1779 by Bonaventura Solari, was officially named "Teatr Narodowy," the National Theater. Its first notable dramatist was the Jesuit priest Franciszek Zablocki, a spokesman of radical, middle-class ideas. He translated Diderot's *Le Père de famille* into Polish and put on the stage Beaumarchais's *Figaro* as an example to the Polish people in their fight for freedom.

In Prague, meanwhile, the art-loving Count Nostic-Rhineck was building a national theater on the Carolinum Square and, in the spirit of Bohemian cosmopolitanism and the centuries-old Prague theater tradition, dedicated it to "every kind of permitted play, no language excepted." The new playhouse opened with great festive pomp on April 21, 1783, with a performance of Lessing's *Emilia Galotti.* The first Czech actors' company was formed in 1786, in an attempt to make Czech the language of the Prague stage. In the sixty years that followed, the idea of a Czech national theater, as Valdimir Prochazka critically observed at a theater congress in Ljubljana in 1963, "degenerated from enlightened rationalism into wretched bourgeois nationalism."

History has taught us to be skeptical of the idea of a national theater. In the course of the following centuries, it has often been invoked for purposes that had little to do with the aspirations of its pioneers. But it has, in fact, also been applied to theaters that really proved to be what the words originally meant. In the period 1767–86, the earliest of these theaters—which included the German national theaters in Hamburg, Vienna, Mannheim, and Berlin—dedicated themselves to "being instruments of humane idealism," and did try to live up to their aims.

At about the same time, the concept of a "world theater" emerged. Goethe championed it at Weimar, and coined the term "world literature": "More and more I am coming to see that poetry is a common possession of mankind," he said in 1827 to Eckermann, "national literature is not of much account nowadays. The epoch of world literature is at hand, and everyone must now contribute to bring it about."

Between Goethe's supreme sense of world citizenship and the originators of the idea of a national theater lay the decades during which the German theater was trying to acquire its own individuality. The path of this development led via Gottsched's *Schaubühne* (*Deutsche Schaubühne nach den Regeln der alten Griechen und Römer eingerichtet*, 6 vols. 1740–45) and Lessing's *Hamburgische Dramaturgie,* to the era of Weimar classicism, and to the echoes it aroused in Berlin and in Vienna.

Gottsched's Dramatic Reforms

If we were to go only by the critical writings of Lessing, the otherwise so unprejudiced trustee of the German theater in the age of Enlightenment, the Leipzig professor of literature Johann Christoph Gottsched would be left with precious little to his credit in matters of the theater. For Lessing wrote,

> In the heyday of Mrs. Neuber, our dramatic writing was in a miserable state. There were no rules, nobody paid attention to any model. Our "heroic dramas" were full of nonsense, bombast, bawdy and vulgar jokes. Our "comedies" consisted of disguises and sorcery, and fisticuffs was their wittiest invention. There was no need to be a particularly subtle or great mind to realize this degradation.

This passage, included in 1759 in *Briefe, die neueste Literatur betreffend,* was the first move in the literary assassination of a man of whom Lessing, in a much-quoted passage, tersely said: "It could be wished that Herr Gottsched had never meddled with the theater. His intended improvements refer either to inessential matter or make things worse."

Admittedly, there would probably have been no common ground even at a more propitious time between the young, clever aesthete and the hidebound professor. But Lessing got to know the literary dictator in Leipzig only when the latter's reforming zeal was already petrified in umbraged pedantry.

Gottsched himself, in his younger days as a university lecturer with a consuming interest in the theater, had ardently approached the task that fired the greatest minds of the century. "The reasonable is at the same time the natural"—that was the aesthetic proposition Gottsched wanted not only to proclaim *ex cathedra,* but to see practiced in drama. This implied, for him, an art of poetry schooled in Boileau's rationalist rules, committed to the law of Aristotle's three unities as much as to the moral principle, not offending either probability or good taste, and based on "the unalterable nature of man and of common sense."

"The poet chooses a moral proposition, which he wishes to impress upon the spectators in a concrete manner. He invents a general fable to illustrate the truth of his proposition," Gottsched explained in his *Versuch einer Critischen Dichtkunst vor die Deutschen* (1730). He discussed the pros and cons of deciding on an Aesopian, comic, tragic, or epic fable. An essential point was that comedy, by exposing vice to ridicule, was to convey not only pleasure, but a lesson as well, namely, salutary laughter about human folly.

Gottsched's theories were largely in agreement with those of the Baroque theorist of poetry Martin Opitz, whose *Buch von der deutschen Poeterey* (1624) remained authoritative well into the eighteenth century.

Invoking Horace, Gottsched banned the "miraculous," all that ran counter to probability, both in terms of poetry and of the stage—and this meant all the "sorcery and spells and jugglery" that beset the Italian stage and the Théâtre de la Foire, and from which even Molière, "to please the crowd," had borrowed many an invention. Another thing that Gottsched disliked in Molière was that, even though his plays were constructed according to the rules and patterns of the ancients, "he often made vice only too pleasant, and virtue all too stubborn, uncivil, and ridiculous."

"Nature—raison—antiquité," demanded Boileau, and Gottsched was likewise guided by this trinity. He went to see the performances of the strolling players, however much they irritated him with their stories and creatures "of a disorderly imagination," and with all the "unbelievable things that have no precedent in nature." But in 1725, a young actress won his approval. In a play called *Das Gespräch im Reiche der Toten,* she played four different roles in men's clothes—a shepherd, an amateur dabbler in Oriental languages, a squabbler, and a gentleman—the sort of tour de force of speech and bearing for which Isabella Andreini had been famous in her time. Gottsched wrote an enthusiastic article about the young actress. She had "so inimitably characterized four lads from the most famous Saxon academies," that he had never seen anything finer in all his life. This review—published on October 31, 1725, in Gottsched's "moral weekly" *Die vernünftigen Tadlerinnen*—was the first printed tribute to Karoline Neuber.

Nothing came of Gottsched's attempt to interest the Haacke-Hoffmann troupe, then playing at Leipzig and to which Karoline Neuber presumably belonged, in his proposed reforms. He pleaded for the adoption of metrical speech after the pattern of French classical tragedy, but the principal, Hoffmann, declared his actors were not used to declaiming verse. Diderot had met with the opposite objection when the Comédie Française was rehearsing his prose play *Le Père de famille.*

By 1727, however, Karoline Neuber and her husband were the principals of a troupe of their own, and she proved sympathetic to Gottsched's ideas. She grasped what advantages were to be gained from collaboration with Gottsched for an improvement in the general level of acting. They agreed on a coordination of theory and practice, to which the German theater came to owe a few important new impulses as well as some spectacular events.

Gottsched entrusted his play *Der Sterbende Cato* to the Neubers' troupe in 1731. It was announced as the "first original tragedy in German" and was a rearrangement of parts taken from Addison and Deschamps, a sort of translation-compilation that later drew from the Swiss art critic Johann Jakob Bodmer the reproach that Gottsched "manufactured his plays with scissors and paste."

The performance was a brilliant success. Frau Neuber had breathed stage life into the anemic product of the professorial mind. She herself played Portia, dressed in the traditional costume of proven popularity, "with a headdress as wide as the street, stiff and in all the colors of a parrot," as Christlob Mylius described her. Friedrich Kohlhardt as Cato solemnly stalked about in wig and clocked stockings.

For Gottsched it was a bitter victory. He had dreamed of Roman costumes, not of a fashion show with plumed hats and dress sword. But on this point Frau Neuber was conservative. She was a sensible and decent woman; she kept order in her troupe's private lives and set a

Frau Neuber as Elizabeth in Essex *by Thomas Corneille. Lithograph by C. G. Bach, after C. Loedel.*

Gottsched and his wife Frau Luise Adelgunde Viktoria, née Kulmus. Anonymous portrait, ca. 1750.

The "Comoedien-Haus" at the Fechthof in Nuremberg, presumably with a performance by the Neuber troupe, which often played there. Heroic tragedy with pair of lovers and four fools. Colored engraving from Angenehme Bilderlust, *Nuremberg, ca. 1730.*

Wing setting for middle-class comedy: scene with Hanswurst as portrait painter; in the foreground, an open prompter's box. Oil painting, ca. 1780. (Munich, Theater Museum.)

good example herself; she appreciated the claims of literature and was an actress through and through. But she was not going to be without her feather hat. She accepted the stage as "a pulpit of moral philosophy" —but not a stage without the effect of costume.

She did join forces with Gottsched in the battle against Harlequin. In another of his "moral weeklies," *Der Biedermann,* Gottsched had declared war on the "licentious Hans Wurste," the popular folk character portrayed by comedians and clowns. Ten years later, Frau Neuber translated Gottsched's repeated intervening attacks on the "vulgar pranks" of the clown into demonstrative action. In a curtain raiser she solemnly banned Hanswurst from the stage. (He was banished, not burned, as Eduard Devrient wrote and as can still be read occasionally today, even though the point was cleared up already in 1854 by E. A. Hagen in his *Geschichte des Theaters in Preussen*). How exactly this was done on the Rossmarkt in Leipzig is not recorded. Presumably, Harlequin and Scaramutz were made to divest themselves of their fool's garb and to leave the stage. For Frau Neuber the episode was spiced with the personal satisfaction of thus getting revenge on her competitors at Leipzig, the troupe of the popular harlequin J. P. Müller.

Lessing regarded the whole thing as the biggest harlequinade of all (No. 17, *Briefe, die neueste Literatur betreffend* [*Letters on New Literature*]), however much, as he said elsewhere, "all German theaters . . . seemed to concur with this banishment. I say 'seemed,' for in truth they had merely got rid of the parti-colored jacket and the name but kept the fool. Frau Neuber herself presented many pieces in which Harlequin was the chief character. But Harlequin was christened Hänschen, and dressed all in white instead of checks." Lessing saw what Gottsched overlooked, namely, that with the banishment of the clown a lot of valuable popular acting heritage had been jettisoned, and, with more flair for comedy, he added: "I think we'd better give him back his colored jacket."

The collaboration between Gottsched and Frau Neuber was interrupted by an engagement in St. Petersburg. When the troupe returned to Leipzig in 1741, disappointed and disillusioned, Gottsched had formed an alliance with the Schönemann company. Frau Neuber wanted a sensational opening. She rehearsed *The Dying Cato,* and intensified to the point of parody what ten years earlier she had rejected, to wit, the "faithfully imitated Roman costume," the best effect of which consisted in nude legs "draped with flesh-colored linen." The public, we are told, "buried the attempt in laughter."

Eventually, on September 18, 1741, Frau Neuber put on a curtain raiser called *Der allerkostbarste Schatz,* in which she put her one-time mentor on the stage in the caricature of a faultfinder, and mocked him

South German Hanswurst in peasant costume. Colored engraving, ca. 1790.

Joseph Ferdinand Müller, principal of the troupe rivaling that of Frau Neuber in Leipzig, as Harlequin. Engraving, middle of the 18th century.

no less aptly than successfully as a bat-winged night watchman. This sealed her breach with Gottsched. What had begun in common zeal for a good cause ended in a petty little scandal of revenge.

But the six volumes of *Die Deutsche Schaubühne*, which Gottsched published between 1740 and 1745, laid the foundation for a future development that won for the theater the middle classes with their cultural aspirations. These volumes contain plays by Holberg, Destouches, Dufresny, and Addison, in translations by Gottsched's Leipzig students, by himself, and by his wife, Luise Adelgunde. Molière is represented only by *Le Misanthrope*. Gottsched also included a wide range of plays by the authors of the early German Enlightenment. Gellert, Borkenstein, Quistorp, Mylius, Uhlich, and Fuchs contributed their "original comedies"; J. C. Krüger, the translator of Marivaux, and J. E. Schlegel were represented, and, of course, also Gottsched himself by his model tragedy and numerous theorizing inserts, ranging from Fénelon's ideas on tragedy to St. Evremond's polemics against opera.

Gottsched's *Deutsche Schaubühne* became the literary stock-in-trade of the German-language theater of the Enlightenment. The theory of moral utilitarianism, later so much abused and pedantically recast by Gottsched himself, called forth forces that had a lasting influence and validated his efforts: although he contributed no original work of quality, he did create the conditions for such work.

The strolling players made it a point of honor to present regular pieces in verse and, referring to "the well-known alliance between Professor Gottsched and Frau Neuber," to demonstrate that they were just as capable as they of satisfying the demands of a choosy and exacting audience. There is evidence of this both in the petitions of a newly founded troupe at Danzig (Gdańsk) and in documents relating to actors' companies in Austria. When the Eckenberg and Hilverding players ventured into verse drama of Gottsched's kind, they earned much applause, it is reported, "although the audience was old-fashioned and partial to Viennese authors."

The plays recommended by Gottsched, with their strict unity of place, were suitable even for theaters equipped only with the most modest stage decorations. If need be, they could make do with a simple podium divided by a central curtain, the basic form of the Baroque strollers' stage. The more accomplished and successful troupes could avail themselves of the customary types of stage sets that provided, in accordance with Opitz's classification of play species, any setting required for tragedy or comedy, such as a hall in a castle, temple with forecourt, dwelling with garden, army camp, or forest.

Gottsched considered it crucial that "the place represented must remain the same throughout the whole tragedy (or comedy)." For, he argued, since the spectator remained in his seat throughout the performance, it would seem improbable if there were a change of place on the stage. This rationalistic rule of probability was the reason for Gottsched's prejudice against both the *théâtre italien* and its Paris offspring the *opéra comique*, and the fairy-tale and fantasy world of opera and *Singspiel.*

But while Gottsched was pontificating with moralizing severity about stilted simplicity, reason was playing a double game in the court theater of the Rococo. Elegant society adorned itself with flower garlands, surround itself with chinoiseries, and enjoyed its frivolous dalliance with the prettified gods of Parnassus. Amor was carving his bow from the cudgel of Hercules.

At Munich the most charming rococo theater was opened on October 12, 1753, on the name day of its patron, the Elector Max Emanuel. It was built by François Cuvilliés in the courtyard of the Residenz palace where it still stands. The inauguration with the opera *Catone in Utica* by Ferrandini, was a gala occasion; the sumptuous draperies, the palmettes of the walls, glowed red and gold in the light of innumerable candles. The hero of the opera was the selfsame Cato of Caesar's time whom Gottsched had forced into the straitjacket of his model tragedy's austere rules.

Lessing and the German National Theater Movement

Lessing's passion for the theater had been awakened under the very eyes of Frau Neuber. His cousin Christlob Mylius had introduced him into the circle of the *Musensöhne* who flocked to the Quandtsche Hof in the Nikolai Strasse at Leipzig to admire the principal and her troupe. Lessing took part in rehearsals, made himself useful as a translator, and learned "a hundred important trifles that a dramatic writer needs to know."

In 1748, Frau Neuber presented Lessing's first comedy, *Der junge Gelehrte.* At the age of nineteen, the young man saw himself fêted by his friends as a future Molière, and it added to his happiness that this success should come his way at Leipzig, the stronghold of contemporary literary life, within the range of vision of the "great Duns" as he labeled Gottsched in his *Literaturbriefe* in 1759 when violently criticizing the latter's "Gallicized theater." But on one matter Lessing was in full agreement with Gottsched, and at the same time anticipated Schiller's concept of the theater as a moral institution: the conviction that comedy is valuable because it brings about laughter (though he objected to the derisive laughter meant by Gottsched). This is the counterpart of the interpretation of Aristotelian catharsis as the transformation of pity and fear into "virtuous accomplishments"—an interpretation that has to be understood in the same moral sense.

While working as a journalist in Berlin, Lessing served as Voltaire's interpreter. He learned to "sift the moral from the purely intellectual," and he sharpened his critical sense, in this contact with the divine and yet not at all divine Voltaire, whose wit did not prevent him from losing his self-control. A quarrel brought the collaboration to an end. Lessing vainly tried to "obtain a philosopher's pardon"; he lost a well-paid position, and Voltaire's secretary Richier de Louvain, who had got it for him, also was let go.

King Frederick the Great heard of the affair, and his recollection of it fifteen years later dashed Lessing's well-founded hopes for the post of head of the royal library. It is to this circumstance that the history of the German theater owes one of its most briiliant documents, Lessing's *Hamburgische Dramaturgie.*

Hamburg, the free Hansa city on the river Alster, had already been an important cultural center in the Baroque period. The English comedians, the beginnings of opera, the plays of Johann Rist, the guest performances of Frau Neuber in the "Comoedienbude in der Fuhlentwiet," the early reception of Holberg and its echo in Borkenstein's *Bookesbeutel* (1742), all these were milestones in Hamburg's theater life. In 1764, the principal Konrad Ackermann obtained permission to tear down the old opera house on the Gänsemarkt and to build on the site a spacious new theater with two galleries for spectators. Friedrich Löwen's allegorical play *Die Comedie im Tempel der Tugend* launched a brief period of success, which began on July 31, 1765 and ended a year later with Ackermann's ruin. He rented the building to a consortium of twelve Hamburg citizens, who took an interest in the theater either for financial reasons or for the sake of its actresses.

The merchant Abel Seyler became business manager, Friedrich Löwen artistic director. With reference to J. E. Schlegel's aspirations, the new venture was named "German National Theater." This so-called Hamburger Enterprise was made up of actors rivaling with each other and businessmen with some prior experience of bankruptcy; it sorely lacked a respectable name and shop sign.

This need was to be filled by Lessing. "I happened to be standing about in the marketplace, with nothing to do; nobody wanted to hire me, no doubt because nobody had any use for me," Lessing recalls at the end of the *Hamburgische Dramaturgie.* The idea of taking part in so promising an enterprise, the good pay, and the disappointment at having been passed over in Berlin, combined to make Lessing accept.

On April 22, 1767, the Hamburg National Theater on the Gänsemarkt opened with J. F. von Cronegk's martyr tragedy *Olint und Sophronia*. On the same day Lessing announced the publication of his *Hamburgische Dramaturgie*. The new enterprise, he promised, would not want for industry and expense; "whether it will want for good taste and judgment, time will tell." He would, he said, "give a step-by-step account of everything done here in both the playwright's and the actor's art." It would, however, not be possible to avoid mediocre plays. "I do not want to raise the public's expectations too high. Both do themselves harm: the man who promises too much and the one who expects too much," concluded Lessing, whose experience had taught him to be skeptical.

Lessing took good care not to fall into either trap. But events proved him right more swiftly than he had feared. The entrepreneurs could not agree among themselves on business and artistic matters, there were intrigues among the actors, and in addition the chief pastor of Hamburg, J. M. Goeze, was preaching against "the sin of the theater." All this impaired the élan and the profitability of the enterprise. And so the performance of Lessing's *Minna von Barnhelm* on September 30, 1767, got a lukewarm reception from the public.

At the repeat performance an attempt was made to amuse the audience by the insertion of acrobatic turns. Lessing's *Dramaturgie* contains no clue about it. His notes were lagging far behind first performances. His high aesthetic demands, his careful appraisal of an art "transitory by nature," his personal integrity, and his sense of responsibility to the project and to himself could not prevent conflict with the actors. His very position in the theater as a critic paid by the management was a contradictory one.

Madame Sophie Hensel, the leading actress of the ensemble and Abel Seyler's mistress, took serious exception to what Lessing had dared say in Section 20 of the *Dramaturgie* about her part in *Cenie*: "Methinks I see a giant drilling with a cadet's gun," and "I'd rather not do everything that I am perfectly capable of doing very well."

While the company was trying to mend its financial fortunes by touring, Lessing discussed the problems of a German national theater and the causes of the—clearly predictable—failure in Hamburg. When he closed the *Dramaturgie* with section 104, he had a bitter statement to make: "We have actors, but no art of acting. If there ever was such an art, we no longer have it; it is lost; it must be invented anew from scratch."

Lessing was in Hamburg for three years. Then he left. The dream of the national theater was over, as regards both its artistic aspirations and its social aims. The actor remained, as before, at the mercy of a nomadic life's vicissitudes. Lessing's disillusionment culminated in

The theater on the Gänsemarkt at Hamburg, built in 1765 by K. Ackermann and managed as a National Theater with Lessing's collaboration, 1767–69. Pencil drawing, 1827.

Décor for the first performance of Schiller's Die Räuber *on January 13, 1782, at the National Theater, Mannheim. Photograph of original settings, which were preserved until 1944.*

mockery about "the good-hearted idea of helping the Germans to a national theater, when we Germans aren't a nation at all. I am not speaking of political constitution, merely of moral character."

Herder agreed with Lessing's complaint. In his prize essay *Über die Wirkung der Dichtkunst auf die Sitten der Völker in alten und neuen Zeiten* ("On the Effect of Poetry on the Morals of Peoples in Ancient and Modern Times") he explained the absence of a national art of poetry by the lack of a common live language, and in pointed allusion to the German rulers' practice of selling their defenseless subjects for service in America, added: "Germany will assuredly have no Homer so long as he would have to sing about his brethren shipped like job-lots of slaves to America."

In Schiller's *Kabale und Liebe* ("Intrigue and Love") Lady Milford's valet relates how a sovereign sold his subjects. There was an outburst of pity and contempt. The optimism of Enlightenment that had governed the first half of the century was submerged by a wave of passionate rebellion against the political and social state of affairs. The young dramatists of the *Sturm und Drang* movement discharged their anti-Enlightenment emotions in a protest against the powers of political compulsion.

"Fullness of heart" and freedom of sentiments were the watchwords of a middle-class, youthful movement espousing self-renewal, taking its inspiration from Rousseau: "Le sentiment est plus que la raison"—sentiment is more than reason. The humanitarian ideal of "natural" man's autonomous personality was emerging. The conflict between what was then in Germany called "original genius" and the current world order tore down the barriers of political, social, and moral taboos, and challenged the complacency of hitherto unquestioned authority. In the drama, it found expression in emphatically dynamic action.

The movement took its name from *Sturm und Drang*, the alternative title C. Kaufmann of Winterthur, an apostle of that movement, had given to Maximilian Klinger's drama *Der Wirrwarr*. Instead of the principles of Aristotle and French classicism, and their adaptation in Gottsched's *Critische Dichtkunst,* Shakespeare was hailed as the new paragon. Sustained by Wieland's prose translation, the Storm-and-Stressers took after him with spontaneous speech and a headlong succession of changing scenes.

J. E. Schlegel had gently mocked the unity-of-place rule with the laconic notice "Place: on the stage," and Justus Möser in *Harlequins Heirath,* with the stage direction "Place: on the spot"; now J. M. R. Lenz, in his *Der neue Mendoza,* declared tersely: "Place: here and there."

Only a little earlier, with the play *Der Hofmeister,* in which a large,

Stage for middle-class drama, ca. 1780. The set has open footlights, prompter's box, and wings with practicable doors and painted windows. Contemporary print.

The National Theater at Mannheim, designed by Lorenzo Quaglio and built in 1778. Drawing by J. F. von Schlichten; engraving by Klauber, 1782.

colorfully varied cast conveys a vivid cross section of the contemporary social structure, Lenz had at least remotely taken account of the scenic possibilities of the stage. *Die Soldaten,* too, was still a play that could be staged, and in his essay *Über die Veränderungen des Theaters im Shakespeare,* Lenz conceded that Shakespeare's changes of scene were always exceptions to the rule, which he sacrificed only to "higher advantages." Lenz entered the plea that the theater was "a spectacle of the senses, not of memory." Armed with this franchise, he pushed the erratic situation technique of *Der neue Mendoza* to excess characterized by Erich Schmidt as "frantic chaos."

The passionate sense of commitment with which these young dramatists challenged their times disdained any concession to convention, and disdained also the limitations of the stage. This meant forgoing the chance of fulfilling the function of satire and social criticism which they had at heart. Bert Brecht adapted *Der Hofmeister* in 1950 in an attempt to renew the play's aspect of social criticism from a twentieth-century viewpoint. The *Frankfurter gelehrte Anzeigen* of July 26, 1774, however, declared: "The whole play exudes knowledge of human nature," and: "Thanks be to the man who has the courage to smash what fettered our mind and heart, and gives us instead what is so rare—real people and true feeling. Thanks be to him for not being deterred when the torrent of his genius overflows. . . ."

One of the few contemporary theater people who opened their doors to the drama of *Sturm und Drang* was Friedrich Ludwig Schröder. In 1771, at the age of twenty-seven, he had succeeded Konrad Ackermann at Hamburg. His artistic canon was to be "true," not "beautiful." He felt attracted by the impetus of the young "genius" dramatists and the "dark dreams of poetic desire," as Merck put it in critical disapproval. He felt it was a summons to him and followed it. He staged Goethe's *Clavigo* and *Götz von Berlichingen* at Hamburg, as also Klinger's *Die Zwillinge* and Lenz's *Der Hofmeister.*

The alternation of short and long stage offered some possibility of doing at least remote justice to the dynamic "here and there" of the *Sturm und Drang* dramatists' limitless mobility. But the example of Schröder, who risked much for scant success, found no imitators. The narrow frame of the peep-show stage was an unyielding constant. In 1786 the young Schiller confessed in a letter to Friedrich Ludwig Schröder in Hamburg: "I now have a pretty good understanding of the boundaries wooden walls and the necessary circumstances of the theatrical principle impose upon the playwright."

GERMAN CLASSICISM

Weimar

> "The theater is one of those businesses that least lend themselves to planned treatment; at every moment one depends upon one's time and contemporaries; what the author wants to write, the actor to play, the public to see and hear, there [matters] tyrannize the managers and deprive them of all discretion of their own.

This passage is taken from the March 1802 issue of *Journal des Luxus und der Moden.* Goethe, who wrote it, was deeply involved in the most systematically planned cultural program ever attempted in the German theater. His theater at Weimar became the nucleus of German classicism. In Weimar, Goethe and Schiller, together, created that harmony between the dramatic work and the stage that England had known in the days of Shakespeare, Spain in those of Calderón, and France at the time of Molière.

Goethe's Weimar stage style had neither the spontaneous vitality of the Elizabethan theater nor the artistic perfection of the Théâtre Français. It was the result of painstaking spadework, an attempt to transfigure the prosaic bricks of an inadequate ensemble into the marble halls of high ideals.

"The Germans, on the average, are solid and decent people, but they do not have the slightest inkling of what originality, inventiveness, distinctive character, harmony and finish mean in a work of art," Goethe complained on February 28, 1790, in a letter to J. F. Reichardt: "Given these conditions, you can imagine what hopes I have of their theater, whoever is in charge." The occasion for Goethe's skeptical remarks was the pending reconstruction, in 1791, of the Weimar Court Theater, of which he was to become the victim and savior. He had no reason for evading this task and probably never any serious intention of doing so.

Since 1775, Goethe had been the heart and soul of the art-happy court society at Weimar, as poet, organizer of entertainments, and actor. His early operettas, skits, and masquerades were meant for the inner select circle and for the Dowager Duchess Anna Amalia. On the makeshift stage of Weimar's Redoutenhaus the first rhythmical prose version of *Iphigenie auf Tauris* was performed on April 6, 1779. Goethe played Orestes, Prince Constantin appeared as Pylades, Seidler, a secretary, as

Scene from Goethe's Iphigenie auf Tauris: *Iphigenia, Orestes, and Pylades. Chalk drawing by Angelika Kauffman. (Weimar, Goethe National Museum.)*

Arkas, and von Knebel, the prince's tutor, as Thoas. The part of Iphigenie was taken by Corona Schröter, the actress Goethe had rapturously admired since his student days at Leipzig.

She set to music and sang the lyrics of Goethe's *Die Fischerin* when it was performed in 1782 in the park of Tiefurt "in the natural setting" —a picturesque rococo-style pastoral under the night sky on the banks of the Ilm.

The spring of 1783 marked the end of Goethe's amateur theatricals. He had to devote himself to the responsibilities of his public offices, especially to the state finances which he had taken on in 1782. From 1784 on, Joseph Bellomo and his "German Players' Company" took care of the city's theater life. During the winter, three performances a week were scheduled at the Redouten- und Comödienhaus at Weimar; in the summer, Bellomo's troupe performed in Thuringia's spas, especially in Lauchstädt where he had acquired a playhouse of his own, and also in Thuringia's cities Eisennach, Gotha, and Erfurt. (In Gotha, his troupe for a time had a rival in the Seyler troupe, headed by Konrad Ekhof, which had survived the bankruptcy of the Hamburger Enterprise.)

Bellomo's license gave him the free use of Weimar's Redouten- und Comödienhaus. Included with the building was the equipment for heating and lighting—and also the scenery and decorations, which, among altogether sixty-nine items, numbering a waterfall painted on cardboard, a tower made of cloth, and a triumphal chariot with two wheels and a shaft. The ducal exchequer contributed forty taler a month toward operating costs. But the most important contribution came in "considerable subsidies from the privy purse of the various members of the ducal family," who, in return, were entitled to reserved seats and free admission at any time.

Weimar's Redouten- und Comödienhaus, built in 1780 opposite the Wittumspalais of the Dowager Duchess Anna Amalia, was a court and town theater such as there were plenty elsewhere, no better and no worse. Its external appearance, if anything, was more modest than that of others: "Not much better-looking than the rectory in our village," the son of the court conductor W. G. Gotthardi said disappointedly when he first came to Weimar.

Such was the situation that Goethe found when, after the dismissal of the Bellomo company in 1791, Duke Carl August asked him to take on the management of the theater. His first reaction was guarded: "I am setting to work very 'piano,' perhaps there'll be something in it eventually for the public and for me."

A new ensemble was put together and made its début under the new management on May 7, 1791, with Iffland's *Die Jäger*, a portrait of rural manners. It was the beginning of an important quarter of a cen-

Performance of Die Fischerin, *by Goethe, in the park at Tiefurt, 1782. Corona Schröter in the title role. Watercolor by G. M. Kraus. (Weimar, Tiefurt Castle.)*

The stage and old decorations at the Lauchstädt theater, where the Weimar Court theater under Goethe's management played in the summer months of the years 1802–06.

tury of German theater history under the administration and artistic guidance of Goethe. The prologue on that opening night told what he was after: "harmonious total effect," and a "team performance making up a beautiful whole."

The great actor-director Ekhof had, some time earlier, talked of "concerting" the performance. Goethe in his turn also liked to derive his metaphors from music, witness the following passage about the art of acting from his novel *Wilhelm Meister*: "Should we not bring as much precision and spirit to our work, since ours is an art much more delicate than any kind of music, since we are called upon to give a tasteful and entertaining representation of the commonest and the rarest of human manifestations?"

The basis of the "Weimar style" as conceived by Goethe was metrical language. A disciplined delivery of verse and a setting so ordered as to form a pictorial whole seemed to him essential to an imaginative presentation on the stage. "Not merely imitate nature, but represent it ideally," was what he expected an actor to do, who, "therefore, should combine truth and beauty in his performance."

To educate oneself through art—that was Goethe's great ideal, which he had himself put into practice. Self-education as understood by the humanist view of Greece was the subject of the novel *Wilhelm Meister*, of the dramas *Iphigenie* and *Tasso* and, ultimately, of *Faust*. Man's vocation for moral freedom and dignity, Winckelmann's "noble innocence and quiet greatness" as a definition of classical beauty—these were ideas upon which masterpieces of creative writing could be constructed. But what, in the meantime, of the prosaic aspects of practical theater work?

The Court Theater at Weimar, in Goethe's time. Engraving by L. Hess.

Goethe's immediate concern was to get the actors gradually out of "the dreadful job-trot style with which most of them just lazily reeled off their lines." He proposed to write a few pieces himself, making reasonable concessions to current taste, and then to see whether the actors could by and by become accustomed to metrical, more sophisticated texts.

Goethe by no means looked upon the Weimar stage as a vehicle for his own dramas. A glance at the repertory shows that even during Weimar's golden period the field was dominated by the manufacturers of plays for the public taste, led by Kotzebue and, at some distance, Iffland, with Goethe, Schiller, Shakespeare, and Lessing bringing up the rear. In the work of the thoughtful actor August Wilhelm Iffland, Goethe saw much of his own striving put into practice; he held up as an example to his company "the intelligence with which this excellent artist keeps his roles apart, makes a rounded whole of each and can portray both what is noble and common, and always artistically and beautifully."

Iffland's one-month season at Weimar in April 1796 was the first great occasion under Goethe's management. Schiller and his wife came over from Jena (where he held a professorship in history at the university), and Goethe's house on the Frauenplan became the center of a great deal of conversation about the theater. Schiller adapted Goethe's *Egmont* specially for Iffland and worked with the actor in studying the part. Naturally, Iffland's star part, Franz Moor, in Schiller's *Die Räuber*, was also on the program. Iffland had created the role at the first performance of *Die Räuber* at Mannheim on January 13, 1782, and all his life felt he had a special right and attachment to this role.

In all, Iffland appeared in fourteen roles, for preference in plays of his own. These were examples of middle-class triviality, which Goethe was prepared to accept more indulgently than Schiller was. The attempt to tie Iffland permanently to Weimar failed after prolonged negotiations. Berlin offered him the management of the Royal National Theater, and he may also have been aware how little the artistic style of Weimar suited him. In fact, Schiller took occasion in 1796, in his parody *Shakespeares Schatten*, to make fun of the manufacturers of tear-jerkers, who instead of Caesar, Orestes, or Achilles put on the stage nothing but "parsons, business men, ensigns, secretaries, or majors of the hussars," and whose greatest ambition it was to be thoroughly folksy, domestic, and middle-class. Schiller was interested in "the majesty of inevitable doom, which exalts man even as it crushes him." The heroes of his tragedies were Fiesko, Don Carlos, Mary Stuart, Jeanne d'Arc, and Wallenstein.

Schiller's *Wallensteins Lager* (paired with Kotzebue's *Die Korsen*) was the play chosen for the gala reopening of the Weimar theater on October 12, 1798, after its reconstruction and redecoration by Professor

Der echte Ring
Vermuthlich ging verloren. ....

Iffland as Nathan in Lessing's Nathan der Weise. *Etching from the series* Ifflands mimische Darstellungen, *by Henschel Brothers, Berlin, 1811.*

Thouret. In December 1799, Schiller moved to Weimar for good. Every evening he and Goethe met, and thus began their direct collaboration in matters of dramatic creation and the theater.

By that time, Goethe had begun to seek for a way of linking up with French classical tragedy. Since the days of the *Sturm und Drang* movement and Herder's influence at Strasbourg, he had indeed esteemed Diderot and Rousseau, but rejected Voltaire. Now he became interested in the latter's *Mahomet* and *Tancrède*. He proposed to Schiller a German adaptation of Racine's *Mithridate* and Corneille's *Le Cid*. The suggestion originally had come from Wilhelm von Humboldt, in a long letter on the theater he had written to Goethe from Paris in August 1799. Goethe published Humboldt's letter in his periodical *Propyläen* in 1800 under the title "Über die gegenwärtige französische tragische Bühne."

What Humboldt wrote about the art of the celebrated actor Talma, who had preserved the tradition of the Comédie Française through the period of the French Revolution, seemed to Goethe a brilliant confirmation of his own aims. "If with other actors one can every now and then notice an isolated beautiful picture, as they say here," Humboldt wrote, "his [Talma's] acting shows an uninterrupted sequence of them, a harmonious rhythm of movement, which brings the whole thing ultimately back to nature, however much this way of acting is, in detail, remote from nature."

What Humboldt especially praised in the French acting style was the aesthetically perfect harmony of movement and gesture with the cadence of the verse, "the painterly aspects of acting," the due proportion of grace and dignity that Goethe strove so single-mindedly to achieve on the Weimar stage.

Goethe's everyday work for the theater is documented in his famous, or notorious, *Regeln für Schauspieler,* the rules for actors that Eckermann collected in 1824 from scattered notes on odd bits of paper and, with Goethe's approval, put together in ninety-one paragraphs. The rules are concerned with such matters as speech technique, recitation and declamation, deportment, team acting and, a point repeatedly stressed, grouping in stylized pictures. Goethe's rules have too many predecessors and successors in the world of the theater to be regarded as unique. There have been rule books for the art of acting in all periods when critical reflection was stronger than vitality in acting, and when the appraising mind carried more weight than spontaneous emotion.

What is irritating in Goethe's paragraphs is neither the fact nor the time of their drafting (Konrad Ekhof, too, had begun his promising though short-lived actors' academy at Schwerin by setting down twenty-four principles)—but the conventional formalism of the rules for posture and movement. Paragraph 43, for instance, says: "A beautiful and thoughtful posture—for example for a young man—is when I remain in the fourth dance position, the chest and whole body turned outward, and I bend my head slightly to the side, fix my eyes on the ground, and let both arms hang down."

But there is an explanation for this apparent pedantry. It must be seen against the background of Noverre, whose famous *Lettres sur la danse* was available in Germany since 1769 in Lessing's translation of excerpts, and of whole volumes of the most various theoretical discussions. Goethe mastered them so thoroughly that, in paragraph 90, he summed them up as follows, quite in the spirit of Diderot: The actor should make "of all these technical rules his own, grasping their meanings, and should always apply them so that they become a habit. Stiffness must disappear and the rule become merely the secret guideline of vivid action."

Goethe was well aware of the danger of frigid mannerism. His principle "First beautiful, then true" led to the sort of stylization that became a straitjacket. Eduard Devrient pointed out an important criterion of Goethe's work for the theater in his *Geschichte der deutschen Schauspielkunst*: Devrient argued that the "poetic and critical approach" dominated, that Goethe, in spite of his fine sense of the art of acting "did not feel its heartbeat."

Goethe's rules on the aesthetics of the theater formed a basic conception of classical stagecraft, and served as a touchstone for later generations. They led to many an outrage as, for instance, in the Weimar Shakespeare adaptations; and they failed completely when an independent spirit confronted the Apollonian striving for harmony. When Kleist's *Der zerbrochene Krug* was given at Weimar on March 2, 1808, it was a catastrophic flop. The division of the tightly constructed one-acter into three acts was only one of the reasons. The inner cause of failure lay in the inflexibility of the Weimar acting style, and in the ineradicable drill of the leading actor's declamation. One of the Weimar company's actors, Anton Genast, wrote, "In spite of all Goethe's nagging at the rehearsals, he [the leading actor] simply could not be deflected from his rambunctious eloquence."

"Seed sown by Goethe. . . ." This was the title of a pamphlet published in 1808 by the actor K. W. Reinhold after his dismissal from Weimar. It is worth mentioning, if for the sole reason that it misled Gerhart Hauptmann, who used it in writing *Die Ratten*. In that play the theater manager Hassenreuter professes "Goethe's actors' catechism" to be the alpha and omega of his artistic convictions. Hassenreuter's dialogue partner, the young theology student Spitta, rejects Goethe's rules as "out-and-out mummified nonsense." Hauptmann's Spitta triumphantly exclaims: "And what are we to make of it when he decrees: 'Every actor, regardless of the character represented, must'—I quote his words—'must show something cannibalistic in his physiognomy'—they are his words—'something which at once brings to mind high tragedy.' "

Hauptmann made his highly theatrical point, but Goethe is innocent of the imputation. The source, as Hans Knudsen has proved, is not Goethe's, but Reinhold's pamphlet *Saat von Göthe gesäet dem Tage der Garben zu reifen. Ein Handbuch für Ästhetiker und junge Schauspieler.*

After Schiller's untimely death (he died in 1805, at the age of forty-six), Goethe continued on the path they had gone together, yielding none of his principles. And so the conflict grew between Weimar and the Hamburg school, whose paramount aim was realistic representation. The leading figure in the Hamburg theater was then Friedrich Ludwig Schröder, the great Shakespeare interpreter and theater director, whose strength was individualization of characters. When Goethe first took over the Weimar theater, he had several contacts with Schröder and was interested in the system of profit sharing the latter had introduced at Hamburg, as well as in his financial arrangements, but so far as Hamburg's individualist and realistic style of acting was concerned, Weimar made no concession. The incompatibility of two so basically different artistic conceptions, both of which left their mark on the century, was the subject of lively debate even in Goethe's and Schröder's lifetime, and long after. "Whether and how the Hamburg and the Weimar schools can be reconciled," Heinrich Laube wrote, "is the substance of all the preoccupations of the German theater's honest and thinking friends ever since the beginning of the century."

Schröder died in 1816. Goethe resigned from the theater in 1817. There was too much intrigue for his liking. When Caroline Jagemann, the leading lady who dominated not only the theater but the Duke's heart, treated herself to the satisfaction of getting Goethe overruled on his rejection of *Der Hund des Aubry de Mont-Didier,* he asked to be relieved of his office with immediate effect. On April 12, 1817, the actor Karsten stood on the stage with his trained poodle, and on April 13, Duke Carl August willy-nilly had to grant the Herr Geheimrat's wish to retire from the management of the court theater. Thus ended the Weimar theater's great age under Goethe's management. During the night from March 21 to 22, 1825, the building burned down.

Goethe took the news calmly; he was by then no longer interested in the practical business of the theater. His ideas were not tied to any house. The goals he expressed and his accomplishments during his years as theater manager continued to exercise a direct and sometimes indirect influence on the German theater. Berlin and Vienna had close connections with Weimar; in the German-speaking countries, both became focal points in the development and destiny of the classical heritage and classicist forms.

Berlin

When Schiller went to Berlin in May 1804, he spent his evenings at the theater, enjoying a metropolitan program that offered lavish productions of Mozart and Gluck, and a dramatic repertory in which the most successful playwright was—Schiller.

Iffland, the manager of the theater, put on his most ambitious productions for the guest from Weimar: *Die Braut von Messina* ["The Bride of Messina"] and the splendidly staged *Jungfrau von Orleans* ["The Maid of Orleans"], which had been a moneymaker for the last three years. The climax of the evening was the fourth act with its neo-Gothic cathedral setting and coronation procession of 200 persons. "The splendor of the production is more than regal," enthused K. F. Zelter, "and, including music and all the rest, of such striking effect that the audience raved ecstatically every time." The dramatic critic of the Berlin *Bürgerblatt* went so far as to use the attribute "sensational." Schiller's reaction was a good deal chillier. The sumptuous coronation parade, he decided, had smothered the play; the public had seen the "procession" and not the "Maid." One hears echoes of Lope de Vega's complaint when his verses were drowned out by Baroque stage machinery.

But for Iffland, since November 1796 manager of the Royal National Theater, lavish spectacle was part of his whole conception. He knew his audience and how to win it. "What is passionate, romantic, and sumptuous affects them all, uplifts the emotions of the better and occupies the senses of the mob," he had written to Schiller on April 30, 1803, and, referring to the *Jungfrau von Orleans,* he drew the author's attention to the fact that since box-office takings stood to gain a lot from spectacles of this kind, the playwrights could expect a larger fee. Iffland suggested that Schiller might with advantage imperceptibly channel his freely soaring mind in the direction of some not unduly abstract subject. "The enormous operating expenses force upon me a businesslike approach to the things of the spirit. I can plead in excuse only that I am trying to combine the interests of the playwright with those of the box office."

These were the frankly admitted principles of a man who was as good a businessman as he was an artist. In return for a salary of 3,000 taler a year and an annual benefit performance, his task, as defined by King Friedrich Wilhelm II in his order in council of 1796, was:

> You are not to devote your exclusive attention either to opera or to drama. Rather, you should, by giving equal consideration to the two kindred arts, try to maintain an overall balance. Both in opera and drama see to variety in the distribution of parts, so as to present acknowledged talents and bring out budding ones, and to save the actor from neglect and the public from ultimate boredom.

Until 1801, the old playhouse in the Behrenstrasse was in use. This is where Lessing's *Minna von Barnhelm* and Goethe's *Götz von Berlichingen* had won their acclaim from the Berlin public, and this is where Carl Theophil Döbbelin began and ended his career as a principal. The king bought out his entire assets for 14,000 taler and made them over to the National Theater.

On January 1, 1802, Iffland moved into a new, spacious playhouse. Its raked stalls and three galleries accommodated 2,000 spectators. It was located on the Gendarmenmarkt and had been built by Langhans the elder—a broadly sited building with classical portico.

Iffland promised his royal patron Friedrich Wilhelm III to produce "the best German theater in the finest German theater building." The king and his wife, Queen Luise, attended the gala opening. Iffland recited a prologue that expressed his gratitude. Then followed a performance of Kotzebue's *Die Kreuzfahrer* ["The Crusaders"]. It gave Iffland

Scene from Schiller's Wallensteins Lager, *first performed on October 12, 1798, at the opening of the reconstructed Weimar theater. Colored engraving by J. C. E. Müller, after G. M. Kraus.*

Scene from the 1778 Berlin Hamlet *production: J. F. H. Brockmann as Hamlet and K. M. Doebbelin as Ophelia. Engraving by D. Berger, after Daniel Chodowiecki, Berlin, 1780. (From:* Deutsche Schauspieler, *Schriften der Gesellschaft für Theatergeschichte, Vol. IX, Berlin, 1907.)*

Coronation procession in Iffland's production of Schiller's Die Jungfrau von Orleans, *of which Schiller said, after his visit to Berlin (1804), that the audience had "seen the procession and not the Maid." Engraving by F. Jügel, after H. Dähling.*

an opportunity to display the full splendor of his effective décor. "The play gives the scene painter an almost uninterrupted and brilliant chance to display his art," we can read in the *Annalen* of 1802. "The countryside of Nicaea is an occasion for romantic and splendid pictures; Verona revealed himself as a master of stage design, for the decorations are powerful, rich, varied, and sparkling."

While Goethe, in the narrow setting and with the stringent budget of Weimar, had to think carefully of balancing expenditure and revenue, Iffland had a free hand. The stage designer Bartolomeo Verona was versatile enough to meet all of Iffland's highly subjective wishes.

Iffland presided over the Berlin National Theater until his death in 1814. He was director and actor and went on tour. In close collaboration with Schiller and Goethe, he made an art out of stage direction. That he packed the program with popular sentimental plays, that he failed to appreciate Kleist, and that he had his reservations about the works of the Romantics—these are shortcomings he shared with Weimar. A year before his death, Iffland called to Berlin Ludwig Devrient, an actor whose art was all bizarre mystery, passion, and demoniac fascination; as such it was in complete contrast to Iffland's own. Iffland, the actor who used his mind, who was out to "paint sentiments," whose concern was with the polyphonic effect of miming and gesture, recognized the genius of this conflict-torn interpreter of horror.

Iffland did not live to see Devrient's début in Berlin. A new Franz Moor stepped onto the stage, "a lurking monster armed with poisons and daggers," a self-destructive genius, an exponent of romantically demoniac zest for life, E. T. A. Hoffmann's boon companion tippling the night away in the Lutter and Wegner wine cellar—Falstaff and Mephistopheles in one.

After Iffland's death, Count Karl Brühl took on the management of the Berlin Theater in 1815. He commissioned stage designs from the

Ludwig Devrient as Franz Moor in Schiller's Räuber. *Contemporary lithograph, Berlin, ca. 1815.*

great classicist architect, city planner, and painter Karl Friedrich Schinkel, tried to adapt the style of costumes to each individual drama, and generally was concerned with "geographical and historical correctness" of the décor, as A. W. Schlegel demanded in his lectures on dramatic art. Such painters as Claude Lorrain, Poussin, and Ruysdael began to be mentioned as models for stage settings.

Schinkel created, in 1816, the décor for Mozart's *The Magic Flute,* and achieved world fame with this majestic, starry firmament, the imposing sphinx, the weird rock architecture enclosing the antique temple hall. What Goethe had designed for the Weimar Theater with the modest intensity of its small scale was lavishly realized in Berlin by Schinkel's scenery. Goethe had sounded the melody, Schinkel elaborated it in a full score. Goethe's sketch of the Ionic temple for *The Magic Flute* calls to mind the portico of the small, antique Temple of Diana at Assisi, the proportions of which seemed perfect to Goethe, while he had not a good word to say about the "Gothic substructions" of the great monastery.

The playhouse built by Langhans the elder on the Gendarmenmarkt in Berlin shared the fate of many of its contemporaries to which tallow candles and chandeliers proved disastrous; it burned down in 1817. To replace it, Schinkel designed a representative classicist building, combining deliberate adherence to the Greek Revival style with functionalism on the grand scale. Goethe followed the construction work with great interest, as evidenced by his correspondence from Weimar with Count Brühl and Schinkel in Berlin. The gala opening on May 26,

Das Neue Schauspielhaus in Berlin, Gendarmenmarkt, designed by Karl Friedrich Schinkel and built in 1821. Drawing by Berger, engraving by Normand Sohn.

1821, was dominated by the triad: antiquity, Weimar, and Berlin. It began with a prologue written by Goethe, followed by his *Iphigenie auf Tauris,* framed by the overture to Gluck's *Iphigenia in Aulis,* and concluded with a ballet called *Die Rosenfee* by Duke Karl of Mecklenburg, brother of Queen Luise. Goethe was invited to honor the occasion by his presence, but, under pretext of his age, he declined (he was seventy-two years old). He had often congratulated his Berlin friends on their far greater possibilities and on "the advantage of belonging to a great state," and he may well have fought shy of personally experiencing the comparison with his own "little world" of Weimar. Prince Hardenberg is reported to have appointed Count Brühl general director of the royal theaters in 1815 with these words: "Make this the best theater in Germany, and tell me what it costs." Schinkel's building on the Gendarmenmarkt crumbled in ruins in 1944; its reconstruction began in 1967.

Vienna

The third center of the German classicist theater triangle was Vienna. There the first steps toward a national theater were taken in Lessing's time. When, in 1776, Emperor Joseph II raised the status of the Haus an der Burg to that of Imperial and National Theater, Lessing hoped for a new sphere of activity on the Danube, for an appointment that would enable him to participate in the shaping of a central institution of culture and cultural advancement in the spirit of humane idealism, such as Klopstock dreamed of.

The emperor charged his theater with the task of "disseminating good taste and refinement of manners." Its management was entrusted to a government committee of five. The actor J. H. F. Müller was sent off on an exploratory trip through Germany to scout for young talent.

He met Lessing at Wolfenbüttel, and was told by him: "I was prejudiced against the Vienna stage, because the descriptions I read in various pamphlets were not of the best. Now I have changed my preconceived opinion, as you have seen yourself. [Lessing had been in Vienna the previous year, 1776, and had had an enthusiastic reception.] It still lacks a lot, but it is better than any other I know." He gave the Vienna national theater project priority over Mannheim, where there was also some talk of getting Lessing's collaboration; for Mannheim, he said, did not have a large enough population to raise the means for such an undertaking.

"Vienna should be for Germany what Paris is for France," Wieland in his turn wrote in his literary review *Der teutsche Merkur*. But Em-

Thurneck Castle. Stage design by Karl Friedrich Schinkel for Kleist's Käthchen von Heilbronn, *performed at the Königliche Schauspielhaus, Berlin, 1824. Aquatint by Dietrich.*

Four-part stage for Nestroy's Das Haus der Temperamente. *Color print by A. Geiger, after J. C. Schoeller, from Adolf Bäuerle's* Wiener Theaterzeitung, *1838.*

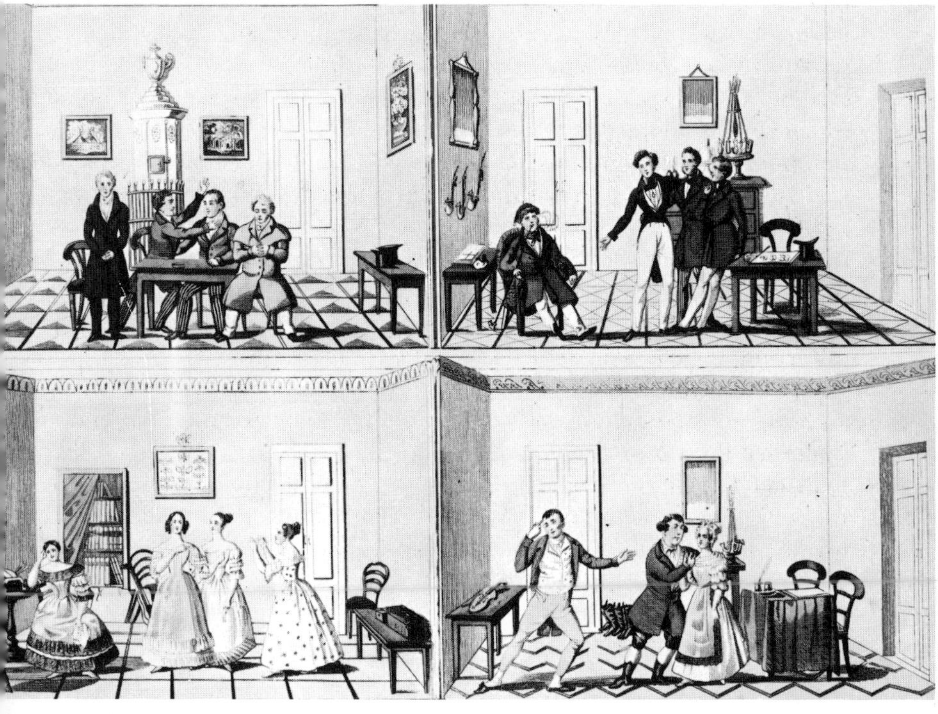

peror Joseph II was shrewd enough, and Viennese enough, not to sacrifice the flowering garden of the popular theater tradition to the new ambitious cultural institution. All the folk figures whom Josef Sonnenfels would so dearly have liked to get rid of, all the Kasperls and Staberls and Thaddädls (indigenous harlequin and buffoon characters), merrily lived on in the suburban theaters—under Laroche in the Theater in Leopoldstadt, and J. A. Gleich and Adolf Bäuerle in the Theater in der Josefstadt and, at the highest level, in the fairy-tale and magic comedy of Raimund and the witty local satire of Nestroy.

Mozart's *Don Giovanni* had a cool reception at the Burgtheater in May 1788. His librettist Lorenzo da Ponte records the emperor's apologetic remark: "The opera is divine, perhaps more beautiful even than *Figaro,* but it isn't meat for the teeth of my Viennese."

Yet it was in the realm of opera that Vienna had to its credit the most outstanding achievements during the early decades of its national theater. It welcomed Gluck's reforms, spread the fame of Mozart and, in 1808, put on a glittering gala performance of Haydn's *Creation.* And the specifically Viennese *opera buffa* combined all those magic and exotic elements which lived on to E. T. A. Hoffmann, Carl Maria von Weber, and Albert Lortzing in Romantic opera, and can still be traced in Beethoven's *Fidelio.*

The decisions concerning the program, recruitment, and contracts rested with the committee of five appointed by the emperor. But he himself had the last word. He took a hand in administration through suggestions and instructions. There were to be more rehearsals, and more intensive ones; in casting important performances provision was to be made for understudies, and seniority rights were to be observed; responsibility for the smooth running of the theater was to rotate according to a weekly schedule, a stage-manager system, incidentally, which Goethe adopted at Weimar.

Improvisation of any kind was strictly banned henceforth from the Hof- und Nationaltheater. In his instructions to the actors Joseph II stated explicitly: "No one is allowed deliberately to add or alter anything in his part or to employ unseemly gestures; everyone, on the contrary, should keep exclusively to the terms prescribed by the author and authorized by the imperial and royal theater censorship; in case of infraction, the offender is fined one-eighth of his monthly salary."

If, however, the playwright's text was to be respected, so was the authority of the censor, which eventually assumed grotesque proportions. Schiller's *Kabale und Liebe* ("Intrigue and Love") escaped being renamed *Kabale und Neigung* ("Intrigue and Affection") by the skin of its teeth. But the censor held fast on another matter: the President had to become Ferdinand's uncle, because his attitude to his son was unworthy of a father. And so Schiller's text had to be amended so that Ferdinand's lines as declaimed in Vienna went like this: "There is a region in my heart whither the word uncle never penetrated. . . ."

While in Berlin under the French occupation Iffland had been allowed freely to appeal to patriotic sentiments with his production of *Wallensteins Lager*, the Napoleonic censor in Vienna suspected conspiracy in *Fidelio*, and permission for the performance was given only at the last moment. (Wieland Wagner did in his Stuttgart production of *Fidelio* in 1954 what the Viennese in 1805 could not afford to do: he gave Napoleonic features to the Governor Don Pizarro.)

Friedrich Ludwig Schröder was recruited from Hamburg in 1781, and he brought to the Burgtheater the passionate ardor of the *Sturm und Drang* style. A wave of artistic problems now beset the Vienna school. "The whole of Vienna is witness to the change that has come over acting here since I came," Schröder wrote in a letter to the Mannheim theater director Dalberg.

Schröder meant to impart to all German actors "nature and truth," those very commandments to which the whole century had dedicated itself. "La nature et le vrai" had been Voltaire's lodestars. But the conflict with Weimar, the seeming incompatibility of Goethe's and Schröder's aims, lost some of its edge in Vienna. Schröder tempered his naturalistic style at the Burgtheater, and he did not miss the opportunity of staging his own middle-class tragedies and adaptations.

An immediate link between Weimar and Vienna was established in the person of Joseph Schreyvogel, dramaturge and artistic guardian of the Burgtheater from 1815 to 1832. He had lived for three years in the Thuringian university town of Jena, written for the *Jenaer Literaturzeitung*, and breathed the spiritual atmosphere of Schiller and Goethe. He had sharpened his judgment on the example of the Weimar theater style and had reflected on the sharp disparity between Goethe's outstanding ability as a poet and the mediocrity of the Weimar theater. But, after two years of his own Sisyphean work in the theater, his judgment mellowed a good deal.

Joseph Schreyvogel systematically built up a repertory in the Vienna Burgtheater on the pattern of Goethe's "world theater." As publisher of the Vienna *Sonntagsblatt*, until 1818, he tried at the same time to educate his public. The great Austrian dramatist Grillparzer acknowledged that he owed his first acquaintance with the intellectual world of Weimar entirely to Schreyvogel and his articles and reviews in the *Sonntagsblatt*.

In matters of practical stagecraft Schreyvogel had his own personal aims. He followed neither the Weimar style of declamation nor the spectacular Berlin style; his idea was "acting from within," and was strongly influenced by Romantic notions. Schreyvogel staged Grillparzer's *Ahnfrau* and his lyrical, melancholy *Sappho.* Sophie Schröder was praised by the Swedish Romantic P. D. A. Atterbom for having grasped "the whole music of poetry in its subtlest shades" and having expressed it in "celestial sound."

Where Goethe failed at Weimar and Iffland in Berlin, Schreyvogel succeeded in Vienna: he established Kleist's dramatic fame. He successfully produced *Der Prinz von Homburg*—under the title *Die Schlacht von Fehrbellin* as insisted upon by the censorship—and thus put on the stage a hero not only radiantly triumphant, but also revealing a human fear of death. Philipp von Stubenrauch, an expert in all period styles who was in charge of décor at Vienna's imperial theaters in the years 1810–48, dressed the cast in uniforms faithfully copied from the time of the Great Elector. But Schreyvogel took the precaution of showing his public not only Kleist the "Prussian," but soon afterward also Kleist the romantically inspired author of *Käthchen von Heilbronn,* which provided simpler fare.

Schreyvogel displayed an unfailing sense of artistic quality throughout his eighteen years as "secretary and consultant" to the Burgtheater, whose repertory was accordingly of a high standard. It included Shake-

Drawing by Franz Grillparzer for the final scene of his Die Argonauten *(second drama of his trilogy* Das goldene Vliess). *Premiere 1824; at the Burgtheater, Vienna.*

speare and Holberg, Goethe and Schiller, Calderón and Goldoni, Sheridan and—the less illustrious Kotzebue. Unexpectedly, Molière's *Tartuffe* in J. L. Deinhardstein's adaptation passed the censorship, even though for only two performances. Emperor Franz allegedly made a point of attending the first performance, for "the censorship might subsequently find a hair in the soup and prohibit the play, and then I wouldn't get to see it."

In its basic principles the Vienna Burgtheater style came very close to the Weimar ideals, and Vienna was equally concerned with pictorial aspects. This is demonstrated in a description of the celebrated actress Sophie Schröder in the review *Europa*: "She was moving and exciting, the latter to the point of terror. Her postures were beautifully calculated; even in the most daring ones she never overstepped the limits of beauty. She always projected a pictorial composition; the play with her cloak, the fall of a fold, all were carefully studied."

Goethe never came to Vienna. But he would have found his own ideals admirably realized by the "harmony of posture and physical expressiveness," which his contemporaries so extravagantly praised in Sophie Schröder.

Schreyvogel's "szenischer [stage design] Realidealismus," as A. W. Schlegel called it, kept to the middle of the road between the tableau style of Weimar and the sumptuous processions of Berlin. The budget was always bemoaned as being too stingy, but could be stretched far enough to provide very respectable productions. It did equip most plays with a décor and costumes of their own and—aided by a sizable "fundus instructus," as the actor Heinrich Anschütz reports—with a permanent stock, especially of costumes.

The stage of the old Burgtheater was nearly 30 feet wide and 40 feet deep, and, with the help of the short and the long scene, could effectively provide an illusion of depth. In addition to the customary diagonal perspectives in the Galli-Bibiena style, the court painter and member of the Imperial Academy of Arts Joseph Platzer, who began to work for the Burgtheater in 1791, developed another illusionist device to masterly perfection. This was the archway backdrop, a perforated canvas flat that could be raised and inserted in front of the painted back wall, thus allowing a multiplication of the perspective effect.

Nineteen of the standard sets created by Platzer for the castle theater at Leitomischl (Litomišl) in Bohemia are still extant. They include a "Gothic hall," whose double backcloth ingeniously continues the diagonal perspective of depth—projected by the six pairs of side wings that are staggered in depth—and leads up to a vista into an open hall. These side wings could be combined with different backcloths to form new sets.

The same system was used by Lorenzo Sacchetti and Antonio de

Pian, stage designers of the Vienna opera, and also by Georg Fuentes at Frankfurt and by his pupil Friedrich Beuther at Weimar. The principle of the short and long stage played an important part until the middle of the century. Some additional technical difficulties were involved in raking, so long as the theater shared its premises with the masked ball, and the stalls were on level ground. This trouble was eliminated with the new practice of building independent playhouses. Now rising stalls offered a good view and enabled the stage, which was moving toward realism, to be raked as required to match the scenery.

ROMANTICISM

A number of often quoted theoretical definitions have been propounded to distinguish between Classicism and Romanticism. Such pairs of contrasts as law and genius, mind and emotion, closed and open form, completion and infinity, objective and subjective art, all touch only partial aspects, as did Goethe's polemic remark: "Classical is what's sound, Romantic what's sick."

Eventually it was agreed to disengage the two concepts from their hostile polarity. And we have ceased to include under Romanticism solely the poetry and painting of the period between 1800 and 1830 as a specifically German art form. More recent scholars have retrieved German Romanticism from its isolated position and assigned it a place in the overall European picture. "From the middle of the 18th century," Klaus Lankheit writes in his book *Revolution und Restauration*, "pre-Romanticism spread from England. It was primarily literary: with Thomson, Young, Burke, and Macpherson in England, with Rousseau in France, with the *Sturm und Drang* in Switzerland and Germany." The most romantic of the German Romantics were the Schlegel brothers, Tieck, Novalis, Wackenroder, the Heidelberg *Dichterkreis*, and E. T. A. Hoffmann. French Romanticism began with Chateaubriand's *Le Génie du Christianisme* (1802) and culminated in Victor Hugo and Alfred de Musset. In Italy, Ugo Foscolo and Alessandro Manzoni were inspired by the ideas of the new literary current. In England, its strongest representatives were Scott, Byron, Shelley, Keats, and Wordsworth. In Sweden, Per Daniel Amadeus Atterbom was the center of the group of Phosphorists. Russian and Polish writing was profoundly influenced by E. T. A. Hoffmann, and Pushkin and Gogol threw a bridge to the mid-century "natural school."

Romanticism flourished everywhere in Europe. In E. R. Meijer's words, it struck the whole Western world "like an epidemic." It was cosmopolitan, and at the same time aroused national impulses in individual countries. "Romantic Poetry is progressive universal poetry," wrote Friedrich Schlegel, "it seeks first to mingle, then to fuse poetry and prose, creative writing and criticism, the poetry of artifice and the poetry of nature." And: "It alone is infinite, just as it alone is free, and its primary law is that the poet's free choice acknowledges no superior law." Novalis gave the cue: "Inward lies the mysterious way."

The theater, on the other hand, is an outward reaching, socializing art, and it was by that time associated with stage techniques and with sociological and organizational patterns, the principles of which seem at first sight to have escaped any major influence from the Romantic movement. All the stronger was its impact on the inner structure of drama and on the art of acting, and ultimately on their representation on the stage.

The court theater and court opera were flanked by municipal and state theaters. The citizens had taken the initiative in setting up these independent theaters and regarded them as their own cultural institutions. They wanted to see their own heroes on the stage. The *Schicksalstragödie*, or "tragedy of fate," which Schiller still saw as the conflict of the free moral personality with the powers of history, became a middle-class family portrait. The Biedermeier period was one when people indulged in writing verse, read about fashion, poetry, and the theater in poetical almanacs and keepsakes, and in their light reading developed a taste for the gruesome, which on the stage took the form of ghost plays.

A parallel development was the increasing commercialization of the theater, which began in the great European cities and fostered a tendency toward stardom on the stage. America entered the scene with attractive guest contracts and lured the great romantic actors, especially from London, to New York, Philadelphia, and Boston.

The cosmic idea, the primacy of the free, creative imagination, the attempt to bridge the chasm between the finite and infinite by romantic irony, the witty play with illusion and poetic self-annulment—all these forms of self-creation and self-annihilation gave the drama of Romanticism its improvisatorial, fragmentary, and arabesque features. The "artistic ego" served as meaning, the multiple refractions justified themselves in the "theater's play with itself." In *Der gestiefelte Kater* ["Puss in Boots"] and *Prinz Zerbino*, Ludwig Tieck brilliantly did away with the identity of stage and public, of play and reality.

The penetration of life with the existential forms of the theater is an aspect of early Romanticism in Germany, which, linking up with the "theatromania" of Goethe's time, found expression in a whole series of theater novels from K. P. Moritz's *Anton Reiser* through Goethe's *Wilhelm Meister* to Jean Paul's *Titan*. It was not so easy, wrote Tieck, to "trifle with the theater, without at the same time trifling with the world, for the two are thoroughly intermingled, especially in our day."

The highest authority for the romantic disintegration of form, as earlier for the *Sturm und Drang*, was Shakespeare. In *Prinz Zerbino* he makes a personal appearance in order to hit Weimar gently below the belt. "Well, so they take you for a wild, sublime spirit," Zerbino greets him, "who has studied nothing but nature, abandons himself wholly to his passion and inspiration, and then just goes ahead and writes, whatever it is, good and bad, sublime and ordinary, all higgledy-piggledy." Shakespeare walks along a bit of the road with Zerbino, but says goodbye as they reach his home, the "garden of poetry," for Zerbino no doubt would like to go further.

The Romantics felt a kinship with "their" Shakespeare precisely in that garden of poetry. And this is how August Wilhelm Schlegel, Ludwig Tieck, and their collaborators achieved the great masterpiece of the German translation of Shakespeare, a congenial recreation in the spirit of the early nineteenth century, a "romanticized" Shakespeare who, riding the wave of cosmopolitan ideas, conquered the whole of Europe. France, Spain, Italy, and Russia learned to admire Shakespeare via the German Romantics.

An active part in all this was played by Madame de Staël. She let herself be guided by A. W. Schlegel's literary advice in praising the imaginative form of the German dramatists, including the Shakespeare and Calderón translations. This she did in her work *De l'Allemagne;* and she made her salon at Château Coppet, on the Lake of Geneva, the meeting place of Europe's intellectual élite. It was here that Zacharias Werner's tragedy *Der vierundzwanzigste Februar* was performed in 1809 in a private literary circle, well before its first public performance at the Weimar Court Theater in 1810; it was here that Benjamin Constant conceived the idea of his *Réflexions sur le théâtre allemand* and of his French adaptation of Wallenstein for the actor François Joseph Talma.

At the same time, Walter Scott and Lord Byron swept Great Britain with the historical, lyrical and satirical phantasmagorias of their cosmopolitan poetry. Goethe created Euphorion in the second part of *Faust* as a monument to Byron, "through whose limbs move the eternal melodies." The stage was unequal to the task of mastering Byron's *Don Juan,* that great epic in verse, which transcends all bounds and satirizes the whole world—just as it was unequal to, say, Tieck's *Prinz Zerbino*.

The great actors of English Romanticism swore by Shakespeare. Charles Kemble and Edmund Kean celebrated their greatest triumphs in his title roles. "To see him act," Coleridge said about Edmund Kean, "is like reading Shakespeare by flashes of lightning." Alexandre Dumas *père* was so fascinated by the acting and the turbulent life of the "titanic soul" Kean that he wrote a drama about him.

In 1818 Edmund Kean starred at the Drury Lane Theatre in London in the drama *Brutus* by the American John Howard Payne. Two years later, he appeared in New York in the same play, and of course also in his famous parts as Richard III, Hamlet, Othello, and Shylock. Kemble's daughter Fanny, Tyrone Power, and W. C. Macready kept up the stream of star actors crossing the Atlantic westward. Kean himself visited the United States a second time in 1825, and in 1828 appeared in Paris, bursting with the primitive force of Romanticism into the measured declamation of the Comédie Française. The ghost of Kean's King Lear seems still to be flitting through Victor Hugo's eerily somber Indian ink drawings. Edmund Kean died in 1833, a year after Ludwig Devrient, the "soaring flame" of romantic acting in Germany.

Strangely enough, Ludwig Tieck had very mixed feelings about the passionate acting of the English Shakespeare interpreters. He went to London in 1817 in search of "genuine" theater. But he felt disappointed. Kemble and Kean, the acclaimed darlings of the London public, seemed to him to be ruining the texts with their hectic acting. Charles Kemble reminded Tieck of Iffland, because of his cerebral approach and doleful recitation, while Edmund Kean seemed to him to be disintegrating his parts by his hasty, erratic manner. Both at Covent

Edmund Kean as Richard III at the Drury Lane Theatre, London, ca. 1815. Contemporary engraving.

Garden and at the Drury Lane, the stage was far too large and the team spirit among the actors far too weak to allow of any "romantic mood" at all.

Nor did Tieck find at Stratford-on-Avon what the theater withheld from him. He went there looking for a beguiling Midsummer Night's Dream landscape; what he found was a neatly built-up, industrial town, bearing witness to manufacturing skill rather than to the moonlit bliss of poetry.

Even the new gas lighting introduced at that time by the Covent Garden and Drury Lane theaters, a pioneering technical achievement, did not redeem the situation in Tieck's eyes. Prince Pückler-Muskau, on the other hand, in his *Briefe eines Verstorbenen,* bestowed poetically measured praise upon the scenery of a dramatically insignificant, but atmospheric "spectacle play" he had seen at Drury Lane in 1827: "It is night, but the moon shines brightly in the blue sky and its pale light mingles with the brightly illuminated windows of the castle and the chapel." It could be the description of a painting by Caspar David Friedrich.

When, after troublesome years as literary adviser to the Court Theater at Dresden, Ludwig Tieck eventually got the chance of doing a production of his own at the court of the Prussian king Friedrich Wilhelm IV in Berlin, it was almost an anachronism.

Tieck, aged seventy by then, together with the composer Felix Mendelssohn, staged *A Midsummer Night's Dream* in 1843 at the Neues Palais at Potsdam as a posthumous model of "Romantic theater."

The arbor in which Titania and Bottom nestled was staged underneath a flight of stairs rising from two sides. Instead of the customary side wings, the stage was bounded by vertically hung rugs. The room in the house of Quince the carpenter was painted on a lowered drop scene.

The production was shown on October 14, 1843, to the court at Potsdam and was then transferred to the Royal Theater in Berlin, where it entered the annals of dramatic criticism as a "literary-theatrical curiosity produced by the poet Ludwig Tieck," in the words of the Leipzig *Illustrirte Zeitung* on December 21, 1844. The reviewer notes with embarrassment that the performance was not consistent with the theoretical principles so often expressed by the poet. Thanks to the excellent music by Mendelssohn, to the décor painted by J. C. Gerst, to the rich and glittering costumes, and to the inclusion of dances, songs, and torchlight processions, it had turned out "a mixture of historical curiosity, fantastic conception, and splendid, balletlike accessories."

Unexpectedly, Tieck's reform ideas had failed just where he felt most confident of his competence, in Shakespeare. An earlier production

Interior of the old Burgtheater on the Michaelerplatz in Vienna, named after 1776 Hof- und Nationaltheater. Colored engraving, early 19th century.

The Covent Garden Theatre in London at the beginning of the 19th century. From Thomas Rowlandson's series of caricatures Tour of Dr. Syntax in Search of the Picturesque, *London, 1815.*

Covent Garden Theatre on tour in Paris, performance of Hamlet *on September 11, 1827, with Charles Kemble as Hamlet and Henrietta Constance Smithson, subsequently married to Hector Berlioz, as Ophelia. Lithograph by Gauguin, after Boulanger and Deveria. (Paris, Bibliothèque de l'Arsenal.)*

Shakespeare on the romantic stage: Ludwig Tieck's production of A Midsummer Night's Dream, *Berlin, 1843. Stage design by J. C. Gerst, incidental music by Felix Mendelssohn. (Lithograph from the* Leipziger Illustrirte Zeitung, *1844.)*

of *Antigone* by Sophocles, with "faithful imitation of the antique *skene*," had entailed fewer problems and had met with an unanimously good reception. Obviously, it was easier to throw a bridge from classicism to historical realism, than to put into effect a romantic stage conception. Karl Immermann had tried it from 1829 onward at Düsseldorf with his model productions for the *Theaterverein*. He seems to have been consistent in excluding "tasteless farce" (even though Romanticism, after all, drew much inspiration from elements of the *Commedia dell'arte* and the idea of the "play within the play"), crude melodrama and translations of "foreign trifles"; but with all his reforming zeal, he was not immune from a certain bias.

The stage effects of illusionism, music, and the mood-creating magic of changing scenery defied any kind of cultural puritanism. E. T. A. Hoffmann, appointed in 1808 to the theater at Bamberg as musical and stage director, indulged in "arousing in the spectator such delight as relieves him of all the torment of this world, of all the depressing weight of everyday life, and of all impure dross." The external conditions with which he had to work at Bamberg and, later, with the Seconda troupe at Dresden and Leipzig, were certainly modest. But Hoffmann managed to lure the clergy of Bamberg to the theater with German versions of *La devoción de la Cruz,* Calderón's "most profound and at the same time most vivid play," and the same author's *El principe constante.* Hoffmann acknowledged his debt to the *Commedia dell'arte* with his *Prinzessin Brambilla* and the ballet suite *Arlequino,* and his fairy opera *Undine,* after Fouqué, in 1816 inspired the Berlin classicist Karl Friedrich Schinkel to create a water-and-castle setting that made him an ally of Romanticism.

If today's art historians speak, with reference to European-wide phenomena, of "romantic classicism," its foremost representative in stage design is Schinkel. His settings for the 1816 Berlin *Magic Flute* or, in 1821, for Spontini's opera *Olympia* (with text by E. T. A. Hoffmann) are, with their fusion of classicist and romantic concepts, the purest "romantic classicism."

Carl Maria von Weber thought a lot of E. T. A. Hoffmann's *Undine* (though it was surpassed by Lortzing thirty years later). Hoffmann in his turn pioneered Weber's *Freischütz.* Friedrich Schlegel's ideal of "progressive universal poetry" was coming true at least to some extent.

The London public of 1845 was treated to the spectacle of four of the world's leading ballerinas appearing together in a *pas de quatre*: Maria Taglioni, Fanny Cerrito, Carlotta Grisi, and Lucile Grahn. Four years earlier, in New York, Fanny Elssler had been paid the highest fee until then recorded in the world, to wit, 500 dollars per evening. The new world knew how to attract and celebrate the stars of Europe's opera and ballet, its dancers and singers. In 1850 Jenny Lind, the Swedish Nightingale, had an ecstatic reception in New York. She had an engagement with P. T. Barnum, and that great showman and business manager on this occasion mounted an early example of the sort of sensational promotion campaign that was later to become a successful technique of the commercial theater. In Paris, meanwhile, the composer Etienne Nicholas Méhul's ballet *La Dansomanie*—which, incidentally, introduced Parisians to the waltz—had in 1800 set the fashion for the postrevolutionary ballet mania. Choreography, subjects, costumes, and style tended toward the "nouveau merveilleux," an offshoot of German Romanticism.

The décor and costumes created for Paris opera and ballet by Cicéri, Desplechin and Joseph Thierry tried to combine the charm of the romantic and marvelous with elements of folklore and history. They became the predecessors of "local color," which in the middle of the century was to lead to romantic realism, to the Meiningers and Makart's luxurious costumes.

When the production of Auber's romantic, historical opera *La Muette de Portici* was being prepared in 1828, Cicéri was sent to Italy to study landscape and architecture. He was also to go to Milan and acquaint himself with the stage techniques of La Scala, built in 1778, which with a capacity of 3,600, was, next to the Teatro San Carlo in Naples, the largest theater in Italy and admired throughout Europe.

To catch the right mood for Meyerbeer's spectacular opera *Robert le Diable* (text by Eugène Scribe and Germaine Delavigne) and the convent ballet it contains, the stage designer Charles Séchan went to Arles and looked at the cloister of Saint Trophime to get ideas for the production scheduled for 1831 at the Grand Opéra in Paris. Spontini and Rossini were rivaling contenders for the conductor's and composer's fame. Meyerbeer's *Les Huguenots* transposed one of history's most brutal acts of violence into a "triumph of virtuosity."

When the Comédie Française on February 25, 1830, first produced Victor Hugo's romantic drama *Hernani,* there was a spectacular battle in the theater. The adherents of the French classics protested against Victor Hugo's free dramatic treatment, but the young cheered him. Indignant cries of "Racine, Racine!" came from the stalls. But Théophile Gautier rose and pronounced the verdict of the new age: "Votre Racine est un polisson, Messieurs"—Your Racine is a scamp, gentlemen.

For French historians of literature the day of the "bataille d'Hernani" marks the final victory of Romanticism. Victor Hugo's *Hernani* became the French romantic drama par excellence. But the failure of *Les Burgraves* in 1843 brought its brief glory to an end. Hugo was the center of the *Cénacle,* a literary group including, besides Théophile Gautier, such other writers as the brothers Émile and Antony Deschamps, Sainte-Beuve and Brizeux; its youngest and, for the stage, most important member was Alfred de Musset, the elegant, elegiac hero of the "mal du sìecle."

Romanticism was capable of forming an alliance both with the Revolution and the Restoration. When Auber's *La Muette de Portici* was given in 1830 on the eve of the Belgian popular revolt in Brussels, the public, on leaving the theater, went to storm the barricades. "Here the theater had played the fine and noble part of the torch which lit the flames of revolution," Alexander Yakovlevich Tairov wrote a century later; "the heartbeat of common purpose, which had awakened in the theater, fired the revolution but extinguished the theatrical action."

In Italy, the main challenge to the classicist tradition came in 1816 from Giovanni Berchet, translator of Fénelon, Schiller and Goldsmith, with his *Lettera semiseria di Crisostomo,* which owes much to G. A. Bürger's ballads. He wanted creative writing "as free as the thought that inspires it, and as bold as the aim to which it aspires." Alessandro Manzoni lived up to this formula in his two dramas *Adelchi* and *Il Conte di Carmagnola.* He deliberately turned his back on classical tragedy to embrace the principle of historical truth instead. He was violently attacked by the learned journal *La biblioteca italiana* of Milan, but Goethe thought *Il Conte di Carmagnola* worth detailed appreciation in his own review *Über Kunst und Alterthum.*

Stendhal aligned himself with Manzoni when, in *Racine et Shakespeare* (1823) he rejected the Aristotelian unities in favor of psychologi-

Sketch by Victor Hugo for his drama Les Burgraves, *Act II. Premiere 1843, at the Comédie Française, Paris.*

La Bataille d'Hernani. *Uproar at the first night of Victor Hugo's* Hernani *at the Comédie Française, Paris, February 25, 1830. Painting by Albert Besnard. (Paris, Musée Victor Hugo.)*

Scene from the fifth act of Il Conte di Carmagnola *by Alessandro Manzoni, first performed in 1828 at Florence. (Engraving from A. Manzoni,* Opere varie, *Milan, 1845.)*

Scene from Boris Godunov, *by Alexander Pushkin, as performed in 1878 at the Alexandrinsky Theater, St. Petersburg.*

cal, prose tragedy conveying a true and accurate picture of human emotions. It was not, he argued, a question of imitating Shakespeare, but of learning from his example "to look at and understand the world in which we live." Efforts to revive interest in Manzoni's works have been undertaken since 1940 by R. Simoni at the Florence Maggio Musicale and since 1960 by Vittorio Gassman at his Teatro Popolare Italiano.

In Russia, Alexander Pushkin chose for his tragedy *Boris Godunov* a historical subject from Russia's strife-filled days. He took his inspiration from Shakespeare and Karamzin, but the theater could not cope with the bold mixture of heroic tragedy and folk elements, illustrated in twenty-three scenes, with its wealth of vivid and contradictory characters and alternations of verse and prose. Pushkin's folk drama shared the fate of most of the great works of Romanticism, in that it made claims on the power of the imagination which the stage, mindful of its limitations, preferred to avoid.

Although *Boris Godunov* was completed in 1825, it was not performed until 1870, at the Mariinsky Theater in St. Petersburg. Four years later, set to music by Mussorgsky, it was produced as a great Russian national opera. The elemental dramatic force of the music of this work set the trend for the future development of the realistic opera style.

Nikolay Gogol made use of an anecdote told him by Pushkin, together with some themes from Kotzebue's comedy *Die deutschen Kleinstädter,* in writing *The Government Inspector.* Tzar Nicholas I is reported to have been present at the first night in the Alexandrinsky Theater in St. Petersburg on April 19, 1836, and to have commented with a laugh: "That was a piece for everyone, but quite especially for me."

But there is more to this play than just making fun of the deceiver deceived and criticizing the corrupt bureaucracy of Russian provincial administration, which so amused the Tzar and helped the play to success on Europe's stages. It is in G. von Wilpert's words, "a sarcastic play with a metaphysical background about man's susceptibility to the temptations of evil and his proneness to listen to the devil, which come to an end with the appearance of the world judge as the representative of incorruptible divine justice."

The playwrights of European Realism adopted the folklore elements of *The Government Inspector,* and Werner Egk made an opera of it in 1957. The stage and figure sketches which Gogol had made by a draftsman friend for his comedy show how much importance he attached to stressing the extent to which his characters are marionettes at the mercy of a superior puppetmaster, in other words, stressing that "inner truth" which, in the spirit of Romanticism, blurs the boundaries between play and reality.

Scene from Adrienne Lecouvreur, *by Eugène Scribe and Ernest Legouvé, as performed in 1849 at the Comédie Française, Paris. Drawing by H. Valentin. (Paris, Bibliothèque de l'Arsenal.)*

Scene from the ballet Swan Lake, *set to Tchaikovsky's music, first performed in 1877 at the Bolshoi Theater, Moscow. Drawing by Gontcharov. (Moscow, Bakhrushin Museum.)*

Drawing made at the instance of Gogol for the final scene of his The Government Inspector. *Premiere 1836, at the Alexandrinsky Theater, St. Petersburg.*

REALISM

Art historians have a legitimate reference point for dating the beginnings of "Realism," to wit, the moment when the term became the watchword of a movement. Its initiator was Gustave Courbet. When the jury of the Paris Universal Exhibition in 1855 rejected two of his paintings, he built a pavilion of his own, apart from the official salon, and over the entrance of it wrote in large letters "Le Réalisme."

In the theater and in literature the concept of realism became an issue much earlier, at least in theoretical terms. In practice, the widest swing of the pendulum is traceable to the performances of the Meiningers and of Charles Kean in London.

As early as 1795 Schiller, in his essay *Über naive und sentimentalische Dichtung,* made a distinction between the realist and the idealist. The realist, he conceded, is conscientious, whereas the idealist "will reconcile himself even with the extravagant and monstrous." He used the image of the realist's "well-planned garden, in which everything has its use" and bears fruit, as against the idealist's world of "nature less utilized, but laid out on a grander scale." This reads like an anticipation of the violent controversy between Stifter and Hebbel.

Goethe and the painter-lithographer Schadow quarreled about what they termed "naturalism." Adolph von Menzel, a master of meticulous historical painting as well as atmospheric magic, declared: "not everything that is timidly copied from nature is true to nature. . . ." Recalling the example of wax figures, "in which the imitation of nature can reach its highest degree," Schopenhauer rejected any semblance of reality which "leaves nothing to the imagination." Otto Ludwig's concept of "poetic Realism" perhaps best characterized the phase of style between Romanticism and Naturalism.

To understand the times and their reality meant also seeing man in his everyday life, in his environment and social commitments. As Alexandre Dumas *fils* puts it, it was the business of realistic theater to uncover social abuse, discuss the relationship between the individual and society and, in the literal as in a higher sense, to prove itself a "théâtre utile."

While Eugène Scribe was still content to write about the "human condition" in witty boulevard comedies, the younger Dumas was more given to moralizing. In his dramas he fights for a cause (especially, e.g., *Le Demi-monde* and *Le Fils naturel*) and denounces the bourgeoisie of his age, its unscrupulous avarice and lust for life, its fake sentiments, its prejudices and outdated conventions. The subject was treated by Dickens, Carlyle, and Thackeray in England, by Dostoevsky, Tolstoy, and Turgenev in Russia, by Büchner and Grabbe in Germany.

The drama of social criticism and historical realism needed a new acting style and new scenery. Stendhal had spoken of the "artist as mirror." The theater critic of the Paris *Journal des Débats,* Jules-Gabriel Janin, attributed to the revolution in dramatic art influences to be perceived in the art both of the written and the spoken word.

The stage became a drawing room. Plush sofas, house plants, marble mantlepieces, ruffled draperies produced the boudoir intimacy required by Sardou and Labiche for their comedy of manners. The extended dramatic monologue was replaced by episodic acting supported by stage props. The characters would sit at the table, drinking tea, or playing patience and, while speaking to their partners rather than to the public, casually reveal their problems. "Today the stage is a drawing room furnished to look just like elegant drawing rooms of our day," Sardou wrote. In the center, the actors sit around the table and converse quite naturally, looking at each other, as people do in reality."

Instead of "la nature et le vrai," as at the time of the Enlightenment and still in Goethe's theater, the new watchword was "le milieu et la réalité." The milieu and reality—and that applied not only to the contemporary play of manners, but also to the historical drama. For his *Théodora,* which is set in Byzantium, Sardou expressly asked for a "milieu as correct from the archaeological point of view" as was produced for modern interiors.

This approach led to all those lavish historical stage designs which became fashionable for both the dramatic theater and opera. Thanks to the combined efforts of choreographer and designer, Hector Berlioz's *Benvenuto Cellini* (1838) gloried in a turbulent Roman masquerade set against a colorful Renaissance background. Charles Gounod's *Philemon and Baucis* (1860) was set between monumental Doric columned halls. Bizet's *Carmen* (1875) offered an opportunity for imaginative Moorish-antique folklore. But the Paris *Tannhäuser* production of 1861 fanned the flames of the controversy between Wagner's fans and opponents. Saint-Saëns's challenge—"Wagneromania is a disease"—became the passionately debated leitmotiv in the development of realistic opera in France.

The *opéra comique* tradition lived on in Jacques Offenbach, whose miniature theater Bouffes Parisiens became the counterpoise to operatic pomp in Paris. Christened "La Bonbonnière" by the public, the vest-pocket premises served well enough for the chamber operettas, developed out of vaudeville, which brought Offenbach world fame. Ludovic Halévy and Henri Meilhac wrote libretti for him, and his music gave an electrifying accent to satire and frivolity, punch-lines and parodoxes. *Orphée aux Enfers, La Belle Hélène, La Périchole* took Paris by storm. Offenbach seemed "as though by chance to have awakened the public's latent emotions," the critic Francisque Sarcey wrote. The pleasure-loving and slightly decadent Paris of the second Empire, and soon the whole of Europe was gripped by the rhythm of the cancan and the waltz. And when Offenbach attended a performance of his *Grand Duchess of Gerolstein* in New York in 1876, the public gave him an enthusiastic ovation such as few European artists had had before him (*Courrier des États Unis).*

Two decades later, American critics lavished their superlatives upon an actress whose star had risen with Sardou's dramas in Paris: Sarah Bernhardt. Her most famous roles were the scandal-clouded Byzantine empress, Justinian's wife Theodora, in Sardou's drama of the same name, and the young Duke of Reichstadt, son of Napoleon I, in Edmond Rostand's *L'Aiglon*. The manager of the Comédie Française, Émile Perrin, recruited Sarah Bernhardt from the Odéon, where she was known to her colleagues as "Madame la Révolte." Together with Mounet-Sully, she introduced a modern, realistic breath into the declamatory acting style of the venerable theater.

In London, Charles Kean took advantage of the pioneering work of English archaeologists in his productions at the Princess's Theatre. When he staged Byron's *Sardanapalus* in 1853, he outdid the continent's historical splendor in authenticity. The then newly published reports of Layard on his excavations on the site of ancient Nineveh served him as a source for a picturesquely magnificent palace setting, which, in the climax of the final destruction scene, collapsed in rubble while the "genuine statute" of the Assyrian king Ashurbanipal crashed down from its pedestal.

Kean was no less renowned for his Shakespeare productions, in which he transposed the contemporary style of history painting onto the stage, surrounded by the ghostly illumination of gas light and torches. He gave himself a free hand with the text of the play, switched scenes around, abridged and deleted, in order to concentrate the course of the play on his sumptuous décor. (George Bernard Shaw considered unpardonable the similar high-handed barbarousness of Kean's successors Henry Irving and Herbert Beerbohm Tree.)

However, Sir John Watson Gordon, the president of the Royal Scottish Academy and doyen of British history painters, considered it an honor to design the décor and costumes of Charles Kean's Shakespeare revivals. Experts were consulted on matters of costume and armor. The stage gave lectures in history so sumptuous and costly that Kean started the system of long runs of up to a hundred consecutive performances. As an actor, Charles Kean did not touch the creative power of his father Edmund Kean. His strength lay in the grandiose overall conception of his productions in the style of his period. He was the foremost representative of the realist theater in England. From 1848 on, he combined his theatrical activities with the office of censor of stage plays under the Lord Chamberlain.

In Germany, Franz Dingelstedt was ambitious in his use of archeological findings in his 1851 Munich production of Sophocles's *Antigone*. Anxious to present exemplary productions on the grand scale, he turned to art and science as guarantors that would be faithful to antiquity. The philologist Friedrich Thiersch edited the text, the stage designer Simon Quaglio was guided by the architect Leo von Klenze, the painter Wilhelm von Kaulbach, director of the Academy, gave advice on costumes and choreography, and the music was provided by Felix Mendelssohn. The setting was Doric and strictly symmetrical, with a foliage-draped altar in the foreground, a flight of stairs rising to both sides in the middle, and at the back a temple portico with four columns.

Dingelstedt had confidence in the scenery's optical power of persuasion. When, in 1859, he produced *Wallenstein* as the climax of the Schiller celebrations at Weimar, he ended the play with a topical tableau: "Seni by the Dead Body of Wallenstein," after Karl von Piloty's famous painting of 1855. (Seni was a character in the play.)

In Cairo, the premiere of Verdi's *Aida* on December 24, 1871, was a

Scene from Mercadet, *by Honoré de Balzac, as performed in 1871 at the Théâtre Gymnase, Paris. Drawing by P. Philipoteaux. (Paris, Bibliothèque de l'Arsenal.)*

Carnival scene from Charles Kean's production of The Merchant of Venice *at the Princess's Theatre, London, 1858. Watercolor by William Telbin. (London, Victoria and Albert Museum.)*

spectacular, festive occasion, combining themes of history and folklore. The opera had been commissioned by the Khedive shortly after the opening of the Suez Canal and, in honor of that event, was to draw on a subject from ancient Egypt. The libretto is based on a story by the Egyptologist Auguste Mariette, who had excavated the necropolis of Memphis, and the action takes place on the sites brought to light by the spade: temple, city gate, and tomb in Memphis and Thebes.

In *Aida,* Verdi created an opera in the grand style, a fusion of French operatic pomp, Italian *bel canto,* and Wagnerian musical drama. The décors came from Paris ateliers. While the stage showed a "Moonlit night on the banks of the Nile," the great river, glittering with a thousand lights, flowed majestically past the doors of the opera house. "To copy reality may be a good thing," Verdi once said, "but to invent reality is better, far better." His *Aida* to this day can hardly be more "real" than it is when performed in the amphitheater of Verona, under the real night sky; there all historicizing attempts at stage realism are shed, and the whole firmament becomes part of the play.

The last major expression of romantic-historical realism was the idea of the theater festival. It moved Richard Wagner to build his Festspielhaus at Bayreuth, which was inaugurated in 1882 with "a State Dedication Festival Play": his opera *Parsifal.* In accordance with Wagner's conception and with an arrangement Schinkel had once proposed for Berlin, the orchestra pit was sunk into what Wagner called "a mystic chasm." Great care was taken to avoid everything that struck Wagner as commonplace. "*Parsifal,* ultimately, can belong only to my creation at Bayreuth," Wagner wrote five months after the premiere. "Henceforth it will be presented exclusively in my festival theater there."

But realistic effects on the stage had their opponents too, and one of the most extreme of them was the German dramatist, critic, and director-producer Heinrich Laube. As early as 1846, in his *Briefe Über das deutsche Theater,* he spoke out against the "exaggeration and bombast" of the contemporary style of décor and acting, and demanded instead that every word and concept should be made clear, and every detail be handled with care so as to compose a great performance.

Laube's *Die Karlsschüler* had its first performance on Easter Monday 1848, in Vienna. Its hero is Schiller, in his schoolboy days, and no other subject could have appealed more to the public at that time. A year later, Laube became producer-director of the Vienna Burgtheater. Adolf Bäuerle's caustically witty *Wiener Theaterzeitung* warned him what to expect: "Pegasus tamed and changed into an imperial parade-ground horse, and instead of the temple of the gods a public hall for aesthetic tea parties."

But Laube knew what he wanted. His theater was not to engage

Mobile scenery at Bayreuth: Gurnemanz and Parsifal on their way to the castle of the Holy Grail. Stage design by Max Brückner for the opening of the Festspielhaus with Parsifal, *July 26, 1882.*

Death of Siegfried. *Final scene of the second part of* The Nibelungen, *by Christian Friedrich Hebbel, produced in 1861 at Weimar by Franz Dingelstedt. Drawing by Carl Emil Doepler. (From the* Leipziger Illustrirte Zeitung, *1861.)*

merely the eye, but the ear and the mind. He based his work on intensive stage direction and diction, on thorough rehearsals. Instead of the staggered side wings, he introduced the box set, representing interiors with side walls. This gave him the optical and acoustic intimacy he needed both for the French conversation piece and for Biedermeier drawing-room comedy. He banned all excess of distracting décor. When the curtain rose to reveal three chairs on the stage, the public could be certain that it was to expect precisely three persons, not one more and not one less. Laube believed that any sort of decorative ostentation encouraged the audience to laziness and thoughtlessness, and was altogether "the archenemy of the chaste, poetic world."

Laube's severe opposition to elaborate scenery indeed was a most profound protest. It was a declaration of war on the influence of opera upon the stage, a declaration of faith in the "bare skeleton of the drama"—a protest against the colorful world of Wagner and Meyerbeer, which buried declamation in a "flowery, musical grave." As a theater director, Laube—though otherwise not opposed to epicurean pleasures—had no taste for the gourmet fare of operatic pomp; he preferred to it even Ernst Raupach's ready-made fare, "the potatoes of the German theater, the daily food of poverty."

Surprisingly, Laube's text-orientated approach failed with one of the greatest dramatists of his time, Friedrich Hebbel. Laube managed much better with the lighter fare of Otto Ludwig's *Der Erbförster* than with Hebbel's *Herodes und Mariamne*. On its first night on April 19, 1849, that somber tragedy played to an almost empty house. The actor Heinrich Anschütz, whose memoirs are in many ways more straightforward and impartial than Laube's own record of his Burgtheater time, explored the reasons for this failure.

He saw them in the political situation, and in the current predominance of Karl Gutzkow and Gustav Freytag, the "Young Germany" dramatists (whose aim it was to found a national and democratic theater), and above all, in Laube himself. Laube's own *Die Karlsschüler*, Anschütz felt, that "first draft of honey from the cup of freedom," had been so seductively easy that it obstructed the audience's receptiveness to Hebbel's heavy and complex spirit. But he believed that a good half of the fault lay with the public, which was so obsessed with materialism and realism that the "canvas world behind the footlights" was bound to lose out.

Laube himself protested against the allegation of having pandered to any "tendentiousness" in his audience. During the seventeen years of his management of the Burgtheater he concentrated more and more on direction of delivery of lines and the cultivation of diction, and he attracted first-class actors and actresses such as Friedrich Mitterwurzer,

Adolf von Sonnenthal, Bernhard Baumeister, Stella Hohenfels, Charlotte Wolter, and Hugo Thimig. In his repertory, he gave Grillparzer the due priority. If his plays proved impossible to cast, he said, that just showed up the gaps in the ensemble and the need to recruit new people.

Rivalry for Grillparzer's heritage brought Laube one of his most bitter defeats. He had left the Burgtheater in 1867 and in 1871 had taken over the Wiener Stadttheater. A year later, the two houses joined battle—both straining to get ready and give the first performance of Grillparzer's *Ein Bruderzwist in Habsburg*. Franz von Dingelstedt, director of the Burgtheater since 1870 and diametrically opposed to Laube in artistic matters, had a double advantage. He had far better technical facilities and, thanks to Laube's earlier work at the Burgtheater, the better actors. The Stadttheater gave Grillparzer's posthumous work on September 24, 1872, the Burgtheater on September 28. Laube had to pay for his four-day lead with the reproach of having made an "impression of shabbiness and improvisation." The Burgtheater, on the other hand, was praised by the *Wiener Extrablatt* for having been "wonderful" and for having made a deep impression, especially in the camp scene.

All the realism and historicism, all the art of stage design, stage direction, and diction that had matured in Europe's theaters reached its last great climax in the style of the Meiningen Players, whose fame and influence spread across the whole continent and Great Britain, and even to the United States. This troupe demonstrated in 2,591 guest performances given in thirty-eight cities what unique stagecraft had been achieved in the tiny ducal capital of Meiningen.

Duke Georg II, who had succeeded to the small dukedom of Saxe-Meiningen in 1866, devoted himself to the court theater. It had been built in 1831 and hitherto had been a modest affair. Duke Georg II now developed it into a model playhouse. Deliberately omitting opera and concentrating on drama, he built up a classical repertory of productions that excelled in an ambitious combination of word and image, precision in style and décor. In this project, he was assisted by the actress Ellen Franz, who received the title Freifrau von Heldburg when she was married to the Duke in 1873.

The actor Max Grube, who was one of the Players, left a record of their work in his *Geschichte der Meininger* (1926). "The Duke's interest in stage direction," he writes, "at first showed itself in a purely pictorial approach. The dramaturgical and literary importance of what was done at Meiningen is primarily attributable to the influence Freifrau von Heldburg exercised on her husband."

In long rehearsals every production was worked out in the most minute detail, and solo and crowd scenes dovetailed and harmoniously

Sketch by Duke Georg II of Saxe-Meiningen: final scene of Romeo and Juliet, *1897.*

Don Juan und Faust, *by Christian Dietrich Grabbe, at the Hoftheater, Meiningen, 1897.*

bridged. Décor and costumes were worked out to be as accurate and "authentic" as the acting, and the Duke himself designed the set and costumes. He chose the color, cut, and material of the costumes, paying attention to every detail. Heavy cloth, precious velvet, pure silk, quality furs instead of the customary rabbit were introducted—no "theater fabrics from Katz in Krefeld," as Max Grube says, but textiles made to special order in Lyons and Genoa. The weapons came from Granget in Paris.

The stage sets, following the Duke's sketches, were executed by the Brückner Brothers in Coburg, who worked also for Bayreuth. The basic color of the scenery was a reddish brown, which set off the lighter colors of the costumes. The Duke had studied with the history painter Wilhelm von Kaulbach in Munich, whose theory of stage composition, inspired by Cornelius and Piloty, became as authoritative for the Meiningen productions as were the effects of English history painting for Charles Kean in London.

But there was one point in which the Meiningers differed sharply from Kean's principles of stage direction: the center of the stage picture was never allowed to coincide with the center of the stage area itself; symmetry was abhorred. The Duke had read his Boileau: "L'ennui naquit un jour de l'uniformité." And his interest in Japanese art taught him that marked asymmetry heightens the optical charm.

For indoor scenes, the Meiningen theater preferred the box set, a room décor complete with ceiling, built-in niches; columns or balus-

Stage design by Duke Georg II of Saxe-Meiningen for the tragedy Papst Sixtus V, *by Julius Minding. Meiningen, 1873.*

trades in the foreground were a prerequisite, suggesting the invisible "fourth wall." This innovation had been introduced in Paris in the early days of realism, and also by Laube in Vienna.

Duke Georg did not use the mobile sets that were creating such a sensation at the time in Vienna and London, though he was impressed by Charles Kean's use of them. In Shakespeare's *King Henry VIII,* Kean had the whole panorama, from London's Westminster Abbey to Grey Friars at Greenwich, rolling by on a cloth panel in the background. Duke Georg, however, stuck to the old principle of keeping the picture static and the choreography moving.

The Meiningen Players, on their extensive tours, brought about changes, as the theater world began to follow their example. Suspended side wings gave way to such elements as pedestals, stairs, or a terraced stage floor, to provide several levels. (As early as 1858, Dingelstedt had used an architectural flight of stairs in the theater at Weimar.) No matter how voluminous the troupe's baggage might be, the Duke never moved without taking along every last item of the stage sets and properties.

Never would the Meiningers recruit an extra on tour, without first training him; no member of the cast, however small his role, was exchangeable. Even silent parts were individually cast, for each part was one of the elements that created the atmosphere of the great, realistically shifting crowd scenes. Today's star might be tomorrow's extra. The finest German actors of the period played with the Meiningers and learned from them—including Ludwig Barnay, Josef Kainz, Max Grube, Friedrich Haase, Arthur Kraussneck, Ludwig Wüllner, and Amanda Lindner.

When the Duke's closest collaborator, the stage director Ludwig Chronegk, collapsed and died, Duke Georg stopped touring. The troupe's last performance abroad was Shakespeare's *Twelfth Night* on July 1, 1890 at Odessa.

But the staging principles of the Meininger Players survived beyond naturalism well into the twentieth century. Stanislavsky in Moscow and Antoine in Paris acknowledged their debt to them, in such matters as historical accuracy, the set's suggestion of a fourth wall, ensemble acting, and the idea that stage direction creates a style.

From Naturalism to the Present

INTRODUCTION

The machine age had begun. Science undertook the interpretation of man as a product of his social origin. Biological factors were recognized as formative forces of society and history. At a time when sociology began to investigate the relationship of the individual to society and to derive new structural theories from the observed changes in community life, historians of civilization clearly also needed new categories of classification.

The view that individual destiny is conditioned by character and instincts, in the context of moral value judgments derived from conflicts of power and interests, governed the *roman experimental* of the great French realists Balzac, Flaubert, and Stendhal, and added new dimensions to fiction in the hands of such writers as Dickens and Thackeray, Dostoevsky and Tolstoy. Hippolyte Taine asked the same "sens du réel" of the dramatist. The latter's duty, he declared, was to put on the stage a reality that explained all human behavior as determined by "race, milieu, and moment." Émile Zola, in his *Le Naturalisme au théâtre* (1881), coined a programmatic password for the new approach that became the slogan of the struggle against the conventional bourgeoisie.

"Art tends to revert to nature. It does so to the extent of its medium and the way of handling it at any given time," said Arno Holz, who was strongly influenced by Zola and championed naturalism in Germany. Subjective imagination was to be eliminated altogether, Holz argued; it had taken the sharp edge off the moralizing criticism of Dumas *fils* in France, even though his concept of a "théâtre utile" in the service of social renewal was topical enough. But for him the demimonde was primarily a milieu rich in contrasts.

In the naturalistic drama the fourth estate itself raised its voice, a voice of accusation, suffering, and revolt. Tolstoy, Gorky, Gerhart Hauptmann went down into the ghettos of the oppressed and ill-treated.

The community rather than the individual was now the hero of the drama: the starving Silesian weavers in Gerhart Hauptmann, the wrecked outcasts of *The Lower Depths* in Gorky, the slum dwellers of Dublin in Sean O'Casey.

The denunciation of the existing social order took on a revolutionary edge. It was sharpened by the expressionists, and even more so in the proletarian and political theater after the First World War. The aggressive spirit shifted from the drama to the staging, as with Meyerhold, Piscator, or the Agitprop theater. Staging against the text led to the controversies around Piscator in the 1920s and after 1965 to the provocative total demolition of the old structure of the play as such.

The director moved into the limelight of the performance and of theater criticism. He set the style, trained the actors, mastered the increasingly complex mechanism of stage techniques. The revolving stage, cyclorama, polychromatic lighting were at his disposal. Modes of style and acting followed each other in rapid succession without a few decades, and overlapped with each other. Naturalism, symbolism, expressionism and conventional theater, tradition and experiment, epic drama and the drama of the absurd, magic theater and mass theater.

Bertolt Brecht posed the dialectic question of whether the theater was to serve entertainment or didactic purposes. Appraising half a century's experiments in nearly all civilized countries, whereby "entirely new subject areas and sets of problems had been conquered for the theater and it had been made into a factor of eminent social significance," he came to the conclusion that these "had landed the theater in a situation where any further development of the intellectual, social (political) experience was bound to ruin the artistic experience." This diagnosis of a crisis has timeless validity far beyond the period 1890–1940 to which it was meant to apply.

Stanislavsky and Max Reinhardt, Toscanini and Stravinsky, Diaghilev and Anna Pavlova rose like meteors in the theater's firmament. People traveled to Paris, London, Berlin, Monte Carlo, and Moscow to see the drama, opera, or ballet that was being talked about. The theater was throwing bridges across frontiers and between continents. America made more and more significant contributions to the twentieth-century theater. The film developed into an autonomous art.

Outmoded, the operetta was superseded by the musical, with its aggressive rhythm, dance, pantomime and scenic display. *Show Boat, Porgy and Bess, West Side Story,* with their American ensembles, circled the globe. Worldwide agencies took Broadway hits to Vienna, the Peking Opera to Paris, the Bolshoi Ballet to London, the Comédie Française to New York. The world's theaters became the common property of the world theater.

NATURALISM

The Théâtre Libre in Paris

Zola had hard words to say about the theater of his time and left no doubt that his chief target was the venerable institution of the Comédie Française. In his 1881 tract *Le Naturalisme au théâtre* Zola sharply condemned conventionally emotional, petrified declamation and declared war on the "mensonges ridicules" of the drawing-room plays with which Émile Augier, Alexandre Dumas *fils,* and Victorien Sardou dominated the stage.

Zola demanded a naturalistic drama, which should meet all the requirements of the stage without clinging to the absolete laws of classical tragedy. As a textbook example he recommended the dramatic adaptation he had written in 1873 of his novel *Thérèse Raquin.* Thérèse and Laurent, fatally at the mercy of their desires, were "human animals." He, Zola the author, had simple performed on two living bodies the dissection surgeons perform on dead ones. The method of the naturalistic dramatist, he said, corresponded to the procedures of scientific research, which the century employed with feverish zeal. Zola worked with the scalpel; coolly and impartially he uncovered the loci of crisis. He took up his knife and began to cut from outside—whereas Dostoevsky placed his heroes in front of an X-ray screen to explore from within what went on in their soul.

In response to the claims of the great Zola and fortified by his benevolence, an unknown clerk of the Paris Gas Company ventured to make the first breach in the perfection of the stereotyped theater. Within a few weeks André Antoine and his group of amateur actors had attracted notice not only in Paris, but throughout Europe.

On March 30, 1887, Antoine's Théâtre Libre made its début before a closed circle of critics and men of letters. The name was borrowed from Victor Hugo's words about "le théâtre en liberté": the premises were in a backyard in the Passage (now Rue) de l'Élysée des Beaux Arts; the program was made up of one-acters by Byl, Vidal, Duranty, and Alexis, plus the decisive element in its success, a dramatization of Zola's short story *Jacques Damour.*

The theater critic of the *Figaro,* Henri Fouquier, wrote a detailed report on this "curiosity," which had been produced in a little out-of-the-way spot in Montmartre, in inexhaustibly astonishing Paris. He hailed it as "one of those lamps lit by a genius or a fool, and which one day will be the source of a new dawn or a conflagration."

Antoine was no genius; but he knew what he wanted. He had learned about stagecraft as an extra at the Comédie Française, and about naturalistic theories of art by listening to Hippolyte Taine's lectures. He was smart enough to take plays from all over Europe into his repertory. The Théâtre Libre was hospitable to contemporary French authors who found no access to the big theaters, but beyond that drew on Ibsen, Strindberg, Tolstoy, Turgenev, Bjørnson, Heijermans, and Hauptmann. Their works "had the effect of a thunderclap on the French stage" (Catulle Mendès).

These playwrights eclipsed the pioneers of the French naturalistic drama. Zola, the brothers Goncourt (whose *Henriette Maréchal* had caused a scandal in 1865), and Henri Becque *(Les Corbeaux)* were already regarded as outdated when they were produced in 1890 by the Théâtre Libre and the Freie Bühne in Berlin.

But the great mainstay of the naturalistic theater was Henrik Ibsen. Within a few years, his *Ghosts* had incited debates about modern drama all over Europe. In 1889, *Ghosts* was on the inauguration program of the Freie Bühne in Berlin. In 1890 it was presented by the Théâtre Libre in Paris, in 1891 by the Independent Theatre in London. It was produced in 1892 by Ermete Zacconi in Florence and in 1896 at Barcelona. Stanislavsky played it in Moscow; Meyerhold presented it in St. Petersburg in 1906—already in a curtainless, deliberately anti-naturalistic production.

Naturalism as a combative program was a flash in the pan. Antoine carefully watched which way the wind was blowing. After a performance of Ibsen's *The Wild Duck* in 1891 he declared that his theater was going to welcome symbolist just as much as naturalistic drama. But he declined to take on Maurice Maeterlinck's *La Princesse Maleine,* with the justified argument that such a play was beyond the range of his theater and that to produce it would involve him in a venture bound to end up in distortion of the author's intent. The pronounced symbolists had a champion in Lugné-Poë, who was to build a bridge to the modern poetic theater.

Antoine's interest turned toward Berlin. He acquired the French rights for Gerhart Hauptmann's *Die Weber,* which the Théâtre Libre produced under the title *Les Tisserands* barely three months after the first performance at the Freie Bühne. Antoine achieved more with this production, according to the Paris critic Jaurès, than did all the "political struggles and discussions."

The play was like a cry of distress and despair. Firmin Gémier played Father Baumert—he projected one single muffled, menacing accusation, with the weavers' song rumbling backstage all through the second act. During the fourth act, in which the weavers break into the manufacturer's house, the audience leapt from their seats. Gerhart

Hauptmann's somber picture of the Silesian weavers' revolt of 1844 fitted the atmosphere of social crisis that pervaded all of Europe in the nineties. It was bound to have a political effect at a time of upheaval, when the stage had, as never before, the acknowledged right to be topical and aggressive. The naturalistic theater took the first step. But in 1896 *Ubu Roi,* Alfred Jarry's caustic farce about usurpers, made use of an entirely different, unnaturalistic style.

When André Antoine wrote his memoirs, he divided them into three phases, dealing respectively with the struggle at the Théâtre Libre in the period 1887–95 against the defenders of conventional theater, with the conquest of the public at large in the Théâtre Antoine in 1896–1906, and with his activities as manager of the government-subsidized Odéon in the years 1906–14.

The important phase for the development of the theater was the first one, the period in which the Théâtre Libre moved from its makeshift premises in the Passage de l'Élysée des Beaux Arts to the Théâtre Montparnasse on the left bank of the Seine and eventually into the Menus-Plaisirs on the Boulevard de Strasbourg.

Antoine's naturalistic stage style, "impregné de réalité," took its inspiration from the Meiningen Players. He traveled specially to Brussels in July 1888 to see them play at the Monnaie Theater for two weeks. Like Stanislavsky in Moscow, he admired the care they took with realistic detail (though he disapproved of the unnecessary expense they went to), and praised the logical consistency of their concept of staging.

"The milieu determines the movements of the characters," Antoine explained, "rather than the other way round." That was the whole secret of the novel approach he had meant to introduce by his experiments at the Théâtre Libre. "Genuine" milieu in the meaning of Zola's "reproduction exacte de la vie" implied, on Antoine's stage, a box set

Ubu roi. *Drawing by Alfred Jarry for his play* Ubu roi. *First performance 1896, at the Théâtre de l'Oeuvre, Paris.*

March of the Weavers. *Etching by Käthe Kollwitz, Berlin, 1897. Inspired by Gerhart Hauptmann's drama* Die Weber, *first produced at the Freie Bühne in Berlin in 1893. Käthe Kollwitz started work on her Weaver's Cycle two years later.*

showing rooms with practicable doors and windows, timber ceilings supported by heavy wooden posts, natural tree trunks, real plaster falling off the walls. His notorious masterstroke was to hang up raw chunks of meat on butchers' hooks on the stage, which he did in a fit of anger when a decorator let him down. It was a short-circuit solution born of ill-temper, not an inherent barbarism born out of his principle.

There is no neat dividing line between the truly realistic and naturalistic heightening of effects and crude, inartistic realism. This is ultimately a matter of personal taste. Ibsen once complimented the stage designer of the Christiania Theater at Oslo, Jens Wang, by telling him that his painted trees were so lifelike that they might fool a dog. Max Reinhardt, in his famous Berlin production of *A Midsummer Night's Dream,* did not resist the temptation of furnishing the revolving stage with a forest of real trees and shrubs. David Belasco, the American pioneer of naturalism, brought to the New York stage what he considered to be faithful copies of the Wild West, with its romantic gold prospectors and bandits. When he staged *The Girl of the Golden West,* which, thanks to Puccini's music, made a brilliant operatic start in 1910, he transformed the stage of New York's Metropolitan Opera House into a "genuine" Californian log-cabin camp. And in the third act, when the noose is put round the neck of the bandit Ramerrez—Enrico Caruso was acclaimed in the part as the star of the evening—the virgin forest trees of the setting were as real as Reinhardt's trees in Berlin.

The second component of Antoine's stage naturalism was the illusory "fourth wall"; that is, when the scene required it, the actor would turn his back to the audience. The foremost law of stage direction was no longer the frontal pictorial effect, facing the spectators—but the relative position of actors required by the course of the action and the dialogue. The most famous textbook example is the Sunken Lane scene in the Meiningen production of Schiller's *Wilhelm Tell,* where the petitioner and her two children, when approaching governor Gessler who is walking frontally forward, turn their backs on the audience.

"Why should not this logical and not in the least expensive novelty replace those intolerable conventional forms we have accepted without knowing why?" asked Antoine. But neither the stars of the Comédie Française, neither Sarah Bernhardt nor Coquelin, would have allowed their appeal to the public to be impaired in this way. For centuries, every great actor had claimed the privilege of occupying the very front of the stage, of addressing his monologues directly to the public and regarding the stage as a decorative foil to his own personal performance. Notwithstanding all changes of style, the principles of the Renaissance theater were basically still unimpaired. They were to survive even in the narrow setting of the boxlike stage, if only for acoustic reasons.

Antoine was successful in directing naturalistic ensemble acting because his actors were amateurs and he therefore was not hindered by bastions of personal ambition. Stanislavsky owed the same success to the devotion of his professional actors to him. There was no such meeting of minds between Shaw and Henry Irving, the guardian of the waning tradition of actor-manager, and the whole approach was eventually drowned out by the wealth of new scenic possibilities opened up by Reinhardt in the first twenty years of the twentieth century.

The time of naturalism was also that of the earliest ventures with the "cinematograph." Charlie Chaplin's and Buster Keaton's films about the little man's struggle against the treachery of things gave the naturalistic emphasis on the material world a twist toward the grotesque and comic. Antoine devoted himself entirely to motion pictures after 1914, first as actor and director, and eventually as critic. He made films using material by Dumas, Hugo, and Zola, and transposed his naturalistic style from the stage to the screen. As René Clair wrote in 1922, it was a simple matter of "applying the doctrine of the Théâtre Libre to the cinema." It was he who became the strongest influence in the movement toward the fantastic and surrealist film, toward paraphrases of dream and intellect, social commitment and romantic irony.

The Freie Bühne in Berlin

In Berlin the naturalistic theater owed its origin to critical revulsion against the stereotypes of the commercial theater and to reaction against tutelage by censorship. Poets and dramatists accepted the challenge to face the problems of their time. Wilhelm Bölsche's *Die naturwissenschaftlichen Grundlagen der Poesie* (1887) was written entirely in Zola's spirit. Karl Bleibtreu in his pamphlet *Revolution in der Literatur* demanded of the poet an active participation in public life and the courage to descend into the gloomy areas of hunger and poverty.

Much as in Paris at the same time, the show business of Berlin lived on the drawing-room play and the comedy of manners. The heavily subsidized Royal Theater limited itself to lip service to the classics. A group of men committed to literature and the drama followed the example of the Paris Théâtre Libre and, in April 1889, founded the theater club Freie Bühne. Here, too, the name expressed the nature of the program: to be free of commercial considerations and free of the compulsion of censorship. The group elected as its president the young literary and dramatic critic Otto Brahm.

The widespread assumption that André Antoine and his ensemble played in Berlin in 1887 and thereby inspired the like-minded venture is erroneous. Antoine's own memoirs say nothing about it. However, Otto

Brahm, the director-manager of the Freie Bühne, had been in Paris in 1888. He had got to know the brilliance of declamation at the Comédie Française and also its reverse side, the unconvincing stereotype, and no doubt had critically considered the potentialities of Théâtre Libre.

The Freie Bühne got its financial backing from the so-called passive members the club acquired. Within a year there were more than a thousand of them. Their contributions covered the expenses for actors and directors, as well as rent for the theater. The theatergoers' organizations that are still common in many European countries follow the same system. One of the first of these was the Freie Volksbühne founded in Berlin as early as 1890 by men in part formerly associated with Brahm.

The Freie Bühne opened with a tribute to "the head of the new realistic school," Ibsen, the grand master of the naturalistic theater. Brahm chose *Ghosts,* the most controversial and celebrated drama of the great Norwegian. It had been shown two years earlier in Berlin, but after the first night had been prohibited by the police censorship. Now, at a Sunday matinée of a closed club, it was safe from the police. A brilliant cast gave weight to the uniqueness of the occasion on September 29, 1889. The playbill proudly announced the distinguished cast: Emmerich Robert of the Vienna Burgtheater portrayed the role of Oswald, Arthur Kraussneck that of Pastor Manders, Marie Schanzer (the second wife of the conductor Hans von Bülow, who had lost Cosima to Richard Wagner) was cast as Mrs. Alving, and the young Agnes Sorma as Regine. Thus the Freie Bühne gave notice that it had not only ambitious aims, but also considerable funds.

The second production became a milestone in the history of German naturalism. It was the first play by a young, hitherto unknown German dramatist, which had just been circulated privately and had alerted the opposition: Gerhart Hauptmann's social drama *Vor Sonnenaufgang.* The play deals with the exploitation of Silesian peasants, with the life and attitudes of the nouveaux riches, with alcoholism and chronic poverty. This famous Freie Bühne production had its spectacular first night on October 20, 1889, at the Lessing Theater. The ensuing uproar had been foreshadowed in anonymous threatening letters to the actors. The hectic excitement in the packed house came to its climax in the fifth act. At the moment when the direction calls for the cries of a woman in labor to be heard from offstage, the physician Isidor Kastan—in the midst of an uproar of applause and protests—rose from his seat and brandished a pair of forceps over his head. (He had planned this demonstration and purposely brought the instrument along. Later he formally apologized for it when the Freie Bühne took him to court.)

With this production, naturalism had burst upon the German stage with a bang. Not only the acting, but the décor, too, was "true to life." The scenery of the second act portrayed a farmyard with every appurtenance, including a well, a dovecote, stables, arbor and front garden, garden bench, garden gate, and half a dozen different doors and gates. "It's a pity they forgot the main item," the critic Karl Frenzel wrote spitefully, "The dungheap with a crowing cock on top." (The attempt to reproduce the odors of the milieu was rejected—because it would have been impossible to get rid of them when changing the scene, and at best they could only have been covered up by different odors.)

All at once, the name of the young dramatist Gerhart Hauptmann was on everybody's lips. Berlin's level-headed, leading drama critic, the novelist and poet Theodor Fontane, defended Hauptmann. He approvingly described him as "the real captain of the black band of Realists," who showed life as it really was, in its full horror, who added nothing, but did not subtract anything either, and who deserved the praise of being a de-illusioned Ibsen.

The Freie Bühne had found "its" author. It became Gerhart Hauptmann's stage, just as Stanislavsky's Moscow Art Theater became Chekhov's house. Neither the performance of the Goncourt brothers' *Henriette Maréchal* nor the Berlin milieu sketch *Familie Selicke* by Arno Holz and Johannes Schlaf, nor the works by Bjørnson, Anzengruber, and Sudermann aroused as much response as Gerhart Hauptmann's plays.

The effect of *Die Weber* ("The Weavers"), however, turned out to be more inflammatory at the Paris Théâtre Libre than in Berlin. This may have been due to personal considerations of Otto Brahm. A public premiere originally planned by Adolphe L'Arronge for the Deutsches Theater was prohibited by the police at the last moment. Thus it was left to the Freie Bühne, as a club free from censorship, to be the first to produce this "most powerful work of the modern literature of accusation." It did so on February 26, 1893. The leading critics noted that, strangely enough, the effect was not as electrifying as might have been expected from reading the play.

Otto Brahm may well have had future plans in mind. A year later (in 1894), he gave up the presidency of the Freie Bühne and took over the Deutsches Theater on Schumannstrasse for ten years. There, on September 25, 1894, he produced for the general public a toned-down version of Hauptmann's *Die Weber*, with Rudolf Rittner, Josef Kainz, and Arthur Kraussneck in the cast. The censorship kept quiet and public success was assured. But for the Freie Bühne the departure of Brahm meant at the same time the loss of its very own author Gerhart Hauptmann, who now of course gave his plays to the Deutsches Theater. The

Setting for Hanneles Himmelfahrt, *by Gerhart Hauptmann, first produced in 1893 at the Königliches Schauspielhaus, Berlin. Watercolor by Eugen Quaglio. (Munich, Theater Museum.)*

Scene from Michael Kramer, *by Gerhart Hauptmann, first produced in 1900 at the Deutsches Theater, Berlin. Max Reinhardt (left) in the title role, Louise Dumont (right) as Michaline Kramer. (From* Bühne und Welt, *Vol. 1900–1901.)*

presidency of the Freie Bühne now passed to Paul Schlenther (who now also became its director-manager). Schlenther was one of the prominent founding members, together with the writers Maximilian Harden, Theodor Wolff, the brothers Heinrich and Julius Hart, and the publisher Samuel Fischer. When Schlenther in 1898 accepted an invitation to the Vienna Burgtheater, he was succeeded by Ludwig Fulda. The Freie Bühne then moved toward the lyrical mysticism of the symbolists. The hard contours of social naturalism became blurred in the poetic valedictory mood of *Die Frau im Fenster* by Hofmannsthal, of *Tote Zeit* by Ernst Hardt, or *Frühlingsopfer* by Eduard von Keyserling.

When, in 1909, the Freie Bühne celebrated its twentieth anniversary with a memorial performance of Hauptmann's *Vor Sonnenaufgang*, the occasion passed without noise or protest. The author was fêted, with Otto Brahm by his side. The theater's history moves fast, and it had long encompassed what twenty years earlier had divided the minds of men.

The Independent Theatre in London

The third center of the naturalistic theater in Europe was London. In 1891 George Bernard Shaw published his essay *The Quintessence of Ibsenism*, a sharp rejection of the star- and business-oriented theater, the "Sardoodledum" intrigue play, and the so-called pseudo-Ibsenists. As the theater critic of the *Saturday Review* Shaw intervened directly in the current polemics about the new drama. The favorite targets of his violent attacks were the well-made realistic problem plays by Pinero, whose *The Second Mrs. Tanqueray* ran to a full house for months.

Shaw measured the qualities of the London principals by their reluctance to put on Ibsen. Henry Irving and Herbert Beerbohm Tree, the two celebrated representatives of the realistic theater, came off very badly. Shaw did not forgive them for cutting Shakespeare at their discretion and destroying the structure of his scenes for the sake of grand pictorial effect. Open war broke out when Irving rejected a one-acter about Napoleon Shaw had written specially for Ellen Terry, *The Man of Destiny* and instead produced another play about Napoleon, Sardou's *Madame Sans-Gêne*.

Just then, in London too, a small amateur theater moved overnight into the public limelight. In 1891, J. T. Grein, a businessman of Dutch origin, founded a theater association with the aim of producing "progressive plays" to which the big theaters remained closed; following the image of the Théâtre Libre in Paris and the Freie Bühne in Berlin, he named it the Independent Theatre Society.

Fourth act of the drama Fuhrmann Henschel, *by Gerhart Hauptmann, at the Lobe-Theater, Breslau, 1899. (From* Bühne und Welt, *Vol. 1899.)*

Stage design for Ibsen's The Vikings at Helgeland: *scene on Iceland. Watercolor by Eugen Quaglio. (Munich, Theater Museum.)*

Grein's intention, too, was to put literary worth above commercial considerations and to circumvent the censorship; logically enough, he first produced a play by the dramatic spokesman of European naturalism, Ibsen. He presented *Ghosts* in 1891, in the Royalty Theatre in Soho he had rented for this occasion. Shaw bestowed liberal praise upon the production and gave Grein his first full-length play, *Widowers' Houses,* which received its first performance in 1892. It was described as an "original didactic-realistic play." Applause and boos ensured plenty of publicity and a repeat performance in the club, which kept the censorship at arm's length. It was all very much like what had happened in Berlin: a start with Ibsen, followed by the *succès de scandale* of a young native author.

But Grein was not Brahm, and Shaw pushed on. While the Independent Theatre struggled to keep alive as best it could until 1897, Shaw set his course for world fame via artistic patronesses. The wealthy Quaker Miss A. E. F. Horniman sponsored the production of *Arms and the Man* in 1894 at the Avenue Theatre. Subsequently, the American actor-director Richard Mansfield took the play, and also *The Devil's Disciple,* to New York, where both had a long and lucrative run.

In the meantime, the energetic Miss Horniman was busy setting up an Irish national theater. In 1904 she founded the Irish National Theatre Society in Dublin. W. B. Yeats, who took part in the project, got from his fellow countryman Shaw the promise to write an Irish comedy. This was *John Bull's Other Island,* a brilliant piece of witty exposure. But Shaw gave it, as well as *Candida,* to the actor-director Harley Granville-Barker. Granville-Barker produced it at the Royal Court Theatre in London, eight weeks before the Irish National Theatre Society made its debut. And so, the curtain of Dublin's Abbey Theatre rose on December 27, 1904, on two one-act plays, one by Yeats and the other by Lady Gregory.

Realism (the Anglo-American term for what was called naturalism in Europe) of a disturbing kind was the aim of the Manchester Repertory Company, another of Miss Horniman's ventures. She put the Gaiety Theatre, Manchester, at the disposal of a daring repertory company for productions of plays by Stanley Houghton, St. John Ervine, and Harold Brighouse. Shaw was never associated with her again. He had less influence on the avant-garde writers of the European theater of his age than on the young American dramatists. His didactic method, learned from Ibsen, provided a simple teaching syllabus. For Shaw modern theater had begun at the moment when Ibsen wrote *A Doll's House,* and his Nora invites her husband to sit down and discuss their marriage. He saw the task of the realistic (i.e., naturalistic) drama in the discussion of psychological and conventional conflicts. The stage became a debating forum. In his prefaces and stage directions Shaw sketched in the background of his plays, the author's own interpretations, in the manner of Ibsen's analytical scenic technique. (This pattern was to be followed by such later playwrights as Eugene O'Neill, Arthur Miller, Graham Greene, and Tennessee Williams.)

In England, the development of modern theater led from T. S. Eliot's *Murder in the Cathedral,* J. B. Priestley's *An Inspector Calls,* and Christopher Fry's *Venus Observed.* Turning away from poetry, away from Restoration comedy, it favored the kitchen, the bed-sitting room, and the accents of the younger playgoers, George Devine, the founder and director of the English Stage Company, determined the course of modern English theater and its dramas of self-analysis with his production of John Osborne's *Look Back in Anger* in 1956 at the Royal Court Theatre, London. Typical of these new plays are Arnold Wesker's *The Kitchen* and his *Chicken Soup with Barley,* which show middle-class life as dominated by politics and resignation, Harold Pinter's *Caretaker,* and Edward Bond's youthful realistic play *Saved.* Most of these plays were first performed, like *Look Back in Anger,* at London's Royal Court Theatre, the dependable host of avant-garde theater. Some, however, like the old pioneering dramas of the naturalistic theater, needed the safety of private-club performances.

As early as 1909 Shaw had violently attacked the censorship, which no one had been able to strip of its powers since the days of the Elizabethan Master of the Revels. When *Mrs. Warren's Profession* was banned, Shaw, who described himself as a specialist in immoral and heretical works, fumed at the insult and the suppression by the theater censor. The result was not a relaxation but a tightening of the screw. It was not until 1968 that the Commons passed a bill, introduced by the Labour government, and abolished the Lord Chamberlain's censorship function.

THE SEARCH FOR NEW FORMS

Stanislavsky and the Moscow Art Theater

In June 1897, a meeting took place at a Moscow restaurant between the writer Vladimir Ivanovich Nemirovich-Danchenko and Stanislavsky, the young, theater-mad son of a Moscow industrialist. The conversation lasted eighteen hours—from two o'clock in the afternoon until eight o'clock the next morning. The result was the foundation of a new private theater enterprise: the Moscow Art Theater.

The care lavished from the outset on the planning of all artistic and organizational details remained characteristic of the Moscow Art Theater throughout its development; no other theater preserved its sense of vocation for decades with such steadfast dedication. Stanislavsky assumed responsibility for theatrical, Nemirovich-Danchenko for literary matters. Funds were contributed by shareholders, from the Moscow Philharmonic Society, which already maintained a theater school where Nemirovich-Danchenko taught acting, and from the Society for Art and Literature, whose amateur performances Stanislavsky had been financing for the past ten years.

Moscow at that time was fortunate in having generous private art patrons. Industrialists and businessmen devoted their fortune to artistic purposes. The brothers Tretyakov fostered painting; opera and concerts were financed by S. I. Mamontov, a man with broad interests in music and the theater. The parents of Stanislavsky (his real name was Constantin Sergeyevich Alexeiev), maintained in their home children's and amateur stages.

When the Meiningen Players came to Moscow in 1885 the twenty-two-year-old Stanislavsky did not miss one of their performances. He admired the "amazing discipline displayed in this great theater feast," but Chronegk's "despotic" methods of direction led him to his first critical assessment of the pros and cons of the director's power and its possible tyrannical effects. Stanislavsky himself never became a tyrannical stage director. He never tired, often through hundreds of rehearsals, of appealing to the understanding of his actors. He never forced his own conceptions upon them, but strove to attune them to the requirements of their part—this was to be the core upon which he later built the unique "Stanislavsky method."

But on the point of historical truthfulness, the Moscow Art Theater fully adopted the Meiningen principles from its very first production. The theater opened with the historical drama *Tsar Fyodor Ivanovich* by Alexey Konstantinovich Tolstoy (distantly related to Leo Tolstoy), which had been written in 1868 and had at the time been banned by the censorship. For months beforehand, Stanislavsky, his wife Lilina, and the stage designer Victor Simov had been visiting historical sites. They looked at the vestments owned by monasteries and churches in the area between the rivers Volga and Oka, ransacked antique shops and flea markets to assemble material for a production of "genuine" emotional power and "genuine" milieu. The rest of the ensemble meanwhile went on with rehearsals in a barn at Pushkino, an excursion center about 20 miles from Moscow.

Blue room: scene from the first act of Turgenev's comedy A Month in the Country, *first produced in 1872 at the Maly Theater, Moscow. Watercolor by Mstislav Dobujinsky.*

Opening night of the Moscow Art Theater, 1898: Tsar Fyodor Ivanovich, *by A. K. Tolstoy, directed by Stanislavsky. Stage design by V. A. Simov.*

On October 14, 1898, the curtain rose for the first time at the Moscow Art Theater. The actor Moskvin spoke the singularly relevant opening words of Tsar Fyodor Ivanovich: "On this enterprise I fasten all my hopes." In this tragedy they came to nought—but they launched the Moscow Art Theater on the road to world fame. The theater's fame was to be bound up with that of "its" great author Anton Chekhov, and was founded on *The Sea Gull*, the second of its productions, which was first shown on December 17, 1898. The play had been a flop a year earlier at the Alexandrinsky Theater in St. Petersburg, and Chekhov was persuaded only with difficulty to present it again.

The production became the touchstone of the Moscow Art Theater. In the case of *Tsar Fyodor Ivanovich*, the major effort had been brought to bear on the scenery; now they concentrated on acting, on the projection of moods, presentiments, intimations, nuances of feeling. Acting set out on the new road of intuition and feeling, as Stanislavsky said, a road "from the outward to the inward, toward the subconscious." This meant total dedication to the play, an almost religious devotion. "We embraced each other as on Easter night," Stanislavsky wrote after the successful first night of *The Sea Gull*.

The Moscow Art Theater had found its author and its style. It became the "house of Chekhov," and henceforth a sea gull with outspread wings became its emblem, to be seen on the curtain, the program, and the tickets. The close artistic and personal connection with Chekhov—he married the actress Olga Knipper—deepened with the subsequent productions of *Uncle Vanya, The Three Sisters*, and eventually *The Cherry Orchard*. Stanislavsky developed a refined impressionistic style. He marshaled all conceivable means of optical and acoustic illusion in order to create the right "mood" in his actors and the public. To create an atmospheric moment, there were sounds of the balalaika and of crickets, of sleigh bells ringing loudly and nearby or faintly in the distance. With disarming self-criticism Stanislavsky admitted that he tended to exaggeration in this area, and he liked to tell the oft-quoted anecdote of Chekhov once saying he would write a new play that would begin as follows: "How wonderfully quiet it is here, not a bird to be heard, not a dog barking, no cuckoo calling, no owl screeching, no nightingale singing, no clock striking, no bells ringing, and not a single cricket chirping."

With Maxim Gorky's works Stanislavsky gained a new dimension, the drama of social criticism and challenge. "External realism" was now worked upon with the same intensity as historical fidelity to the milieu, which had led Stanislavsky to send a group to Cyprus before his *Othello* production, and Simov the stage designer to Rome for *Julius Caesar*, or to order furniture from Norway for an Ibsen production.

During the rehearsals for *The Lower Depths*, Stanislavsky sent his actors to the Khitrov market in a Moscow district where vagrants used to hide out. They ate with vagabonds, and Olga Knipper shared a room with a prostitute in order to "get the feel" of the role of Natasha. The creation of a part from reality—"to act means to live"—is one of the essentials of the much-vaunted (and equally often misunderstood) Stanislavsky method. This earned Stanislavsky the reproach that he underestimated the capacity of the imagination. In point of fact, however, Stanislavsky meant his "method," so often misunderstood as an abracadabra of the actor's art, to be a flexible guide leading to the collaboration of director and actor. Stanislavsky, too, took a middle position in the controversial question of identification, which has been debated ever anew from Riccoboni to Brecht. Is the actor what he plays, or does he play something he knows he is not? Ultimately, Stanislavsky's system was a delicate balancing act. He warned his actors not to abuse the stage for private confessions. Personal emotions, he argued, do not enrich the actor's art; an actor who himself is experiencing jealousy does not make a better Othello, but a worse one.

Michael Chekhov (Anton Chekhov's nephew), whose notes on his work at the Moscow Art Theater studios under Stanislavsky were used in the early thirties by the New York Group Theatre, summed up the essence of the Stanislavsky method by the formula: "The materials of imagination are always taken from life."

Stanislavsky himself, however, worked with the two concepts of "physical action" and "super-objective," that is, agreement on a creative basic thesis for the interpretation of a stage work. As an example he chose *Hamlet* (Gordon Craig's production of it in 1911 was of profound and lasting influence). *Hamlet,* Stanislavsky maintained, could be played as a family drama from the aspect: "I want to honor my father's memory." It could be interpreted as the tragedy of a man intent on exploring the secrets of existence. Finally, there is the possibility of the highest "super-objective": "I want to save mankind."

But, if Shakespeare's tragedy is interpreted in terms of applied politics—"I want the feudal state to be abolished"—then the principle of the "super-objective" is in dangerous water. The director, at his discretion, can put the "super-objective" at the service of humanitarian ideals or of the powers-that-be. In a totalitarian state, the full expression of art is balanced on a knife's edge.

For a time, Stanislavsky's "thoroughly bourgeois ideology" was as suspect in Russia as was the rousing "Sire, give us freedom of thought," pronounced by Marquis Posa in Schiller's *Don Carlos,* or the Rütli oath in his *Wilhelm Tell* in the Germany of 1940. The upheavals of the 1905 revolution already made Stanislavsky feel he was at a dead end. And after the October Revolution in 1917 he kept aloof. Luckily, A. V.

Lunacharsky, the first People's Commissar for Education, kept a protective hand over him. From September 1922 to August 1924 the ensemble of the Moscow Art Theater was on tour abroad, honoring long-standing commitments in Europe and America. "We had to gain distance," Stanislavsky wrote in his autobiography *My Life in Art,* which was first published in 1924, "distance from an atmosphere of disorganization." This refers to the time when the revolutionary storm in the theaters had reached gale force, and the Moscow Art Theater was not at all looked upon with favor. Actually, it was not only the government itself that disapproved, but also those theater people who closely followed the party line.

The leading theater artists of the day—Vsevolod Meyerhold, Evgeni Vakhtangov, and Alexander Tairov—had come from Stanislavsky's school, from the experimental studios of the Moscow Art Theater. As early as 1905, Meyerhold had tried to interest Stanislavsky in the principles of stylized scenery. But the 1905 revolution put an end to the studio on Povarskaya Street before Meyerhold had any practical results to show.

Systematic experiments were undertaken by the so-called First Studio of the Moscow Art Theater under the director L. A. Sulerzhitsky and, after the latter's death in 1916, under Vakhtangov. Maxim Gorky gave the Studio his notes on the methods of improvisation used by the Neapolitan *Commedia dell'arte* which he had studied intensively during his voluntary exile on the island of Capri. The initially very makeshift character of the Studio's room-stage imposed unconventional combinations with pedestals and movable platforms. Stanislavsky invented a metal grid to be fixed below the ceiling, so that decorative cloth panels could be hung from it as desired.

On the miniature scale of these studio improvisations, Stanislavsky tried out stage techniques that the revolutionary theater later transposed onto a vast scale. There are detailed records, for instance, of his use of black velvet in settings for Symbolist plays. In Andreyev's play *The Life of Man,* he had used hangings of this material to suggest a forest, and a transparency likewise covered with black velvet but with little holes for light cut in it, to give the illusion of station lanterns glimmering afar.

Abroad, Stanislavsky's stage direction was known only through classical productions of the Moscow Art Theater in their highest degree of perfection, with every detail refined through decades of repertory performance. Their effective use of the suggested "fourth wall"—as for instance in the second act of *The Sea Gull,* when a bench is placed before the footlights, and the seated actors turn their backs to the audience—became exemplary staging for the whole world.

Experiments with new forms were limited to the studios, which became the storehouse of the modern Russian theater. The First Studio was followed by the Second, the Third (today's Vakhtangov Theater) and the Fourth, as well as by a Musical Studio under Nemirovich-Danchenko. Stanislavsky had a personal part in the development of the Studio of the Hebrew Habimah players, where at his request Vakhtangov taught for some years and he himself gave courses on his method. The artistic climax of this studio was Vakhtangov's 1922 production of *The Dybbuk,* S. Ansky's dramatization of a Hassidic legend. After touring Europe and America, the Habimah players went to Palestine in 1928, later settled there and, when the State of Israel was founded in 1948, became the Hebrew State Theater of Tel Aviv.

Other groups working with Stanislavsky's methods were the Armenian Studio in Moscow, the Polish Reduta founded in 1919 in Warsaw, the studio set up in Kiev by the Polish actress S. Wysocka, and the Bulgarian National Theater in Sofia under the direction of N. O. Massalitinov, a pupil of Stanislavsky's. All these theaters of the Stanislavsky method formed a chain, the links of which, through Michael Chekhov, reached as far as the United States.

Symbolism—Imagination and Stage Lighting

State realism as a program originated in Paris, and in France, too, now originated the deliberate rejection of naturalism: symbolism. Stéphane Mallarmé, "le prince des poètes," protested in the name of poetry against the view that all that was to be expected of the poet was a mere copy of what meets the eye of the uninitiated. The poet's task, Mallarmé maintained, was not to name an object, but to conjure it up with the power of his imagination. Mallarmé dreamed of "a marvelously realistic theater of our imagination," a theater "from within," just as the Romantics had looked for the "inward way."

Baudelaire spoke of the "forest of symbols." For him the visible universe was a treasure-house of images and symbols, to which only the poetic imagination could assign their status and value. Valéry said poets must take back from music what belonged to poetry. And so poetry and music together gave the theater of Symbolism its most convincing justification. The age-old rivalry between word and music was to be the subject of Richard Strauss's last opera, his sharp and polished *Capriccio.*

Naturalism was a program, but not necessarily a limitation for the creative personality. Ibsen had to get away from *Peer Gynt,* from the national atmosphere of Norwegian Romanticism, before he could write *Ghosts* and *A Doll's House.* Later, he, too, left pure naturalism behind

Stage design by Joseph Wenig for Macbeth, *Nationaltheater, Prague, 1914.*

Stage design by Eduard Sturm for Die Bürger von Calais, *by Georg Kaiser, directed by Gustav Lindemann and Louise Dumont, Schauspielhaus, Düsseldorf, 1928. (Düsseldorf, Dumont-Lindemann-Archiv.)*

and created the mysterious symbolism of *The Wild Duck.* Gerhart Hauptmann had already gone beyond doctrinaire harshness in *Hanneles Himmelfahrt,* and entered the neoromantic world of myth with *Die Versunkene Glocke* and *Und Pippa tanzt.* Chekhov's young Konstantin in *The Sea Gull* craves for new forms, for forces that should put an end to the routine of the contemporary theater and to its pathetic efforts "to fish a moral out of trite pictures and phrases." But Konstantin Treplev founders in the chaos of his dreams and figures. Chekhov, himself standing on the boundary line between naturalism and symbolism, recognized the danger to art and life alike from an escape into the dissolving realm of dreams, from that journey into the nowhere of emotional states in which Maeterlinck's *Tintagiles* loses itself.

One of the youngest of the Paris Symbolists, Paul Fort, turned against the realism of the Théâtre Libre as early as 1890. With the support of a group of like-minded writers, he founded the Théâtre d'Art and appointed as its artistic director the actor Alexandre Lugné-Poë, who had started with Antoine. The intellectual atmosphere in the theater, torn by the conflict of styles, was well characterized by Lugné-Poë at that time: "My confused mind reeled from Realism to Symbolism, and in both mangers found but meager fare."

The Théâtre d'Art concentrated on the symbolist Maeterlinck, on the lyrical drama of loneliness and melancholy. The good response to *Pelléas et Mélisande* in May 1893 encouraged Lugné-Poë to found a stage of his own, the Théâtre de l'Oeuvre. In this venture he had the support of the writer and critic Camille Mauclair. It opened in October 1893 with Ibsen's *Rosmersholm.* In his search for stronger fare, Lugné-Poë came across *Ubu Roi,* a play by the young Paris bohemian Alfred Jarry. This schoolboy farce with its bitter social criticism had its premiere on December 10, 1896, and ended in a riot such as Paris had not seen since *Hernani.* Firmin Gémier played Ubu, and his very first word—*"Merde"*—shattered the audiences' postprandial comfort.

The stalls were filled by the elite of the symbolist cult of beauty. There were Mallarmé and Henri Ghéon, W. B. Yeats and Arthur Symons—and before their eyes was born the avant-garde theater of the coming century. Here the road was opened from the symbolist to the surrealist drama, and, eventually, to the drama of the absurd, via Roger Vitrac's *Victor, ou Les Enfants au pouvoir* as far as Ionesco, Beckett, and Audiberti.

Nearly fifty years later, Henri Ghéon, in his retrospective essay *L'Art du théâtre* (1944), still praised *Ubu Roi* as "a hundred percent theater," which "at the borderline of reality created another reality with the help of symbols"—an interpretation that demonstrates how close the divergent attitudes really were to each other. (In 1958 Jean Vilar rediscovered the stage-worthiness of *Ubu Roi* when he produced it at the

Théâtre National Populaire as a grotesquely aggressive mask play. A Czech adaptation was shown throughout Europe after 1960 by the Prague Balustrade Theater.

But in practice, the theater kept its distance from the critics' controversies about style, as is proved by the fact that in March 1908, Gémier also appeared as Pére Ubu at the Théâtre Antoine.

This simultaneity of apparent contradictions became the mark of future developments. Even as the traditional dramatic conventions were being shattered, the stage itself began to break through its now customary peep-show frame. The first to take the initiative were the symbolists with their refusal to be enslaved by realistic detail. In Ibsen's *The Wild Duck* young Ekdal's life as a photographer is a deception; it glosses over the tissue of lies of a convenient arrangement. The camera has become an instrument of self-deception.

For the symbolists the photographic approach of the drama of naturalism was a screen obstructing the view to deeper insight. The stage was not to depict a real milieu, but to explore zones of feeling. Its task was not description, but incantation. Lighting acquired an important function, and the word was aided by music and dance. In a few lucky instances the symbolists did succeed in transposing inner moods rooted in lyricism to the public realm of the stage. That the Symbolist drama survived without injury such revelations of the "état de l'âme" was solely due to music.

It was Claude Debussy's music that won Mallarmé's poem "L'Après-midi d'un Faune" a place on the stage and in the concert hall. With Nijinsky's choreography, it became in 1912 one of the high points of the Russian ballet in Paris. And it was Debussy's music which conferred upon Maeterlinck's elfin love drama *Pelléas et Mélisande* a degree of poetic transfiguration beyond the reach of the nonoperatic theater. Hugo von Hofmannsthal found a congenial partner in Richard Strauss. And Gabriele d'Annunzio's symbolist whirl of sound and color drew life from the dark, suggestive melody of Eleonora Duse's diction.

This was the time when Auguste Rodin sculpted his lovers in white marble, when Rainer Maria Rilke wrote the *Sonnette an Orpheus,* when *Jugendstil* and *art nouveau* reveled in decoratively writhing ornaments, when Isadora Duncan danced Aphrodite clad in tunic and strap sandals and declared with naïve, cosmic gush: "My soul was like a battlefield where Apollo, Dionysos, Christ, Nietzsche, and Richard Wagner disputed the ground."

The Western world was taking stock. For the opera, this had been done by Richard Wagner. His ideal of the *Gesamtkunstwerk,* the integral work of art, kept the aestheticians of Europe and America busy. In 1892 the Swiss stage designer Adolphe Appia made a series of sketches

Stage design for the symbolist fairy-tale play The Blue Bird, *by Maurice Maeterlinck, Paris, 1923. (Paris, Bibliothèque de l'Arsenal.)*

Alfred Roller: design for the Feldmarschallin's bedroom in Der Rosenkavalier, *by Richard Strauss, first produced at the Hofoper, Dresden, 1911.*

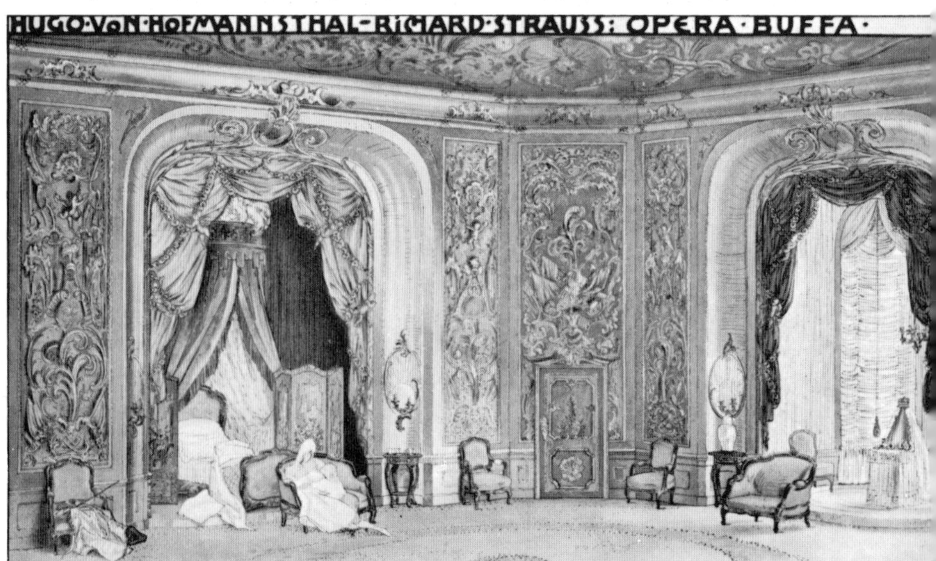

and maquettes for *Das Rheingold,* and in 1896 for *Parsifal.* He assigned to light a task of which the stage had so far made no use, namely, to cast shade, to create space by producing depth and distance. Appia built up architectural shapes of heavy blocks, cubes, and wedges into the broad surfaces of what he called "interior scene," according to his principle of the three-dimensional stylized stage with spotlights. But the invitation to Bayreuth never came. Cosima Wagner safeguarded the master's testament, with Valhalla and the Castle of the Holy Grail made of papier-mâché, realistic mobile panoramas, and the wheeled platforms that carried the Rhine Maidens. The first radical break with these conventions had to wait half a century, for Wieland Wagner, who would rid the Bayreuth stage of the old sets and was to realize the light-space visions that the two great symbolist stage reformers—Adolphe Appia and Edward Gordon Craig—had had in mind.

However much the designs and ideas of Appia had in common with the poetic sensibility of the symbolists, he was given little chance to try them out in practice. At the private theater of the Comtesse de Béarn in Paris, Appia had an opportunity in 1903 to create nonrealistic settings for parts of Bizet's opera *Carmen,* and for Byron's *Manfred,* which was set to music by Robert Schumann. Appia's meeting with Émile Jaques-Dalcroze led to the series of designs that he called *Espaces Rythmiques* —optical counterparts to the concept of eurhythmic stage direction as developed by the Swiss Institut Jaques-Dalcroze at Hellerau near Dresden.

Appia's *Tristan und Isolde* for Milan's La Scala, a collaboration with Jean Mercier and Arturo Toscanini, his *Ring des Nibelungen* for the Stadttheater in Basel under the direction of Oskar Wälterlin, and his scenery for Paul Claudel's *L'Annonce faite à Marie* for Hellerau went even further in the striving for metaphysical transcendence. Its ultimate utopian culmination, divorced from the theater, was the "Cathedral of the Future."

Appia's first prerequisite was to keep the stage free of everything that impairs the physical presence of the actor. "The human body does not need to bother trying to give a pretense of reality, for it is, itself, reality. The sole purpose of stage decoration is to set off reality to best advantage."

This was the conviction of Edward Gordon Craig, too. But in his designs he treated the figures on the stage and their movements as components of the graphic whole. The stretched-out arms of Electra, the bent back of Lear, the slender silhouette of Hamlet are not an accessory, but an a priori element of the scenic vision. In the Moscow *Hamlet,* spears, lances, and flags rise steeply to stress the monumentally vertical aspect, and, lowered, transpose the tragic end into optical terms.

As the son of the actress Ellen Terry, Craig was familiar with the

Adolphe Appia: Moonlight, *from the series* Espaces rythmiques, *suggested by his work with Emile Jaques-Dalcroze, 1908–12. In 1913 Appia designed settings for Claudel's* L'Annonce faite à Marie *and for Gluck's* Orpheus *at the Institut Jaques-Dalcroze at Hellerau near Dresden.*

Adolphe Appia: Götterdämmerung, *second act. 1925. Stylized space stage for Oskar Wälterlin's production of Wagner's* Ring *at the Stadttheater, Basel.*

Design by Edward Gordon Craig for King Lear, *Act III, Scene 2. Woodcut from the periodical* The Mask, *January 1924.*

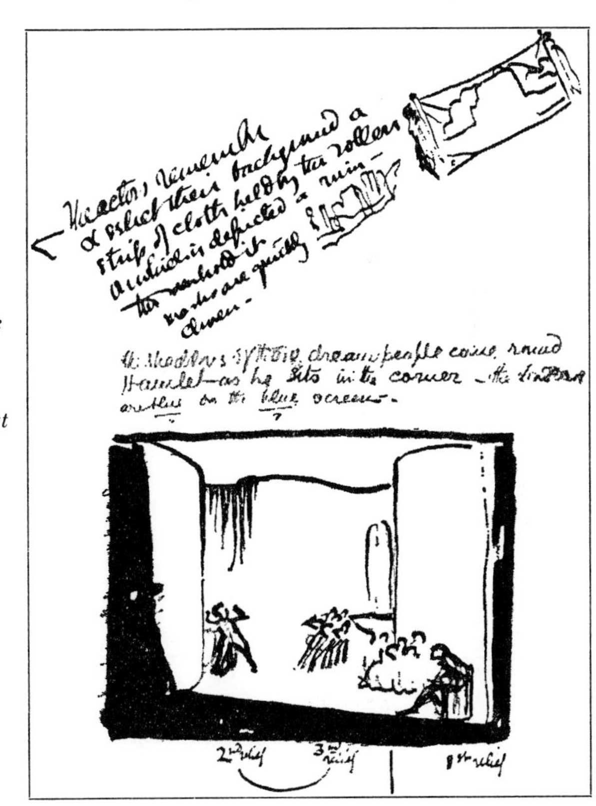

A page from Craig's note book, with instructions for the Hamlet *production at the Moscow Art Theater, 1911. Hamlet and the Players, in Act II, Scene 2: the first player is reciting "The rugged Pyrrhus" lines.*

stage from childhood. He learned to know, and act, Shakespeare from Henry Irving. He considered himself Irving's heir, however much he differed from him in artistic matters, from the veneration of Shakespeare to the rejection of Shaw. Craig preferred dramatists with a grand emotional sweep. It fascinated him to translate mystical and tragic lines about human destiny into light and space, to "spirit away" stage realism.

When Craig, in 1900, together with his friend Martin Shaw (no relation to G.B.S.) produced the opera *Dido and Aeneas,* the décor consisted of nothing but a simple blue background. But this blue expressed the soul, "l'état de l'âme," of Purcell's opera: shining clarity, paling twilight, and in the background a distant, delicate filigree of ships' masts. The sketch for Ibsen's drama *The Vikings at Helgeland* looks like an anticipation of the 1953 Bayreuth *Parsifal.*

When producing Hofmannsthal's lyrically symbolic play *Das gerettete Venedig* (after Thomas Otway's *Venice Preserved*) at the Berlin Lessing Theater for Otto Brahm, Craig limited himself to long, colored curtains. Pools and intersecting beams of light created the illumination magic that was to become such a distinguishing feature of the expressionist theater, and was further developed by Kokoschka and Cocteau—by the latter even for motion pictures—in their own specific optical-dramatic manner. (In 1954 the London stage director Peter Brook entered a protest against scene painting with light. He maintained that Craig had overestimated the importance of the spotlight. Brook felt that even color screens could only soften the light by degrees and could not rival the painter's brush either in subtlety, or in shading and coloring.)

Craig conceived of his stage not merely in terms of the symbolic medium of light, but also of architecture. The movable screens he used for the famous *Hamlet* production at Stanislavsky's Moscow Art Theater in 1911 were meant to achieve more than just monumentality. They were at the same time to cancel the visual effect of the traditional peep-show stage, to give an imposing mobile foil to the acting, and to provide changing openings for the shifting lights.

We have Stanislavsky's own record of the joint preparations for the memorable production:

> Craig dreamed of having the entire performance take place without intermissions or the use of the curtain. The audience was to come to the theater and see no stage whatsoever. The screens were to serve as the architectural continuation of the auditorium and were to harmonize with it. But at the beginning of the performance the screens were to move gracefully and their lines were to take on new combinations. At least they

Edward Gordon Craig: Design for Macbeth, *1909. (From: Craig,* Towards a New Theatre, *1913.)*

Edward Gordon Craig: scenery with movable screens, designed for the 1911 Hamlet *production at Stanislavsky's Moscow Art Theater. Design for the last act.*

> were to grow still. From somewhere there would be light that would give them a new picturesqueness, and all present in the theater were to be carried away in their dreams to some other world which was only hinted at by the artist, but which became real by virtue of the colors of the imaginations of the spectators.

It is interesting to read in Stanislavsky's autobiography how he deplores that the stage has only "coarse and primitive means" for satisfying man's "best spiritual longings which rise from the purest aesthetic depths." Stanislavsky and his stage director Sulerzhitsky were left with the difficult task of fitting the model designed and demonstrated by Craig into the inadequate technical facilities.

One of his personally most happy stage successes came Craig's way at Florence in December 1906, when he produced Ibsen's *Rosmersholm* with Eleanora Duse. She wrote him a letter of thanks on the day after the premiere: "I played as in a dream last night—and far away. I was conscious of your help and your strength. . . ."

Craig's dream of having a theater of his own never came true. His theater school at Florence, too, lasted only a few years. But his theoretical writings were read throughout the world, both his fundamental book *The Art of the Theatre* (1905) and his magazine *The Mask*, which, with some interruptions, he published at Florence from 1908 to 1929. It was a well-illustrated review, dealing with all aspects of the theater. Illusion, Naturalism, and scenic stylization were discussed, as also the age-old actors' problem: identification or detachment. Craig developed his theory of the super-marionette, of the mask play, which alone, he said, could eliminate all traces of egotism and so, ideally freed of flesh and blood, would "aim to clothe itself with a deathlike beauty while exhaling a living spirit." Some of his ideas recur in Meyerhold, O'Neill, and Brecht.

Craig's mystique of light found a follower in the American stage designer Robert Edmond Jones, whose designs for the Hopkins-Barrymore productions of *King Richard III* and *Macbeth* in New York in 1920 and 1921 were greatly influenced by Appia and Craig. Three tall arches against a black background served as the optical equivalent of Macbeth's ambitions. They collapsed when the curve of Macbeth's fortunes dipped.

In Europe, the young abstract painters of the late twenties drew on symbolist ideas for reform. Naum Gabo and Antoine Pevsner with their 1927 Paris production of *La Chatte*, and László Moholy-Nagy with his 1928 *Tales of Hoffmann* production at the Krolloper in Berlin tried, in the spirit of Craig, to make space out of light and shade. The wings became mere devices for casting shade, everything was transparent, and all this transparence culminated in an organization of space "superabundant, but still comprehensible."

The shaping of the stage and of the acting by a sole creative personality, which the symbolists had demanded in the name of poetry and Craig in the name of the magic of space and light, was to come with the great stage directors of the twentieth century: with Konstantin Stanislavsky (1863–1938) in Moscow; with Max Reinhardt (1873–1943) in Berlin, Vienna, Salzsburg, and New York; with Jacques Copeau (1879–1949) in Paris; with Elia Kazan (born 1909) in New York. The great actor-director Jean-Louis Barrault (born 1910) of Paris has paid Craig the supreme compliment: "Craig's work was my catechism and he himself the theater's most accomplished artist."

Expressionism, Surrealism, and Futurism

Since the days of antiquity intellectual controversy portrayed on the stage is as much part of the theater's tradition as the provision for festive splendor. Aristophanes took the Athenians' breath away with his polemics and provocations. At all times controversies and quarrels aired in the theater were the yeast in the dough. They became more frequent as art began to oppose the leveling pressure of industrialized mass society. Technical progress and the competition for world markets had led to the First World War and its mania of destruction. The individual was degraded, sank to a nonentity, defenseless at the mercy of uncontrollable powers.

"We are puppets whose wires are pulled by unknown masters," says Büchner's Danton, in *Dantons Tod.* German Expressionist drama responded to the crisis of self-destruction with a scream. Nightmares and utopias, the determinism behind the individual's decisions, the socialist vision of the future, the conflict between uninhibited instinct and emasculated vestiges of religion—all these added up to a load so heavy that it disrupted coherent language. Ecstasy, confession, protest exploded in tattered phrases, in a frenzied condensation of language, in strident dynamics of sound—in the scream. Such plays as August Stramm's so-called *Schrei-Dramen* ("Scream Dramas") and Reinhard Goering's *Seeschlacht* ("Sea Battle") which begins with a scream—all seem to groan with the agony of being lost. In his one-act play *Ein Geschlecht* ("A Generation"), in front of a macabre graveyard wall, Fritz von Unruh cast the accounts of horror; his play was an incantatory, ecstatic denouncement of war and its atrocities, a summons to humanity and brotherhood in harsh hammering iambic pentameters.

The generation of the fathers became the target of prophetically

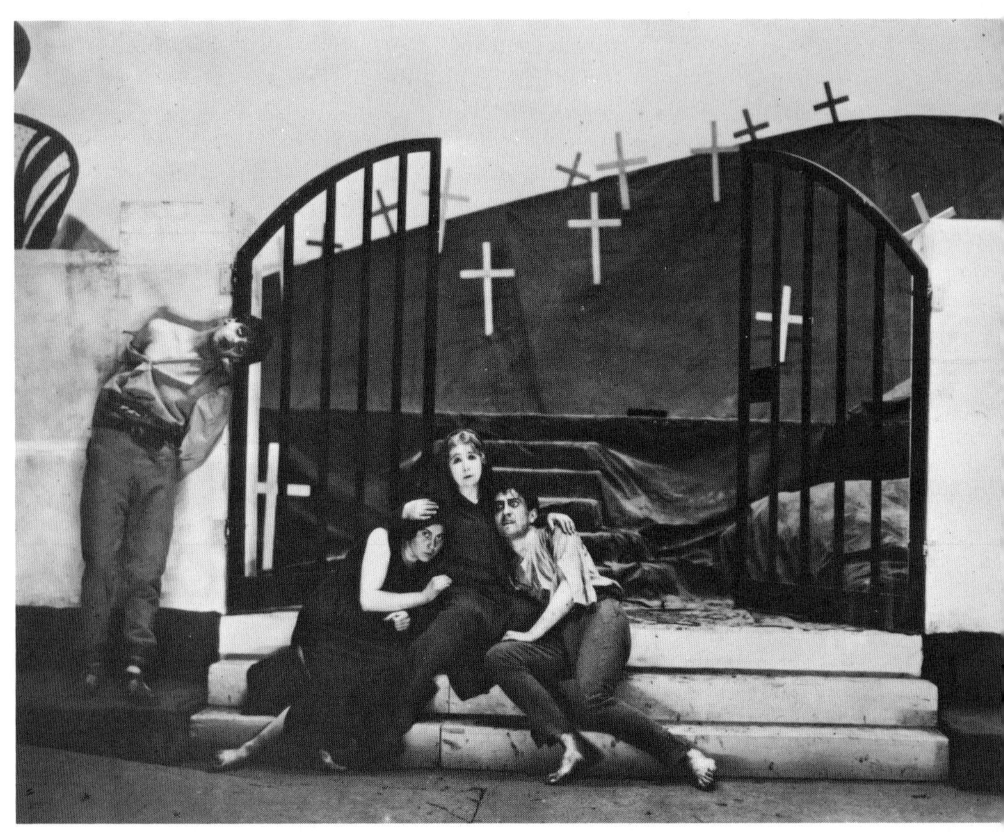

Photograph of a scene from the tragedy Ein Geschlecht, *by Fritz von Unruh, first produced in 1918 at the Schauspielhaus, Frankfurt am Main. Direction, Gustav Hartung; scenery, August Babberger. Rosa Bertens as Mother, Gerda Müller as Daughter, Carl Ebert as Son.*

aggressive poets and dramatists of the asphalt jungle. The strife between young and old, between son and father, erupted in manifestos and on the stage. The old conflict, in Carl Sternheim's comedies *Der Snob* and *1913,* still the subject of caustic satire vented against the philistine middle classes, now was whipped up to the point of bloody execution, in such plays as *Der Sohn* ("The Son") by Walter Hasenclever, *Dies irae* by Anton Wildgans, *Der Bettler* ("The Beggar") by Reinhard Johannes Sorge, right down to *Vatermord* ("Patricide") by Arnolt Bronnen and *Die Krankheit der Jugend* ("The Sickness of Youth") by Ferdinand Bruckner.

The stage had only one means of handling the scenery for this onslaught of the expressionist dramatists, those "waking sleepers" with their "burden of dreadful immediacy," as Alfred Kerr once called them. This was to make use of the full potential of lighting as a means of visual expression, as a storm signal of the intellectual, emotional, and political crisis. As early as 1911, Oskar Kokoschka wanted for his drama *Der brennende Dornbusch* ("The Burning Bush") a moonlit room, "large and full of shifting shadows that draw figures on the floor." Cones of light were to seek each other out, to cross and to form a halo around the dying man. Kokoschka saw the scene as a painter. But the uproar caused by the Berlin performance in 1919 was attributable more to the rank imagination of his language than to his visual images.

In his turn, Reinhard Sorge, when the literary society "Das junge Deutschland" gave his drama *Der Bettler* in 1917 at Max Reinhardt's Deutsches Theater, asked for moving spotlights that would pick out a single figure or a group from amid the nocturnal darkness. In Richard Weichert's 1918 Mannheim production of Hasenclever's *Der Sohn,* a spotlight falling vertically upon the stage achieved the degree of stark isolation which the playwright intended. In Ernst Toller's ecstatic drama of humanity *Die Wandlung* ["The Transfiguration"], which Karl Heinz Martin produced in 1919 at the Berlin Tribüne, the stage was lined with dark cloth and the few inconspicuous settings deferred to the furioso of the word.

Ernst Barlach's plays made plain the connection between Expressionist drama and Expressionist painting. So did Ernst Stern in his décors for the 1919 Berlin production of *Die Wupper* by Else Lasker-Schüler, in which factory chimneys slanted up over rust-red workmen's houses, and violent color contrasts emphasized the realistically expressive moods of the play.

Another devotee of colored light as a means of stage setting was Herwarth Walden, editor of *Der Sturm.* A production of August Stramm's *Sancta Susanna* in the Berlin Künstlerhaus marshaled the whole spectrum as a background for a church interior: a semicircle of

Stage design by Otto Reigbert for Der Sohn, *by Walter Hasenclever, intended for the Stadttheater Kiel, 1919.*

Death in the Tree. *Design by César Klein for Victor Barnowsky's production of the expressionist drama* Von morgens bis mitternachts *by Georg Kaiser, at the Lessingtheater, Berlin, 1920.*

HEBBEL „HERODES U. MARIAMNE" V. AKT. GERICHT.

Stage design by Otto Reigbert for Otto Falckenberg's production of Herodes und Mariamne, *by Friedrich Hebbel, Deutsches Theater, Berlin, 1921.*

The Jessner stairs. Stage design by Emil Pirchan for Leopold Jessner's production of Shakespeare's King Richard III, *Staatstheater am Gendarmenmarkt, Berlin, 1920.*

deep red, above it concentric rings of yellow, blue, purple, and finally black. The primary colors were repeated in the costumes. Later, Oskar Schlemmer in his production of *Das Triadische Ballet* at the Bauhaus also played with rhythmic color and form contrasts.

The great state theaters with their representative program of classics could hardly afford stage experiments with expressionist dramatists, except at literary matinees. But the principles of abstraction by means of light and color found their master in Leopold Jessner, director of the Berlin Staatstheater on the Gendarmenmarkt. Jessner came to Berlin from Königsberg, and in 1919 took charge of the Schinkel building, in succession to a hitherto markedly traditional management. On December 12, 1919, he staged a *Wilhelm Tell* which strictly shunned the glories of the Swiss mountain landscape. An austere system of steps against a background of dark curtains was all the setting; and there was Albert Bassermann as Tell, a Goliath of the type portrayed in Hodler's paintings, and Fritz Kortner as Gessler, in martial makeup and hung with medals. There was no "smiling lake," no "sunken lane," but instead Bassermann's stentorian call to order from the ramp to the stalls, when the continuation of the performance was threatened by tumult and uproar: "Throw out the paid hoodlums!"

The situation was saved and the performance continued; Jessner had held his own in the witches' cauldron of theater intrigues. And the flight of steps he used in this production became his artistic trademark. For Shakespeare's *King Richard III* Emil Pirchan designed for Jessner a broad, frontal stairway, slightly narrowing toward the top—a visual interpretation of the rise and fall of the murderous and domineering king, portrayed by Fritz Kortner in suitably, well-tried diabolic fashion. Emotions and factions were indicated by red, black, and white.

Jessner's steps sent a precedent. They lent themselves well to being interpreted as an expression of cosmic conceptions and thus testified to intellectual pretension. They also were easy to imitate, could be used for almost any purpose, and presented no difficulty even to a technically primitive stage. When Jessner, on his return from a visit to a number of provincial theaters, was asked for his impressions, he gave the much-quoted answer: "Stairs, nothing but stairs." Much later—in 1960—during a discussion in Munich, Fritz Kortner was asked again about that "cosmic" flight of steps. He gave an evasive answer: if the Staatstheater had had a revolving stage, there would have been no need to resort to stairs for getting one's effect. Whatever the reasons, to make an artistic principle out of necessity is the stage director's opportunity. And the use of stairs on the stage goes back to Piranesi, Juvara, the Meiningers, and Appia.

Jacques Copeau, the reformer of French acting, similarly formalized the stage by combinations of stairs. He asked Francis Jourdain to create for the stage of the Théâtre du Vieux Colombier in Paris, which he opened in 1913, a fixed architectural frame with a neutral playing podium in front of it. His model was the Elizabethan stage, his aim the "retheatricalization of the theater": a clear, simple, well-proportioned stage; an inconspicuous sounding board for the dramatic text, which required no more than "an empty platform."

Copeau had contacts with Appia, Craig, and Stanislavsky, and out of his school came such directors as Louis Jouvet and Charles Dullin and, later, when he was codirector of the Comédie Française in 1944, also Jean-Louis Barrault and Jean Vilar. Copeau's original interest lay in literature. His ideal was the humanization of the theater through the word. He was one of the founders of the *Nouvelle Revue Française*, in the September 1913 issue of which he published the announcement of his own theater and of his artistic aims, under the title "Le Théâtre du Vieux Colombier."

The first occasion on which Copeau created a stir was his dramatization of Dostoevsky's last novel, *The Brothers Karamazov*, in 1910. (The production made such a lasting impression that in 1927 the Theatre Guild asked him to stage it again in New York.) Copeau's influence is woven into the fabric of the modern French theater. It can certainly be traced in Giraudoux and Anouilh, but also in some unexpected places, like, say, the biblical play *Noé* by André Obey, director of the Comédie Française after 1946. This play owed its stage success in 1931 to Copeau's nephew and pupil Michel Saint-Denis. Pierre Fresnaye played the title role in New York, John Gielgud in London. Many of Copeau's ideas contributed to the development of the English theater via Saint-Denis, who became director of the Old Vic dramatic school.

The Théâtre du Vieux Colombier closed its doors in 1924. But Copeau's teachings remained alive in the "Cartel des Quatre," known as the "Big Four"—a group that was founded in 1926 and lasted until the Second World War. It consisted of the most outstanding private theater managers of Paris: Louis Jouvet, Charles Dullin, Gaston Baty, and Georges Pitoeff. However much they differed by origin and temperament, they had in common Copeau's aim of producing unconventional theater, humanizing the art of the stage, and opposing the trend toward increasing artificiality. Soon the reproach was heard that the Big Four were out to overstress the role of the director. But this was a natural development at a time when the pluralism of creative possibilities was greater than ever before.

Stage direction presupposed critical discrimination and required an ability to fuse the most heterogeneous elements in one internally consistent form of art. The choice began with stage techniques and did not stop at the play itself. Otto Brahm had made himself the advocate of Gerhart Hauptmann, Stanislavsky's Moscow Art Theater was the house of Chekhov, and Louis Jouvet suggested and actively fostered Giraudoux's switch from novel to drama. At the Comédie des Champs-Elysées in 1928 Jouvet produced Giraudoux's *Siegfried,* a "dialogue with Germany, that paroxysm of landscape and passion, to which the soul alone can give fullness."

Gaston Baty, principal of the "Compagnons de la Chimère," moved in the area between religion tinged with symbolism and the feather-light verbal wit of Labiche. Armenian-born Georges Pitoeff, who had settled in Paris in 1922, not only staged Russian and Scandinavian authors, but also Pirandello, Shaw, and Ferdinand Bruckner. When Charles Dullin produced *King Richard III* at the Théâtre de l'Atelier, he stylized the battle scenes in the manner of ballet—a slap in the face of the traditional way of dealing with the classics.

The dramatic qualities of ballet were not doubted since Serge Diaghilev. *Schéhérezade* (1909) and *Petrouchka* (1911) asserted themselves as independent, choreographic and musical works of art. Léon Bakst and Alexandre Benois gained fame overnight with their designs for scenery and costumes. The prima ballerina, sole heroine of the evening in the nineteenth century, now shared her acclaim with the painter and choreographer. To have taken part in a Diaghilev production in Paris, London, or Monte Carlo was the first step of the ladder of international fame.

Jean Cocteau scored his first *succès de scandale* in 1917 in Rome, with a ballet called *Parade.* Its music was by Eric Satie, the décor by Pablo Picasso, and its style was described in the program by a word coined by Guillaume Apollinaire: Surrealism. Here was a new slogan for a form of art that wanted to be unnaturalistic, unrealistic, superrealistic. The word first occurred in the subtitle of Apollinaire's fantastic shocker *Les Mamelles de Tirésias,* which his friends staged as a "drame surréaliste" on June 24, 1917, at the Théâtre Maubel in Montmartre. The Paris critics' reaction was lukewarm. There was not enough either for success or scandal. Apollinaire's concepts had a more lasting influence on the theater than his plays. He was the originator, too, of the term "rayonism" for the specifically Russian variant of futurism (the -isms began to multiply) which achieved world recognition thanks to Diaghilev's collaborators Nathalie Gontcharova and her husband Michael Larionov.

Ballet and music were emancipating themselves fast, and the impetus of this movement found expression in the group known as "the Six"—that is, the six composers Georges Auric, Louis Durey, Darius Milhaud, Francis Poulenc, Germaine Tailleferre, and Arthur Honegger. Their attacks on the followers of Wagner and Debussy entailed for the latter, as Cocteau who was an ally of the Six quipped with malice, the danger of being taken seriously.

Cocteau himself was very angry indeed when the public refused to go along with him. But he was most irritated, not by the reception of his surrealist films from *Le Sang d'un poète* to *Orphée,* or of his dramas *La Machine Infernale* or *Bacchus,* so much as by that of the Munich production in 1962 of *L'Aigle à deux têtes,* which Cocteau had personally sponsored. The young protested. But the reason was not at all a belated misunderstanding of Cocteau's surrealism; the protest in this case was due to the inadequacies of cheap historical melodrama.

Cocteau's great achievement on the threshold of surrealism was to have interested the painters of the Paris School in the theater. Picasso, Matisse, Braque, Utrillo, Juan Gris, Giorgio de Chirico, André Derain, Delaunay, Max Ernst, and Joan Miró designed décors and scenery for Stravinsky and Prokofiev, for Maurice Ravel and Manuel de Falla, for Albeniz and Richard Strauss.

The stage became the vehicle for avant-garde pictorial compositions on the grand scale. The Russian Ballet, risen to new glory after 1917 at the Paris Opera, and the Swedish Ballet at the Théâtre Hébertot after 1920, celebrated triumphs of highly expressive décor. For Manuel de Falla's *Le Tricorne,* which the Russian Ballet brought to London in 1919, Picasso tipped the Miller's pond onto the vertical and lined up cubist elements. Fernand Léger derived the scene for *Skating Rink* from cubist color dynamics, and de Chirico built into the background for *La Jarre* the calm expanses of his painterly perspective—both for memorable productions of the Swedish Ballet in Paris, in 1922 and 1924 respectively. Stimulating ideas from this heyday of ballet can still be traced in the ballet interlude of Arthur Honegger's dramatic oratorio *Jeanne d'Arc au bucher.* Honegger's world fame, however, goes back to 1921 and his music for *Roi David,* given at the avant-garde festival of the brothers René and Jean Morax, whose Théâtre du Jorat at Mézières near Lausanne aimed at close collaboration between the stage and the audience.

In Italy futurism started in the plastic arts and developed into a radical rejection of tradition. F. T. Marinetti made clear in his *Proclama sul teatro futurista* (1915) what the tenets of his Futurist manifesto implied for the stage. The criteria for the theater of the future were to be the dynamics of the machine, the mechanization of life, the functional principle of the automaton. For the actor this meant a staccato of acoustically conditioned verbal *montages,* marionettelike movements intensified into acrobatics, and reduction of his own person to a smoothly working cogwheel of the "teatro sintetico."

The décor, too, had to be "dynamic." The scene must become part

Stage design by Pablo Picasso for the ballet The Three-Cornered Hat, *b[y] Manuel de Falla, choreography by Léonide Massine. Russian Ballet und[er] Diaghilev, at the Alhambra Theatre, London, 1919.*

Stage design by Enrico Prampolini: Metaphysical Architecture, *1924.*

of the rhythm of movement, according to Enrico Prampolini's *Scenografia futurista.* Léger adopted this principle to some extent. In his designs for the ballet *La Création du Monde* (1923), some surfaces in the strangely colored geometrical composition were intended to be in perpetual motion. As a later variant we have Oskar Schlemmer's *Figurales Kabinett,* intended for a jazz band and designed in 1927 for the Bauhaus at Dessau.

The machine-age experiments with the new form found effective expression in the new art of motion pictures. The painter Robert Wiene in 1919 used for his horror film *Das Kabinett des Dr. Caligari* an expressionist décor, tricks of lighting and shock reflexes to suggest the nightmare visions of a pathological split personality. René Clair in his short film *Entr'acte* brought to the surface the flickering subconscious of a ballerina struck with stage fright—a tribute to the Swedish Ballet, for which the film was meant, as the name suggests, as an entr'acte. In *Le Sang d'un poète* Jean Cocteau demonstrated with picturesque and intellectual fantasy what could be done with the film as "a realistic document of unreal events." His surrealistic use of the camera was later inexhaustibly repeated in the films *Orphée* down to *Testament d'Orphée.*

Max Reinhardt: Magic and Technique

The century of the great directors produced a second trump card after Stanislavsky: Max Reinhardt. His artistic conceptions, too, followed the changing styles of his age. He once called himself a "mediator between dream and reality." A true heir to the spirit of the Austrian Baroque, Reinhardt liked to abandon himself without reservations to the festive magic of the theater. It was part of the nature of his art and of his personality to draw generously on rich resources, to spread out on the stage all the conceivable riches of mood and color, of intellectual and visual expression.

In its turn, the theater at that very moment was equipped with the new technical means by which hitherto undreamed-of metamorphoses could be wrested from the traditional clumsy apparatus of stage decoration. In 1896, at Munich, Karl Lautenschläger had invented the revolving stage and thus created the practical conditions for realizing an old dream of the theater. In the East, the Japanese *kabuki* had other, primitive predecessors, and, in Milan, Leonardo da Vinci had constructed revolving scenery in 1490; but the revolving stage did not become the common, practicable property of the theater until Lautenschläger invented the electrically operated turntable. The cyclorama, multicolored

Stage design by Oskar Schlemmer for Don Juan und Faust, *by C. D. Grabbe, Nationaltheater, Weimar, 1925. Two-setting scene in Rome: left, a street; right, Faust's study on the Aventine.*

Stage design by Alexandra Exter for The Merchant of Venice, *1927.*

Stage design by Emil Pirchan for Georg Kaiser's Gas, *at the Schillertheater, Berlin, 1928.*

Karl Lautenschläger: electrically operated revolving stage, first used in 1896 at the Nationaltheater, Munich.

lighting, skydome, and effect projectors completed the equipment for the new magic, and Max Reinhardt became a master in its use.

He supervised the renovation of the Kleines Theater in Berlin in 1905, and his instructions on that occasion illustrate the significance of technical devices for the stagecraft of the future. The lighting system was to have "rich possibilities, a lot of colors and projectors." It was to replace the stage decorations, for Reinhardt was going to do without any for the time being. Whatever else happened, the revolving stage must be built: "I attach the greatest possible importance to that revolving stage."

The flies must go, "those miserable rags"; nor had Reinhardt any use for the grid: "What comes from up there is usually rotten." He placed his faith in the revolving stage, on which three-dimensional scenery for the whole play was, if possible, to be installed in advance, and above it all was a vaulted skydome.

Max Reinhardt came to Berlin via Vienna, Bratislava, and Salzburg, where Otto Brahm saw him in 1894 as Franz Moor and invited him to the Deutsches Theater. He appeared there together with Josef Kainz, Agnes Sorma, and Albert Bassermann. But the protestant Otto Brahm's cool, objective, and undeviating naturalism could not satisfy Reinhardt in the long run. He wanted transformation. He looked for the theater's other, more luxuriant, more spell-binding possibilities, the higher, sensual reality rather than its desecrated copy.

Reinhardt's launching pad was the literary cabaret. He threw in his fate with a group of young artists which called itself "Schall und Rauch" (Sound and Smoke) and began to draw attention to itself in 1901 first with short sketch numbers and soon with full-length plays. (It all began with a benefit performance for the poet Christian Morgenstern, sick and no longer able to pay for his stay in a Swiss sanatorium.) Max Reinhardt disengaged himself from Brahm. The erstwhile actor became a stage director, and the stage director within a few years the most passionate artistic driving power and entrepreneur of the Berlin theater. New plans, new stages, rebuilding, enlarging to ever-increasing size, mass theater, arena, festivals—Max Reinhardt's infectious energy overcame every obstacle.

At the end of February 1903, he took on the management and direction of the Neues Theater am Schiffbauerdamm. His masterpiece there was a racy, parodistic production of Offenbach's *Orphée aux Enfers* with Alexander Moissi as Pluto-Aristeus and the young Otto Klemperer wielding the conductor's baton. In the Kleines Theater, Unter den Linden, the modernized hall of "Schall und Rauch," Gorky's naturalistic, somber play *The Lower Depths* was followed by a no less naturalistic glimpse of fairy-land, Shakespeare's *A Midsummer Night's Dream*, with real trees on a green carpet of grass, trees behind which a moon rose and upon which stars shone down from the skydome. In full view of the audience, the forest wheeled about, as did the carpenter's room and the palace. Reinhardt staged *A Midsummer Night's Dream* about a dozen times in all, and always differently—the last time being in 1935 as a film, in Hollywood, together with Wilhelm Dieterle—but never did he gain as much acclaim as with the revolving stage and the real trees in Berlin.

In the summer of 1905, Reinhardt moved to the Deutsches Theater on Schumannstrasse as its manager-director, and a few months later bought it from its founder Adolphe L'Arronge, the writer of comedies. It was the same theater in which Reinhardt had acted under Otto Brahm; one of the most prominent German theaters then, it became so again after 1945, when Gustaf Gründgens, Paul Wegener, and Horst Caspar lent new luster to the name "Max Reinhardts Deutsches Theater."

After Reinhardt had rebuilt a dance hall next door into the Kammerspiele, he used these smaller premises for plays by Sternheim, Wedekind, Ibsen, and Strindberg, keeping the main theater chiefly for the classics. Strindberg came in person and was thrilled by the elegant, intimate atmosphere of the Kammerspiele and the intimate contact between stage and audience, unobstructed by any ramp. In 1907, he founded the Intimate Theater in Stockholm on Reinhardt's model. It seated only 160 persons and thus offered the desired guarantee for the psychological subtleties and nuances which, under the direction of August Falck, eventually brought success to *Miss Julie* in Stockholm, too.

For Max Reinhardt, the Kammerspiele was merely a chord in the orchestra of his plans—a chord he stuck with the exquisite delicacy befitting this auditorium that, with its dark paneling and easy chairs, seemed as private as a drawing room. For the opening on November 8, 1906, he chose Ibsen's *Ghosts* with stage designs by the Norwegian painter Edvard Munch.

Reinhardt also secured the services of the painters Max Slevogt, Lovis Corinth and, for Hebbel's *Genoveva,* of Max Pechstein. Ernst Stern, César Klein, and Emil Orlik collaborated with him for years. He established contact with Edward Gordon Craig and was energetic and self-assured enough to put into effect the theater of the future as Romain Rolland and Craig saw it, that is, a spectacle for the masses, a huge auditorium in which the crowds would gather as they did in antiquity or on the marketplace of the Christian Middle Ages.

Reinhardt hired the Zirkus Schumann, which held 5,000 people, to stage Sophocles's *Oedipus Rex* in Hugo von Hofmannsthal's new adaptation. Alfred Roller built him an imposing stairway to carry the an-

Ibsen's Ghosts, *produced by Max Reinhardt for the opening of the Kammerspiele in Berlin, November 8, 1906. Stage design by Edvard Munch. (Basel, Kunsthalle.)*

Max Reinhardt at a rehearsal for Sophocles' Oedipus Rex, *Zirkus Schumann, Berlin, 1910. Aquatint by Emil Orlik.*

tique tragedy right down into the arena. As chorus, Reinhardt organized a crowd in monumental movements. He mastered the art of handling a crowd, and he won the acclaim of his audience, first with *Oedipus Rex* in 1910, and a year later, also at the Zirkus Schumann, with the *Oresteia* by Aeschylus. That same year, 1911, he transformed the great hall at the Olympia, in London, into a Gothic cathedral for Karl Vollmöller's *Miracle*. Stained-glass windows, ogival arches and columns, designed by Ernst Stern, masked the austere steel structure and suffused the entire hall in a magic twilight. The public was drawn into the medieval, mystic atmosphere, to which the music of Engelbert Humperdinck also contributed.

Similar attempts at a theater of the masses were made by the French director Firmin Gémier at the Cirque d'Hiver in Paris. There he produced, in 1919, *Oedipe, Roi de Thèbes,* an Oedipus drama full of religious symbolism by Saint Georges de Bouhélier. But the stage designer Emile Bertin drew on Roman rather than Greek models, furnishing the circus floor with an arena in the style of Orange. This production was followed in March 1920 by *La Grande pastorale,* a Christian play by Charles Hellem and Pol d'Estoc, produced by Gaston Baty.

But Reinhardt went further still. The public was to take part not only passively, but actively. And so he produced his famous, and notorious, *Danton* by Romain Rolland. This was at the Grosses Schauspielhaus in Berlin, in 1920. Seated among the audience, about 100 actors kept shouting interruptions during the revolutionary assembly, leaping up from their seats with wild gesticulations. The entire huge hall, transformed by Hans Poelzig into a monstrous vault of stalactites, became the Tribunal.

"And then entered Paul Wegener as Danton, tall, broad, massive; he stood under a bright light at the ramp of the railed-in tribune, which was pushed out in front of the stage into the stalls," reported Paul Fechter. He was one of the few who were willing to admire Reinhardt even at this critical crossroad in 1920. The conservative audience entered a veto. The "total theater," barely half a century later the familiar slogan of all experimenters, began in Germany with Max Reinhardt's imposing failure in the Grosses Schauspielhaus, Berlin.

In October 1920 he withdrew from the management of the Deutsches Theater (his old-established collaborator Felix Hollaender replaced him for two years) and went to Vienna. In the autumn and winter 1922–23 he staged a number of productions at the Wiener Redoutensaal and the Deutsches Volkstheater, and in 1924 took over the Theater in der Josefstadt. He opened it on April 1st with Goldoni's *Servant of Two Masters*—Reinhardt's declaration of love to the *Commedia dell'arte,* a declaration he never tired of repeating in many variants.

Reinhardt production at the Olympia, London, 1911: The Miracle, *by Karl Vollmöller, with music by Engelbert Humperdinck; stage arrangements and setting by Ernst Stern. Drawing by J. Duncan. (London, Victoria and Albert Museum.)*

Reinhardt's "Total theater" at the Grosses Schauspielhaus, Berlin, 1920: Danton, *by Romain Rolland, with Paul Wegener in the title role. Drawing by Ernst Stern.*

Reinhardt found the simplest form of stage as challenging as the most elaborate. Over and over again he reexamined and tested the range of his creative powers. He found it tempting to take untrodden paths, to cast his Circean spell over actors he did not know. In 1929 he welcomed the first participants of his seminar on acting and stage direction at the Schönbrunner Schlosstheater in Vienna, with these words: "It is not the world of make-believe that you are entering today, it is the world of being." Here in a nutshell is Reinhardt's own faith in the higher truth of the theater.

Max Reinhardt did not stick exclusively either to particular stylistic forms or to particular authors. He introduced Ludwig Thoma and Ludwig Anzengruber to Berlin. He made room for the pacifist expressionists at the Sunday matinees of the Deutsches Theater and in his periodical *Das junge Deutschland.* He loved Shakespeare, Hebbel, and Kleist, and he captured a glimmer of the Far Eastern theater with a production of *Sumurun* at the Berlin Kammerspiele in 1910, where the leading actor made his entry on a flower path that ran at the height of the heads of the audience, as in the Japanese *kabuki* theater.

On June 16, 1933, Max Reinhardt wrote what is perhaps the most moving letter ever written by a successful man of the theater upon turning his back on a totalitarian regime. The Nazis had expropriated his theaters, the management of which he had handed over in 1931 to Rudolf Beer and Karl Heinz Martin. Now Reinhardt formally acknowledged the situation:

> With these I lose not only the fruits of thirty-seven years of work but also the soil that I have cultivated all my life and on which I have grown up. I lose my home. . . . But since the fiat of the State has created a situation in which there is no longer any appropriate place for my work, and since it has therefore become impossible for me to pursue my life's work any further and to fulfill the obligations this would entail, I must regard it as a matter of course to leave all of this work to the State. . . . In addition to its paramount task of keeping its doors open to the living currents of the time and displaying the nation's drama, the Deutsches Theater has acquired an incomparable international reputation by numerous guest performances in all the great capitals of the world. . . . The satisfaction of having given of my best in contributing to this result, tempers the bitterness of my farewell.

Reinhardt, sent copies of this letter to several government offices in Berlin. None of them replied.

Dantons Tod, *by Georg Büchner, produced by Max Reinhardt at the Kammerspiele, Munich, 1929: V. Sokoloff as Robespierre. Drawing by Peter Trumm.*

The Festival Idea

The name of Max Reinhardt is associated not only with Berlin and Vienna, but also with Salzburg, the city of his early life and the city of the Festival. The idea of making a festival town of Salzburg came to him in 1903. It was a beautiful, intellectual, and gay city, and the combination of charming natural surroundings with splendid architecture in so conveniently central a location seemed to him ideal for an artistic Mecca. Under the banner of Mozart he meant to recover for the theater the "festive and holiday mood, the uniqueness," which "is the mark of all art, and which the theater of antiquity possessed."

Hugo von Hofmannsthal supported the idea. Reinhardt wrote pressing letters to arouse the cultural and economic interest of the Salzburg city fathers. At last, in the summer of 1920, it was all set up, and the first festival was arranged. On August 22, the call of *Everyman* was heard for the first time across the square in front of the Baroque cathedral façade, and the fortress of Hohensalzburg threw back the echo. Reinhardt had mobilized his biggest guns for Hofmannsthal's new version of the late medieval mystery play. Alexander Moissi played Everyman, Wilhelm Dieterle the Good Fellow, Heinrich George took the part of Mammon, Werner Krauss those of Death and the Devil, Hedwig Bleibtreu was Faith, Johanna Terwin was Sensual Love, and Helene Thimig, Reinhardt's wife, Good Works. Salzburg has guarded this first festival production like a legacy. Today, almost half a century later, it still is sacrosanct as one of the mainstays of the program—often changed in the cast, but faithfully preserved in style.

Two years after *Jedermann,* in 1922, Reinhardt produced *Das Salzburger Große Welttheater,* Hofmannsthal's Baroque religious play after Calderón. He staged it in a church, the Kollegienkirche. The setting that Reinhardt had to conjure up in an austere hall for Vollmöller's *Miracle,* the atmosphere of a sacred place, was all ready for him here. Reinhardt subordinated himself to the majestic architecture of Fischer von Erlach. He chose stylized canopies and glowing red cloth panels as the only additions to the cool white of the plinths, columns, and pilasters.

But the important thing in 1922 was that the tone was set for the future musical complexion of the Salzburg Festival. For the first time, four Mozart operas figured on the program, and each had four performances; they were *Don Giovanni, Così fan tutte, The Marriage of Figaro* and *The Abduction from the Seraglio.* (Salzburg had known music festivals with works by Mozart since 1877.) This was the beginning of a shift toward opera, which was reinforced by the construction of the festival playhouse and its enlargement in 1926 by Clemens Holzmeister.

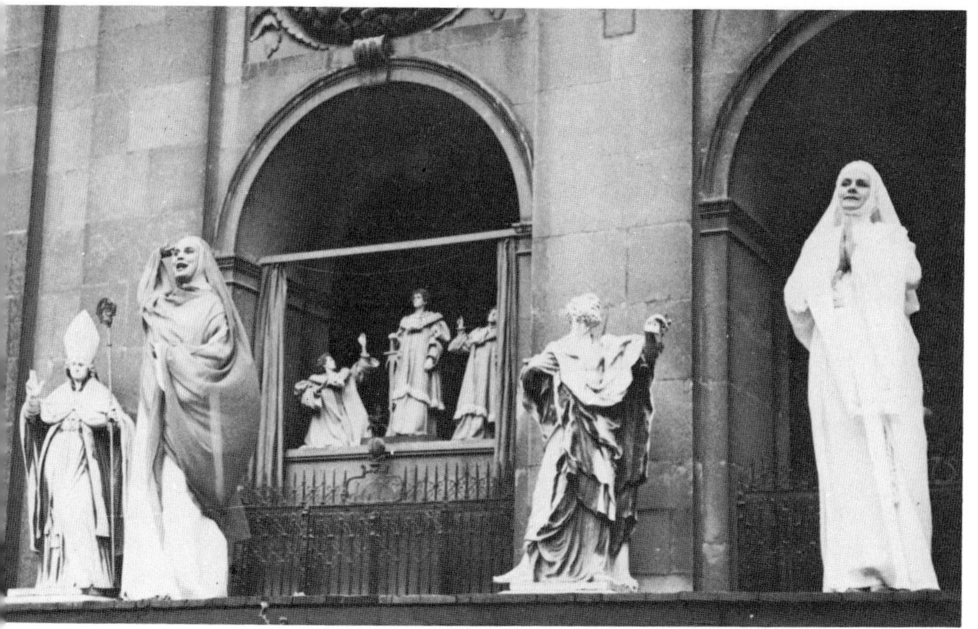

Jedermann, *by Hugo von Hofmannsthal, on the Salzburg Cathedral square, 1920. Reinhardt's production opened the Salzburg Festival, which he originated together with Hofmannsthal.*

Das Salzburger grosse Welttheater, *by Hugo von Hofmannsthal, first staged in Salzburg in 1922 at the Kollegienkirche, was repeated in 1925 at the Festspielhaus: scenery with Gothic canopy.*

Conductors included Richard Strauss, Arturo Toscanini, Bruno Walter, Clemens Krauss, and Wilhelm Furtwängler. The major roles were sung by stars from Vienna, Milan, and New York. The picturesque Felsenreitschule, the old riding school, accommodated opera and drama, oratorio and ballet. The old playhouse became too small for the crowd of visitors. Clemens Holzmeister designed a new, ultramodern building, deeply embedded in the rocks of the Mönchsberg. Its inauguration in 1960 also initiated the era of Karajan, which was rich in artistic achievements and administrative setbacks, and took a new turn in 1968 with the Easter Festival suggested, and largely financed, by Herbert von Karajan.

Together with Bayreuth, Munich, and Vienna, Salzburg forms the core of Europe's musical summer festival, surrounded by a host of the most diverse other festival localities. Their name is legion, and they attract artists of international renown. To mention but a few examples: there is the Holland Festival in Amsterdam; the Berlin Festwochen; the Maggio Musicale at Florence; the Musical at Bordeaux; the Festival de Musique at Aix-en-Provence; the Festival Gulbenkian de Musica in Portugal; the International Festival at Edinburgh; the Norwegian Festival at Bergen; the Finnish National Theater weeks in Helsinki—and the festivals at Athens, Epidaurus, Avignon, and Stratford-on-Avon, which are devoted predominantly to drama. In addition, there are all the summer performances in monastery ruins, cloisters, and open-air theaters, which are trying to hold their own on the margin of the great festival competition. Some have not much more to offer than the picturesque natural setting which Reinhardt originally sought, namely, to be outside the bustle of the metropolis. But however lavish or modest their efforts, they all have their justification and their merit, so long as their concern is with the theater and not with mere tourism.

To complete the picture, mention must be made of the local pageant plays, the grandly staged festival performances common especially in Switzerland, from the open-air *Tell* plays at Altdorf or Interlaken to the traditional vintners' feast at Vevey, where thousands take part in the procession and plays.

THE THEATER OF COMMITMENT

Soviet Russia: "October in the Theater" Movement

The October Revolution brought about a radical and lasting break with tradition in the Russian theater. In the years immediately following 1917, enormous pressure was brought to bear upon the theater to harness itself for political propaganda purposes. The theater was to celebrate the revolution and serve the dissemination of communist ideals. Mass rallies with speaking chorus and songs, with thundering tanks and guns were given a theatrical aspect—half popular festival, half pageant play. Specially trained *agitprop* ("agitation propaganda") cadres and experienced theater people took over the organization of the mass events directly sponsored by the central Party authorities in the capital cities—and also of the no less strictly controlled "improvised events" throughout the country. At this time, Meyerhold declared that the purpose of the theater was not "to present a finished work of art, but rather to make the spectator take part in the creation of drama."

"[On our stage], we must present the spirit of the people," Vakhtangov wrote in 1918, "in every event it is the crowd itself that acts. . . . It storms the obstacles and overcomes them. It triumphs. Buries its dead. Sings the world's song of freedom."

One of the most imposing mass entertainments of the period was "the Storming of the Winter Palace," staged in Petrograd on November 7, 1920, as a dramatic, theatrical celebration of the historical events of the Revolution on its third anniversary. Guns were fired, there were fanfares, and searchlights; a white and a red platform served as stages for the presentation of the crushed Czarists and the victorious Bolsheviks; there was shellfire, then the storming of the palace; a great, transparent red Soviet star was displayed—and the whole assemblage sang the *Internationale,* while fireworks concluded this vast nocturnal open-air spectacle. The event was directed by Nikolai Evreinov, who had at his disposal some 15,000 participants, consisting of Red Army men and a number of actors. The spectators are reported to have numbered around 100,000. "Theatricalization of life"—this is how Evreinov described these mass spectacles, for which the holidays of the Red calendar offered annually recurring opportunities.

The same motto governed the work of the three outstanding stage directors of the Revolution, who channeled the overflowing stream of the mass event into the more limited dimensions of the drama, that is, Meyerhold, Vakhtangov, and Tairov. All three came from the Moscow Art Theater, from Stanislavsky's tradition of middle-class humanism.

On the imperial stages of St. Petersburg, Meyerhold had begun soon after the turn of the century to develop an avant-garde style of his own, together with the actress Vera Kommisarzhevskaya. Instead of the sensitive attunement at which Stanislavsky aimed, Meyerhold established the reign of rationality. His direction of every movement, every gesture was the result of precise mathematical calculation; beyond that it acquired symbolic significance in the terms of his "biomechanics"—reminiscent of the East Asian theater, and of Brecht's "effects of alienation."

Meyerhold introduced his method in 1918, when he staged at Petrograd Vladimir Mayakovsky's *Mystery-Bouffe* and Sergei Tretyakov's *Earth Turning*. He used film projections, jazz and concertina, whipped up the pace with the noise of machines and engines and wheels revolving, used metal constructions as scenery, had his extras sprint to the stage through the stalls, climb up scaffolds, and slide down rope ladders. Meyerhold swept away the last vestiges of the bourgeois theater; he was concerned not with atmosphere, but with propagandistic agitation.

As a stage repeat of the Revolution he concluded Tretyakov's war play *Earth Turning* with a scene in which Red Army soldiers storm the stage, the auditorium and the foyer, plant red flags and intone the *Internationale*. In Tretyakov's *Roar China*, Meyerhold underscored the ideological conflict between coolies and colonists by having the Europeans wear masks and behave in operetta fashion, in provocative contrast to the realism of the coolies' poverty. For effects of pure pantomime, acrobatics, or clowning, Meyerhold dressed his actors in uniform overalls, the plain working clothes being the consistent counterpart to the illusionless workers' stage. Nothing was to distract attention, nothing to embellish the "biomechanic" action in the austere setting of turntables, traps, hoists, and riggings.

Meyerhold's anti-illusionism knew no limits. Yuri Elagin, eyewitness of the revolution in the Russian theater, reported in his book *Taming of the Arts* (1951) that he never subsequently saw on the stages of Europe and America any scenic trick that Meyerhold had not already used. This, he added, applied not only to the years after 1917, but also to Meyerhold's prior experiments with Maeterlinck's "mystic" theater, to stylistic contacts with the Münchner Künstlentheater with Max Reinhardt in Berlin, with the marionette and puppet play (whose internationally famous Russian master Sergei Obratsov is a man of abundant wit and feeling) and, above all, with the *Commedia dell'arte*, the techniques of which Meyerhold had chosen in 1912–13 as subject matter for one of the teaching studios.

Max Reinhardt's turbulent 1920 production of *Danton* at the Grosses Schauspielhaus in Berlin looks much less isolated and unique when seen in the context of the Russian revolutionary theater. There is a parallel both in theme and in style. Reinhardt's choice of a subject from the French Revolution is explained by the political situation. That he chose for his mass theater not Büchner's *Dantons Tod* but *Danton* by Romain Rolland, who was an advocate of organized popular spectacles, confirms how close Reinhardt was to Meyerhold. The line could be traced further through Piscator's Berlin productions during the twenties to points beyond, for instance the 1937 Orson Welles production of *Julius Caesar* at the Mercury Theater on Broadway. Shakespeare's Romans

Backdrop for V. Meyerhold's production of Earth Turning, *by Sergei Tretyakov, Leningrad, 1918.*

Scenery with spiral staircase for V. Meyerhold's production of the comedy The Forest, *by Alexander Ostrovsky, Moscow, 1924. Stage model by Feodorov.*

appeared in modern, ready-made clothes. Orson Welles played Brutus. The stage was without decoration. In the freely adapted text, the New York critic Burns Mantle detected something reminiscent of a conspiracy against a dictator of the Mussolini type.

In the thirties, Meyerhold had a "relapse into bourgeois imitations." While the ideas of his agitatorial propaganda theater were avidly taken up wherever there was ferment, he himself now paid his respects to the theater of illusion. He produced *La Dame aux Camélias* by Dumas *fils* in a subtle and intimate setting. Marguerite Gauthier, played by Zinaida Raikh, loved and suffered among genuine mahogany furniture, valuable Sèvres china, and mournful velvet curtains. Meyerhold explained that beautiful old things radiate an ambiance, which he hoped would ennoble the sensitivity of the actors. He was back in the realm of Stanislavsky, with primary emphasis on a differentiated dynamic style.

Improvisation and perfection were the two poles between which moved the work of another Russian stage director of that time, Evgeni Vakhtangov. As a member and, from 1916, head of the Moscow Arts Theater's First Studio, he had taken part in certain experiments suggested by Maxim Gorky, namely, to revive the notion of the *Commedia dell'arte* that the actors have a creative function and are to "shape the plays" as they go along. In 1918 Vakhtangov organized a group temporarily known as the Popular Art Theater, and there found himself caught up in Constructivism and Meyerhold's mania for improvisation. But his most successful, and most personal, production was that of Carlo Gozzi's *Princess Turandot,* in 1922 at the Moscow Art Theater's Third Studio, which soon afterward was renamed Vakhtangov Theater. Vakhtangov, already under the shadow of death, once more summoned to the stage all the magic of fairyland, the charm and droll grace of marionettes. The actors entered the stage in evening dress, and with the help of a few colored draperies transformed themselves into a charming, improvised chinoiserie. Quickened by Sisov's music and dominated by young Boris Shchukin's Tartaglia, the fable, in a half dreamlike, half anti-illusionist conception, seemed to have the quality of a musical box. Any actors with nothing to do for the moment mingled with the public in the stalls, commented on the performance with improvised jokes, and put into effect the principle Vakhtangov had in mind: "Remind the spectators once more at the climax of the dramatic action that it is a play and not reality, that it should not be taken too seriously, for the theater is not life."

Tairov, the third of the great stage directors of the revolutionary theater, developed a rigorously rationalized *l'art pour l'art.* He was a formally strict aesthete, whom even the storm of the revolution could

Stage model for Vakhtangov's 1922 production of Gozzi's Princess Turandot *at the Moscow Art Theater's Third Studio, which shortly afterward was renamed Vakhtangov Theater. Design by Vakhtangov and Nivinsky.*

Stage model for A. Y. Tairov's 1924 production of The Hairy Ape, *by Eugene O'Neill, at the Moscow Kamerny Theater, founded by Tairov in 1914 as an experimental theater.*

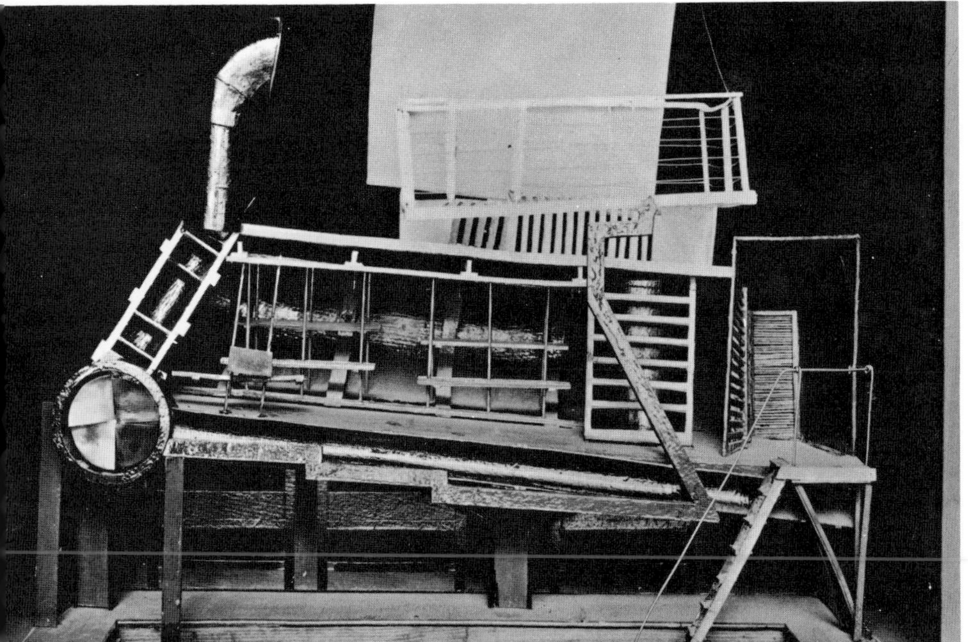

not carry away beyond the bounds of the theater. Tairov believed that theater ceases when it is overwhelmed by reality.

As an example, Tairov adduced the historical occasion when the Brussels performance of Auber's opera *La Muette de Portici* in 1830 had given the signal for the Belgian rebellion. "Here the theater had played the fine and noble part of the torch that kindled the flames of the revolution, but the performance came to an end. The heartbeat of common purpose, which had awakened in the theater, fired the revolution but extinguished the theatrical action."

The consequence of this insight meant for Tairov "theatricalization of the theater." He expected an actor to master all means of expression equally well. At the Moscow Kamerny Theater, an experimental playhouse run by Tairov from 1914 on, the company had to be able to act, sing, and dance, handle solemn liturgical and eccentric variété situations, display soul and fireworks, brutal greed, and enigmatical fantasy. This concept is behind the title of Tairov's book, *The Theater Unchained,* which became the label for the "October" theater.

Tairov was decidedly a literary stage director. He opened the Moscow Kamerny Theater with Kalidasa's *Shakuntala.* Clearly, he was as fascinated by the old Indian drama as was Lugné-Poë in Paris, who got Toulouse-Lautrec to design the scenery for his 1895 production of *Le Chariot de terre cuite.* Tairov improved the *Commedia dell'arte* with Goldoni plays, and for his first postrevolutionary production chose a fantastic harlequinade after E. T. A. Hoffmann's *Prinzessin Brambilla.* He played Claudel, and discovered in O'Neill's early dramas not only social criticism but the psychological confusion of the modern approach to life, which gave him an opportunity to try out the concept and effect of his *Emotionsgeste.*

In contrast to the "proletarian" theater of that time, Tairov's Kamerny Theater was of an "academic" type. So were, as historical institutions, the Bolshoi Opera, the Maly Theater, the Korsch Theater that had been built by the art patron Bakhrushin, and Stanislavsky's Moscow Art Theater. Prominent on the opposite side was the "prolet cult theater" of Sergei Eisenstein, with its eccentric, acrobatic style of an "emotionally saturated" theater: "Gesture is intensified into gymnastics, fury is expressed by a somersault, excitement by a *salto mortale.*" Eisenstein admitted that these tendencies, applied directly and literally, did not logically find their way into drama, but "became known through buffoonery, eccentricity, and circus turns." They linked up with the slogans of Meyerhold and Tairov: from emotion to the machine, from overexcitement to the trick, from the stage to the circus ring. Eisenstein later broke loose and went his own ways. In the motion picture he found a medium from whose formal and visual dynamics he

Pantomime espagnole. *Stage construction by Alexandra Exter for Tairov's Kamerny Theater in Moscow, 1926.*

wrested such masterpieces as his *Potemkin* in 1925. By means of effective cuts and montages Eisenstein achieved in his films a heightening of mass scenes and of detail, and succeeded in going beyond accustomed dimensions that could never have been achieved on the stage.

Piscator and the Political Theater

The Russian Revolution attempted to assert a new principle that would unite all peoples. Many European workers and intellectuals were intoxicated with the ideal of a classless and stateless society. "Russia is the rock in the surge of world revolution," Erwin Piscator wrote in 1919 in his manifesto addressed to the workers of Berlin and calling for the creation of a "Proletarian Theater." It was in Berlin on the river Spree, that the squalls from Moscow blew most violently. Piscator harnessed them for a theater of propagandistic agitation. The aim of his enterprise was not to produce art, but effective propaganda, to win over the politically still wavering and indifferent masses. The halls and premises used for meetings in Berlin's working-class district were his field of action. The masses were to be tackled where they lived, as in Russia by the theatrical *agitprop* cadres. Shabby stages, primitive decorations, tobacco smoke and beer fumes were overcome by the impetus of the purpose.

Piscator's "proletarian theater" was an instrument of the class struggle. He appealed to the spectators with political, economic, and social argumentation. His purpose was pedagogical, as Brecht's was to be later. In Piscator's case this meant successful propaganda.

For the Parliamentary elections in 1924 Piscator, on Party orders, produced the *Revue Roter Rummel* with texts by himself and his future collaborator Gasbarra. "Much of it was put together crudely, the text was quite unpretentious, but it was just that which made room for topical insertions right to the end," Piscator recalled in his book *Das politische Theater* (1929); "and we indiscriminately used every possible means: music, songs, acrobatics, quickly sketched cartoons, sport, projected images, film, statistics, acted scenes, speeches."

Piscator's technique, unburdened by structural considerations, of hammering in the constantly repeated political leitmotiv with a barrage of examples, was known as "direct action," a word much in vogue at the time. The provocative break with the middle-class dramatic form had begun earlier in Berlin with the Dadaist performances and their hullabaloo described by Piscator as *Klamauk* ("ear-splitting noise").

In France, at the same time, Antonin Artaud proclaimed a theory of theater as "action" pure and simple—no longer illustration of a literary text, but "made up on the stage." Artaud's concept of the "theater of cruelty" has been much misunderstood; it really meant something quite different, namely the unrestrained use of all theatrical means, giving over the stage to an eruptive vitality that turns the scenic action into a contagious and at the same time a curative focus of unrest. The effects with which Artaud made his points were the same as Piscator's.

Alfred Kerr, the devil's advocate among Germany's drama critics, wrote as early as 1910: "In the future, many a drama will be no more than a pretense at drama (in the old sense) . . . but in fact a newspaper parceled out in stage roles."

Not only the theater of Piscator and the Russian Revolution took this direction. Around 1935, the so-called Living Newspaper, a theater form of topical stage reporting, developed in the United States. In the 1960s its first cousin, the documentary play, made an internationally recognized, if controversial, place for itself.

In 1925, Piscator ran into trouble with the authorities because of his documentary mass drama *Trotz alledem*. The title was taken from a remark made by Karl Liebknecht after the suppression of the Spartakus rebellion. John Heartfield took care of the scenic montage of printed speeches, articles, newspaper clippings, manifestos, leaflets, photographs and films, printed dialogues between historical personages, and arranged scenery. The performance took place in Berlin's Grosses Schauspielhaus, where Max Reinhardt had produced his spectacular *Danton* in 1920 and lost so much sympathy among a large section of the conventional theater audience. Piscator noted with satisfaction that Reinhardt's activation of the participating masses had not gone beyond the "good idea" to motivate it. After the second performance of *Trotz alledem* the censorship intervened. When, in 1926, Piscator used Schiller's *Die Räuber* as a vehicle for political agitation and had Paul Bildt as Spiegelberg wear a Trotsky mask, there was an uproar.

An even more tumultuous uproar followed Piscator's production, a year later, of Ehm Welk's *Gewitter über Gotland* for the Volksbühne. Notwithstanding his early misgivings, Piscator had taken on the direction of the Berliner Volksbühne in 1924. He took advantage of the opportunity to produce revolutionary, political theater with a first-class company.

The subject of Ehm Welk's *Gewitter über Gotland* is the fight of the pirate Klaus Störtebeker against the Hanseatic League, which ended in 1401 with Störtebeker's execution. Piscator gave it a topical twist, placed the political accent on the Hanseatic Asmus, who wore a Lenin mask, and thus glorified the first leader of the Soviet Union, who had died in 1924. He interpreted the play as "the revolt of the sentimental revolutionary Störtebeker, who would probably be a National-socialist today, against Asmus, the sober man of action, the typical rational revolutionary best exemplified by Lenin."

Inevitably, there was an outcry. Neither Heinrich George as Störtebeker nor Alexander Granach as Asmus, nor the film material, contributed by Curt Oertel to establish the association with Lenin, could justify the massive violation of the historical material. Ehm Welk's own objection had been of no avail. Resigned, he sided with the critics who declared: "a grandiose production, a gigantic success of stage direction against the play."

Piscator and the Volksbühne parted company. Piscator had plans for setting up an agitatorial stage of his own and in his unique, grand, impressionistic style. The actress Tilla Durieux found him financial backers. Walter Gropius, head of the Bauhaus in Dessau, was enthusiastic about the idea. He designed for Piscator an ultramodern "total theater," a boldly conceived all-purpose playhouse with swiveling parquet and adaptable to almost any scenic requirement. It could be used as an amphitheater, as an arena with a central stage, or else with peripheral acting and entry ways circling the auditorium. The model Gropius made was exhibited in Paris in 1930 and was much admired, but never carried out. It remained a glorious project, a pipe dream like Meyerhold's similarly extravagant plans for an avant-garde total theater in Moscow.

Piscator rented the Theater am Nollendorfplatz in Berlin and opened it on September 3, 1927, with Ernst Toller's antibourgeois play *Hoppla, wir leben* in a highly technicalized production, in which Piscator assigned to the film part a pronounced didactic function. Toller was one of the late Expressionist dramatists whose antiwar plays combine accusation with radical socialist sympathies. Twenty years later, Wolfgang Borchert wrote a play similar in style and accusation, his *Draussen vor der Tür,* which may be regarded as the first important topical drama presented in Germany after the Second World War. It was the frenzied, urgent outcry of the deceived, uprooted war generation returning to ruins. Piscator gathered up the last offshoots of the Expressionist drama, which he had violently opposed in 1920, and tried to charge them with political high tension.

From Piscator's half-failures and failures there arose in 1927 his undisputed masterpiece, the production of the epic satire *Die Abenteuer des braven Soldaten Schwejk.* Bert Brecht, Felix Gasbarra, Leo Lania, and Piscator himself had adapted the novel by the Prague writer Jaroslav Hašek for the stage—an undertaking that had its problems, given the purely epic nature of the work. Its ingredients—a passive hero, continual change of scene, and passages of commentary as vehicles of the satirical content—are not suitable for a drama in the conventional sense, but rather for "epic" theater.

Piscator hit upon a brilliant device for keeping the action moving and welding as many episodes as possible together in seamless continuity: the conveyor belt. Modern assembly-line processes of manufacture

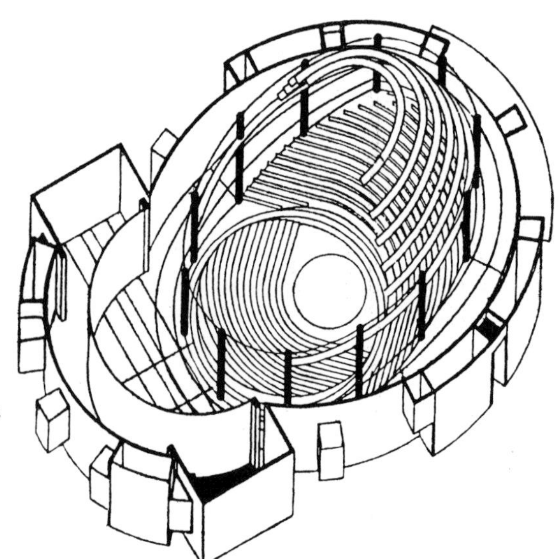

Totaltheater. *Design by Walter Gropius for Erwin Piscator, 1927.*

Piscator stage in Berlin, 1927: transparent multi-story construction for Hoppla, wir leben, *by Ernst Toller, with central screen for the combination of stage and film. (Montage with silhouette of Piscator, by Sasha Stone.)*

Marionette scenes by George Grosz for the "conveyor belt" in Piscator's production of Die Abenteuer des braven Soldaten Schwejk, *after the novel by Jaroslav Hašek, Berlin, 1927.*

gave him the idea; he used two conveyor belts, drawn across the stage from left and right in opposite directions. Mounted upon them were flat sections showing Schwejk's environment: "the petrified types of political and social life in old Austria," a grotesquely satirized world in which Schwejk finds himself defenseless, the "only human being." Piscator's original intention had even been to give only the title role to an actor and to contrast him with an exclusively mechanical apparatus.

The painter George Grosz designed the trick sets and marionettes, giving both the stage properties and the figures a super-caricature, clownlike comic function. (His designs ended up on the public prosecutor's desk and landed him in a trial for blasphemy.) For the Prague street scenes Piscator used as background a film shot on the spot. For the march to Budějovice he had drawings of rows of trees copied on nature stills drawn across the stage as an optical representation of the endless road. The great actor Max Pallenberg played Schwejk. He gave him his human substance and, beyond that, entirely according to Piscator's intentions, "something reminiscent of the variety show and Charlie Chaplin." Pallenberg came from Max Reinhardt's stable, and Piscator boasted proudly of the immense inner effort he had induced Pallenberg to make in order "to do justice to this new, mathematical kind of acting."

Piscator repeatedly discussed the question of how to define his specific style. His purpose, he explained, was utmost intensification of effect by the use of extra-theatrical means. Crucial to the degree of effect was that, given the correct choice of subject, it should be identical with the political effect. The desired propaganda effect could not be achieved in the absence of a sufficiently strong play, nor with a technical setting conveying merely an aesthetic object lesson. This criterion is still controversial now, forty years later.

Kerr's remark about the "newspaper parceled out in stage roles," dating from 1910, retains its validity in the rhythm of crisis generations. It proved true in the theater of the early thirties in the United States, when the economic temperature chart of the New Deal was climbing to its peak. The dramatist Elmer Rice was the driving power behind the Federal Theatre Project, the only government-subsidized stage, which took on the double task of giving employment to several hundred out-of-work actors and of taking issue with the economic problems of the time. Elmer Rice used the current stage documentation of the "Living Newspaper" for social and sociological criticism. *Power* was the name of one of the documentary dramatizations by which he put political issues on the stage. In this case sparks were struck from questions of the development and ownership of electric power. Another edition dealt with the problem of abolishing slums; it was called *One-Third of a Nation*, with reference to that third of the American people which Roosevelt had said was ill-housed. Epic, episodic, and pedagogic passages, speaking choirs, commentaries, lyrics and musical inserts were the motive elements of the "Living Newspaper." Washington soon afterward stopped the government subsidies to this controversial venture and so it came to an end.

The relationship between theater and politics has been tense for two and a half thousand years. Aristophanes campaigned from the stage against the demagogues and the advocates of the Peloponnesian War; he did it in the sovereign art form of Attic comedy, which remains fascinating as an original theatrical form even when the polemic allusions are not understood. But when the sole purpose is political attack, there is no need of the stage.

Artaud talked of the "impotence of the word," as compared with the vitality of direct action, of the ritual and rhythmic *coup de théâtre*. He spoke of the strength of the play whose action is spatially laid out toward the four cardinal points, is split up by paroxysms and then gathered together by light, and again fanned out. He regarded the scream as the primary element of direct action, a scream uttered at the far end of the space of the theater hall and transmitted from mouth to mouth in a wild *accelerando*. The group productions of The Living Theatre as well as the work of the Polish stage director Jerzy Grotowski owe much to Artaud's ritual of movement and gesture. His total theater of "direct action" contributed to the shattering of form in the political theater of the second half of this century.

The stage director's motto for today's political theater is: action. To the extent that the underlying text is regarded as binding at all, it is merely raw material. It can be replaced by collages of film, billposters, newspaper reports, signals, or transparencies—by the "use of extra-theatrical means," as Piscator said.

The documentary play has its place in a formally restrained, intermediate zone, ranging, say, from Herman Wouk's *The Caine Mutiny Court Martial* (based on his novel), to Rolf Hochhuth's *Der Stellvertreter* ("The Deputy"), and Heinar Kipphardt's *In der Sache J. Robert Oppenheimer* ("In the Matter of J. Robert Oppenheimer") to Peter Weiss's *Die Ermittlung* ("The Investigation"). Weiss's play is an "oratorio"-like, stark documentary about the inferno of the Nazi holocaust. He noted that it contains "nothing but facts as they emerged in the court proceedings."

From factual documentation the political theater of the sixties moved on to committed information, as in *Vietnam Report* by Peter Weiss, *MacBird* by Barbara Garson, Aimé Césaire's play about Patrice Lumumba *Une Saison au Congo,* Michael Hatry's *Notstandsübung,* or the Bremen revue collages of Wilfried Minks. Elagin's remark about

Meyerhold—that no one in the European or the American theater could think up a stage trick that Meyerhold had not already used—could also be applied to Piscator for today's theater still draws on his store of "extratheatrical means."

Brecht and the Epic Theater

The stage took on the rhythm of our time, the "tempo" of the twentieth century. While the agitatorial refashioning of the play was still going on, the new drama found an author in Bertolt Brecht. Brecht, in his collaboration with Piscator, came to realize that the revolutionary theater depended not only upon the play, but also on stage direction. But "activating" direction remained for Brecht a provisional solution, valid only so long as there was no genuine radical reshaping of the theater. He accepted neither the naturalistic "milieu as destiny" nor the expressionist "hail Man!" emotionalism, and he had his reservations about purely agitatorial direction. He did not wish to arouse emotions, but to appeal to the critical intelligence of the spectator. His theater was to convey knowledge, not experiences.

The drama of the scientific age, as Brecht saw it, looks at man as part of the calculable mechanism that keeps history moving, treats man as an instrument of executive organs that manipulate him at their discretion. Enter the packer Galy Gay, a harmless man who goes out one morning to buy some fish, falls into the hands of soldiers on the way and is transformed into a "human fighting machine." Galy Gay, the recast hero of Brecht's *Mann ist Mann,* became the textbook example of the new didactic theater.

Peter Lorre played the part in 1931 at the Berlin Staatstheater (while at the same time working under Fritz Lang on the crime thriller *M*). He made of the sequence of separate incidents the "inventory of arguments" Brecht had at heart. Lorre, he said, had convincingly achieved the "most objective possible exhibition of a contradictory inner process as a whole." The scene, in this case India, is not crucial to the action. Brecht is out to generalize an individual case. The "exhibition" character of his theater is something on which Brecht kept harping. It refers to the specific dramaturgical form, the principle of epic theater. Its external characteristics are inserted commentaries on the action spoken by a narrator, "chapter" headings on large boards, masks, and projected images.

The conceptual and didactic origin of the epic theater go back to the Piscator circle. Lion Feuchtwanger, who in 1924 collaborated with Brecht on a rationalized, topically updated version of Marlowe's *Edward the Second,* attributes the invention of the epic principle to Brecht. Alfred Kerr claimed to have defined it as early as 1910, when he spoke of the drama of the future as a "newspaper parceled out in stage roles." Brecht himself accepted the attribution of primacy with the self-assurance of the creative writer receptive to the signs of his time, and he processed them in the style of his time. Influences of American behaviorist psychology and the connection it establishes between the production of goods and mass consumption have left their mark on his plays, just as have the theories of the Russian *agitprop* stage, the "productive" theater based on agitatorial and organizational functions.

But Brecht looked further afield for the roots of his stylistic principles. "As to its style," he wrote in the early thirties, "the epic theater is nothing particularly new. In its use of 'exhibition character,' and its stress on the artistic it is akin to the age-old Asian theater. Such didactic tendencies are evident in the medieval mystery plays, as well as in the classical Spanish drama and the Jesuit theater."

It was from his study of the Chinese style of acting that Brecht derived the essential features of direction and production in his epic theater: the effect of alienation. It is grounded in a complete neutralization of the traditional means of theatrical representation. To keep distance is the first commandment, both for the actor and for the audience. No "hypnotic fields" must be allowed to form between the stage and the auditorium. The actor is not to arouse emotions in the spectator, but to awaken his critical faculty. "Not at any moment will he [the actor] allow himself to be completely absorbed by the character," Brecht wrote in 1948 in *Kleines Organon für das Theater.* The Aristotelian tradition is as untenable as Schiller's idea of the stage as a moral institution, where every individual "enjoys the delight of all" and "his heart has room for only one emotion, to be a human being." Brecht throws them both on the scrap heap.

Brecht's anarchist play about soldiers coming home from the front, *Trommeln in der Nacht* ("Drums in the Night"), was staged by Otto Falckenberg in 1922 first at the Munich Kammerspiele and soon afterward in Berlin. The author wanted posters to be hung in the auditorium with such aphorisms as "Inside his own skin every man is the best man," or the much-quoted "Don't make such romantic goggle-eyes." They culminated in the categorical statement: "The theater is not a dispensary of substitutes for unlived experiences."

In his notes for the opera *Aufstieg und Fall der Stadt Mahagonny* Brecht for the first time drew up the antithetical schedule of the "dramatic" and "epic" forms of the theater. The table has become famous since then, and, with slight modifications, was used again by Brecht in *Vergnügungstheater oder Lehrtheater?* (1936). It is as follows.

Stage design by Otto Reigbert for Trommeln in der Nacht, *by Bertolt Brecht, first produced by Otto Falckenberg at the Kammerspiele, Munich, September 30, 1922.*

Dramatic Theater	*Epic Theater*
The stage impersonates an event	it narrates it
involves the spectator in an action and	makes him an observer, but
uses up his activity	awakens his activity
enables him to feel emotions	forces him to make decisions
conveys to him experiences	conveys to him knowledge
the spectator is immersed in an action	he is confronted with it
the method is suggestion	the method is argument
emotions are preserved as such	carried to the point of knowledge
man is assumed as known	man is the subject of investigation
man is unalterable	man is alterable and alters
suspense directed to the end	suspense directed to the course
one scene leads to another	each scene for itself
events move in a linear course	in curves
natura non facit saltus	facit saltus
the world as it is	the world as it becomes
what man should do	what man must do
his instincts	his motives
thought determines existence	social existence determines thought

For rehearsal work, Brecht recommended three aids: to transpose the actor's lines into the third person; to transpose it into the past; and to include, in the reading of the lines, the stage directions.

Every action that is represented automatically takes on the character of a model. Thus *Dickicht der Städte* ("In the Jungle of Cities" —written in 1924) demonstrates "the struggle as such," exemplified in the dogged trial of strength between two men against the background of the great city of Chicago. Brecht announces his didactic intent in the very introductory sentences: "Don't worry your head about the motives of this struggle, but share the human effort, judge the fighting form of the opponents without bias, and direct your interest to the finish."

This note to the spectators anticipates the whole of Brecht, the pedagogic function and artistic methodology of his theater, his forgoing psychology in favor of examples, his appeal to critical objectivity. It is a logical consequence of his aims that he preferably demonstrates them in negative heroes, such as can be found in the early *Dickicht* (1924), through his work of the thirties, and to his great late works. *Mutter Courage und ihre Kinder*—first performed in 1941 under Leopold Lindtberg at Zürich, that courageous refuge of the German-language theater in exile—is not meant to arouse pity, but to promote knowledge and condemnation of war profiteering. When Mother Courage dips into her pocket in order to give away her last coins for the funeral of her last child, she quickly puts some of them back, for the war goes on and:

For war's just business is the end,
Instead of cheese there's lead to trade.
If costs are more than you can spend,
You just won't make the V-Day grade.

Therese Giehse in Zurich and Munich, and Brecht's wife, Helene Weigel, at the Berlin Theater am Schiffbauerdamm, have made Mother Courage an unforgettable character, unmatched in her aggressive, topical urgency. The model performance of the Berliner Ensemble with Helene Weigel has been filmed and is thus available as a record.

Critical objectivity is also the intent of *Leben des Galilei,* of *Herr Puntila und sein Knecht Matti,* and of the 1943 Schwejk play. Transposed from Hašek's original Prague milieu into a total dictatorship at war, the hero of *Schweyk im Zweiten Weltkrieg* is one of those that march to Stalingrad, who must take their skin to the battlefield and so furnish the hide for the drum. Brecht called him a counterpart to Mother Courage and was much sharper on this occasion than in Piscator's 1927 montage production of the original Hašek play,*The Good Soldier Schweik.* Brecht's play was first performed, with songs set to music by Hanns Eisler, in Warsaw in 1957, a year after Brecht's death.

Songs played an important part in Brecht's plays from the outset. They interrupt the action, mark a pause that sometimes is announced by a gong. In *Die Dreigroschenoper* ("Threepenny Opera") and in *Aufstieg und Fall der Stadt Mahagonny* ("Mahagonny") they add up to "epicurean" music theater, though Brecht meant it to be "antiepicurean." The 200-year-old *Beggar's Opera,* with a brand-new didactic function, made a brilliant comeback in 1928 as *Dreigroschenoper.* At the Theater am Schiffbauerdamm in Berlin Lotte Lenya, Erich Ponto, and Roma Bahn ensured a great success for Bertolt Brecht and his composer Kurt Weill. But it was a triumph contrary to Brecht's intentions. The raised forefinger was swept aside by the audience's delight in the romanticism they saw in gangster and brothel life. It was all great fun, the songs were a hit, but the challenge fell flat. Brecht's didactic purpose had been to parody the middle-class, romantic opera with its own means, and to turn it from an entertainment into an information medium. This purpose failed. Brecht the artist had defeated Brecht the theoretician.

The scandal and controversy that failed to materialize on this occasion came two years later, with Leipzig premiere of *Aufstieg und Fall*

Helene Weigel as Mother Courage in the 1949 production at the Theater am Schiffbauerdamm, Berlin.

Bertolt Brecht—with raised forefinger—directs his Mutter Courage *at the Kammerspiele, Munich, 1950. Scenery by Teo Otto.*

Charles Laughton in the author's production of Brecht's The Life of Galilei *at the Coronet Theater, Los Angeles, 1947.*

Bert Brecht's Dreigroschenoper *at the Kammerspiele, Munich, 1929. Director: Hans Schweikart, with Kurt Horwitz as Macheath, Therese Giehse as Mrs. Peachum, Maria Bard as Polly, and Berta Drews as Jenny. Scenery by Caspar Neher.*

der Stadt Mahagonny. Brecht's deliberate aggressiveness broke through the opera-entertainment packaging. The cynical denouncement of capitalist society made its point. Forty years later, when Brecht's works had become classics of the modern theater—with "the classics' penetrating lack of effect," as Max Frisch quipped—directors were very fond of going back to Brecht's "epicurean" operas, e.g., Günther Rennert's Stuttgart production of *Mahagonny* in 1967, with Anja Silja, Martha Mödl, and Gerhard Stolze.

With brilliant dialectic Brecht denied in the end that he meant to "emigrate from the realm of pleasantness." He laconically conceded that the didactic character of his epic theater need not necessarily exclude the bourgeois categories of beauty and enjoyment. He made peace between the estranged sisters "theater" and "entertainment," for "our theater should awaken pleasure in knowledge, motivate fun in the recognition of the changes that take place in reality."

Brecht, above all, did not decisively change the social function of the theater so much as the theater and the drama themselves. His purpose of denouncing and abolishing the economic and social contradictions of bourgeois society did, after all, presuppose convention as the indispensable opponent who was to be challenged—and the spectator had to be transformed from an entertained onlooker into a speculative partner. Accordingly, "our plays are not final, or let us say frankly, they are unfinished," the reason being that "whole conceptual complexes necessary for their understanding are still quite hazy and must be unfinished until the whole substructure of these ideologies is forcibly altered."

Brecht's system of the open form, that is, an optionally extendable future, defies ideological dogmatism. He intends his dramatized incidents to be understood as exhibited situations of a "societal accident," as incidents that can be prolonged at will. "We feel let down, and with dismay we stare as the curtain falls, and our questions are left hanging in the air," as he says in the epilogue to the parable play *Der gute Mensch von Sezuan* ("The Good Woman of Setzuan").

Brecht's plays demonstrate no solutions, they unmask facts. The lesson is presented in multiple ironic refractions and leads through stretches of rich and rough poetry. Brecht often resorts to parable, which is one method of breaking out of illusion—a method Max Frisch and Friedrich Dürrenmatt also pursued, each in his own way.

Techniques of the Epic Theater: The Stage on the Stage

The dramaturgical disruption of the stage illusion, the play within the play, the insertion of direct address to the public, the recital of critical or didactic statements or songs—all these are devices the theater had known and used for thousands of years, from the *parabasis* of old Attic comedy to the Solomon song in *Die Dreigroschenoper*. In romantic irony the drama had made the best of the gap between the infinite and the finite, and had used the play within the play for topical polemics. "If I am to say what I really believe, I regard the whole thing as a trick to spread opinions and insinuations among the people. You'll see whether I'm right or not. A revolutionary play, to the extent that I understand it, with horrible monarchs and ministers. . . ." These lines occur, not in a twentieth-century political play, but in 1797, in a parodistic attack on the Berlin Enlightenment, *Der gestiefelte Kater* ["Puss in Boots"], a play by Ludwig Tieck.

The *Commedia dell'arte* characters and the mask play function as timeless, anti-illusionist forces, whether in their own name, as in the famous Goldoni and Gozzi productions of Max Reinhardt, Evgeni Vakhtangov, or Giorgio Strehler, or as interchangeable, depersonalized and neutralized clownlike figures, as in Samuel Beckett's nihilistic *Waiting for Godot* (1954).

On the threshold of the modern, anti-illusionist theater we find Luigi Pirandello. As early as 1918, his parable play *Così è (se vi pare)* ("Right You Are If You Think You Are") raised the ultimately insoluble question of illusion versus reality. The problem of split identity led him through the drama *Enrico IV* to the best-known and most successful of his works, *Sei personaggi in cerca d'autore* ("Six Characters in Search of an Author"). The six characters are members of a come-down, middle-class family—conceived as dramatic raw material and not fully elaborated—who intrude upon the stage during a rehearsal. They act out their own destiny for the theater people, and the rehearsing cast now try in their turn to reproduce "real life." Two, three, and even four levels of consciousness overlap. The conflict between reality and illusion, between life and form, is thrown wide open. When the director at the end sends away the spectators, in order to go on rehearsing behind the curtain "the play that is yet to be made," the question of human "truth" remains as unanswered as Brecht's question regarding the future revision of social relationships.

Pirandello's formal device of setting his action in the frame of a stage rehearsal has been taken over by many playwrights. The American dramatist Maxwell Anderson borrowed it for *Joan of Lorraine*. Into the doubts and misgivings of the leading lady at rehearsal he fades in the human problems of the historical Joan of Arc together with those of her modern interpreter, and finds timeless, recurring parallels in past and present.

Another example is furnished by Günter Grass in his "German tragedy" of June 17, 1953, *Die Plebejer proben den Aufstand.* ("The

Plebeians Rehearse the Uprising"). Grass works on three levels. On the stage in the theater a rehearsal of Shakespeare's *Coriolanus* is going on; the director is the "Chief," meaning Bertolt Brecht who wrote an adaptation of *Coriolanus*; outside in the street, is the workers' uprising, and some of the demonstrators break in upon the rehearsal. The "Chief" distributes the rebels among his cast, tries to turn their emotions into theater, and chooses to regard reality as raw material for his production.

Peter Weiss used a kindred device in *Die Verfolgung und Ermordung Jean Paul Marats, dargestellt durch die Schauspielgruppe des Hospizes zu Charenton unter Anleitung des Herrn de Sade,* where the very title warns us of the two levels of a play, culminating in the hysterical riot of lunatics stripped of all inhibitions.

To put a stage on the stage offers an opportunity for presenting the familiar as the strange, placing it at a distance in Brecht's meaning, giving it an ironic refraction, interpreting it "epically" with the help of the director, announcer, narrator, or chorus. The two outstanding twentieth-century dramatists who go along with Brecht's epic principle are Thornton Wilder and Paul Claudel, both diametrically opposed to Brecht in their general philosophy and, for that matter, differing from each other.

Wilder has a background of humanistic-religious, quietist convictions, and this is the direction to which he points. But as regards the de-illusioning of the stage he is, if anything, stricter than Brecht. He prefers a stage entirely without decoration, makes do with a table and a few chairs which, as in children's games, serve as motorcar or railway. The narrator explains the scene and the events, introduces the cast, and deciphers the episodic incidents of everyday life to reveal them as little parables of the great course of all existence.

In *Our Town* (1938) Wilder gave us the world in a nutshell in the small town of Grover's Corner; in *The Skin of Our Teeth* (1942) he showed us the drama of mankind through five thousand years of world history. The ice age, the flood, and world-war bombing are the great disasters which Wilder's prototype family escapes by the skin of its teeth, and after which it pulls itself together again and gathers up the wreckage that is left, goes on to a new beginning, to old conflicts. In postwar Europe, bled white as it was, this thoughtful and relevant play, in which the actors keep breaking out of their part into reality, made a great impression. Karl Heinz Stroux staged it in 1946 at the Hebbel Theater and no one who saw the performance, amid the ruins of Berlin, is likely to forget it.

Paul Claudel's dramaturgical experiments with the epic theater go back to the year 1927. When, at the request of Max Reinhardt and as a librettist for Darius Milhaud, Claudel began to write his *Christopher Columbus,* he chose to have a mediator between stage and auditorium in the person of a narrator. He placed him to the side of the stage, with a reading desk bearing an open book: *Le Livre de Christophe Colomb* (this is the title of the revised version produced by Jean-Louis Barrault and published at Bordeaux, in 1953). The explorer is split into two characters, an ailing old man who steps up beside the narrator and sits in judgment over himself on a "neutralized" space-time level, and the young navigator who sets sail to discover America. A solemn Hallelujah is sung by the chorus to conclude the allegory, while on a film screen the pilgrim James and the Mother of God appear.

Claudel's *Christopher Columbus* was long regarded as the model example of total theater aimed, unlike the revolutionary drama, at putting across a religious view of the world with modern means. This approach recurs, on a vast scale, in *Le Soulier de satin* ["The Satin Slipper"]; here Claudel, taking his inspiration from the Spanish Baroque drama, roams between mystery and farce in a powerful masterpiece of imagery and language. Pantomimes, dance and sketch numbers, allegorical and philosophical interludes range between the seventeenth-century religious play and modern forms of expression. It is left to the director's discretion (and his financial means) to concentrate on the text on a bare stage or to turn the play into a grand spectacle with the help of all the technical resources of the modern stage.

SHOW BUSINESS ON BROADWAY

Max Reinhardt's pithy formula for the New York theater was "entertainment as business." Comparing it with four leading European theatrical centers, he noted that artistic pleasure was uppermost in Paris, that sensuous pleasure dominated the stage in Vienna, that in Berlin "extremely hard work went into preparing the battle between the actors and a critical audience," and that in Moscow both actors and public had an almost religious dedication to the art of the theater.

As regards both form and substance, for two centuries the theaters of North America drew on European models. But they soon showed a greater skill in making the theater succeed as a commercial venture. In the words of Irving Berlin's famous lyric, Americans found that "there's no business like show business."

Various aspects of American drama have been discussed previously in relation to the different dramatic genres, but the following section is briefly concerned with the theater as "show business" in the sense that it has come to be exemplified by Broadway.

Though for better or for worse New York is now the undisputed

Scenery by Wolfgang Znamenacek for Friedrich Domin's production of The Satin Slipper, *by Paul Claudel, at the Kammerspiele, Munich, 1947.*

theatrical center of the United States and few plays can succeed without the cachet of a production there, the origins of American professional theater are to be found in the neighboring, and for a long time rival, city of Philadelphia. Indeed it was there that Thomas Godfrey, Jr.'s *The Prince of Parthia,* the first play written in America to be produced by a professional company of actors, opened in 1767 at the Southwark Theatre, the first permanent theater in the United States. A verse tragedy with an exotic setting, it dealt, in a manner that clearly betrayed its Shakespearean inspiration, with the princely rivalry of two brothers. It was given a single performance.

Prophetically enough, however, New York was the scene of America's first native *comedy,* Royall Tyler's *The Contrast* (1787). In it the author flattered his recently independent compatriots with a tale involving the romantic competition between Billy Dimple, an anglophile of upsettingly easy ways with the ladies, and Colonel Manly, a true-blue revolutionary officer, for the love of a pure American girl. A still playable but not very often played comedy, its popularity and importance were due to the introduction into drama of the first typically American stage character, Colonel Manly's manservant Jonathan. The latter's unspoiled, hardheaded, and rural view of life were to make him the prototype for hundreds of similar figures in fiction, drama, films, and musical comedies.

Though it is now fashionable to say that Broadway theater is as old as the movies and emerged under similar conditions, its origins are in fact considerably older. Broadway's business practices, management, perfectionism, star principle and long-run system were fully developed in the nineteenth century. Great actors and singers whose appearance could assure a sensational success were invited from Europe. Through the years and on into the twentieth century stars such as the Kembles, Sarah Bernhardt, Coquelin, Jenny Lind, Eleanora Duse, Caruso, and Richard Tauber repeated their European triumphs on the American stage.

Comedians and colonists had crossed the Atlantic together. The theatrical contingent was led by the pioneer principals, and its troupes soon came thick and fast: 1750, Murray and Kean; 1751, Robert Upton; 1752, William and Lewis Hallam. In George Washington's day—an advocate of the theater during his lifetime, he was later to be the glorified hero of numerous unsuccessful plays—New York could already boast several permanent theaters, including the John Street Theatre, where *The Contrast* was given its premiere by the American Company, the literarily ambitious Park Theatre, and the Ricketts Circus, hailed as the "new and commodious amphitheater."

It was at the Park Theatre that William Dunlap, playwright and author of the pioneering *History of the American Theatre* (1832), presented the city's most stimulating theatrical bill of fare. His big box-office attraction was Kotzebue, whose plays were regarded as object lessons in the ideas of the French and the American Revolutions. In the 1799–1800 season fourteen Kotzebue plays were given in New York. The anonymously produced *The Italian Father,* one of Dunlap's successes in 1799, was also widely assumed to be by Kotzebue until Dunlap acknowledged his debt to Thomas Dekker's *The Honest Whore.* Dunlap also adapted Schiller's *Don Carlos,* Pixerécourt's *La Femme à deux maris,* and a variety of plays by popular European authors. There was in addition a constant stream of Shakespearean revivals.

It was not customary for any theater to concentrate exclusively either on drama or opera. Each put on whatever promised a full house. An Italian opera group under Montrésor filled New York's Richmond Hill Theatre for three months in 1832, giving 35 performances in all. The artistic adviser for the venture was Lorenzo da Ponte, erstwhile friend and librettist of Mozart.

In Louisville, Kentucky, in 1828, actor Thomas D. Rice, assigned to play a Negro fieldhand in a local melodrama, observed an old Negro singing and dancing outside the theater. He was so taken with the performance that he incorporated it into his part, and from his successful black-face rendition of the song "Jump Jim Crow" was born the minstrel show. The rage spread like wildfire, and in 1843 a new competitor in show business, the Virginia Minstrel Show, made its debut at New York's Bowery Amphitheater. The program was a sentimental mixture of ballads, musical numbers, and short dialogues; the music was supplied by banjos, violins, castanets, and tambourines. Soon minstrel shows were being given all over the country. White performers in black face entertained audiences with a parody of Negro life that was to become a tradition difficult to destroy.

In 1847 the state of New York theater was such that Walt Whitman, writing in the *Brooklyn Eagle,* branded all theaters with the exception of the Park as "low places where vulgarity (not only on the stage, but in front of it) is in the ascendant, and bad taste carries the day with hardly a pleasant point to mitigate its coarseness." Even the Park provided only "third-rate imitation of the best London theaters. It gives us the cast-off dramas, and the unengaged players of Great Britain; and of these dramas and players, like garments which come second-hand from gentleman to valet, everything fits awkwardly."

Whitman was perhaps somewhat unfair, but he did put his finger on the two motive forces of American theater in his time: the too-overwhelming and lingering English tradition, and a tendency to rely on "the *star* system." "Some actor or actress flits about the country, playing a week here and a week there, bringing as his or her greatest recommendation, that of *novelty*—and very often having no other." In the intervals between these virtuoso performances theaters were often empty, in spite of the fact that excellent local stock companies were often doing plays of interest.

Despite Whitman's castigations American drama had shown considerable vitality and an ability to make use of indigenous elements. At Philadelphia's Chestnut Street Theatre James Nelson Barker had presented his *The Indian Princess, or La Belle Sauvage* (1808); a tale of Pocahontas, it was the first produced American drama to make use of Indian characters. The following year the play was done at the Park and thereafter at theaters all over the country. Its fame was such that it even achieved the distinction of a doctored and pirated production at London's Drury Lane in 1820. In addition to many adaptations of European plays, novels, and poems, Barker also wrote *Superstition* (1824), a drama of Puritan intolerance.

Because of the already powerful star system, many of the best early American plays were written as vehicles for famous actors. In addition, exotic settings were still very much in order. Before he found that the absence of copyright laws made the playwright's livelihood a precarious one, Robert Montgomery Bird, one of the best of the early romantic playwrights, wrote for Edwin Forrest such plays as *The Gladiator* (1831), a tale of Spartacus and ancient Rome in which abolitionist sentiments predominated, and *The Broker of Bogota* (1834), a tumultuous drama set in Colombia.

The "imported" drama continued to hold sway on Broadway, however. This preference is reflected in the prologue of Anna Mowatt's "unequivocally brilliant success" *Fashion, or Life in New York* (the description is the author's own, but justified), which packed the Park for several weeks in 1845. Scanning a newspaper announcement of the play, the Prologue comments in verse: "Bah! homemade calicoes are well enough,/But homemade dramas *must* be stupid stuff./Had it the *London* stamp, 'twould do . . ." The play was not only homegrown, but written by a *woman*!

Drawing inspiration from Tyler's *The Contrast* and Sheridan's *The School for Scandal,* Mrs. Mowatt presented an intrigue in which native virtues are contrasted with foreign deviousness. Honest Adam Trueman, the rural guest of the muddleheaded Mrs. Tiffany, who hopes to marry her daughter to Count Jolimaitre—"a fashionable European importation"—is a recognizable reincarnation of Tyler's Jonathan.

Bucking the trend of comedy, exotic melodrama, and celebrations of democratic virtues, were the patrician verse tragedies of George Henry Boker, who developed the tradition inaugurated in Philadelphia with Godfrey's *The Prince of Parthia.* Himself a Philadelphian, Boker followed the advice he gave poet Richard Henry Stoddard: "Get out of your age as far as you can." The best of his plays is undoubtedly *Francesca da Rimini* (1855), which remains the finest treatment in English drama of Dante's doomed lovers.

As Whitman had noted, novelty and virtuoso performances continued to dominate the theater in New York. When, for example, Edwin Booth, in partnership with a Boston businessman, opened his new theater in 1869, New Yorkers scrambled for tickets, which were auctioned at prices up to $125. Opening night at Booth's Theater provided a triple sensation: the magnificence of the playhouse, the promising technical equipment—which included hydraulic traps—and the memory of Edwin's brother John Wilkes Booth, the assassin of President Lincoln.

Described with American fondness for hyperbole as "the world's greatest hit," the dramatization of Harriet Beecher Stowe's abolitionist novel *Uncle Tom's Cabin* had been launched at the Museum Theater in Troy, New York, in 1852. A hit indeed, it was transferred the following year to Purdy's National Theatre in New York. A perennial favorite, over the years this sprawling six-act attack on slavery developed a life of its own. Its theme of man's inhumanity to man was coated over by a variety of spectacular stage effects, and accompanied by dances and banjo songs it was eventually given in 1881 in a production by P.T. Barnum and James A. Bailey, of circus fame. It thus becomes in a way an ancestor of America's great contribution to the stage: the post–Civil War development of the musical.

However, the true source of this indigenous genre is probably Charles M. Barras's *The Black Crook,* which opened in 1866 to the delighted applause of New Yorkers at Niblo's Garden. The production came about as the result of a fortuitous accident that stranded a corps de ballet in New York after the theater they hoped to perform in had burned down—a common contemporary occurrence. By combining the beauteous and scantily clad—for the time—dancers with a melodrama involving spectacular scenic displays, the manager of Niblo's Garden contrived a formidable show business success that held the stage off and on for the next three decades, in spite of fulminations from the pulpit and the press.

Designed with the requirements of Broadway in mind, the musical was to thrive there, along with the variety show in which singing, dancing, and short acts of various types were strung together with no attempt to develop a story line. It was at the recently opened theater of Florenz Ziegfeld, whose spectacular *Ziegfeld Follies* had in 1907 begun to "glorify the American girl," that the American musical reached a new peak with *Show Boat* (1927). Based on Edna Ferber's sentimental novel of the previous year, it featured a libretto by Oscar Hammerstein and music by Jerome Kern. Its hit song, "Ol' Man River," was on its own to earn millions for the theater and record companies.

Its success, however, was to be overshadowed in 1943 by *Oklahoma!* which was based on Lynn Riggs's 1931 folk comedy *Green Grow the Lilacs*. It introduced a trend in which choreography played an increasingly important role. Because of the fabulous combination of dialogue, lyrics, ballet, and enticingly orchestrated rhythms, *Oklahoma!* broke all box-office records, running for 2,250 performances in New York alone. In the interval between *Show Boat* and *Oklahoma!* there had been the sparkling musical comedies by George Gershwin: *Strike Up the Band* (1930) and *Of Thee I Sing* (1931)—with a libretto by George S. Kaufman—the first musical to win a Pulitzer Prize.

The American musical achieved international success and carried the day against the vestiges of the "silver age" of operetta when the works of Johann Strauss, Franz Lehar, Franz von Suppé, Nico Dostal, and Emmerich Kalman flourished at the Carlstheater and the Theater an der Wien in Vienna, and at the Metropol in Berlin.

In developing the musical, Broadway bowed to the public's desire for a specifically American form of expression. As Gideon Freud put it, it is a form that "America has thought up in order to let off steam on the grand scale. Its style fluctuates and has not as yet reached any kind of finality. It is as new, as loud, and as much outside any beaten track as the continent which fathered it."

Realizing that nothing more was to be squeezed out of the old, sentimental clichés, Broadway bethought itself of the libraries and took to literary models, reinterpreting the classics for contemporaries: *Kiss Me Kate* (1948, based on Shakespeare's *The Taming of the Shrew*), *West Side Story* (1957, inspired by his *Romeo and Juliet*), and *My Fair Lady* (1956, after G.B. Shaw's *Pygmalion*). *Candide* (1956), based on Voltaire's satirical novel, featured a book by Lillian Hellman, a score by Leonard Bernstein, and lyrics by Richard Wilbur, John Latouche, and Dorothy Parker. Though it attained new heights of literacy and wit, it was a financial failure. It continues however to enjoy an underground life as a recording.

Attempts to bring the Broadway musical closer to opera—Gershwin's *Porgy and Bess* (1935, based on Dubose Heyward's novel *Porgy*) and Kurt Weill's *Street Scene* (1947, based on Elmer Rice's play of the same name and supplied with lyrics by poet Langston Hughes)—originally met with limited financial success, but are nevertheless still revived. In 1950, *Porgy and Bess* successfully toured Europe with an all-black cast that even performed in Moscow. In recent years, American musicals that achieved international success include *Fiddler on the Roof* (1964)—based on Sholem Aleichem's immortal stories about the life of Tevye the Milkman in a pre-World War I Russian village, directed and choreographed by Jerome Robbins, and *Hair* (1969), a rock celebration of the hippie world's mysticism and protest.

Broadway produces at least ten new musicals annually and has recently shown a tendency to produce little else. Investments can easily go to over half a million dollars for actors, musicians, decor, and choreography. Very few succeed. Try-outs in smaller cities are no foolproof indication of how Broadway will react, and New York openings are a nervous affair for the "angels," the financial backers. If the first night is a flop, all is lost; if it is a smash hit, profits snowball. The gamble is between success and utter failure: "There's no business like show business."

Somewhat less spectacular than that of the musical was the post–Civil War development of the drama. It begins in a sense with the brilliant success a year before the war of Dion Boucicault's *The Octoroon* (1859), a drama of the love between a white man and a free mulatto girl. An Irish actor-author who came to New York after having established his reputation in London, Boucicault had a sure sense of the theater as entertainment. Though his play dealt with social problems that continue to haunt the United States, its emphasis—like much of the social theater that was to follow—was on sentiment. In addition, it offered a number of spectacular scenes ranging from a slave auction to a burning steamship.

Boucicault also had a hand in one of the most famous successes of the American stage when he collaborated with Joseph Jefferson III on the latter's adaptation of Washington Irving's classic story *Rip Van Winkle*. The play originally opened in London in 1865 but was soon transferred to New York and then to other parts of the country. Over the course of years Jefferson, following in the footsteps of his famous father and grandfather who had presented earlier adaptations of Irving's tale, altered the play many times.

Realism in the American theater can be said to date from James A. Herne's "daring" treatment of the consequences of adultery in *Margaret Fleming* (1890), which received a single matinee performance in New York's Palmer Theatre a year after its initial performances in Lynn, Massachusetts. A passionate admirer of Ibsen, actor-author Herne had stripped his drama of too many of the theatrical conventions of his day to find favor with Broadway audiences, and the play was seldom revived, even after he rewrote the last act to suggest a possible reconciliation between husband and wife. Earlier in his career, Herne had shared the stage with David Belasco, the brilliant actor, director, and playwright whose more flamboyant notions of realism were to dominate the Broadway stage for some time. Belasco is now chiefly remembered for Puccini's operatic adaptations of his *Madame Butterfly* (1900) and *The Girl of the Golden West* (1910).

Realism in the sense of dramas of social criticism and satire found a more successful exponent in Clyde Fitch, who had originally established his reputation with romantic comedies such as *Beau Brummell* (1890) and *Captain Jinks of the Horse Marines* (1901). In plays such as *The Climbers* (1901), *The Truth* (1906), and *The City* (1909), Fitch turned his ethical New England conscience on questionable aspects of American society.

Four years after the triumph of Belasco's romantically "realistic" drama about the American far west, William Vaughn Moody presented in *The Great Divide* (1909), an adaptation of his earlier verse play *The Sabine Woman* (1906), an interesting drama that focuses on the conflicting values of the Puritan East and the rough and ready West. Alone in her brother's Arizona cabin, Ruth, a girl raised in the East, is besieged by three ruffians. She saves herself by appealing to one of them to make her his own. Stephen Ghent "buys" her from his companions, and when Ruth has earned the money to "repurchase" herself, she returns to New England. But essentially she rejects the cultivated men of her milieu and longs for the untamed mate to whom she has shown life's possibilities. *The Faith Healer* (1909), though possibly a better play, met with little success because of its mystical theme in which man's innate spiritual power is pitted against rationalism and conventional religion.

The contrast between East and West in the United States was taken up somewhat less profoundly in Rachel Crothers's *The Three of Us* (1906), the first of a series of dramas and comedies in which the author examined social questions from the feminine viewpoint: *As Husbands Go* (1931), *When Ladies Meet* (1932), and *Susan and God* (1937). After 1922 Philip Barry kept Broadway alternately amused and bemused with a series of sparkling social comedies and mystically oriented dramas, including *Holiday* (1929), a young man's revolt against the "sensible" life; *The Animal Kingdom* (1932), an examination of the true nature of marriage; *Here Come the Clowns* (1938), a fascinating—but commercially unsuccessful—investigation into the deep-rooted sources of human motivation; and *The Philadelphia Story* (1939), a hilarious and barbed account of a restive society woman on the eve of a second marriage. At about the same time Maxwell Anderson attempted in plays such as *Elizabeth the Queen* (1930), *Mary of Scotland* (1933) and *Winterset* (1935)—inspired by the Sacco-Vanzetti case—to revive verse drama.

During the 1930s Broadway rose to the challenge of the Depression and the gathering war clouds with a series of vigorous dramas that examined the basic assumptions of American society. Perhaps the most representative of these was Clifford Odets's *Awake and Sing!* (1935), in which a young man is passionately exhorted to "Go out and fight so life shouldn't be printed on dollar bills." Sidney Kingsley's *Dead End* (1935) gave Broadway audiences a grim glimpse into New York's crime-breeding slums. In *Idiot's Delight* (1936) Robert E. Sherwood portrayed the forces that were driving the world to a major conflict and called upon the common man to resist them. Somewhat less aggressively, but no less entertainingly—because in spite of his moral fervor, Sherwood had not forgotten that Broadway's essential function was to entertain—William Saroyan pitted the modern forces of good and evil against each other in *The Time of Your Life* (1939), romantically choosing a San Francisco honky-tonk as the scene of his encounter. In that same year Lillian Hellman examined the roots of American capitalism in *The Little Foxes,* in which the southern aristocratic tradition is shown giving way to the forces of industrialism.

The 1940s saw the emergence of the two playwrights who—along with Edward Albee, after the success of *Who's Afraid of Virginia Woolf?* (1962)—remain to this day the most representative of Broadway theater in its "serious" mood: Tennessee Williams and Arthur Miller. In *The Glass Menagerie* (1944) Williams autobiographically mused on the pitiful pretenses of the remnants of the southern tradition and showed sensitivity taking refuge from the harshness of the modern world in dreams and withdrawal. The theme was expanded on in *A Streetcar Named Desire* (1947), in which the decadent sensitivity of Blanche is pitted against the brutal vigor of her brother-in-law Stanley. Williams continued in this vein with increasingly grotesque variations on his theme.

While Williams's criticism of American life seems in a sense to come from an outsider, Miller's examination of businessman ethics in *All My Sons* (1947) unconsciously accepts many of the ground rules of capitalism—so much so that performances were suspended in the USSR—and merely criticizes infractions. It was not until *Death of a Salesman* (1949) that Miller offered a more fundamental criticism of American values in the story of Willy Loman's destruction by the illusions that had guided his life. In some of his later plays Miller changed his emphasis from social criticism to psychological study: *A View from the Bridge* (1955, revised 1957), *After the Fall* (1964), *The Price* (1968).

At the present time the Broadway stage is almost completely dominated by light comedy and above all the musical—almost no subject seems to be resistant to song-and-dance treatment.

THE EXPERIMENTAL THEATER IN AMERICA

In 1900, the monthly illustrated magazine *The Theatre* was founded in New York. It informed its readers of American productions, published the theories and designs of the European stage reformers Appia and Craig, and criticized the commercialism of the Broadway theater. In 1913 it published a cry of alarm: "What's wrong with the American stage?"

The solution, it seemed, lay off Broadway—out of reach of the commercial theater's dictatorship—in decentralization, and in the courage to experiment. The age of the little theaters dawned. In the lead were those of the 1912 vintage, the Toy Theater in Boston, the Little Theater in New York, and the Chicago Little Theater. They were American counterparts to the Russian studio, experimental theaters that went in for repertory rather than long runs, and offered young avant-garde authors and artists an opportunity to try out new plays and new staging techniques.

At the same time, university campuses came alive with new theater projects. At Harvard, Professor George Pierce Baker set up his 47 Workshop in 1913, and this was soon followed by numerous similar drama and theater departments at other universities throughout the United States. The artistic, practical, technical, and organizational aspects of the theater entered the syllabus. Amateur college groups gave public performances and thereby exercised an indirect influence on the professional theater. Professor Baker's workshop was decades ahead of similar European ventures such as, say, the Théophiliens, a group founded in Paris by Gustave Cohen, who took their name from, and in 1933 made their début with, Rutebeuf's *Miracle de Théophile*. Baker was equally far in advance of the experimental stages nowadays attached to nearly all drama departments of European universities. Out of his 47 Workshop emerged the American dramatists Eugene O'Neill, S. N. Behrman, Sidney Howard, Philip Barry, Percy MacKaye, and Thomas Wolfe.

Eugene O'Neill, the first U.S. dramatist of international stature, within the compass of his own works raced through all the phases of contemporary European drama. He wrote naturalistic plays and symbolist ones, plays of social criticism and depth psychology, realistic-romantic and expressionist plays. His development and his choice of subjects are symptomatic of his contemporaries and succeeding generation of dramatists.

Subject and milieu are taken from personal experience: a broken home, casual employment, gold prospecting, going to sea, strolling players, the sanitarium, and, in between, applied theater in the Workshop. The Provincetown Players, one of the outstanding experimental theaters since 1915, produced O'Neill's drama of the sea *Bound East for Cardiff*; in 1921, the then two-year-old Theatre Guild staged *Beyond the Horizon* and gave O'Neill his first Broadway success. Three years later, *The Moon of the Caribbees* was produced by Piscator for the Berlin Volksbühne, the expressionist drama *The Hairy Ape* and soon afterward *Desire under the Elms,* by Tairov at the Moscow Kamerny Theater.

O'Neill once said that he wrote plays in order to make plain the bit of truth that it was given to him to achieve. His work is the melancholy exploration of private life, the exposure of its falsehoods—an application of Freudian teachings in the disclosure of psychoanalytical casualties.

One of the more interesting post-World War II experimental theaters was the short-lived Artists' Theatre, which between 1953 and 1956 produced sixteen original plays by men who were primarily poets. Determinedly turning its back on the box office, the group encouraged a collaboration of writers, painters, and composers who would, in the words of Herbert Machiz, director of these productions, "experiment with new vistas for themselves and offer fresh experiences to an audience." The plays eschewed the realism that dominated the "serious" Broadway stage and ironically viewed the situation of modern man in a complex world that lent itself to no single and simple interpretation. Many of the plays—Frank O'Hara's *Try! Try!,* John Ashbury's *The Heroes,* and James Merrill's *The Bait*—were written in verse, but their simplicity and directness were in sharp contrast to the self-consciously "poetic" theater of Maxwell Anderson. Perhaps the most interesting was Lionel Abel's *Absalom,* a prose retelling of the Bible story in which the dramatist attempted to introduce to the American stage the kind of philosophical drama that had been popularized in France by Sartre and Camus.

The immediate post-war off-Broadway theater was for some time concerned largely with the revival of classics, both ancient and modern. This was to a certain extent true of the Living Theater formed by the intrepid Judith Malina Beck and Julian Beck, who staged their first performances in their own apartment. Nevertheless, the group's first productions included such exotically noncommercial items as Gertrude Stein's *Dr. Faustus Lights the Lights* and William Carlos Williams's *Many Loves.* Eventually, the Becks introduced into their repertoire experimental works by young and unknown American playwrights. The most outstanding of these were Jack Gelber's *The Connection,* a two-act, free form drama that focused on the elements of narcotics addiction and jazz—giving the effect of a brutal improvisation—and Kenneth Brown's *The Brig*, a terrifyingly realistic recreation of a day in a U.S. Marine prison compound.

In the early sixties, after some stormy disagreements with the U.S. Internal Revenue Service about unpaid taxes, The Living Theater went into "exile" in Europe for several years. It was during this period that the group developed a new concept of theater in which the playwright as such seemed to be abandoned and the work presented evolved from collaboration and innovation on the part of various members of the company. In discussing productions such as *Frankenstein* and *Paradise Now* the Becks put great stress on the fact that their "free theater" was inseparable from their anarchist and pacifist orientation, and that it was the direct result of the group's community style of living.

The Living Theater itself appears to have disbanded, but the Open Theatre, one of the most vigorous experimental groups in the United States today, is one of its enduring offshoots. It was begun in 1963 by Joseph Chaikin, who initiated a series of workshops devoted to new experiments in form. Once again the final result was to stem from "collaboration" between the group and the author. Among the better-known productions of the Open Theatre were Megan Terry's *Viet Rock* and Jean-Claude van Itallie's *America Hurrah* and *The Serpent*.

In the tradition of Ionesco's and Beckett's theater of the absurd was Edward Albee's *The American Dream*, which was first performed in New York's off-Broadway York Playhouse. In it Albee proceeded to a cool diagnosis and exposure of the "American way of life," of the grotesque triviality and banality of the stereotyped idols of average people, the hopeless isolation of the individual in the hothouse of neuroses.

The effort to get away from the restrictions of Broadway has led to the foundation—often ephemeral—of a great number of off-Broadway and off-off-Broadway companies. Special mention must be made of the Bread and Puppet Theater, a politically radical street theater group directed by Peter Schumann, which utilizes such elements as grisly ballads and parables and borrowings from mystery plays and circuses, and of Ellen Stewart's La Mama Experimental Theater Club, whose influence on acting techniques has been so extensive that it is reflected in experimental theater groups in Europe and Japan.

THE THEATER IN CRISIS?

The twentieth century is not alone in asking whether its theater is in a crisis. Seneca in Rome and Lessing in Hamburg questioned the meaning and form of their contemporary theater. But it is rather alarming that so much pessimism has been voiced since 1950 in so many different circles: by the public, at theater congresses, by those responsible for theater grants, by theatergoers' clubs, critics, and dramatists.

Today's theater is so fragmented in its formal aspects, and so uniform in its tendencies, that the barometer reading is equally high or equally low in New York and London, in Paris and Berlin. Today the world's theater is truly a world theater. Thanks to the mass media, to radio, film, and television, it has an almost unlimited audience. At the threshold of the atomic age, it is an international phenomenon. It is a seismograph of the intellectual and political state of mankind at a moment in history that, at the cost of devastating disasters, gives us no more than a deceptive partial peace between new centers of crisis.

Called upon to serve as the test pit for a new order, the theater piles up the rubble on the one side, and the narrow veins of ore on the other, in front of a measuring rod marked with the most contradictory scales: place of amusement or propaganda institute, the promised land or a debating forum, timeless "as if" of a higher reality or x-ray screen of a lower one, moral institution in Schiller's sense or "active reflection of man about himself" in the words of Novalis, launching pad for discussions about ethics, ideology, and philosophy or museum for classically fixed stars, the individual's path to his inner self or uninhibited exposure of his emotions. So many slogans, so many serious, superficial, conservative or provocative arguments surround a phenomenon that cannot be controversial enough.

Hamlet's description of the theater as "the abstracts and brief chronicles of the time" was perhaps never more true than today. The brief chronicle of the atomic age that has just begun is brimful with problems, with social, sociological, psychological, and political controversy, with deceptive self-assurance on the one side and malaise and protest on the other, with the soft radiance of the men of good will and the turbulent wake of those who drive the world into a new catastrophe.

The theater stands right in the middle of all this. In Germany, among the ruins of the Second World War, it had to satisfy the pent-up demand for international drama. During the last ten years, it has moved into modern multipurpose buildings of glass and concrete. In New York, the Metropolitan Opera and theater and concert halls make up the Lincoln Center complex. In London a great new art center is emerging on the south bank of the Thames, with an art gallery and three concert halls already completed and a new national theater just begun. In Australia, Sydney is to have an imposing opera house in the shape of a great sailing ship, placed on a spit of land in the harbor, and designed by the Danish architect Jorn Utzon.

The theater has become both more sensuous and more spartan than it ever was, it is more intellectual and more subjective, it likes to shock and to pose as anti-theater. It is trying out how far it can go in questioning its own validity. It has the choice between taking advantage of every conceivable modern stage mechanism or proving, on the contrary, that it does not need any props at all. The theater may owe its impulses to a dramatist, a director, a manager, a subsidizing body, or a commercial company.

But when the public speaks of a theater crisis, it does so with reference not so much to the external conditions, but to the substance of theatrical representation. It cannot make head or tail of the modern drama, and so the stage appears as a distorting mirror reflecting an image the public is not prepared to accept.

Ionesco once said that the most characteristic trait of people in our time is that they have lost any profound sense of destiny. The drama must necessarily render a tragicomic picture of life, in an age in which we cannot evade the question of what we are doing on earth and how we can bear the crushing burden of the world of things.

The theater of the absurd is a logical consequence of these considerations. It was introduced with a rude shock in 1895 by Jarry's *Ubu Roi,* and Ionesco and Beckett firmly established it on the mid-twentieth-century stage. Albert Camus explained in *Le Mythe de Sisyphe* (1942) how the modern awareness of absurdity came to the surface: "A world which can be explained, albeit with inadequate reasons, is a familiar world. But in a universe which suddenly is deprived of illusions and of the light of reason, man feels a stranger. . . . This separation of

The opera house now under construction (to open in 1973) in Sydney, Australia. Sketch of the project designed in 1956 by the Danish architect Jorn Utzon.

man from his life, of the actor from his background, that, precisely, is the sense of absurdity."

Ionesco wrote much the same in 1957, in an essay on Kafka (*Cahiers de la Compagnie Madeleine Renaud – Jean-Louis Barrault*): "Something is absurd when it is aimless. When man is cut loose from his religious, metaphysical, and transcendental roots, he is lost, everything he does becomes senseless, absurd, useless, is nipped in the bud."

What counts is psychological reality. The stage becomes a space without any identifiable place in it, the visualized nightmare of emptiness. A desolate plateau with one last, bare tree, in front of which Vladimir and Estragon, in senseless self-deception, wait for Godot; a sandy desert into which Winnie keeps sinking more and more deeply; two trash cans in which Nagg and Nell waste away in expectation of the miserable end of the *Endgame*—that is Samuel Beckett's stage world of the absurd.

The promised "message" of Ionesco's *Chairs* is a farce: the orator who is to announce it turns out to be a deaf-mute, a pathetic personification of grotesque helplessness.

Ionesco's characters are adrift in a disconnected world, coffined in their fears, caricatures of themselves, macabre clowns of a tragic Punch-and-Judy show. Ionesco talks of the dramatist's creative process as "research." He does not claim to be a discoverer of virgin land. On the contrary, the aim of the dramatic avant-garde must be to rediscover, not to invent, the eternal forms and the forgotten ideals of the theater in their purest form.

"We must break through the clichés," he continues, "get away from hidebound 'traditionalism'; we must rediscover the sole true and live tradition." The theater of the absurd is the *Commedia dell'arte* of nihilism, the *grand guignol* of a world of paradoxes.

THE THEATER AND THE MASS MEDIA

"Rediscovery" under other aspects became characteristic of the twentieth century's theater, and the film as well. Brecht's derivation of the epic principle from the "exhibition character" of the "age-old Asian theater" is as pertinent as, say, Eisenstein's statement that he owed the idea of film montage "first and foremost to the basic principles of the circus and the music hall," for which he had had a passion ever since he was a child.

The first forward step in cinematic technique was that of fantasy

Nell and Nagg in the trash cans, in Endgame, *by Samuel Beckett, first performance April 3, 1957, at the Royal Court Theatre, London. Director: Roger Blin. C. Tsingos as Nell, G. Adet as Nagg.*

and trick, achieved by Georges Méliès; the second was the slapstick farce; the third was the action tableau, which originated in the nineteenth-century theater.

When Henry Irving in 1882 produced *Romeo and Juliet* in London he sought to create a photographic reproduction of the time and the place by means of settings and action tableaux. Thirty years later, when Louis Mercanton produced his film *Queen Elizabeth,* he worked with stage scenery and stage business: Sarah Bernhardt not only took her curtain call on the screen, as Nicholas Vardac writes, "but her final plop into a pile of pillows directly towards the camera at the climax of the death scene seemed nearer slapstick than drama."

The challenge offered by *Queen Elizabeth* and by the Italian productions of G. Pastrone was accepted by D. W. Griffith. His *Judith of Bethulia* was based on the spectacle of the same name by T. B. Aldrich, which was currently successful on the stage. But it was with *Intolerance* and *The Birth of a Nation* that Griffith brought an end to the nickelodeon days. At this point large motion-picture houses had to be built or theaters had to be taken over for the showing of the new films.

René Clair rejected any rapprochement between the two unequal sisters, theater and film. He claimed for the screen the privilege of breaking through the dogma of realism—as, for instance, Robert Wiene did in his *Cabinet of Dr. Caligari* (1919)—and of expressing a "subjective truth." René Clair maintained that theater and film are governed by entirely different artistic laws and ought to be kept separate. As late as 1950 he declared, consistently: "I have not joined those who always regarded the film as a mere instrument for the dissemination of stage plays." He had a simple and basic formula for distinguishing the two categories: "In the theater, the word guides the action, while optics is of secondary importance. In the film, the image has primacy, and sound and the spoken word take second place. I am tempted to say that a blind man could get his money's worth with the drama, and a deaf one with the screen."

In their turn, the elements and possibilities of the film had an artistically stimulating effect on stage scenery. When Jo Mielziner in 1949 designed the scenery for the New York production of Arthur Miller's *Death of a Salesman* (directed by Elia Kazan), he put on the stage the skeleton of a one-family house standing wedged-in among skyscrapers, but shown in the midst of sunlit trees in the flashbacks of the action. A thin muslin veil with translucent rows of windows painted on it was lit up from behind to give an impression of gloomy house-walls; with the rear lights extinguished and the tenement milieu thus eliminated, a yellow-green foliage projection bathed the same picture in a bright spring atmosphere.

In 1947, for Tennessee Williams's *A Streetcar Named Desire,* directed by Elia Kazan, Mielziner used transparent walls which, with the help of light and shade, made possible a fluid transition between indoor and street scenes. This kind of scene painting was the most fascinating of all in Mielziner's view. Through him the ideas of Appia and Craig, which had reached the United States via Robert Edmond Jones, came back to Europe in a new, differentiated forms owed to the film. Their most direct influence can perhaps be seen in the designs made in the early fifties by Wolfgang Znamenacek for the Munich Kammerspiele, such as those, say, for Dürrenmatt's *Die Ehe des Herrn Mississippi* ["The Marriage of Mr. Mississippi"] or, since the sixties, by the Czech stage designer Josef Svoboda. For a production of Sophocles's *Oedipus Rex* at the Prague National Theater in 1963, Svoboda built a thirty-foot-wide staircase with semitransparent steps, which rose from the bottom of the orchestra pit up to the grid. The music was heard through perforations in the staircase.

Another kind of convergence between the artistic techniques of the theater and the motion pictures came with the miniature-space stage that became popular in Europe after 1945 under various names best rendered as "intimate" or "room" theater. In a small room and on a bare podium the actors faced the audience as immediately as they did the camera and the microphone in the film studio. Any excess in voice, gesture, or miming was registered by the spectator sitting close by, just as the photographic lens, though with the difference that subsequent correction was ruled out.

At a distance, on the peep-show or box stage, or in the arena, the actor has to rivet the spectator's attention across 60 or 100 feet and to bring him into the area of the dramatic action. In the intimate chamber theater, he has to follow opposite rules—withdrawal of emotion, simplicity and, if anything, underemphasis in the delivery of the text; he will use no makeup, intensive instead of extensive acting. This is the origin of meaningful understatement based on constant awareness of the "close-up." When this acting technique is transferred to the usual box stage at a distance, audibility is sometimes badly impaired.

The heyday of contemporary chamber theater was the middle of the twentieth century. Picasso's farce *Le Désir attrapé par la queue* ("Desire Caught by the Tail") was first performed during the Second World War, in 1944, by the small circle around Jean-Paul Sartre and Simone de Beauvoir. It was a private studio reading, held by the prominent literati of Paris in an apartment in Saint-Germain-des-Prés—a "happening" in the tradition of Dada, surrealism, and the "Cabaret Voltaire." Camus and Queneau were among the participants.

In Germany, the first chamber theater was organized in 1947 by

Stage design by Jo Mielziner for Elia Kazan's production of Death of a Salesman, *by Arthur Miller, first performance February 10, 1949, Morosco Theatre, New York.*

Scenery by Wolfgang Znamenacek for Hans Schweikart's production of Die Ehe des Herrn Mississippi, *by Friedrich Dürrenmatt, first performance March 26, 1952, at the Kammerspiele, Munich.*

Helmuth Gmelin, on the upper floor of his house in Hamburg; soon afterward it moved into a neoclassic patrician building, where, among other works, Günther Rennert of the Hamburg Opera staged *Waiting for Godot*. Berlin, Frankfurt (under Fritz Rémond), Wiesbaden, Düsseldorf, Bonn, and Cologne followed with chamber theaters; Munich in 1949 with a studio theater in Schwabing, its artists' quarter. Luigi Malipiero set himself up in the gate tower of Sommerhausen, a Franconian village. Two miniature versions of the "space stage" were established in 1953 in Milan—the Teatrangolo organized by the professor of literature Francesco Prandini in his own dining room, and soon afterward in the Teatro Sant'Erasmo. In many cases the effort to make an artistic virtue out of material necessity succeeded. Several university towns still have active chamber theaters today; they have developed their own style and are holding their own—about half-way between stage and film.

Jerzy Grotowski says:

> There is only one element which film and television cannot rob the theater of—the closeness of the living organism. Because of this, each challenge from the actor, each of his magical acts (which the audience is incapable of reproducing) becomes something great, something extraordinary, something close to ecstasy. It is therefore necessary to abolish the distance between actor and audience by eliminating the stage, removing all frontiers. Let the most drastic scenes happen face to face with the spectator so that he is within arms' reach of the actor, can feel his breathing and smell his perspiration. This implies the necessity for a chamber theater.

The pioneers of the motion picture bemoaned its transitoriness, the lack of durability of its material. In the present state of technology, it is at least possible to make plenty of copies of any film before it perishes, and so to retain documentary evidence both of the early motion pictures and of theatrical events. Admittedly, a filmed theater performance is a hybrid, but it is at any rate repeatable and transportable. It makes room for comparisons, which can be fascinating and instructive even when wear and tear begins to be visible. A case in point is the television film of Giorgio Strehler's Milan production of *Arlecchino, servitore di due padroni,* with Marcello Moretti. Today Ferruccio Soleri plays the title part—almost imperceptibly, but, as the telescreen shows, in detail often quite markedly different from his teacher and predecessor.

Sir Laurence Olivier had his *Hamlet* filmed in 1948 as a record of an impressive sequence of stage scenes in front of mobile sets; this compromise between stage and screen won four Oscars and the Gold Lion of Venice. In the filmed version of the Hamburg *Faust* production, with

Gustaf Gründgens as Mephisto and Will Quadflieg as Faust, the camera came so close to the actors' faces that what was meant for the closeness of the theater appears brutally coarsened. But for posterity the *Faust* film is as invaluable as, say, the one made of the Salzburg *Don Giovanni* conducted in 1950 by Wilhelm Furtwängler in the old Festspielhaus, or the screen version made by Palitzsch and Wekwerth of the Berlin Ensemble's model production of *Mutter Courage* at the Theater am Schiffbauerdamm (1960).

Akira Kurosawa's Japanese Samurai film *Rashomon* is without doubt incomparably more impressive than the four-version story imitated in some German theaters, and thanks to Peter Brook's production Peter Weiss's *Marat/Sade* has achieved on the screen a haunting effect that would be hard to match on any stage.

None of this does away with the fact that the theater and the motion picture rest on entirely different artistic premises. Filmed theater is most convincing when the film adheres to its own law, which is visual expression. With the emergence of television as a new mass medium, the antinomies were accentuated. Hundreds of suburban movie houses have had to close their doors, but hardly a single theater has been affected. Theater, perhaps because of its social function, is holding its own against the television screen. There are TV transmissions of parts of first nights, or, for that matter, of whole festival or opera performances. Theater directors stage TV shows. Dramatists write for broadcasting and television, and elaborate radio and TV plays into full-length works for the stage. Max Frisch expanded his *Biedermann und die Brandstifter,* and Martin Walser added a second act to *Die Zimmerschlacht* at the suggestion of Fritz Kortner. "The subject of the play seemed a little too private to me," Walser admitted in explanation of his détour via the mass media, "I thought the theater should concern itself in the first place with political issues."

In 1967, Martin Walser attacked the theater as "a bathhouse for the soul." In this essay he writes:

> If we look at the action of plays for the legitimate theater, that is, the sum of traditional and current dramaturgy, we see that the result is a ritual sequence of events, which is, as necessary, recharged and updated with mild imitative functions and thus dished up to a long-specialized audience. How can we break out of this rut? One might begin like the young West German playwright Handke (born 1943) with *Publikumsbeschimpfung* ("insulting the audience") and *Selbstbezichtigung* ("self-accusation"). But it is to be hoped that we can go on performing something with action in it.

The protest against the cultivated theater led on the one hand to the above-mentioned "speech plays" by Peter Handke, or in the opposite direction to bare action, to the combination of action and noise designed to shock: the "happening."

Ionesco already had described his *La Cantatrice chauve* ["The Bald Soprano"] as an anti-play. Raymond Queneau went to the extreme of witty nonsense with his *Exercices de Style,* a parodistical juggling with language. His novel *Zazie dans le métro* reached wide circles through the movies; his exercises in style were first given a pantomimic stage interpretation in 1948 by Yves Robert, and in 1966–67 made the round of German and Swiss theaters as choice tidbits for linguistic gourmets. René de Obaldia took the disarming perfection of banality further along the track of the absurd. The simpleton now speaks tongue-in-cheek: "The accidental has become permanent," says Zephyrin in Obaldia's farce *Le Cosmonaute agricole.*

In Ionesco's *Scène à quatre* we are told that people talk in order to say nothing. Peter Handke, in his "speech plays" and, in 1968, in *Kaspar,* tries to use the creaky vehicle of language for the contrary purpose, to make man aware of himself. When the mysterious Nuremberg foundling Kaspar Hauser says: "Ich möcht' ein solcher werden, wie einmal ein anderer gewesen ist" (I'd like to become such a one as another has once been) the sentence turns into linguistic torture, into a resounding, booming beat exercise.

At this point Handke—or his stage director—joins up with the "happening" invented by the musicians and painters. "The medium is the message," according to Marshall McLuhan. Since 1958, Al Hansen's painting studio and John Cage's music class at the New School for Social Research in New York have been putting on happenings as antitheatrical events. The motto is "flight into reality" instead of the conventional flight from reality. Cool jazz, overturned pots of paint, frenetic rhythms, background noises, rags and scraps of packing paper are the ingredients of the happening, and its result is a collage of charades, a Pop- and Op-style perverted scarecrow imitation of the modern consumer society and *ersatz* world.

"We want to outrage the public, shock it into direct participation," Jean-Jacques Lebel declared when he arranged a week of happenings at the American arts center in Paris in 1964. His German comrades-in-arms, such as, say, the initiators of a once-only happening in Ulm in 1966, proclaimed they were going to "overcome banality" by disconnecting and alienating concrete processes from their normal context. The Dadaists come to mind as relatively harmless precursors, and Marinetti's aestheticization of artillery barrages and detonations offers a discordant parallel. The *tabula rasa* Lebel demands as a point of departure for a new "theater" met with a lively, but short-lived response in Barcelona, Amsterdam, Belgrade, and, in Scandinavia.

Among musicians, Karlheinz Stockhausen, John Cage, and Mauricio Kagel are trying to master the paradoxes of the age of fear by means of spatial music, concerts for watering cans, aleatory random manipulations, and silent perambulation with a walking-stick obbligato.

The painter Max Ernst, one of the founders of Dada in 1919, has a poor opinion of breaking up form in the old manner. He says skeptically: "Dada was a bomb. Is it conceivable that half a century after its explosion anyone should bother to look for its splinters and stick them back together?"

The private theatergoer is free to decide from case to case whether and how far he is willing to be drawn into the problems of the "theater." The managers of theatergoers' clubs and organizations worry about what they can offer and recommend to their members, or in the last resort expect them to put up with. Standards originally taken for granted are discussed at conferences, such as "Does a Christian theater exist?"—or "Should the theater be a forum of time or a place of timelessness?" The Munich theater critic Hanns Braun in 1956 examined the situation of theater and drama from the point of view of the thesis that both must come to an end when, in addition to uncertainty about meaning and purpose, they lose their form. "At this stage the theater of the autonomous director no longer defends its dramatic substance," he wrote, "it has neutralized itself: the novelty of a production appears more important than anything else."

For the last fifty years, theatergoers' organizations have been major clients of the repertory theater. German theaters with municipal or stage subsidies today owe some 20 to 40 percent of their takings to a public affiliated with the *Volksbühne* and *Theatergemeinde*.

The subscription system and the renting of boxes or orchestra stalls go back to the early days of the Venice opera houses and to the times of the court and city theaters. In many European countries, the sale of season tickets is still the only arrangement between the theaters and the public. The first theater association to be founded in Germany was the *Freie Volksbühne*, set up in 1890 (to be distinguished from the naturalistic *Freie Bühne*, a society for the production of new plays). An offshoot of it, the *Neue Freie Volksbühne*, in 1914 moved into a playhouse of its own, the Theater am Bülowplatz in Berlin, and under a cartel agreement admitted also the members of the parent organization. In 1920, a joint society was incorporated under the name of *Volksbühne*, with which a second independent venture, the Theater am Schiffbauerdamm (today the Berliner Ensemble) was affiliated in 1926.

In addition, the *Bühnenvolksbund* was set up in 1919, with the explicit purpose of promoting, on a Christian religious basis, an understanding for all fields of artistic life among all classes of the population. Both associations were discontinued after 1933. They were revived in 1949 in the *Verband der Deutschen Volksbühnenvereine,* and in the *Bund der Theatergemeinden,* founded in 1951 to succeed the *Bühnenvolksbund.* Similar theatergoers' organizations exist in Austria and in Switzerland.

THE DIRECTORS' THEATER

At the beginning of the 1960s, six different productions of *Tartuffe* were running in Paris during the same season in six different theaters. Critics had to specialize in "comparative analysis of stage direction." They still often have to go in for this sort of thing, not only in the case of classical plays, but of new ones too. Peter Weiss's *Die Ermittlung* ["The Investigation"] got a simultaneous first performance in sixteen theaters on October 19, 1965, and at the end of January 1968 Max Frisch's play *Biografie* was staged more or less at the same time in four cities.

The question of *how* eclipses the question of *what.* The interpretation of the classics is a touchstone today in all countries that have a major theater tradition. When Roger Planchon, director of the Théâtre de la Cité at Villeurbanne, near Lyons, prepared to produce Molière's *Tartuffe,* he discovered that two distinguished interpreters had taken an exactly opposite view of the play: Coquelin used it to attack religion, Fernand Ledoux in support of religion. In Stanislavsky's terminology we would say, "It all depends what super-objective I assign to the play."

It is the director's task to distribute the weight. The scenery creates an atmosphere that can be as reflexive and internally refracted as the production. When, in 1967, Kurt Hübner produced *Macbeth* at Bremen, Wilfried Minks did the stage out in rusty brown. A horizontal transversal upper stage was fitted with an ornamental strip of colored neon tubes, the cyclorama had a reddish glow. Apart from dark wooden sliding walls in the background, the means of transforming the scene was change of lighting. Craig's ideas are clearly still about, and the Meiningers are far away.

It was with reference to the Meiningers however, that Stanislavsky in his time first thought about the question of a "director's despotism."

Classical Walpurgis night in Faust, *Part II: scenery by Teo Otto for Gustav Gründgens' production at the Schauspielhaus, Hamburg, 1958.*

Berlin premiere of Die Ermittlung, *by Peter Weiss, Freie Volksbühne, October 19, 1965. Director: Erwin Piscator; music by Luigi Nono; scenery by H. U. Schmückle. Left, the accused; right, defense counsel; in front, Hilde Mikulicz as fifth witness and Martin Berliner as eighth witness.*

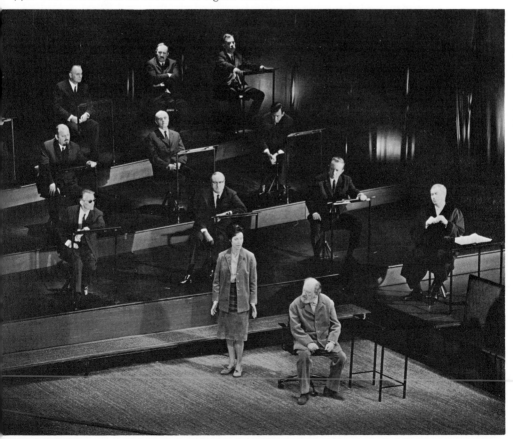

What he had in mind was the problem of discipline with regard to the actors rather than that of subjectivism in the production. In the case of Max Reinhardt, his personal temperament set the style of direction and scenery. Leopold Jessner introduced the creative reduction of external means, Erwin Piscator started directing "against the play." Jürgen Fehling and Fritz Kortner eliminated the actor's own conception in order to reshape him from scratch according to their own view. Gustaf Gründgens brought the cool, limpid passion of his intellect both to the creation of his roles and to his staging.

The great aristocrat of the British theater, Sir Laurence Olivier, since 1962 artistic director of the National Theatre in London, the new Old Vic, cultivates a style of conscientious diction, subtle inconspicuousness, and intensive attention to every last extra's part. In 1966, he produced at the National Theatre *Juno and the Paycock,* Sean O'Casey's drama about the Irish civil war, and did so without any external display —as a warning that fanatic nationalism and second-rate phraseologies must not be allowed to claim a senseless and cruel sacrifice of life.

For his own great Shakespeare roles, Olivier liked to play under the direction of Peter Brook, about twenty years his junior. At Stratford-on-Avon he also worked with Peter Hall. Olivier's Archie Rice in John Osborne's *The Entertainer,* 1957 in London and 1958 in New York, as well as his Bérenger in Ionesco's *Rhinoceros* at the Royal Court Theatre in London, 1960, were highlights of contemporary dramatic interpretation. At the latter theater, the foremost experimental stage in London, Roger Blin produced Beckett's *Endgame* in 1957. He himself played Hamm, with a handkerchief over his face, sitting in an armchair like the faceless dignitaries of the English painter Francis Bacon.

Edmund Husserl, the phenomenologist philosopher, speaks of "intuitive evidence" and of the need to "keep hold of the entire range of variations." These terms might have been specially coined for the twentieth century's staging conceptions. Questions of style are today no longer conditioned by the period, but by the individual; they remain at the director's personal discretion. Karl Heinz Stroux at Düsseldorf; Boleslaw Barlog in Berlin; Oscar Fritz Schuh at Cologne, Hamburg, and at the Salzburg Festival; Gustav R. Sellner at Darmstadt and in Berlin; Heinz Hilpert at Göttingen—all these, as theater managers and directors, have devoted themselves to the entire range of the pent-up demand after 1945, of the aggressive modern drama and the international classics. Stage designers like Caspar Neher, Wolfgang Znamenacek, Helmut Jürgens, Rochus Gliese, Teo Otto, and Emil Preetorius took care of "the entire range of variations" in scenery. Filmlike transparency of the elements of décor, cool stylization and imaginative irreality on the visual side contributed much to the style of staging.

Otto Schenk's production of Verdi's Macbeth, *with Anja Silja, Nationaltheater, Munich, 1967. Stylized technical setting by Rudolf Heinrich.*

Stage design by Caspar Neher for Shakespeare's Coriolanus, *1925.*

Scenery by Franz Mertz for G. R. Sellner's production of Sophocles' Oedipus Rex *at the Landestheater, Darmstadt, 1952. An example of stylized classical Greek drama on the modern stage.*

Jean Vilar for many years favored a bare, black-lined stage which he peopled with a colorfully costumed ensemble that captivated by the perfection of its gestures and diction. When he opened his Théâtre National Populaire in 1951, in the Palais de Chaillot opposite the Eiffel tower in Paris, he had on the playbill two star parts for Gérard Philipe: Corneille's *Cid,* and Kleist's *The Prince of Homburg.* Through the Festival d'Art Dramatique at Avignon, Vilar tried, as did later Roger Planchon at Lyons, to renew the French theater by work in the provinces. In 1967 he undertook, at the instance of André Malraux, to work out a radical reform of the state opera houses in Paris.

The Italian stage and motion-picture director Luchino Visconti, sometimes in collaboration with Roberto Rossellini, is regarded as the founder of neorealism. He got Salvador Dali to design for a Shakespeare production in Rome, he produced operas by Bellini and Verdi at La Scala, Milan, at Spoleto, in Paris and in Berlin. His *Falstaff* in Vienna was conducted by Leonard Bernstein, his *Rosenkavalier* in London by Georg Solti. Social commitment, detached and objective obsession with, and passion for the elementary are characteristic of Visconti's films, too, as indicated even by such titles as the early *Ossessione* (1943) and *La terra trema* (1948).

His fellow countryman Franco Zeffirelli won first prize at the 1965 Théâtre des Nations season in Paris for his production of *Romeo and Juliet* with the ensemble of the Florence theater. A year earlier Zeffirelli gave proof of his artistic versatility by staging Albee's *Who's Afraid of Virginia Woolf?* at Venice and *Tosca* at the Paris Opera, with Maria Callas in the title role.

Two of today's internationally known directors started with the stage and went on to devote themselves predominantly to the screen. They are, in the United States, Elia Kazan, who was responsible both for the first production of Tennessee Williams's *A Streetcar Named Desire* (1947, Barrymore Theatre, New York) and for the 1951 film version of it with Marlon Brando and Vivien Leigh—and, in Sweden, Ingmar Bergman. While Kazan was shooting *On the Waterfront,* Bergman created the somber, melancholy *Sawdust and Tinsel.* After his successful production of Stravinsky's opera *The Rake's Progress* at the Royal Opera of Stockholm in 1961, Bergman made plans for a Swedish repertory theater of international status, but nothing came of them in the end. The magic, or the lure, of the motion picture prevailed.

In Prague, Jan Grossman of the Balustrade Theater developed an individual form of stylization, which proved highly impressive in such productions as *Ubu Roi* by Jarry, and *The Trial,* after Kafka's novel. The Polish director Tadeusz Kantor professed his faith in the "circus as elementary basis" with his 1966 production in Germany of *Der Schrank,* by S. I. Witkiewicz—after the original *W malym dworku* ("In a Small Countryhouse").

In Moscow, Ruben Simonov carried on the tradition of his teacher Vakhtangov. He revived the latter's last production, the famous *Princess Turandot* and won unanimous acclaim with it at the Vienna and Zurich Festival Weeks in 1968.

But loyal adherence over decades to a particular theatrical conception, such as is likewise exemplified in the Salzburg *Jedermann,* is the exception nowadays, standing out in isolation against the modern theater's efforts at innovation and subjectivization.

What can, and should, be the director's task? The first answer that comes to mind is the traditional one: to serve the play. The second answer is: to carry the play further. The third: to defy the play. The boundaries are blurred. Seemingly only to serve the play, to explore its possibilities and make plain its unretouched core may, in disturbed times, actually amount to defiance. During the Second World War, from 1939 to 1945, the Schauspielhaus at Zürich stood out on the continent of Europe as the last island of cosmopolitan, free, German-language theater. Under Oskar Wälterlin, Leonard Steckel, and Leopold Lindtberg it opened its doors to modern works that had no access to the stage elsewhere in Europe. It was here that the first performances took place of Georg Kaiser's *Soldat Tanaka* (1940), Brecht's *Mutter Courage* (1941), and *Der Gute Mensch von Sezuan* (1943).

John Steinbeck's *The Moon Is Down* (an adaptation of the novel) had its German-language premiere at Basel in 1943. The performances at the Basel Stadttheater sold out days ahead. In Switzerland, Steinbeck's play was understood as a contribution to the country's own spiritual defense. Oskar Wälterlin, who otherwise was hard to interest in an outspoken political play, chose khaki-colored, imaginary uniforms and placed the main accent on "men acting as tools of the powers behind them," in a struggle in which "brutality is defeated by the spirit" (G. Schoop). All his effects were brought out from within. His success was all the more resounding. In serving the play, he demonstrated its importance for the time, intensified by the director's responsible, personal declaration of faith.

Wälterlin wrote in 1947,

> the theater serves the play, but the play must be infused with the spirit of a present-day, living performance that rejects any attempts to turn it to a purpose. The performance must bring out the drama's inner view and attitude. Without that, it is a mere textbook, occasioning a movement, which is the independent work of stage representation at any given moment. We

are faced not with a static situation of once-and-for-all validity, but with a process.

The same approach can be found in Piscator, notwithstanding the wholly different results of his staging.

> The director simply cannot be a mere "servant" of the play [he wrote], because the play is not something rigid and final, but, once launched into the world, becomes rooted in time, acquires a patina, and assimilates new contents of consciousness. It is the director's task to find the viewpoint from which he can uncover the roots of the dramatic creation. This viewpoint cannot be discovered by excogitation nor chosen arbitrarily. Only to the extent that the director feels himself to be the servant and exponent of his time, will he succeed in fixing the viewpoint which he has in common with the crucial forces that shape the nature of an age.

The second possibility of creative direction, that of carrying the play further, may in lucky cases lead to very satisfactory results. When Jean-Louis Barrault in 1942 was preparing a production of Claudel's *Le Soulier de satin* ("The Satin Slipper") from the Comédie Française in Paris, he was in constant contact with the author. His original idea, which Claudel approved, to divide the monster play between two evenings, was rejected by the committee of the Comédie Française. The only thing to do was to cut, cut, cut . . . with resulting breaks in the text and meaning. Claudel himself came to rehearsals. Barrault proposed changes, and he has told how carefully Claudel was prepared to consider them: "Next day I was at the Comédie Française at eight o'clock. A telephone call: Claudel has had an inspiration overnight and has rewritten the whole scene. At nine he's there, in tears. The sixty-six-year-old author weeps like an eighteen-year-old . . . We locked ourselves into a small room in the theater, and he read to me what he had written down all in one piece during the night."

The joint "version pour la scène" was included in the collected edition of Claudel's works with the note: "cut, rewritten, and arranged in collaboration with Jean-Louis Barrault."

But there are examples of the contrary, too. In 1967 Rudolf Noelte undertook to direct Max Frisch's new play *Biografie* at Zürich. Rehearsals started in the presence of both author and director, but then differences of opinion developed between them. Leopold Lindtberg took over from Noelte. Noelte in his turn brought an action claiming that alterations due to his suggestions should be indicated as such. Frisch refused.

There is less chance of conflict when the author in question is

Open Theatre, New York, during rehearsal for Peter Feldman's production of The Masks, *with one-acters by Brecht, Ionesco, and others.*

Scenery by Teo Otto for Kurt Hirschfeld's production of Andorra, *by Max Frisch, first performance November 2, 1961, at the Schauspielhaus, Zürich. Final scene with Peter Brogle as Andri.*

already dead. Giorgio Strehler produced Pirandello's unfinished play *I giganti della montagna* ["The Mountain Giants"] with a third act, in pantomime, added. He took his cue from a report by Pirandello's son, who related to him that during the night before his father's death, the latter had told him of his intention to end the play with a pantomime and had explained to him the whole conception of the cryptic play.

In the first production, in 1930, of Reinhard Goering's *Die Südpol-expedition des Kapitäns Scott,* Leopold Jessner placed the third act before the second. Rudolf Noelte, when directing Chekhov's *The Three Sisters* at Stuttgart in 1965, reduced the whole play to one setting; a subtle change of lighting transposed the lyrical, melancholy drama into a realm of strident loneliness, in which total resignation was tantamount to nihilism.

Not only directors, but dramatists, too, give new and different interpretations to the plays of others. Jean-Paul Sartre adapted Euripides' *Trojan Women*; Peter Hacks, Aristophanes' *Peace* (the *Eirene*). At about the same time, Karolos Koun, touring with his Greek Art Theater of Athens, introduced his version of the classical drama. He saw it as "deeply rooted in its soil, universal, and eternal." In the 1968 classical Greek version of Carl Orff's *Prometheus*—produced in Stuttgart by G. R. Sellner and in Munich by August Everding—the composer surpassed his *Oedipus* and *Antigone*. He drew from the classical tragedy new musical and scenic effects bridging the span between ancient times and the present.

Theater, when it reaches perfection, is both the most ancient and the most contemporary representation of man's vulnerability in the face of unfathomable forces.

For generations, there has been much heated discussion on how to direct and produce the classics. Shaw in his day was greatly agitated by the arbitrary rearrangement of scenes when Beerbohm Tree and Henry Irving produced Shakespeare on their realistic and gorgeously equipped London stages. Their objective, as Charles Kean's before them, was to achieve impressive tableaus. Thus they translated Shakespeare's scenic fantasy into their own concept of realistic theatrical style.

In the twentieth century works by Shakespeare and Schiller served to explore another problematic aspect of theatrical direction: to bring out provocation within the framework of the play. The results were not infrequently scandal and shock. Piscator, in 1926 in Berlin, politicized Schiller's *Die Räuber* and had Spiegelberg (an ambitious villain) wear a mask representing Trotsky. Hansgünther Heyme, in 1966 in Wiesbaden, went so far as to rework *Wilhelm Tell* to make it express "the inhumanity of all mass revolts."

In search of a new approach to Shakespeare's historical dramas, Peter Palitzsch, in Stuttgart in 1967, forced the *Henry VI* trilogy into a format that spread over two evenings. He presented this monumental chronicle as *The Wars of the Roses* (with sets by Wilfried Minks) —and interpreted it as a programmatic example of unscrupulous greed for power. The limping, hunchbacked Richard of Gloucester announces in a monologue (excerpted from *Richard III* and rearranged as prologue) toward what end his ambitions were driving him. A year later, Palitzsch logically followed up with a new production of *Richard III*—a parallel to the Shakespeare cycle *The Wars of the Roses* produced at Stratford-on-Avon by Peter Hall, whose vast and rich achievement drew on assassination, politics, intrigue, and war.

Thomas Mann once joked about *Die Räuber* and said that the play could be regarded as a sort of superior "Western." This is roughly what Peter Zadek did with his 1966 production at Bremen. He transposed the play into today's world of mass consumption. Wilfried Minks designed a cyclorama with comic strips, after a painting by Roy Lichtenstein. A year later, Zadek produced Shakespeare's *Measure for Measure* as an example of "intuitive, subjective direction," as he himself explained. On an empty stage, edged by Minks with a braid of colored electric bulbs, Zadek showed "what happens in the imagination on reading the play." Asked at a conference at Munich where the limits of subjective direction lay, Zadek answered with disarming frankness: "When the public refuses to follow us, we've got to stop."

Peter Brook sums up the problem in terms of an added dimension, the crucial relationship between theater and society: "A stable and harmonious society might need only to look for ways of reflecting and reaffirming its harmony in its theatres. Such theatres could set out to unite cast and audience in a mutual 'yes.' But a shifting, chaotic world often must choose between a playhouse that offers a spurious 'yes' or a provocation so strong that it splinters its audience into fragments of vivid 'nos.' "

So long as audiences do not forget that they are creative partners in the theater and not mere passive consumers, so long as they assert their right to take a spontaneous part in the performance by their approval or protest, so long will the theater continue to be an exciting element in our life.

Kosinsky scene in Peter Zadek's production of Schiller's Räuber, *Bremen, 1966. Scenery by Wilfried Minks, with background projection after Roy Lichtenstein.*

Bibliography

Standard Works and Dictionaries

Altman, G., et al., *Theater Pictorial: A History of World Theater as Recorded in Drawings, Paintings, Engravings and Photographs.* Berkeley, 1953.

d'Amico, S., *Storia del teatro drammatico.* 4 vols. Milan, 1950 ff., 1968.

Bentley, E., *The Life of the Drama.* New York, 1964.

Bowman, W. B., and Ball, R. H., *Theatre Language: A Dictionary of Terms in English of the Drama and Stage from Medieval to Modern Times.* New York, 1961.

Braga, T., *Historia do teatro portuguez.* Porto, 1870 ff.

Brockett, O. G., *History of the Theatre.* Boston, 1968.

Cheney, S. W., *The Theatre: Three Thousand Years of Drama, Acting and Stagecraft.* New York, 1952.

Cheshire, D., *Theatre: History, Criticism and Reference.* 1967.

Chujoy, A. and P. W., *The Dance Encyclopedia.* New York, 1967.

Clark, B. H., ed., *European Theories of the Drama.* Newly revised by H. Popkin. New York, 1965.

Dějiny Českého Divadla. Vols. I–IV. Prague, 1968 ff.

Devrient, E., *Geschichte der deutschen Schauspielkunst.* 1848. New edition by H. Devrient. Berlin, 1905.

Dubech, L., *Histoire générale illustrée du théâtre.* 5 vols. Paris, 1931 ff.

Enciclopedia dello spettacolo. 9 vols. and supplement. Rome, 1954–62, 1966.

Ewen, D., *The Complete Book of the American Theatre.* New York and London, 1959.

Fergusson, F., *The Idea of a Theater.* Princeton, 1949.

———, *The Human Image in Dramatic Literature.* Garden City, N.Y., 1957.

Freedley, G., and Reeves, J. A., *History of the Theatre.* New York, 1968.

Gascoigne, B., *World Theatre: An Illustrated History.* Boston, 1968.

Gassner, J., and Quinn, E., editors, *The Reader's Encyclopedia of World Drama.* New York, 1969.

Gregor, J., *Weltgeschichte des Theaters.* Zurich, 1933.

Hartnoll, P., ed., *The Oxford Companion to the Theatre.* London, 1951, 1967.

Hartnoll, P., *A Concise History of the Theatre.* London, 1968.

Hewett, B., *Theatre USA, 1668–1957.* New York, 1959.

Hilleström, G., *Theatre and Ballet in Sweden.* Stockholm, 1953.

Histoire des spectacles. Encyclopédie de la Pléiade. Paris, 1965.

Hughes, G., *A History of the American Theatre, 1700–1950.* New York, 1951.

Hürlimann, M., ed., *Atlantisbuch des Theaters*. Zurich, 1966.
Kindermann, H., *Theatergeschichte Europas*. (9 vols. Vienna, 1957 ff. published so far)
Knudsen, H., *Deutsche Theatergeschichte*. Stuttgart, 1959, 1969.
Kutscher, A., *Grundriß der Theaterwissenschaft*. Munich, 1949.
Laver, J., *Drama: Its Costume and Decor*. London, 1951.
Macgowan, K., and Melnitz, W., *The Living Stage*. New York, 1955.
Mantzius, K., *A History of Theatrical Art*. London, 1903.
Melchinger, Siegfried, and Rischbieter, H., *Welttheater*. Braunschweig, 1962.
Nagler, A. M., *Sources of Theatrical History*. New York, 1952.
Nicoll, A., *Masks, Mimes and Miracles*. London, 1931.
———, *The Development of the Theatre*. London, 1949, 1966.
———, *World Drama from Aeschylus to Anouilh*. London, 1949.
Prat, A. V., *Historia del teatro español*. Barcelona, 1956.
Prideaux, T., *World Theatre in Pictures*. Philadelphia, 1953.
Roberts, V. M., *On Stage: A History of the Theatre*. New York, 1962.
Schöne, G., *Tausend Jahre deutsches Theater*. Munich, 1962.
Schwanbeck, G., *Bibliographie der deutschsprachigen Hochschulschriften zur Theaterwissenschaft von 1885–1952*. Berlin, 1956. Continued for the years 1953–1960 by H. J. Rojek. Berlin, 1962.
Shergold, N. D., *A History of the Spanish Stage from Medieval Times until the End of the 17th Century*. Oxford, 1967.
Southern, R., *The Seven Ages of the Theatre*. New York, 1961.
Stamm, R., *Geschichte des englischen Theaters*. Bern, 1951.
Taylor, J. R., *The Penguin Dictionary of the Theatre*. London and New York, 1966.
El Teatro: Enciclopedia del arte escénico. Barcelona, 1958.
Varneke, B. V., *History of the Russian Theatre*. New York, 1951.
Wilson, G., *A History of American Acting*. Bloomington, 1966.
Young, S., *The Theatre*. New York, 1937.

The Primitive Theater

Albright, W. F., *Von der Steinzeit zum Christentum*. Munich, 1949.
Cornford, F. M., *The Origin of Attic Comedy*. London, 1914.
Eberle, O., *Cenalora: Leben, Glaube, Tanz und Theater der Urvölker*. Olten, Switzerland, 1954.
Frazer, J. G., *The Golden Bough: A Study in Magic and Religion*. London, 1911.
Freud, S., *Totem und Tabu*. Vienna, 1913.
Havemeyer, L., *The Drama of Savage Peoples*. New Haven, 1916.
Hunningher, B., *The Origin of the Theater*. New York, 1961.
Lommel, A., *Masken: Gesichter der Menschheit*. Zurich/Freiburg, 1970.
Oesterley, W. O. E., *The Sacred Dance*. Cambridge, 1923.
Reich, H., *Der Mimus*. Berlin, 1903.
Wilson, A. E., *The Story of Pantomime*. London, 1949.

Egypt and the Ancient East

Brunner-Traut, E., *Der Tanz im alten Ägypten*. Hamburg-New York, 1938.

Gaster, T. H., *Thespis: Ritual, Myth and Drama in the Ancient Near East*. New York, 1950.

Horovitz, J., "Das ägyptische Schattentheater," by F. Kern. Appendix to *Spuren griechischer Mimen im Orient*. Berlin, 1905.

Sethe, K., *Dramatische Texte zu altägyptischen Mysterienspielen*. Leipzig, 1928.

Soden, W. von, "Ein Zwiegespräch Chammurabis mit einer Frau." *Zeitschrift für Assyrologie*, 15. New series, 1950.

The Islamic Civilizations

And, M., *A History of Theatre and Popular Entertainment in Turkey*. Ankara, 1963.

Jacob, G., *Das Schattentheater in seiner Wanderung vom Morgenland zum Abendland*. Berlin, 1901.

Pelly, Sir Lewis, *The Miracle Play of Hasan and Husain*. Collected from oral tradition by Colonel Sir L. Pelly. 1879.

Rezvani, M., *Le Théâtre et la danse en Iran*. Paris, 1962.

Indo-Pacific Civilizations

Ambrose, K., *Classical Dances and Costumes of India*. Introduction by Ram Gopal. London, 1950.

Anand, M. R., *The Indian Theatre*. London, 1950.

Bacot, J., *Zugiñima*. Paris, 1957.

Bharata, *Natyasastra*. Translated by M. Ghose. Bengal, 1950.

Gargi, B., *The Theatre in India*. New York, 1962.

Gupta, C. B., *The Indian Theatre*. Banaras, 1954.

Iyer, K. B., *Kathakali: The Sacred Dance-Drama of Malabar*. London, 1955.

Keith, A. B., *The Sanskrit Drama in its Origin, Development, Theory and Practice*. Oxford, 1924.

Kindermann, H., ed., *Fernöstliches Theater*. Stuttgart, 1966.

Konow, S., *Das indische Theater*. Berlin-Leipzig, 1920.

Lévi, S., *Le Théâtre indien*. Paris, 1890, 1963.

Mathur, J., *Drama in Rural India*. New York, 1964.

Mellema, R. L., *Wayang Puppets: Carving, Colouring, Symbolism*. Amsterdam, 1954.

Schuyler, M., *A Bibliography of the Sanskrit Drama with an Introductory Sketch of the Dramatic Literature of India*. New York, 1906, 1965.

Wilson, H. H., *Select Specimens of the Theatre of the Hindus*. Calcutta, 1955.

Zoete, B. de, and Spies, W., *Dance and Drama in Bali*. London, 1938.

China

Alley, R., *Peking Opera*. Peking, 1957.
Arlington, L. C., *The Chinese Drama from the Earliest Times until Today*. Shanghai, 1930.
Chen, J., *The Chinese Theatre*. London, 1949.
Granet, M., *Danses et légendes de la Chine ancienne*. 2 vols. Paris, 1926.
Johnston, R. F., *The Chinese Drama*. Shanghai, 1921.
Kalvodovà-sis-Vanis, *Schüler des Birngartens: Das chinesische Singspiel*. Prague, 1956.
Laufer, B., *Oriental Theatricals*. Chicago: Field Museum of Natural History, 1923.
Lee Hae-ku, "Korean Mask Drama." *Korean Journal*. Seoul, November 1961.
Obraszow, S., *Das chinesische Theater*. Velber by Hannover, 1965.
Roy, C., *L'Opéra Pekin*. Paris, 1955.
Scott, A. C., *The Classical Theatre of China*. London, 1957.
———, *An Introduction to the Chinese Theatre*. London, 1959.
Tsong-nee Ku, *Modern Chinese Plays*. Shanghai, 1941.
Winsatt, G., *Chinese Shadow Shows*. Cambridge, Mass., 1936.
Yang, R. F. S., *The Social Background of the Yüan Drama*. Mon. Serica, vol. XVII. 1958.
Zucker, A. E., *The Chinese Theatre*. Boston, 1925.
Zung, C. S. L., *Secrets of the Chinese Drama*. New York, 1964.

Japan

Araki, J. T., *The Ballad-Drama of Medieval Japan*. Berkeley/Los Angeles, 1964.
Arnott, Peter, *The Theatres of Japan*. London, 1969.
Bowers, F., *Japanese Theatre*. Introduction by Joshua Logan. New York, 1951.
Brandon, J. R., *The Theatre of Southeast Asia*. Cambridge, Mass., 1967.
Ernst, E., *The Kabuki Theatre*. London, 1956.
Haar, F., *Japanese Theatre in Highlight: A Pictorial Commentary*. Tokyo, 1952.
Halford, A. and G., *The Kabuki-Handbook*. Rutland-Tokyo, 1956.
Hironaga, S., *Bunraku: Japan's Unique Puppet Theatre*. Tokyo, 1964.
Kawatake, S., *An Illustrated History of Japanese Theatre Arts*. Tokyo, 1955.
———, *Kabuki: Japanese Drama*. Tokyo, 1958.
Keene, D., *Major Plays of Chikamatsu*. Translated by D. Keene. New York, 1961.
———, *Bunraku: The Art of the Japanese Puppet Theatre*. Tokyo, 1965.
Kincaid, Z., *Kabuki: The Popular Stage of Japan*. London, 1925.
Lucas, H., *Japanische Kultmasken*. Kassel, 1965.
Miyamori, A., *Masterpieces of Chikamatsu, the Japanese Shakespeare*. New York, 1926.
Muccioli, M., *Il teatro giapponese*. 2 vols. Milan, 1962.
O'Neill, P. G., *A Guide to Nô*. Tokyo, 1953.

———, *Early Nô Drama*. London, 1958.
Ortolani, B., *Das Kabuki-Theater: Kulturgeschichte der Anfänge*. Tokyo, 1964.
Peri, N., *Le Nô*. Tokyo, 1944.
Pound, E., and Fenollosa, E., *The Classic Noh Theatre of Japan*. New York, 1959. New edition of *Noh or Accomplishment: a Study of the Classical Stage of Japan*. 1917.
Sakanishi, S., *Kyôgen*. Boston, 1938.
Scott, A. C., *The Kabuki Theatre of Japan*. London, 1955.
Shaver, R. M., *Kabuki Costume*. Tokyo, 1966.
Waley, A., *The Nô Plays of Japan*. London, 1921.

Greece and Rome

Allen, J. T., *Greek Acting in the Fifth Century before Christ*. Berkeley, 1916.
———, *The Greek Theatre of the Fifth Century before Christ*. Berkeley, 1920.
Arnott, P. D., *An Introduction to the Greek Theatre*. London, 1961.
———, *Greek Scenic Conventions in the Fifth Century B.C.* Oxford, 1962.
Beare, W., *The Roman Stage*. London, 1964.
Bernhart, J., *Bibel und Mythus*. Munich, 1954.
Bieber, M., *The History of the Greek and Roman Theatre*. Princeton, 1961.
Breitholz, L., *Die dorische Farce*. Uppsala, 1960.
Bulle, H., and Wirsing, H., *Szenenbilder zum griechischen Theater des 5. Jahrhunderts v. Chr.* Berlin, 1950.
Duckworth, G. E., *The Nature of Roman Comedy*. Princeton, 1952.
Fiechter, E., *Antike griechische Theaterbauten*. 9 vols. Stuttgart, 1930 ff.
Flickinger, R. C., *The Greek Theatre and Its Drama*. Chicago, 1936.
Hamilton, E., *The Roman Way*. New York, 1932.
———, *The Greek Way*. New York, 1952.
Hanson, J. A., *Roman Theatre-Temples*. Princeton, 1959.
Kitto, H. D. F., *Greek Tragedy*. New York, 1952.
Norwood, G., *Greek Tragedy*. London, 1920.
———, *Greek Comedy*. London, 1931.
Pickard-Cambridge, A. W., *The Theatre of Dionysus in Athens*. Oxford, 1946.
———, *The Dramatic Festivals of Athens*. Oxford, 1953.
———, *Dithyramb, Tragedy and Comedy*. Oxford, 1962.
Rees, K., *The Rule of the Three Actors in the Classical Greek Drama*. Chicago, 1908.
Rockwood, J., *The Craftsmen of Dionysus: An Approach to Acting*. Chicago, 1966.
Schadewaldt, W., *Antike und Gegenwart: Über die Tragödie*. Munich, 1966.
Webster, T. B. L., *Greek Theatre Production*. London, 1956.
Whitman, C. H., *Sophocles: A Study of Heroic Humanism*. Cambridge, Mass., 1966.

Byzantium

Beckwith, J., *Art of Constantinople.* London: Phaidon, 1961.
Dölger, F., *Die byzantinische Dichtung in der Reinsprache.* Berlin, 1948.
Houston, M. G., *Ancient Greek, Roman and Byzantine Costume and Decoration.* 2d ed. London, 1947.
La Piana, G., "The Byzantine Theatre." *Speculum, a Journal of Mediaeval Studies* 11. April 1936.
Morey, C. R., *Early Christian Art.* Princeton, 1953.
Sherrard, P., *Constantinople.* London, 1965.
Theocharidis, G., *Beiträge zur Geschichte des byzantinischen Profantheaters im IV. und V. Jahrhundert.* Saloniki, 1940.
Vogt, A., "Le Théâtre à Byzance dans l'empire du IVe au XIIIe siècle." *Revue des questions historiques* 59. 1930.
———, "Etudes sur le théâtre byzantin." *Byzantion* VI. 1931.

The Middle Ages

Anz, H., *Die lateinischen Magierspiele.* Leipzig, 1905.
Borcherdt, H. H., *Das europäische Theater im Mittelalter und in der Renaissance.* Leipzig, 1935.
Brooks, N. C., "The Sepulchre of Christ in Art and Liturgy." *University of Illinois Studies in Language and Literature* VII, 2. May 1921.
Carey, M., The Wakefield Group in the Towneley Cycle. Göttingen, 1930 (*Hesperia.* Supplement, no. 11).
Catholy, E., *Das deutsche Lustspiel: Vom Mittelalter bis zum Ende der Barockzeit.* Stuttgart, 1969.
Chambers, E. K., *The Medieval Stage.* 2 vols. Oxford, 1903.
Cohen, G. *Geschichte der Inszenierung in geistlichen Drama des Mittelalters in Frankreich.* Leipzig, 1907.
Craig, H., *English Religious Drama of the Middle Ages.* Oxford, 1960.
Craik, T. W., *The Tudor Interlude: Stage, Costume and Acting.* Leicester: The University Press, 1958.
Donovan, R. B., *Liturgical Drama in the Medieval Spain.* Toronto, 1958.
Evans, M. B., *The Passion Play of Lucerne.* New York, 1943.
Frank, G., *The Medieval French Drama.* Oxford, 1954.
———, *The Medieval Drama.* Oxford, 1960.
Gardiner, H. C., *Mysteries' End: An Investigation of the Last Days of the Medieval Religious Stage.* New Haven, 1946.
Hardison, O. B., *Christian Rite and Christian Drama in the Middle Ages: Essays in the Origin and Early History of Modern Drama.* Baltimore, 1965.
Herrmann, M., *Forschungen zur deutschen Theatergeschichte des Mittelalters und der Renaissance.* Berlin, 1914.
Hunningher, B., *The Origin of the Theatre.* New York, 1961.

Ludus Coventriae (or the Plaie called Corpus Christi, Cotton Ms. Vespasian D. VIII), by K. S. Block. London, 1922.

Michael, W. F., *Die geistlichen Prozessionsspiele in Deutschland.* Baltimore, 1947.

———, *Frühformen der deutschen Bühne.* Berlin, 1963.

Paecht, O., *The Rise of Pictorial Narrative in the Twelfth Century.* Oxford, 1962.

Salter, F. M., *Medieval Drama in Chester.* Toronto, 1955.

Sharp, T., *A Dissertation on the Pageants or Dramatic Mysteries Anciently Performed at Coventry.* 1825.

Shergold, N. D., *A History of the Spanish Stage from Medieval Times until the End of the 17th Century.* Oxford, 1967.

Shoemaker, W. H., *The Multiple Stage in Spain during the Fifteenth and Sixteenth Centuries.* Princeton, 1935.

Southern, R., *The Medieval Theatre in the Round.* London, 1957.

Stratman, C. J., *Bibliography of Medieval Drama.* Berkeley, 1954.

Stuart, D. C., *Stage Decoration in France in the Middle Ages.* New York, 1910.

Weiner, A. B., *Philippe de Mezières' Description of the "Festum Praesentationis Beatae Mariae".* Translated from the Latin and introduced by an essay on the Birth of Modern Acting. New Haven, 1958.

Wickham, G., *Early English Stages, 1300–1660.* 2 vols. London, 1959/63.

Williams, A., *The Drama of Medieval England.* East Lansing: Michigan State University Press, 1961.

Young, K., *The Drama of the Medieval Church.* 2 vols. Oxford, 1933.

The Renaissance

Adams, J. C., *The Globe Playhouse: Its Design and Equipment.* Cambridge, 1942. 2d ed. New York, 1961.

Adams, J. Q., *Shakespearean Playhouses: A History of English Theatres from the Beginning to the Restoration.* Boston, 1917.

Baldwin, T. W., *Organization and Personnel of the Shakespearean Company.* Princeton, 1927.

Beckerman, B., *Shakespeare at the Globe, 1599–1609.* New York, 1962.

Bentley, G. E., *The Jacobean and Caroline Stage.* 5 vols. Oxford, 1941–56.

Beutler, E., *Forschungen und Texte zur frühhumanistischen Komödie.* Hamburg, 1927.

Boas, F. S., *University Drama in the Tudor Age.* Oxford, 1914.

———, *An Introduction to Stuart Drama.* London, 1946.

Bowers, F. T., *Elizabethan Revenge Tragedy, 1587–1642.* Princeton, 1940.

Bradbrook, M. C., *Themes and Conventions of Elizabethan Tragedy.* Cambridge, 1935.

———, *The Growth and Structure of Elizabethan Comedy.* London, 1955.

Bradley, A. C., *Shakespearean Tragedy.* London, 1904.

Brooke, C. F. T., *The Tudor Drama.* Boston, 1911.

Campbell, L. B., *Scenes and Machines on the English Stage during the Renaissance.* Cambridge, 1923. Reprinted, New York, 1960.

Catholy, E., *Fastnachtspiel.* Stuttgart, 1966.

Chambers, E. K., *The Elizabethan Stage.* 4 vols. Oxford, 1923.

Chesnaye, N. de la, *La Condemnacion de Bancquet.* New York, 1965.

Crawford, J. P. W., *Spanish Drama before Lope de Vega.* Philadelphia, 1937.

Ellis-Fermor, U., *The Jacobean Drama: An Interpretation.* London, 1936.

Gildersleeve, V., *Government Regulation of the Elizabethan Drama.* New York, 1908.

Harbage, A., *Shakespeare's Audience.* New York, 1958.

Hathaway, B., *The Age of Criticism: the Late Renaissance in Italy.* Ithaca, N.Y., 1962.

Herrick, M., *Italian Comedy in the Renaissance.* Urbana, Ill., 1960.

———, *Italian Tragedy in the Renaissance.* Urbana, Ill., 1965.

Herrmann, M., *Entstehung der berufsmäßigen Schauspielkunst im Altertum und in der Neuzeit.* Berlin, 1962.

Hewitt, B., ed., *The Renaissance Stage: Documents of Serlio, Sabbattini and Furttenbach.* Coral Gables: University of Miami Press, 1958.

Hodges, C. W., *The Globe Restored.* London, 1953.

———, *Shakespeare's Theatre.* London, 1964.

Hotson, L., *Shakespeare's Wooden O.* New York, 1960.

Jacquot, J., ed., *Les Fêtes de la Renaissance.* 2 vols. Paris, 1956/60.

———, *Le Lieu théâtral à la Renaissance.* Paris, 1964.

Jeffery, B., *French Renaissance Comedy, 1552–1630.* Oxford, 1969.

Joseph, B., *Elizabethan Acting.* London, 1951.

Kennard, J., *The Italian Theatre.* 2 vols. New York, 1932.

Kernodle, G. R., *From Art to Theatre: Form and Convention in the Renaissance.* Chicago, 1944.

Knights, L. C., *Drama and Society in the Age of Jonson.* London, 1937.

Köster, A., *Die Meistersingerbühne des 16. Jahrhunderts: Ein Versuch des Wiederaufbaus.* Halle, 1921.

Kott, J., *Shakespeare Our Contemporary.* London, 1964.

Lawrence, W. J., *The Elizabethan Playhouse and Other Studies.* 2 vols. Stratford-on-Avon, 1912–13.

———, *Pre-Restoration Stage Studies.* Cambridge, 1927.

Lynch, J. J., *Box, Pit and Gallery: Stage and Society in Jonson's London.* Berkeley, 1953.

Maassen, J., *Drama und Theater der Humanistenschulen in Deutschland.* Augsburg, 1929.

Merchant, W. M., *Shakespeare and the Artist.* London, 1959.

Moulton, R. G., *Shakespeare as a Dramatic Artist.* London, 1893.

Nagler, A. M., *Shakespeare's Stage.* New Haven, 1958.

———, *Theatre Festivals of the Medici, 1539–1637.* New Haven and London, 1964.

Nicoll, A., *Stuart Masques and the Renaissance Stage.* New York, 1938, 1963.

Ornstein, R., *The Moral Vision of Jacobean Tragedy.* Madison/Milwaukee, Wisc., 1960.

Phialas, P. G., *Shakespeare's Romantic Comedies: The Development of Their Form and Meaning.* Chapel Hill, N.C., 1966.

Reynolds, G. F., *The Staging of Elizabethan Plays at the Red Bull Theatre, 1605–1625.* New York, 1940.

Ribner, I., *Jacobean Tragedy: The Quest for Moral Order.* New York, 1962.

Schanzer, E., *The Problem Plays of Shakespeare.* New York, 1963.

Schmidt, P. E., *Die Bühnenverhältnisse des deutschen Schuldramas und seiner volkstümlichen Ableger im 16. Jahrhundert.* Berlin, 1903.

Schöne, G., *Die Entwicklung der Perspektive von Serlio bis, Galli-Bibiena: Nach den Perspektivbüchern.* Leipzig, 1933.

Skopnik, G., *Das Straßburger Schultheater: Sein Spielplan und seine Bühne.* Frankfurt, 1935.

Smith, I., *Shakespeare's Blackfriars Playhouse. Its History and Its Design.* New York, 1964.

Sprague, A. C., *Shakespearean Players and Performances.* Cambridge, Mass., 1953.

Sumberg, S., *The Nuremberg Schembart Carnival.* New York, 1941.

Tillyard, E. M. W., *Shakespeare's History Plays.* London, 1944.

Vitruvius, *The Ten Books of Architecture.* Translated by M. H. Morgan. Cambridge, Mass., 1914.

Weimann, R., *Shakespeare und die Tradition des Volkstheaters.* Berlin, 1967.

Weisbach, W., *Trionfi.* Berlin, 1919.

The Baroque

Alasseur, C., *La Comédie française au 18e siècle.* Paris, 1967.

Attinger, G., *L'Esprit de la commedia dell'arte dans le théâtre français.* Paris, 1950.

Aubrin, C. V., *La Comédie espagnole (1600–1680).* Paris, 1966.

Avery, E. L., *The London Stage, 1700–1729.* Carbondale/Edwardsville, Ill., 1968.

Avery, E. L., and Scouten, A. H., *The London Stage, 1660–1700.* Carbondale/Edwardsville, Ill., 1968.

Baesecke, A., *Das Schauspiel der englischen Komödianten in Deutschland.* Halle, 1935.

Baur-Heinhold, M., *Baroque Theatre.* London and New York, 1967.

Beijer, A., *Court Theatres of Drottningholm and Gripsholm.* Malmoe, 1933.

Berthold, M., "Joseph Furttenbach," *Ulm und Oberschwaben* XXXIII. Ulm, 1953.

Biach-Schiffmann, F., *Giovanni und Ludovico Burnacini.* Vienna-Berlin, 1931.

Bjurstrom, P., *Giacomo Torelli and Baroque Stage Design.* Stockholm, 1961.

Burckhardt, J. C., *The Civilization of the Renaissance in Italy.* New York, 1950.

Duchartre, P. L., *The Italian Comedy: The Improvisation, Scenarios, Lives, Attributes, Portraits and Masks of the Illustrious Characters of the Commedia dell'arte.* Translated by R. T. Weaver. London and New York, 1929.

Duchartre, P. L., *La commedia dell'arte et ses enfants.* Paris, 1955.

Elwin, M., *The Playgoers Handbook to Restoration Drama.* New York, 1928.

Flemming, W., *Andreas Gryphius und die Bühne.* Halle, 1921.

Fujimura, T. H., *The Restoration Comedy of Wit.* Princeton, 1952.

Gotch, A., *Inigo Jones*. London, 1928, 1968.

Hadamowsky, F., *Barocktheater am Wiener Kaiserhof (1625–1740)*. Vienna, 1955.

Hilleström, G., *Theatre and Ballet in Sweden*. Stockholm, 1953.

Hinck, W., *Das deutsche Lustspiel des 17. und 18. Jahrhunderts und die italienische Komödie*. Stuttgart, 1965.

Holland, N., *The First Modern Comedies*. Cambridge, Mass., 1959.

Hubert, J., *Molière and the Comedy of Intellect*. Berkeley, 1962.

Klingler, O., *Die Comédie-Italienne in Paris nach der Sammlung von Gherardi*. Strasbourg, 1902.

Kutscher, A., *Vom Salzburger Barocktheater zu den Salzburger Festspielen*. Düsseldorf, 1939.

Lancaster, H. C., *Sunset: A History of Parisian Drama in the Last Years of Louis XIV, 1701–1715*. Baltimore, 1950.

Lawrenson, T. E., *The French Stage in the XVIIth Century: A Study in the Advent of the Italian Order*. Manchester, 1957.

Lea, K. M., *Italian Popular Comedy*. 2 vols. Oxford, 1934.

Lough, J., *Paris Theatre Audiences in the Seventeenth and Eighteenth Centuries*. London, 1957.

Manifold, J. S., *The Music in English Drama from Shakespeare to Purcell*. London, 1956.

McGowan, M., *L'Art du ballet de cour en France*. Paris, 1963.

Mayor, A. H., *The Bibiena Family*. New York, 1945.

Nicoll, A., *A History of Restoration Drama, 1660–1700*. Cambridge, 1923.

———, *A History of Early Eighteenth Century Drama, 1700–1750*. Cambridge, 1925.

———, *The World of Harlequin*. Cambridge, 1963.

Niklaus, A., *Harlequin Phoenix*. London, 1956.

Odell, G. C. D., *Shakespeare from Betterton to Irving*. 2 vols. New York, 1920.

Oreglia, G., *The Commedia dell'arte*. New York, 1968.

Pandolfi, V., *La commedia dell'arte: Storia e testo*. 6 vols. Florence, 1957.

Rasi, L., *I comici italiani*. Florence, 1897.

Rennert, H., *The Spanish Stage in the Time of Lope de Vega*. New York, 1909.

Rolland, R., *Histoire de l'opéra en Europe avant Lully et Scarlatti*. Paris, 1931.

Rommel, O., *Die Alt-Wiener Volkskomödie*. Vienna, 1952.

Rudloff-Hille, G., *Barocktheater im Zwinger*. Dresden, 1954.

Scholz, J., *Baroque and Romantic Stage Design*. New York, 1962.

Schwartz, I. A., *The Commedia dell'arte and Its Influence on French Comedy in the Seventeenth Century*. Paris, 1933.

Scouten, A. H., *The London Stage, 1729–1747*. Carbondale/Edwardsville, Ill., 1968.

Smith, W., *The Commedia dell'arte*. New York, 1964.

Tintelnot, H., *Barocktheater und barocke Kunst*. Berlin, 1939.

Turnell, M., *The Classical Moment: Studies in Corneille, Molière and Racine*. New York, 1948.

Vasari, G., *Vasari's Lives of the Artists*. New York, 1957.

Vossler, K., *Die romanische Welt: Gesammelte Aufsätze*. Munich, 1965.

White, J., *The Birth and Rebirth of Pictorial Space*. London, 1957.
Wiley, W. L., *The Early Public Theatre in France*. Cambridge, Mass., 1960.
Worsthorne, S. T., *Venetian Opera in the 17th Century*. Oxford, 1954.

The Rise of the Middle-Class Drama

Arvin, N. C., *Eugène Scribe and the French Theatre, 1815–1860*. Cambridge, Mass., 1924.
Bernbaum, E., *The Drama of Sensibility: A Sketch of the History of Sentimental Comedy and Domestic Tragedy, 1696–1780*. Cambridge, Mass., 1915.
Boas, F. S., *An Introduction to Eighteenth Century Drama, 1700–1780*. New York, 1953.
Booth, M. R., *English Melodrama*. London, 1965.
Brown, T. A., *History of the New York Stage, 1836–1918*. New York, 1923.
Bruford, W. H., *Theatre, Drama and Audience in Goethe's Germany*. London, 1957.
———, *Culture and Society in Classical Weimar, 1775–1806*. Cambridge, 1962.
Burnim, K., *David Garrick, Director*. Pittsburgh, 1961.
Carlson, M., *The Theatre of the French Revolution*. Ithaca, N.Y., 1966.
Cibber, C., *An Apology for the Life of Mr. Colley Cibber*. London, 1740 (many reprints).
Cole, J. W., *The Life and Theatrical Times of Charles Kean*. 2 vols. 1859.
Cook, J. A., *Neo-Classic Drama in Spain: Theory and Practice*. Dallas, 1959.
Davies, T., *Memoirs of the Life of David Garrick*. 2 vols. London, 1780.
Disher, M., *Melodrama. Plots That Thrilled*. New York, 1954.
Findlater, R., *Six Great Actors: Garrick, Kemble, Kean, Macready, Irving, Forbes-Robertson*. 1957.
Grube, M., *Geschichte der Meininger*. Berlin, 1926.
Hawkins, F., *The French Stage in the Eighteenth Century*. 2 vols. London, 1888.
Hill, W., *Die deutschen Theaterzeitschriften des 18. Jh.*, Weimar, 1915.
Hogan, C. B., *The London Stage, 1776–1800*. Carbondale/Edwardsville, Ill., 1968.
Hommel, K., *Die Separatvorstellungen vor König Ludwig II. von Bayern*. München, 1963.
Hotson, L., *The Commonwealth and Restoration Stage*. Cambridge, Mass., 1928.
Jourdain, E. F., *Dramatic Theory and Practice in France, 1690–1808*. New York, 1921.
Kindermann, H., *Theatergeschichte der Goethezeit*. Vienna, 1948.
Knudsen, H., *Goethes Welt des Theaters*. Berlin, 1949.
Krutch, J. W., *Comedy and Conscience after the Restoration*. New York, 1949.
Lancaster, H. C., *French Tragedy in the Time of Louis XV and Voltaire, 1715–1774*. Baltimore, 1950.
Lucas, F. L., *The Decline and Fall of the Romantic Ideal*. New York, 1936.
Mander, R., and Mitchenson, J., *The Artist and the Theatre*. London, 1955.
Matthews, B., and Hutton, L., *Actors and Actresses of Great Britain and the*

United States, from the Days of David Garrick to the Present Time. 5 vols. New York, 1886.

Melcher, E., *Stage Realism in France from Diderot to Antoine.* Bryn Mawr, 1928.

Mindlin, R., *Zarzuela: Das spanische Singspiel im 19. und 20. Jahrhundert.* Zurich, 1965.

Moody, R., *America Takes the Stage: Romanticism in American Drama and Theatre, 1750–1900.* Bloomington, 1955.

Nicoll, A., *A History of Late Eighteenth Century Drama, 1750–1800.* Cambridge, 1927.

———, *A History of Early Nineteenth Century Drama, 1800–1850.* 2 vols. Cambridge, 1930.

———, *A History of Late Nineteenth Century Drama, 1850–1900.* 2 vols. Cambridge, 1946.

Odell, G. C. D., *Shakespeare from Betterton to Irving.* 2 vols. New York, 1920.

———, *Annals of the New York Stage.* 15 vols. New York, 1927–49.

Oman, C., *David Garrick.* London, 1958.

Palmer, J. L., *The Comedy of Manners.* London, 1913.

Pascal, R., *The German Sturm und Drang.* Manchester, 1953.

Pedicord, H. W., *The Theatrical Public in the Time of Garrick.* New York, 1954.

Quinn, A. H., *A History of the American Drama from the Beginning to the Civil War.* 2d ed. New York, 1943.

———, *A History of the American Drama from the Civil War to the Present Day.* 2d ed. New York, 1949.

Rowell, G., *The Victorian Theatre.* London, 1956.

Scholz, J., *Baroque and Romantic Stage Design.* New York, 1962.

Sherbo, A., *English Sentimental Drama.* East Lansing, Mich., 1957.

Sichardt, G., *Das Weimarer Liebhabertheater unter Goethes Leitung.* Weimar, 1957.

Slonim, M., *Russian Theatre from the Empire to the Soviets.* Cleveland, 1961.

Southern, R., *The Georgian Playhouse.* London, 1948.

———, *Changeable Scenery: Its Origin and Development in the British Theatre.* London, 1952.

St. Clare Burne, M., "Charles Kean and the Meininger Myth." *Theatre Research* VI, 3. 1964.

Stone, G. W., Jr., *The London Stage, 1747–1776.* Carbondale/Edwardsville, Ill., 1968.

Summers, M., *The Restoration Theatre.* London, 1934.

Waldo, L. P., *The French Drama in America.* Baltimore, 1942.

Wittke, C., *Tambo and Bones: A History of the Minstrel Stage.* 1931.

From Naturalism to the Present

Antoine, A., *Memories of the Théâtre Libre.* Translated by M. Carlson. Coral Gables, Florida, 1964.

Appia, A., *The Work of Living Art and Man Is the Measure of All Things.* Coral Gables, Florida, 1960.

Archer, W., *The Old Drama and the New.* London, 1923.

Artaud, A., *The Theatre and Its Double.* New York, 1958.

Atkinson, B., *Broadway Scrapbook.* New York, 1957.

———, *Broadway.* New York, 1970.

Bablet, D., *Edward Gordon Craig.* New York, 1967.

Bablet, D., and Jacquot, J., *Le Lieu théâtrale dans la société moderne.* Paris, 1963.

Balakian, A. E., *Surrealism.* New York, 1959.

Baumol, W. J., and Bowen, W. G., *Performing Arts—The Economic Dilemma.* New York, 1966.

Bentley, E., *The Playwright as Thinker.* New York, 1946.

———, *Bernard Shaw.* New York, 1947.

———, *In Search of Theatre.* New York, 1953.

Bernheim, A. L., *The Business of the Theatre.* New York, 1932.

Birdoff, H., *The World's Greatest Hit: "Uncle Tom's Cabin".* New York, 1947.

Blum, D., *Great Stars of the American Stage: a Pictorial Record.* New York, 1952.

Bowers, F., *Broadway, USSR. Theatre, Ballet and Entertainment in Russia Today.* New York, 1959.

Bradshaw, M., ed., *Soviet Theatres 1917–1941.* New York, 1954.

Braulich, H., *Max Reinhardt. Theater zwischen Traum und Wirklichkeit.* Berlin, 1966.

Brook, R., *The Empty Space.* London, 1968.

Brown, J. R., *Effective Theatre. A Study with Documentation.* London, 1969.

Brustein, R., *Theatre of Revolt.* Boston, 1964.

Byrne, D., *The Story of Ireland's National Theatre.* Dublin, 1929.

Carter, H., *The New Spirit in the European Theatre, 1914–1924.* New York, 1925.

Carter, L. A., *Zola and the Theatre.* New Haven, 1963.

Chekhov, A. M., *Stanislavski's Method: New Theatre.* 1935.

———, *To the Actor on the Technique of Acting.* New York, 1953.

Cheney, S., *The New Movement in the Theatre.* New York, 1914.

Chiari, J., *The Contemporary French Theatre: The Flight from Naturalism.* London, 1958.

———, *The Theatre of Jean-Louis Barrault.* Translated by J. Chiari. 1961.

Clurman, H., *The Fervent Years: The Story of the Group Theatre in the Thirties.* New York, 1957.

Cole, T., and Krich, H., *Actors on Acting.* 1950.

Cole, T., ed., *Playwrights on Playwrighting: The Meaning and Making of Modern Drama from Ibsen to Ionesco.* New York, 1961.

Cole, T., and Chinoy, H., *Directors on Directing.* 1963.

Copeau, J., *Souvenirs du Vieux-Colombier.* Paris, 1931.

Cornell, K., *The Symbolist Movement.* New Haven, 1951.

Corrigan, R., *The Modern Theatre.* New York, 1964.

Craig, E. G., *On the Art of the Theatre.* London, 1911.

———, *Towards a New Theatre.* London, 1913.

———, *The Theatre Advancing.* London, 1921.

———, *Scene.* Oxford: University Press, 1923.

———, *Henry Irving.* London, 1930.

———, *Ellen Terry.* London, 1931.

Dahlstrom, C. E. W. L., *Strindberg's Dramatic Expressionism.* Ann Arbor: University of Michigan Press, 1930.

Diebold, B., *Habima: Hebräisches Theater. 32 Bilder mit einer Einführung von B. Diebold.* Berlin, 1928.

Dietrich, M., *Das moderne Drama.* Stuttgart, 1963.

Disher, M. W., *Fairs, Circuses and Music Halls.* London, 1942.

Driver, T. F., *Romantic Quest and Modern Query: A History of the Modern Theatre.* New York, 1970.

Edwards, C., *The Stanislavski Heritage.* New York, 1965.

Elagin, Yuri B., *Taming of the Arts.* New York, 1951.

Esslin, M., *Brecht: The Man and His Work.* New York, 1960.

———, *The Theatre of the Absurd.* New York, 1961.

Fay, G., *The Abbey Theatre.* Dublin, 1958.

Felheim, M., *The Theater of Augustin Daly: An Account of the Late Nineteenth Century American Stage.* Cambridge, Mass., 1956.

Fowlie, W., *Age of Surrealism.* Bloomington, 1960.

———, *Dionysus in Paris. A Guide to Contemporary French Theater.* New York, 1960.

Fuerst, W. L., and Hume, S. J., *Twentieth-Century Stage Decoration.* New York, 1928, 1967.

Gaipa, E., *Giorgio Strehler.* Berlin, 1963.

Gassner, J., *The Theatre in Our Times.* New York, 1954.

———, *Form and Idea in Modern Theatre.* New York, 1956.

———, *Directions in Modern Theatre and Drama.* New York, 1965.

———, *Dramatic Soundings.* New York, 1968.

Gorchakov, N. A., *The Theater in Soviet Russia.* New York, 1957.

———, *Stanislavski Directs.* Translated by M. Goldina. New York, 1954.

Gorelik, M., *New Theatres for Old.* New York, 1940.

Gregor, U., and Patalas, E., *Geschichte des Films.* Gütersloh, 1962.

Gropius, W., ed., *Oskar Schlemmer, Laszlo Moholy-Nagy, Farkas Molnàr: Die Bühne am Bauhaus.* Mainz, 1965.

Grossvogel, D. I., *The Self-Conscious Stage in Modern French Drama.* New York, 1958.

Grotowski, J., *Towards a Poor Theatre. Odin Teatrets Forlag,* 1968.

Guicharnaud, J., *Modern French Theatre from Giraudoux to Beckett.* New Haven, 1961.

Hainaux, R., ed., *Stage Design throughout the World since 1935.* New York, 1956.

———, *Stage Design throughout the World since 1950.* New York, 1964.

Hartwig, E., *Kulisy Teatru.* Warsaw, 1969.

Henze, H., *Otto Brahm und das Deutsche Theater zu Berlin.* Berlin, 1920.

Houghton, N., *Moscow Rehearsals. An Account of Methods of Production in the Soviet Theatre*. New York, 1936.

———, *Return Engagement. A Postscript to "Moscow Rehearsals"*. New York, 1962.

Ihering, H., *Von Reinhardt bis Brecht: Eine Auswahl der Theaterkritiken von 1909–1932*. Reinbek by Hamburg, 1967.

Jacobs, L., *The Rise of the American Film*. New York, 1939.

Jolivet, A., *Le théâtre de Strindberg*. Paris, 1931.

Jones, M., *Theatre-in-the-Round*. New York, 1951.

Jones, R. E., *Drawings for the Theatre*. New York, 1925.

———, *The Dramatic Imagination*. New York, 1941.

Kienzle, S., *Modern World Theater: A Guide to Productions in Europe and the United States since 1945*. Translated by A. and E. Henderson. New York, 1970.

Kirby, M., *Happenings*. New York, 1965.

Knellessen, F. W., *Agitation auf der Bühne—Das politische Theater der Weimarer Republik*. Emsdetten, 1970.

Knowles, D., *French Drama of the Inter-War Years, 1918–39*. New York, 1968.

Krutch, J. W., *The American Drama since 1918*. Rev. ed. New York, 1957.

Larson, O. K., ed., *Scene Design for Stage and Screen Readings on the Aesthetics and Methodology of Scene Design for Drama, Opera, Musical Comedy, Ballet, Motion Pictures, Television and Arena Theatre*. East Lansing, Mich., 1961.

Ley-Piscator, M., *The Piscator Experiment. The Political Theatre*. New York, 1967.

Macgowan, K., and Jones, R. E., *Continental Stagecraft*. New York, 1922.

Mackay, C. D., *The Little Theatre in the United States*. New York, 1917.

Magarshack, D., *Chekhov the Dramatist*. New York, 1960.

Magriel, P., *Chronicles of the American Dance*. New York, 1948.

Meisel, M., *Shaw and the Nineteenth-Century Theater*. Princeton, 1963.

Melcer, F. H., *Staging the Dance*. Dubuque, 1955.

Melchinger, S., *The Concise Encyclopedia of Modern Drama*. New York, 1964.

Metz, C., *Essais sur la signification au cinéma*. Paris, 1968.

Mielziner, J., *Designing for the Theatre*. New York, 1965.

Miller, A. I., *The Independent Theatre in Europe, 1887 to the Present*. New York, 1931.

Moderwell, H. K., *The Theatre of To-day*. New York, 1925.

Nemirovich-Danchenko, V., *My Life in the Russian Theatre*. London and Boston, 1936.

Nicoll, A., *Film and Theatre*. London, 1936.

Nicollier, J., *René Morax (Théâtre du Jorat)*. 1958.

Novick, J., *Beyond Broadway: A Quest for Permanent Theatres*. New York, 1968.

Palmer, J., *The Future of the Theatre*. 1913.

Plummer, G., *The Business of Show Business*. New York, 1961.

Poggi, J., *Theatre in America: The Impact of Economic Forces, 1870–1967*. Ithaca, N.Y., 1968.

Price, J., *The Off-Broadway Theatre.* New York, 1962.
Pronko, L., *Theatre East and West: Perspectives toward a Total Theatre.* Berkeley, 1967.
Reinhardt, M., *Max Reinhardt. Sein Theater in Bildern. Herausgegeben von der Max-Reinhardt-Forschungsstätte Salzburg.* Velber by Hannover, 1968.
Rotha, P., *The Film till Now.* London, 1960.
Rühle, G., *Theater für die Republik, 1917–1933, im Spiegel der Kritik.* Frankfurt, 1967.
Rühle, J., *Das gefesselte Theater. Vom Revolutionstheater zum sozialistischen Realismus.* Cologne-Berlin, 1957.
Ruhnau, W., *Versammlungsstätten.* Gütersloh, 1969.
Ruppel, K. H. (ed.), *Wieland Wagner inszeniert Richard Wagner.* Konstanz, 1960.
Sayler, O. M., ed., *Max Reinhardt and His Theatre.* New York, 1926.
Schlemmer, O., *The Theatre of the Bauhaus.* Middleton, 1961.
Schley, G., *Die Freie Bühne in Berlin.* Berlin, 1967.
Schmidt-Joos, S., *Das Musical.* Munich, 1965.
Schoop, G., *Das Zürcher Schauspielhaus im zweiten Weltkrieg.* Zurich, 1957.
Selden, S., and Sellman, H. D., *Stage Scenery and Lighting.* 3d ed., New York, 1959.
Seltzer, D., ed., *The Modern Theatre: Readings and Documents.* Boston, 1967.
Shaw, G. B., *The Quintessence of Ibsenism.* London, 1913.
———, *Our Theatre in the Nineties.* 3 vols. London, 1932.
Shaw, L. R., *The Playwright & Historical Change: Dramatic Strategies in Brecht, Hauptmann, Kaiser, and Wedekind.* Madison/Milwaukee/London, 1970.
Simonson, L., *The Stage is Set.* New York, 1932.
———, *The Art of Scenic Design.* New York, 1950.
Smith, C., *Musical Comedy in America.* New York, 1950.
Sokel, W. H., *The Writer in Extremis: Expressionism in Twentieth-Century German Literature.* Stanford, Calif., 1959.
Sondel, B. S., *Zola's Naturalistic Theory with Particular Reference to the Drama.* Chicago, 1939.
Southern, R., *The Open Stage.* New York, 1959.
Spalter, M., *Brecht's Tradition.* Baltimore, 1967.
Spolin, V., *Improvisation for the Theatre.* Evanston, 1963.
Stanislavski, C., *My Life in Art.* London, 1924.
———, *An Actor Prepares.* New York, 1936.
———, *Building a Character.* New York, 1949.
———, *Creating a Role.* New York, 1961.
Stein, J. M., *Richard Wagner and the Synthesis of the Arts.* Detroit, 1960.
Stone, E., *What Was Naturalism? Materials for an Answer.* New York, 1959.
Stratman, C. J., *Bibliography of the American Theatre, Excluding New York City.* Chicago, 1965.
Strickland, F. C., *The Technique of Acting.* New York, 1956.
Styan, J. L., *The Dark Comedy: The Development of Modern Comic Tragedy.* Cambridge, 1962.

Tairow, A., *Das entfesselte Theater. Aufzeichnungen eines Regisseurs.* Potsdam, 1927.

Taylor, J. R., *Anger and After: A Guide to the New British Drama.* London, 1962.

Theaterarbeit: 6 Aufführungen des Berliner Ensembles. Berlin, 1967.

Ulanov, B., *Masks of the Modern Theatre.* New York, 1961.

Vardac, A. N., *Stage to Screen: Theatrical Method from Garrick to Griffith.* Cambridge, Mass., 1949.

Veinstein, A., *La mise en scène théâtrale et sa condition esthétique.* Paris, 1955.

Volbach, W. R., *Adolphe Appia, Prophet of the Modern Theatre: A Profile.* Middletown, Conn., 1968.

Waxman, S. M., *Antoine and the Théâtre Libre.* New York, 1964.

Weales, G., *American Drama since World War II.* New York, 1962.

Weigand, H. J., *The Modern Ibsen.* New York, 1925.

Wigman, M., *The Language of Dance.* Middletown, Conn., 1966.

Willett, J., *The Theatre of Bertolt Brecht.* New York, 1959.

———, *Brecht on Theatre.* Translated by J. Willett. New York, 1965.

Young, S., *Theatre Practice.* New York, 1926.

Zucker, A. E., *Ibsen, the Master Builder.* New York, 1929.

Zwanzig Jahre Komische Oper: Eine Dokumentation. Berlin, 1967.

Index

The illustrations are listed under the individual chapter titles. The half-tone plates are indicated by roman page numbers and the line drawings by italicized page numbers.